Praise for Best Places® Guidebooks

"Best Places *are the best regional restaurant and guide books in America.*"
—THE SEATTLE TIMES

"Best Places *covers must-see portions of the West Coast with style and authority. In-the-know locals offer thorough info on restaurants, lodgings, and the sights.*"
—NATIONAL GEOGRAPHIC TRAVELER

"*. . . travelers swear by the recommendations in the* Best Places *guidebooks . . .*"
—SUNSET MAGAZINE

"*For travel collections covering the Northwest, the* Best Places *series takes precedence over all similar guides.*"
—BOOKLIST

"Best Places Northwest *is the bible of discriminating travellers to BC, Washington and Oregon. It promises, and delivers, the best of everything in the region.*"
—THE VANCOUVER SUN

"*Not only the best travel guide in the region, but maybe one of the most definitive guides in the country, which many look forward to with the anticipation usually sparked by a best-selling novel. A browser's delight,* Best Places Northwest *should be chained to dashboards throughout the Northwest.*"
—THE OREGONIAN

"*Still the region's undisputed heavyweight champ of guidebooks.*"
—SEATTLE POST-INTELLIGENCER

"*Trusting the natives is usually good advice, so visitors to Washington, Oregon, and British Columbia would do well to pick up* Best Places Northwest *for an exhaustive review of food and lodging in the region. . . . An indispensable glove-compartment companion.*"
—TRAVEL AND LEISURE

"Best Places Southern California *is just about all the inspiration you need to start planning your next road trip or summer vacation with the kids.*"
—THE FRESNO BEE

"Best Places Alaska *is the one guide to recommend to anyone visiting Alaska for the first or one-hundredth time.*"
—KETCHIKAN DAILY NEWS

"Best Places Northern California *is great fun to read even if you're not going anywhere.*"
—SAN FRANCISCO CHRONICLE

TRUST THE LOCALS

The original insider's guides, written by local experts

COMPLETELY INDEPENDENT

- No advertisers
- No sponsors
- No favors

EVERY PLACE STAR-RATED & RECOMMENDED

★★★★   The very best in the region

★★★   Distinguished; many outstanding features

★★   Excellent; some wonderful qualities

★   A good place

NO STARS   Worth knowing about, if nearby

MONEY-BACK GUARANTEE

We're so sure you'll be satisfied, we guarantee it!

HELPFUL ICONS

Watch for these quick-reference symbols throughout the book:

   FAMILY FUN

   GOOD VALUE

   ROMANTIC

   EDITORS' CHOICE

BEST PLACES®

ALASKA

The Locals' Guide to the Best
Lodgings, Outdoor Adventure, Sights,
Shopping, and Restaurants

Edited by
KATE RIPLEY

EDITION

SASQUATCH BOOKS
SEATTLE

Printed in the United States of America
Published by Sasquatch Books
Distributed by Publishers Group West

Third edition
09 08 07 06 05 04 03   5 4 3 2 1

ISBN: 1-57061-374-5
ISSN: 1095-9777

Cover and Interior design: Nancy Gellos
Cover photograph: Paul Souders
Interior composition: pdbd
Maps: Lisa Brower/Greeneye Design

SPECIAL SALES

BEST PLACES guidebooks are available at special discounts on bulk purchases for corporate, club, or organization sales promotions, premiums, and gifts. Special editions, including personalized covers, excerpts of existing guides, and corporate imprints, can be created in large quantities for specific needs. For more information, contact your local bookseller or Special Sales, BEST PLACES Guidebooks, at the address below.

Important Note: Please use common sense when visiting Alaska's wilderness. No guide-book can act as a substitute for experience, careful planning, and appropriate training. There is inherent danger in all the outdoor activities described in this book, and readers must assume responsibility for their own actions and safety, even when using a guide or outfitter. Changing or unfavorable conditions in weather, roads, trails, waterways, wildlife, etc. cannot be anticipated by the editors or publisher, but should be considered by any outdoor participants. The editors and publisher will not be responsible for the safety of users of this guide.

SASQUATCH BOOKS

119 South Main Street, Suite 400
Seattle, WA 98104
206/467-4300
books@sasquatchbooks.com
www.sasquatchbooks.com

CONTENTS

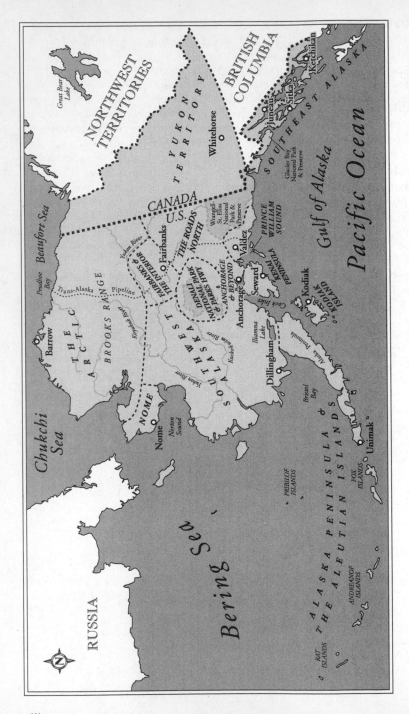

Contributors and Acknowledgments

A diverse mix of Alaskans researched and wrote this book.

All of us are professional writers—several with book credits to our names. We are mountain climbers (two of us even summitted McKinley), kayakers, fishers, photographers, dog mushers, sailboaters, hunters, wildlife watchers, wilderness explorers, philosophers, log cabin builders, river runners, skiers, berry pickers, and snowmachiners. We are up and coming young turks, but also old grandmas and grandpas, mothers, fathers, curmudgeons, and optimists. Some of us have family roots in Alaska that go back generations. The newest comer of the bunch has been here 10 years.

All of us call Alaska our home. Some of us chose to live here; others were born here. Most of us never want to leave. We love this wild and wonderful place, and we're sharing a slice of it with you, through this book, in the hope that you too will view this land and its people with awe and respect.

"We" are Dave Kiffer and Charlotte Glover (Ketchikan, Prince of Wales Island, Misty Fjords National Monument); Bill Sherwonit (Sitka, Icy Strait, Gustavus, Glacier Bay, Nome, the Southwest, and Alaska Peninsula/Aleutians Islands); Robert Tkacz (Juneau); Dimitra Lavrakas (Skagway, Haines, the Yukon); John Kooistra (The Roads North); Natalie Phillips (Prince William Sound, Anchorage and Beyond); Peter Porco (Chugach State Park); McKibben Jackinsky (Kenai Peninsula); Susan Jeffrey (Kodiak Island); Kris Capps (Denali National Park, Denali Highway); Matt Hayes (Wasilla–Talkeetna); Dermot Cole (Pipeline sidebar); Tom Walker (the Arctic) and myself, Kate Ripley (Alaska Cruises, Fairbanks/Interior, Barrow, Wrangell/Petersburg, Wrangell–St. Elias National Park, and Kennicott/McCarthy).

Thanks also to contributors of past editions of *Best Places Alaska,* and to my loving and supportive family.

—Kate Ripley
Editor, *Best Places Alaska* (Third Edition)

About Best Places® Guidebooks

People trust us. Best Places® guidebooks, which have been published continuously since 1975, represent one of the most respected regional travel series in the country. Each guide is written completely independently: no advertisers, no sponsors, no favors. Our reviewers know their territory, work incognito, and seek out the very best a city, state, or region has to offer. Because we accept no free meals, accommodations, or other complimentary services, we are able to provide tough, candid reports about places that have rested too long on their laurels, and to delight in new places that deserve recognition. We describe the true strengths, foibles, and unique characteristics of each establishment listed.

Best Places Alaska is written by and for locals, and is therefore coveted by travelers. It's written for people who live here and who enjoy exploring the state's bounty and its out-of-the-way places of high character and individualism. It is these very characteristics that make *Best Places Alaska* ideal for tourists, too. The best places in and around the state are the ones that denizens favor: independently owned establishments of good value, touched with local history, run by lively individuals, and graced with natural beauty. With this third edition of *Best Places Alaska*, travelers will find the information they need: where to go and when, what to order, which rooms to request, how to find the best guides and outfitters, where the best festivals, shopping, and other attractions are, and how to find the state's hidden secrets.

We're so sure you'll be satisfied with our guide, we guarantee it.

NOTE: *Readers are advised that places listed in the previous edition may have closed or changed management, or may no longer be recommended by this series. The reviews in this edition are based on information available at press time and are subject to change. The editors welcome information conveyed by users of this book. A report form is provided at the end of the book, and feedback is also welcome via email: bestplaces@sasquatchbooks.com.*

How to Use This Book

All evaluations in this book are based on numerous reports from local and traveling inspectors. BEST PLACES reporters do not identify themselves when they review an establishment, and they accept no free meals, accommodations, or any other services. Final judgments are made by the editors. Every place featured in this book is recommended.

STAR RATINGS Restaurants and lodgings are rated on a scale of zero to four stars, based on uniqueness, loyalty of local clientele, performance measured against the establishment's goals, excellence of cooking, cleanliness, value, and professionalism of service. Reviews are listed alphabetically, and every place is recommended.

★★★★ The very best in the region

★★★ Distinguished; many outstanding features

★★ Excellent; some wonderful qualities

★ A good place

NO STARS Worth knowing about, if nearby

(For more on how we rate places, see the Alaska Star Ratings box, on page xii.)

PRICE RANGE Prices for lodgings are based on peak season rates for one night's lodging for two people (i.e., double occupancy). Off-season rates vary but can sometimes be significantly less. Prices for restaurants are based primarily on dinner for two, including dessert, tax, and tip. Call ahead to verify, as all prices are subject to change.

$$$ Expensive (more than $100 for dinner for two; more than $150 for one night's lodgings for two)

$$ Moderate (between expensive and inexpensive)

$ Inexpensive (less than $35 for dinner for two; less than $80 for one night's lodgings for two)

ACCESS AND INFORMATION At the beginning of each chapter, you'll find general guidelines about how to get to a particular region and what types of transportation are available, as well as basic sources for any additional tourist information you might need. Also check individual town listings for specifics about visiting those places. **ALASKA WILDERNESS RECREATION AND TOURISM ASSOCIATION (AWRTA)** is a group of more than 200 outdoor-oriented businesses throughout the state. Their trip planner, *Alaska Source Book: Trip Planning Info for Independent Travelers to Alaska*, is available by contacting AWRTA (2207 Spenard Rd, Ste 201, Anchorage AK 99503; 907/258-3171, fax 907/258-3851; awrta@alaska.net; www. alaska.net/~awrta).

WILDERNESS LODGES For some visitors, the best way to experience Alaska is to stay at a remote wilderness or fishing lodge. There are hundreds of such lodges throughout the state, but we have tried to include here only those establishments that have proved to be dependable operations. They are not star-rated because they vary widely in terms of location and of overall experience versus fishing poundage. Please be aware that many of these places require expensive Bush flights to reach, minimum stays during the peak season, and charge an all-inclusive rate by the day or week.

ADDRESSES AND PHONE NUMBERS Every attempt has been made to provide accurate information on an establishment's location and phone number. But it's always a good idea to call ahead and confirm. Please note that many Alaska businesses observe seasonal closures, operating only certain months of the year. The establishments in this edition are open year-round unless otherwise noted.

CHECKS AND CREDIT CARDS Most establishments that accept checks also require a major credit card for identification. Note that some places accept only local checks. Credit cards are abbreviated in this book as follows: American Express (AE); Carte Blanche (CB); Diners Club (DC); Discover (DIS); Japanese credit card (JCB); MasterCard (MC); Visa (V).

EMAIL AND WEB SITE ADDRESSES We've included email and Web site addresses for establishments, where available. Please note that the World Wide Web is a fluid and evolving medium, and that Web pages are often "under construction" or, as with all time-sensitive information, may no longer be valid.

MAPS AND DIRECTIONS Each chapter in the book begins with a regional map that shows the general area being covered. Throughout the book, basic directions are provided with each entry. Whenever possible, call ahead to confirm hours and location.

HELPFUL ICONS Watch for these quick-reference symbols throughout the book:

 FAMILY FUN Family-oriented places that are great for kids—fun, easy, not too expensive, and accustomed to dealing with young ones.

 GOOD VALUE While not necessarily cheap, these places offer you the best value for your dollars—a good deal within the context of the region.

 ROMANTIC These spots offer candlelight, atmosphere, intimacy, or other romantic qualities—kisses and proposals are encouraged!

EDITORS' CHOICE These are places that are unique and special to Alaska, such as a restaurant owned by a beloved local chef or a tourist attraction recognized around the globe.

 Appears after listings for establishments that have wheelchair-accessible facilities.

INDEXES All restaurants, lodgings, town names, and major tourist attractions are listed alphabetically in the back of the book.

READER REPORTS At the end of the book is a report form. We receive hundreds of reports from readers suggesting new places or agreeing or disagreeing with our assessments. They greatly help in our evaluations, and we encourage you to respond.

MONEY-BACK GUARANTEE See "We Stand by Our Reviews" at the end of this book.

ALASKA STAR RATINGS
(A Disclaimer)

First of all, if you equate four stars to the best that Paris has to offer, be aware that our stars relate to nobody else's stars in the world! Our rating system is strictly "Alaska Bush Style." Character rates highly. In many places in this far northern state, assigning stars is like trying to compare Belgian chocolates and tropical mangos. Sometimes, the *best* place is the *only* place—and you're darn happy to be there, particularly if the rain is blowing horizontally in your face or the temperature has dropped to -50°F.

While we do have some wonderful places to eat and sleep—places which rival the best in the world—if you are on a serious four-star gastronomic mission and your toes cannot possibly be pampered outside a world-class hotel, we suggest you keep flying north over the pole to Paris. A singular quest for the finest food and lodging should not be the sole reason you come to Alaska.

While in most major cities you could learn a dozen different languages just by studying the menus, in Alaska, outside of a few towns, the only foreign word you'll see on a menu is *deluxe*—and it usually follows "cheeseburger." Ah, but do not dismay. There are also hundreds of places all over Alaska to eat (and sleep) which are so extraordinary and so outrageously magical that you will remember them all the days of your life. You cannot make a reservation. They have no maitre d' or concierge. They have no walls. As one of our writers so eloquently says, "The most exquisite meal is the country itself."

—The Editor

SOUTHEAST ALASKA

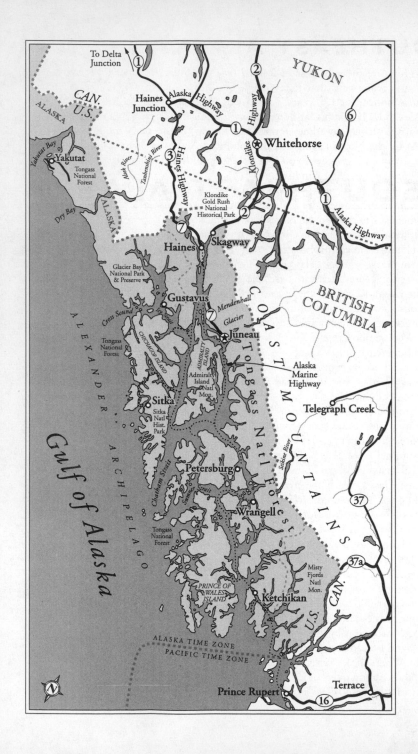

SOUTHEAST ALASKA

Named for Alexander II, czar of Russia, the Alexander Archipelago is a series of islands and waterways that today define Southeast Alaska. Once, it was part of Russian America; for 126 years, Alaska was under the imperial Russian flag until Czar Alexander II sold his far-flung colony to the United States in 1867.

A narrow strip of coastline, bounded on the east by steep, icy mountains and on the west by the North Pacific Ocean, Southeast Alaska is often called "The Panhandle." You can see why if you look at a map of the rest of Alaska, which looks somewhat like the frying pan itself.

If you were to fly over it, you would see islands, mountains, fjords, icefields, glaciers, more islands, and more ice-covered mountains rising like a crescendo to some of the highest summits on the North American continent.

Southeast Alaska is rich in culture. The original peoples to inhabit the land were predominantly Tlingit (pronounced klink-it). Today, three major Native groups live in the Southeast—Tlingit, Haida, and Tsimshian. Because the weather here is mild and the sea and forest rich with food, the peoples of Southeast Alaska had more time than the Eskimos and Indians of the north to create great art—carved totem poles, clan houses, wooden suits of armor, priceless blankets, great headdresses, masks, and silverwork. Many Native artists today are producing stunning works, blending both the contemporary and the traditional.

Although early inhabitants of Southeast Alaska considered the climate so mild that they did not have tailored clothing, this is not a wise custom to practice today. Southeast weather, even at the best of times, is usually cool. At its worst, it's downright bone-chilling. The sunniest months, although not necessarily the warmest, tend to be April, May, and June. Be forewarned: there is still plenty of snow then, at least in the mountains. But whenever you come, if you get two days of sun in a week, consider yourself fortunate. After all, there's a reason why all this country looks so green in the summer. You are traveling in a rain forest.

The Tongass National Forest, a temperate rain forest, covers 17 million acres of Southeast Alaska, nearly the entire Panhandle. It is the largest national forest in the United States. There are nearly 1,000 islands under its banner. This is one of the country's last old-growth forests. The trees are primarily Sitka spruce and western hemlock interspersed with red and yellow cedar. The water between the islands and the mainland is known as the Inside Passage—summer home for cruise ships, fishing boats, ferries, skiffs, kayaks, and rowboats of all sorts.

Water is an extension of everyone's life in the Southeast. There are few roads and rarely do they link one community to another. So water serves not only as the transportation corridor, but also as the place of livelihood and recreation. Indeed, the official name of the state's ferry system is the Alaska Marine Highway. The only other way to get around is by air—bush plane, jet, or helicopter.

The land is dramatic. Carved by glaciers, the valleys have that telltale, U-shaped contour. Where the ice retreated, the sea rushed in to create deep, spectacular fjords. Today, those grand rivers of ice tumble down to the ocean. Warmed by the Japanese current, the sea itself does not freeze, even in winter, but glaciers are constantly kicking out icebergs, which you can see floating in the water or tossed up on a sandbar.

Magnificent whales, chubby harbor seals, swooping eagles, wild salmon, and the great Alaska brown bears are just a few of the alluring creatures that call the Southeast home.

Towns and villages along the coast have their own special characters, founded on fishing, fur, gold, timber, or tourism. Native peoples have lived here for untold centuries. White settlers arrived within the past 300 years—Russian fur traders, Yankee whalers, European explorers, navigators, sailors, fishermen, and gold prospectors have all made their way here. Names on the map hint at the rich stories of a few of those early travelers who came before you.

Ketchikan

Visitors to Ketchikan, Alaska's fourth largest city, are usually surprised that the century-old community appears to be a work in progress. New buildings and construction are everywhere. Old buildings frequently wear scaffolding, and get new roofs and new coats of paint. This is partly true because of the town's infamous "Chinese water torture"—150 INCHES OF ANNUAL RAINFALL—which takes a toll on buildings. But it's also true because Alaska's "First City" is always reinventing itself.

For centuries, the Tlingit people had summer camps at the mouth of Ketchikan Creek, but the inclement weather caused them to build permanent villages elsewhere. Still, the millions of salmon that returned to the area each year were a powerful draw for white settlers. In the late 1880s, the first saltery was built and a small village grew up. The influx of people drawn by the Klondike Gold Rush to the north gave the village a boost, as did a decision to move a Customs Station from Mary Island to Ketchikan. A brief mining boom helped the town grow in the early 1900s, but by the 1920s the fishing industry was king and Ketchikan was the "Salmon Capital of the World." More than a dozen canneries lined the waterfront, packing millions of cases of salmon. Locals still refer fondly to the cannery days when the smell of money was literally in the air. By the 1950s, use of fish traps had decimated the salmon runs, but Ketchikan succeeded in getting one of the world's largest pulp mills built at Ward Cove, 6 miles north of town. The timber industry dominated the area until economic and political forces collided in 1997, causing the mill to close. Both the timber and fishing industries continue to play roles in the Ketchikan economy, albeit smaller ones.

All along, tourism had been a steady but relatively minor part of the local economy. That changed in the 1990s, when the Alaska cruise industry exploded. Cruise visits increased from four or five ships a week to four or five ships a day, and the ships themselves grew from several hundred passengers per boat to upwards of 2,000 plus crew members. The May to September cruise season now brings more than 600,000 visitors a year. Consequently, downtown can occasionally look like a giant tourist trap. But savvy visitors learn that the real Ketchikan still lives on just beyond the false front buildings and the curio and jewelry stores near the cruise ship docks.

With more than 14,000 people, Ketchikan serves as an administrative, transportation, and economic center for the southern part of Southeast Alaska (an area roughly the size of New England). There are numerous outlying areas that make interesting day or overnight trips. Like elsewhere in Alaska, the wilderness is just a short boat or plane ride away.

ACCESS AND INFORMATION

As is typical in the state's island-dotted Panhandle, Ketchikan can only be reached by boat or plane. The community, which sits on the edge of Revillagigedo Island, has daily JET SERVICE year-round via Alaska Airlines (800/252-7522 or 907/225-2145; www.alaskaair.com). The airport is located on the neighboring island of Gravina, a short ferry ride from Ketchikan. The ferry costs $4 per person and connects up with bus and taxi service. Another option is the Airporter van service that will take you from the airport ferry terminal to any point in Ketchikan for $15.

The ALASKA MARINE HIGHWAY SYSTEM (907/225-6181 or 800/642-0066; www.alaska.gov/ferry) stops in Ketchikan several times a week. The airport ferry terminal and the marine highway ferry terminal are approximately 2 miles north of downtown. Public buses ($1.50) run from Wal-Mart (3 miles north of downtown) to Saxman (2 miles south), but many visitors opt for a rental car to explore sites along the 30 miles of road outside the city. Call ALASKA CAR RENTAL (2828 Tongass Ave; 907/225-5000 or 800/662-0007; www.akcarrental.com). They also have an office at the airport and have courtesy pickup.

There are several small locally based air services that provide scheduled and chartered flights to the surrounding communities. The best of these airlines are PROMECH AIR (1515 Tongass Ave; 800/860-3845; www.promechair.com), TAQUAN AIR (1007 Water St; 800/770-8800; www.taquanair.com) and PACIFIC AIRWAYS (1007 Water St; 907/225-3500; www.flypacificairways.com).

Ketchikan is an extremely spread out community. The 3,000-foot mountains pin the city to the shoreline; the town is truly no more than a few blocks wide at some points. Since the city is spread out along nearly 30 miles of coastal road, it's a good idea to get oriented at the city center. The KETCHIKAN VISITORS BUREAU (131 Front St, just off the cruise ship docks; 907/225-6616 or 800/770-3300; info@visit-ketchikan.com; www.visit-ketchikan.com) has maps and plenty of information about what is going on in town. For a great overall introduction to the region, visit the SOUTHEAST ALASKA DISCOVERY CENTER (50 Main St; 907/228-6214; www.fs.fed.us/r10/tongass/districts/discoverycenter). Completed in 1995, this world-class center features exhibits on the Native peoples of the area (most notable are three specially carved totem poles representing the Tlingit, Haida, and Tsimshian tribes), the industries that built the Southeast, and a rain forest recreation exhibit. There is also an exceptional natural-history bookstore and a room where visitors can get trip planning information for the Tongass National Forest. A theater also offers a short film about the people and places of the Tongass. During the summer admission is $4 per person or $12 per family. It's free during winter months.

5

EXPLORING

CREEK STREET / Although much of downtown has been overrun by the seasonal tourist stores, there is one area that has always been a hub of commerce. Creek Street was the area's red-light district from the early part of the twentieth century, when local officials sought to contain illicit activities by making them semilegal in the Creek section of what was then called Indian Town, until the 1950s when prostitution was outlawed. Known as either "Alaskan's Tenderloin" or the "Barbary Coast of the North," locals joked that it was the only place in the world where both fish and fishermen went up the creek to spawn. It also was a center for illegal liquor sales during Prohibition. More than a few prominent families can trace their grubstake to money earned running either speakeasies or brothels on Creek Street, which actually isn't a street at all but rather buildings atop pilings, linked together by boardwalks (it's quaint, and the most photographed sight in town). Today you can visit several of the former houses of ill repute. **DOLLY'S HOUSE** (24 Creek St; 907/225-6329), the home of Ketchikan's most famous madam, Dolly Arthur, is a must-see museum. The Five Star Building (named for the star on its large dance floor) houses the **PARNASSUS BOOKSTORE** (907/225-7690), which has the best local selection of books as well as the ambience of a wonderful independent bookstore. Owner Lillian Ferrence is a local treasure. Like the good old days, Creek Street remains a commerce center, although few of the remaining shops have any connections to the past. Prices for the standard visitor fare here are lower than at the cruise ship docks.

MARRIED MAN'S TRAIL / Although most visitors to Creek Street cross over bridges from the downtown side of the district, there is a more scenic route. The Married Man's Trail was completed in the last few years and brings visitors from the Park Avenue Bridge or the Cape Fox Hotel. The short trail through the woods commemorates the fact that many "married men" used to visit the Creek surreptitiously rather than "publicly" from the waterfront. This trail gives a scenic and less crowded view of the salmon pooling in the creek below the falls.

WALKING AND BUS TOURS / The best way to see downtown Ketchikan is via foot. Ketchikan has two **HISTORIC WALKING TOURS,** one that covers the downtown and one that covers the area just north of downtown, called the West End. You can pick up copies of the numbered tour maps at the Ketchikan Visitors Bureau (see Access and Information, above) and other locations around town. The **DOWN-TOWN TOUR** (approx. 90 minutes) starts at the visitors bureau and quickly moves beyond the bustle of the cruise ship docks into the heart of Ketchikan. The first stop is the **LIQUID SUNSHINE GAUGE,** which measures the annual precipitation. It topped out in 1949 at nearly 17 feet. Another accurate weather gauge is to look up at the peak of Deer Mountain. Locals say that if you can't see the peak, it's raining. (And if you can see the peak? It means it's going to rain.) The tour continues up Ketchikan Creek into the Nickeyville residential area, the City Park, and the **TOTEM HERITAGE CENTER** (601 Deermount St; 907/225-5900; museum@city.ketchikan. ak.us), which houses an extraordinary collection of old totem poles that were carved a century ago in neighboring villages. Nearby is the **DEER MOUNTAIN TRIBAL HATCHERY AND EAGLE CENTER** (1158 Salmon Rd; 907/225-6026 or 800/252-5158; kichatch@ktn.net). Visitors can watch workers tend to the more than 350,000 salmon and trout that are raised and released each year. Just about 2 percent of the raised salmon survive the wild to return to Ketchikan Creek. The Eagle Center cares for wounded eagles and other birds. The walking tour then snakes around through the Deermount residential area and back toward the Thomas Basin waterfront where visitors can get a close-up view of Ketchikan's fishing fleet, with fishermen preparing for their next trip out. A short walk out the Thomas Basin breakwater offers the best photo opportunities in the downtown area. Farther along the tour, anglers crowd the Stedman Street dock hoping to snag a salmon on its way up Ketchikan Creek. Across the creek are the **TONGASS HISTORICAL MUSEUM** (629 Dock St; 907/225-5600; museum@city.ketchikan.ak.us) and the **KETCHIKAN PUBLIC LIBRARY** (629 Dock St; 907/225-3331; www.firstcitylibraries.org), which have great views of the salmon attacking the lower falls on Ketchikan Creek. The walking tour then cuts upland past Edmonds Street (one of Ketchikan's few remaining stairway streets) and then into what is called Nobb Hill, Ketchikan's original "mansion" district, in which many of the houses date from the first decade of the 20th century. There is a great view from upper Front Street, looking out over a section of Ketchikan called Newtown, the second oldest part of the community just north of the tunnel. The downtown tour ends at Ketchikan's **FAMOUS TUNNEL,** once listed in the *Guinness Book of World Records* as the only tunnel in the world that one can drive through, over, and around.

The **WEST END WALKING TOUR** (two hours) starts at Casey Moran Float in Newtown. The tour heads out into the lovely neighborhoods of Water Street and the West End. Here is where the visitor learns that, despite less than perfect weather, Ketchikan boasts numerous enthusiastic gardeners who tend a great variety of flowers and even a few green lawns. The bird's-eye views of the waterfront from upper Water Street are spectacular, as evidenced by the dozens of bald eagles and ravens that roost in the trees, always on the lookout for their next meal from the fish processors below. The trail passes by White Cliff School—the oldest operating school in Alaska—and down into the West End commercial area. It then winds its way back along the waterfront toward downtown, passing several working fish plants and floatplane docks.

If you prefer a more sedate way of exploring Ketchikan, there are dozens of tours available with everything from **DOUBLE-DECKER BUSES** to **HORSE-DRAWN TROL-LEYS.** You can also **RENT TAXIS** by the hour. Adventurous visitors can even rent **KAYAKS OR BICYCLES** from several purveyors (ask for contact info at the visitors bureau). Two of the more interesting excursions are **THE KETCHIKAN DUCK TOUR** (907/225-9899; www.alaskaamphibioustours.com/tours.htm) and **CLASSIC TOURS** (907/225-3091; lois@classictours.com). The 90-minute duck tour (adults $34, children ages 3–12 $19, children under 3 free) is a large amphibious vehicle that not only hits the land-based highlights but also enters the water for a boat tour of the harbor. "Classic Tours in a Classic Car with a Classy Lady" is the billing for Lois Munch's personalized '55 Chevy tours of the community. At $60 per person (two person minimum), you will be regaled with the "real" history of Ketchikan for two hours. Longer and custom tours also available.

SHOPPING

The oldest department store in Ketchikan is **TONGASS TRADING** (312 Dock St; 907/225-5101), at 100 years strong. You'll also want to check out the local kitchen and bath store **SILVER BASIN** (2525 Tongass; 907/225/2284) and **MAGGIE'S FINE APPAREL AND GIFTS** (312 Mission; 907/225-6244). The 80-year-old **KETCHIKAN FIVE AND DIME** (500 Mission; 907/225-4433) offers a wide selection of household items, Alaska-themed curios and souvenirs, and vacuum-packed salmon.

The farther you get from the cruise docks, the more likely you'll find a shop with local connections. The exception to that rule is the **SALMON LANDING MARKET** (5 Salmon Landing; 907/225-3299), a two-story shopping market adjacent to the docks. Locals often refer to this area as the Spruce Mill, because it was a sawmill property for more than 80 years. Inside you'll fine toys, teas, fabric, and bead shops and artwork.

Having been named one of the "200 Best Art Towns in America" it comes as no surprise there are several world-class art and craft galleries in Ketchikan. One of the oldest and best is **SCANLON GALLERY** (318 Mission St; 800/690-4730; www. Scanlon.com), featuring originals by Alaskan favorites Rie Muñoz, Byron Birdsall, and George Estrella. After visiting Scanlon's, cross Mission Street and choose from dozens of hand-dipped chocolates, fudge, and truffles made from family recipes at **KETCHICANDIES** (315 Mission St; 907/225-0900; www.ketchikandies.com). **EXPLORATION GALLERY** (633 Mission St; 907/225-4278; dave@exploration gallery.com) has original—primarily local—art that is carefully selected by owner Dave Dossett and expertly framed by his wife Jane, who works upstairs at **THE FINISHING TOUCH** (same phone number as gallery). Inside the gallery you'll find the work of more than 45 Alaskan artists in mediums ranging from paint to print to glass, silver, and pottery, as well as a large selection of Northwest Coast art. Exploration also has the largest local selection of antique maps and printed Alaskana.

If you're looking for contemporary and eclectic art, don't miss **THE SOHO COHO** (No. 5 Creek St; 800/888-4070; www.trollart.com), owned and operated by Ketchikan's most famous local artist, Ray Troll, whose carefully detailed and often comical looks at fish and fishermen have brought him national fame. Stop by the gallery on a Saturday and you'll likely find Ray at the register, happy to talk art or sign copies of his numerous books, including the latest, the children's book *Sharkabet*. Besides Ray's art and T-shirts (Spawn 'til You Die and Ain't No Nookie like Chinookie), you'll find $1 toy fish squirters to fine ceramics worth thousands of dollars. The gallery also represents linocut artist and children's book author Evon Zerbetz, ceramacist Carla Potter, photographers Hall Anderson and Chip Porter, and painters such as Mary Ida Hendrickson.

THE BLUE HERON (123 Stedman St, Ste B; 907/225-1982) offers art and handicrafts made in Alaska. The little shop is packed and truly has something for everyone, from walrus teeth to trade beads to one-of-a-kind jewelry and art. It's also the local distributor for fossil and stingray-coral patterned limestone items from Prince of Wales Island, including bookends, pens, and knives. Across the hall is **GOLDEN EAGLE GIFTS** (123 Stedman St, Ste A; 907/225-5404), where the ever helpful Elaine Johnson features such great items as ulu knives, historic local posters, Theobroma Chocolates, and Raven's Brew Coffee, a locally roasted java.

Just over the Stedman Street bridge is **HERRING COVE ORIGINALS** (229 Stedman St; 907/225-COVE (2683); www.sharronhuffman.com/linocuts.htm), a working studio and gallery owned by artist Sharron Huffman that features linocuts and gyotaku (fish rubbings) on a variety of fabrics and handmade papers.

Ketchikan is also at the forefront of the Native arts and crafts revival. Works by carvers and basket makers can be found throughout the city and on-site demonstrations are common in the summer. Tlingit carver Norman Jackson owns the charming **CARVER ON THE CREEK** (28 Creek St; 907/225-3018; www.norman jackson.com), near the Stedman Street bridge. Inside the small shop are outstanding masks, bowls, baskets, and moccasins from the finest Northwest Coast artists working today. Tshimshian artist and carver Ken Decker sells his beautiful prints, carvings, and original T-shirts at **CRAZY WOLF STUDIOS** (418 Mission St; 907/247-1661).

ADVENTURES

FISHING CHARTERS / Looking at the salmon in Ketchikan Creek inspires many visitors to try their luck at catching one. Several outlets offer fishing poles for rent near the creek and in Thomas Basin. There are also dozens of charter boats ready to take visitors out on the water for half-day and full-day excursions ($200–$400 per person). The visitors bureau (see Access and Information, above) has a list of charter operators. Another good source is **KETCHIKAN CHARTER BOATS INC.** (907/225-7291; www.ketchikancharterboats.com). The migratory salmon arrive at different times of the season, so it is best to plan your trip around what you want to catch. Freshwater trout fishing starts late in the spring, with steelhead catches best in April and May. King salmon season is May through early July, while cohos (silvers) are prominent in July and August. Pinks are caught mostly in August and September.

SAXMAN TOTEM PARK / Saxman is a Tlingit village 2 miles south of Ketchikan on the South Tongass Highway. It was created when several smaller outlying villages were abandoned in the early part of the 20th century and is named after a missionary who drowned while trying to find a site for the new village. The center of the 350-person village is a clan house and one of the world's largest collection of totem poles. The totem poles were originally carved at outlying villages and many were restored by local carvers and the federal government in the 1930s. Most of the local tour companies offer side trips to Saxman. **CAPE FOX TOURS** (tours should be booked through travel agents or cruise lines)—a subsidiary of the village corporation of Saxman—offers the most comprehensive one, with a two-hour guided tour of the poles, a carving shed, and the clan house, where visitors are treated to Native songs and dances.

TOTEM BIGHT STATE HISTORICAL PARK / Although Totem Bight (907/247-8574; www.dnr.state.ak.us/parks/units/totembgh.htm) is not an original village, it does give a sense of what the early Native communities looked like. Located on a pretty cove 10 miles north of Ketchikan on the North Tongass Highway, the site features a clan house and a large collection of totem poles, most of which were brought from old village sites as part of an effort to save the rapidly rotting poles. Traditionally, poles—made out of the relatively soft cedar wood—were not repaired once the climate began to rot them after about 50 years. It is only in recent years that old poles have been saved and pole restoration has taken place. Year-round tours at the park are self-guided and free.

DEER MOUNTAIN TRAIL / There are several trails in the area but the most popular—and one of the most strenuous—is the Deer Mountain Trail that climbs a spectacular ancient volcanic cone 3,000 feet over downtown Ketchikan. The trailhead is about a 30-minute hike—uphill—from downtown, but taxis are always available to get you there. The 3-mile trail itself rises through a series of steep switchbacks with several overlooks, the first about 50 minutes into the hike. The first two hours of the hike are spent mainly in the dark old-growth forest populated by eagles, ravens, deer, and bear. Above tree line, sunny-day views are incredible with all of Ketchikan and miles of the surrounding islands and mountains before you. There is usually snow on the upper reaches of the mountain into late July, and it can be steep and slippery. It is also not safe to wander far from the trail, as the mountain has precipitous drop-offs.

WARD LAKE RECREATION AREA / The best introduction to hiking in the area is the 1½-mile, mostly flat trail around Ward Lake, 6 miles north of Ketchikan (www.fs.fed.us/r10/naturewatch/southeast). There are numerous interpretive signs that explain the nature in the old-growth forest and visitors will often see a variety of wildlife, including swans, spawning salmon, and otters. Bears frequent the area when the salmon are running in late summer, but usually only late at night. The trail also has several picnic sites and crosses **SIGNAL CREEK CAMPGROUND** ($10 per night). A new trail is being built that will connect the Ward Lake area with the **LAST CHANCE CAMPGROUND** farther up Ward Creek. Also nearby is the 3-mile **PERSEVERANCE LAKE TRAIL**, which is primarily a boardwalk with a moderate grade.

SETTLER'S COVE STATE PARK / Near the end of the North Tongass Highway, 17 miles north of Ketchikan, is one of the local jewels. This state park has one of the best beaches in Ketchikan and several campsites ($15 per night). A brand new bridge offers spectacular creek and waterfall viewing just ¼ mile from the parking area. A series of new trails is opening up the area north of Settler's Cove for walkers and hikers. Call 907/247-8574 for information.

PUBLIC-USE CABINS / The Tongass National Forest offers dozens of recreational cabins that can be rented for a few days; there are more than 50 in the Ketchikan/Prince of Wales Island area. Rates vary between $25 and $40 a night and the most popular cabins are usually rented out months in advance. The main cost is transportation to the more remote ones. Although some can be reached by hiking trails or by boat, many require floatplane charter flights, which cost in the neighborhood of $200–$800 per person, round-trip. The cabins offer unparalleled wilderness activities such as fishing and hiking and, in some cases, nearby hot springs. Contact the Southeast Alaska Discovery Center (see Access and Information, above), or make reservations at 877/444-6777 or www.reserveusa.com.

FESTIVALS AND EVENTS

CELEBRATION OF THE NORTH / Held in February each year, this monthlong festival features concerts, plays, special programs, arts events, and poetry readings. The celebration begins with one of the favorite yearly events, the Wearable Art Show, where Ketchikan residents parade down the runway in costumes almost too spectacular to describe. Past highlights have included the Spamurai Warrior and the Hootchie Coo. Contact the Arts and Humanities Council (907/225-2211).

CELEBRATION OF THE SEA / Generally held the first week in May, this celebration is pulled together by volunteers each year and usually features tours of boats, an art contest, search-and-rescue displays, the blessing of the fleet, and historical presentations. Ask around or look for announcements.

KING SALMON DERBY / At 54 years, it's the oldest derby in the Southeast, usually held on the last weekend in May and the first two weekends in June. The winning fish is frequently in the 60-pound range and the grand prize is usually worth more than $10,000. Nearly 1,000 fishers take part each year. Contact Ketchikan Cabaret, Hotel, Restaurant and Retailers Association (907/225-2077; www.ketchikancharr.com).

FOURTH OF JULY / The big town celebration features carnival booths, a parade, a logging rodeo, model-plane demonstrations, and the legendary St. John's Church pie sale. The fireworks display has to wait until nearly midnight for enough darkness to fall. Contact the Ketchikan Chamber of Commerce (907/225-3184; www.ketchikanchamber.com).

BLUEBERRY ARTS FESTIVAL / Held the first Saturday in August, right about the time the local blueberries have reached perfection, this festival features dance (the superb Gigglefeet Festival) and music, an art show, the community spelling bee and trivia contests, numerous craft booths, the slug race, and a pie eating contest. Contact the Ketchikan Area Arts and Humanities Council (907/225-2211; www.Ketchikanarts.org).

FISH PIRATE'S DAUGHTER / Ketchikan's homegrown musical melodrama (first staged nearly 40 years ago) is held on Friday nights in the summer. Ketchikan's First City Players (907/225-4792; www.ketchikanarts.org/firstcityplayers.html) stage this "history" of Ketchikan's sporting past that features fish pirates, bootleggers, prostitutes, and, of course, a hero (Sweet William Uprightly) and a heroine (Little Nell Swenson). Audiences are encouraged to boo, hiss, and cheer to their heart's content. There is even an end of the season "gender bender" in which cast members switch roles with those of the opposite sex. Not to be missed. Call for performance dates. The theater group also gives performances of other plays during the year including the big town musical every fall. Costs vary, depending on venue.

THE GREAT ALASKAN LUMBERJACK SHOW / This show caused a few people to roll their eyes when it first opened on the downtown docks. Many a wag noted the irony in "fake" loggers celebrating an industry that was being squeezed out of the woods by changes in forest laws. But the two-hour ($30) show has become one of the most popular summer attractions with both visitors and locals alike. Sure, the competition between the American and "Canadian" loggers is pretty hokey, but there is no denying the impressive skills of the lumberjacks in such events as speed climbing, sawing, and log rolling. Lumberjacking is a fast-growing sport. The Ketchikan show was even featured on ESPN. For information, call 888/320-9049 or visit www.lumberjackshows.com/alaska/.

THE MONTHLY GRIND / No single event can define Ketchikan, but this long-running show that takes place the third Saturday of each month, September through

11

May, at the Saxman Tribal House, comes close. It resembles a community talent show in which everyone—including the audience—is a winner. Music, dance, storytelling, poetry readings, comedy, and other acts impossible to classify are wrapped around the most sinful dessert intermission imaginable. The admission is $5 per person, but if you bring a homemade dessert you'll get your money back. Contact the Ketchikan Area Arts and Humanities Council (907/225-2211; www.Ketchikan arts.org).

WINTER ARTS FAIRE / Held the weekend after Thanksgiving, this is the premier pre-Christmas shopping and crafts show. Many local artisans gear their work toward sales at this huge event that fills the Ted Ferry Civic Center each year. Contact the Ketchikan Area Arts and Humanities Council (907/225-2211; www. Ketchikanarts.org).

RESTAURANTS

Burger Queen / ★

 512 WATER ST, KETCHIKAN; 907/225-6060 Don't let the plain exterior of this small place fool you; the Burger Queen consistently serves up the tastiest fast food in town. The big, juicy burgers drip with a variety of condiments, the onion rings are piping hot and dusted with parmesan cheese, and the deep-fried halibut sandwiches are a revelation with their cornmeal-breaded fish topped with grated cheddar. The colorful side salads and fries are equally good. During peak hours there is usually a wait for one of the three booths, so call ahead or ask for free delivery. On sunny days, take your meal across the street to the waterfront park at Casey Moran Float. *$; MC; V; local checks only; lunch and early dinner Mon–Sat (summer), lunch only Mon–Tues (winter); no alcohol; next to the tunnel on Water St.* &

Diaz Cafe / ★

335 STEDMAN ST, KETCHIKAN; 907/225-2257 The Diaz family has been feeding Ketchikan families for more than half a century. Open the tiny door and step back into an old-fashioned Filipino-American diner with sparkling clean linoleum floors and Formica tables. Locals—who crowd the place for the daily lunchtime specials—joke that the yellow and red color scheme separated by a black line, matches the hot mustard/ketchup/soy sauce condiments. The chicken adobo on Wednesdays is one of the best meals in town and Thursdays bring indescribably delicious boneless pork, marinated to fork tenderness. Cheeseburgers are served with the unusual choice of fries or sweet-and-sour rice. On a rainy day, nothing beats the gigantic bowl of green soup, with its chunks of fresh ginger, pork, and egg. The sweet-and-sour halibut is also outstanding. *$; No credit cards; local checks only; lunch, dinner Tues–Sun (closed for a month from Christmas through mid-Jan); no alcohol.*

Heen Kahidi Restaurant / ★★

800 VENETIA AVE, KETCHIKAN; 907/225-8001 Located on a hillside overlooking downtown and the Tongass Narrows, the Cape Fox is blessed with one of the best views in Alaska. The lodge-style dining room, with its open beams and glass architecture, warm woods and central fireplace is the most welcoming in town. The service is warm and attentive and the large menu offers some nice variations on the usual surf and turf. This is the place to go for king crab legs, fresh oysters, and Halibut Olympia. *$$; AE, DC, DIS, MC, V; local checks only; breakfast, lunch, dinner every day; full bar; reservations recommended on weekends; in the Westcoast Cape Fox Lodge, take the tram from Creek St.* &

The New York Cafe / ★★

211 STEDMAN ST, KETCHIKAN; 907/225-0246 After several menu changes in recent years, this lively restaurant adjacent to the historic New York Hotel has finally found a winning combination. Squeeze into one of the tiny tables and enjoy fluffy pancakes, homemade bread of the Deer Mountain Deluxe, a mountain of homefries, tomatoes, onion, spinach, cheddar, and eggs. Lunch offers a delicious halibut wrap or a savory oriental chicken. Vegetarians will find the most options in town here, such as roasted seasonal vegetables over pasta, black bean burritos, or garden burgers. In the evening, enjoy the daily menu plus specially prepared dishes that usually feature local fish and fresh vegetables. In between meals, stop by for fresh pastries and the largest menu of espresso and fountain drinks in town. *$; AE, MC, V; local checks only; breakfast, lunch, dinner every day; beer and wine; just past the Stedman St bridge.*

Salmon Falls Resort / ★★

16707 N TONGASS HWY, KETCHIKAN; 907/225-2752 When you make the drive out to this lodge and restaurant, bring your binoculars; you're almost guaranteed to see seals and other marine life from the windows of this spacious octagonal restaurant overlooking Behm Canal and several small islands. The comfortable seating and carefully prepared food invite guests to linger until the sun goes down. The menu is standard Ketchikan steak-and-seafood fare, but the service is excellent and many a wedding or other special occasion is celebrated here. *$$; AE, MC, V; local checks only; breakfast, lunch, dinner every day (open mid-May to mid-Sept); full bar; reservations recommended; 16 miles north of Ketchikan on the North Tongass Hwy.* &

LODGINGS

ALASKA TRAVELERS (907/247-7117 or 800/928-3308; www.alaskatravelers.com/ketchikan.htm) is a regional reservation service offering lodging and fishing charters for several towns in the Southeast including Juneau, Sitka, and Ketchikan. Each listing provides full information on accommodations, rates, special features, and meals, accompanied by color photographs of the interiors and exteriors. You can book with confidence using the information on the Web site or call the local number to speak with the Ketchikan agent.

Blueberry Hill Bed and Breakfast / ★★

500 FRONT ST, KETCHIKAN; 907/247-2583 OR 877/449-2583; FAX 907/247-2584 This Ketchikan favorite recently changed owners and Vicki and John Zahler have continued the tradition of offering fine food and lodging in their beautifully restored 1917 residence. Vicki is a former decorator and has infused the house with a cheerful shot of color. The location, just three blocks from downtown on a quiet street, can't be beat. The first floor offers a spacious living area and break-fast room for guests to enjoy, while the four distinctive guest rooms are on the second floor. The John Muir room, a former library with built-in bookcases, is the largest. It's a corner room with a partial water view, queen-size bed, sofa sleeper, writing desk, and extra large private bath. The other rooms are smaller but have private baths and comfortable beds with vibrant quilts and cozy corners for relaxing. A hearty breakfast is served downstairs each morning and the outdoor garden is a lush oasis on nice days. Rates are $80–$145, depending on the room and the season. No smoking. $$; D, MC, V; checks OK; Stay@blueberryhillbb.com; www.blueberry hillbb.com; above the tunnel on upper Front St.

Captain's Quarters Bed and Breakfast / ★★

325 LUND ST, KETCHIKAN; 907/225-4912 Centrally located between the down-town and West End, the Captain's Quarters is within walking distance of shops, restaurants, and groceries, if you don't mind a couple of hills. Perched three streets above sea level, this attractive home features outstanding water views from the two upstairs rooms, which are decorated in soothing pastel colors with queen beds. Downstairs, there is a new room with a full kitchen. Each has a private bath, cable TV, and phone. Rates are some of the best in town, at $85 for a double in the summer and lower in the winter. No smoking. $$; MC, V; local checks only; captbnb @ptialaska.net; www.ptialaska.net/~captbnb; in a residential neighborhood near downtown, call for directions.

New York Hotel and Cafe / ★★

207 STEDMAN ST, KETCHIKAN; 907/225-0246 This tastefully restored his-toric inn (built in the 1920s) is ideally located just a few paces from the busy attractions of Creek Street. Climb the narrow stairs and you'll find eight charming rooms. Each features original woodwork, antiques, inviting queen beds covered with quilts, and gleaming tiled baths, some with claw-foot tubs. Modern amenities include phone, cable TV, and dataports. The hotel is usually full in the summer, so reservations are a must. The front rooms have nice views of Thomas Basin and the harbor while the back rooms are away from the noise of busy Stedman Street. Singles run from $69 and doubles $79 per night in the summer, less in the off-season. A fresh continental breakfast is included. The cafe serves breakfast, lunch, and dinner every day, and beer and wine is available. $; AE, MC, V; local checks only; www.thenewyorkhotel.com; downtown, just past the Stedman St bridge.

Westcoast Cape Fox Lodge / ★★★

800 VENETIA WY, KETCHIKAN; 907/225-8001 OR 800/544-0970 (RESERVA-TIONS); FAX 907/225-8286 After more than a decade in business, the Cape Fox has achieved a reputation as one of the finest hotels in Alaska. Maybe it's the gorgeous views from all sides or the genuinely nice staff. Perhaps it's the tasteful lodge-style architecture or even the fun funicular tram that deposits you in the middle of Creek Street. Whatever it is, locals and visitors love this hotel. Located at the top of a tree-covered hillside, with Deer Mountain rising behind, the Cape Fox offers a scenic getaway in the heart of downtown. The unusually large rooms are decorated with Shaker-style furniture and attractive tapestry print fabrics.

Amenities include cable TV, coffeemakers, hairdryers, ironing boards, and data-ports. Rooms overlooking the city and the harbor cost more, but the ones in back offer equally spectacular views of the snow-covered Ketchikan "alps." Room rates generally are $139 for a double, but there are a variety of discounts available. Ask about weekend specials. The hotel also features stunning displays of Alaskan Native art and handicrafts, including work by Nathan Jackson, one of Alaska's most prominent carvers. No courtesy van, so take a taxi from the airport or ferry. If you have a car, there is ample free parking at the hotel. *$$; AE, DC, DIS, MC, V; local checks only; www.capefoxcorp.com/cflodge1.html.*

WILDERNESS LODGES

Salmon Falls Resort

16707 TONGASS HWY, KETCHIKAN; 907/225-2752 OR 800/247-9059 Salmon Falls is the rare wilderness resort that is easily accessible; approximately 16 miles north of Ketchikan. Named for its spectacular adjacent waterfall, the resort offers a variety of guided and unguided fishing options as well as sight-seeing. Located up scenic Behm Canal there is a large number of resident wildlife and it is one of the few places near Ketchikan where whales are common in the summer. It is also inexpensive by lodge standards, with three-day stays beginning at just under $1,000 per person. Courtesy transportation is available and its restaurant is one of the best in Ketchikan, with stunning sunset views. *$$$$; AE, MC, V; local checks only; closed mid-Sept through mid-May; www.salmonfallsresort.net; 16 miles north of Ketchikan, near the end of North Tongass Hwy.*

Waterfall Resort

PO BOX 6440, KETCHIKAN AK 99901; 907/225-8530 OR 800/544-5125 If world class is what you're looking for, Waterfall Resort is for you. The restored cannery is a favorite of celebrities and captains of industry who cheerfully stay in the sumptuously renovated cabins that once housed the lowly cannery workers. The largest salt-water resort in Alaska has a staff-to-guest ratio of 1 to 1 for each of the 84 guests. Here you can fish for salmon—truly world-class salmon fishing, capped off by a $100,000 tourney that is usually won by king salmon in the 70-pound range. But even though the lodge caters to the super-serious sports fishermen, it also does right by the novices, who are happy to catch their fish, get their picture taken with it, and then go on to other activities. Three days of world-class fishing, world-class dining, and world-class service will generally set you back at least $3,000 per person, but visitors in early June can often stay at the resort for as little as $1,700 per person, which includes the 60-mile floatplane trip from Ketchikan. *$$$$; Cash only; closed Sept to May; www.waterfallresort.com.*

Yes Bay Lodge

PO BOX 8660, KETCHIKAN AK 99901; 907/225-7906 OR 800/999-0784; FAX 907/225-3816 Originally built in the 1950s as a casino and brothel (before both were outlawed at statehood in 1959), the Yes Bay Lodge is one of Alaska's finest small lodges, with no more than 24 guests a time. Located a 20-minute floatplane ride from Ketchikan, on the western end of Behm Canal, prices begin at $2,700 per person for a four-day stay. Cost includes the floatplane trip. All rooms have private bathrooms, and there is a dining room overlooking beautiful Yes Bay, a game room, gift shop, and exercise room. *$$$; No credit cards; checks OK; closed Sept through late May; info@yesbay.com; www.yesbay.com.*

Misty Fjords National Monument

When this 2.3-million-acre preserve, 20 miles east of Ketchikan, was set aside by presidential decree in 1978, many people wondered what value a large tract of mostly wilderness would have to the area economy. Now, as dozens of floatplanes carry hundreds of visitors each summer day to see the monument, they have their answer.

The cliffs of the deep-water fjords that were carved by glaciers 10,000 years ago rise to heights of 3,000 feet and above and are frequently shrouded in mist, thus the name of the monument. **PUNCHBOWL COVE,** with its vertical granite walls, is called the Yosemite of the North. Unfortunately, the area's sudden popularity is coming at the expense of its spectacular solitude. The popular areas of the monument do indeed resemble the popular areas of Yosemite, and the Forest Service is working on plans to limit the flight-seeing and small-cruise-boat visitors.

ACCESS AND INFORMATION

For the time being, there are a variety of flight-seeing and boating options for the monument. The best flight-seeing companies are **ISLAND WINGS AIR SERVICE** (888/854-2444; www.islandwings.com), **FAMILY AIR TOURS** (800/380-1305; www.familyairtours.com), and **SOUTHEAST AVIATION** (907/225-2900; www.southeastaviation.com). Prices range from $150–$300 round-trip. **ALASKA CRUISES** (800/228-1905; www.goldbelt.com/subsidiaries/ak_cruises.html) offers a variety of boat/plane or boat round-trip tours, from $150–$200 per person. **SOUTHEAST EXPOSURE** (907/225-8829 or 907/783-2377 mid-Oct to early Apr; www.southeastexposure.com) offers four- and eight-day sea kayak trips ranging from $700–$900 per person.

For information about Misty Fjords and cabin-use in the monument, contact the **U.S. FOREST SERVICE** (3031 Tongass Ave, Ketchikan AK 99901; www.fs.fed.us/r10/tongass/) or the **SOUTHEAST ALASKA DISCOVERY CENTER** (see Ketchikan, Access and Information). Nearly all of Misty Fjords is wilderness area, and there are **NO VISITOR FACILITIES** here. You must bring everything you'll need for wilderness camping, including plenty of rain gear, even if the weather looked good back in town. Consult with locals on weather, water, boats, safety, itinerary, and the skills necessary to enjoy the area.

Prince of Wales Island

Residents of Ketchikan often refer to Prince of Wales as "the big island." At more than 2,200 square miles, it is larger than some states and is the third largest island under the American flag. Only Kodiak Island and the Big Island of Hawaii are larger.

But more importantly, Prince of Wales Island has a larger road system (more than 1,500 miles) than all the other communities in Southeast Alaska combined.

This road system is the key to enjoying an island that residents consider the "real Alaska"—small, previously isolated communities just beginning to experience the interconnectedness of more urban parts of the state. Because of this, Prince of Wales couples small-town charm with a visitor industry just starting to provide services. That means accommodations may not be four star outside the communities of Craig or Klawock. Indeed, accommodations frequently are very rustic. But visitors will find a truly authentic Alaskan experience.

The original inhabitants of the island were the Tlingit Indians who have lived throughout Southeast Alaska since the last Ice Age. In the last 250 years, Haida Natives from the Queen Charlotte Islands crossed over Dixon Entrance to establish villages on the southern shores of Prince of Wales and neighboring islands. Shortly after the United States purchased the territory from Russia in 1867, one of the first canneries in the state was built in Klawock. Like other parts of the region, there was a lot of mineral exploration and, over the years, communities sprang up and usually passed quickly over gold, copper, and uranium strikes. There have also been significant marble quarries on the island that have provided stone for many public buildings throughout the western United States.

The real growth of Prince of Wales Island (which approaches 8,000 residents) is due to fishing and timber. The older communities—primarily on the island's west side—are tied to the fishing industry, which boomed in the first half of the 20th century. Many of the smaller east-side communities—such as Coffman Cove, Whale Pass, Hollis, and Thorne Bay—began life as logging camps in the 1950s and 1960s.

There are three significant **NATIVE VILLAGES** on Prince of Wales; Klawock, Hydaburg, and Kasaan. Klawock has one of the largest collections of authentic totem poles in Alaska. Kasaan's Chief Son-I-Hat's Tribal House was recently added to the National Register of Historic Places. And Hydaburg was formed when three smaller villages were combined early in the last century. All three communities have active fishing fleets.

The island's lengthy **ROAD SYSTEM** is a direct benefit of the timber industry. Visitors arrive at the Inter-Island Ferry Terminal in **HOLLIS** and can drive 30 miles south to **HYDABURG,** 30 miles west to **CRAIG** and **KLAWOCK,** 50 miles northeast to **THORNE BAY,** and nearly 100 miles north to the **EL CAPITAN** area. When these roads were first built, they were narrow, bumpy logging roads. A 30-mile trip could take several hours. But now the Federal Highway Administration is in the process of improving them. Hollis to Hydaburg and Hollis to Craig are paved, making the journey a comfortable 40 minutes. Work is currently taking place on the road between Klawock and Thorne Bay, with paving expected in the next two years. North of Thorne Bay toward Whale Pass, Naukiti, and El Capitan, roads remain rugged at best, and a four-wheel-drive or high-clearance vehicle is a necessity.

Since these roads were created for the timber industry, they often cut through areas that were heavily logged in the last 50 years. Sometimes the view is not as pretty as one would like. On the other hand, the oldest cuts, near Hollis, are some 50 years old and have experienced significant growth. It is also worth noting that logging on the island's public lands has been drastically reduced due to changes in federal forest policy in the last decade. Visitors are unlikely to see any new logging under way, except on private land owned by the regional and village Native corporations. There also remains significant wilderness on Prince of Wales, some of which is accessible from the road system. The Forest Service also has numerous cabins and several campgrounds that can be reached by road.

ACCESS AND INFORMATION

In the past, visitors to Prince of Wales had to rely on expensive charter planes or boats to reach the island, but the new **INTER-ISLAND FERRY AUTHORITY** (866/308-4848; www.interislandferry.com) has made the island a viable option for travelers in all price ranges. The ferry authority provides one round-trip each winter day between Ketchikan and Hollis and two round-trips daily between May and September (the trip is 30 miles and takes three hours). **PACIFIC AIRWAYS** (877/360-3500; www.flypacificairways.com) also offers daily service to the island.

For the most up-to-date information, check out the **PRINCE OF WALES CHAMBER OF COMMERCE** (PO Box 497, Craig AK 99921; 907/826-3870; www. princeofwalescoc.org). Businesses offering accommodations and other services are in their infancy, and go out of business or change hands and services frequently. Always call ahead and make reservations well in advance. The chamber also publishes a yearly guidebook that covers all the communities on the island (and a few on neighboring islands) that is extremely helpful in planning a trip to the area.

ADVENTURES

CAMPING AND PUBLIC-USE CABINS / Prince of Wales has 19 Forest Service cabins and several fine campgrounds. Craig, Klawock, and Coffman Cove also have RV accommodations. The **HARRIS RIVER CAMPGROUND** (located on the Hollis-Craig Highway) is particularly scenic and is also near the junction for the road to Hydaburg. For more information about camping options, contact the **CRAIG RANGER DISTRICT** (907/828-3271) or the **THORNE BAY RANGER DISTRICT** (907/828-3309).

TRAILS / There are 16 developed hiking trails on the island, as well as scenic canoe routes at Sakar and Honker Divide. One of the most spectacular natural resources of Prince of Wales Island is its system of caves in the El Capitan area in the northern part of the island. Between late May and early September, the caves are open to the public. The Forest Service gives guided tours of the **EL CAPITAN CAVE** (one of the deepest in the world) during summer months, but be warned: the trail is steep and strenuous and features 370 boardwalk steps. Reservations must be made at least two days in advance with the Thorne Bay Ranger District (see above). Contact either Forest Service district for more information on hiking trails (see above).

FESTIVALS AND EVENTS

THE PRINCE OF WALES ISLAND INTERNATIONAL MARATHON (contact the Prince of Wales Chamber of Commerce, above) takes place along the road between Hollis and Craig on Memorial Day weekend, attracting several hundred runners. For fishing enthusiasts, the **CRAIG/KLAWOCK SALMON DERBY** (907/826-3579) takes places from April to July each year. The **THORNE BAY SALMON DERBY**

(907/828-3455) takes place from May to June. The **CELEBRATION OF THE SEA ARTS AND CRAFTS FAIR** (contact Craig Parks and Recreation; 907/826-2575) is held in late May, and is one of the island's biggest shopping events. **THE PRINCE OF WALES FAIR AND LOGGING SHOW** (contact Prince of Wales Chamber of Commerce, above) is the island's largest celebration, drawing residents from all over the island. It usually takes place the last weekend in July in Thorne Bay and offers one of the best small timber shows anywhere. **THE BLACK-TAILED DEER HUNTING SEASON** runs from August to December and draws large numbers of hunters taking advantage of the logging roads; **BLACK BEAR HUNTING SEASON** runs from September to May. For more information contact the Alaska Department of Fish and Game (907/826-2560).

RESTAURANTS

Dockside Café

154 FRONT ST, CRAIG; 907/826-5544 Inside this small log cabin, you'll find a handful of tables and the best home cooking in town: standard short-order fare, hamburgers, sandwiches, steaks and chops, and the best pies in the Southeast. Owner Karen Howard perfected her recipes years ago in Sitka and now offers up to 13 pie varieties daily, including a wonderful chocolate-peanut confection. *$; AE, MC, V; checks OK; breakfast, lunch every day, dinner Thurs–Sat; no alcohol.*

Papa's Pizza

WESTWIND PLAZA, CRAIG; 907/826-2244 This Craig favorite serves appetizers, salads, hot sandwiches, and delicious hand-tossed pizza. The freshly prepared toppings are plentiful and varied. The Pesto Gourmet with garlic and artichoke hearts is a yuppie favorite. Hearty eaters enjoy the combo with everything or the imaginative New York Blue that pairs steak, onions, and mushrooms with blue cheese dressing. You can dine in the casual restaurant, take out, or have the meal delivered. *$; MC, V; lunch, dinner every day (longer hours on weekends); wine and beer.*

LODGINGS

In recent years, many B&Bs have sprung up in Craig and other island communities. There are also several hunting and fishing resorts. The best accommodations can be found on the **PRINCE OF WALES CHAMBER OF COMMERCE** Web site (www.prince ofwalescoc.org). Another good source is **ALASKA RENTALS** (907/826-3468 or 800/720-3468; www.alaskarentals.com), which features a wide variety of vacation homes and charter boats.

Dreamcatcher Bed & Breakfast

1405 HAMILTON DR, CRAIG; 907/826-2238; FAX 907/826-2250 When Alaskans come to Craig this is their favorite B&B. Owners Ken Owen and his children Alexandra and Lewis Owen offer three rooms in their spacious home, which is conveniently located near downtown just steps from a waterfront park and walking path. Step upstairs to your private entrance to find inviting king or queen beds covered with crisp hunter green–checked bedding, cable TV, phone, and a spotless private bath. Two of the rooms also have a double futon for additional guests. The modest rates, $65–$95 depending upon the number of guests and the season, include a self-serve continental breakfast. No smoking. *$; AE, MC, V; checks OK; dreambb@aptalaska.net; www.AlaskaOne.com/dreambb.*

Lupine Pension

607 OCEAN VIEW, CRAIG; 907/826-3851 OR 888/546-3851 Hosts Dave and Pauline Johnson rent a small apartment with a separate entrance in their spacious home that is ideal for families or larger groups traveling to Craig. The apartment has a living room with a sofa sleeper, full kitchen, and two bedrooms. The decor is not fancy, but you'll find everything you need to set up housekeeping, including complementary instant beverages. Rates are $75–$120 per night, depending on the season and the number of guests. *$–$$; MC, V; local checks only; rkjohn@aptalaska.net; www.aptalaska.net/~rkjohn/.*

McFarland's Floatel

PO BOX 19149, THORNE BAY AK 99919; 888/828-3335 Located 2 miles from Thorne Bay, the Floatel is an accessible yet remote experience. You either arrive by boat or plane, but Jim and Jeannie McFarland will make sure you can get there once you arrive in Thorne Bay. There are four deluxe beachfront cabins with lodge-style accoutrements, kitchen supplies, propane stoves, refrigerators, and modern bathrooms with showers. B&B accommodations are also available. The Floatel itself, at the end of a 200-foot dock, has evolved from accommodations into a marine, sporting goods, and basketry store. A 30-foot boat is available for charter, and skiffs can be rented. Tours of the local beaches are also offered. Rates range from $80 per night for B&B rooms to $240 to rent one of the deluxe cottages. *$–$$; MC, V; local checks only; floatel@aptalaska.net; www.mcfarlandsfloatel.com.*

Ruth Ann's Hotel and Restaurant

FRONT ST, CRAIG; 907/826-3378 Ruth Ann's is the lone traditional hotel on the island and dominates the downtown Craig waterfront. In 25 years, the operation has grown to encompass three buildings. The main building houses a special honeymoon suite and a full-service restaurant (fine dining but high priced) that offers spectacular waterfront views and a bar. Across the street is a building with four spacious suites, with a common deck and a waterfront view. Each has a kitchenette and two queen beds. If you have an aversion to dead animal heads staring back you, ask for one of the rooms with the fish motif. The renovated cannery bunkhouse is half a block away and contains 10 cozy rooms decorated with old-fashioned pink and green floral prints, wicker, and quilts. All rooms have private bath, refrigerator, cable TV, and phone. Double occupancy rates range from $75–$125. *$$; MC, V; checks OK; RuthAnns@aptalaska.net.*

Sitka

To fully appreciate this lovely town on the western edge of Baranof Island, it is important to know something of its rich history. When Chicago was merely a fort town in the middle of the prairies and San Francisco a small mission, Sitka was hailed as the "Paris of the West." Ships docked here from all over the world. Today only 8,500 people live in Sitka year-round. But the modest population is a large part of her charm.

For many years, Sitka was the capital of Russian America. In the center of town, dominating the low skyline, is the onion-shaped dome of the old wooden church known as St. Michael's Cathedral. As the ironies of history often unfold, the fortunes and legacy of an empire here rose and fell on a funny, bewhiskered fellow—the sea otter.

Alaska was once a treasure chest of sea otters. To the Russian hunters, this creature's fur was known as "soft gold," and the pelts brought high prices in the courts of China. But as the sea otters began to disappear, hunted to near extinction, Russia's interest in her far-flung colony began to wane. In 1867, the advice given the czar was "Sell! Sell the colony before someone takes it by force." So after 126 years of rule in this wilderness outpost, Russia sold her colony to the Americans under a storm of controversy here at home. There were many who thought Russia had sold us "a sucked orange," a land of icebergs and polar bears, a wasteland of no consequence. But history has proven much to the contrary. The purchase price of Alaska—$7.2 million—has been recouped many times over—in furs, fish, timber, gold, oil, and, today, tourism.

Sitka was home to the Tlingit Indians before the Russians, however, and today it is the blending and preservation of the history of both cultures that gives the town its unique flavor. Sitka's economy is now founded primarily on fishing and tourism. It has a beautiful setting, with sparkling waters, emerald islands, rocky beaches, and a safe harbor for ships. Even though thousands of cruise ship tourists land on shore every week in the summer, Sitka manages to maintain its individual character and charm.

ACCESS AND INFORMATION

Sitka lies on the west side of Baranof Island. As with most Southeast towns, there are no roads to Sitka. Access is **BY AIR** or sea. Alaska Airlines (800/252-7522; www.alaskaair.com) has scheduled flights daily, north and south, summer and winter. The **ALASKA MARINE HIGHWAY** (907/747-8737 or 800/642-0066; www.alaska.gov/ferry) has ferry service to Sitka throughout the year from ports in Alaska, Canada, and Washington. (It takes about three days of cruising to reach Sitka from Bellingham, Washington, 88 miles north of Seattle, and about 18 hours from Prince Rupert in Canada.) The ferry terminal is located about 6 miles north of town, near the end of Halibut Point Road. From downtown Sitka, the road extends about 7 miles in either direction. Rental cars are available at the airport. The airport is only 5 minutes or so from downtown Sitka, and there is a limousine service that runs year-round ($5 round-trip). A local **AIR CHARTER** operation is Harris Air Service (907/966-3050; harrisaircraft@worldnet.att.net; www.harrisaircraft.com).

Stop first at the **HARRIGAN CENTENNIAL HALL VISITORS INFORMATION** booth (330 Harbor Dr; 907/747-3225; fax 907/747-8495; donk@cityofsitka.com; www.cityofsitka.com). It is located in the heart of downtown, inside the Centennial Hall at the edge of the harbor. For more information, contact the **SITKA CONVENTION AND VISITORS BUREAU** (303 Lincoln St, PO Box 1226, Sitka AK 99835; 907/747-5940; fax 907/747-3735; scvb@sitka.org; www.sitka.org). **OLD HARBOR**

BOOKSTORE (201 Lincoln St, Sitka AK 99835; 907/747-8808; fax 907/747-8813; oldharbr@ptialaska.net) in the downtown district has a wonderful array of books on Sitka, the Southeast, and Alaska, and also sells nautical charts.

The **TONGASS NATIONAL FOREST'S SITKA RANGER DISTRICT** (204 Siginaka Wy, Sitka AK 99835; 907/747-6671; fax 907/747-4331; www.fs.fed.us/r10/tongass/districts/sitka/sitka.html) has information about recreational opportunities and a brochure about public-use cabins on beaches, mountain lakes, and remote islands in the national forest. Cost for cabin rentals is $35–$45 per night—a great deal. For cabin reservations, call the national reservation line (877/444-6777) or check www.reserveusa.com. The **ALASKA DEPARTMENT OF FISH AND GAME** (304 Lake St, Rm 103, Sitka AK 99835; 907/747-5355 or 907/747-5449; www.state.ak.us/local/akpages/fish.game) is a good source of information on fishing and hunting in the area, regulations, seasons, and licenses.

EXPLORING

ALASKA RAPTOR REHABILITATION CENTER / Volta collided with a powerline. Contact hit an airplane. Elder got trapped in barbed wire while trying to steal ducks. Beauty is from Kodiak and Midi can't fly. While these five unfortunates are all bald eagles, many other raptors live here, including golden eagles, and a variety of hawks, owls, and falcons. "Help Us Help the Birds!" is the slogan used by the center, which receives no state or federal funding. Your contributions support the work at Alaska's premier raptor rehab center and help these "patients" return to the wild. About 80 percent of the injuries these birds have suffered are human-caused by such things as bullets, traps, oil slicks, and the like. Presentations and tours are given 8am–4pm, Monday through Friday, May through September. The center is located along Sawmill Creek Road, a 10-minute walk from the historical park (see below). Cost is $10 for adults; $5 for children. *1101 Sawmill Creek Rd; 907/747-8662; fax 907/747-8397; programs.alaskaraptor@alaska.com; www.alaskaraptor.org.*

BALD EAGLE SIGHTINGS / OK, get ready. We're about to—gasp!—give **MCDONALD'S** Golden Arches its first four-star rating ever (at least in this guidebook series). It's not, however, for its Big Mac, but for its parking lot, which is the best place in town to see wild bald eagles. The tree and beach at low tide are often jammed with 30 or more eagles. Head north from town (about 1.5 miles) on Halibut Point Road. This area is also great for sunsets.

SHELDON JACKSON MUSEUM / On the campus of Sheldon Jackson College, 5 minutes from Sitka National Historical Park (see below), the Sheldon Jackson Museum is an octagonal treasure box crammed full of beautiful Native tools, art, boats, and clothing, the artistry of which you may not find anywhere else in Alaska. Despite its close physical association with the college, the museum is actually part of the Alaska State Museum system. Both college and museum are named for the 5-foot-tall, feisty Presbyterian missionary Sheldon Jackson, who came to Alaska in 1877. He lobbied vigorously in Congress for funds to educate Native peoples; he was responsible for the "school ma'am schooner," which transported teachers into rural Alaska; and he helped import the first reindeer herds to what was then the Territory of Alaska to fend off widespread starvation in the villages. Many of the treasures in this museum come from his early journeys to Native villages. The cost is $4 for adults, free for those 18 or younger. *Open daily 9am–5pm mid-May through mid-Sept, 10am–4pm Tues–Sat the rest of the year; 104 College Dr; 907/747-6233; fax 907/747-3004; www.museums.state.ak.us.*

SITKA NATIONAL HISTORICAL PARK / Do not miss this gem of a national park, located at the end of town, about a 10-minute walk from the cruise ship dock. A **MUSEUM** houses beautifully displayed cultural treasures, but the real treasure is along the 2-mile trail through the **TOTEM POLE PARK,** which weaves through the coastal rain forest and along the beach. The carved cedar totem poles blend so well into the woods that the faces of frogs, ravens, whales, and other creatures appearing out of the mist seem magical. Most of the totems standing along the park's trails are reproductions of the original poles brought to Sitka at the start of the 20th century by Territorial Governor John G. Brady. There's also a large, open meadow where a Tlingit fort once stood. Adding to the forest's magic are the screech of eagle, caw of raven, and warbled song of hermit thrush and winter wren. The **VISITOR CENTER** is also home to master artists from Southeast Indian clans. You can watch them working—making mountain goat wool, spruce tree roots, abalone shells, and cedar bark into masks, ceremonial regalia, robes, jewelry, and other traditional artworks. The park and visitor center are open year-round.

One of the few surviving examples of Russian colonial architecture in North America, the **RUSSIAN BISHOP'S HOUSE** is also part of the park. It stands near the heart of downtown on Lincoln Street. Built in the 1840s by Finnish shipwrights, the house was elaborately restored in the 1980s at a cost of $5 million, all from private donations. The first resident of the house was Ivan Veniaminov, known as Bishop Innocent, and later canonized as St. Innocent. The bishop was an impressive man. Wherever he was, he learned the local dialects, paddled hundreds of miles by kayak to the farthest islands of his parish, and built chapels; later he built St. Michael's Cathedral. Note the clock he invented and built, which keeps accurate time with the dripping of water. From May to October, the Bishop's House is open daily; in winter, it is open by appointment. For more information, contact Sitka National Historical Park (106 Metlakatla St, Sitka AK 99835; 907/747-6281; fax 907/747-5938; www.nps.gov/sitk).

SITKA WALKING TOUR (GUIDED) / This is not a generic title, so don't get confused. Of all the guided tours in Sitka, this is the best. With her love of stories and nature, longtime resident Jane Eidler gives her walking tours a personable and humorous twist. She worked for both the National Park Service and the U.S. Forest Service in Alaska as a ranger/naturalist before settling in Sitka more than 20 years ago to raise her family. The tour is historical and anecdotal, which, to quote that time-honored newsman Paul Harvey, tells "the rest of the story." Rain or shine, Jane or substitute guide Lisa Busch will give you the behind-the-scenes of Sitka, and then point you in the right direction to explore the Sitka National Historical Park on your own. Tours start at the Centennial Hall; times vary. Cost is $10 per person for the one-hour tour. For information, call Jane at 907/747-5354.

SITKA WALKING TOUR (SELF-GUIDED) / If you miss Jane's tour or prefer to strike out on your own, here are a few of the highlights of any walk around Sitka. First, look for the unmistakable onion-shaped dome spires of **ST. MICHAEL'S**

CATHEDRAL (on Lincoln St, in the center of town; 907/747-8120). The cathedral burned to the ground in a 1966 fire. Bucket brigades saved precious icons, and 10 years later it was rebuilt to the original design. The **HARRIGAN CENTENNIAL HALL** (Harbor Dr, on the waterfront, next to Crescent Harbor) offers some wonderful shows throughout the summer, including the Sitka Summer Music Festival and the all-women New Archangel Dancers (see Festivals and Events, below) who celebrate the town's Russian past with folk dances from the old country. Next door is **THE LIBRARY** (next door to Centennial Hall), is a haunt of bookworms and, believe it or not, brides. With a beautiful view of Sitka Sound through its windows, the library is popular for weddings as well as an attractive place to read or do research.

A 5-minute walk along Harbor Drive and up the stairs to **CASTLE HILL** offers a commanding view of the sea, mountains, and islands. This was the original village site for the Tlingit people before the arrival of the Russian invaders. Old Russian cannons punctuate the circular stone wall where once stood the governor's residence known as Baranov's Castle, named for the first governor of Russian America. Baranov himself never lived here. But many of the 13 Russian governors who followed him to Alaska did. The **SITKA PIONEER HOME** (the corner of Lincoln and Katlian) is a state nursing home for elderly Alaskans. The gardens are brilliant with colorful flowers and visitors are always welcome. Up the hill is the **RUSSIAN BLOCKHOUSE** (behind the Pioneer Home on Katlian St); built of logs, it's a replica of the blockhouse that was part of the fort and stockade dividing the Tlingit and Russian sections of Old Sitka. Surrounding it is the peaceful **RUSSIAN GRAVEYARD**. Look for the old stone Russian crosses.

GOVERNORS WALK is the old name for the promenade along Sitka's main street (Lincoln St) from Castle Hill along the waterfront to the woods by Indian River; the walk takes about 15 minutes. This forested area is now **SITKA NATIONAL HISTORICAL PARK** (see above). On the way, you will pass the **BISHOP'S HOUSE** and **SHELDON JACKSON MUSEUM** (see above).

STA (SITKA TRIBE OF ALASKA) COMMUNITY HOUSE: SHEET'KA KWAAN NAA KAHIDI / The name means "House for All the People of Sitka." Owned by the Sitka Tribe of Alaska, the Community House hosts dance and storytelling performances throughout the summer. As one young Native guide explained, "This was a 200-year dream of the Tlingit people of Sitka. We celebrated the first anniversary of the Community House completion in 1998 with sacred songs and dances to thank the tree spirits since we had taken a lot of wood for the building. We try to stay in balance with nature—bad things happen when one is not in balance with nature." The building is lovely, with an impressive entrance and totems and carvings. Designed in the style of the traditional clan house, it features tiered seating inside around a fire pit and a house screen in the back. In 1879, clan houses would have lined Katlian Street. Here, you will hear history from the Tlingit point of view. For instance, Castle Hill was known as "Noow Tlein" and used to have a clan house sitting on top before the Russians came; Old Sitka was known as "Gajaa Heen," the name of the river where salmon return. *200 Katlian; 907/747-7137 or 907/747-7290; fax 907/747-3770; www.sitkatribal.com; a short walk from the center of downtown.*

SHOPPING

Named for the Sitka rosebush that blooms out front, the **SITKA ROSE GALLERY** (419 Lincoln St; 907/747-3030; sitkarosegallery@alaska.com; www.sitkarose gallery.com) is a lovely little gallery situated in a quaint Victorian house across from the harbor. The little turreted building is 100 years old and a piece of art in itself. Owners Eugene Solovyov and his wife, Barbara Kendall, feature sculpture, painting, and Native art, representing 100 artists around Alaska. **"THE ROSE BUD"** (120 Lincoln St) is the nickname of a smaller version of the gallery located four blocks west.

For the best chocolate in Southeast Alaska, stop in the **CHOCOLATE MOOSE** (104 Lincoln St; 907/747-5159; chomoose@ptialaska.net). They have a variety of freshly made fudge, chocolate fish, specialty teas, and good espresso. Owner Cay Wood also runs a florist shop, **SITKA FLOWERS,** in the same downtown location.

With its rich assortment of Russian and Alaskan handicrafts, **THE RUSSIAN AMERICAN COMPANY** (407 Lincoln St; 907/747-6228; www.russianamerican company.com) is upstairs at the MacDonald Bayview Trading Company in downtown Sitka. A tribute to one part of Sitka's heritage, it has some gorgeous and colorful items, from handpainted lacquered boxes to religious icons and nesting dolls.

Hands down, the **NUGGET RESTAURANT** (907/966-2480 or 800/764-2480) at the Sitka Airport has the best pies in town. You often will see folks boarding planes with the telltale bakery boxes tucked under their arms for pie-lovers back home. Some of the most popular, available in season, are strawberry, banana-coconut, blackberry-rhubarb, chocolate "moose," and cherry crisp.

Step into the old bowling alley, **LANE 7 SNACK BAR** (331 Lincoln St; 907/747-6310), in the heart of downtown and belly up to the bar for the best milkshakes in town. At **HIGHLINER COFFEE CO.** (Seward Square Mall, 327 Seward St; 907/747-4924; highlinercoffee@gci.net), one block north of the Shee Atika Hotel, you can drink fresh-roasted espresso (they roast their own coffee here) and choose from a selection of yummy treats, while you check your e-mail. The baked goods are homemade and delicious. Try Norwegian krumkaka, Pumpkin Extreme Cake, or the popular "mookies," which are a cross between a muffin and a cookie, with cranberries, oatmeal, and walnuts. A **CYBER CAFE** as well as an upscale coffeehouse, Highliner, through both its name and the photos on the walls, is a tribute to Sitka's fishing industry. Its high-energy owner, Melissa Thorsen-Broschat, is a fourth-generation Alaskan and former fisherwoman from Petersburg.

ADVENTURES

BIKE AND SCUBA GEAR RENTALS / If you love to bike and are looking for a different kind of adventure, call Bill Hughes, the enthusiastic and imaginative owner of **YELLOW JERSEY CYCLE** (across from Centennial Hall, 101 Harbor Dr; 907/747-6317; yellow_jersey_cycles@yahoo.com; www.geocities.com/yellow_jersey_cycles). He'll rent you top-quality mountain bikes and gear and point you in the direction of some wonderful excursions, past black sand beaches, up the cylinder cone of an extinct volcano, or on old logging roads watching for brown bears and nesting eagles. Bikes rent for $25 a day at this full-service bike shop. Want to get under the water you biked by? **SOUTHEAST DIVING AND SPORTS** (near the Russian Bishop's House off Lincoln St, 105 Monastery St; 907/747-8279) can outfit and advise you (call for rates). The waters can be very colorful in spring, when the plankton are blooming, but visibility is best in winter months, say locals. The water is always cold. The shop also rents mountain bikes for knocking about town.

KAYAK RENTALS / Get out on the water. Go anywhere. With all the islands in Sitka Sound and the proximity to Olga and Neva Straits, the paddling around Sitka is quite protected, despite its location on the outer coast of the Panhandle. Rent a kayak from Eric Stromme at **BAIDARKA BOATS** (320 Seward St; 907/747-8996; fax 907/747-4801; www.kayaksite.com), in business since 1977. Reasonable rates range from $35 (single kayak, half day) to $95 (folding double kayak, full day); higher-cost multiday rentals are also available. They give a good orientation on paddling and safety skills, and they can also arrange fly-in trips with their folding kayaks.

HIKING / Whether you go on a short hike or a long one, plan for wet, cool weather. And remember: this is **BROWN BEAR COUNTRY**. Don't let that keep you from enjoying the woods, but be alert. The buddy system always makes good sense. If you do go alone, sing, recite poetry, whistle, or make other noise occasionally, particularly in deep grass, thick brush, bends in the trail, or when the streams are filled with salmon and the hills are covered with berries. Bears love both. Unless you surprise them, mistakenly get between a mother and her cubs, stumble on a bear's food cache, or have the great misfortune to encounter a bear with a toothache, for the most part, any bear will be more frightened of you than you are of it. With that in mind, here are some popular hikes in the Sitka area. The **U.S. FOREST SERVICE, SITKA RANGER DISTRICT** (204 Siginaka Wy; 907/747-6671; www.fs.fed. us/r10/tongass/districts/sitka/sitka.html) has a full listing of hikes and directions.

GAVAN HILL TRAIL will get you up high into the forested mountains that overlook Sitka. The trail begins at the edge of downtown; the marked trailhead is just past the house at 508 Baranof Street. It takes about three hours to make the steep climb to the summit, at 2,505 feet. A plank trail, mainly wooden stairs, has been built all the way up, and the kids in town call it "The Stairmaster." Watch your knees going up and down. You are pretty much in the trees until about three-quarters of the way up. But at the top are gorgeous, flowered alpine meadows and a beautiful view of the water and islands. (*Gavan* in Russian means "harbor.")

HARBOR MOUNTAIN RIDGE TRAIL is the hike to do on a clear day. The views are spectacular. Drive 4 miles north of town along Halibut Point Road, turn right, and go 5 miles up Harbor Mountain Road, which was built during World War II as an access to a military lookout. The trail begins where the road ends and wanders 2 miles along ridges and alpine meadows. It takes two hours one-way. The end of the trail intersects with the Gavan Hill Trail (above). If you really want to make it a day, you can continue down Gavan Hill and end up back in Sitka. If you have buddies who want to start from the opposite direction, you can pass car keys and meet back in town for a beer.

If it's a cloudy day, the **INDIAN RIVER TRAIL** is the perfect riverside hike. You can walk to the trailhead from downtown. Head east along Sawmill Creek Road to Indian River Road (the next road east of the Troopers Academy driveway). The trail begins just west of the pumphouse, about ½ mile along the road. The trail is flat, wandering through typical, lush rain forest and alongside muskeg meadows. The falls are about 5 miles in. Walk softly and you may see deer or sometimes bear.

MOUNT EDGECUMBE TRAIL leads to the top of Mount Edgecumbe, the volcano that is one of Sitka's most stunning landmarks. This hike is good on a sunny day, but don't try to do the approach and hike in one day. You need a skiff to get to the trailhead on Kruzof Island, about 10 miles west of Sitka. Ask at the visitor center in Sitka about rentals. The trail begins behind Fred's Creek Cabin and is wet and muddy in places and steep for the last 3 miles. It's about 7 miles one way and will take you about five hours to get to the summit. Reserve the cabin through the U.S. Forest Service's national reservation line or Web site (877/444-6777; www.reserve usa.com) for a few nights, so you won't have such a long journey back. The best time to go is mid-July, when the snow in the crater has all melted and leaves a warm, shallow lake for swimming. Too early, it's all snow; too late, and it's all evaporated.

TO THE ENDS OF THE ROAD / From downtown Sitka, the road runs about 7 miles to the north and 7 miles to the east. If you have access to wheels, it's great for biking or a scenic drive. To the north, **FOLLOW HALIBUT POINT ROAD**. Near the end of the road is the site of the Russians' first fort on the island. Nature and bird lovers won't want to miss the **STARRIGAVAN BIRD VIEWING PLATFORM**, on the right side of the road, just past Old Sitka. (*Starrigavan* in Russian means "old harbor.") There is a beautifully designed boardwalk and interpretive trail about the life of the estuary at Starrigavan Bay.

To the east of downtown Sitka, follow **SAWMILL CREEK ROAD**, which extends about 5 miles out to Herring Cove. Near the end of the road, there is a dirt road to Blue Lake, then, at the very end, another dirt road that continues to Green Lake. It's a perfect mountain-bike ride. **WHALE PARK**, 3 miles out, sits on the edge of the cliff and is an excellent spot for peaceful picnicking and whale-watching. Frolicking whale sculptures welcome you to a series of artful wooden gazebos, boardwalks, and stairways to the beach.

GUIDES AND OUTFITTERS

HARBOR MOUNTAIN TOURS / If it's a beautiful day and you're not into serious aerobic activity, consider taking a ride with a former fisherman who survived one of Alaska's wildest fishing adventures. Your guide, Howard "Howie" Ulrich, is not only famous, but a character to boot. He also has the only Forest Service permit to drive you up the old military dirt road for spectacular views of Sitka and the surrounding jagged mountains and islands. The trip lasts about three hours. If you want, he'll drop you off so you can hike back down to Sitka on the Gavan Hill Trail (see Hiking, above) or he'll take you and your bike up to the top of the gravel road and you can fly "like a bomber on two wheels" back down to sea level. All combinations are possible. Because of snow at upper elevations, the mountain tour takes place only from July through mid-September. Ulrich also does two-hour historic tours of Sitka from mid-May through mid-September. Cost for each tour is $25. *1210 Edgecumbe Dr; 907/747-8294; fax 907/747-4888; hgulrich@worldnet. att.net.*

MARINE WILDLIFE TOURS / Discover the nature of Southeast Alaska aboard a comfortable 60-foot diesel cruiser owned and run by **RAVEN'S FIRE INC.** Join Capt.

Barbara Bingham and her crew for half- and full-day birding and wildlife tours to St. Lazaria Island seabird colony, inhabited by puffins, rhinoceros auklets, pigeon guillemots, murres, murrelets, storm petrels, and black oystercatchers. Guests are also likely to see whales, sea otters, sea lions, and bears. Day trips can also be arranged to nearby Goddard Hot Springs. The cost for half- to full-day trips ranges from $90–$195 per person, with a minimum of 6 and maximum of 25 passengers. Raven's Fire also specializes in weeklong, live-aboard, Inside Passage cruises that emphasize natural history and outdoor adventure. The cost is $370 per person per day; these extended trips can accommodate 6 to 8 people. *403 Lincoln St, Ste 234, PO Box 6112, Sitka AK 99835; 907/747-5777 or 888/747-4789; fax 907/747-5963; captbarb@ravensfire.com; www.ravensfire.com.*

SITKA WILDLIFE QUEST / Though it specializes in tours with cruise ship passengers, **ALLEN MARINE TOURS** also does two-hour trips with independent travelers. Morning and evening cruises are scheduled every week from late May through the end of August. The wildlife quest takes visitors near St. Lazaria Island, a world-famous bird sanctuary with puffins, petrels, and murres. Sea otters and whales may also be seen. Trips depart from Crescent Harbor in downtown Sitka, near Centennial Hall. Fare is $49 for adults; $30 for children 3–12. *PO Box 1049, Sitka AK 99835-1049; 907/747-8100 or 800/747-8101; www.allenmarine.com.*

TLINGIT CULTURAL TOURS / Tlingit Indians have lived continuously in Sitka since the end of the last Ice Age. Through their eyes, "Sitka's history is a steady drumbeat, a rhythm, a song 10,000 years old." The Tlingit peoples of Sitka invite you to tour the area from their perspective and then enjoy the songs, language, and dance regalia of their people. The $29 tours are one–three hours. Call **TRIBAL TOURS** (888/270-8687) or contact their umbrella organization, **SITKA TRIBAL ENTERPRISES** (200 Katlian St, Sitka AK 99835; 907/747-7290; fax 907/747-3770; ttours@sitkatribal.com; www.sitkatribal.com).

FESTIVALS AND EVENTS

TLINGIT DANCE PERFORMANCES / In a replication of the old-style Tlingit clan house called Sheet'ka Kwaan Naa Kahidi Community House (see Exploring, above), there are stories and dance performances by the Tlingit people of Sitka twice daily in summer when larger cruise ships are in town or by prearrangement at other times. Cost is $6 per adult, $4 for children 12 or younger. *200 Katlian St; 907/747-7290; www.sitkatribal.com.*

RUSSIAN DANCE PERFORMANCES / More than 30 years ago, so the story goes, eight women in Sitka who loved to dance started a Russian folk-dance troupe and tried to entice men in town to join. No way, said the men! Undaunted, the women formed the New Archangel Dancers, taking the old Russian name for Sitka (and taking on the men's dance parts as well). In the ensuing years, they also took their show on the road, performing all over the world. Now men ask to audition. But the dance troupe still preserves its all-women status—entertaining tourists in the summer with such popular dances as the Cossack Horsemen's Dance and the Moldovian Suite. Choreographers from New York, Russia, and the Ukraine come to teach the group new dances every year. Performances are in Centennial Hall near the harbor and coincide with the cruise ship schedules, beginning in early May. The cost is $6. *907/747-5516; newarchangel@att.net.*

SITKA SUMMER MUSIC FESTIVAL / If you love music and beauty and beautiful music, come to Sitka in June for a festival that began in 1972. Internationally renowned musicians come back year after year and consider it an honor to be asked to play here. The people of Sitka love "their" musicians and they treat them like visiting royalty with down-home style. It's all very contagious. The grandeur of the stage at the Centennial Hall frames the concerts to perfection. The backdrop is all windows out to ice-streaked mountains and Sitka Sound. Look particularly for the performances of a lively, bearded, elflike violinist who answers to the name of Paul Rosenthal. A former student of Jascha Heifetz, Rosenthal is the genius behind the festival and a delightful character to boot. *PO Box 3333, Sitka AK 99835; 907/747-6774; director@sitkamusicfestival.org; www.sitkamusicfestival.org.*

SITKA SYMPOSIUM / This popular gathering coincides with the music festival in the middle of June. Though it began in the 1980s as a writer's conference, you do not have to be a writer to participate. You just have to love ideas, the written word, the interrelationships of story, culture, and nature, and discussions of the values and forces that influence our global village. Every year, the **ISLAND INSTITUTE** (PO Box 2420, Sitka AK 99835; 907/747-3794; island@ak.net; www.islandinstitutealaska. org) in Sitka pulls together a small faculty—including writers, poets, scientists, philosophers, and always one leader who is an Alaska Native—and organizes the weeklong forum around a current topic of interest. Writers are invited to have their manuscripts critiqued. The symposium features public readings ($8) and faculty presentations ($35). Participation in the entire symposium, which includes much more than the readings and presentations, is $300.

WHALES AND HERRING / From mid-September to mid-January, Sitka is a seaside cafe for dozens and dozens of **HUMPBACK WHALES.** These huge creatures make winter migrations to the warmer climates of Hawaii and Mexico, but they hang around the rich marine waters of Sitka Sound, bulking up for the journey by feeding on herring. The first wave of humpback whales returns to Alaska in March from their winter breeding grounds. By the third week or so of March, there is another marine-life extravaganza when the **HERRING RETURN**—millions and millions of herring. The Department of Fish and Game sometimes opens this fishery to fishermen for just a matter of minutes. Dozens of boats congregate in anticipation in the sound, like runners waiting for the starter's pistol to go off in the 100-yard dash. The opening is calculated to occur at the moment before the female herring is ready to release her eggs, and fortunes are made and lost with one set of the net. The Japanese particularly prize the eggs as a delicacy that is salted and eaten on New Year's Day. You can view the fishery from Halibut Point Road or charter a boat into the sound to watch the action.

NIGHTLIFE

PIONEER BAR / Also known as "The P-Bar," this is an old-time Alaska establishment. Windows overlook the harbor, and the walls are plastered with photos of boats and fish, with this maxim overhead: "There is nothing, absolutely nothing, half so much worth doing as simply messing about in boats." It can get smoky, but it's a friendly meeting place. And, as one resident says, "Any gossip you missed out at the Backdoor Cafe, you can pick up later at the P-Bar." For live action, go Friday night. *Open every day; 212 Katlian St; 907/747-3456.*

RESTAURANTS

The Backdoor Cafe / ★★★

104 BARRACKS ST, SITKA; 907/747-8856 This is "the real Sitka," as one resident says—"a verbal message board"—and the best place for espresso drinks and gossip in town. Anybody who's anybody in Sitka comes in here. At the back door of the Old Harbor Bookstore, the little cafe is cozy, welcoming, and appropriately has a buzz from all the conversations going on. It's a great place to meet someone or hang out at a corner table with a good book or journal. There's an array of coffee drinks, make-your-own bagel sandwiches, and baked goods such as cranberry-walnut scones or poppy-seed cake. Nonsmoking. *$; No credit cards; local checks only; breakfast, lunch every day; no alcohol; no reservations; walk through the Old Harbor Bookstore or go around the alley to the back door.*

Bayview Restaurant / ★

407 LINCOLN ST, SITKA; 907/747-5440 This bright, pleasant, second-story cafe has large windows overlooking a million-dollar view—the islands, mountains, boats, and sparkling waters of Sitka Sound. There's something for everyone's taste buds here; the four-page menu features an eclectic mix of choices, from Russian borscht to seafood, gourmet burgers, reindeer sausages, pastas, and sirloin steak. Breakfast features crispy hashbrowns, and espresso drinks are served throughout the day. *$-$$; AE, DIS, MC, V: local checks only; breakfast, lunch, dinner Mon–Sat, breakfast, lunch on Sun; beer and wine; reservations recommended; downtown on the 2nd floor of the Russian Trading Company building, at the corner of Lake and Lincoln Sts, across from the Shee Atika Hotel.* ﾖ

Channel Club / ★★

2906 HALIBUT POINT RD, SITKA; 907/747-9916 Three miles from downtown, the Channel Club is for serious carnivores. They serve the best steaks in town. As one resident said, "If you really want to stuff yourself, this is the place to go." Bill and Dotty Aragon have owned it for more than 25 years. They serve "corn-fed Nebraska beef, which is fresh cut on the premises and has never been frozen." They also serve plenty of fresh seafood and boast a salad bar with 35 salads. The windows look out to Sitka Sound and the interior is bush Alaska, complete with moose antlers, crab shells, and glass net floats hanging from the walls. Limited seating for nonsmokers. *$$-$$$; AE, DC, DIS, MC, V; local checks only; dinner every day (closed 3 weeks in Jan); full bar; reservations recommended; 3 miles out along Halibut Point Rd (call a taxi or the Channel Club's courtesy van).*

Mojo's / ★★

203 LINCOLN ST, SITKA; 907/747-0667 Mojo's and the Backdoor Cafe are hand-in-glove operations, almost next door to each other. All the baked goods for the Backdoor Cafe are made at Mojo's and delivered there early in the morning. The interior is bright, casual, and chummy, with bar

stools by the front windows, hanging plants, and several cheerful tables. They serve all kinds of coffee drinks—espresso, lattes, and the powerful Buzzsaw—along with baked goods. But lunch is where they really excel, with a rich and inventive menu of soups and sandwiches that are flavored with Asian and Indian spices and chutneys. The sandwiches are huge; half is plenty. They also have fresh juices such as carrot, ginger, and celery. The owners, Bernadette Rasmussen and Darryl Rehkopf, say their specialty is that they make everything from scratch using as many organic ingredients as possible. Nonsmoking. *$; No credit cards; local checks only; breakfast (baked goods only) and lunch every day; no alcohol; no reservations; downtown, on Lincoln St beside the Old Harbor Bookstore.*

The Raven Dining Room / ★★★

330 SEWARD ST, SITKA; 907/747-6465 If you want a romantic candlelit dinner, the Raven Room in the Westmark Shee Atika (see Lodgings review) is your best choice. In the heart of town, the restaurant has a great view of the mountains and harbor and reflects Sitka's friendly, small-town atmosphere. The staff is welcoming, the service prompt, and the menu original. They serve reindeer sausage, a variety of steaks, and the best eggs Benedict in town. Seafood dishes include tiger prawns coated with almonds with an orange marmalade dip, a shrimp and crab fettuccine, broiled tropical halibut topped with pineapple salsa and a splash of tequila, the local favorite beer-battered halibut, and salmon, cucumber, and spinach salads. *$$–$$$; AE, DC, DIS, MC, V; checks OK; breakfast, lunch, dinner every day; full bar; reservations recommended; www.westmarkhotels.com; in the center of town.* &

Van Winkle & Sons / ★★

205 HARBOR DR, SITKA; 907/747-7652 Located on the second floor of the former Marina Building, this restaurant has large glass windows that give it an open feel, while providing excellent views of Sitka Sound and the forested coast. The menu offers a variety of steaks, salads, and pasta dishes, but the specialty is seafood. They usually have the freshest fish in town—halibut or rockfish and sometimes salmon caught just that day—and they often grill it, adding an extra flavor of the outdoors. Their fish-and-chips is by far the most popular and their Mud Pie is famous—the best in town. *$$; AE, MC, V; checks OK; lunch Mon–Fri, dinner every day; full bar; reservations recommended; kirkvw@ptialaska.net; a short walk from the Centennial Hall and Crescent Harbor.*

LODGINGS

Crescent Harbor Hideaway / ★★

709 LINCOLN ST, SITKA; 907/747-4900 A stone's throw from the water's edge and a short walk from the center of town, this charming historic home overlooks Crescent Harbor and Sitka Sound. One of Sitka's longtime B&Bs, it has two guest units each with private bath and entrance; one is a full apartment with fully equipped kitchen, living room, and patio. Rates range from $110–$150, double occupancy. Visitors interested in marine mammals, ocean birds, and the Southeast rain forest will enjoy talking with host Susan Stanford, a longtime Alaskan and naturalist who's very familiar with the area's wildlife. She is also a gifted glass-bead artist. Non-smoking. *$$; No credit cards; checks OK; bareis@ptialaska.net; www.ptialaska.net/~bareis; directly across from Crescent Harbor, downtown.*

Karras Bed and Breakfast / ★

230 KOGWANTON ST, SITKA; 907/747-3978 The Karras's home reflects a delightful mixture of Greek and Tlingit cultures, homey atmosphere, and has some great views of Sitka Sound. The B&B's four rooms share a bath but have private entrances. Bertha is Tlingit and Pete is Greek, and at Christmas he sometimes moonlights as Jolly Old Saint Nick. It's almost like having Santa Claus and Earth Mother running a B&B. In summer, Pete wields a fishing rod and a spatula. He's a great breakfast cook, preparing meals that range from sourdough hotcakes, to soufflés, sausage, and muffins; occasionally he'll cook up a locally caught salmon. Rates for a double are $85. No smoking or alcohol allowed. *$$; AE, MC, V; checks OK; up the hill from the Pioneer Bar.*

Rockwell Lighthouse / ★★★

SITKA SOUND, SITKA; PHONE-FAX 907/747-3056 One of Sitka's most famous landmarks, the picturesque white-and-red lighthouse sitting on a small rock island out in the bay was not originally designed as a beacon for ships but built as a mock lighthouse back in the 1980s by one of Sitka's most eccentric and well-loved characters, Burgess Bauder, the local veterinarian. Four stories high, the lighthouse, made of brick, cedar, fir, mahogany, and black walnut, can bunk two people on each level. With two bathrooms and a fully equipped kitchen, if you have eight in your party, it's the cheapest place to rent in town. Locals rent it for all kinds of events and celebrations. Renting a skiff costs extra, but Bauder will take you over and pick you up, and the ride with him is worth the price of admission. It's good for those who enjoy relaxing. There's no television and the hot tub is often broken. Rates for two to eight run $125–$200 in winter and $150–$340 in summer. Warning: The lighthouse books up fast in summer, so plan well ahead. *$$–$$$; No credit cards; checks OK; PO Box 277, Sitka AK 99835; accessible by boat from the harbor.*

Westmark Shee Atika / ★★

330 SEWARD ST, SITKA; 907/747-6241 OR 800/544-0970 (RESERVATIONS); FAX 907/747-5486 *Shee Atika* is an old name for Sitka. It is the name the Tlingit people gave to their home here, long before the arrival of the Russians. *Shee* is Baranof Island. *Shee Atika* means roughly "the settlement on the outside of Shee." Some translate it as "the village behind the islands." Today, this friendly downtown hotel is owned by the Tlingit people of the region, under the aegis of the Shee Atika Corporation, and managed by Holland-America/Westours. The hotel is decorated with Tlingit motifs and artwork, and the hotel's Raven Dining Room serves excellent food (see review above). For the best views, reserve a room on the fourth or fifth floors, middle to the west wing, overlooking the water. The fourth and fifth floors are non-smoking. Double occupancy rates are $149. *$$; AE, DC, DIS, MC, V; checks OK; www.westmarkhotels.com; in the center of town.* &

WILDERNESS LODGES
Baranof Wilderness Lodge

EAST SIDE OF BARANOF ISLAND; PHONE-FAX 907/738-3597, MAY TO SEPT; 530/582-8132, OCT TO APR; 800/613-6551, YEAR-ROUND This wilderness fishing lodge is located 20 air miles over the mountains from Sitka, on the east side of Baranof Island, and the flight alone will stop your heart from beating. Jagged peaks, glaciers, and mountain passes sail past until you descend, swooping over a roaring river and a spectacular waterfall, to land on floats at the head of Warm Springs Bay. You'll fall in love with this bay and the lodge, originally built in the 1980s by the grandson of Alaska's most beloved territorial governor, Ernest "Pop" Gruening. Cabins sit close to the water, meals are family-style and delicious, and the fishing is great. Mike Trotter owns it now and offers remote fishing expeditions as well as lodge stays. Anglers can fish saltwater bays and estuaries or freshwater streams and lakes for a variety of species, from halibut to five species of Pacific salmon, cutthroat trout, Dolly Varden, Arctic char, and grayling. Trotter and his professional guides encourage catch-and-release fishing in fresh water, but anglers are welcome to keep saltwater catches. Several weeks each summer, the lodge features guest instructors with specialties that range from fly-fishing to wildlife photography and outdoor adventure. Per person rates range from $1,185 guided, $585 nonguided (two nights) to $3,550 (five nights). *$$$$; No credit cards; checks OK; closed Oct through Apr; Summer address: PO Box 2187, Sitka AK 99835; winter address: PO Box 42, Norden CA 95724; mtrotter@flyfishalaska.com; www.flyfishalaska.com.*

Wrangell

At the northern tip of Wrangell Island, far from the popular *Love Boat* circuit of the Inside Passage, nearly 90 miles north of Ketchikan and 150 miles south of Juneau, the small community of Wrangell (pop. 2,300) sits amid wilderness splendor. It's an unpretentious little town that, until recently, relied heavily on the timber industry for its livelihood. This is the more typical Southeast Alaska town of the not-so-very-long-ago, when only a few small cruise ships and the Alaska ferry tucked into the dock. (On any given summer day, cruise ship passengers can double—even triple—the population of some of these small Southeast towns.)

Wrangell is older than its neighbor, Petersburg, with a history that weaves together the ancient Tlingit culture and the cultures of three world powers—Russia, Britain, and the United States—who have occupied the region in more recent times. When Wrangell's sawmill, the largest private industry in town, closed in 1994, it took a big chunk out of the local economy. Recently, the mill has been revived on a smaller scale, exporting cedar, spruce, and hemlock and supporting independent woodsmen and artisans in town. The small fishing fleet still pulls in salmon, halibut, shrimp, crab, and herring. While the town is trying hard to develop a tourist industry, it still retains its original character.

Although Wrangell was founded by Russian traders in the early 1800s, the Tlingits long dominated the region. Perhaps the greatest carver in the history of the Tlingit nation lived here 200 years ago. The museum holds four of his totem poles, thought to be the oldest Tlingit house posts in existence. A replica of a clan house on Shakes Island, in the city harbor, contains copies of the old posts, crafted by modern master carvers.

Wrangell is the gateway to the Stikine River, a wild and spectacular waterway with headwaters in Canada. The Tlingit people named it *Stik-Heen,* which means "great river." Nearby is the Anan Creek Wildlife Observatory, famous for its bears which come to feast on spawning salmon.

ACCESS AND INFORMATION

Wrangell has daily **JET SERVICE** year-round via Alaska Airlines (800/252-7522; www.alaskaair.com). One of the two flights per day goes north; the other one south. The state ferries also make frequent stops here; call the **ALASKA MARINE HIGHWAY SYSTEM** (800/642-0066; www.alaska.gov/ferry) for reservations. Pick up information at the **WRANGELL CHAMBER OF COMMERCE** (PO Box 49, Wrangell AK 99929; 907/874-3901 or 800/367-9745; www.wrangellchamber.org), located at the end of the city dock, on Stikine Avenue.

EXPLORING

GARNETS / Through land deeded to "the children of Wrangell," local kids are allowed to travel to the Garnet Ledge on the Stikine River delta to "mine" for garnets. The ledge is not really a ledge, but an outcropping where raw garnets are literally right there in the ground. Sometimes due to a harsh winter, the garnets must be dug up or even blasted out. These are not gem quality, but a deep red wine color and genuine souvenir of any Wrangell visit. Don't worry about finding the children—they'll find you. They usually set up shop on the docks whenever a ship or ferry is in.

PETROGLYPH BEACH / Three-quarters of a mile north of the ferry dock (look for the signs) is a beach where ancient artists—for reasons unknown today—carved symbols, faces, fish, and seashell spirals into the rocks. Several thousand years old, these carved rocks perhaps served as territorial markers or pointed the way to good fishing on the Stikine River. Perhaps they were ritual carvings to invoke the spirit helpers of the animals killed in the hunt.

SHAKES ISLAND / Chief Shakes Tribal House—there were eight chiefs named Shakes—on Shakes Island in City Boat Harbor, is a wonderful replica of an original clan house. It's so wonderful, in fact, that it's on the National Register of Historic Places. It was built by a Civilian Conservation Corps crew in the 1930s. You must call for an appointment to view inside the tribal house, though it's usually open if a cruise ship or state ferry are in town for any length of time. Cost is $2 per person for groups of 10 or more; groups less than that pay a flat $20 fee. Even if you don't see inside, walking around the outside is peaceful, and the intricately carved totem poles surrounding the hand-hewn structure are beautiful by themselves. Only one thing is mandatory on a visit to Shakes Island—bring a camera. *907/874-2023; www.wrangell.com.*

WRANGELL MUSEUM / It's worth a visit to this museum to see the original Shakes totem poles and artifacts from the early days of Russian, British, and American settlement. While the museum is currently on the lower floor of the Community Center (318 Church St), plans to move into a greatly expanded and much anticipated space are in the works. The new museum building will be right on the waterfront, next to Bob's IGA within a short walk from the downtown dock. Admission is $3 for adults; children 16 and under are free. *Open Mon–Fri in summer, weekends if a ship is in; 907/874-3770; www.wrangell.com.*

ADVENTURES

ANAN WILDLIFE OBSERVATORY AND CABIN / Thirty miles southeast of Wrangell in Anan Bay, large runs of pink salmon returning to Anan Creek attract a bevy of black bears, brown bears, bald eagles, and harbor seals. The Forest Service maintains a popular rental cabin here for $35 a night during the summer season, by permit only (877/444-6777; www.reserveusa.com). There also is a covered platform at the falls, a mile upstream from the cabin via trail, so that visitors can watch in relative comfort as bears feed. A staircase leading down to the creek itself allows visitors an even closer look, though only five or six are allowed at that spot at any given time. Forest Service interpreters are at the sight during the spawning season, which starts around July 1, until Labor Day. The best time for viewing the bears and other wildlife is July and August. Anan is accessible only by boat or floatplane. Commercial charters are allowed to the site by permit—check with the Wrangell Ranger District for a list of permitted guides who can get you there. Other guides not permitted are allowed to "transport" visitors to Anan, but cannot accompany them to the viewing platform. In these cases, visitors should be familiar with wilderness travel and bear habits. *U.S. Forest Service, Wrangell Ranger District, 525 Bennett St, PO Box 51, Wrangell AK 99929-0051; 907/874-2323; www.fs.fed.us/r10/tongass/ (follow links to Anan Creek).*

GOLFING / Golf enthusiasts will be happy to find Muskeg Meadows in Wrangell, an 18-hole golf course that likes to point out its "unique hazards." This is golfing Southeast style. One such hazard was so common they came up with a rule for it, appropriately called "the raven rule." It goes like this: if a raven steals a ball, it will be replaced without penalty, provided there's a witness who can vouch for you. Guest rates for adults are $25 for 18 holes; youth 13–17 pay $10; youth 12 and under are free with paying adult. *PO Box 2199, Wrangell AK 99929; 907/874-4653; www.wrangellalaskagolf.com; off the Airport Loop Rd, look for the sign.*

HIKING / There are many good hiking trails around Wrangell, as well as old logging roads that make for interesting exploration. Two favorites are the 3-mile trip to **RAINBOW FALLS,** a fairly steep but gorgeous hike in lush rain forest, and the ½-mile climb to **DEWEY HILL.** The trail is steep—starting out as stairs—but you gain a good view of the town and surrounding area. If you want a local expert to show you around, consider **RAINWALKER EXPEDITIONS** (907/874-2549; www.rain walkerexpeditions.com). Guide Marie Oboczky leads nature hikes, and walking and adventure tours, with an emphasis on ecology. Her two-hour hike to Rainbow Falls is $30 per person, and includes lunch. A half-day "island explorer" trip includes several stops in the **TONGASS NATIONAL FOREST,** including a hike into **LONG LAKE** ($65 per person, includes lunch). She also rents kayaks, canoes, and bikes.

STIKINE RIVER / From its headwaters in British Columbia, the Stikine River flows for 400 miles, entering salt water just a few miles north of Wrangell, with a delta that stretches 16 miles wide. It is a popular destination for birders (120 species of migrating birds stop here in the spring and fall), fishermen, and river runners. Depending on the time of year, you can see hooligan running, sea lions feeding, and thousands of bald eagles perched on trees and stumps.

The river's name comes from the Tlingit Indian word *Stik-Heen,* which translates to "great river." It served as a transportation route into Canada during the Stikine, Cassiar, and Klondike Gold Rushes between 1861 and 1898. Sixteen miles upriver, the Forest Service maintains **CHIEF SHAKES HOT SPRINGS,** a fantastic natural hot springs that features two tubs—one outdoors, surrounded by decking, and one inside a screened-in shelter. Folks who stop here adjust the temperature of the water in the tubs simply by adding cold or hot from two different pipes. Just getting to the springs is an adventure in itself. There are no signs, but locals and guides know where to go (Hot Springs Slough, it's called, off Ketili Slough). Low water can sometimes mean you'll have to hike in, but other times, you can pull your boat right up to the dock near the tubs. There are times you'll come up and have the springs all to yourself. Other times, it seems half the town of Wrangell is there, soaking and living it up. Respect the beauty of the place; what you bring in, pack out.

Near the mouth of the river is **GARNET LEDGE,** where the children of Wrangell mine the garnets they sell you in town. The Stikine is fast flowing, averaging 8 knots per hour. River runners (see Guides and Outfitters, below) who venture onto the Stikine usually start in Wrangell, and can take you all the way to **TELEGRAPH CREEK** (pop. 300), in British Columbia. It is the only inland town along the river and about 130 miles from Alaska tidewater. Above Telegraph Creek is the Stikine's spectacular **GRAND CANYON,** where cliff walls jut up to 1,000 feet straight up from the river's edge. The canyon is about 55 miles long and considered dangerous and unnavigable.

PUBLIC-USE CABINS / The U.S. Forest Service, Wrangell Ranger District, maintains 22 public-use cabins near Wrangell, including 13 on the Stikine River and delta. They can be reserved for $25–$35 a day (877/444-6777; www.reserveusa.com). The Forest Service also sells maps showing Stikine River canoe and kayak trails. For information, contact the Wrangell Ranger District (see Anan Wildlife Observatory and Cabin, above).

GUIDES AND OUTFITTERS

For such a small town, Wrangell has a wealth of professional guides, charter-boat operators, and outfitters to choose from. Most of them do jet-boat trips up the Stikine River, as well as guided day trips to Anan Creek, fishing charters, and water-taxi service, in which they provide transport for adventure seekers who are out on their own. Others specialize in whale-watching, hunting, and glacier trips. For large groups interested in trips up the Stikine River, the **STIKINE RIVER JET BOAT ASSO-CIATION** (907/874-2300) can help book your tour. For smaller groups, such as couples or families, it's best to contact the guides individually.

Providing unique multiday "river safaris" to Telegraph Creek ($727–$825 per person) in British Columbia is **ALASKA WATERS** (907/874-2378 or 800/347-4462; www.alaskawaters.com). The trips include stays at either a wilderness homestead or historic hunting lodge, as well as Riversong Lodge at Telegraph Creek. Capt. Jim Leslie also does day trips up the Stikine, as well as guided trips to Anan and fishing charters. **BREAKAWAY ADVENTURES** (888/385-2488; www.breakawayadventures.

com) has perhaps the most economical trip up the Stikine, at $80 per person for a four-hour trip (most trips are about double that, but they are full-day affairs). Capt. Eric Yancey takes guests on guided trips to Anan Creek and specializes in day trips to the LeConte Glacier and Petersburg. **ALASKA CHARTERS AND ADVENTURES** (907/874-4157 or 888/993-2750; www.alaskaupclose.com) offers guided Stikine and Anan trips, and specializes in logistical support for kayak club and canoe excursions. Capt. Ed Garrison also does fishing charters. Capt. Mark Galla at **ALASKA PEAK AND SEAS** (907/874-2454; www.wedoalaska.com) provides guided Stikine and Anan trips, as well as guided hunting and fishing excursions. Capt. Tom Leslie operates **TIMBER WOLFE CHARTERS** (907/874-2893), specializing in fishing charters, Stikine River tours, Anan trips, and water-taxi transport to remote cabins or other locations.

FESTIVALS AND EVENTS

TENT CITY DAYS / Held in early February, this is Wrangell's most unique celebration, commemorating the gold rushes with such silliness as a beard contest, bed races, long-john contest, and a tall-tales contest. The festival's roots are the courageous men and women who came to Wrangell in the late 1800s and early 1900s, establishing tent cities as staging areas before trekking up the Stikine River to the Cassiar gold region of British Columbia or inland to the Klondike goldfields. Up to 10,000 people lived here then, mostly in tents. The three-day celebration culminates in a "fancy dress" ball. *Wrangell Chamber of Commerce, PO Box 49, Wrangell AK 99929; 907/874-3901 or 800/367-9745; www.wrangellchamber.org.*

GARNET FESTIVAL / This April celebration marks the arrival of spring and the annual spring migration of bald eagles on the Stikine River delta. There's workshops, birding trips, and lots of family activities. *www.wrangell.com*

KING SALMON FISHING DERBY / Over the years, winning fish have weighed between 44 pounds and 74 pounds. There are often thousands of dollars in cash and prizes. The derby is usually held over a monthlong period, from about mid-May to mid-June. There's a tagged fish out there, and if caught, it's worth $50,000 to the lucky fisherman. Check the Wrangell chamber's Web site, www.wrangellchamber.org, for the latest rules.

FOURTH OF JULY / Like many small towns across the country, Wrangell goes all out for its Fourth of July celebration. You'll find the parade, a carnival, logging show, and what's billed as the "largest, best, most spectacular" fireworks display in all of Southeast Alaska.

RESTAURANTS

J & W's Fast Food

FRONT ST, WRANGELL; 907/874-2120 This is the spot for the most delicious, deep-fried shrimp burgers you'll ever taste—shrimp caught right in Wrangell waters. You'll also find fish-and-chips, made with locally caught halibut, charbroiled beef and chicken burgers, and wonderful milk shakes homemade with hard-packed ice cream. This is mostly a take-out place, but there are tables both inside and out. *$; No credit cards; checks OK on approval; lunch, dinner every day; no alcohol; no reservations.*

Waterfront Grill / ★

IN THE STIKINE INN, WRANGELL; 907/874-2353 This establishment has the best view in town—it's right on the water with a panoramic view of Zimovia Strait. You may even see a pod of killer whales right from your dinner table. For such a small town, this restaurant has an extensive menu, everything from handmade pizza, calzone, and pasta dishes to locally caught seafood and Angus beef steaks. One unique dish is the hot seafood salad, made with prawns, scallops, and halibut in a white-wine sauce with zucchini and sundried tomatoes. Breakfast also runs the gamut, from omelets to Belgian waffles. There's a little cafe section, where you can buy hard ice cream or eat a casual meal, and there's the more formal dining area overlooking the water. The only down side, if you care to look at it that way, is there's no alcohol. But several Wrangell watering holes will be happy to take care of you after your meal. *$$; AE, DIS, MC, V; checks OK; breakfast, lunch, dinner every day; no alcohol; no reservations.*

Zak's Café

FRONT ST, WRANGELL; 907/874-3355 This is a convenient spot for lunch, with a variety of soups, salads, and wraps, as well as burgers, sandwiches, fish-and-chips, and chicken strips. Dinner features seafood, steaks, stir-fry, and assorted pasta and chicken dishes. *$–$$; MC, V; checks OK on approval; lunch, dinner every day (closed Sun in winter); no alcohol; no reservations.*

LODGINGS

Grand View Bed and Breakfast / ★★☆

MILE 2 ZIMOVIA HWY, WRANGELL; 907/874-3225 This B&B has what one resident describes as the most gracious host in Wrangell. They have three rooms, one with a queen and double bed; two with one queen bed each. All have private baths and entrances, and two of them have waterfront views. Two of the rooms have their own telephones and televisions, while the third room has those amenities in a common living area (separate from the hosts' living area). Rates are $85–$100, double occupancy. A full home-cooked breakfast is served each morning, with a varied menu dependant on the desires of each guest. A coin-operated laundry is available, and courtesy van transportation is included. *$$; No credit cards; checks OK; www.grandviewbnb.com; drive 2 miles out of town on the Zimovia Hwy, on the uphill side of the road.*

Rain Haven ★★

CITY BOAT HARBOR, WRANGELL; 907/874-2549 This is a truly unique lodging, a thoughtfully appointed houseboat either tied up dockside, or taken to a private bay or cove nearby for total relaxation. Rain Haven's cozy interior can sleep up to five, but two will be extremely comfortable here with feather beds, a galley stocked with staples, hot showers, a library, and sunny atrium and covered deck on the bow. Details include dry bags for your personal gear and a picnic basket for day excursions. This is a Coast Guard registered vessel, equipped with personal floatation devices and marine radios, plus other safety equipment. Double occupancy rates are $114 dockside, or $354 for a remote experience (two-night minimum stay), including transportation. Packages including jet-boat tours and a canoe rental are also available. *$$; No credit cards; checks OK in advance; www.rain walkerexpeditions.com/.*

Rooney's Roost / ★★

206 MCKINNON ST, WRANGELL; 907/874-2026 The six rooms in this B&B are inside a nicely renovated, 100-year-old house, warmly decorated in antiques with a hint of French Provençal. Three of the rooms have private baths, while three share a bath. There are two common areas, and the entrance to the B&B section of the house is completely separate. Rates are $75–$95, double occupancy, and there's courtesy transportation for guests' arrivals and departures. The full, home-cooked breakfast features such mouth-watering dishes as halibut hash and crab quiche (made with locally caught seafood), as well as baked goods made with handpicked berries. Within a half block is the trailhead to Dewey Hill, a steep but short trail that offers glorious views of the city and surrounding area on a nice day. *$–$$; MC, V; checks OK; www.rooneysroost.com; 1 block off Front St.*

Zimovia Bed and Breakfast

319 WEBBER ST, WRANGELL; 907/874-2626 This is a B&B with many personal artistic touches, such as a sauna with a stained-glass window and a little kitchenette with handcrafted cabinets and tilework. A slate floor is inlaid with garnets—even the drain in the shower is lined with garnets. The two rooms are adjoining, and you may want to consider renting both, as they are quite small ($65 per night for the larger room, which has the sauna and bathroom, and $40 a night for the smaller room). A private entrance to the B&B is wooded, with a nice garden. A continental breakfast is provided in the room, and the host brings down homemade baked goods each morning, everything from cinnamon rolls to fresh baked loaves of bread. There's courtesy transportation for arrivals and departures, which includes a homey orientation to the town. *$; No credit cards; checks OK; www.zimoviabnb.com; close to downtown.*

Petersburg

The fishing town of Petersburg (pop. 3,200) is quite prosperous, capitalizing on its abundant salmon, natural beauty, and Scandinavian charm. While Petersburg welcomes visitors, like Wrangell it is not a mainstay on the cruise ship circuit.

Petersburg was founded just before the turn of the century by sturdy Norwegian immigrants who were drawn here by plentiful salmon and halibut and an inexhaustible supply of natural ice from nearby LeConte Glacier, in which they packed their catch. Many of them were fishermen from the fjord country of western Norway who found a landscape of tall mountains and deep waters remarkably like their homeland. A century later, Petersburg is still dominated by a Scandinavian aesthetic and work ethic. The homes are square, wooden, and solid. Descendants of the early immigrants are raising their families here, and some of the boats you see in the harbor are operated by fourth- and fifth-generation Petersburg fishermen and women.

Above all, Petersburg is an authentic fishing community, untouched by the big-business tourism that has radically changed such places as Juneau and Ketchikan. You won't find mega–cruise ships, and shops filled with trinkets and T-shirts. Instead, you'll experience a bustling seaport going about the business of catching, processing, and selling seafood. And you'll find a few nice visitor amenities.

If you're comfortable in rain jacket and rubber boots, you're sure to enjoy Petersburg. More than 100 inches of rain falls every year, moisture that nurtures salmon streams and gives the rain forest a thousand shades of green. Consider yourself blessed when the sun breaks through and reveals the stunning coastal mountain range with its jutting pinnacle, Devil's Thumb.

ACCESS AND INFORMATION

Petersburg is served by **ALASKA AIRLINES** (800/252-7522; www.alaskaair.com) daily jet service. It's possible to leave San Francisco in the morning and arrive in Petersburg in the afternoon. **ALASKA MARINE HIGHWAY** (800/642-0066; www. alaska.gov/ferry) vessels also make frequent stops here.

Stop in at the **PETERSBURG VISITOR INFORMATION CENTER** (907/772-4636; www.petersburg.org) at the corner of First and Fram Streets downtown, to pick up information; open daily in summer, reduced hours in winter. **SING LEE ALLEY BOOKS** (No. 11 Sing Lee Alley, on the way to the south harbor; 907/772-4440) is a great little bookstore, with the feeling of a corner bookstore in a much larger city. It's open daily, featuring field guides, Alaskana, and a lot of other good reading.

ADVENTURES

FISHING CHARTERS / Try your luck at hauling in an Alaska salmon or halibut aboard the 32-foot cabin cruiser *The Getaway* with **TERRY'S UNFORGETTABLE CHARTERS AND EXPEDITIONS**. Terry, with 35 years of fishing experience, specializes in multiday trips with groups of four or five. A three-day trip costs $4,000 per group, all meals included, but day trips are also available. *Mile 9.7 Mitkof Hwy; 907/772-2200 or 907/227-6203; www.terrysfishing.com.*

HIKING / There are several good hiking trails. **THREE LAKES TRAIL** is a delightful hike, completely on boardwalk, that connects three lakes named Sand, Hill, and Crane. Go to Mile 21 on Mitkof Highway, then turn on Three Lakes Road. The trail begins at the sign for Crane Lake. A new addition to the trail takes you to Ideal Cove, on the southeast side of Mitkof Island, often offering a glimpse of LeConte Glacier and icebergs. The **OHMER CREEK TRAIL** starts a couple of miles beyond the Three Lakes turnoff on Mitkof Highway. You walk 2 miles one-way through a deep, green, old-growth forest, across a floating bridge over a series of pools, and into a wildflower meadow. The **RAVEN'S ROOST TRAIL** is more challenging. It's 8 miles round-trip to a rustic cabin, and views of Frederick Sound are great. The trail begins 2 miles from downtown, near the airport. The cabin, about $30 per night, requires a permit from the U.S. Forest Service (877/444-6777; www.reserveusa.com).

KAYAKING / Rent a boat or take a guided trip. With **TONGASS KAYAK ADVENTURES** trips range from afternoon paddles to Petersburg Creek ($65 per person) to multiday trips to LeConte Glacier, Frederick Sound, or weeklong tours to the Stikine

River or Tebenkof Bay. *PO Box 2169, Petersburg AK 99833; 907/772-4600; www.tongasskayak.com.*

WALKING AND BOATING EVERYWHERE / Stroll the boardwalks that cross Mitkof Island's muskeg meadows. Wander along the harbor. Get up early, buy a latte at **ALASKAFE**, upstairs from Coastal Cold Storage on Nordic (see Restaurants review, below), and park yourself on a bench overlooking the Old Boat Harbor, a block off Main Street. During salmon season, you'll see cannery laborers hurrying to jobs, fishing crews readying their gear, and boats of all kinds coming and going. All this activity may inspire the more adventurous to rent a skiff and motor down Wrangell Narrows—really the best way to get a feel for how people live here. Scandia House (downtown; 907/772-4281) has 18-foot Lunds (people in Alaska probably own more Lunds than folks anywhere else) with 40-horsepower outboards for rent for $135 for hotel guests, or $160 for others. Call ahead.

WHALES, ICEBERGS, AND MOUNTAINS / Classic Petersburg excursions are whale-watching in Frederick Sound; a visit to LeConte Glacier, the southernmost tidewater glacier in North America; and flight-seeing around Devil's Thumb. **VIKING TRAVEL** (101 N Nordic Dr; 907/772-3818 or 800/327-2571; www.alaska-ala-carte.com or www.alaskaferry.com) books charters and tours with such offerings as humpback whale-watching, LeConte Bay boat tours, helicopter flight-seeing, and glacier walk, and half-day kayak adventures. **PACIFIC WING** (907/772-4258 or 907/772-9258; www.pacificwing.com) is the best for flight-seeing or air charters. Their most popular trip, a 45-minute ride to LeConte Glacier aboard a Cessna 185, is $270 for three people.

FESTIVALS AND EVENTS

LITTLE NORWAY FESTIVAL / This festival takes place the third weekend of May and commemorates Syttende Mai (May 17), the day in 1814 when Norway declared its independence from Sweden. The celebration includes smorgasbords for sampling Scandinavian delicacies, displays of traditional crafts, and a community pageant that's a kitschy mix of old-country dancing and corny Norwegian humor. *Petersburg Chamber of Commerce, PO Box 649, Petersburg AK; 99833; 907/772-3646; www.petersburg.org.*

PETERSBURG'S SALMON DERBY / This fishing derby takes place Memorial Day weekend. What sets it apart from all the other derbies in the Southeast is the level of competition. Casual sportfishers will find themselves competing with the most competitive and successful commercial fishermen anywhere. But that doesn't mean the skipper of a 78-foot seiner has a leg up. It's still a matter of luck. Contact Petersburg Chamber of Commerce (see above).

RESTAURANTS

Alaskafe / ★★

306 N NORDIC DR, PETERSBURG; 907/772-JAVA (5282) Funky gourmet coffee house by day, bistro by night, this is the best place in town for a latte or any kind of steaming coffee drink. Sit outside at the outdoor tables on a nice day. You'll find grilled gourmet panini sandwiches, soups, salads, and pastas for lunch and fresh seafood dinners. Fresh-baked muffins and pastries, along with the coffee, will help wake you up in the morning. *$–$$; No credit cards; checks OK on approval; breakfast, lunch Tues–Sat, dinner Wed–Fri (summer), limited reservation-only dinner in winter; no alcohol; no reservations; upstairs from Coastal Cold Storage.*

Coastal Cold Storage / ★★

306 N NORDIC DR, PETERSBURG; 907/772-4177 This small seafood processing plant and take-out restaurant is a favorite of locals and visitors alike. They offer delicious halibut and salmon salad sandwiches, soups, and homemade pasta salads. There are a few picnic tables where you can sit down to eat. You'll also find fresh crab (they have two "live" tanks), shrimp, and other delicacies of the sea to take home and cook yourself. There's no alcohol served here, but you can take your food to the Harbor Bar next door if you like. *$; AE, DC, DIS, MC, V; checks OK; lunch, dinner every day; no alcohol; no reservations; coastal@alaska.net; 1 block from the waterfront, downtown.*

Pellerito's Pizzeria / ★

1105 S NORDIC DR, PETERSBURG; 907/772-3727 If you're hungry for pizza, this is the place. Choose between 20 different combinations, or build your own. This is hand-thrown pizza, with a thick Sicilian-style crust. You can get it whole or by the slice, and they also serve spaghetti, lasagna, sandwiches, and calzone. Most of the menu is offered to go, but there are a few small tables. In the summer you can take your food upstairs, to Ole's Bar, and have a beer or your favorite cocktail. Delivery by local taxi companies available with $5 charge. You can also buy a pizza "take and bake." *$; MC, V; checks OK with proper ID; dinner every day; no alcohol; no reservations; across from ferry terminal.*

LODGINGS

Nordic House B&B / ★★

806 S NORDIC DR, PETERSBURG; 907/772-3620 You can't get any closer to the water unless you're on a boat. This B&B, on pilings over the water with an incredible view of the small floatplane dock and harbors, offers homey comforts such as feather beds, kitchens, and decks. Upstairs is a suite suitable for four people, as well as three rooms with a common living area and shared bath, perfect for couples traveling together. Downstairs are two more rooms with a shared bath. The continental breakfast is a help-yourself affair with stocked kitchens. Rates run $88–$120, double occupancy. *$$; MC, V; checks OK; www.nordichouse.net; 1½ blocks from ferry terminal on the waterfront.*

Broom Hus / ★★

BETWEEN THE FERRY TERMINAL AND DOWNTOWN, PETERSBURG; 907/772-3459 Sylvia Nilsen's house is one of the solid old Norwegian places that make Petersburg distinctive. The location is terrific—midway between the ferry terminal and downtown—making it a short walk in either direction. The downstairs suite is completely separate from her home, with a pretty garden entrance. From the boat harbor across the street, you can walk to town entirely on the floats. The rate for two is $85 per night, but the suite can sleep up to six people comfortably for $140. The breakfast is continental, with homemade breads and muffins. *$$; No credit cards; checks OK; PO Box 427, Petersburg AK 99833; www.alaska.net/~broomhus.*

Scandia House / ★★★

DOWNTOWN, PETERSBURG; 907/772-4281 OR 800/722-5006 When the Scandia House burned down in 1994, Petersburg lost its oldest, funkiest hotel. But the new Scandia House is clean, quiet, and comfortable and retains the central downtown location. There are 33 rooms, with many different configurations. All have baths; many have kitchenettes. There's no hotel restaurant, but there's a coffee shop right next door. Rates are $100–$185 for a double. *$$–$$$; AE, DC, DIS, MC, V; checks OK; PO Box 689, Petersburg AK 99833.*

Water's Edge Bed and Breakfast / ★★

SANDY BEACH RD, PETERSBURG; 907/772-3736 OR 800/868-4373 Barry and Kathy Bracken's B&B is on the bottom level of their split-level seaside home on Sandy Beach Road, about 1½ miles from downtown. They have two rooms—the Beach Room, with a panoramic view of Frederick Sound, and the Creekside Room, tucked in the woods overlooking a creek with a partial view of the beach. The rooms ($85–$95 double) each have a private bath and share a common living area, making them perfect for couples traveling together. Barry, a biologist, offers naturalist excursions aboard his 28-foot cruiser in the summer, specializing in whale-watching and glacier viewing. A daylong whale-watching trip runs $180 per person, though B&B guests get a discount. *$$; No credit cards; checks OK; PO Box 1201, Petersburg AK 99833; www.alaska.net/~bbsea; follow Nordic Dr until it turns into Sandy Beach Rd, 3 miles from ferry terminal.*

WILDERNESS LODGES

Rocky Point Resort

PO BOX 1251, PETERSBURG AK 99833; 907/772-4405 Only 12 miles from town, this family-owned and -operated lodge still feels remote even though you can drive to it. It caters to serious sportfishers. From June to September, guests fish for the region's best: salmon, lingcod, halibut, and trout. Up to 22 guests stay in six cabins, and eat in a main dining lodge. The $295 per person price includes three hearty meals a day, gear, and use of skiffs. Guided fishing trips are available for $75 per person extra each day. The lodge will wrap and store your catch in their walk-in freezer until you head home. Airport pickups available. *$$$$; No credit cards; checks OK; closed Sept to May; 12 miles from Petersburg, call for pickup or directions.*

Juneau

Juneau is the only state capital in the United States that you can't drive to in your car. That's because the nearest road leading out of the state ends about 60 miles away, between mountains, beneath avalanche chutes, and across oceans. Whether or not to complete that final land link is among the fiercest of local debates, but while it's unsettled the lack of road access endows Juneau with what actor Spencer Tracy once called "the charm of distance."

Juneau's local roadways stretch barely 50 miles, more or less south to north, along Gastineau Channel and Lynn Canal. The city limits comprise treed mountains, flinty granite ridges, glaciers, and vast icefields, but all of Juneau's 30,000 residents live within little more than a mile or less of salt water, with the single exception of those in the upper reaches of the Mendenhall Valley.

Whatever visitors may be looking for, they discover an almost furtively modern community that wears its barely 120-year-old past like a favorite pair of blue jeans or, with upwards of 90 inches of rain per year, a well-used nylon and microfiber raincoat. Downtown Juneau retains the wood-framed flavor of its gold-mining, boomtown past, complete with jewelers ready to turn your nugget into a ring, and a few occasionally rowdy honky-tonks. Juneau is sometimes called the San Francisco of the north—actually, only by summer tour guides, but it is a place of hills, narrow wooden stairways, and well-maintained parking brakes.

Ranging up the hills in converted-to-offices antique houses and hidden among Sitka spruce groves, is the modern apparatus of a state and federal government center still deeply involved in the management and development of a frontier as well as the provision of traditional urban services.

Internationally recognized fisheries and environmental managers and a scrappy fishing fleet of several dozen vessels work out of Juneau's three downtown harbors. The fishing boats provide almost daily summer deliveries of salmon, halibut, and other species, depending on the season, to two local seafood processors, grocery stores, and restaurants. You can buy live Dungeness crab and shrimp in season directly from fishing boats at prices nearly as mouthwatering as the wriggling purchases if you keep on eye peeled for impromptu, hand-lettered billboards posted at the harbor entrances.

Beside its role as workplace, the sea is also Juneau's playground. Two salmon derbies—in May targeting the spring king salmon run and in August when silver salmon return—give anglers a chance to hone their fishing and storytelling skills. When the summer solstice provides the Southeast region with nearly 20 hours between sunrise and sunset each day, the Juneau Yacht Club hosts the Spirit of Adventure sailboat race. The 200-mile-long competition around neighboring Admiralty Island is the longest coastal sailing race in the country, and the high point of the wind-driven fleet's racing series.

Though it is literally difficult to turn your back on the sea in Juneau, those who do face hundreds of miles of hiking trails into the Coast Mountains, whose 4,000-foot peaks mark the border between Alaska and British Columbia. Dozens of trails ranging from near-technical climbs up the steepest slopes to boardwalked strolls through emerald woods double as cross-country skiing trails in the winter and are easily accessible from trailheads throughout town.

The Last Chance Basin, barely a 15-minute walk from the front doors of the state capitol, is the trailhead for a variety of hikes. It is also the source of Gold Creek, where Auk Indian Tribe Chief Cowee led sourdoughs Joe Juneau and Richard Harris to the 1880 gold strike that resulted in the start of a settlement on the shores of

Gastineau Channel. "Juneau City" was established in 1881 when the Committee on Town Laws chose that name over "Harrisburg" and "Rockwell." In 1882, the U.S. Postal Service dropped the word "city," making "Juneau" the official name, and in 1900 the City of Juneau was incorporated and became the territorial capital. Gold mining and milling was also expanding across Gastineau Channel, where the City of Douglas was also established in 1881. Once larger than Juneau, Douglas's growth was stunted by major fires in 1911 and 1937. In 1970, Douglas and Juneau unified as the City and Borough of Juneau.

Although there is currently no active gold mining on an industrial scale in the Juneau region, some locals still take their (now plastic) pans to the braided streams of Last Chance Basin and other waterways in the hills. On a good day, modern-day miners come away with a little flake gold.

As with many other parts of Alaska, the tourism business provided Juneau's latest boom, growing at almost 10 percent annually during much of the 1990s. When the last cruise ship leaves, not long after Labor Day, the city has a couple of months to itself before it begins to shift into political gear for the four-month session of the Alaska legislature that begins each January. With a legislature of 40 house members and 20 senate members, the session draws upwards of 500 winter residents, including lawmakers' families and staffs, plus a continuous stream of lobbyists, local officials, and activist citizens from other communities.

With its weather dominated by moisture-laden winds off the Pacific Ocean, the capital city is not the place to go for your Alaskan dog-mushing adventure. Weather patterns along the entire Southeast are distinctly milder than the brutally cold winters of the Interior and Arctic regions of the state. Juneau enjoys a couple of days each summer when the mercury tops 80°F, and the average high in July is 64°F, but the year-round average high is only 47°F. The average low is 34°F, while in January it's a balmy (for Alaska) 18°F. There is enough white precipitation up in the north Douglas Island mountains, across Gastineau Channel from Juneau proper, for some of the best snow conditions in the country in a good year. The same stuff comes down as rain closer to sea level, and most of the time.

ACCESS AND INFORMATION

Arriving in Juneau is an accomplishment in itself whether you fly in on a brilliantly sunny day with Auke Bay sparkling below, emerge from a gray mattress of clouds between the lush green folds of the mountainsides, or stride down the gangway of a state ferry or cruise ship. Not many people find themselves in Juneau because they were just passing through.

The sky and the sea are the only roads to Juneau. **ALASKA AIRLINES** (800/252-7522; www.alaskaair.com) is the only major carrier offering daily, year-round service. **AIR NORTH** (800/764-0407 in the United States or 800/661-0407 in Canada; www.flyairnorth.com) flies from Juneau to Whitehorse, Yukon Territory, once each Wednesday, Thursday, Friday, and Sunday afternoon. Regional carriers including **WINGS OF ALASKA** (907/789-0790; fax 907/789-2021; info@Wings OfAlaska.com; www.WingsOfAlaska.com) and **LAB FLYING SERVICE** (907/789-9160) offer scheduled or charter service between Juneau, regional villages, and Glacier Bay or any remote beach or lake of your choice.

Juneau is the headquarters of the **ALASKA MARINE HIGHWAY SYSTEM** (907/465-3941 or 800/642-0066; fax 907/277-4829; www.alaska.gov/ferry). Ferries arrive in Juneau several days a week during the summer from Bellingham, Washington, and Prince Rupert, British Columbia via various Southeast communities and continue on to Haines or Skagway, where roads connect with the rest of North America. Reserve well in advance if you want a cabin or are driving on; walk-ons are assured passage almost any time and can pitch a tent on the stern decks or unroll a sleeping bag on a chaise lounge on the solarium deck or in out-of-the-way corners in the public lounges during the evening. Showers are available on mainline vessels, and all ships offer cafeteria-style restaurants or snack bars, depending on their size. Bicycles and kayaks can also be accommodated. Once each summer month the ferry MV *Kennicott* makes a round-trip passage (36 hours each way) from Juneau across the Gulf of Alaska to Valdez, in Prince William Sound, and Seward, on the Kenai Peninsula south of Anchorage. The system also operates a western route between the Kenai, Kodiak, and the Aleutian Island city of Unalaska.

Juneau is also a port of call for some 40 **CRUISE SHIPS** ranging from 900-foot, 2,500-passenger leviathans of the international cruise lines to 100-foot pocket cruisers carrying fewer than 50 guests. In addition, a mosquito fleet of scheduled, crewed, and bare-boat charters has developed in Juneau in recent years. Commonly offering gourmet cooking, they offer regional cruises. Check with your travel agent or at the **JUNEAU CONVENTION AND VISITORS BUREAU** (see below) for details (also see the Alaska Cruising chapter).

On shore the cheapest way to get around is the city's **CAPITAL TRANSIT** bus system (907/789-6901; www.juneau.org/pubworks/captrans/). Buses run from the south end of downtown to Auke Bay, an easy ½-mile walk from the state ferry terminal and even closer to the **UNIVERSITY OF ALASKA SOUTHEAST** campus (on the shore of Auke Lake). The system operates on a 30-minute schedule from 7:30am–11pm weekdays, 9am–6pm on weekends. Buses have bicycle racks and the fare is $1.25, exact change please.

Juneau's **TAXI FLEET** is available for tours and most of the national car rental agencies operate out of the airport terminal. **RENT-A-WRECK** (907/789-4111; sonnie@gci.net) offers courtesy pickup throughout the city and also rents trucks.

Once you're in town don't bother looking for the historical **DAVIS LOG CABIN**. Once a church, then a brewery office, the former visitor information center is now history. It was torn down in 2002 after rot got the better of the 1800s-era structure. The new **JUNEAU CONVENTION AND VISITORS BUREAU** (907/586-1737 or 800/586-2201; info@traveljuneau.com; www.traveljuneau.com) is housed in **CENTENNIAL HALL**, the big wood-paneled exhibition center on Egan Drive just across the street from the **GOLDBELT HOTEL**. The expanded visitor center took over much of the space formerly occupied by the **U.S. FOREST SERVICE**, which maintains a small booth there during the summer only. The Forest Service has more substantial facilities at the **MENDENHALL GLACIER VISITOR CENTER**, about 13 miles from the city center (see Mendenhall Glacier in Exploring, below).

To get a feel for Juneau, check out www.juneauphotos.com, a fun Web site by Juneau photographer Pat Costello. He updates it every other day.

EXPLORING

ALASKAN BREWERY CO. / Founded in 1986, Alaskan Brewery Co. has won more than 25 national and international awards for their continually expanding variety of handcrafted ales, porters, and stouts. Free tours are offered (11am–5pm daily May to Sept, 11am–4:30pm Thurs, Fri, Sat the rest of the year), but under state law all persons 20 and younger must be accompanied by a parent or legal guardian, and all visitors may be requested to show identification. *5429 Shaune Dr; 907/780-5866; www.alaskanbeer.com; in Lemon Creek, a few miles north of Juneau.*

GLACIER GARDENS RAINFOREST ADVENTURE / One of Juneau's most unique attractions, this 50-acre natural and fantasy botanical garden opened in 1998. Guided tours on covered golf carts take visitors through environments from sea level to the 580-foot overlook on Thunder Mountain, passing through primeval rain forest drenched in every shade of green imaginable and rainbow galleries of the brilliantly colored flowers and muted lichens, mosses, and ferns. The garden's "flower towers," a.k.a. upside-down trees, offer a unique perspective on hanging gardens. The Wild Berry Cafe demonstrates that the forest can taste as good as it looks. Adults $17.95; children 6–12 $12.95; 5 and under free. *Open May 1 to Sept 30, 9am–9pm Mon–Sat and 10am–5pm Sun; 907/790-3377; www.glaciergardens.com; off the Old Glacier Hwy, about a ½ mile from Fred Meyer store.*

JUNEAU PUBLIC LIBRARY / You may not be in Juneau long enough to get a library card, but the library's main branch is worth a visit on two counts. One is the 15-foot-high stained-glass window you can't miss as you get off the elevator. The other is the view from the balcony on the Gastineau Channel side of the building. Often as not in summer, you can peer down into the staterooms and mid-decks of a cruise ship moored at the pier—or up, in the case of the new giant ships, but that can provide some interesting perspectives as well. It's smack in the middle of downtown and built on the top floor of the city parking garage (don't ask!). *Open 11am–9pm Mon–Thurs and noon–5pm Fri–Sun; 292 Marine Wy; 907/586-5267.*

MACAULAY SALMON HATCHERY VISITOR CENTER / Whether you like salmon as a magnificent sea and river dweller, or grilled with lemon and butter, a visit to the hatchery when the salmon are running is educational and fun. DIPAC (Douglas Island Pink and Chum) is a non-profit organization that runs several salmon hatcheries and is dedicated to helping stock the area's sport fishery. It was founded in large part by the late Ladd Macaulay. The facility raises millions of king, chum, coho, and pink salmon to fingerling size for release into the ocean, where they mature before returning to spawn in two to five years, depending on the species. Salmon begin returning to the hatchery in early July, and during the late-summer peak, thousands can be seen schooling in the local harbors during slack tide and fighting their way up the fish ladder into "raceways." Hatchery staff sort the salmon by sex and species and "milk" the females for their eggs, which are then fertilized with milt (sperm). The carcasses, still delicious eating, are often given away to the public when the annual returns are larger than expected. The visitor center saltwater aquarium provides a close look at a wide range of common sea life in the waters around Juneau, and hatchery staff can probably tell you anything you care to ask about salmon. Admission is $3 for adults and $1 for children. *Open in summer 8am–6pm Mon–Fri and 10am–5pm on weekends; 2697 Channel Dr; 907/463-4810; www.dipac.net/*

JUNEAU THREE-DAY TOUR

DAY ONE: Head to sea in the most intimate way possible in Alaska's cold waters: by kayak. If you didn't bring your own kayak or camping and fishing gear, arrange with **ALASKA BOAT & KAYAK** for rental and transportation to Auke Bay, Tee Harbor, or anywhere else along the 45 miles that take you to **ECHO COVE** at the end of Juneau's road system. Time your departure with the flood or ebb tide and head for 10-mile-long **BERNERS BAY,** just north of the road's end. The somewhat protected waters of the bay make it easy for novice paddlers (as long as you stay close to shore) and provide endless opportunity for marine-mammal watching, with ready beaches to put in if the weather turns nasty or you just get tired of paddling. The Lace, Berners, Gilkey, and Antler Rivers all empty into the north end of the bay, offering additional exploratory options, plus sites for fly-fishing and total tranquility once you've pitched your campsite. Take standard bear-country precautions with food and especially with any fish you catch.

DAY TWO: If you really want to return to civilization already, head south toward Juneau to your pickup point or to Auke Bay Harbor. If you're the type who finds yourself suddenly starving, stoke up when you reach shore with a blueberry malt and salmon burger at the **HOT BITE.** If you want to eat off a plate, try **CHAN'S THAI KITCHEN,** just across the street from the harbor. If you're still into the wilderness thing, you can hike 2 miles and a bit north from the harbor to the U.S. Forest Service **AUK VILLAGE CAMPGROUND** (Juneau Ranger District, 8465 Old Dairy Rd, Juneau, AK 99801; 907/536-8800). Tent sites cost just $8 a night, but there are only 12, so get there early. Piped water and outhouses are the only amenities. On the way there, on the uphill side

MUSEUMS / Permanent exhibits in the **ALASKA STATE MUSEUM** (395 Whittier St, around the corner from Centennial Hall; 907/465-2901; www.museums.state. ak.us; 8:30am–5:30pm daily in summer, 10am–4pm Tues–Sat in winter) tell the history of Russian America, the stories of the diverse Native peoples, and the rich natural history of Alaska. The eagle nesting tree is not to be missed. Admission in summer is $5 for visitors over 18, but drops to $3 in winter. The **JUNEAU-DOUGLAS CITY MUSEUM** (4th and Main Sts; 9am–5pm weekdays and 10am–5pm weekends in summer, noon–4pm Tues–Sat in winter) focuses on the region's mining history and life in the frontier city. Year-round admission is $3 for adults 19 and older.

WALKING TOUR OF TOWN / Juneau's vertical orientation allows you to combine a healthy workout with a leisurely stroll as you explore the sights. Free walking tour maps are available at the city visitor center in **CENTENNIAL HALL** (on Egan Dr, next to the Goldbelt Hotel), the visitor information kiosk in **MARINE PARK** (at the cruise ship dock downtown), or at the city and state museums (see above).

The **STATE CAPITOL** (4th and Main Sts; 907/465-2479; free guided tours 9am–4pm daily, self-guided tours 8:30am–5pm) is hard to miss since it's the only building in town with four two-story marble pillars in front. The seat of the federal

of the road, you'll pass the trailhead to **SPAULDING MEADOWS**. It's a 3-mile hike with an 1,800-foot increase in elevation to the public-use cabin. Take water once the snow is gone. If Auk Village is full, head for the **MENDENHALL LAKE CAMPGROUND** (same as above) where there are 60 tent sites at $10 a night, as well as showers and full hook-up RV sites. You can take the **CAPITAL TRANSIT** bus from the harbor to **MONTANA CREEK ROAD;** the campground is barely ½ mile from there. For sore muscles or just a little luxurious cleansing, go to **NORTHERN HOT SPOTS** (2055 Jordan Ave; 907/789-9251) for a soak in a Jacuzzi hot tub; $25 per hour before 5pm, $31.50 after; open 7am–9pm weekdays and 9am–8pm weekends.

DAY THREE: Ditch the camping gear or dump it in the corner of your hotel room. If you want to hang out with other swarthy just-back-from-the-wilderness types, check in at the **ALASKAN HOTEL** (167 Franklin St; 800/327-9347), where you can get a "Scandinavian style" room (bath and toilet down the hall) for $60 a night, or one with a private bath for $80. Smack in the middle of downtown Juneau, you can trade tall tales over fresh **ALASKAN BREWERY** ale on tap or take your pick from downtown's range of restaurants and nightspots. If you've built up an Alaska-size appetite from the past two days, try the **THANE ORE HOUSE SALMON & HALIBUT BAKE** (907/586-3442). They'll send their bus to bring you to their beach lodge 4 miles south of downtown. The menu is all-you-can-eat fish, barbecued beef ribs, salad bar, and side dishes. Open 11am–9pm with a lunch menu until 4pm. Darts and horseshoe pits are available if you want to work off some of your meal, or you can relax by the fireplace.

—*Bob Tkacz*

government during Alaska's territorial days, it was inherited by the 49th state upon statehood and houses the governor and legislature. The fifth floor hall walls are worth a look—framed newspaper front pages depict historic events.

Kitty-corner from the capitol is the **STATE OFFICE BUILDING**, affectionately known as the "S.O.B." The eighth floor atrium balcony provides a great view of Gastineau Channel and the off-downtown vicinity. Recitals on an antique pipe organ are presented at noon on Friday. Exit the S.O.B.'s main entrance on Calhoun Street, turn left, and you'll come to the **GOVERNOR'S MANSION,** with its white-columned entrance and a mosquito totem pole, just across the next corner. On your way, keep an eye out for **BLACK BEARS** that actually graze on the slope just below you. The mansion isn't open for tours, but if it's December you may be able to catch the governor's annual holiday open house. Anything from Gore-Tex to "Juneau tennis shoes" (knee-high rubber boots) is proper attire. The governor is likely to greet you at the door.

Next, head to the top of Main Street, turn right and come to **WICKERSHAM HOUSE** (213 7th St; 907/586-9001), once the residence of Alaska's first territorial delegate to the U.S. Congress, Judge James Wickersham, and now a museum. Open for free tours (donations accepted) daily, 10am–noon and 1pm–5pm. Closed Wednesdays.

Across and farther along Seventh Street find a stairway down to **COPE PARK,** home of the only public tennis courts in downtown Juneau. The park is bordered on the far side by Gold Creek. Head upstream to a stand of Sitka spruce and hemlock, and then downstream where you might find a modern sourdough panning for flake gold. Exit on lower Calhoun Avenue.

Or, from Wickersham House, head to **LAST CHANCE BASIN,** the heart of the original prospecting that led to the creation of Juneau. Bear left from Seventh Street onto Basin Road, a wooden trestle hugging the rocky mountainside. Watch for bears—they occasionally cruise the slope across Gold Creek. In fact, all of Juneau is prime bruin habitat, so be prepared to encounter a bear at any time while hiking on official trails or in wooded areas, especially after dark and during late summer.

Downhill from where Basin Road ends, take the bridge across the creek to the **LAST CHANCE MINING MUSEUM** (907/586-5338; mid-May to late Sept, subject to weather conditions, 9:30am–12:30pm and 3:30pm–6:30pm daily). It's located in some of the original gold-rush mine buildings; $3 admission. If gold mining history is your passion, tour the **AJ MINE/GASTINEAU MILL ENTERPRISES,** in part of the vast (more than 200 miles) tunnel complex inside Mount Roberts (Princess Tours; 907/463-3900). The two-hour excursion includes almost an hour underground, with demonstrations and explanations of jack-leg drilling and other mine operations. Tours run in coordination with cruise ship schedules, starting roughly hourly until mid-afternoon. Rates for non–cruise ship visitors are $49 per person; $24.50 per child 12 and under. Reserve at least a day in advance.

Heading uphill from the end of Basin Road will put you on the **PERSEVERANCE TRAIL,** probably the most-hiked trail in the Juneau system. Rated "easy" in the Juneau Trails guide (see Mendenhall Glacier in Adventures, below), the route dead-ends in 3 miles at Silver Bow Basin. On the way you'll pass **EBNER FALLS,** and the **MOUNT JUNEAU** and **GRANITE CREEK TRAILS,** all signed. If it's been raining for any length of time, a pair of rubber boots can be a must and will greatly expand your ability to cross or explore the well-braided creek.

Left from Last Chance Basin, continuing on Basin Road to another left at **SIXTH STREET** (just look to the left and up), will bring you to the **MOUNT ROBERTS** trailhead, a beckoning wooden staircase. It's 4½ hours to the 3,800-foot summit on a trail that curls around the mountain through shadowed forest, reaching the tree line well after you're back on the Gastineau Channel side of the mountain.

SHOPPING
Juneau is the shopping center for Panhandle residents and by extension has become the region's tourism "mall," in contrast with the specialty shops of neighboring communities. But you can still find some gems. The Southeast's long, rainy winters nurture reading in Alaska. **HEARTHSIDE BOOKS** (254 Front St; 907/586-1726), with a second location in the **NUGGET MALL SHOPPING CENTER** (in the Mendenhall Valley; 907/789-2750), has a wide selection of Alaska books, the latest best-sellers, and a colorful children's section. **RAINY DAY BOOKS** (113 Seward St; 907/463-BOOK (2665)) specializes in used books. **THE OBSERVATORY** (200 N Franklin St;

907/586-9676; fax 907/586-9606; www.observatorybooks.com) is also stacked with used books, but specializes in rare books, maps, and prints. Owner Dee Longenbaugh can track down titles on request.

WILLIAM SPEAR DESIGN (174 S Franklin St; 907/586-4132; www.wmspear. com) is a necessary stop for pin collectors. You won't find the standard chamber of commerce pin, but eclectic pieces of lapel jewelry that illustrate wildlife, comedy, social commentary, politics, and even autobiography (ask to see "The night my goddamn drink caught on fire" pin). Doll collectors will want to visit **MEMELUCK DOLL FACTORY** (126 Seward St; 907/463-2627), which features Eskimo and other porcelain fur-clad dolls, fur hats and slippers, and other small fur and leather items.

Diversity and high quality are the foundation of the Alaska Native art collection at **THE RAVEN'S JOURNEY** gallery (439 S Franklin St; 907/463-4686), an educational oasis in a sea of T-shirt shops. Owners John and Kathy Ellis are personally acquainted with every artist whose masks, carvings, baskets, Chilkat weavings, whalebone carvings, earrings, and other works they display. Joy in the everyday life of rural and Native Alaska is central to the work of **RIE MUÑOZ**. Her works are available throughout Alaska, but her own gallery of prints, posters, silkscreens, tapestries, books, and cards is squirreled away across the street from the Jordan Creek Mall, about 2 miles from the Juneau International Airport near the McDonald's (Rie Muñoz Gallery, 2101 N Jordan Ave; 907/789-7411; info@riemunoz.com; www. riemunoz.com). **ANNIE KAILL'S FINE CRAFTS GALLERY** (244 Front St; 907/586-2880) in the heart of downtown displays a variety of wood, clay, glass, crystal, fabric, and other gifts. It's an especially good place to find a wedding gift with an Alaska flair.

In need of tougher clothing, replacement fanny pack clasp (or a whole new pack), pitons, crampons, ski wax, or sun block? The **FOGGY MOUNTAIN SHOP** (134 N Franklin St, across from the Baranof Hotel; 907/586-6780) is the likeliest place in Juneau to find it, and the only serious gear store downtown. **NUGGET ALASKAN OUTFITTERS** (8745 Glacier Hwy, Ste 145; 907/789-3635), in the Nugget Mall Shopping Center, offers an equally good selection of heavy duty work and play clothes and a better variety of marine foul-weather gear. **OUTDOOR HEADQUARTERS** (9131 Glacier Hwy; 907/789-9785), in the Airport Shopping Center farther down the road, is the only army surplus store in Juneau, and in case you've really overpacked, a pawnshop to boot. A Capital Transit bus runs on Glacier Highway.

ADVENTURES

BIKING / Located about ½ mile past the Grants Plaza shopping center in the Lemon Creek neighborhood, **CYCLE ALASKA** (5454 Jenkins Dr; 907/321-BIKE (2453)) is Juneau's only bicycle shop. Mountain bikes go for $30 a day and $20 for a four-hour half day; rentals can be delivered to you anywhere in Juneau. The shop also offers tours Sunday through Friday. They last about four and a half hours and take in the sites at an easy/moderate pace. The **"BIKE & BREW"** tour ($50 per person) stops, near its conclusion, at the prize-winning **ALASKAN BREWERY CO.** (see above).

HIKING / Juneau is a hiker's paradise. Within 15 minutes of leaving any downtown hotel or B&B you can be on a trail through an emerald forest, up a mountain, or headed toward the wonders of the intertidal beach zone. If you head out Juneau's 45-mile road toward its dead end, you'll find many more trails following very fishable streams or through medieval forests. If socializing is part of your hiking style, the JUNEAU PARKS & RECREATION DEPARTMENT (in City Hall at 155 S Seward St; 907/586-5226 or 907/586-5330 for recorded information) sponsors group hikes guided by local volunteers, every Wednesday and Saturday beginning around 9am. The recorded message also lists commercially guided hikes.

MENDENHALL GLACIER / All glaciers are overwhelming by virtue of their massive presence. The Mendenhall Glacier is that and more because of its accessibility as one of five "drive-up" glaciers in Alaska. A short drive north of town, the MENDENHALL GLACIER VISITORS CENTER (8465 Old Dairy Rd; 907/789-0097; www.fs.fed.us/r10/tongass/, follow links; 8am-6:30pm daily in summer, 10am-4pm Thurs-Sun in winter) has an observatory, exhibit hall, theater, and Alaska natural-history bookstore. Telescopes offer a close look at the massive ice formation from a comfortably warm and dry vantage point, and you can sometimes find a family of mountain goats feeding on the highest of the surrounding ridges. Admission is $3.

For a more strenuous encounter with the glacier, the East Glacier Trail will lead you to the glacier itself in about 3½ miles and 2½-3½ hours round-trip. Start from the stairway behind the visitors center. The total elevation gain is 400 feet, but all of the ups and downs will make it feel like a lot more. It is rated as "more difficult" in the very worthwhile JUNEAU TRAILS, the Tongass National Forest Juneau Ranger District hiking guide, available at the visitors center and area bookstores. The WEST GLACIER TRAIL, also rated "more difficult," is just under 3½ miles, but takes 5-6 hours round-trip because you gain 1,300 feet. The trailhead is located across Mendenhall Lake from the visitors center. It is also accessible on foot from the Mendenhall Lake Campground. Both the trailhead and campground are well-marked off Montana Creek Road.

For those more inclined to let their pocketbooks do the heavy lifting, you can land, hike, and even go dog-sledding on the one of the several glaciers that are part of the 1,500-square-mile Juneau Icefield. NORTHSTAR TREKKING (907/790-4530; fax 907/790-4419; www.glaciertrekking.com) offers a combination flight-seeing/glacier hike ($319 per person). The four-hour trip includes two hours on the ice, fully equipped with the appropriate clothing, boots, ice ax, and crampons and accompanied by seasoned mountain guides. No previous glacier experience is necessary, but moderate agility is recommended. Book at least 14 days in advance during the peak summer season. TEMSCO HELICOPTERS (907/789-9501; www.alaskaone.com/temscoair/) offers a one-hour Mendenhall Glacier tour that includes a brief landing on the icefield, or a "pilot's choice" trip that includes two landings on two glaciers or on the icefield (up to $269 per person). Heli-skiing trips are also offered during ski season. ERA HELICOPTERS (907/586-2030; www.era-aviation.com) offers various tour/landing packages, including a stop at their seasonal dog mushing camp. For $349 per person, fly over four glaciers and spend an hour at the camp, staffed by veterans of the famed Iditarod Trail Sled Dog Race.

MOUNT ROBERTS TRAMWAY / Ascend 2,000 feet to alpine meadows in six minutes. Painted in Tlingit motifs of gleaming red and black, the Eagle and Raven tram cars make continuous trips from 9am to the last descent at 9:30pm. Waiting at the top is the **CHILKAT THEATER**, presenting a documentary film on Southeast Native history and culture, the full-service **TIMBERLINE BAR & GRILL**, an observatory, and the **GASTINEAU GUIDING NATURE CENTER** (907/586-2666). The **GASTINEAU GUIDING COMPANY** (see Guides and Outfitters, below) is one of the premier guided hike businesses in the Southeast. The tram complex is still almost 2,000 feet below the summit, and interpretive trails lead through various loops in the vicinity or to the top, where you can go for miles on more-or-less ridgetop jaunts with views of eagles soaring over Gastineau Channel or sightings of hoary marmots, mountain goats, wolves, Sitka black-tailed deer, and, of course, bears. The meadows below the ridge are the favored launch site for a squadron of brave **PARASAILERS**. An all-day ticket for the tram costs $21.95 for adults, $12.60 for children 7–12; children 6 and under are free. If you want to hike from the bottom, one-way descent tickets are $5 with any $5 purchase from the tram complex. *907/463-3412 or 888/461-8726; www.alaska.net/~junotram; look for the tram terminal on S Franklin St.*

GOLFING / Golfing isn't a major sport in the Panhandle due to the shortage of flat, wide-open spaces, the rain, and, to a lesser extent, the moving black and brown hazards (a.k.a. bears), but you can play a few rounds most summer days at the **MENDENHALL GOLF COURSE**. Between ball-stealing ravens and a rough that resembles the fairways where the Scots invented the game, "winter rules" are played year-round. If you bring your own clubs the greens fee is $10; if not, $25 covers it, plus clubs, balls, tees, and a cart. *Open at 8am weekdays, 7am weekends, subject to weather, with last tee-off at 5pm; 2101 Industrial Blvd; 907/789-1221.*

SKIING / City-owned and -operated **EAGLECREST SKI AREA** was the training ground of Juneau native and Olympic silver-medalist Hilary Lindh. It features a 1,400-foot vertical drop and is geared for experienced skiers, with 12 black-diamond routes. The 640 acres include 31 alpine runs and 8 kilometers of groomed Nordic trails and are rated 20 percent novice, 40 percent intermediate, and 40 percent expert. The Eagle's Nest warming hut at the top of the Ptarmigan chairlift is 2,600 feet above sea level and at the top of a 2-mile run. *Open Thanksgiving through Apr, on a good year; 907/790-2000 or call 907/586-5330 for conditions; www.juneau.org/eagle crest; about 9-miles on Douglas Hwy, turn left on Fish Creek Rd, and go another 5 miles up the road to the ski area.*

FLIGHT-SEEING / For jaw-dropping views (and prices), flight-seeing is the ticket. Locally-owned **COASTAL HELICOPTERS INC.** (907/789-5600; www.coastal helicopters.com) offers two glacier tour packages. The Icefield Excursion is an hour-long pilot-guided tour with a 20-minute landing on the ice ($168 per seat). The Adventure Tour is an hour of flight-seeing and an hour on the ice ($275 per seat; three-passenger minimum). Tours begin on the hour, with the last flight at 6pm; courtesy van pickup at convenient locations in the downtown dock area.

WINGS OF ALASKA (907/789-0790; info@WingsOfAlaska.com; www.Wings OfAlaska.com), just behind Merchants Wharf at the foot of Main Street, offers two floatplane trips. The takeoff and landing are experiences in themselves. Both trips take you over five different glaciers. The Icefield Excursion is a 45-minute flight with 20 minutes on a glacier ($135 per person; every hour on the half hour). The three-hour Adventure Tour begins with the same flight and landing, followed by a king-salmon feast at Taku Lodge, a remote outpost on the Taku River ($199 per person; five departure times throughout the day in summer).

FISHING / Juneau's fleet of fishing charter boats grows and shrinks by a few vessels each year, but many have lengthy records of bringing home satisfied anglers with coolers full of salmon, halibut, and the increasingly popular rockfish. **ALASKA FLY' N' FISH CHARTERS** (907/790-2120; akbyair@ptialaska.net; www.alaskaby air.com) owners Butch and Sarah Laughlin use floatplanes to offer any combination of freshwater fishing, bear, and whale-watching adventures. David and Cynthia Hansen, both U.S. Coast Guard licensed captains, run **ALASKA ACCESS CHARTERS & TOURS** (907/780-2232 or 888/432-4282; www.juneaucharterboats.com), which specializes in salmon and halibut fishing. **FLYWATER ADVENTURES** (907/789-5977; flywater@alaska.net; www.flywateradventures.com) specializes in fly-fishing and variety. Their Angler's Retreat provides a guide/host who can take you to small creeks, coastal rivers, estuaries, and lakes to target the species and conditions of your choice.

WHALE-WATCHING AND GLACIER CRUISES / Humpback whales are the most common species of great whale in Alaska waters. Majestic and serene, even at their adult size of up to 50 feet and 40 tons, they are playful and acrobatic. They may be seen any time of year in any of the open waters of the Southeast. If you're on a **STATE FERRY**, the north Frederick Sound area around The Brothers and Five Finger Islands is a good place to find pods of humpbacks. Chasing a meal during spring herring runs, they even come up Gastineau Channel and have been seen north of the Douglas Island bridge. Dall porpoise and orcas are also common.

ADVENTURE BOUND ALASKA (215 Ferry Wy; 907/463-2509 or 800/228-3875; www.adventureboundalaska.com) combines whale- and seal-watching in a leisurely trip to the Sawyer and South Sawyer Glaciers, 25 miles deep in the Tracy Arm Fjord, about 40 miles south of Juneau. Each voyage includes close to an hour spent about ¼ mile (a reasonably safe distance) from the 10-story-high face of each glacier. The continuous crackling sounds that echo off fjord walls often presage a calving. You can also watch scores of seals hauled out on the ice floes that surround you. In early summer, mother seals give birth to pups on the ice, sometimes before your eyes. The 56-foot MV *Alaska Adventure* departs from Marine Park daily at 8am and returns at 6pm ($99 for adults, $59 for children 12 and under; 10 percent discount if booked a day in advance). Complimentary snacks and coffee are served, with sandwiches, snacks, and soft drinks for sale. Kayak drop-off and pickup can also be arranged.

AUK NU TOURS (76 Egan Dr; 907/586-8687 or 800/820-2628; www.goldbelt. com/subsidiaries/AukNu.html) offers whale-watching and glacier cruises accompanied by trained naturalists. The Tracy Arm Glacier Cruise departs Tuesday, Thursday, and Saturday at 9am from its downtown dock (across from the Goldbelt Hotel) and returns at 5pm ($110.25 per person; includes hot lunch and beverages). The Icy Straits Whale-Watching Cruise leaves at 9am on Sunday, Monday, Wednesday, and Friday, taking you to Point Adolphus, a humpback whale gathering area west of Admiralty Island off the north coast of Chichagof Island. Return is at 8:30pm ($195 per person; includes lunch and beverages).

For shorter trips, **DOLPHIN TOURS** (907/463-3422; www.dolphintours.com) offers daily whale-watching cruises in custom-built jet boats that spend two hours on the waters out of Auke Bay, three hours total including pickup from downtown locations ($95 per person). **ORCA ENTERPRISES** (907/789-6801 or 888/733-6722; www.alaskawhalewatching.com) launches four Whale Watching Adventures daily, guided by marine biologist and researcher Capt. Larry Dupler. Cruises depart several times a day with a sunset cruise at 6pm, depending on the weather. The $99 per person package includes two and a half hours on the water and smoked salmon and other Alaskan snacks.

SEA KAYAKING / Owner Nancy Peel of **ALASKA PADDLE SPORTS** (800 6th St; 907/789-2382) has been guiding for 17 years and her students have included professional guides and park rangers. She offers intensive daylong classes in one-person-kayak operation, including paddling skills, flipping boats, and getting in and out of capsized boats. Classes are limited to 10 students ($135 or $110 if you have your own boat). Rentals also available.

ALASKA BOAT & KAYAK (Auke Bay boat harbor; 907/789-6886 or 907/321-5026; www.juneaukayak.com; closed mid-Sept to mid-May) is as close as you can come to one-stop shopping for a trip on the water. Former commercial crabber and licensed 100-ton-vessel master Kerrie Kirkpatrick offers kayak, skiff, and camping equipment and fishing tackle rentals, basic vessel operation instruction, and kayak transport. One-hour, by-appointment classes cost $25 and will give you the knowledge you need to operate a kayak in the protected waters of Auke Bay. Boat rentals range from $110–$150 per day with discounts for multiday use. They also rent 16- and 18-foot Lund skiffs, complete with 25- to 50-horsepower outboards, VHF radios, and signal flares. Kayak transport and storage also available; they can meet you at the state ferry terminal or other arrival point and transport your boat to a put-in anywhere along the road system. To assure pickup at the time of your choice, call at least a week in advance.

AUK TA SHAA DISCOVERY (76 Egan Dr, in the Goldbelt Seadrome Bldg; 907/586-8687 or 800/820-2628) offers excursions down the glacier-fed Mendenhall River several times daily ($89 per person round-trip; includes transportation from Juneau, lunch, and equipment). Although the river is nothing for white-water enthusiasts to write home about, it can make for a mildly exciting ride after a week of rain has swollen the stream to its banks.

CHARTERS / If you're looking for a little more luxury than a kayak can provide, Juneau has several crewed and bare-boat charter companies that allow you to explore, whale-watch, or fish at your own pace. **ADVENTURES AFLOAT** (907/789-0111 or 800/3-AFLOAT (323-5628); valkyrie@ptialaska.net) owners Francis and Linda Kadrlik operate the 106-foot MV *Valkyrie,* which offers eight staterooms and a 1,500-mile cruising range. Sea kayaks, seacycles (two-person paddle boats), and fishing gear are available for cruises and in the off-season. When there are no charters booked, the *Valkyrie* is operated as a floating hotel for overnight guests.

ALASKA YACHT ADVENTURES (907/789-1978 or 800/725-3913; dennis@ alaskayacht.com), based in Auke Bay, and **SEAWIND CRUISES** (907/586-6641; seawindak@aol.com), in Douglas Harbor, both offer crewed day or long-term charters. If you're ready to head to sea with your own crew, **ALASKAN BEAR YACHT CHARTERS** (907/780-8685; fax 907/780-4473; www.alaskanbear.com/charter) and **ABC ALASKA YACHT CHARTER** (907/789-1239 or 800/780-1239; www.abcalaska. com/) both have fleets of 32- to 45-foot motor yachts, accommodating four to eight persons, available for charter.

RENT A LIGHTHOUSE / Well, that might be a bit ambitious, but you could get lucky. Of the dozens of lighthouses that once dotted the Pacific Northwest most have been automated. In the Panhandle several of the properties that included substantial structures have been privatized and are being turned into B&Bs or lodges. As of 2002, none were open for business, but some offer charter tours or trade volunteer labor in exchange for visits. For information try the **JUNEAU LIGHTHOUSE ASSOCIATION** (907/364-3632; fax 907/586-2636; juneaulight@earthlink.net; www. 5fingerlighthouse.com), **SENTINEL ISLAND LIGHTHOUSE** (907/586-5338; fax 907/586-5820), or **ALASKA LIGHTHOUSE ASSOCIATION** (907/364-2410).

PUBLIC-USE CABINS / The Forest Service rents public-use cabins in the Juneau area for $25–$45 per night. Cabins with propane stoves and plywood bunks for up to eight persons can be reserved up to 180 days in advance by phone (877/444-6777) or online (www.reserveusa.com). Cabin rentals and permits for bear viewing at **PACK CREEK** on Admiralty Island may be obtained from the **JUNEAU RANGER DISTRICT OFFICE** (8465 Old Dairy Rd, 907/790-7488; fax 907/586-8808; www. fs.fed.us/r10/tongass/), or by calling the national reservation service (877/444-6777; www.reserveusa.com).

ALASKA STATE PARKS (400 Willoughby Ave, 4th floor, Juneau AK 99801; 907/465-4563; www.dnr.state.ak.us/parks) maintains three cabins that can be reserved up to two months in advance. You can check availability online, but reservations can be placed only in person or by mail. The Cowee Meadow and Blue Mussel Cabins, both near Point Bridget, 39 miles out Glacier Highway from downtown Juneau, can sleep up to eight persons and are available for $35 per night. The Oliver Inlet cabin, which sleeps four and cost $25 nightly, is located about 23 miles south of Juneau on Admiralty Island, accessible only by plane or boat. If you time the flood and ebb tides in Gastineau Channel right, the trip to Admiralty Island makes for a relatively easy kayak trip from the downtown harbors. However, crossing open water from south Douglas Island to Admiralty can be difficult for novice paddlers, depending on sea conditions.

GUIDES AND OUTFITTERS

ALASKA DISCOVERY WILDERNESS ADVENTURES / This is one of the oldest and most respected wilderness expedition guiding companies in the state, with quality trips led by knowledgeable and enthusiastic guides. The company emphasizes "leave no trace" camping and donates 10 percent of its profits to environmental organizations working toward the preservation of Alaska's special places. The Southeast is home, and the company offers 1- to 12-day canoeing, sea kayaking, and rafting trips to see glaciers, wild rivers, bears, and other wildlife. Not a budget operation, Alaska "Disco" prices range from $125 per person for a one-day Gustavus kayak tour to $495 per person for a daylong floatplane, bear viewing, and hiking excursion on Admiralty Island. Multiday wilderness trips are, of course, even more expensive.

5449 Shaune Dr, No. 4, Juneau AK 99801; 907/780-6505 or 800/586-1911; akdisco@alaska.net; www.akdiscovery.com.

ALASKA RAINFOREST TOURS / This is a travel agency for independent travelers staffed by agents who have been on all the trips they recommend. They can make your connections for wilderness travel, whale-watching, remote lodges, bed-and-breakfasts, charter fishing boats, kayaking trips, and more. Their 72-page catalogue is available on their Web site. *1873 Shell Simmons Dr, Juneau AK 99801; 907/463-3466; rainforest@alaska.com; www.alaskarainforesttours.com; at the Juneau International Airport.*

GASTINEAU GUIDING COMPANY / They offer three Juneau-area hikes ranging from a two-hour tour of the interpretive trails at the top of the Mount Roberts Tramway to a 4- to 6-mile "guide's choice" trek on a route in the Juneau area. Prices range from $46 per person for the "tram 'n trek," which includes an all-day tram ticket, to $69 per person for the guide's choice. Details are available at the company's nature center (907/586-6421) at the top of the tram. *PO Box 240576, Douglas AK 99824; 907/586-2666; fax 907/586-3990; hikeak@ptialaska.net; www.ptialaska. net/~hikeak/.*

FESTIVALS AND EVENTS

ALASKA FOLK FESTIVAL / This is a springtime, cabin-fever-curing, musical jamboree that goes on for 10 days in April. A master folk musician headlines the largest free music festival in the United States, but anyone (almost) who signs up in time gets 15 minutes on the stage during continuous performances from 7 to 11 every evening. Daylong weekend concerts run concurrent with workshops, folk, rock, and ethnic dances, and pretty much every stage in town has jam sessions throughout the weekend. It's a great time. *907/463-2658; www.juneau.com/aff/.*

JUNEAU JAZZ & CLASSICS / This May festival features live professional jazz and classical performances, musical workshops, special cruises, and events for the whole family. Tickets—$5 per person for family concerts to $50 per person for evening cruise concerts—can be bought at Hearthside Bookstores. *907/463-FEST (3378); music@juneau.com; www.juneau.com/music/.*

FOURTH OF JULY / Juneau is the first city in the United States to shoot off its fireworks each Independence Day. Owing to the need to wait until after 11pm for the sky to get good and dark, they light the fuse at midnight at the start of July 4th, on a barge that slowly cruises the downtown harbor. The booming echoes bouncing between the mainland and Douglas Island mountains make the blazing light show even more spectacular. After a few hours rest, Juneau enjoys an old-fashioned holiday in the best small-town American tradition. Tons of saltwater taffy and other sweets are tossed to the crowd by Juneau parade participants. After the Juneau parade, most floats and participants head across the bridge to the old city of Douglas for another parade through that community's main thoroughfare (old Douglasites still like to think of themselves as separate from Juneau). Then the action shifts to Savikko Park, on Douglas Island, for the dog Frisbee, volunteer fire department hose-coupling, and sand castle–building contests. Look for courtesy marine shuttles across Gastineau Channel.

SALMON DERBIES / Early or late in the summer you can fish for potential profit, as well as fun. The **SPRING KING SALMON DERBY** (907/586-1432) runs for the entire month of May, with top prizes including a new pickup truck or cash. Participants in the **GOLDEN NORTH SALMON DERBY** (907/789-2399), the third weekend in August, go after a tagged coho salmon as well as the biggest fish for like prizes. Record fish are in the 50-pound range. Proceeds from both competitions, including ticket prices and the sale of donated fish, fund college scholarships for local students.

THE GALLERY WALK / If you happen to be in Juneau the weekend after Thanksgiving, this is an opportunity you shouldn't miss. Numerous downtown galleries host a floating holiday reception and art show with seasonal snacks. Begun by Annie Kaill at her Front Street gallery (907/586-2880).

NIGHTLIFE

BAR SCENE / Tourists go to the **RED DOG SALOON,** which specializes in afternoon sing-alongs. Locals go to the **ALASKAN HOTEL,** featuring open-mike night on Thursdays. **THE TRIANGLE** is the place to go for a ballpark-style hot dog and is a popular hangout of legislative staff and other political types when the Alaska legislature takes over the town for the winter. **THE VIKING** lounge is gaining as a watering hole for political denizens and has the newest pool tables in town in a recently remodeled second floor. All are in a two-block stretch of Franklin Street.

Downtown's other "hot spot" is **MERCHANTS WHARF,** that two-story powder blue wooden building at the foot of the Main Street hill. A semihistorical structure, still on its original piling foundation, The Wharf was a seadrome that housed Juneau's first flight services, all floatplanes. It now houses shops, tanning and hair salons, restaurants, and the **CHILKAT CONE KITCHEN & JUICE BAR** (10am–10pm Mon–Sat, noon–9pm Sun), the only downtown ice-cream parlor. The Kitchen bakes its own waffle cones and will blend any fruit or veggie drink you can dream up if they've got the ingredients.

PERSEVERANCE THEATRE / Juneau has its own Broadway in the bush in this internationally renowned professional, multicultural theater. The Perseverance stage was the birthplace of *How I Learned to Drive,* winner of the 2000 Pulitzer Prize for playwriting, and it has been the site of more than 50 world premiers, including *In the Blood* by 2001 Pulitzer winner Suzan-Lori Parks. Director Peter DuBois was called "one of 15 up-and-coming directors under 30" by *American Theater* magazine. Perseverance specializes in Alaskan and new plays and performers and the mainstage season runs September through May. Preparations for construction of a new theater on property next to its Douglas Island home were nearing completion in 2002. Call for performance schedules. *914 3rd St, Douglas AK 99824; 907/364-2421; www.perseverancetheatre.org.*

RESTAURANTS

Chan's Thai Kitchen / ★★☆

11820 GLACIER HWY, JUNEAU; 907/789-9777 This spot is popular with students from the University of Alaska Southeast campus uphill behind it and with hungry sailors arriving at Auke Bay Harbor just across the street. Ambiance is correspondingly casual, but Chan's varied menu is authentic Thai basics like spring rolls and pad thai, plus varied creations. Waiting lines are common at prime time on weekends. *$; MC, V; local checks only; lunch, dinner Tues–Sun; no alcohol; no reservations; across from public harbor in Auke Bay at the end of the Capital Transit bus route.*

The Fiddlehead Restaurant and Bakery & Di Sopra / ★★★

429 W WILLOUGHBY AVE, JUNEAU; 907/586-3150 Sold in the late '90s, the Fiddlehead Restaurant and Bakery continues as the ground-floor restaurant, still featuring a creative menu that treats vegetarian cuisine with respect without scaring away carnivores. For example, the Mexican Rice Grande (melted cheddar over salsa and brown rice with sherried black beans, sour cream, and guacamole) would go well with Porterhouse Pork Chops (grilled with a chipotle barbecue sauce). The slightly more upscale Di Sopra, upstairs, features an Italian cuisine that takes advantage of living in Alaska. Dinner menu offerings include Pernod steamed Alaskan clams, roasted halibut cheeks with prosciutto di parma and rosemary, and fresh Alaskan salmon encrusted with hazelnuts. Also 80 wines including 15 selections by the glass. Prices upstairs are a bit steeper than the more casual downstairs. *$$–$$$; AE, DIS, MC, V; checks OK; breakfast, lunch, dinner every day downstairs; dinner every day upstairs; beer and wine; reservations recommended downstairs, required upstairs.*

Hangar on the Wharf / ★★

2 MARINE WY, STE 106, JUNEAU; 907/586-5018 The Hangar offers the best views of the harbor in town. Floatplanes land just outside the windows, seeming to play dodge 'em with the lightering craft moving passengers between anchored cruise ships and the city dock. The casual atmosphere tends toward loud as the clientele morphs from diners to nightclubbers as the start of live music approaches at 10pm. Seafood influence is strong on the menu (halibut tacos are a popular lunch item), but the jambalaya is reasonably Cajun and you can get a steak cooked to order. If you're there for the night scene, there are pool tables upstairs and 108 beers, ales, porters, and stouts behind the bar, including 24 on tap. *$$; AE, DIS, MC, V; local checks only; lunch, dinner every day; full bar; reservations recommended; downtown in Merchants Wharf.*

Heritage Café / ★★

174 S FRANKLIN ST, JUNEAU; 907/586-1087 One of two local coffee houses, Heritage is also a great soup-and-sandwich lunch spot with front window seats to watch the street scene. Homemade pastries, soups, sandwiches, teas, and, of course, its own roasted coffee, plus a variety of car mugs and travel thermoses. The cafe sells 14-ounce bags of coffee. (So does the roasting house, but it's hard to find; look behind the Salvation Army Thrift Shop at 538 Willoughby Ave). *$; AE, DIS, MC, V; local checks only; breakfast, lunch, dinner every day; no alcohol; no reservations.*

The Hot Bite / ★★

AUKE BAY HARBOR, AUKE BAY; 907/790-2483 Well hidden from those whose Juneau visit only includes downtown, the Hot Bite serves the best malts in town. With burgers—including halibut burgers—fries, and onion rings, this is the last stop for serious junk food before heading "out the road," or out to sea. *$; No credit cards; local checks only; lunch every day (winter), lunch, dinner every day (summer); no alcohol; take a left downhill into the harbor parking lot, then past the harbormaster's shack, just above the ramp to the mooring floats.*

Olivia's de Mexico / ★★

222 SEWARD ST, JUNEAU; 907/586-6870 Take a tip from Olivia's countrymen—the Mexican crews off the cruise ships come here for a taste of home. Diners get the genuine article—chili verde and chilies rellenos are popular, and Olivia makes daily specials such as *posole*, a meat and hominy stew. During the legislative session you may have to wait for a lunch table. *$; MC, V; local checks only; lunch Mon–Fri, dinner Mon–Sat; beer and wine; dinner reservations recommended; downtown.*

Paradise Lunch & Bakery / ★★

245 MARINE WY, JUNEAU; 907/586-2253 The fresh-baked fragrance of breads and morning pastries, all from scratch, can help you find this tiny cafe across the street from Marine Park. On a sunny day they'll have their sidewalk cafe furniture out. Fare may include Paradise sausage, black olive zucchini soup, tortilla wraps with meats roasted in-house, pastas, and potato salads. *$; No credit cards; local checks only; breakfast, lunch Mon–Sat. (summer), Mon–Fri. (winter); no alcohol; no reservations.*

Pel'Meni / ★★

 MERCHANTS WHARF, 2 MARINE WAY, JUNEAU; 907/463-2630 Billing itself as "the underground midnight cafe," Pel'Meni's only menu item is *pel'meni*, a little, meat-filled Russian dumpling served in a tangy red sauce with heavy brown bread, all made fresh daily, and all the sour cream you want. Not only are Pel'Meni's *pel'meni* tasty, but it's the only place downtown to find a bite to eat after 10pm (they're open until 1:30am weeknights and until 3:30am Friday and Saturday). If the line is long after bar-closing time you can pass the time playing tunes from the eclectic record collection—real vinyl platters on a turntable. *$; No credit cards; checks OK; lunch, dinner every day; no alcohol; no reservations.*

Pizzeria Roma / ★★★

MERCHANTS WHARF, 2 MARINE WY, JUNEAU; 907/463-5020 Pizza for adults (a lot more than tomato sauce and cheese), some of the best oil-and-vinegar salads in town, and a home for garlic-lovers. *$; All major credit cards; Alaska checks only; lunch, dinner every day; beer and wine; no reservations.*

The Twisted Fish & Alaska Grill / ★★★

550 S FRANKLIN ST, JUNEAU; 907/463-5033 The four-foot-long, neon-painted fish hanging from the wood beams help put a ceiling on this airy restaurant at the south end of the downtown waterfront. Their seafood comes from the Taku Fisheries/Taku Smokeries processing plant, which shares the same building. The only way to get it fresher is to walk across the yard to the pier where fishing boats unload their catch. If you catch some sunny weather there's no better Alaskan dining experience in Juneau than dinner alfresco. Seafood pastas are a local favorite, and it's the only place in town to get a salmon pizza. It can be a noisy place. *$$; AE, MC, V; local checks only; lunch, dinner every day (May to mid-Sept); beer and wine; reservations recommended; across the parking lot from the Mount Roberts Tramway.*

Valentine's Coffee House & Bakery / ★★

111 SEWARD ST, JUNEAU; 907/463-5144 Everything is baked from scratch. There are good coffee drinks, exceptional coffee cakes, interesting and tasty sandwiches, and some of the best coffee T-shirts you'll find anywhere. Occasionally hosts a poetry slam or traveling musician. *$; No credit cards; local checks only; breakfast, lunch every day (closed Sun in winter); no alcohol; across the street from the side door of McDonald's.*

LODGINGS

Aurora View Inn / ★★★

2917 JACKSON RD, JUNEAU; 907/586-3036 OR 888/580-VIEW (8439) Located more than 800 feet up the slopes of Mount Troy on Douglas Island and featuring a 35,000-acre backyard, the Aurora View Inn is a minilodge with a focus on your comfort. Accommodations include rooms and suites. All have private baths, entrances, phones with Internet connections, coffeemakers, and refrigerators. Suites include kitchenettes and a sitting room. Full breakfast is served in your room. Prices range from $129–$200, double occupancy. Add $10 for each additional person. *$$$; AE, MC, V; no checks; auroravu@ptialaska.net; www.ptialaska.net/~auroravu.*

The Baranof / ★★

127 N FRANKLIN ST, JUNEAU; 907/586-2660 OR 800/544-0970; FAX 907/586-8315 Built in 1939, the Baranof remains the premier hotel in Juneau, as much for its importance as a gathering place as for its accommodations. Located three blocks from the state capitol, the Baranof is particularly busy during the winter legislative season. It hosts almost nightly political receptions and provides a home away from home for lobbyists parachuting in for an emergency. In summer, it's all tourists and is easy walking distance from everything downtown. Rooms are small. Rates range from $79 for a "nothing fancy" double with two twin beds, to $229, double occupancy, for a suite on an upper floor. We recommend the corner, water-view suites on the sixth and seventh floors. *$$$; AE, DC, DIS, MC, V; checks OK; www.westmark hotels.com/locations/juneau/juneau.html; near the capitol.*

Goldbelt Hotel Juneau / ★★★

51 EGAN DR, JUNEAU; 907/586-6900 OR 888/478-6909; FAX 907/463-3567 Owned and operated by Goldbelt, the local Native corporation, the hotel is staffed largely by young Native men and women who radiate enthusiasm tempered with folksy small-town charm. Remodeled after being bought from the Westmark Hotel chain, the Goldbelt lobby and restaurant, Chinooks, are airy, light places adorned with museum-quality Tlingit and Haida artwork. Staff can tip you to hot fishing spots if you're going to be in town long enough to "wet a line." The Chinooks menu is mostly standard fare but their salmon platter is a great snack or a light meal; open daily for breakfast, lunch, and dinner, and brunch on Sunday. Half

of the 105 rooms have great harbor views and five of six bedroom floors are non-smoking. Rates range from $169, double occupancy, for a room facing the back to $179, double occupancy, for a room facing the channel. Add $15 for each additional person. Lower rates are available in winter. *$$$; AE, DC, DIS, JCB, MC, V; checks OK; www.goldbelt.com; downtown, directly across from the Goldbelt Seadrome Bldg charter and tour center.*

Juneau International Hostel / ★★★

614 HARRIS ST, JUNEAU; 907/586-9559 For budget traveling, this is probably the top hostel in Alaska and ranks with the best in the world, especially when it comes to cleanliness. Hiking boots or sandals come off at the door. Located high enough (six blocks) above downtown to escape the tourist frenzy, the hostel is close enough to two of the most popular hiking trailheads to see snack-hunting bears stroll by late at night. Free Internet access for guests, plus lockers and laundry. Midnight curfew is strictly enforced. The hostel operates year-round, but is often virtually empty during winter. Reservations via mail with deposit are highly advisable in summer. And you can't beat the prices: $10 for adults; $5 for children 6–17; under 5 free with paying adult. Open for check-in and room access 7am–9am and 5pm–midnight only. *$; No credit cards; checks in U.S. currency OK; www.juneauhostel.org.* &

Pearson's Pond Luxury Suites & Garden Spa / ★★★

4541 SAWA CIRCLE, JUNEAU; 907/789-3772 OR 888/658-6328 This is one of the best of the "mini-inns" that are defining the difference between one- and two-guest B&Bs and larger but still intimate guesthouses. Pearson's Pond is located deep in Mendenhall Valley. You're away from the downtown hubbub and can be assured of very peaceful nights, but you need wheels for convenient travel around the city. On the other hand, the amenities don't provide a lot of reason to leave the premises. They include a massage room, music room/library, outdoor hot tub, a rowboat on the pond, skis, mountain bikes, and, for those who can't leave the world behind, a business center with high-speed Internet access. All guest rooms have private entrances and stocked kitchenettes for continental breakfast whenever you want it. Rates are $210–$270, double occupancy (two-night minimum). *$$$; AE, DIS, MC, V; no checks; book@pearsonspond.com; www. pearsonspond.com.*

Whale's Eye Lodge / ★★★

SHELTER ISLAND, NEAR AUKE BAY; 907/723-2920/2921 If you're looking for someplace to stay in Juneau that caters to hard-core anglers, or for true isolation, the Whale's Eye Lodge may be the place you're searching for. Built on 9-mile-long Shelter Island, about 30 minutes by boat from the Auke Bay Harbor, the lodge guarantees "at least 8 hours of fishing per day" if that's your desire. Guests stay in private cabins with bathrooms, fish off the lodge's 26-foot Bayliner cabin cruiser, and dine family-style in the lodge overlooking Saginaw Channel, Admiralty Island, and the Chilkat Mountains. It's a little on the pricey side at $770 per person for two nights. All meals, transportation, and fishing tackle is provided, but the price does not include cost of fishing license, shipping and processing of your catch, or alcoholic beverages. *$$$$; no credit cards; checks OK; PO Box 21066, Auke Bay AK 99821; whaleseye@starband.net; www.whaleseye.nu.*

BED-AND-BREAKFASTS

There's around a hundred B&Bs in Juneau ranging from classic Alaska log cabins to the room that used to be the kids' before they moved to Seattle. That gives you the opportunity to find accommodations on the waterfront, on a mountainside, or in the middle of downtown Juneau. At **CASHEN QUARTERS** (303 Gold St, Juneau AK 99801; 907/586-9863; fax 907/586-9861; cashen.quarters@acsalaska.net; www.cashenquarters.com), located halfway between downtown and the multiple hiking trailheads in Last Chance Basin, you'll find single rooms and suites, all with private entrances and kitchenettes. An expansive continental breakfast is available throughout the day from 7am. No smoking, check before bringing pets. Cost is $85–$155, double occupancy, plus $15 for each additional guest (AE, DIS, DC, MC, V; checks OK).

Literally perched at the top of the most upslope neighborhood in the downtown area, **CLIFF HOUSE B&B** (124 W 6th St, Juneau AK 99801; 907/586-2179; fax 907/463-3893; jhoman@ptialaska.net; www.juneaucliffhouse.com) is an easy walk to everywhere you can go downtown without getting on a boat. Amenities include complete kitchen, laundry, and barbecue grill on the deck. Continental breakfast includes fresh fruit and fresh-baked muffins. No smoking. Call for rates (no credit cards; checks OK).

A little less than midway between downtown and the Mendenhall Valley, the **ALASKAN BEAR B&B** (4436 Glacier Hwy, Juneau AK 99801; 907/780-6420; kgilmore@ptialaska.net) offers private rooms with or without private baths in communal accommodations that include microwave oven and a fully furnished kitchen. It's an easy bicycle ride to downtown and the Capital Transit bus stops nearby. No smoking. The Black Bear, Polar Bear, and Kodiak deluxe suites cost $55–$175, double occupancy. Add $10 for each additional person (MC, V; checks OK with credit card guarantee).

Peaceful, simple accommodations in residential Douglas is what **GOULD'S ALASKA VIEW B&B** offers (3044 Nowell Ave, Juneau AK 99801; 907/463-1546; fax 907/463-3810; tci@gci.net; www.bedandbreakfast.com/bbc/p604346.asp). It's located a block above the main Douglas Island highway and the bus stop; a mile from downtown Juneau; and maybe 4 miles from Sandy Beach on the island, with hiking trailheads nearby. The single suite sleeps up to three and there's a private entrance and phone, as well as laundry facilities. Full breakfast is served 8am–9:30am. No smoking or pets. Rates are $110–$125 per night for one–three persons (two-night minimum), plus $15 for each additional person (no credit cards; checks OK).

Thane is the neighborhood at the dead end of the road that runs 5 miles south from downtown Juneau. Folks moved there for the peace and quiet, and **SALMONBERRY INN B&B** (5025 Thane Rd, Juneau AK 99801; phone-fax 907/586-3451; paula@salmonberryinn.net; www.salmonberryinn.net) offers just that, smack in the middle of towering Sitka spruce on the slopes of Mount Roberts. Continental or full breakfasts, including homemade breads and jams, are offered and special dietary needs can be accommodated with advance notice. Bicycles and fishing tackle are ready for use, as is the hot tub. Children and pets OK with notice. Double occupancy rates are $85 for one of two rooms that share a bath, $160 for a suite with private bath (no credit cards; checks OK).

If you're happy with a peaceful, roomy apartment with a fabulous view of Mendenhall Glacier, crab quiche and blueberry waffles for breakfast, and easy access to Mendenhall Lake and hiking trails up the side of the glacier, you should consider **GLACIER TRAIL B&B** (1081 Arctic Circle Dr, Juneau AK 99801; 907/789-5646; fax 907/789-5697; stay@juneaulodging.com; www.juneaulodging.com). Fresh-cooked breakfast is served at 8:30am only; in-room continental is anytime. Apartments are for two or up to five in the Bear Den. Both have private baths, with whirlpool bathtub. No smoking. Rates are $120 and $145, double occupancy, plus $20 for each additional person (MC, V; checks OK).

Gustavus and Glacier Bay National Park

Gustavus is unique in the Southeast, tucked into the forest and spreading out on a flat outwash plain created by glaciers that receded long ago. It is also on the edge of **GLACIER BAY NATIONAL PARK AND PRESERVE**. A 10-mile road connects the tiny town and park headquarters at Bartlett Cove. If you are flying into the park, you land in Gustavus.

Tlingit Indians built camps and smokehouses here for many generations. Then, in 1914, the first wave of white homesteaders arrived and called the settlement Strawberry Point because of the abundance of wild strawberries. A second wave of homesteaders arrived in the 1960s and 1970s, armed with the *Whole Earth Catalog* and a desire for back-to-the-land lifestyles. Gustavus (pop. 430) exudes small-town friendliness. People wave at each other, and pickup trucks still outnumber cars.

BARTLETT COVE offers a very different experience from Gustavus. While Gustavus appeals to independent travelers who want free time along with sight-seeing, visitors who stay at Bartlett Cove are generally on package tours designed to put the maximum amount of wilderness scenery in front of their video camera viewfinders. Besides park headquarters, Bartlett Cove is home to the only developed campground in the area, as well as the Glacier Bay Lodge, where all manner of excursions may be arranged.

When Capt. James Cook sailed up Icy Strait more than 200 years ago, there was no Glacier Bay, only a huge wall of ice stretching across the opening to what we know today as the bay. In this blink of geologic time, the ice has receded and opened up a treasure of fjords and cascading rivers of ice—one of our most precious national parks. You can now travel 60 miles up the bay into the West Arm, which is the park's most dramatic and glacially active area. This is the route the cruise ships take. But the best way to see the bay is slowly, over 10–14 days, by small boat, paddling or under sail. Watch for seals, puffins, whales, and bears.

ACCESS AND INFORMATION

AIR TAXIS in Juneau, Sitka, Skagway, and Haines offer scenic flights to Gustavus. For those who prefer to do their flight-seeing in a Boeing 737, **ALASKA AIRLINES**

(800/252-7522; www.alaskaair.com) has daily jet service in the summer. The **GLACIER BAY FERRY** (907/586-8687 or 800/820-2628; www.goldbelttours.com), based in Juneau, runs daily between Juneau and Bartlett Cove. The three-hour trip will cost you about $70 one-way. If you need taxi service while in Gustavus or Bartlett Cove, call **TLC TAXI** (907/697-2239; tlctaxi@glacierbaytravel.com); they'll even transport your bike or kayak. TLC Taxi's owners also run a travel agency, Glacier Bay Travel (907/697-2475; www.glacierbaytravel.com). For those who want to drive themselves around the area, there's **BUD'S RENT-A-CAR** (907/697-2403; fax 907/697-2789); the rate is $60 a day.

Contact the **GUSTAVUS VISITORS ASSOCIATION** (PO Box 167, Gustavus AK 99826; info@gustavusalaska.org; www.gustavusalaska.org) for area information. **GLACIER BAY NATIONAL PARK** (PO Box 140, Gustavus AK 99826; 907/697-2230; www.nps.gov/glba) headquarters and visitor information are located in Bartlett Cove.

ADVENTURES

EXPLORING BY BIKE / Most bed-and-breakfasts have old one-speed cruisers for biking through town. At the hub of Gustavus is a re-created 1930s-era gas-station-cum-English-cottage-flower-garden, the perfect symbol of Alaskans' two loves—the internal combustion engine and Mother Nature. **THE GUSTAVUS DRAY** (907/697-2481; fax 907/697-2355) has petroleum memorabilia inside as well as a gift shop and, most years, ferry tickets for sale. Pedal about ½ mile north from the gas station to **FIREWEED GALLERY** (907/697-2325), open afternoons in summer. Longtime Gustavus resident Jim Healy has a small gallery displaying local and Alaska sculpture and paintings. Go ½ mile south from the gas station to **GUSTO BUILDING SUPPLY** (907/697-2297), where you can get a fishing license. Then stop in at the **BEARTRACK MERCANTILE** (907/697-2358), a well-provisioned general store, to pick up a visitor's map or the booklet *Trails of Glacier Bay and Gustavus* for a list of off-road hikes. For another splash of local color, cycle over to artist Carole Baker's **FLAMINGO GALLERY** (907/697-2283; caroleterrybaker@hotmail.com). Go south off Main Road just west of the Salmon River Bridge and turn right at the flamingo sign. Pedal another mile to the dock, which juts into Icy Passage and offers a 360-degree panorama of everything Southeast—mountains, islands, forests, dunes, and ocean surf. The Gustavus dock is the best place to watch the sunset and sunrise. The salt air is a bracing tonic.

FISHING AND WHALE-WATCHING / The chief attractions in Gustavus, besides relaxing, are fishing and whale-watching. A **HALIBUT** of more than 400 pounds was caught on sport gear just a few miles from the Gustavus dock. Nearby **POINT ADOLPHUS** is summer home to **HUMPBACK WHALES.** You may want to book your outdoor trips after you arrive and check the weather; kayaking or sailing in rain or heavy ocean swells can be miserable. (See Guides and Outfitters, below, for some trip options.)

GOLFING / Within walking distance of the ferry dock, the nine-hole, par-36 **MOUNT FAIRWEATHER GOLF COURSE** (907/697-2214) is not hoity-toity golf, but it offers a good old seaside game on the links nonetheless. There's beach, rampant weeds, and even real grass; Kentucky blue grass is used on the greens. Put your cash

($15) in the money jar and grab a set of brand-new clubs. If it's a clear day with the Fairweather Range in view, you won't find a prettier course in all of Alaska. Watch out for bears and moose, and be forewarned that the first hole in mid-July might take at least two hours because everyone is down on their knees picking wild strawberries.

GUIDES AND OUTFITTERS

ALASKA DISCOVERY / The fully equipped, guided sea-kayak tours of Bartlett Cove and the Beardslee Island Archipelago are for adventurous, but inexperienced, day trippers ($125 per person). The company also guides 5- to 11-day kayaking and camping expeditions into Glacier Bay at, of course, a higher cost. *907/697-2411, summer; 800/586-1911, year-round; fax 907/780-4220; info@akdiscovery.com; www.akdiscovery.com.*

GLACIER BAY CRUISELINE / Day cruises on the *Spirit of Adventure* travel into Glacier Bay National Park, where the magnificence of the Ice Age is still at work. Cost is about $160 per person, including lunch. From mid-May to early September, the *Spirit of Adventure* also serves as a camper/kayaker ferry service, with four drop-off/pickup points that change from year to year. The vessel has space for 150 passengers and 30 kayaks. Cost one-way is about $90 per person. Make reservations at the front desk of the Glacier Bay Lodge (see Lodgings review, below) in summer, at the Goldbelt Tour Center (800/820-2628) in Juneau, or on the reservation line out of Seattle (800/451-5952). *www.glacierbaycruiseline.com.*

GLACIER BAY SEA KAYAKS / Rent seaworthy kayaks and gear for exploring the waterways around Gustavus. This is the National Park Service concession in Glacier Bay for "do-it-yourself" camping and kayaking trips. The fiberglass kayaks rent for $35–$40 per day for singles and $40–$60 per day for doubles. They also will arrange drop-offs in the West and East Arms of Glacier Bay. *907/697-2257; fax 907/697-2414; kayakak@he.net; www.glacierbayseakayaks.com.*

GUSTAVUS MARINE CHARTERS / Capt. Mike Nigro runs these highly recommended trips, excellent for small yacht tours of Glacier Bay National Park and Icy Strait. If at all possible, set aside a minimum of three days to fully absorb the wonder and the subtlety of the park. *907/697-2233; fax 907/697-2414; gmc@mars.he.net; www.gustavusmarinecharters.com.*

KELLY BAY YACHT CHARTERS / This outfit is the first choice for those who want the ultimate custom trip—picnicking on a wilderness beach overlooking Icy Strait, or serious fishing for trophy salmon or halibut. You name it, and you can do it in complete comfort on their motor yacht, equipped with skiff for beachcombing excursions. Hosts Mike and Connie Mills can also put you up in their sweet little log-cabin Spruce Tip Lodge (see Lodgings review, below). *907/697-2215; fax 907/697-2236; sprucetiplodge@hotmail.com.*

SEA OTTER KAYAKS / Rent single and double Necky kayaks and gear for half-day paddles or longer expeditions. Reservations are recommended. Located near the Gustavus dock on Dock Road. *907/697-3007; seaotter@he.net; www.he.net/~seaotter.*

SEA WOLF WILDERNESS ADVENTURES / Using their 65-foot motor yacht *Sea Wolf* as a moveable base camp, hosts Rusty Owen and Pamela Jean Miedtke take their clients on a variety of five- to eight-day custom trips, which may include whale-watching, hiking, kayaking, glacier gazing, and birding. Nights are spent on the yacht anchored in remote bays, often near glaciers. Rusty and Pam are both U.S. Coast Guard, 100-ton-vessel license holders with years of experience piloting the waters of the Southeast. *907/697-2416; alaska@seawolf-adventures.com; www.seawolf-adventures.com.*

SPIRIT WALKER EXPEDITIONS / This outfit offers complete one-day, guided sea-kayak excursions to Pleasant Island ($125) or Icy Strait ($319), just outside Glacier Bay, and longer trips to nearby wilderness areas. *907/697-2266 or 800/529-2537; fax 907/697-2701; kayak@he.net; www.seakayakalaska.com.*

PONY CART RIDES / For those who prefer a more festive arrival in Gustavus or a special honeymoon trot down the beach, Kate Boesser (wife of Fritz Koschmann of Woodwind Sail Charters) can often be enticed to garland up her pony cart with flowers and meet your plane or take you on a sunset ride. *907/697-2282; kate boesser@mail.com.*

RESTAURANTS

Bear's Nest Cafe and Cabins

NO. 2 WHITE DR, GUSTAVUS; PHONE-FAX 907/697-2440 Tucked into the forest, this little cafe is the home (upstairs) to artist Lynne Morrow and her husband, musician Philip Riddle. Downstairs is a warm, creative cafe with artistic touches such as straw baskets hanging from the ceiling, handmade paper menus, a lot of windows, and green plants. Specializing in organic, homemade foods, the owners serve fresh crab, vegetarian enchiladas, salmon stir-fry, hot sausage sandwiches, almond butter and jam sandwiches, espressos, Italian sodas, Alaska-brewed beers and organic wines, along with decadent homemade desserts. They even have a fun B&B a stone's throw away, with two cabins: The Round House ($95 per night for two) and the A-frame ($85 per night for two). Additional roommates can join you for $25 each. The price includes breakfast. *$–$$; DIS, MC, V; checks OK; lunch, dinner every day; beer and wine; no reservations; PO Box 216, Gustavus AK 99826; lynnemorrow @hotmail.com or bearsnest@starband.net; www.gustavus.com/bearsnest; just off Wilson, ¼ mile from Four Corners, the center of Gustavus.*

LODGINGS

Glacier Bay's Bear Track Inn / ★★

255 RINK CREEK RD, GUSTAVUS; 907/697-3017 OR 888/697-2284; FAX 907/697-2284 Bears are not just stuffed decorations for the interior of this huge log lodge, but are much alive, lumbering through the meadows and down to the slough to feast on salmon. (The National Park Service wanted to make all of Gustavus a black-bear preserve because there are so many bears here.) Sitting on 17 acres at the end of the road, this lodge is peaceful, but on a grand log scale—a huge lobby with walk-around fireplace, expansive windows looking out on Icy Strait and Pleasant Island, and 14 spacious guest rooms with double beds. The on-site restaurant features a choice of fresh seafood, beef, or steak, with a medley of desserts including home-made berry ice creams, apple tarts, and Whiskey Fudge Pie. Beer and wine are also available. Dinner is open to the public ($32 per person; call before noon for reservations). One night's lodging is $454 per person, double occupancy. All activities are extra, but the inn provides all ground transportation to and from the inn and its activities. $$$; DIS, MC, V; checks OK; open May to mid-Sept; PO Box 255, Gustavus AK 99826; beartrac@aol.com; www.beartrackinn.com; at the end of Rink Creek Rd, about 7 miles from the center of town. &

Glacier Bay Country Inn / ★★★★

PO BOX 5, GUSTAVUS AK 99826; 907/697-2288 OR 800/628-0912; FAX 907/697-2289 The original owners of the inn once dreamed of having a hay farm here, but it wasn't very practical, so they turned it into a country inn and welcomed visitors from around the world. The cleared hay fields—in summer beautiful meadows filled with flowers—give the inn an unusual pastoral setting with lovely views of the Bear Track and Chilkat Mountains. Current owners Sandi and Ponch Marchbanks have done a wonderful job to enhance the character of the original inn. There are four guest cabins and six rooms. Tea is served on the big outdoor deck. Chef Noon Gaffney's specialties are Asian and vegetarian dishes. Meals feature fresh Alaska seafood, with intriguing twists such as a Greek-inspired sautéed halibut muffaletta or the visually lovely salmon roulade where the fish is cut open, stuffed, and rolled into spirals. Beer and wine are also offered. Many activities may be arranged through the inn, such as fly-fishing, deep-sea fishing, whale-watching, kayaking, and day trips to Glacier Bay. Someone from the lodge will meet you at the airport or dock. The cost is $185 to $195 per person per night, including meals. $$$; AE, DIS, MC, V; checks OK; open May 18 to Sept 10 (until Sept 30 for fly fishers only); info@glacierbayalaska.com; www.glacierbayalaska.com; 4 miles from the center of town. & (with limitations)

Glacier Bay Lodge / ★★

GLACIER BAY NATIONAL PARK, GUSTAVUS AK 99826; 907/697-2226, SUMMER; 800/451-5952, YEAR-ROUND A handsome cedar, glass, and stone structure with wide porches and a massive stone fireplace, this is the only lodge located within Glacier Bay National Park. A boardwalk connects the guest rooms to the lodge. Excursions and tours are available as part of package tours sold by the lodge operator or can be arranged once you get to the lodge. Nature walks, fireside programs, guided or on-your-own kayaking, sportfishing, whale-watching, day and overnight cruises into Glacier Bay, and flightseeing are some of the options. In the warmth of a rare sunny summer evening, it's a pleasure to sit out on the deck for drinks and hors d'oeuvres. There are rustic, modern rooms ($189 for a double), but campers who have spent too many nights in the rain can also choose to stay in dorms with room for six men and six women ($30 per person). $-$$$; AE, DC, DIS, MC, V; checks OK; open mid-May to mid-Sept; www.glacierbaycruiseline.com; at Bartlett Cove, inside the park.

Good River Bed and Breakfast / ★

 PO BOX 37, GUSTAVUS AK 99826; 907/697-2241; FAX 907/697-2269 On part of the old homestead once settled by Abraham Lincoln Parker, this homespun three-story guest house is made of Sitka spruce timbers salvaged from an old fish trap. Each log has been painstakingly chiseled with a decorative bevel and perfectly dovetailed at the ends. Inside, hand-thrown ceramic tiles surround the woodstove, simple homemade patchwork quilts top the beds, and paintings by Alaskan artists grace the walls. The craftsmanship continues at breakfast: homemade granola, flapjacks served with spruce-tip syrup, wild berry jams, and smoked salmon. The four guest rooms are not spacious, but the living room (with harpsichord) and deck are cheerful places to relax. For those who desire more privacy, a snug, rustic cabin with cooking facilities is also available. The cabin has no indoor plumbing, but many guests think of the "one-holer" as another addition to their life list of Alaska experiences. Rooms are around $95 for double occupancy, $85 for the cabin. They also have wild, rainbow-painted bicycles for the borrowing or to ride in the Fourth of July parade. *$; MC, V; checks OK; open mid-May to mid-Sept; bandb@goodriver.com; www.goodriver.com; off Good River Rd, 3½ miles from the Gustavus airport.*

Gustavus Inn / ★★★★

ON THE SALMON RIVER NEAR AIRPORT, GUSTAVUS; 907/697-2254 OR 800/649-5220; FAX 907/697-2255 More than 25 years ago, Jack and Sally Lesh began the transformation of their family's homestead on the Salmon River into a small, comfortable country inn—no small feat considering there was no electricity, no telephone, no stores, only sporadic mail and barge service, and eight children to raise. At the time, Gustavus was considered a featureless backwater, but Sal's good cooking and the unpretentious charm of the old homestead earned the inn a loyal following among Alaska cognoscente. Today, their son Dave and his wife, JoAnn, continue the tradition of offering the best of country living. Guest rooms look onto the stunning garden or across hay fields to Icy Strait. They might serve their popular Halibut Caddy Ganty, a concoction of halibut and sour cream, or black cod steamed in sake and topped with wild morel mushrooms from the woods nearby, accompanied by salads with greens and carrots from the garden and a choice of beer or wine. Dessert might be homemade ice cream or lemon meringue pie with homegrown sweet red raspberries. (Dinner is available for nonguests by reservation.) This is one of Alaska's very best. $150 per person per night, double occupancy, which includes all meals and local transfers; singles pay $210 per night with private bath. *$$$; AE, MC, V; checks OK; open mid-May to mid-Sept; PO Box 60, Gustavus AK 99826; dave@gustavusinn.com; www.gustavusinn.com; 1 mile from the Gustavus airport.* &

Spruce Tip Lodge / ★★

NEAR THE DOCK, GUSTAVUS; 907/697-2215; FAX 907/697-2236 Open year-round, this small charming log cabin lodge, designed barn-style, is cozy, warm, and friendly—just what you'd expect in a picture postcard of Alaska. Much of the furniture is handmade from local wood, with cheerful quilts on the beds. Prices start at $130 per person per day, which includes three meals a day and all ground transportation. Alcohol is not provided with the meals, though guests are welcome to bring their own. The lodge is within walking distance of the beach, the dock, and the heart of town. The owners, Mike and Connie Mills, also run a first-class boat charter business called Kelly Bay Yacht Charters, and they provide ground transportation. *$$; AE, DIS, DC, MC, V; checks OK; PO Box 299, Gustavus AK 99826; sprucetiplodge@hotmail.com; in the heart of Gustavus.*

Icy Strait

Icy Strait is the watery divide separating Glacier Bay National Park and Gustavus from Chichagof Island. The Icy Strait area has escaped much of the hype surrounding Glacier Bay, although in many people's minds it's every bit as beautiful, and has just as much wildlife as the national park. The tiny outposts of Elfin Cove, the Hobbit Hole, and Gull Cove in Icy Strait are beginning to look toward tourism, but commercial fishing, subsistence, and rugged self-reliance are still their heart and soul.

Until a few years ago, **ELFIN COVE** (winter pop. 32) could have passed for the set for the Popeye movie, with its handful of weathered houses perched on a boardwalk and rafts of fishing boats in the harbor. Unfortunately, plywood siding has made significant inroads in recent years, and a small cruise ship occasionally drops anchor here in the summer. Still, the setting is wild and magnificent. Trophy-size salmon and halibut are abundant, and enough salty ambience remains to charm the most jaded tourist. You can buy the best smoked salmon in Icy Strait at Patti Lewis's smokehouse above the inner harbor, and a short walk down the boardwalk brings you to Augusta Clement's cabin, where she sells homemade jams. Look for the faint handwritten sign on an old cabin saying "Jams for Sale" or ask directions from anyone on the boardwalk. (The jams are self-serve, honor system, outside her cabin.)

On a small, forested island, in a sheltered bight, lies the **HOBBIT HOLE** (see Lodgings review, below), named in the 1970s for the hobbit dwellings in Tolkien's mythological stories. As you approach, the only sound you may hear is the haunting song of a hermit thrush deep within the forest. Wood smoke curls from the stovepipe of a rustic home, perfuming the air with cedar. The land was originally homesteaded in the 1920s by F. R. Townsend; the current owners recently began welcoming visitors to their Alaska paradise.

After a day of kayaking, the two lodges at **GULL COVE** are a welcome sight. On a private inholding in the Tongass National Forest, the lodges are the only development between Elfin Cove and Hoonah, a distance of about 35 miles. Although they are next to each other and have similar layout (three beachside cabins with baths and a main cookhouse), the personalities of the owners make each place unique. You can't go wrong staying at either place (see Lodgings, below).

ACCESS AND INFORMATION

For **AIR CHARTER SERVICE** from Juneau, try Alaska Seaplane Services (907/789-3331 or 800/478-3360; fax 907/463-4453; akseaplanes@alaska.com; www.akseaplanes.com), Alaska Fly 'n' Fish (907/790-2120; akbyair@gci.net; www.alaskabyair.com), or Wings of Alaska (907/789-0790; fax 907/789-2021; info@WingsOfAlaska.com; www.WingsOfAlaska.com). From Gustavus, try Air Excursions (907/697-2375; fax 907/697-2376; airex@ptialaska.net; www.airexcursions.com) or Wings of Alaska.

CROSS SOUND EXPRESS (phone-fax 907/697-2726 or 888/698-2726; csetaz@ hotmail.com) can take up to 23 passengers and gear by boat to Icy Strait destinations from Juneau or Gustavus. DOUG OGILVY (phone-fax 907/697-2409) can quickly transport people and kayaks anywhere in Icy Strait from Gustavus. The kayak drop-off services in Juneau don't usually run all the way to Elfin Cove—too far and not enough demand.

ADVENTURES

GUIDED TRIPS / SPIRIT WALKER EXPEDITIONS (907/697-2266 or 800/529-2537; fax 907/697-2701; kayak@he.net; www.seakayakalaska.com) leads small groups on lodge-to-lodge kayak trips in Icy Strait. For hardier sorts, they offer two- to seven-day camping/kayaking expeditions along the northern shore of Chichagof Island and to Point Adolphus. ALASKA DISCOVERY (907/697-2411, summer; 800/586-1911, year-round; fax 907/780-4220; info@akdiscovery.com; www.akdiscovery.com) also leads multiday kayak trips to Point Adolphus. If you'd rather use horse-power instead of arm power to explore Icy Strait, charter operators in Gustavus, Pelican, Elfin Cove, or Hoonah can arrange custom trips in their cabin cruisers.

SEA KAYAKING / If you have good outdoor gear and sea kayaking or skiffing experience, you can enjoyably explore Icy Strait on your own. Be aware that under certain conditions South Inian Pass becomes a nightmare of standing rooster tails and whirlpools, and the crossing from Point Adolphus to Pleasant Island can be treacherous. In Gustavus, rent kayaks from GLACIER BAY SEA KAYAKS (907/697-2257; fax 907/697-2414; kayakak@he.net; www.glacierbayseakayaks.com) or SEA OTTER KAYAKS (907/697-3007; seaotter@he.net; www.he.net/~seaotter). Both companies give thorough instructions before turning paddlers loose on the water.

LODGINGS

Gull Cove Lodge / ★

IN IDAHO INLET, GULL COVE; PHONE-FAX 907/697-2720, SUMMER; 907/789-0944, WINTER Paul and Tammy Johnson's lodge features guided sportfishing and hunting trips, although nonhunters and nonfishers would feel comfortable here too. It is, perhaps, a little less rough around the edges than South Passage Outfitters (reviewed below). Gull Cove is 80 miles west of Juneau on Icy Strait; guests arrive by charter aircraft or boat. The cost of $500 per person per night includes lodging, meals, and boat transportation from Gustavus. $$$$; No credit cards; checks OK; open mid-May to mid-Sept; summer address: PO Box 22, Elfin Cove AK 99825; winter address: 22891 Glacier Hwy, Juneau AK 99801; mowich@alaska.net; wwwgullcove.com; 25 minutes by boat from Elfin Cove.

The Hobbit Hole Guest House / ★★

INIAN ISLANDS, ELFIN COVE; 907/723-8514 Guests stay in a bright and airy cabin, named the Hobbit Hole Guest House, on the beach and can either prepare their meals in the cabin or join owners Jane Button and Greg Howe for delicious home-cooked meals. Jane is a treasure and a great cook; Greg is, in his words, "a crusty old fisherman," with a sense of humor. The setting is quintessential Southeast Alaska and offers visitors a unique glimpse at modern homestead life.

Don't be put off by first impressions; there are always construction materials and some gear on the dock and beach. They rent skiffs and kayaks, too, and are very savvy about local waters and weather conditions. The Hobbit Hole is on the largest of the Inian Islands near Elfin Cove, and someone will meet guests at Elfin Cove with prior arrangement. If you're arriving by boat, call VHF 14 or 16 for directions. Charter flights are available out of Juneau and Gustavus. The cost is $200 per night for the cabin, for up to four people; add $25 for each additional person. Add $50 a day for three home-cooked meals. *$$–$$$; MC, V; checks OK; closed Jan to Feb; Inian Islands, PO Box 9, Elfin Cove AK 99825; www.hobbitholealaska.com; 4 miles by boat from Elfin Cove.*

South Passage Outfitters / ★

EAST OF ELFIN COVE; 907/723-4561, SUMMER; 360/385-3417, WINTER Peggy McDonald and Dennis Montgomery cater to experienced campers, fishers, and kayakers. They rent skiffs and kayaks and are extremely knowledgeable about local waters. This is a remote, pristine setting—still a little rough around the edges. Indoor plumbing and a futon seem luxurious when you've been kayaking for a week but would seem pretty basic if you've been traveling by private yacht. Guests arrive by charter aircraft or boat. The wildlife watching is good, both for coastal birds and marine mammals, especially whales and sea otters. The cost of $200–$225 per person per night includes lodging, meals, and use of a skiff and kayak. *$$$; No credit cards; checks OK; open mid-May to mid-Sept; summer address: PO Box 48, Elfin Cove AK 99825; winter address: PO Box 1967, Port Townsend WA 98368; info@icystrait.com; www.icystrait.com; E of Elfin Cove about 8 miles.*

Tanaku Lodge / ★★

ACROSS THE HARBOR FROM ELFIN COVE; 907/239-2205 OR 800/482-6258; FAX 907/239-2253 At the entrance to the inner harbor, Tanaku Lodge is the best bet for quiet accommodations for the independent traveler, although sportfishermen are the big kahunas here. Cushy guest rooms have views of both harbor and town; ask for a room overlooking the water. Easy-maintenance decor is the theme of the lounge, with a wraparound window looking out over the town and the Fairweather Range. Tanaku is on the opposite side of the "gut" into the inner harbor from downtown Elfin Cove, and it is quieter and less congested as a result. The philosophy here is ecotourist friendly. Lodge staff will meet guests; if you're coming by boat, the lodge dock is clearly marked. The cost ranges from $2,695 for three nights to $2,995 for five nights; price includes lodging, meals, and guide services. *$$$; AE, MC, V; checks OK; open May to mid-Sept; PO Box 72, Elfin Cove AK 99825; tanaku@msn.com; www.tanaku.com.*

Haines

Haines has what every Southeasterner often pines for—*sun!* Haines only gets 60 inches of rainfall annually, while Ketchikan receives a whopping 160 inches and Juneau is drenched with 90 inches. (Skagway receives only 30 inches of annual rainfall, but beware the wind.) Both Haines and Skagway are in the rain shadow of the Fairweather Range, which catches much of the precipitation blowing off the Gulf of Alaska.

Beyond the benefits of being a bit drier, Haines also is one of the most picturesque towns in all of the Southeast, sleeping peacefully in unbelievable mountain splendor, where road meets sea. From the 1940s until the 1980s, before Skagway was linked to the Alaska-Canada Highway, Haines had a unique feature in Southeast life: a road that actually went somewhere. In its commanding position at the head of the Inside Passage, Haines was the beginning (or the end, depending on your perspective) of the road to the Interior. It sits on the edge of the forests and fjords of Southeast Alaska and the wide glacial valleys, mountain kingdoms, and more severe climates of the north. Its population is made up of resilient old-timers who have done it all and young adventurers who are trying to do it all with boundless enthusiasm for everything this mountain-ocean playground offers.

At 90 miles north of Juneau—the same latitude as Oslo, Norway—Haines lies on a peninsula between the mouths of two rivers, the Chilkat and the Chilkoot. Situated at the edge of a deep fjord called Lynn Canal, the town and surrounding Chilkat Valley have a population of about 2,300. The Tlingit people called it *Deishu,* or "End of the Trail"; traders called it Chilkoot; the missionaries called it Haines.

The architectural centerpiece of Haines is striking and one of a kind. Sitting just up the hill from the water, framed by breathtaking snowy mountains, is a grassy parade ground ringed by old Victorian buildings. This is historic Fort William H. Seward, once known as the Chilkoot Barracks, a former U.S. Army post built in the early part of the 20th century and deactivated in the 1940s. A group of returning World War II veterans bought the fort years ago and today the buildings include private homes, a hotel, and an art center. In the old days, the parade ground was the place where new recruits, on skis for the first time, learned to discharge their firearms (preferably without killing anyone). Now, this grassy arena serves as a popular summer location for salmon bakes, dance performances, and informal football.

Haines is so picturesque that in recent years the Walt Disney Company, the National Geographic Society, the British Broadcasting Corporation (BBC), and wildlife photographers from around the world have "discovered" it. Jack London's classic story *White Fang* was filmed here in 1990. Almost everybody in town was an extra, and had a jolly good time.

ACCESS AND INFORMATION
Haines is linked to the Alaska Highway, also known as the Alaska-Canada (Alcan) Highway, by a 160-mile road built in the 1940s called the **HAINES HIGHWAY**. This means that from Haines you can drive anywhere the roads go in Alaska or, at Haines Junction, turn right and go back to the Lower 48 (through Canada, of course). Be aware that you will pass through U.S. Customs at Mile 42 on the Haines Highway. Haines is also linked to the **ALASKA MARINE HIGHWAY SYSTEM** (907/766-2111, Haines office; 800/642-0066, reservations; www.alaska.gov/ferry). The MV *Malaspina* (all state ferries are named after glaciers) runs throughout the summer between Juneau, Haines, and Skagway. If you want to sail between Haines and

Skagway, **CHILKAT CRUISES** (907/766-2100 or 888/766-2103; www.chilkat cruises.com) has daily passenger shuttle service from May through September, with a resident Native naturalist/interpreter on board for about $39 round-trip. **ALASKA FJORDLINES** (907/766-3395 or 888/766-3395; www.lynncanal.com) also has daily, round-trip passenger service from Haines or Skagway to Juneau with a wildlife tour. Several small flight services fly in and out of Haines. The best are **WINGS OF ALASKA** (907/766-2646; info@WingsOfAlaska.com; www@WingsOfAlaska.com) on Main Street, which has scheduled service to Haines, Juneau, Gustavus, and Hoonah, as well as Glacier Bay flight-seeing and charters in Alaska and Canada, and **SKAGWAY AIR SERVICE** (907/983-2218; www.skagwayair.com).

THE HAINES VISITOR INFORMATION CENTER (907/766-2234; fax 907/766-3155; www.haines.ak.us), located on Second Avenue near Willard Street in downtown Haines, is open daily in summer. For information year-round, contact the **HAINES CONVENTION & VISITORS BUREAU** (PO Box 530, Haines AK 99827; 907/766-2234 or 800/458-3579; hcvb@haines.ak.us). For a copy of the *Visitor's Guide to Haines,* published annually, write the *Chilkat Valley News* (PO Box 630, Haines AK 99827; www.chilkatvalleynews.com). For **WEATHER FORECASTS AND MARINE CONDITIONS** around the clock, call 907/766-2727.

If you want to see Haines the way it was, put your speed shoes on. This town is fast becoming an outdoor mecca not only for the young and go-for-the-gusto crowd, but also for seniors off the huge cruise ships that started docking here in 1995. Their arrival doubles or even triples the population of the town in a single day.

EXPLORING

AMERICAN BALD EAGLE FOUNDATION / This small museum is a labor of love. A tribute to the bald eagle, it's also filled with the wildlife of the Chilkat Valley (once alive, but now stuffed) and resides just around the corner from the Mountain Market, close to the center of town. Cost is $3. *PO Box 49, Haines AK 99827; 907/766-3094; CHILKATEAGLE@wytbear.com; www.baldeagles.org.*

CHILKAT DANCERS STORYTELLING THEATER / Performing in traditional regalia, this troupe presents Northwest Coast mythology with masks and puppets. These Native dancers have been an inspiration to other Southeast Native communities for keeping traditional dance an integral part of life. They perform at the Tribal House on the parade grounds at Fort Seward (907/766-2160; www.alaskaindian arts.com). Call for a schedule of performances and times for the salmon bake, billed as the **PORT CHILKOOT POTLATCH.** Grilled over an alderwood fire, the all-you-can-eat salmon is truly delicious. **HOTEL HALSINGLAND** also has an all-you-can-eat salmon bake (907/766-2000 or 800/542-6363 for times).

SHELDON MUSEUM AND CULTURAL CENTER / One of five accredited museums in the state, this tiny museum at the corner of Main and Front Streets will give you a feel for the history of Haines, its Native peoples and their traditional art, shipwrecks along the Inside Passage, early pioneers of the region, and more. Admission is $3 for adults and is free for kids under 12. *Open daily in summer, 1pm–4pm Mon–Fri in winter; PO Box 269, Haines AK 99827; 907/766-2366; curator@ sheldonmuseum.org; www.sheldonmuseum.org.*

SHOPPING / There are probably 100 traditional and contemporary artists making a living off their art in Haines (quite extraordinary in a town this size). Spend some time poking around. **ALASKAN INDIAN ARTS** (907/766-2160) and **WILD IRIS** (907/766-2300) are both located in the historic building on the west side of the Fort Seward parade ground. **SEA WOLF GALLERY** (907/766-2540) on the parade ground, and **WHALE RIDER GALLERY** (907/766-2540), on Portage Street, feature the work of Tresham Gregg. His signature style can be seen in wonderful masks such as the mythical sea wolf, a tiny mosquito mask, a raven encircled with rabbit fur, or a wolf-head mask with fur tails. A block or so from the visitor center downtown is **FORM AND FUNCTION GALLERY** (907/766-2539). Most of these shops and galleries are open year-round. Haines also has a charming little bookstore on Main Street called **THE BABBLING BOOK** (907/766-3356).

ADVENTURES

ALASKA CHILKAT BALD EAGLE PRESERVE / Located between Mile 10 and Mile 26 on the Haines Highway, this area is known as the **VALLEY OF THE EAGLES**. About 200 eagles live here year-round. But in the fall and early winter their ranks swell to nearly 4,000, lining the sandbars and filling the cottonwood trees. Warm water, which wells up from the bottom of the Chilkat River, keeps part of the river ice free all winter, allowing these birds to feast on the carcasses of salmon. It's the largest gathering of eagles in the world. A 5-mile stretch along the Chilkat River called the **EAGLE COUNCIL GROUNDS**, between Mile 18 and Mile 22, is the main eagle-viewing area. The greatest concentrations of eagles gather in the fall, peak in November, and taper off by February. *907/766-2202; www.dnr.state.ak.us/parks/ units/eagleprv.*

BIKING / Haines is so small, and the country around it so grand, that you'll find biking is a nice way to get around, from Chilkat Inlet to the west to Chilkoot Lake to the north. You can't lose. Both directions provide intense beauty. Rent mountain or road bikes at **SOCKEYE CYCLE** (Portage St, Fort Seward; 907/766-2869; sockeye@cyclealaska.com; www.cyclealaska.com).

CAMPING / Two exquisite campgrounds lie at the ends of the roads running out of town. To the northwest is **CHILKOOT LAKE STATE RECREATION SITE** at the head of Lutak Inlet. To the south, across the peninsula and along Mud Bay Road, is **CHILKAT STATE PARK**. It sits at the edge of the ocean and has knockout views across to the water to the Davidson and Rainbow Glaciers. For information call 907/766-2292.

FISHING CHARTERS / Just to be out on the water is a treat. Haines and Skagway are not the richest fishing grounds in Southeast Alaska, but they're still good compared to most other places in the world. Several charter companies offer trips for both saltwater and freshwater fishing. Try **JIM'S JAUNTS** (907/766-2935). For more information, call the **ALASKA DEPARTMENT OF FISH AND GAME** in Haines (907/766-2625).

FLIGHT-SEEING / **WINGS OF ALASKA** (see Access and Information, above) on Main Street in downtown Haines, offers flights over Glacier Bay National Park, a short distance to the west. **MOUNTAIN FLYING SERVICE** (132 2nd Ave; 907/766-3007 or 800/954-8747), also operates out of Skagway. This small airline, which has gotten special kudos from passengers and other Southeast pilots, can take you on several unusual aerial adventures, such as beach landings in the remote wilderness of the Gulf Coast or glacier landings in their fixed-wing aircraft equipped with skis.

HIKING / The mountain that rises directly behind Haines, **MOUNT RIPINSKI** (3,610 feet), is a rigorous but wonderful climb on a clear day. Make noise in the forest, as bears abound. The smaller **MOUNT RILEY** (1,760 feet), also with good views is the highest point on the Chilkat Peninsula and rises south of town in Chilkat State Park. For a forest and beach walk, head to Chilkat State Park and the 6.5-mile **SEDUCTION POINT TRAIL**, which has beautiful views of water, glaciers, and mountains and the chance to see bears, whales, seals, and sea lions. Check tides before setting out on this trail, which crosses tidal flats.

KAYAKING / Experienced paddlers can rent kayaks, after a safety review, from **DEISHU EXPEDITIONS** (425 Beach Rd; 907/766-2427 or 800/552-9257; paddle@ seakayaks.com; www.seakayaks.com). They run the gamut from guided trips to kayak and powerboat rentals to skills instruction.

THE GOLDEN CIRCLE ROUTE / You'll find 360 miles of indescribable beauty by road and 15 miles of scenic cruising over water along what is known as the Golden Circle Route. You can drive a car, or go slow and savor the scenery while riding a bicycle. If you want a **GUIDED BIKE TOUR**, call Sockeye Cycle (see Biking, above, for contact info). Four times a summer, the company runs a fully supported summer expedition along this route, which takes nine days. By car or bike, follow the Haines Highway to Haines Junction, on the rim of Kluane National Park; turn right on the Alaska Highway, head toward Whitehorse in the Yukon, and then ride back through the mountains on the Klondike Highway to Skagway in Alaska. At this point, just a few miles of water at the head of Lynn Canal separate Skagway from Haines. You can take the ferry or a water shuttle back to Haines.

GUIDES AND OUTFITTERS

ALASKA MOUNTAIN GUIDES AND CLIMBING SCHOOL INC. / For those looking for a guide service, climbing school, and custom expedition outfitter, Alaska Mountain Guides is your best bet. Its instructors and guides have worked on mountains all over the world. The school offers a five-day Mountain School as an introduction to the basics of safe mountaineering. The groups are limited to six people, with two instructors. Activities include glacier travel and guided climbs. Longer mountaineering and wilderness trips will take you on the Tsirku Icefield Traverse or combine sea kayaking, ice climbing, glacier trekking, skiing, and river rafting. *PO Box 1081, Haines AK 99827; 907/766-3366 or 800/766-3396; climbs@alaskamountain guides.com; www.alaskamountainguides.com.*

CHILKAT GUIDES / The folks at Chilkat Guides specialize in river trips. They offer a scenic and peaceful half-day float through the Chilkat Bald Eagle Preserve (see Adventures, above) along the Chilkat River, with daily departures. Chilkat Guides also offers 2-day adventures, but their crème de la crème trips are the 10-day and 13-day expeditions down the Tatshenshini and Alsek Rivers, which flow through two spectacular wilderness areas, and the Stikine River, a short distance from the island town of Wrangell farther down the panhandle. *PO Box 170, Haines*

AK 99827; 907/766-2491; fax 907/766-2409; www.chilkatguides.com; Raft Alaska@chilkatguides.com.

DEISHU EXPEDITIONS / For kayaking adventures to suit all comers, look no further. This company—"dedicated to safety, ecotourism, and preserving the Alaska wilds"—offers half-day, full-day, or overnight trips to the Davidson Glacier and even 50 percent, money-back-guaranteed whale trips (mid-July through Sept) in search of the great whales. Prices range from $85, plus tax, per person for a half-day trip with a snack, to $125, plus tax, per person for a full-day trip with lunch. *425 Beach Rd; 907/766-2427 or 800/552-9257; paddle@seakayaks.com; www.sea kayaks.com.*

GLACIER VALLEY ADVENTURES / See seven glaciers from where you're standing once you land at this tour base. It's an awesome sight. The folks at Glacier Valley Adventures will take you by plane up and over Glacier Bay's northern escarpment, the Tatshenshini-Alsek Preserve and into the Tsirku River valley. The tour ranges from $210–$310 per person, and there are several methods of getting there: fly in and airboat up to the DeBlondeau Glacier, or fly in and raft out, fly round-trip, or airboat in and out. Snacks are available, and you'll surely require some comfort food after guide Al Gilliam tells some of his hair-raising bear tails. *Phone-fax 907/767-5522; akcroscountry@wytbear.com; www.glaciervalleyadventures.com; call for pickup location.*

RIVER ADVENTURES / If you prefer jet-boat travel, River Adventures will take you into the Chilkat Bald Eagle Preserve (see Adventures, above). Trips depart daily in summer. Cost is $85 per person with lunch, or $75 without. *907/766-2050 or 800/478-9827; karenhess@whytbear.com; www.AlaskaRiverTours.wytbear.com.*

FESTIVALS AND EVENTS

MAYFEST / Mother Nature puts on this show. In May, everything is waking up after a long winter's sleep. It's a fabulous time to be anywhere in the Southeast, but particularly in Haines. Long days make for great cross-country skiing in Chilkat Pass. The first two weeks of May, hooligan are running upriver, followed by a whole bevy of sea lions; the sky is white with sea gulls. Whales are returning. Native folks dipnet for fish. People from the Yukon come to the coast with moose meat for trading. Hooligan oil is a prized commodity. The Native peoples of the Interior use it for dipping meats and dried fish. (In the old days, it was so valuable that the routes to the Interior were often called "The Grease Trail.") Good places to watch nature's show, particularly the hooligan and sea lions, are at Mile 4 on the Haines Highway, alongside the Chilkat River, and at the bridge over Lutak Inlet, on your way to Chilkoot Lake.

KLUANE TO CHILKAT INTERNATIONAL BIKE RELAY RACE / Held on the weekend closest to the summer solstice (June 21), this bicycling event has taken off like a rocket since its inception in 1993. More than 1,000 cyclists participate, either as individuals or in bike relay teams of two to eight people. Racers roar off in a mass start from Haines Junction in the Yukon, and then follow the road over the pass to the ocean at Haines, about 153 miles. The terrain is rugged and demanding, but competitors like the nice local flavor and say the race has not yet been invaded by big-time serious racers from Outside (meaning non-Alaskans). Watch for bears crossing the road—no kidding! For information, call the Haines Convention & Visitors Bureau (800/458-3579).

SOUTHEAST ALASKA STATE FAIR (AND BALD EAGLE MUSIC FESTIVAL) / For five days near mid-August, folks from all over the Southeast and the Yukon gather in Haines for a good old-fashioned fair, featuring big names in the music world and talented musicians from around the state. There are also the famous pig races (usually), contests from log rolling to ax throwing, a parade, great food, and dancing, of course. Never mind that it often rains some of the days; everybody loves the fair. For more information, call 907/766-2476.

ALASKA BALD EAGLE FESTIVAL / The gathering of bald eagles on the Council Grounds of the Chilkat River from October to December is the largest concentration of eagles in the world. In their honor, Haines puts on a festival of local artists and musicians, usually the second weekend of November, but the really big-name, flamboyant performance artists here are white-headed, wear more than 7,000 feathers, and weigh in at about 13 pounds each. Contact the Haines Chamber of Commerce, PO Box 1449, Haines AK 99827; 907/766-2202 or 800/246-6268.

NIGHTLIFE

THE OFFICER'S CLUB LOUNGE (907/766-2002) is a dignified bar in the **HOTEL HALSINGLAND** (see Lodgings review, below) and a popular watering hole for locals. Located smack on the water's edge is the **LIGHTHOUSE RESTAURANT** (Main and Front Sts; 907/766-2442) whose claim to fame is its fantastic buttermilk pie— "Alaska slices at Alaska prices." (That translates as big and expensive.) Thirty-three miles "out the road" toward the Interior (otherwise known as the Haines Highway) is the historic **33 MILE ROADHOUSE** (907/767-5510). Everybody in Haines goes to Milepost 33 for the "best burgers in town." The pies are pretty good, too. Since it's 7 miles before the Canadian border, they also advertise it as "the last gas in America." Open every day; closed Tuesday in winter.

RESTAURANTS

The Commander's Room Restaurant

HOTEL HALSINGLAND, FORT SEWARD, HAINES; 907/766-2000; FAX 907/766-2060 The commander of the fort once lived here; today you can eat here. The original menu was a replica of the writing portfolios used by the army at Fort Seward; it celebrated past characters such as a beer-guzzling bear, a dog named Gus who once flew co-pilot with the commander and wolfed down steak every night, and the commander's wife, Eleanor, who either through stroke of genius or perverseness composed the music to Alaska's Flag Song. (Genius? Because only the best voices in the state can actually sing this song. Perverse? Because the rest of us make it painful to your ears.) The new menu has sadly left off the old characters, but features a creative Pacific Northwest cuisine highlighting fresh Alaska seafood. If they're offering fresh Dungeness crab when you're there, order it—it's entertainment unto itself. *$$; AE, DC, MC, V; local checks only; breakfast, dinner every day (closed Oct to March); full bar; no reservations; www.hotelhalsingland.com.* &

Fort Seward Lodge Restaurant & Saloon / ★

39 MUD BAY RD, HAINES; 907/766-2009 OR 800/478-7772 The seasonal specialty is all-you-can-eat crab, plucked right from the waters of Lynn Canal. Service is friendly, the atmosphere cozy, and from some tables you have a view of the water. While you're waiting for dinner, make a homemade dart with an autographed dollar bill and fire it at the ceiling. It is wise here to go for the house specialties—prime rib or crab. *$–$$; MC, V; local checks only; dinner every day in summer and 5 nights in winter, days vary (closed a few weeks in Jan); full bar; no reservations; part of historic Fort Seward.*

Just for the Halibut / ★★

142 BEACH RD, HAINES; 907/766-3800 OR 877/766-2800 On a pretty day in Haines, if you're waiting for the shuttle ferry to Skagway or even if you're not, this is a fun place to eat out on the sunny deck just off the dock, but over the water, looking out at beautiful Lynn Canal. This little cafe boasts a simple, tasty menu: ale-battered fish-and-chips ("best in town" say many residents), grilled halibut kebabs, and espresso drinks. *$; MC, V; local checks only; lunch, dinner every day (closed winter); no alcohol; no reservations; portage@klukwan.com; www. portage.klukwan.com; on the dock at the Portage Cove Adventure Center.* &

Mountain Market / ★★

151 3RD AVE S, HAINES; 907/766-3340 Thoughtful, wholesome food is served in this combination deli–health food store. Except for the sandwiches, the cuisine is largely vegetarian, with great muffins, good homemade soups, fresh salads, tortilla wraps, basil-pesto pasta, and daily specials. They boast the best coffee drinks in town with creations like Mocha Margarita—tastes just like a milkshake. It's a grab-and-go kind of place, but on any given day you'll also find fishermen, kayakers, mountain climbers, cabin dwellers, artists, and alternative-lifestyle folks holding court here. *$; MC, V; local checks only; breakfast, lunch, dinner every day; no alcohol; no reservations; corner of 3rd Ave and Haines Hwy.* &

Weeping Trout Sports Resort

144 2ND AVE S, HAINES; 907/766-2827 OR 877/94TROUT (948-7688); FAX 907/766-2824 On Saturday evenings in summer, the lodge has a special dinner open to the public. The resort is in a beautiful location on the edge of Chilkat Lake. Getting to dinner—which takes about half an hour from town—is half the fun and adventure as you bump over roads by car and then take prop and jet boats to the lodge; or you can fly in. Set menus are published a month ahead—you can check them out and make reservations at Yeshua Tours on Second Avenue (907/766-2334). Many Haines residents say it's a fun outing for a special dinner. For the price of about $50 per person including transportation to the resort, the meal is a set entree, and varies from lamb to seafood, with salad, dessert, a good wine list, and a full bar. Seating for dinner is at 6pm and the dining room looks across the lake. You can always go earlier on Saturday morning—fish, golf (Alaska-style), hike, and then eat dinner if you want to make a day of it. *$$–$$$; MC, V; local checks only; dinner Sat*

in summer; full bar; reservations recommended; PO Box 129, Haines AK 99827;
trout@weepingtrout.com; www.weepingtrout.com.

The Wild Strawberry / ★★★

138 2ND AVE S, HAINES; 907/766-3608 In a charmingly handcrafted wood
house with scalloped gables, turrets, large deck, and gazebo, the Wild Strawberry is a delightful new addition to Haines cuisine. A fishing family for more
than 25 years, owners Jim and Pam Moore specialize in seafood from the barbecue,
fresh halibut sandwiches, homemade soups, an array of meat and vegetarian sandwiches served on focaccia, and, for dessert, giant ice-cream cones or a beautiful selection of chocolates, like a Mount Ripinski and Turtles. They also serve Belgian
waffles, espresso, and decadent "candy bar drinks." *$; MC, V; local checks only;*
breakfast, lunch, dinner every day (closed Nov to March); beer and wine; no reser-
vations; downtown, 4 doors south of the visitor center. &

LODGINGS

Hotel Halsingland

FORT SEWARD, HAINES; 907/766-2000 OR 800/542-6363; FAX 907/766-2060
Overlooking Lynn Canal, with mountains in all directions, the hotel is part of historic Fort Seward. The old Victorian buildings and the rooms have a kind of faded
gentility to them. The hotel itself, once home to the fort's commanding officer, has
60 rooms with either private or shared baths. The former owner, an immigrant from
Sweden, named the hotel after a province of her native homeland. Bought in 2002
by Juneau hotelier Jeff Butcher, you can expect some innovative changes. The
Officer's Inn B&B has 13 guest rooms and is up the hill from the hotel. The hotel's
economy rooms are $69 for a single or a double. At the Officer's Inn B&B, rates are
$109 for a double. Add $10 per person after that. *$$; AE, DC, DIS, MC, V; checks*
OK; closed Nov to May; PO Box 1649, Haines AK 99827; reservations@hotel
halsingland.com; www.hotelhalsingland.com; on the east side of the Fort Seward
parade ground. &

River House on the Chilkat / ★★

1 MILE OUT OF TOWN, WHERE THE CHILKAT RIVER RUNS INTO THE SEA,
HAINES; 907/766-3215 OR 888/747-RHBB (7422) A sweet, luxury rental cottage
beside the Chilkat River, this place has a third-floor tower bedroom with skylights
for watching the stars, and a private garden, deck, and sauna. This lovely oasis fea-
tures views of mountains, glaciers, and the river, and is a happy getaway for a night
or a week. Rent the first floor unit or the second and third floor unit for $115–$165
per night in the summer (double occupancy), or the whole cottage for $195 (double
occupancy) per night in the summer. It's fully equipped with espresso machine, VCR
and video library, telephone, fax machine, and stereo. The entire cottage can accom-
modate up to seven people. No smoking. *$$; MC, V; no checks; PO Box 1173,*
Haines AK 99827; www.rhvacation.com.

A Sheltered Harbor Bed & Breakfast / ★

57 BEACH RD, HAINES; 907/766-2741 With big picture windows, this B&B offers waterfront accommodations on Portage Cove, which lies at the foot of Fort Seward in downtown Haines directly across from the Port Chilkoot cruise ship dock. Several of the rooms have excellent views of the Lynn Canal and the surrounding mountains. As the rooms are located two flights over the Orca Arts & Crafts Gift Shop, you get an extra workout hauling your luggage upstairs. The rooms are cozy, tidy, and nicely decorated. Each has private bath, TV, and phone. Your hosts, Byron, Laura, and Mary Rettinger, serve a hot, all-you-can-eat Alaska breakfast each morning. *$$; AE, MC, V; no checks; PO Box 806-B, Haines AK 99827; ashelter@aptalaska.net; www.asheltered@yahoo.com.*

Summer Inn Bed and Breakfast / ★★

117 2ND AVE, HAINES; PHONE-FAX 907/766-2970 A five-bedroom historic house, this simple but charming inn has pretty views of Lynn Canal from the upstairs front bedrooms. It was built by Tim Vogel, a member of Soapy Smith's notorious gang of hoodlums, who skedaddled out of Skagway when Soapy was gunned down around the turn of the century. Quite a dandy, and known as a ladies' man, Vogel was a colorful character in the history of Haines. In the evening, you can take a bubble bath in the scoundrel's original tub, circa 1912. The inn is cheerful, homey, and in a great location. They serve a hearty breakfast here and in the afternoon offer homemade cookies and tea. Summer rates are $70 for a single, $80 for a double, and $100 for a triple; winter rates are $10 lower. *$–$$; MC, V; checks OK; PO Box 1198, Haines AK 99827; summerinnb&b@wytbear.com; www.summerinn.wytbear.com; downtown, 2 blocks off Main St.*

Skagway

In the fall of 1896, a prospector named George Washington Carmack was panning for gold on a tributary of the Klondike River in Canada. Something glittered. He brushed away the gravel, and there was the first taste of the gold that would electrify the world. "I felt," he said later, "like I had just dealt myself a royal flush in the game of life."

The rush was on. Skagway, on the Alaska side of the coastal mountains, provided access to the quickest route into the Canadian Klondike, up and over Chilkoot Pass. From bank presidents to lowly clerks, oyster pirates to boardinghouse matrons, everywhere around the globe, people lured by gold walked out of their jobs, bound for the Klondike. Most of the gold claims were already staked by the time the masses had clambered and clawed their way over glaciers and peaks to get there. But not a soul forgot the glory days of the gold rush and its grand, unparalleled adventures as immortalized in Robert Service's poem "The Spell of the Yukon." Years later, many of their private journals would record it as the highlight of their lives.

For every man who came to dig gold from the ground, hundreds more followed to dig it from his pocket. In those wild days, it was written about Skagway that a man could come into town from the Klondike with a fortune one night, and the next morning find himself scraping for a meal. One visitor wrote in 1898: "I have stumbled upon a few rough corners of the globe in my wandering, but I think the most outrageously lawless quarter I ever struck was Skagway."

One of the most lawless fellows could be found in Clancy's Saloon, headquarters for the notorious Soapy Smith gang. As a two-bit con man down south, Soapy picked up his nickname, as well as some extra cash, by using a trick involving soap to swindle the unsuspecting out of their dough. But when he arrived in the north, he hit the big time, and locals were soon calling him the King of Skagway. It was a glorious but brief reign, for Soapy eventually pinched one poke too many. On July 8, 1898, the *Skagway News* headlines read: "Soapy Smith's Last Bluff; Shot Through the Heart by Frank Reid."

Now visitors say this is the friendliest place they experience in the Inside Passage. Locals number 867, but the population swells to about 1,200 with seasonal workers. When the last cruise ship sails down Lynn Canal in late September, folks start boarding up their shops and heading for Bali, Boston, Washington, or Tahiti. The population shrinks back, and residents get the chance to recover from the busy summer and socialize, go outdoors and play, and get into the holiday spirit. Skagway is very wheelchair accessible with its flat valley floor and wide boardwalks that make for easy access to establishments.

ACCESS AND INFORMATION

Skagway can be reached year-round by scheduled and chartered air services out of Juneau and Haines. **SKAGWAY AIR SERVICE** (907/983-2218; www.skagway air.com), with the dance-hall queen doing the high-step on the tail flaps and the motto "We can can-can," is a good first choice. In summer, there's water transportation between Skagway and Haines with **CHILKAT CRUISES HAINES-SKAGWAY SHUTTLE FERRY** (907/766-2100 or 888/766-2103; www.chilkatcruises. com) and **ALASKA FJORDLINES** (907/766-3395 or 888/766-3395; www.lynn canal.com). The **ALASKA MARINE HIGHWAY SYSTEM** (the Southeast's marine road) has one ferry, the **MV MALASPINA** (907/983-2941, Skagway; 800/642-0066, reservations; www.alaska.gov/ferry), which runs between Juneau, Haines, and Skagway all summer. Call for recorded arrival/departure information in Skagway. If you're coming by road, from the Alaska Highway, it's 110 miles on the **SOUTH KLONDIKE HIGHWAY**. To rent a car, contact **AVIS** (3rd and Spring Sts; 800/331-1212), located in the lobby of the Westmark Hotel, for daily or weekly rates.

The best place to start exploring is at the old railroad depot, now home to the **KLONDIKE GOLD RUSH NATIONAL HISTORICAL PARK** (see Adventures, below). Located in the heart of town, on Second Avenue and Broadway, the park's visitor center is open daily in the summer, with scaled-back hours in winter. The visitor center offers films, exhibits, walking tours, ranger talks, and the latest information on conditions on the Chilkoot Trail—all for free. **SKAGWAY CONVENTION & VISITORS BUREAU** (Broadway and 2nd Ave; 907/983-2854; fax 907/983-3854; www.skagway.org) in the historic, driftwood-covered Arctic Brotherhood Hall has a great brochure, *Skagway Walking Tour,* for a do-it-yourself guided trip. **THE SKAGWAY NEWS DEPOT** (264 Broadway; 907/983-3354; www.skagwaybooks. com) is the town's largest bookseller, open year-round.

EXPLORING

Whether on foot, by buggy, or in a vintage car, tours abound. The National Park Service offers **WALKING TOURS OF HISTORIC SKAGWAY** (907/983-2921) that depart several times daily from its visitor center at the old railroad depot. A marvelous raconteur and performer, Steve Hites runs a fleet of red, replica, vintage cars, **SKAGWAY STREET CAR COMPANY** (907/983-2908). His drivers are dressed in flamboyant costumes of the gold rush era and entertain you with story after story of yesteryear as they toot about town. "Show me your bloomers," is the cry of the visitor wanting to take a picture of the tour drivers. If you want to get from here to there in a turn-of-the-century taxi, just flag down the **KELLER'S CURIOS LIMO,** a horse and buggy with costumed driver.

ADVENTURES

BIKING AND HIKING / The **KLONDIKE SUMMIT TO SEA CRUISE** is a two-hour guided bike trip offered by **SOCKEYE CYCLE** (5th Ave off Broadway; 907/983-2851; open daily 9am–6pm May to Sept; www.cyclealaska.com). They'll drive you up to White Pass; then you "coast" back down to the sea. You won't lack for speed or beauty on this trip. The quickest and easiest trails up into the mountains are those that go to **LOWER AND UPPER DEWEY LAKES.** If you have only a few hours, hike to Lower Dewey Lake, a beautiful ½-mile jaunt with a 500-foot elevation gain. The trail begins behind the Westmark Hotel employee housing on Spring Street and Fourth Avenue. Ask for directions. If time allows, continue to Upper Dewey Lake, a round-trip of 7 miles.

 KLONDIKE GOLD RUSH NATIONAL HISTORICAL PARK / This park is unique among national parks in that it encompasses both historic downtown Skagway (the beginning—and the end—of the trail of gold) and the routes and mountain passes that thousands of gold seekers flowed over to get to the goldfields of the Canadian Klondike. Included in the park, miles and miles away from Alaska, is an historic section of Seattle, Washington, which was an integral outfitter for the gold rush up north. Over the years, the National Park Service has restored many of the old buildings, breathing life into the stories of the characters who once proliferated here. Visit, for instance, the **OLD CABIN OF CAPT. WILLIAM MOORE,** the founder of Skagway, who predicted gold would soon be discovered in the creeks of the Yukon River; **THE MASCOT SALOON,** a hop and a skip down Broadway; or nearby **JEFF SMITH'S PARLOR,** the gambling dive and hangout of the nefarious Soapy Smith.

 Two routes led into the Klondike from Skagway: the 33-mile **CHILKOOT TRAIL,** which you can still walk today, and the **WHITE PASS TRAIL,** the route followed by the trains of the White Pass & Yukon Railroad. The park is managed through the international cooperation of the national park services of both the United States and Canada.

 THE CHILKOOT TRAIL / For those who love history and mountains, a hike along the Chilkoot Trail from Dyea to Lake Bennett is a wonderful adventure. Go prepared. While the distance (33 miles) may not look overly intimidating, the route is rugged and there's plenty of snow, even in July. The park service can give you maps, information, latest trail conditions, and an excellent brochure, *A Hiker's Guide to the Chilkoot Trail.* The trail crosses the international boundary between the United

States and Canada at the top of the infamous "Golden Stairs"—Chilkoot Pass. Although you are required to register on the U.S. side, currently the permit is free. However, Parks Canada currently charges $35 CDN per adult and $7.50 CDN for children younger than 15 and limits the number of hikers coming into Canada over Chilkoot Pass to 50 per day. This restriction is for the protection of natural and cultural resources as well as the quality of visitors' experiences. If you are on a tight schedule or have an organized group, advance permit reservations are strongly recommended ($10 CDN per person; see contact below). Only eight permits per day are reserved for hikers who arrive with no reservations. The busiest season is July to early August.

Currently, a train operates Monday, Tuesday, Thursday, and Saturday, June through August, from the end of the trail at Lake Bennett back to Skagway for around $65 per person or $30 to the Fraser border station in British Columbia. But that service has not been consistent in the last several years, so be sure and check with the White Pass & Yukon Railroad (see below) or the park services so you'll know whether you have to hoof it about 15 miles to the road or nearest train stop. For more information on **FEES AND RESERVATIONS,** contact Parks Canada (205-300 Main St, Whitehorse, YT, Y1A 2B5 Canada; 867/667-3910 or 800/661-0486, within Canada and U.S. mainland). On the U.S. side, contact Klondike Gold Rush National Historical Park (PO Box 517, Skagway AK 99840; 907/983-2921; www.nps.gov/klgo).

THE WHITE PASS & YUKON RAILROAD / They said the route was "too steep for even a billy goat," but they hadn't counted on Michael J. Heney, a brilliant engineer known for getting the job done. His famous rallying cry was "Give me enough snoose and dynamite, and I'll build you a road to Hell!" The route followed the old White Pass Trail and took miners into the Klondike. From the beginning of May to the end of September, the train departs twice daily for White Pass Summit, returning to Skagway three hours later. Round-trip fare is $82 for adults and $41 for children 3–12. *907/983-2217 or 800/343-7373; fax 907/983-2734; www.white passrailroad.com.*

GUIDES AND OUTFITTERS

THE MOUNTAIN SHOP/PACKER EXPEDITIONS / Look for the mural of Alfred Packer or stampeders going up the Golden Stairs on the Chilkoot Trail on either side of their building at Fourth Avenue and Broadway. **THE MOUNTAIN SHOP** rents and sells packs, tents, backpacks, sleeping bags, kayaks, snowshoes, skis, fuel, camping and climbing gear—everything you need to get up and over the Chilkoot Trail and just about anywhere else. Or, stop into the shop to sign up for a guided tour with **PACKER EXPEDITIONS.** Their 15 or so personable guides can take you up some of the best trails in the area, complete with majestic waterfalls, second-growth forests, and hanging glaciers. The half- or full-day **HELI-HIKING** tour to Laughton Glacier choppers out of Skagway, flies over the Juneau Icefield, lands on the White Pass & Yukon Railroad tracks (don't worry there's no trains in sight), and sets you on your way up a nice soft trail with snacks and water to a lookout. From there, you can continue on a more strenuous hike up a riverbed, over a jumble of moraine onto the Laughton Glacier itself. Hikers are often split into pace-specific groups. All the guides are Emergency Medical Technicians and are in radio contact with the Skagway base for hikers' safety. After the tour there's a private White Pass car awaiting you, stocked with refreshments and memorable salmon pâté. They'll also tailor, supply, and guide tours over the Chilkoot Pass. *907/983-2544; fax 907/983-3544; packer@aptalaska.net; www.packerexpeditions.com.*

FESTIVALS AND EVENTS

THE BUCKWHEAT CLASSIC / Started by one of the town's great characters, the classic is a cross-country skiing event (with associated hoopla) the third weekend of March for serious and not-so-serious racers and kids. Courses range from 5 to 50 kilometers. Rooms book up fast for the popular event, so reserve early and share! And don't miss the Miss Buckwheat Contest (no long-legged beauties need apply, this is for babes under the age of 10). For more information, call the Skagway Convention & Visitors Bureau (907/983-2854).

FOURTH OF JULY / Four days after Soapy Smith rode his white stallion down Broadway at the head of the Fourth of July parade in 1898, he lay dead, shot through the heart in the shoot-out with Frank Reid. Skagway holds a wonderful small-town Fourth with an historic theme. The parade marches a few blocks down Broadway; and, just in case you didn't get a good look, turns around and marches right back again.

KLONDIKE TRAIL OF '98 INTERNATIONAL ROAD RELAY / This is a wildly popular relay race (on foot), which starts at night and runs up and over the mountains the 110 miles from Skagway to Whitehorse. It's a fun team event for those who love to punish themselves with sleep deprivation and heavy, heart-pumping exercise up long hills through heavy fog. Hallucinatory aide stations have themes that can run from Klondike Gold Rush to a Hawaiian vacation. The race began in 1983 with 6 teams to commemorate the gold rush. Now there are more than 130 teams from all over the country. Part of the competition seems to be coming up with the most unusual team name, such as Midnight Claim Jumpers, Take No Prisoners, Wild Women Do, Out of the Ooze & Born to Cruise, Food Factory Flamethrowers, Vestigial Appendages, and One Knight Stands. The relay usually takes place the first week in September. For more information, call the Skagway Convention & Visitors Bureau (907/983-2854) or Sports Yukon in Canada (867/668-4236).

VICTORIAN YULETIDE / As the dark and wintry days of December roll around, Skagway gets decked out in lights to celebrate an old-fashioned Victorian Christmas. The tree is lit in the center of town, sometimes followed by a parade of lighted boats in the harbor (depends on how bad the wind is howling). There are organ recitals, sing-alongs, teas, tours of restored Victorian homes, and a Yuletide Ball. Santa and Mrs. Claus arrive on the ferry for the children's carnival. Festivities occur during the first two weeks of December. For more information, call the Skagway Chamber of Commerce (907/983-1898) or the visitors bureau (907/983-2854).

NIGHTLIFE

Skagway's local character—**BUCKWHEAT DONAHUE**—with his merry grin and trademark howl ("Howling is good for you," he says) will dance, sing, and recite his way into your heart. Almost every summer, he has a one-man show, performing Robert Service favorites like "The Cremation of Sam McGee," along with other rousing tales of the North. He might even pull you up on stage to help him act it out. Look for notices of his show about town or follow the howl bouncing down the boardwalk. The **DAYS OF '98**—"Longest Running Show in the North," or so the town claims—is a historic musical comedy about Skagway and legendary con man Soapy Smith. Catch a matinee or evening show, with mock gambling in the Deadhorse Saloon, in the Eagles Hall on Broadway at Sixth Avenue (907/983-2545 for tickets).

Afterward or before (or any other part of the day), head on down to the **RED ONION SALOON** (Broadway at 2nd Ave; 907/983-2222) for toe-tapping honkytonk piano or live music and dancing. This was once a brothel. Legend has it there's the ghost of a "fallen dove" roaming around up there named Lydia. Dance-and music-wise, things really get revved up on Saturday nights. Thursdays are Jam Night, when world-class musicians off the cruise ships play the music they want to play—jazz.

RESTAURANTS

Haven Café / ★★★

9TH AVE AND STATE, SKAGWAY; 907/983-3553 There's a panini sandwich for each meal of the day. Dry grilled on a hot panini press with focaccia bread, there's no fat involved. Favorites are the brie with pesto and the chicken caliente. Fresh baked goods sniffed when you go in for your morning coffee are a lure to return in the afternoon. Exacting espresso handling transports you to Seattle, even though the special blend is roasted in the Yukon. In summer, locals come to avoid the cruise ship crowd on Broadway. Plus, there's a great view of Mount Harding and its glacier. *$; MC, V; checks OK; breakfast, lunch, dinner every day; no alcohol; no reservations; jabajaba@aptalaska.net; between 8th and 9th on State St.* &

Olivia's at the Skagway Inn / ★★★

7TH AVE AND BROADWAY, SKAGWAY; 907/983-3287 A charming little restaurant in the historic Skagway Inn, Olivia's specializes in fresh seafood and is renowned for its French onion soup with sherry, cognac, and lots of garlic; its broiled portobello mushrooms with fresh herbs and feta cheese; and its signature dessert—a delicious white-chocolate bread pudding soaked in rum sauce. The philosophy of chef Wendell Fogliani, a longtime Skagway resident trained at the Culinary Institute of Nevada, is this: "Simple is better. People still like seafood, meats, and greens, and we have more healthy ways now of preparing dishes with lots of herbs and olive oil." Dinner is prix fixe—a fixed price for the whole meal. A new addition to the Inn is Greg's Bistro, serving espresso and light fare of fresh greens and soups and sandwiches for breakfast and lunch. The Inn can arrange an "Alaska Garden Gourmet tour," offered daily with a tour of town, the Skagway Inn garden, and live cooking demonstrations using the garden's produce and fresh Alaska seafood. *$$–$$$; AE, DIS, MC, V; local checks only; lunch Mon-Fri, dinner every day (open June to mid-Sept]; full bar; reservations recommended; 5 blocks down Broadway from the old railroad depot.* &

Ristorante Portobello & Pizzeria / ★★★

111 BROADWAY, SKAGWAY; 907/983-3459 Want to practice your Italian, Arabic, Spanish, or French? Or just love the ambiance of international flavors and spicy conversation? Then stop in this popular gathering place where the pizzas and focaccia are as flavorful as the accents—full of the spices of the Mediterranean. This comes as no surprise, when you learn that the gregarious owner, Farid Hosni, of Tunisian and Italian descent, began his 26-year culinary career in Florence, Italy, and came to Skagway via Paris, London, and Juneau. His initial small pizzeria became so popular that he expanded into a new building on Broadway in the summer of '99, and the menu grew into full ristorante fare with his own favorite—linguine with fresh clams. For Alaska fare, there's the memorable halibut burger on a big onion roll accompanied by crispy French fries with the skins on. We think it's the best in town. *$$; MC, V; local checks only; lunch, dinner every day (open May to late Sept); beer and wine; no reservations; on Broadway in the heart of town.* ⅄

Skagway Fish Company / ★★★

201 CONGRESS WY, SKAGWAY; 907/983-3474 Right next door to the Stowaway, this restaurant grew from a little take-out and fresh-fish market to a covered outdoor porch eatery, which was then enclosed and now houses a bar and a full restaurant. It's the best fish-and-chips in town—light and not too greasy. We've tried them all over and we go back here for more. This is a favorite after-hours hangout for locals. Owners Dan and Eileen Henry, when not working their tails off, are gregarious and friendly. Dan is particularly sassy. *$–$$; AE, DIS, MC, V; checks OK; lunch, dinner every day (closed in winter); beer and wine; reservations recommended; sfc@aptalaska.net; overlooking the small-boat harbor, on the road out to the railroad dock.* ⅄

Stowaway Café / ★★★

205 CONGRESS WY, SKAGWAY; 907/983-3463 If the sun's shining, sit out on the deck and enjoy waterfront dining. The food is tasty, creative, and thoughtful, from Mom's Incredible Spinach Salad and Hilbo's Hot Scallop and Bacon Salad to seafood filé gumbo (as close to Louisiana gumbo as you're going to get this far north), mesquite-grilled halibut, and blackened salmon. You can start with pot stickers with orange-ginger dipping sauce or baked brie with pesto and pecans. For dessert, there's a heavy Southern leaning with pecan pie and bread pudding in bourbon sauce, a local favorite. *$$–$$$; MC, V; local checks only; dinner every day (closed in winter); beer and wine; reservations recommended; overlooking the small-boat harbor, on the way out to the railroad dock.* ⅄

Sweet Tooth Café / ★★

3RD AVE AND BROADWAY, SKAGWAY; PHONE-FAX 907/983-2405 A comfy place for breakfast, this cheerful cafe is a gathering spot for locals. Early in the morning listen to the lively political debate at "The Table." Buttermilk pancakes, homemade bread, doughnuts, and French toast are the main fare. For lunch, go for the halibut burger, lightly grilled in egg batter. Of course, if you have a sweet tooth, their specialties are sundaes and ice-cream floats. *$; MC, V; local checks only; breakfast, lunch every day (shorter hours in winter); no alcohol; no reservations.*

LODGINGS

Alaska Sojourn / ★★

8TH AVE AND MAIN ST, SKAGWAY; 907/983-2030; FAX 907/983-3686 This home hostel opened in 2002 and is housed in an almost century-old cabin that's been added on to—a very Alaskan touch. Proprietor Janilyn Heger made it her business to sample other hostels to determine the best for her guests. There's one couple's room in the main house, with a two-story bunkhouse in the yard with gender-specific rooms. The main house's kitchen, dining room, living room, porch, and bathroom are available to guests as well as free Internet service, local reference books and brochures, and board games. Heger will shuttle you free to and from the ferry, the White Pass & Yukon Railroad, and the Chilkoot trailhead. She has it all covered. The couple's room is $40 a night and bunks are $20. *$; MC, V; checks OK; PO Box 564, Skagway AK 99840; ijourneynorth@hotmail.com; www.alaskansojourn.com.*

At the White House / ★★★☆

8TH AVE AND MAIN ST, SKAGWAY; 907/983-9000; FAX 907/983-9010 An historic building from 1902, the White House became a boardinghouse, then officers quarters and a hospital during World War II, then a boardinghouse and a hotel again until a fire destroyed it in 1978. The Tronrud family—two brothers and their wives—bought it, renovated it, and opened it as a B&B in 1997. It's quiet, with a lovely lawn, flower gardens, and beautifully refurbished inside. The 10 rooms are fairly large so it's a good choice for families or for winter guests with a lot of gear. All rooms have private baths ($108 for a double, summer; $75 and up for a double in winter; $95 for four in winter). The morning breakfast is a delicious selection of hot egg casseroles, French toast, bagels, muffins, and fresh fruit. In winter, it's a continental breakfast. *$–$$; AE, DIS, MC, V; checks OK; PO Box 41, Skagway AK 99840; whitehse@aptalaska.net; www.atthewhitehouse.com.* ੬

Chilkoot Trail Outpost / ★★★

MILE 8.5 DYEA RD, SKAGWAY; 907/983-3799; FAX 907/983-3599 This is the closest place to the Chilkoot trailhead to stay and not be in a tent or an RV. The log-cabin lodge and eight log cabins were a labor of love for owner Kathy Hosford. You'll really appreciate its convenience when you come off the trail, tired and funky. There are bikes, a gazebo with a barbecue, and hiking trails on the property. It also boasts a natural spring with the sweetest water you ever tasted; folks come here with buckets for it. A bunk and breakfast is $35, but you need to bring a sleeping bag. There's a wheelchair-accessible cabin for $88 a night, and the suite cabins are $100–$125, with breakfast. Every cabin has all the amenities: fridges, microwaves, coffee pots, and bathrooms. A 50 percent deposit is required for reservations, but if you come off the trail there will probably be a bunk with your name on it. *$–$$; AE, DIS, MC, V; checks OK; closed in the winter; PO Box 286, Skagway AK 99840;*

khosford@aptalaska.net; www.chilkoottrailoutpost.com; easy to spot on the right of Dyea Rd, past the National Park Service campgrounds. &

Gold Rush Lodge / ★

6TH AVE AND ALASKA ST, SKAGWAY; 907/983-2831 OR 877/983-3509; FAX 907/983-2742 Simple and comfortable, this small lodge sits on the edge of Skagway's recently upgraded airfield and the wilderness at the edge of town. It has rustic wood doors and pine-accented rooms with handmade, Northwest-theme quilts on the beds. The rooms are small but cozy, with phones, VCRs, cable TV, small refrigerators, microwaves, coffee pots, hairdryers, and outside entrances. More like a motel but with the personal attention of a B&B, the lodge has fresh-baked cookies every day at the reservation desk. If you are fascinated by small bush planes, there's a whole flotilla—a kind of Alaska entertainment while drinking your morning coffee or sipping an evening beer. *$; AE, DIS, MC, V; checks OK; open May to Sept; PO Box 514, Skagway AK 99840; info@goldrushlodge.com; www.goldrushlodge.com; at the edge of the airfield.* &

Historic Skagway Inn Bed and Breakfast / ★★★

7TH AVE AND BROADWAY, SKAGWAY; 907/983-2289 OR 888/752-4929; FAX 907/983-2713 In 1897, this now-historic inn was a brothel that stood in the red-light district a few blocks off Broadway. Moved to its present location in 1916, the original inn has 12 rooms, each named for a different woman who might have once lived there. (It is said that in two of the rooms, their ghosts linger on.) While you're waiting for the spirits of these gentle, tarnished doves, this is as comfortable, friendly, and charming a place to tuck in as you will find anywhere in this part of the country. Six bathrooms for the 12 rooms are shared. Prices range from $109–$129 for a double in summer, which includes a full, hot breakfast at Olivia's (see Restaurants review). Innkeepers Karl and Rosemary Klupar are in the process of adding on six rooms—with private, half bathrooms with a shared bath and shower, but still in keeping with the nostalgia of the original inn. *$$; AE, DIS, MC, V; local checks only; PO Box 500, Skagway AK 99850; stay@skagwayinn.com; www.skagwayinn.com; 5 blocks down Broadway from the old railroad depot.*

Mile Zero Bed & Breakfast / ★★

9TH AVE AND MAIN ST, SKAGWAY; 907/983-3045; FAX 907/983-3046 Built in 1995, Mile Zero has a warm and friendly atmosphere, halfway between a B&B and a motel. The rooms are bright, contemporary, and easily accommodate four people, with a few homey touches like an antique steamer trunk or bureau, but mostly quite simple and spacious, with phones and private baths. Each room has a private outside entrance, but there's also a front entrance and common room for socializing, which makes it convivial. As one happy guest said, "Mile Zero is user-friendly." There's a help-yourself continental breakfast of fresh fruit, cereals, and muffins. No children, please; and no smoking. Rates are $105 for a double and $25 for each additional guest. *$–$$; DIS, MC, V; checks OK; PO Box 165, Skagway AK 99840; mile0@aptalaska.net; www.mile-zero.com.*

Skagway Bungalows / ★★★
MILE I DYEA RD, SKAGWAY; 907/983-2986 OR 877/983-2986; FAX 907/983-3986
Get out of town! Tucked in the woods, these two log cabins with their distinctive raven and eagle carvings were carefully built by proprietor Nan Saldi's husband, Mark. The Eagle Cabin has a king bed and the Raven Cabin has a queen and a double futon. Both have electric kettles with complimentary tea, coffee, and hot chocolate and microwaves, refrigerators, and complete baths. Sit on your deck and enjoy the view of cascading Reid Falls high above the town. Both cabins are $99 a night for two people, with an extra $10 for each additional guest. There's another cabin in the works. *$–$$; No credit cards; checks OK; open April to Oct; PO Box 287, Skagway AK 99840; saldi@aptalaska.net; www.aptalaska.net/~saldi; take the first right off Dyea Rd and continue up the rise to a barn-red house with deep purple trim.*

THE ROADS NORTH

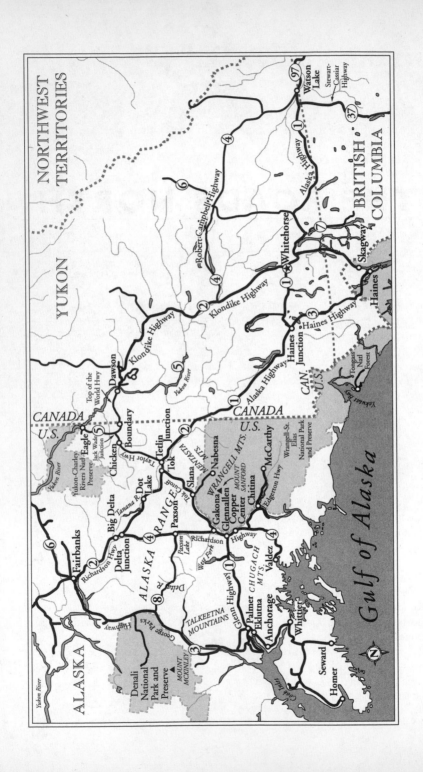

THE ROADS NORTH

When visiting Alaska, you will surely want to drive. Some people have the time to drive from the Lower 48 all the way to Alaska on the Alaska-Canada Highway (a.k.a. the Alcan, or simply the Alaska Highway). If you choose this option, you will be a road warrior by the time you cross the border. Others arrive in Haines or Skagway in Southeast Alaska via the Alaska Marine Highway and drive the 400 miles to Interior Alaska through Canada or the 800 or so miles to Anchorage. If you choose this option, be sure to reserve ferry space well in advance, as it is booked solid in the summer. You also can fly to Anchorage and rent a car.

In Alaska, the road map, like the average menu, is limited to **BASICS,** and if you don't like the options, that's tough. Even Anchorage, Alaska's largest city, has just two roads: one going north and one going south. Fairbanks does better with three, but in deep winter many residents suspect that all three go in and none out. Indeed, when the temperature is minus 40°F or minus 50°F, a long car trip is serious business and one packs basic survival gear.

Be sure to carry *The Milepost* (www.themilepost.com) with you. Billed—correctly—as the "Bible of North Country Travel," it takes you mile marker to mile marker down all the roads of Alaska. It's available at nearly any grocery store or bookstore in the state. A note about lodging and food along the route: the watchword is "practical." Many of the operative words like "best" and "cuisine" become tongue-in-cheek in the Alaska outback. If you need to sleep and shower, there is probably a place to do it. One alternative to be considered for those with energy and equipment is camping. It's cheap, you can pick your spot and otherwise control your destiny.

The Alaska Highway

In the old days, the Alaska Highway nominally began in Dawson Creek, British Columbia, at Mile 0. It really began where the pavement ended in Fort St. John 50 miles later. From there, the trip hovered between novelty and tedium, with novelty predominating in the beginning and intense tedium at the end. It was like being trapped inside a house that was being drywalled for five days. Dust hung in the air inside the vehicle. Opening windows only sucked it in faster through the trunk or tailgate. There was no way to get fresh air without stopping and getting out of the car. If you followed another car at any distance of less than half a mile, dust was a steady entree. The real knuckle-blancher was seeing a semi-truck bearing down, stones sparking out from the wheels as dust in great churning petticoats billowed out behind. These were both IFR (Instrument Flight Rating) situations with religious overtones.

The road tightly wound around the contours of hills, lakes, and rivers, with sharp, steeply banked turns. One developed empathy for the magnitude of this wartime project of 1942, which punched a road through some of the most unforgiving terrain and climate in the world in less than a year. Typically, the traveler prepared for the arduous journey with extra tires and gas. It was harder to prepare psychologically. You knew that the trip was long and that none of it would be lost. So you tried to settle in behind the wheel and be patient. But after a couple of days, you just wanted to get it over. You drove faster and faster, taking on the turns by using both lanes, hoping no one else would appear. This backslide into recklessness was made even more palpable by the white crosses—little wooden obituaries that stood at the places where fatalities had occurred.

Now, the highway is **PAVED**. Where it used to resemble a dropped rope, the worst stretches have been eliminated. There are **AMPLE GAS AND AMENITIES,** and having a sign on your vehicle that states "Alaska or Bust" says more about you than the trip. Even the crosses are gone, removed after people complained that they gave the drive a macabre tone. Still, it is a long stretch of driving, and some of the same psychology that held in the old days colors responses today. You become very anxious to arrive at the Alaska border, and it is a relief to see the solitary little customs compound show up in the middle of nowhere (unless either you or your car gets treated to a strip search).

Canadian Border to Tok

As if to say "Welcome back to the States," the road widens and becomes a flowing river of blacktop. Gas drops below two bucks a gallon and looks like a bargain. Tok, your first "real" Alaska town, is just 90 miles down the road. Things are looking up. If you're not immune to the **SPARE BEAUTY** of the landscape by this time, there is much to appreciate.

You are now in Alaska, a huge state that once spanned four time zones. More precisely, you're in Interior Alaska. The destination no longer recedes like a carrot on the horizon, and there is time to take it all in. From the border all the way to Fairbanks, the road follows the **TANANA RIVER** drainage. The climate is continental, protected from moderating ocean influences by the Wrangell-St. Elias Mountains to the south. Temperatures vary with the amount of daylight, reaching as high as 90 degrees in the summer and as low as 60 below zero in winter. Precipitation averages about 12 inches a year, only slightly more than arid. Any that falls as snow from early October on is part of the scenery until spring. In June and July, the sun makes a wide arc around most of the sky, rising in the north and setting there roughly 20 hours later. In winter, it's the other way around: the sun rises in the south and sets there perhaps 4 hours later, little more than an ornament for the cold.

For a relatively new civilization, the country has a strangely historical feel to it. The immensity and barrenness of the northern landscape lend a sense of timelessness that is unrelenting. Since each day lengthens or shortens by up to six minutes a day, one does not become absentminded. The sense of urgency is caught nicely by all the **MIGRATING WATERFOWL,** as well as in the miner's reference to the first snow on the mountaintops as "termination dust." This usually comes in late August and used to mean that it was time to head out before the rivers froze and the last boat left for the south.

Speaking of miners, it was mining that opened up the Interior to the white man and that was the raison d'être for almost every town here. What is a "real" Alaska

THE DRUNKEN FOREST

At first sight, the trees seem to weave—first to the left, then to the right. No, it's not your eyes playing tricks on you. The trees really are leaning. Most of the land in northern Alaska consists of permanently frozen ground or "permafrost." During the summer, the top few inches of soil above the permafrost thaw out. It is in these few inches of moist soil that plants extend their roots. Trees growing in a permafrost zone can put down only shallow roots. The frozen soil inhibits further growth. Thus, their anchors are shaky and unstable. They often will grow at an angle, listing first this way, then that. Scientists call this "the drunken forest."

—*Nan Elliot*

town? The typical Alaska town was created around one natural resource and defined by it. A "real" Alaska town might, therefore, be a fishing town, a mining town, a trading town, or, more recently, a tourist town. Alternatively, it may have always been here, as in the case of aboriginal villages built around traditional food sources. If the reason for being here disappears, these towns become ghosts. There are no ghost towns in Ohio, but there are plenty in Alaska. So there is a strong feeling for history in Alaska—for time inexorably moving on.

Tok

The first Alaska town you arrive in after crossing the border is Tok. Its reason for being there is incorporated in its old name, Tok Junction. Not a town of obvious grace and beauty, Tok occurs in a floodplain of thousands of acres. Its only defining characteristic is that two roads join, making it a logical place to sell needed things to travelers passing through on the way to or from mining districts such as Valdez, Anchorage, and Fairbanks, and from the Lower 48. A town naturally sprang up.

Tok had its beginnings as a **CONSTRUCTION CAMP** on the Alaska-Canada Highway in 1942, when the road was being pushed through as part of the defense effort against an anticipated Japanese invasion. One story about the origin of Tok's name is that it is an abbreviation of "Tokyo Camp." The population today is 1,250, and the mean monthly temperature in January is truly mean: 19 degrees below zero. In July, it is 59 degrees above.

ACCESS AND INFORMATION

First, stop at **TOK MAINSTREET VISITORS CENTER** (Box 389, Tok AK 99780; 907/883-5775 or 907/883-5887; open daily May to Sept) located at the junction of Alaska Highway and Tok Cutoff. The **ALASKA PUBLIC LANDS INFORMATION CENTER** (907/883-5667) is next door to the visitors center and open daily in summer. Managed under the auspices of the U.S. Fish and Wildlife Service is **TETLIN WILDLIFE REFUGE** (907/883-5312), which is across the highway from the Public Lands Information Center and is open weekdays, year-round.

RESTAURANTS

Fast Eddy's

MILE 1313.3, ALASKA HWY, TOK; 907/883-4411 Fast Eddy's is connected with Young's Motel, one of the clean, modern motels in Tok. There's a salad bar, sandwiches, pizza, Alaska seafood, and steaks. No new wrinkles here, but the food is well prepared. The place is busy, always a good sign. *$; AE, DIS, MC, V; no checks; breakfast, lunch, dinner every day; beer and wine; no reservations; PO Box 482, Tok AK 99780; ¾ mile east of the junction.*

Tok Gateway Salmon Bake / ★

MILE 1313.1, ALASKA HWY, TOK; 907/883-5555 Like most places in Alaska, it's billed as a salmon bake, but the fish is grilled. No matter. Essentially, this is a barbecue with ribs, buffalo burgers, reindeer sausage, king salmon, and halibut. One advantage of a limited menu is that the establishment can pay attention to the few items it serves. Fresh salmon and halibut, grilled just right, are hard to top. *$$; MC, V; checks OK; lunch Mon–Sat, dinner every day in summer; no alcohol, but you may bring your own; no reservations; PO Box 577, Tok AK 99780; slammingsalmon@ pocketmail.com; ⁷⁄₈ mile east of the junction.*

LODGINGS

Cleft of the Rock Bed and Breakfast / ★★

MILE 1316.5, ALASKA HWY, TOK; 907/883-4219 OR 800/478-5646; FAX 305/425-7901 One of the first things you notice as you drive in is a real lawn and an absence of the usual Alaska collection of extra cars and odds and ends that might someday rise again like the old South. The guest rooms in the house are located in the daylight basement and share a bathroom ($85–$125 for two). They are clean and acceptable, but the stars are awarded for the five log cabins you pass on the way in, complete with running water and bathrooms. The largest one sleeps up to five adults and has a kitchen, loft, and bath. The cabins are nicely situated on the lawn, among scattered trees, and come with lawn chairs begging to be used after a long day's drive. Reserve ahead. Full, hot breakfast served. The B&B also rents mountain bikes. *$$; AE, DIS, MC, V; checks OK; PO Box 122, Tok AK 99780; info@cleftoftherock.net; www.cleftoftherock.net; off Alaska Hwy, 3 miles west of Tok, turn right on Sundog Trail and go ½ mile.*

The Tok Cutoff

Technically, this road is part of the Glenn Highway, running from Tok south to Anchorage, but the first 125 miles have always been called the Tok Cutoff. It was built from Tok on the Alaska Highway to Gakona Junction on the Richardson Highway—a shortcut from one highway to another.

Be prepared for a lot of frost heaves and cracks on this portion of highway. It's nearly impossible to put a road surface down over permafrost that lasts beyond a couple of seasons. It isn't that Alaska refuses to put money into highways; it just can't keep up with ongoing deterioration.

A magnitude 7.9 earthquake in November 2002 also wreaked havoc on the road; be on the lookout for construction in the 2003 season, particularly from Milepost 75 through 82.

The first 10 miles of road south out of Tok are straight, true, and well-surfaced. From there, you can kiss the straight and well-surfaced goodbye and the scenery hello, as you are in the mountains for about the next 50 miles. The road follows the Tok and Little Tok Rivers most of the way to Mentasta Summit. **EAGLE TRAIL STATE RECREATION SITE,** 15 miles out of Tok, has 40 campsites in a forest of large spruce. It's on the old trail that ran from Valdez to Eagle, a section of which has signed hiking trails.

The road continues on in quiet grandeur through the mountains. The food and lodging on this route, even though they do not merit stars, still can be part of a great adventure. **MINERAL LAKES RETREAT** (HC72, Box 830, Tok AK 99780-9410; 907/883-5498), 35 miles south of Tok, has cabins overlooking the lakes, but with no running water or electricity. You do get a memorable view of the Mentasta Mountains and a chance to go fishing. There's a canoe and motorboat for rent. **MENTASTA LODGE** (HC01, Box 585, Gakona AK 99586; 907/291-2324), 47 miles south of Tok, has cabins and a bar and cafe. When people live year-round in such extreme climate and geography, a special resonance may occur that also deserves stars. Call it character.

Beyond Mentasta Lodge, the road runs beside the **SLANA RIVER.** On this side of Mentasta Summit, the rivers flow south into the Copper River and Prince William Sound instead of north into the Tanana River and then finally the Yukon. As you emerge from the Mentasta Mountains, if the weather is clear, you'll get your first glimpse of **MOUNT SANFORD** (16,237 feet). Welcome to the Wrangell Mountains. The country opens up, but the scene is always dominated by Mount Sanford, 35 miles away.

The **NEBESNA ROAD** branches off to the southeast at **SLANA** and allows access into the **WRANGELL-ST. ELIAS NATIONAL PARK AND PRESERVE** (see below). A park ranger station, ¼ mile down the road, offers information about the park and road conditions. The road is paved for the first 4 miles and gravel thereafter. Twenty-eight miles out, the road becomes rough and fords several streams. The area is open to camping. The road ends after 45 miles at the old mining town of **NEBESNA,** which is pretty much of a ghost town, although various population figures for the area say "less than 25." The last 3 miles are the roughest. Don't expect a chocolate shake at the end.

From Slana to **GAKONA JUNCTION** the road is less than exciting, unless you're looking for the perfect frost heave or road fissure to facilitate signature head-prints in the roof of your vehicle. The highway is relatively straight, as there is nothing for it to go around and much of the country is permafrost. You come to **CHISTOCHINA,** one of the more beautiful Alaska names to the ear. Besides Mount Sanford and **MOUNT DRUM** (to the right of Sanford at 12,010 feet), startling scenery is absent, except if you travel at sunrise, sunset, full moon, first snow, first leaves, or first love, in which case the magic will be there with no help needed from terrestrial aberrations.

About 3 miles before the Tok Cutoff joins the Richardson Highway at Gakona Junction, the road drops into the shallow canyon created by the Copper River.

RESTAURANTS

Gakona Lodge / ★

MILE 2, TOK CUTOFF, GAKONA; 907/822-3482 Gakona Lodge is an old roadhouse, built in 1905. It was added to the National Register of Historic Places in 1977 and makes an interesting stop. It is one in a series of roadhouses that once ran up the old Richardson Trail, spaced about a day's travel apart. Most of the roadhouses have burned down now. Gakona Lodge and Rika's Roadhouse at Big Delta are still operating as historic places, while Black Rapids Lodge, at Mile 227.4, is standing but in serious decline. At Gakona, a cluster of mostly log buildings includes the old carriage house, which is now a restaurant, and the main lodge. The historic feel has been maintained. The dining room is dark and comfortable. The log walls come complete with mounted animal heads and old-time Alaska tools. The menu consists of steaks and seafood with salad bar. Bring your poke. *$$; MC, V; local checks only; dinner every day (closed in winter); full bar; PO Box 285, Gakona AK 99586; by the bridge in Gakona.*

Tok to Delta Junction

The last chunk of the Alaska Highway runs from Tok to Delta Junction, where it joins the Richardson Highway for the trip into Fairbanks. It covers a scenic 100 miles. The road out of Tok runs for 15 miles, with hardly a bend until the road gets close to the **MENTASTA MOUNTAINS.**

A rustic and scenic camping spot, the **MOON LAKE STATE RECREATION SITE** comes at Mile 1331.9. A lovely spot, ¼ mile off the highway, it has swimming and a small sandy beach.

Jan Lake Road turns off to the south at Mile 1353.7. **JAN LAKE** is ½ mile back, nestled among the mixed birch- and spruce-covered hills. It's a pretty location and a good picnic spot. The lake is small and stocked with small rainbows. In the fall, if you're lucky, you'll see hundreds of sandhill cranes fly over in wavering filaments, sun reflecting off their beating wings as if from waves.

The road crosses the Johnson River Bridge at Mile 1380.5. You'll cross bridges over several rivers, most of which have access roads that allow for a more intimate look and possible campsites (no amenities). **JOHNSON RIVER** is especially nice in this regard. In a few miles, the road leaves the mountains and goes straight over flat land for 40 miles, right into Delta Junction. It is still a beautiful drive, but the beauty now comes with distance. To the south, there's a line of mountains. The closer ones are soft, while those farther back are white and craggy—the beginnings of the Alaska Range. The rivers are glacial and run in braids across broad shallow beds. At Mile 1403.6, Sawmill Creek Road takes off to the north, right through the **DELTA BARLEY PROJECT,** an agricultural project. There's an interpretive sign explaining the project, and you can decide if you want to face a gravel road to see more.

Although you expect to see signs for moose and caribou crossings, it is a surprise to see a sign warning you to watch out for **BISON**. A herd of bison was transplanted from Montana in the 1920s to see how they'd do. They've done fine, much to the chagrin of the farmers who have been feeding them whether they wanted to or not. The Bison Range, 70,000 acres of grassland for fall and winter grazing, was established south of the highway to reduce agricultural losses. The last 25 miles into Delta is all new blacktop and has wide shoulders, a welcome stretch after all the frost heaves one enjoys as part of the Alaska road package.

Delta Junction

Delta Junction was established as a construction camp on the Richardson Highway in 1919. It is the official end of the Alaska Highway, and from here you have the choice of heading south to Valdez or Anchorage or taking the Richardson on into Fairbanks. Delta Junction's population is listed as 736. If you want to put your finger on the pulse of the town, go to the **IGA FOOD CACHE** (907/895-4653), located on Main Street. It all happens here. There's an espresso cart and fresh-made doughnuts from the bakery. The homemade soups come after the coffee-and-doughnut rush subsides. No yuppies here, just farmers mumbling about getting the rest of the hay in and other folks in work clothes and quilted jackets. The weather is the topic in the fall, with all the geese and cranes filtering through in long strings; but it's also the topic the rest of the year because, well, there's always weather.

The Taylor Highway

Alaskans know most of the roads by heart. They still excite us, but the prospect of a fresh road is like spring. One road not heavily traveled, even by Alaskans, is the **ROAD TO EAGLE**. Eagle has a mystique about it. Alaskans know it as a checkpoint on the 1,000-mile Yukon Quest International Sled Dog Race between Fairbanks, Alaska, and Whitehorse, Yukon Territory, and as a town that cannot be reached by road in winter. It is a town for real Alaskans, for folks who don't need a bank or the security of an international airport within taxi distance. The name itself inspires. A town named "Finch" or "Dove" wouldn't have the same draw. Chicken, on the same road, catches the ear too, but its mystique is so bound by absurdity it never gets off the ground. So Eagle it is, with a Chicken thrown in. If you venture down this road, your heart will soar like a hawk.

Most people travel to Alaska in summer, when the long, magic days open up possibilities limited only by stamina. If you drive to Eagle in late September with the days getting short, you get a sky full of stars in place of the same number of mosquitoes. And the northern lights! Also, a nearly empty road. If you do go in late September, there are no services until you get to Eagle. The highway is not maintained by the state beyond mid-October, the time of the general onset of serious snow. Before then, people from Eagle make their last drives of the year out to the big cities of Anchorage and Fairbanks for winter supplies.

CHICKEN

Chicken, at Mile 66 on the Taylor Highway, is an obvious draw. Who could resist such a burlesque name? And why "Chicken"? The story goes that early miners wanted to name the town "Ptarmigan" because of the bird's abundance there, but no one knew how to spell it. So they settled for Chicken. To our eye, a ptarmigan does not much resemble a chicken but then, that's the charm of the story. The best thing to do in Chicken is to get the Chicken postmark on your letters at the post office, a small log building with flower boxes and a flagpole outside. Mail service to Chicken (pop. 37) is by air twice a week, weather permitting. If there is any more economic belt-tightening, Chicken's tiny post office, which was established in 1903, may be eliminated—a notion that worries the postmistress. So buy your year's worth of stamps in Chicken from someone who cares, and keep Chicken's mail service from getting fried.

—*John Kooistra*

The **TAYLOR HIGHWAY** runs from Tetlin Junction to Eagle, 160 miles of unpaved road marked with mileposts. **FROM TETLIN JUNCTION,** the road begins to ascend mountains appropriately called "domes." They are old and soft hills when compared to the brash, rugged, snow-covered Wrangell-St. Elias Range to the south, which contains some of the highest mountains in North America. Within 2 or 3 miles, you ascend enough to get a view of the hills, which is exciting after all the valley travel on the Alaska Highway. You truly start to feel "on top of the world," especially after about 25 miles, at the point where the road goes above timberline and skirts **MOUNT FAIRPLAY** (5,541 feet), the second-highest point on the way to Eagle.

Gold was discovered in this area in 1886. This is the **FORTYMILE COUNTRY,** named after the old town located where the Fortymile River enters the Yukon, a few miles east of the border. Chicken Creek and Wade Creek were also rich finds. In many places, the Taylor Highway runs right over the top of or right beside the old horse-and-wagon road that was built and used by the miners and freight haulers.

At Mile 34.4, there is a pullout on the left (west) and a mind-altering view. Food, gas, and "likker" are available in **CHICKEN** (Mile 66) during the summer. Blueberries and crowberries are everywhere.

Beyond Chicken, rivers are a big part of the scenery. From Mile 76 to Mile 80, the road rises high above **WALKER FORK,** which cuts an average of 800 feet into solid rock. It is one of the most scenic stretches of the highway. Pull over, peer into the canyon, and listen to the river far below. (During summer traffic this would not be a safe practice, so exercise due caution.)

Mile 96 brings Jack Wade Junction and a parting of the ways: east into Canada and Dawson City via the appropriately named **TOP OF THE WORLD HIGHWAY** or north to Eagle. The route to Dawson City is part of the popular **KLONDIKE LOOP,** traveled by more than 20,000 people each summer. It leaves the Alaska Highway at

Whitehorse, goes to Dawson City and Jack Wade Junction, and reconnects with the Alaska Highway 12 miles east of Tok at Tetlin Junction via the first leg of the Taylor Highway. Though the road west from Dawson City is gravel, the Klondike Loop is better suited to heavy traffic than the Taylor Highway spur to Eagle; the Canadian section has been improved, with heavy visitor traffic in mind.

From Jack Wade Junction to Eagle, the Taylor Highway is 65 miles of narrow, winding, eminently cursable, and memorable road. It was finally punched through in 1953, after eight years of construction. This stretch takes you back decades to the bad old Alaska Highway days, something to be considered before making the drive. The road is less than two lanes wide in those places where it hugs the mountainside in tight turns as it follows various river valleys. We cannot recall a single guardrail. It would not be a comfortable jaunt for a large motor home towing a getaway car. One Eagle resident said the trip out to Tetlin Junction used to take seven hours; now it takes four, with more than half devoted to the Eagle spur. This is four hours for someone who has and means business, not someone who's there to savor the sights and the feel of the country. For touring, better stick with the original seven hours, with lots of stops.

On this section the scenery is terrific, and when the road is not "threading" its way through the gorges and valleys, it is up on top of the world overlooking a landscape that goes on like a clear conscience. A sunset looks small up here: it's so far away and takes up so little of the horizon. If you want photos, bring a disposable panoramic camera. The wide-angle bite will still be too narrow, but several overlapping vistas can be put together to catch some sense of that space.

After 10 miles on "the roof," the road descends toward the **FORTYMILE RIVER BRIDGE**, a place for putting in your raft or canoe for running the river. For much of the next 30 miles the road hugs **O'BRIEN CREEK** with lots of tight places and turns in the road. There are no guardrails and some of the drop-offs are precipitous. When the road leaves the valley around Mile 136, things open up and you're on top of the world again, traversing **AMERICAN PASS**. A few miles away only one tiny building is visible, making it seem lonelier still. The sign in front announces "American Summit Liquor," surely one of the world's most isolated liquor stores.

Eagle

Eagle was named in 1897 for the eagles that nested on the nearby bluff. At the time there were only 28 miners, but by spring of 1898, there were 1,700 people in Eagle— 10 times the number who live here today. In 1899, the army established **FORT EGBERT**, just west of the town, to maintain law and order; to build roads, trails, and the telegraph; and to help unfortunate civilians. Judge James Wickersham presided over the first federal court in the Alaska Interior here: the Third Judicial District, which covers 300,000 square miles. Eagle was the commercial, judicial, and military center for the Interior during the Klondike gold rush.

Today, Judge Wickersham's original courthouse serves as a museum, and Fort Egbert's military buildings have been completely restored. And there's the town itself—a cluster of old buildings and cabins, an old school, and a library, as well as the Yukon River. The town is squeezed down to the river by the mountains in two levels. Most of the town is on the second level—the sensible level—protected from the vagaries of the river.

EAGLE VILLAGE is an Athabascan settlement on the banks of the Yukon, 3 miles upstream. On your way, you'll pass the town's primary airport, marked by signs displaying the silhouette of a Boeing 747, a droll touch. If a 747 ever lands in Eagle, it won't be a scheduled stop. Eagle Village is less than a mile down the road from the airport. The houses line the riverbank, and empty chairs sit waiting along the edge of the bluff. This is the best show in town. All the action is on the river.

Both the town and the residents have personality to spare. The impact of tourism is evident, but this community has not turned itself inside out catering to it. Few places take credit cards, and the nearest bank is in Delta Junction, 275 miles away, so come prepared. Most impressive, though, is the absence of a bar or liquor store, a notoriously profitable business in a state where many folks head for the bar to wait for spring. Unless you want to winter in, start driving out before termination dust settles for good on Mount Fairplay.

ADVENTURES

HISTORICAL TOUR / Given by the **EAGLE HISTORICAL SOCIETY**, the tours meet at the courthouse daily, 9am, Memorial Day through Labor Day. *PO Box 23, Eagle AK 99738; 907/547-2325; fax 907/547-2232.*

FLOAT TRIPS / Float the Fortymile or Yukon River, but know what you're doing. Canoes can be rented in Dawson City or in Eagle at **EAGLE CANOE RENTALS** (907/547-2203). You can float through the **YUKON-CHARLEY RIVERS NATIONAL PRESERVE** to Circle on the road system north of Fairbanks. Get any of your buddies driving north to pick you up.

RESTAURANTS

Riverside Cafe

FRONT ST, EAGLE; 907/547-2250 The best restaurant in town also happens to be the only restaurant. The log cafe with central woodstove is attractively situated, overlooking the Yukon. It is warm and friendly and supplies the town coffee table. You bring the conversation. Gravy-sogged rolls and canned fruit notwithstanding, the core of the dinners is straightforward and ample. Pies are homemade. *$; No credit cards; local checks only; breakfast, lunch, dinner every day (open mid-May to early Nov); no alcohol; no reservations; Box 36, Eagle AK 99738-0036.*

LODGINGS

Eagle Trading Co. Motel

ON THE RIVERFRONT, EAGLE; 907/547-2220 This basic motel, right next to the store and cafe, has 18 rooms (9 are in an annex). During summers, the 9 rooms just behind the store have their own bathrooms, including showers, but in winter, guests must use a common bathhouse. The annex rooms have a common bathhouse year-round. The rooms are simple, with two queen beds, but comfortable. Double occupancy rates are $70, year-round. *$; No credit cards; checks OK; PO Box 36, Eagle AK 99738-0036; www.eagletrading.com.*

The Glenn Highway

This route to Glennallen lies east out of Anchorage, a journey of about 200 miles. Half an hour out of town, the Athabascan village of **EKLUTNA** is on your left and a beautiful mountain lake of the same name is 14 miles up a dirt road, off the highway to the right. Just before the bridge, look to the left and you'll see sofas and chairs lined up on the bluff overlooking the highway, where the locals lounge around watching the traffic flow.

Right before the Knik River Bridge is the old road into **PALMER,** a scenic detour through this agricultural valley. After the bridge, you cross the **PALMER HAY FLATS.** Be on the lookout for moose, particularly in the early morning. **PIONEER PEAK** rises behind you, dominating the valley. It was named for the midwestern pioneers who came here in the 1930s to start a new life, fleeing the Dust Bowl during the Depression. Some of the most fantastic cold-weather vegetables are grown here—70-pound cabbages and foot-long carrots. If you're in the area during late August and the first of September, stick around for one of the state's most popular events—the **ALASKA STATE FAIR** (see Anchorage and Beyond chapter). You'll pass the fairgrounds on the right as you head toward Palmer.

To visit the **MUSK OX FARM** (907/745-4151), turn at Mile 50.1, just past Palmer. These marvelous creatures can even be your namesake. For a modest donation of $50, you can have a musk ox named after you or your best friend. Contrary to their name, it's not the musk for which these animals are famous. In fact, they have no musk glands. Furthermore, they're not even oxen. They're really related to the goat and antelope family. But their great treasure is their underhairs, called qiviut, which are finer, lighter, and warmer than cashmere. Hats and scarves from qiviut make truly lovely, if expensive, gifts. The farm is open daily, May through September, with tours every half hour (see also Anchorage and Beyond chapter).

The next stretch of highway provides scenery of matchless beauty. The road follows the **MATANUSKA RIVER,** and then climbs the outer fringe of the **TALKEETNA MOUNTAINS,** with the **CHUGACH MOUNTAINS** off to the right across the valley. As is true elsewhere in Alaska, many of the peaks in the Chugach are still unnamed, a reminder that this is still a young country, only recently explored. The stark and rugged mountains are interspersed with glaciers, including **MATANUSKA GLACIER,** which appears soon in this journey, off to the west. Meanwhile, you climb through a forest of aspen interspersed with evergreen: a lovely sight at any time, but if you hit it at the height of fall colors, it's a vision of golden beauty. **CHICKALOON** is summer home to NOVA (Mile 76 Glenn Hwy; 800/746-5753; www.novalaska.com), white-water river-rafting guides who will take you on half-day trips down the Matanuska River. They offer everything from peaceful floats to wet-and-wild rides, depending on your thrills-to-chills quotient. Trips cost $60–$90 per person.

KING MOUNTAIN, one of the few named peaks in the area, rises with majesty to the south. Up above the confluence of the Chickaloon and Matanuska Rivers, there is a fine view over the valley. The road follows the shore of Long Lake and brings you to Matanuska Glacier.

THE CIRCULAR ROUTE

ANCHORAGE-GLENNALLEN-VALDEZ-WHITTIER-ANCHORAGE, WITH A SIDE TRIP TO CHITINA AND MCCARTHY A journey by land and sea, this route combines a series of scenic dramas. You can go in either direction. In essence, this is a spectacular drive out of Anchorage to Glennallen along the Glenn Highway, turning right onto the Richardson Highway, peeling off shortly (if you have a few extra days for a side trip to historic Kennicott and McCarthy, reached via the Edgerton Highway), then back to the Richardson Highway and heading south to the port town of Valdez. Explore Valdez (see the Prince William Sound chapter), then take the ferry, part of the Alaska Marine Highway System, through Prince William Sound to the port town of Whittier (about seven hours). Drive your car off the ferry and onto the train flatcars or, if the toll road is open, you can drive straight through the tunnel in the mountains and come out on the Seward Highway, just an hour or so south of Anchorage. And voilà! The circle is complete. Allow at least four or five days for the trip, the longer the better. The mountains and rivers beckon to the hiker, backpacker, fisherman, or rafter. And a side trip to McCarthy always offers a good time.

—John Kooistra

Beyond **SHEEP MOUNTAIN**, the road climbs to **EUREKA SUMMIT** (Eureka Lodge is a possible pie stop), and the scenery changes dramatically. The Chugach Mountains fall away to the south, as Mount Drum and the Wrangells appear in the east. A tundralike plain opens up, studded by several lakes and stunted trees—the "drunken forest" in local parlance (see "The Drunken Forest" in this chapter). The vast **NELCHINA GLACIER** interrupts the dark range of the Chugach and gives its name to the caribou herd that frequents this area. Keep a lookout for these wild reindeer.

LODGINGS

Sheep Mountain Lodge / ★★★

MILE 113.5 GLENN HWY, PALMER; 907/745-5121; FAX 907/745-5120 As you climb up to Sheep Mountain, the trees thin out and it's possible to catch glimpses of Dall sheep high up on the mountains. The best place to break your trip or, for that matter, to stop for several days of adventure is Sheep Mountain Lodge, run by David Cohen and his wife, Diane Schneider. It is the best—and the only—place of this superb quality for many, many miles. Rustic and charming, the lodge is right on the highway. The entry is set off by a brilliant bank of lovingly tended flowers, which provide a special touch of class to this wilderness outpost. Individual cabins are sturdy and tastefully designed with comfort in mind. Views are stunning—wide-open country, glaciers, light woods. The hospitality is warm, and the lodge's dining room provides generous Alaska fare with a spicy Southwest touch. There is also a bunkhouse for larger parties or those on the cheap. *$$; MC, V; local checks only;*

open May to Oct (some years open earlier for spring skiing); HC03, Box 8490, Palmer AK 99645; sheepmtl@alaska.net; www.alaska.net/~sheepmtl.

Glennallen

For a taste of local color, tune into the radio message board *Caribou Clatter* on KCAM (AM 790, 7am, noon, 5pm, and 9pm). In other regions of Alaska, this same radio message program has been called *Ptarmigan Telegraph, Tundra Drums,* and *Cabin Trapline.* The messages you hear are sometimes strange and wondrous, and always full of local color. Call to send a message yourself (907/822-3306).

In Glennallen, at the junction of the Glenn and Richardson Highways, is the **GLENNALLEN VISITORS INFORMATION CENTER**, a charming log cabin, dripping with flowers, open only in summer.

LODGINGS

New Caribou Hotel

CENTER OF TOWN, GLENNALLEN; 907/822-3302 (800/478-3302, IN-STATE); FAX 907/822-3711 An attractive place to stay if you get sleepy in Glennallen. The rooms are standard motel, but cheerful. It is on the tour-bus circuit, so it can be a mob scene when the buses arrive. On the average, rooms run about $140 for a double. They do have a few suites and apartments to accommodate families or larger groups traveling together. Also, for bicyclists or hikers trying to make it on the cheap but wanting a shower and a bed, there is an economy section with beds for $49 per night. The hotel is almost completely nonsmoking. *$$; AE, DIS, MC, V; local checks only; PO Box 329, Glennallen AK 99588.* &

The Richardson Highway

Unless you are agoraphobic, it is hard to imagine not liking driving the roads of Alaska. There is space, something hard to get away from in Alaska. Most of the time, the scenery will knock your eyeballs out. But there are also miles of wet lowlands. The country around Glennallen has stretches of lowland permafrost stuff, marshy bogs with trees like pipe cleaners. You've got about 40 miles of this to drive through until you get to more exciting parts. The redeeming features are the distant regal mountains—**SANFORD** (16,237 feet), **WRANGELL** (14,163 feet), and **DRUM** (12,010 feet)—which form a postcard backdrop.

Glennallen to Fairbanks

For the first 30 miles, the Richardson Highway north from Glennallen is utilitarian. It's relatively straight with sections of generous frost heaves. The scenic attractions are caribou, if you're lucky, and views of the Gulkana River Gorge on the west side of the highway. The **GULKANA RIVER** is a good salmon and rafting river. It runs out of Paxson and Summit Lakes. The float from Paxson Lake to Sourdough Campground at Mile 147.6 is popular for experienced river runners.

Your first good look at the **ALASKA RANGE** comes when you round Hogan Hill and encounter a row of shark's teeth running all the way across the horizon. The range begins near Tok, running west and then southwest through Denali National Park, ultimately becoming the Aleutian Chain. Mount McKinley (20,320 feet) is the highest mountain of this range and the highest in North America.

Here in the foothills of the Alaska Range, you can see the **TRANS-ALASKA PIPELINE,** curving and silver, winding its way across the terrain like a sculpture, sometimes aboveground and sometimes under. **PAXSON LAKE** appears west of the highway—a long, deep lake, famous for lake trout.

Paxson Lake was named after the owner of **PAXSON LODGE,** at Mile 185.5, one of the early roadhouses. The original lodge burned, but the new lodge goes by the same name. The town of **PAXSON** has a population of 33. Before 1972, the year the George Parks Highway was completed, the only way to drive to Denali National Park, then known as Mount McKinley National Park, was to take the Denali Highway west from Paxson for 135 miles. If you wanted to drive to Fairbanks at that time, you also went through Paxson.

The road continues north from Paxson, climbing right alongside the Gulkana River, by now a sprightly creek that runs between Summit and Paxson Lakes. **SUMMIT LAKE** is at the divide, where the waters run either north or south. The elevation here is 3,210 feet. Midway along the lake, a blackened hole and standing chimney mark the spot where Summit Lake Lodge stood until 1993, another piece of history turned into firewood.

For the next 40 miles, the road makes its way through the Alaska Range. You'll find serious mountains and scenery here, and the road is some of the best highway in Alaska. A canyon curves alongside the headwaters of the Delta River, with the Alaska pipeline showing up here and there as if it were shadowing you. At Mile 204, there's a pullout where springwater gushes through a pipe out of the side of the mountain. Fill up there and save the freight from France.

At Mile 227.4, you'll see the old **BLACK RAPIDS ROADHOUSE** on the east side of the road. It was one of the roadhouses on the Valdez Trail, and the part now falling down dates from 1905. It originally was called "The Black Rapids Hunting Lodge." The old roadhouses have been replaced by pump stations for the Alaska pipeline, a sign of the times.

The mountains get bigger as you drive. To the west, you see three of the great peaks of the Alaska Range: **DEBORAH** (12,339 feet), **HESS** (11,940 feet), and **HAYES** (13,832 feet). They don't look that big until you find out they're 40 miles away and dominate the horizon a good portion of the way into Fairbanks (See Fairbanks and the Interior chapter). The last 20 miles into Delta Junction puts you down on the flats. It might sound like a letdown, but it's not. The scenery now comes as a marvel of straightness.

At the junction of the Richardson Highway and the official end of the Alaska Highway is **DELTA JUNCTION.** The Delta River, which you have followed from its source in the mountains down to the floodplains, runs right beside the town. People seem to be on their own time here, as well as having some to share.

The Richardson Highway continues into Fairbanks, 100 miles to the northwest, following first the Delta River and then the Tanana, which it joins at **BIG DELTA,** 10 miles down the road. If you have time, take the gravel road that runs along the river to Big Delta. There are good views of the milewide riverbed and the Alaska Range as the road follows the bluff. Take the first turn to the left after passing the sign for Jack Warren Road, 2 miles out of Delta.

Big Delta State Historical Park

In 1909, the Alaska Road Commission installed a ferry across the Tanana River on the old Valdez-to-Fairbanks trail to accommodate traffic to the goldfields. This was a natural place for a roadhouse, and John Hajdukovich built one that year. In 1917, he hired a Swedish immigrant, Rika Wallen, to run it for him. She bought it in 1923, and it became known as Rika's. She had a large garden and raised animals and poultry to supply the table. Rika operated the roadhouse into the late 1940s and lived there until her death in 1969, at the age of 94. After the ferry was replaced by a bridge, people no longer had to stop as they did in the past. More than 2,000 people crossed the river by ferry in 1925. Now, people don't even slow down.

In 1986, **RIKA'S ROADHOUSE** (Big Delta, Mile 275 Richardson Hwy; 907/895-4201; fax 907/895-4787) was reopened as a living history homestead, after being restored by the Alaska Division of Parks and Outdoor Recreation. Admission is free. During the tourist season, the restaurant is open daily until 5pm and features home-baked goods. Just before crossing the Big Delta bridge, you'll see a parking area and interpretive display for the Trans-Alaska Pipeline, which makes an impressive sight as it crosses the river, especially in winter when it's all lit up. Only 90 miles remain to Fairbanks—Alaska's second-largest city with 80,000 people—and the terminus of the Richardson Highway.

Glennallen to Valdez

Turn right from the Glenn onto the Richardson Highway and head south. In a few miles you'll see the signs for the Copper Center Loop, a small road that swings you into the community of **COPPER CENTER** and back out to the main road again. Along the way is the ranger station for **WRANGELL-ST. ELIAS NATIONAL PARK,** open daily in the summer, with books, maps, and information. If you are going on to McCarthy and Kennicott, check here for McCarthy Road conditions.

Traveling south on the Richardson Highway alongside the **TONSINA RIVER,** the most intriguing sight—apart from spectacular nature—is a section of the oil pipeline, which transects Alaska, running 800 miles from the Arctic Ocean to the North Pacific, from Prudhoe Bay to Valdez. At various points, the pipeline parallels the road, crosses it, and recrosses it. Shortly before descending into the port town of **VALDEZ,** often called Little Switzerland because of the spectacular mountains and icefields, you'll pass the site of the World Extreme Skiing Championships, held in March every year at Thompson Pass (see the Prince William Sound chapter).

LODGINGS

Copper Center Lodge / ★★

MILE 101 RICHARDSON HWY, LOOP RD, COPPER CENTER; 907/822-3245 OR 888/822-3245; FAX 907/822-5035 This very cozy hotel is an old historic roadhouse brought up to date for comfort and still in operation. The roadhouse, on the banks of the Copper River, opened its door to travelers in 1898 and has been welcoming them ever since. It's a warm, family-run enterprise, with breakfast, lunch, and dinner served every day. The owners say their sourdough starter is more than 100 years old—test it out. Try the sourdough pancakes or popular homemade berry pies. Beer and wine are also available. *$$; MC, V; local checks only; closed mid-Sept to mid-May; Drawer J, Copper Center AK 99573.* &

Copper River Princess Wilderness Lodge

MILE 102 RICHARDSON HWY, COPPER BRENWICK RD, COPPER CENTER; 907/822-4000 OR 800/426-0500; FAX 907/822-4480 This is yet another Princess hotel in Alaska (we're at five, and counting), with all the amenities and familiar elegance a Princess regular would expect. The company's latest offering is an 85-room retreat, located on 200 acres at the junction of the Klutina and Copper Rivers, with views of Mounts Wrangell, Drum, and Blackburn. The chief draw is the lodge's proximity to Wrangell-St. Elias National Park, the largest national park in the United States. There's a restaurant and bar, and the hotel's tour desk can arrange rafting or fishing trips down the Gulkana and Klutina Rivers, flight-seeing tours, horseback riding, Copper River jet boat tours, or tours to the abandoned Kennicott copper mine. There's only one room style, which goes for $189, double occupancy. *$$$; AE, DC, DIS, MC, V; checks OK; closed mid-Sept to mid-May; www.princess lodges.com; from Mile 102 Richardson Hwy, turn onto Copper Brenwick Rd, go 1 mile, you can't miss it.* &

Tsaina Lodge / ★★

MILE 34.7 RICHARDSON HWY, VALDEZ; 907/835-3500; FAX 907/835-5661 Even if you're not staying, stop in to sample the cuisine—it's adventurous and definitely a surprise from what you'd normally expect at the side of the road in Alaska. An historic old roadhouse, with hand-hewn logs on the interior, this little place has had new life breathed into it by its young, enthusiastic outdoorswoman-proprietor Lisa Wax, who bought it in 1994. About 40 miles from Valdez, with the massive Worthington Glacier out the window and an array of breathtaking peaks, this is the land of extreme skiers, snowboarders, heli-hikers, and paragliders. You can rent a bed in a log cabin, yurt, or the bunkhouse; camping is free. Meals (breakfast, lunch, dinner every day, and full bar) aim for healthy ingredients, with fresh seafood, pastas, and homemade soups high on the list. *$$; MC, V; no checks; open for spring ski season, Feb to June; SR 80, Valdez AK 99686.*

Wrangell–St. Elias
National Park and Preserve

The Wrangell–St. Elias region is a 13-million acre, mountain-and-ice kingdom of extraordinary beauty. It is the largest national park in the United States and has some of the highest peaks and the most extensive sweep of glaciers on the North American continent. It is mind-boggling. Thirteen mountains rise more than 14,000 feet; four of them are higher than 16,000 feet. Mount St. Elias (18,008 feet) is the second-highest peak in Alaska, next to Mount McKinley (20,320 feet). There are 75 named glaciers and many more unnamed. Together with its neighboring park Kluane National Park in Canada, this region has been designated a World Heritage Site by the United Nations. Signed by 111 member nations, the World Heritage Convention declares such sites to be of such exceptional interest and such universal value that their protection is the responsibility of all mankind.

While several of the high peaks such as Mounts Sanford, Drum, and Blackburn and the still-active volcano of Mount Wrangell can be viewed from the highways that skirt the park's borders, this is just a hint of what lies beyond.

This is a park for the wilderness seeker. There are relatively **FEW VISITOR FACILITIES**. Only two unpaved roads penetrate the park at all: the McCarthy Road in the west and the Slana-Nebesna Road in the north. The National Park Service stresses that in this mountainous region where help is often days away, visitors need to be skilled in backcountry travel and carry proper survival gear. You need to be both self-motivated and self-sufficient. A new **PARK VISITOR CENTER** (Mile 106.8 Richardson Hwy, PO Box 439, Copper Center AK 99573; 907/822-5235; www.nps.gov/wrst) features exhibits, a theater, and plenty of tour and trail information. It's open daily during summer months and weekdays during the winter. There is also a ranger station at Nebesna (907/822-5238), and one in the little town of Chitina (907/823-2205).

The Edgerton Highway

A terrific side trip en route to Valdez begins when you peel off on the Edgerton Highway (at Mile 82.6 Richardson Hwy), which takes you to Chitina. From there, continue along the McCarthy Road to the Kennicott River, park the car, walk across the bridge, and visit the historic mines and old ghost town of Kennicott and the picturesque town of McCarthy nearby.

Chitina

Tundra gives way here to meadows and trees of middling size. **LIBERTY FALLS,** a short distance off the road, is quite lovely, with clear cascading water and a scramble up the hillsides for the more energetic. From here, head on to Chitina (pronounced chit-nah), which sits at the end of the gravel road under the shadow of Spirit Mountain. The year-round population here is about 50, but on a summer weekend, when the salmon are running in the Copper River and the dipnetters running right behind them, the population can sometimes balloon to 3,000 folks.

EXPLORING

RAVEN DANCE (Mile 32.5 Edgerton Hwy; 907/823-2254; closed Sept to mid-May) offers espresso and pizza at the near end of town, called "uptown Chitina."

On the main road in Chitina you'll find a charming art gallery, **SPIRIT MOUN-TAIN ARTWORKS** (Box 22, Chitina AK 99566; 907/823-2222; spiritmountain@starband.net; open summers—call first in the off-season, Oct to May), the creation of Art Koeninger. He bought the building for a song, intending to use parts for salvage, then became entranced by it, secured some federal grants, spent a fortune, renovated it, and now it's on the National Register of Historic Places. It's a fun gallery of fine Alaska art. "Husbands Welcome" says the sign out front. More than 100 Alaska artists are featured here. Art himself is a custom jeweler, working in silver and gold and other materials. He's also a storehouse of knowledge.

Now the fun begins. As you drive through imposing walls of rock, you are entering the **MCCARTHY ROAD,** built along the old railroad bed of the Copper River and Northwestern Railway, 59 miles of dirt washboard and potholes. When you can spare time from the futile effort of trying to avoid these pitfalls, enjoy the lovely forest, but keep your eyes peeled for other drivers careening around the corners and for miscellaneous old railroad spikes. These are not good for your tires. Although it's only 59 miles, it will take you at least three hours. In the height of summer, it can be a long, dusty ride.

Above the trees, the Wrangell Mountains rise stark and bare, and you can spot the sharp division between the lighter limestone on top and the darker volcanic rock below. That division is where the metals—copper and gold—are to be found. On the ground, the erratic spruce hen or ptarmigan may scuttle across your path as you bounce along at a comfortable 20mph. About 15 miles out, the road narrows somewhat just before you get to the **KUSKALANA BRIDGE,** but the change is not dramatic. The bridge is! It is an old railway trestle that has been reinforced. The view into the river gorge is heart-stopping and should be the biggest thrill you get on the way. If you want more thrills, some people bungee-jump here(!).

If you avoid a flat (a minor miracle—so do carry mounted spares) or other mishap, you should reach the end of the road at **COPPERPOINT,** a minuscule encampment on the banks of the Kennicott River. Now you are faced with fording whitewater rapids. Do not attempt this in your car unless it is winter and 40 below zero.

The McCarthy Road ends at the white water of the Kennicott River, and the next stage of the journey involves a little more physical labor. Until just a few years ago, residents and visitors alike pulled themselves and their gear hand-over-hand across the river in an open aerial tramway. But, sadly, the tram has slipped into a footnote of history and today you can see where it once reigned supreme. Now, there are two footbridges over the river to the other side.

McCarthy and Kennicott

Copper was discovered in these hills in the 1860s. Some mining took place in the last part of the century, but with the completion of the Copper River and Northwestern Railway in 1911, which ran from Cordova on the coast 200 miles into the mountains, business really boomed. The story of that railroad, built across the face of two moving glaciers by the brilliant engineer and wild Irishman Michael J. Heney, is a saga of great proportions.

The ore that came out of the **KENNECOTT MINES** high up on the hills here was about 80 percent pure copper in the early days. It was the richest and purest deposit of copper in the world. But the large costs of transportation required that it be further refined on the spot and, as the percentage of copper in the native ore declined in later years, refinement became increasingly important.

Refining was performed in the multistoried, red building that you can still see framed dramatically against the hillside today. The ore was brought down from the mines and decanted into a vertical process where, level after level, it was crushed, pulverized, shaken, washed, and sifted until it was ready to be tipped into waiting railroad cars. To this mechanical operation, the mine added a chemical separation process in the 1920s. This took place in a separate building across the road. Both of these buildings, as well as the vast steam plant for generating electricity, can be seen on a guided tour (see Adventures, below), which takes a couple of hours. As you climb up the 192 steps in the processing plant, you will be astonished at the solidity of this rundown building. Much of the machinery has been ravaged by past salvage operations, but nonetheless this journey into the past is quite special.

Kennicott was once a boomtown with more than 800 workers, until the price of copper fell and the operation was abandoned. Today it is a ghost town, with the exception of one or two hardy souls who live here in cabins year-round.

The little town of McCarthy sprang up at the edge of the Kennicott River, just across from the recently deceased tramway. It was a place for miners' relaxation in the old days. Only a handful of folks live here now, but it is a popular destination for Alaskans all summer long, particularly for celebrations on the Fourth of July and Labor Day. Five miles up the hill is the ghost town of Kennicott and the Kennicott Lodge.

(So you will not be confused or think we are bad spellers, note that the spelling of Kennicott Glacier, named for Robert Kennicott, early explorer and geologist, is spelled with an *i*. The lodge spells its name the same way, as does the settlement of Kennicott. But you will see that Kennecott Mines is spelled with an *e*. This is what is known as a historical mistake, now historical fact. Someone from those yesteryears misspelled Kennicott, and it stuck.)

ACCESS AND INFORMATION

Drive the roads from Anchorage to McCarthy, or take the fast route with regularly scheduled air service from Anchorage through Gulkana to McCarthy on **ELLIS AIR TAXI** (907/822-3368; 800/478-3368). Service is year-round, Wednesday and Friday departures and return. **MCCARTHY AIR** (907/554-4440) has charters. **WRANGELL MOUNTAIN AIR** (McCarthy No. 25, PO Box MXY, Glennallen AK 99588;

907/554-4411 or 800/478-1160; www.wrangellmountainair.com) offers two daily flights between Chitina and McCarthy, for $140 round-trip. A van service, to save driving the McCarthy Road, is available in summer, departing from Chitina and Glennallen seven days a week in summer. Call **BACKCOUNTRY CONNECTION** (907/822-5292 or 866/582-5292, in-state only; www.alaska-backcountry-tours.com).

Wrangell-St. Elias National Park and Preserve puts out an informative annual newspaper called *K'elt'aeni,* about travel in the park. For a list of mountaineering, rafting, backpacking, horsepacking, hunting, and fishing guides permitted to offer commercial trips into the park/preserve, contact **PARK HEADQUARTERS** in Copper Center (907/822-5235).

ADVENTURES

FLIGHT-SEEING / In this mountain kingdom of castle peaks, glaciers, and stunning valleys, flight-seeing is a fantastic experience not to be missed. A tempestuous sea of wild and jagged peaks spreads before you (and the pilot carefully misses them all) as you fly up bare rocky passes. The multicolored cliffs are reminiscent of southwestern deserts. Glaciers tumble from the brilliant snowfields down icefalls to black crushed rock below. As your eyes get used to the dimensions of aerial vision, you may spot herds of mountain goats. A good charter air service flying trips out of McCarthy is **WRANGELL MOUNTAIN AIR** (see Access and Information, above). They have four different tours, ranging from $60–$140 per person.

GUIDES AND OUTFITTERS

COPPER OAR / These guides specialize in white-water rafting, river float trips, hiking and kayaking expeditions, and canoe trips. Among the great variety of trips offered, the shortest and most affordable is the half-day "paddle and peddle," a rafting and mountain-bike trip for $70–$85 per person, depending on group size. A full-day rafting trip down Class II and Class III rapids concludes with a spectacular 30-minute flight-seeing tour for $245–$265 per person, depending on group size. They do custom trips and much, much more during the river season, May through September. *Box MXY-McCarthy, Glennallen AK 99588; 907/554-4453(May to Sept), 800/523-4453 (year-round); www.copperoar.com.*

ST. ELIAS ALPINE GUIDES / This highly respected guide service, owned by Bob Jacobs, does everything from two-hour walking tours of the old Kennecott Mine ($25 per person) to major backcountry and mountaineering expeditions, including first-ascent attempts in the Wrangells. Popular choices for those with limited time are half-day glacier hikes ($50 per person) and daylong ice climbing trips ($100 per person). They have offices both in McCarthy and Kennecott. *PO Box 111241, Anchorage AK 99511; 907/277-6867, winter, 907/554-4445, summer; www.stelias guides.com.*

LODGINGS

Kennicott Glacier Lodge / ★★★

5 MILES UP THE ROAD FROM MCCARTHY, KENNICOTT; 907/554-4477, SUMMER; 800/582-5128, YEAR-ROUND; FAX 907/248-7975 This is a fine wilderness resort, dedicated to the pleasure of hikers, river rafters, and all outdoorsmen and -women. The veranda has a breathtaking view that extends from the Chugach Mountains to

Mount Blackburn, the highest mountain in the Wrangells, and takes in Kennicott Glacier. Descended from the draftsmen's quarters or bunkhouse of the old mining days, it is still painted in the symbolic red and white colors of the day. Bathrooms are shared. Dining is family style with simple but hearty meals (beer and wine available). And the staff couldn't be friendlier. The lodge accommodates only 50 guests (25 rooms), so book early. Rates are $179 for a double. *$$$; AE, MC, V; checks OK; closed mid-Sept to mid-May; www.kennicottlodge.com; 5 miles from McCarthy, at the site of the old Kennicott mine and next to Kennicott Glacier.*

McCarthy Lodge / ★★

DOWNTOWN, MCCARTHY; 907/554-4402; FAX 907/554-4404 You can't get much more classic Alaska than this moose-horn-bedecked lodge in the center of town. It's the centerpiece of innumerable photos of McCarthy and boasts a more laid-back, easygoing, T-shirts-and-beer crowd than the lodge higher up on the road. Although built in 1916, the hotel does have modern bathrooms. It offers group bookings for winter getaways in the Wrangells. The rate of $130 a night for a double includes a free breakfast, transportation to the mine, and a pickup at the bridge. They also have free Internet service. Dining facilities include breakfast, lunch, and dinner, and there's a full bar as well as a package store. The lodge is owned by McCarthy Ventures, which also operates a backpacker hotel, a saloon, and other properties in town. *$$$; MC, V; local checks only; closed Oct to May; PO Box MXY, McCarthy AK 99588; www.mccarthylodge.com; go over the river and through the woods, following the signs.*

ANCHORAGE AND BEYOND

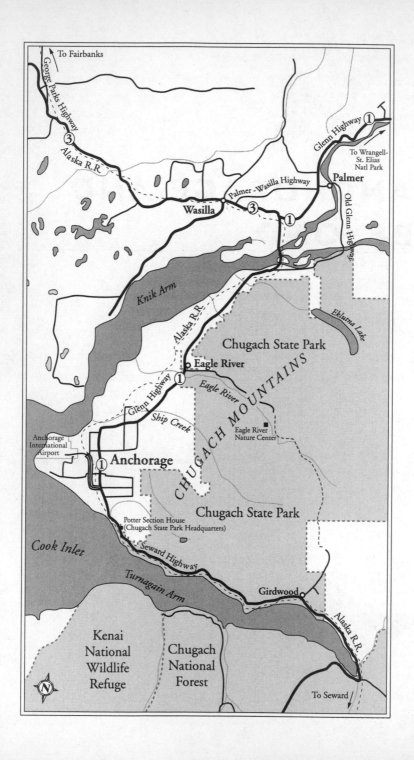

ANCHORAGE AND BEYOND

For many people, the greater Anchorage area is where you can get it all: a city with a small but enthusiastic nightlife, good restaurants, and Broadway musicals—plus access to the half-million-acre Chugach State Park, with its streams, glaciers, bears, moose, and more than 100 miles of trails. To the north, the wilderness playgrounds of the Susitna and Matanuska Valleys give way to views of the Chugach and Alaska Ranges. If the weather cooperates, Mount McKinley, which locals simply call Denali or "The Mountain," juts above the horizon. And in the right season, salmon run so thick you have to watch your step crossing a stream.

Seasons are alternately fleeting and harsh. Summer is short and intense. In September, the leaves turn a vibrant gold. Not long after, you'll see snow (euphemistically called "termination dust") capping local mountains. By mid-October, downtown Anchorage is usually under a layer of snow, which stays well into April. Temperatures can drop to below zero for a week or two at a time, but usually stay in the teens and 20s. By mid-May, the land comes alive again: migratory birds travel through to their nesting grounds in the Arctic and western Alaska, the six hours of winter sunlight nearly triple, and summer is just a few weeks away. Not that the region has what most people from the Lower 48 would call "summer." Temperatures rarely get above 70°F—the Anchorage July average is about 57°F—and rain is common. But on days when the sun shines until midnight and the Chugach Mountains scream with color, this place is spectacular.

Anchorage

People who live in Anchorage often say the best thing about it is that it's 20 minutes from the real Alaska. Built on the fortunes of the railroad, war, and oil, it began in 1915 as a tent city on the banks of Ship Creek. Today, almost half of the state's population—about 260,000 people—live in this metropolis. A center for business, the arts, and political power, it's also a gateway for adventures into Alaska's outback.

The Park Strip, on the south flank of downtown, was once the very edge of town. In the 1920s, it was a combined airfield and golf course. Today it defines the edge of downtown and hosts late-night softball games, during which an outfielder is as likely to watch the midnight sunset in awe as to watch the play. Though few in number, highly trained chefs prepare the world's best seafood with aplomb. Anglers pull 40-pound king salmon out of Ship Creek, a river of wildlife on downtown's north flank, in the shadow of glass-skinned office buildings. In early March, a visitor can see the start of the most famous sled-dog race in the world, cross-country ski to lunch, and then go to a Broadway musical in the evening.

ACCESS AND INFORMATION
Most people **FLY** to Anchorage. As is the case elsewhere in the state, Alaska Airlines (800/252-7522; www.alaskaair.com) is the predominant airline. Some drive the **ALASKA HIGHWAY** through Canada from the Lower 48. Be sure and pick up a copy of **THE MILEPOST** (www.themilepost.com) if you are making this adventure. Others arrive by **CRUISE SHIPS**. Once here, as in all big cities, you can choose between

rental cars and public transportation. The bus system, called **THE PEOPLE MOVER** (907/343-6543; www.peoplemover.org) can get you about town. The **ALASKA RAILROAD** (907/265-2494; www.alaskarailroad.com), a 5-minute walk from downtown, will take you north to **DENALI NATIONAL PARK** (www.nps.gov/dena) or south to Seward on Resurrection Bay. **ALASKA BACKPACKER SHUTTLE** (907/344-8775 or 800/266-8625) can take you north to Denali and Fairbanks or south to Seward. Call for friendly, reliable service.

With its cascades of flowers, the charming little **LOG CABIN INFORMATION CENTER** (907/274-3531) is located in the heart of downtown on Fourth Avenue and F Street, and is run by the **ANCHORAGE CONVENTION AND VISITORS BUREAU** (907/276-4118; www.anchorage.net). The first kiosk for a self-guided tour of old Anchorage's colorful past stands directly outside. Kitty-corner, in the old Federal Building, is the **ALASKA PUBLIC LANDS INFORMATION CENTER** (907/271-2737; www.nps.gov.aplic/center/), with its marvelous displays and information on parks, refuges, forests, hikes, cabins, wildlife, and more. The *Anchorage Daily News* (www.adn.com) publishes an arts/entertainment guide called "8" that appears every Friday and contains information on food, music, theater, and special events around town. For another sprightly look at the local arts scene, pick up a free copy of the *Anchorage Press* (www.anchoragepress.com) at coffeehouses and outdoor boxes around town. Anchorage restaurants and businesses have gone "smoke free." So if you want a cigar with that scotch, find a bar.

EXPLORING

ANCHORAGE MUSEUM OF HISTORY AND ART / This is the only major venue for sculpture and painting in the area. The upper floor is devoted to the history of Alaska. During tourist season, the museum hosts major touring exhibits, such as the Smithsonian's "Crossroads of Continents" or glass art by Seattle artist Dale Chihuly. The Children's Gallery provides an interactive, hands-on exploration of the arts and is free admission for both children and adults. *121 W 7th Ave; 907/343-4326; www.anchoragemuseum.org; downtown.*

ALASKA NATIVE HERITAGE CENTER / Opened in 1999, the Heritage Center provides an opportunity to appreciate the vastness of Alaska and the richness of her cultures. Situated on 26 acres on the outskirts of town, the Welcome House is filled with exhibits and demonstrations. Traditional village settings have been re-created around a small lake, one for each of the five indigenous peoples in Alaska, from the Inupiat in the north to the Tlingits of Southeast. This is a living museum with artists and craftspeople at work—building kayaks, carving totems, sewing mukluks, weaving baskets, drying fish, singing, and dancing. The original dream of the center was to celebrate, perpetuate, and share these traditions. The former president of the center, Perry Eaton, who was born on Kodiak into the Aleut/Alutiiq culture, says, "Alaska is unique in American Indian experience because people still live in original traditional villages, not removed to reservations." The entrance fee is $20 for adults, $18 for seniors, and $15 for children under 12. *Open every day in summer; winter hours differ with educational programs offered; 907/330-8095 or 800/315-6608; www.alaskanative.net; at the intersection of Muldoon Rd and the Glenn Hwy.* &

FRESH ART FIRST FRIDAY / The first Friday of the month features gallery receptions where you can meet some of Anchorage's finest artists, rub elbows with the up-and-coming, and purchase a piece of innovative Alaska art. Sometimes there are as many as 10 art openings about town on First Friday. The best local galleries include **DECKER/MORRIS GALLERY** (621 W 6th Ave; 907/272-1489), Anchorage's most professional gallery of original art, and **ARTIQUE LTD.** (314 G St; 907/277-1663), which offers original fine arts and crafts as well as prints. The best source of information on gallery openings is the *Anchorage Press* (www.anchoragepress.com), which also lists addresses, phone numbers, and hours.

MUSIC AND THEATER / Located in Town Square, **THE ALASKA CENTER FOR THE PERFORMING ARTS** (800/478-7328; www.alaskapac.org) is the hub of dance, music, and theater performances in town. You can't miss it. In summer, the little park in front is ablaze with colorful flowers. In winter, it's lit up with Christmas lights. It covers the ground between E and G Streets and Fifth and Sixth Avenues. The box office has a display showing each season's events and sells tickets, or you can reserve them through **CARRSTIX** ticket outlets (907/263-2787).

Anchorage has its own symphony orchestra, opera company, and concert association. With the dark winters, community theater has also been important in the far north. Some of the most successful and ambitious in recent years have been **VALLEY PERFORMING ARTS** (907/373-9500), headquartered in the Matanuska Valley; **CYRANO'S BOOKSTORE & OFF CENTER PLAYHOUSE** (413 D St; 907/274-2599); the **UNIVERSITY OF ALASKA ANCHORAGE THEATRE/DANCE DEPARTMENT** (907/786-1792 or 907/786-4721, box office); **OUT NORTH CONTEMPORARY ART HOUSE** (1325 Primrose St; 907/279-8200; www.outnorth.org).

SHOPPING

From Nordstrom to Wal-Mart, boutique to department store, Anchorage has it all. But it wasn't always this way. With the exception of Nordstrom, none of the retail standards made their way north until the mid-1990s. For the best one-stop shopping for the basics, try **THE FIFTH AVENUE MALL** downtown.

If you have come all the way to Alaska, consider skipping what you can find at home and shop for **NATIVE ART** instead. In Anchorage, that's tough. But if you ask around, you can find Athabascan beaded mukluks, Yupik grass baskets, soapstone and ivory carvings, or a baby-soft "smoke ring," a neck gaiter knit from the spun, lightweight undercoat of musk ox called qiviut (pronounced kiv-ee-ute). To learn more about qiviut, check out a co-op of 250 Native women called **OOMINGMAK** (604 H St; 907/272-9225 or 888/360-9665; www.qiviut.com). Locals have long known that **ALASKA NATIVE MEDICAL CENTER,** on E Tudor Road near Bragaw Street, has some of the best selections of and prices for Native arts and crafts, and the displays alone make it a worthy trip. The **ANCHORAGE MUSEUM OF HISTORY AND ART** (121 W 7th Ave; 907/343-4326; www.anchoragemuseum.org) also sells Native art. Do beware of fraud when buying Native crafts; look for the silver-hand logo for authentic, made in Alaska, Native art. To assure authenticity, buy something made with marine mammal parts, including whale baleen or bone, which only Natives can harvest. Grass baskets are also a pretty sure bet—no one has figured out how to mass produce those.

ANCHORAGE THREE-DAY TOUR

DAY ONE: Start the day with coffee and pastries at **SIDE STREET ESPRESSO** (412 G St; 907/258-9055), or a hearty omelet or cheese blintze breakfast at the **DOWNTOWN DELI AND CAFE.** Walk off breakfast on the **HISTORIC WALKING TOUR,** an award-winning stroll that follows a trail of kiosks from the Log Cabin Information Center to Silk Stocking Row and through Bootlegger's Cove, once honeycombed with whiskey tunnels. When finished, drive to the intersection of Muldoon Road and the Glenn Highway and spend the rest of the morning at the **ALASKA NATIVE HERITAGE CENTER** exploring the history and culture of five Native Alaska peoples. Drive back into Anchorage for lunch at the **GLACIER BREWHOUSE** or **MOOSE'S TOOTH PUB & PIZZERIA.** If it's a nice day, rent a bike at **DOWNTOWN BICYCLE RENTAL** and cruise the **TONY KNOWLES COASTAL TRAIL** that winds through downtown and into the nearby wilderness. Try a culinary adventure for dinner at **SACKS CAFE AND RESTAURANT,** where chefs dream up new dishes every night. For a more boisterous atmosphere and some top-notch pub food, swing by **HUMPY'S GREAT ALASKA ALEHOUSE.** After dinner, don't miss The Whale Fat Follies at the legendary **FLY BY NIGHT CLUB,** and stick around for the hoppin' house band that plays blues after the show. Finally, collapse into bed in your quaint room at the **ANCHORAGE HOTEL,** the oldest hotel in the city.

DAY TWO: Fuel up with pancakes or a plate of eggs at **GWENNIE'S OLD ALASKA RESTAURANT** (4333 Spenard Rd; 907/243-2090), and then spend the morning exploring the **ANCHORAGE MUSEUM OF HISTORY AND ART,** which often hosts expansive special exhibits in summer. From here, it's time to take one of the most scenic drives in the country on the **SEWARD HIGHWAY.** As you head south toward Girdwood, **TURNAGAIN ARM** will be on your right. It has the second-highest tides in North America; watch for beluga and killer whales. Dall sheep also hang out on the roadside rocky cliffs and the peaks of the **KENAI NATIONAL WILDLIFE REFUGE** and **CHUGACH STATE PARK** create a spectacular backdrop. Break for tasty soups and sandwiches at **THE BAKE SHOP** in Girdwood, located on the Alyeska Boardwalk. After lunch continue driving on the highway and watch for the turnoff to **PORTAGE GLACIER.** Park at the **BEGICH, BOGGS VISITOR CENTER** (907/783-2326; www.fs.fed.us/r10/chugach) and explore glacial-history exhibits and watch icebergs float around the lake. (For more about the Begich, Boggs Visitor Center, see the Prince William Sound chapter.). Unfortunately that's all that's visible from shore, but you can see the glacier by joining a tour boat for a ride nearer the terminus. On the way back to Anchorage, Girdwood is worth another stop, this time for dinner at the spirited **DOUBLE MUSKY** for impeccable pepper steak and gargantuan Cajun portions. Or, if the evening is clear, get your dinner with a side of scenery at **SEVEN GLACIERS RESTAURANT AND LOUNGE,** an elegant restaurant sitting high on Mount Alyeska. Then stay the evening at the **ALYESKA PRINCE HOTEL.**

DAY THREE: Eat breakfast at the hotel and then get ready for some outdoor adventure. Drive north on the Glenn Highway to **EKLUTNA LAKE,** about 40 miles northeast of Anchorage. Spend the afternoon hiking and taking in the beautiful mountains via the **TWIN PEAKS TRAIL,** a strenuous hike from lakeside with wonderful views. If you feel like camping, pitch a tent at the state parks' Eklutna Lake Campground, or rent the Yuditna Creek Cabin, about 3 miles from the trailhead, also operated by state parks. If you don't feel like hiking or physically aren't able to, spend the day in the gorgeous Matanuska-Susitna Valley instead. Drive out toward Knik–Goose Bay to the headquarters of the **IDITAROD TRAIL SLED DOG RACE** and learn what the fuss over Alaska's official sport is all about. Then take a guided tour of the **MUSK OX FARM** in Palmer and splurge on the downy softness of hand-knit qiviut. If camping doesn't strike your fancy, drive back to Anchorage and spend the night at **BED & BREAKFAST ON THE PARK,** a quaint historic inn that used to be a log-cabin church. And since you're in the city anyway, treat yourself to a delicious meal at **MARX BROS. CAFÉ.**

If it's books you're looking for, check out **COOK INLET BOOK COMPANY** (415 W 5th Ave; 907/258-4544; www.cookinlet.com) for one of the largest selection of books on Alaska and the North. Around the corner is the small, slightly disorganized but intriguing **CYRANO'S BOOKSTORE** (413 D St; 907/274-2599). **BARNES & NOBLE BOOKSELLERS** (200 E Northern Lights Blvd; 907/279-7323) is huge and located in Midtown. **BORDERS BOOKS & MUSIC** (1100 E Dimond Blvd; 907/344-4099) is also an event in itself, located at the south end of town. For an amazing selection of used books and a cozy experience try **TITLE WAVE USED BOOKS** (1360 W Northern Lights Blvd; 907/278-9283; www.wavebooks.com).

Check out **SATURDAY MARKET,** every Saturday in summer on the old "buttress" area of downtown (3rd Ave and E St), a huge outdoor market of vendors selling produce, food, homemade crafts, and art. If it's strictly **FRESH PRODUCE** you're after, try the summer market in the parking lot of the *Anchorage Daily News* (1001 Northway Dr, near the intersection of Bragaw and DeBarr Sts). As the summer progresses, farmers from the Matanuska Valley haul in their giant cabbages and zucchinis, huge sweet carrots, herbs, peanut potatoes, and delicious snap peas.

ADVENTURES

ALASKA BOTANICAL GARDEN / Established in 1993, the Alaska Botanical Garden is set in a boreal forest on 110 acres, east of town, at the foot of the Chugach Mountain range. About 11 acres have been developed with pathways through perennial, herb, native flower, and rock gardens, with more than 480 varieties of cultured plants in all. There are almost always classes, tours, or events going on during the weekends, but no phone; check the Web site for the schedule. *Open 9am–9pm daily* *during summer; www.alaskabg.org; drive east on Tudor Rd to Campbell Airstrip Rd, turn right and you'll see the sign.*

ALASKA ZOO / This nonprofit zoo got its start in 1968 after a local grocer won a contest and the prize was a 2-year-old Asian elephant. Nestled in the woods on 25 acres are many animals you would expect to find in the Alaska wild, including lynx, brown and black bear, caribou, and harbor seals. But you will also find llamas, camels, Siberian tigers, and Maggie the elephant. Oreo, a brown bear, and Apun, a polar bear, have been housed together since they were cubs and their antics can be mighty entertaining. The zoo boasts that it is one of the most visited places in the state. It's popular with locals too. And don't feel sad about those caged bald eagles—most of the animals housed at the zoo have been injured and rescued, and wouldn't be able to survive in the wild. $8 for adults; kids under 3 free. *Open daily in summer until 6pm; 4731 O'Malley Rd; 907/346-1088; www.alaskazoo.org; take Seward Hwy south, exit on O'Malley, head east.*

THE COASTAL TRAIL / Bike, walk, blade, jog, or ski the Tony Knowles Coastal Trail, which runs for miles along the shores of Cook Inlet. Named after Anchorage's former mayor and the state's former governor, this trail is one of the great treasures of the city, coursing like a lifeline from downtown neighborhoods to the airport to wilderness trails. Everybody uses the trail, including porcupines, moose, and bears. Once you get to Kincaid Park, the wilderness trails there are a mecca for running in the summer and skiing in the winter and are the site of world-class cross-country ski races. Rent bikes at **DOWNTOWN BICYCLE RENTAL** (333 W 4th Ave, No. 206, Anchorage AK 99501; 907/279-5293; www.alaska-bike-rentals.com). Rent skis at **REI** (1200 W Northern Lights Blvd; 907/272-4565), which has interesting weekly programs covering everything from mountain climbing to ski waxing.

HISTORIC WALKING TOUR / Look for the blue, three-sided kiosks downtown, and follow them on this award-winning stroll filled with gossip, stories, and photographs from yesteryear. The first kiosk stands in front of the Log Cabin Information Center on Fourth Avenue. Visit **SILK STOCKING ROW** and see where the fancy folks lived, or wander down by the water through **BOOTLEGGER'S COVE,** once honeycombed with whiskey tunnels. "The only thing more prevalent than the fine dust which clogs the air is the raw whiskey with which they wash it down," observed one disgusted federal bureaucrat in Anchorage's early days, thoroughly unimpressed by the new railroad town and the moral fiber of its inhabitants.

PARKS

More than 200 parks can be found in Anchorage. Many of the parks are linked by a maze of more than 200 miles of trails that lace the city. About 120 miles are paved; the rest are gravel or dirt-packed trails. Some stretches are lit for winter nighttime skiing. The **NORDIC SKI ASSOCIATION OF ANCHORAGE** (www.alaska.net/~nsaa/) relies on club-member donations to groom more than 90 miles of skiing trails. The parks at Goose Lake and Jewel Lake have sand beaches with lifeguards on duty. While the Tony Knowles Coastal Trail might get the heaviest use, the 1,500-acre **KINCAID PARK** on the city's west side, and the 4,000-acre **FAR NORTH BICENTENNIAL PARK,** which sits on city and federal land, are the places to go to get lost in the woods. At Bicentennial, also known as Campbell Tract, the trails are shared by horseback riders, mountain bikers, hikers, dog walkers, and skiers. And unlike steep, mountain trails in neighboring **CHUGACH STATE PARK** (see Chugach State Park section in this chapter), the trails in Bicentennial are fairly level.

GUIDES AND OUTFITTERS

ALASKA SNOW SAFARIS / If you have only a day or two in Anchorage, Rudi and Natasha von Imhoff, both lifelong Alaskans and outdoor enthusiasts, and their staff of experienced guides can take you out of the city into wilderness on your own snow-machine expedition for a few hours, a half day, or overnight ($95 to $1,400 per person). They also can arrange dog-sledding excursions and heli-skiing packages. In the summer, they run guided sea-kayaking tours in Prince William Sound through their summer business, Alaska Outdoor Adventures. Their boats are top of the line, both single and double kayaks. Morning and day trips ($60 to $99 per person) begin out of Whittier. *DIS, MC, V; checks OK; 9400 Vanguard, Ste B, Anchorage AK 99507; 907/276-2628 or 888/414-7669; fax 907/222-1898; info@akadventures. com; www.akadventures.com.*

BIRD WATCHING TOURS OF ANCHORAGE / Spend four hours tracking down some of the 100-plus bird species that make the Anchorage bowl home. The area is unique because the coast to the west draws shoreline birds and the mountains to the east are home to high-alpine species. This operation is pretty new, but it taps local birding talent to lead tours. Binoculars and field guides are provided and the cost is about $75. *Tours depart at 8am, 1pm, and 6pm, or by arrangement for groups; 4030 Gallactica Dr, Anchorage AK 99517; 907/248-7282; www.anchoragebirding.com.*

NOVA / For 25 years, Nova has been taking folks rafting down Alaska's rivers on day trips. If your time is limited (and even if it's not), this is one way to experience the thrill and beauty of the outdoors a few hours away from Alaska's biggest city. North, in the Matanuska Valley, they float the Matanuska River, Class II to Class IV rapids. South, on the Kenai Peninsula, at Granite Creek and Six-Mile Creek, you can experience Class IV and Class V rapids. Choose your level of excitement. *800/746-5753; www.novalaska.com.*

FESTIVALS AND EVENTS

SKI FOR WOMEN / Founded in 1997 and held on Super Bowl Sunday in January, this is the largest cross-country ski race for women in North America. The race is 5 km with both classic and skating divisions. All you need are some skis and a partner—any and all women are encouraged, whether beginner, recreational, racer, Olympian, mother, daughter, or grandmother. If you're shy or just visiting, race organizers will find you a partner. In recent years, the youngest competitor was 4 years old; the oldest was 77. Participants come dressed in old prom dresses, hula skirts, racing silks, or black lycra if they succumb to that competitive edge. The spirit is fun-filled, enthusiastic, and contagious, and the effort draws attention to and supports a good cause—AWAIC (Abused Women's Aid in Crisis). *907/279-9581 or 907/345-1913; www.alaskaskiforwomen.org.*

FUR RONDY / To see the real Anchorage, visit in mid-February for the Fur Rendezvous, fondly known to locals as the Fur Rondy. That's French, Alaska-style, for a fur get together. Originally, trappers came in from the bush to sell their pelts and spend some money. Today, the cabin-fever festival features all that's great and strange about Anchorage. On opening night, a spectacular display of fireworks lights up the winter sky (Anchorage goes all out here because on the Fourth of July the long daylight hours make fireworks nearly invisible). Over the next several days, people participate in more than 100 contests ranging from ice bowling to oyster slurping. *907/274-1177; www.furrondy.net.*

IDITAROD TRAIL SLED DOG RACE / This famous race kicks off from Fourth Avenue in downtown Anchorage, the first Saturday of every March. The city is packed with television cameras, howling dogs, racing colors, and fur-clad mushers. For a brief moment, it all feels very glamorous. But in a couple of hours the teams are out of here and on their way across the wilderness, 1,049 miles to Nome, and the city quiets down again (many people fly out along the trail to watch the teams or go to Nome for the grand finale). For information, contact the Iditarod Trail Committee (Mile 2.2 Knik–Goose Bay Rd, PO Box 870800, Wasilla AK 99687; 907/376-5155; www.iditarod.com). For great tales and insight into the race go to race sponsor Cabela's Web site at www.cabelasiditarod.com. It's not the official site, but it's the best.

TOUR OF ANCHORAGE / This race sponsored by the Nordic Ski Association of Anchorage gets everybody out on skis. Usually held around the first weekend of March, more than 1,700 skiers line up to race 50K, 40K, or 25K. Sometimes race weekend coincides with the start of the Iditarod Trail Sled Dog Race, so skiers who come from out of town get an extra treat. The starts are scattered about town, but the finish for everyone is almost simultaneous at Kincaid Park. *907/276-7609; www.tourofanchorage.com.*

THREE BARON'S FAIR / For more than 10 years, lords and ladies have been gathering for the first couple of weekends every June to celebrate the Renaissance of days gone by, and to dance, sing, act silly, and say a lot of things that Shakespeare might have said. More than 100 performers wander in the make-believe Hillshire village on the Alaska Pacific University campus, and artisans and craftsmen vend their wares. *907/868-8012; info@3barons.org; www.3barons.org; at the corner of Bragaw St and University Lake Dr.*

MAYOR'S MIDNIGHT SUN MARATHON / This premiere 30-year-old running event held around the summer solstice (late June) draws nearly two-thirds of its field of 4,000 from out of state. The race starts in the mountains on the city's east side and winds along city trails to the Coastal Trail. There are half-marathon and 5-mile options. *907/343-4474; www.mayorsmarathon.com.*

NIGHTLIFE

Spenard, once the racier part of Anchorage, is home to **CHILKOOT CHARLIE'S** (2435 Spenard Rd; 907/272-1010), a bar with the infamous motto "We cheat the other guy and pass the savings on to you." Chilkoot's has a loyal crowd and a lot of one-timers who come to catch live bands, drink beer, and walk around on wood chips in what's billed as a rustic Alaska saloon.

Don't miss the **FLY BY NIGHT CLUB** (3300 Spenard Rd; 907/279-7726), with *The Whale Fat Follies,* billed in their ads as "the show the Alaska Chamber of Commerce doesn't want you to see." It'll tell you more about the inside humor of Alaska than you'll learn anywhere else. After the show, a house band plays some rockin' blues.

RESTAURANTS

Bear Tooth Grill & Theatre Pub / ★★

1230 W 27TH AVE, ANCHORAGE; 907/276-4200 This is a hopping place brought to you by the same boys who opened the popular Moose's Tooth Pizzeria (below). Catch a classic movie while enjoying burritos and beer delivered into the dark to your table. In addition to the movie theater, you can eat in the cafe or in the recently added grill. All are kid friendly, but check the movie rating before dragging the young ones in there. Both the cafe and grill feature Mexican fare with a flare; the grill tends toward Nuevo Mexicana—halibut tacos, fresh-filled burritos, and spicy enchiladas—but also serves up pasta dishes and build-your-own salads. Try the spicy habanero chicken skewers for starters, and wash them down with made-from-scratch margaritas. The cafe is open for lunch and dinner, the grill only at night; entrees are reasonable, from $8 to $12. *$$; DIS, MC, V; local checks only; lunch, dinner every day except major holidays; full bar; no reservations; a block off Spenard Rd.*

Campo Bello Bistro / ★★

601 W 36TH AVE, ANCHORAGE; 907/563-2040 Campo Bello (meaning "beautiful field") offers a fine menu featuring delicate pastas, chicken, and seafood dishes. Its gentle, white-tablecloth, candlelit interior provides a wonderful backdrop for fine art, promising food, and quiet conversation. The service is good with a friendly staff. The bread is delicious, baked next door at Europa Bakery. Appetizers are particularly inventive, and the lively calamari scaloppini with capers and lemon comes to the table fork-tender. Follow a light meal of tasty homemade soup with a winning Caesar salad, loaded with grilled chicken and roasted sweet peppers. Then kiss the evening good night with a celestial combination: heavenly chocolate-raspberry cake. *$$; DC, MC, V; local checks only; lunch Mon–Fri, dinner Tue–Sat; beer and wine; reservations recommended; in a strip mall near Arctic Blvd and 36th Ave.* &

Club Paris / ★★

417 W 5TH AVE, ANCHORAGE; 907/277-6332 If you look up at the dizzying Eiffel Tower, which has graced the exterior of the little Club Paris for decades, you will see the false-front architecture typical of an old Wild West frontier town. The idea was to make the building look grander and more permanent than it really was, as if folks were seriously planning on staying, when instead they would be moving on when the gold or work was gone. The funny thing is, Club Paris has indeed stayed on and been a dining institution for more than 40 years. This is old Anchorage, with a devoted clientele, and not even the new kid on the block can ruffle their feathers. Some of the staff from that "other steak house" even eat at the Club and sing its praises. The filet mignon with blue-cheese stuffing will melt in your mouth. But, if you top it off with their famous homemade Key lime pie or New York–style cheesecake, you'd better hike a couple of mountains before dinner. *$$; AE, DC, MC, V; local checks on approval; lunch Mon–Sat, dinner every day; full bar; reservations recommended; www.clubparisrestaurant.com; between E and D Sts on 5th Ave.*

Corsair / ★★

944 W 5TH AVE, ANCHORAGE; 907/278-4502 This is dining in the old-world style—a continental cuisine rich with sauces and butter, everything tossed, flamed, or carved tableside by tuxedoed waiters. Go ahead, splurge on that good bottle of Burgundy; they've got probably the best cellar in town. Hans Kruger and crew also do rich things with oysters, such as topping them with pâté and béarnaise sauce. The charbroiled rack of lamb Armenonville is exquisite. *$$$; AE, DC, DIS, MC, V; checks OK; dinner Mon–Sat; full bar; reservations recommended; www.corsair restaurant.com; west end of 5th Ave, downtown.* &

Crow's Nest / ★★★★

939 W 5TH AVE, ANCHORAGE; 907/276-6000 The bird's-eye view, fancy service, feeling of elegance, and light French cuisine make dinner here a pleasure. The wine list is one of the finest in Anchorage. Feel pampered when they serve your entree from under a dramatic silver dome, and enjoy one of the best views downtown. Be sure to specify which view you'd like: take the inlet in the summer and the city in winter's darkness. If you're not ravenous, one of the loveliest places for a quiet tête-à-tête is the bar, which offers the same exquisite views and a fun sampling of exotic hors d'oeuvres. *$$$; AE, DC, DIS, MC, V; checks OK; dinner Mon–Sat (summer), Tue–Sat (winter); full bar; reservations recommended; www.captaincook.com; at the top of the Hotel Captain Cook.* &

Downtown Deli and Cafe

525 W 4TH AVE, ANCHORAGE; 907/276-7116 One of the few spots to open early and close late, the comfortable Downtown Deli is often packed with summertime tourists. In winter, locals stop by for breakfasts of lox and bagels, omelets, and filling cheese blintzes, or schedule working lunches built around bagel sandwiches and matzo-ball soup. Butcher-block tabletops, lots of room, and quick service are draws, but so is the fact that former Alaska Governor, and former Anchorage mayor, Tony Knowles owns the place. The deli is a testament to how little space separates the average Alaskan from the pinnacles of power. *$; AE, DC, DIS, MC, V; local checks only; breakfast, lunch, dinner every day; beer and wine; no reservations; on 4th Ave, near the Log Cabin Information Center.* &

F Street Station / ★★

325 F ST, ANCHORAGE; 907/272-5196 For a quick, delicious meal at a good price, cruise into this freewheeling, casual bar. With a surprisingly good kitchen, F Street has redefined bar food in Alaska. The cheeseburgers, served with crisp, hand-cut fries, are the best in the city. Calamari is tender and the sautéed scallops are worthy. Go for the daily special, whether it's a saffron-infused seafood chowder, a piece of halibut topped with black bean–fruit salsa, or a steak sandwich cooked rare and served with wild mushrooms on a baguette. A lot of pilots and lawyers hang out here and it can get a bit cliquish. Note the huge block of Tillamook Sharp cheese at the bar with the careful sign "For Display Only. Do Not Eat." Note also that everybody is eating it. It's a good conversation piece—ask for the story.

Avoid crowds by heading in for a late lunch or supper. *$; AE, MC, V; local checks only; breakfast on weekends, lunch, dinner every day; full bar; no reservations.* &

Gesine's / ★★★

6700 JEWELL LAKE RD, ANCHORAGE; 907/243-0507 Gesine Marquez creates fantastic lunches and elegant dinners in what started years ago as a corner soup-and-sandwich cafe. The presentation is beautiful, the appetizers delicious, and the entrees inventive. Ones that regulars won't let Marquez retire include house-smoked artichokes served with garlic aioli, Jamaican jerk-beef skewers, crawfish étouffée and double-cut, house-smoked, and roasted pork chops dressed a little differently every year. Complementing the unusual cuisine is an atmosphere splashed with color—yellow and purple tablecloths. Ask for a table with a view of the Chugach Mountains. *$$; AE, MC, V; local checks only; lunch, dinner Tue–Fri; beer and wine; reservations recommended; www.gesinesrestaurant.com; corner of Jewell Lake and Raspberry Rds.* &

Glacier BrewHouse / ★★

737 W 5TH AVE, ANCHORAGE; 907/274-BREW (2739) The BrewHouse is one of the most popular places to eat in town, with tasty food, award-winning beers, a nice wine list, and friendly bartenders. In fact, the whole atmosphere of this open warehouse–exposed beams interior is warm and inviting and packed year-round. (Don't go for quiet conversation.) Particular favorites on the menu are barbecued silver salmon, herb-crusted halibut, roasted chicken, spit-roasted pork loin chops, and all manner of pizzas. The bread alone will make you a convert. If you're traveling by yourself, it's a happy, comfortable place to go sip a glass of wine at the bar and eat a Caesar or blue-cheese salad. And parents—kids will always find something they like on the menu here. *$$; AE, DC, MC, V; checks OK; lunch Mon–Sat, dinner every day; full bar; reservations recommended; www.glacierbrewhouse.com; between G and H Sts.* &

Humpy's Great Alaska Alehouse / ★

610 W 6TH AVE, ANCHORAGE; 907/276-BEER (2337) Is it the location? The boisterous nature? The 40-plus beers on tap? Or the bar food? Who knows? Ever since it appeared on the scene, Humpy's has been a smash hit. This dark, crowded brewpub has two time zones. At lunch and early dinner it is congenially filled with office workers and bicycle fanatics; later on in the evening and weekends, it's packed with 20-somethings and frat boys gone to seed. Stick with what they do best, like the halibut tacos, Humpy Fettuccini, or Teriyaki Tid Bits. Live music every night. *$; AE, DC, DIS, MC, V; local checks only; lunch, dinner every day; full bar; no reservations; www.humpys.com; across from the Alaska Center for the Performing Arts.* &

Ichiban Japanese Restaurant / ★

2488 E TUDOR RD, ANCHORAGE; 907/563-6333 Those in the know, including several distinguished chefs about town, sneak off to Ichiban to drink cold sake and eat what they deem "the best sushi in town." It has the freshest fish and the best prices. The Ichiban Roll is our favorite, made with eel, shrimp, *tabiko* (flying fish eggs), sprouts, and cucumber slices. The Super California Roll is delicious, stuffed with crab meat and cooked eel on top. If you want a momentary diversion from raw fish, try the fantastic Kalbi Ribs. *$; AE, MC, V; local checks only; lunch Mon–Sat, dinner every day; beer and wine; reservations recommended; on Tudor Rd near Lake Otis.*

Jens' Restaurant / ★★★★

701 W 36TH AVE, ANCHORAGE; 907/561-5367 Jens Hansen, of the restaurant that bears his name, is a wild Dane who is at once enchanting, zany, and incredibly knowledgeable about food. He'll eat caviar by the tablespoonful and dance on his wine bar, but when it comes to serious cooking, he's the man. No one else in the city has such a way with black cod, salmon, or halibut. His menu will always reflect his heritage: cabbage, root vegetables, smoked or cured fish, and light veal and pork meatballs called *frikadeller*. Mussels in season with a mustard sauce make a nice nosh with a glass of wine, or go all out with a traditional rack of lamb or the pepper steak favored by locals. Inexpensive but tasty wines and crack waiters make for a nice evening. If you're feeling rich and rowdy, stick around after dinner and party with the well-to-do but silly crowd that pools in the wine bar next to the restaurant. *$$$; AE, DC, DIS, MC, V; local checks only; lunch Mon–Fri, dinner Tues–Sat (closed Jan); beer and wine; reservations recommended; www.jensrestaurant.com; in the strip mall on the corner of 36th Ave and Arctic Blvd.* &

Kumagoro / ★

533 W 4TH AVE, ANCHORAGE; 907/272-9905 Kumagoro is one of the oldest Asian restaurants in downtown Anchorage and today serves primarily Japanese cuisine, although there are touches of other North Pacific cultures on the menu. They have a lovely little sushi bar where you can warm up from the winter cold with miso and a bottle of hot sake. Or sit at one of the little tables (which are all quite close together) and order a spicy appetizer of tasty meat dumplings called *gyoza,* dipped in a fiery hot oil. Kumagoro makes fresh udon and ramen noodles. The soups are big, hearty, and healthful. When the weather is chilly and you're up for a warm and lingering meal, try their *shabu shabu*—vegetables, tofu, and meat in a broth that you cook at your own table—a marvelous dish for sharing with friends. *$$; AE, DC, DIS, MC, V; local checks only; lunch, dinner every day; beer and wine; downtown.*

Marx Bros. Café / ★★★★

627 W 3RD AVE, ANCHORAGE; 907/278-2133 For more than two decades, this little historic house downtown, built during the early railroad era on Silk Stocking Row, has been home to some of the city's most innovative cuisine, a signature style of that flamboyant "galloping Greek," chef Jack Amon. In the summer, greens and edible flowers from the garden garnish delicious Alaska seafood such as halibut baked with a macadamia nut crust or roasted poblano chiles rellenos stuffed with Alaska king crab. In winter, fixed-price ethnic nights feature cuisine from the likes of Tuscany and Provence. Begin a delightful evening with a *melitzano salata,* roasted eggplant pâté with Greek olives and pita bread. Then try a Caesar salad whipped up tableside by master artist Van Hale, co-owner and keeper of the impressive wine cellar with 500 labels, one of the top cellars in town. Don't miss the crème caramel made with rum and coconut milk. Candlelight and sweet views of

Cook Inlet (ask for a view table when you make a reservation) only add to the panache. *$$$; AE, DC, MC, V; checks OK; dinner every day (closed Sun in winter); beer and wine; reservations recommended; www.marxcafe.com; downtown.*

The Middle Way Cafe and Coffeehouse / ★★

1200 W NORTHERN LIGHTS BLVD, ANCHORAGE; 907/272-6433 This small cafe is very much into healthy, delicious fare. Start off with a jolt from the espresso bar or a soothing mixture called Inner Balance (fresh orange juice, strawberries, banana, and ginger) from the juice bar. Wraps here are a good choice. They have winning fillings such as humus and pistachios, rounded out with red bell pepper–lemon yogurt dressing. Sandwiches and soups, both meat and vegetarian, are equally yummy. The atmosphere is mellow, with a crowd sporting everything from pierced body parts to pinstripes. *$; No credit cards; local checks only; lunch Mon–Sat; no alcohol; no reservations; Spenard Rd and Northern Lights Blvd.* &

Moose's Tooth Pub & Pizzeria / ★★

3300 OLD SEWARD HWY, ANCHORAGE; 907/258-2537 Two climbers, Rod Hancock and Matt Jones, started this popular pub in the summer of 1996 and named it after an extraordinary pinnacle of granite in the Alaska Range. At first it was chiefly a climbers' haunt, but its popularity has skyrocketed to include the young and active to families with children to older professionals and outdoor types. It has a simple picnic-table approach, fresh salads, the best pizza in town, and handcrafted ales from their own microbrewery. Often there's a long line at the door in the evening, but they'll take your name and usually can seat you in about 30 minutes. So order your gourmet pizza and sip a beer while you wait. There's pizza to suit everyone's fancy, from Aloha Escape to Pepperoni Supreme. A good choice for a post-hiking or -biking adventure with buddies or a quick bite before the movies. *$$; DC, DIS, MC, V; checks OK; lunch, dinner every day; beer and wine; no reservations; www.moosestooth.net; turn right off New Seward at 36th and backtrack on Old Seward Hwy.* &

Organic Oasis / ★★

2610 SPENARD RD, STE B, ANCHORAGE; 907/277-7882 For the growing population of vegans, this is a new haven, opened in the spring of 1999. An open, peaceful space with a long juice and espresso bar, the Oasis also has dining tables gathered around a fountain. You can get a shot of wheat grass juice and a Ginger Blast or a Palm Desert Smoothie to go with the brimming-with-health salads, sandwiches, soups, and hot specials. Everything, with the exception of a few teas, is organic. And while you pay a little extra, it's definitely worth it. *$; DC, MC, V; local checks only; lunch, early dinner Tue–Sat; beer and wine; no reservations; in a strip mall off Spenard Rd.* &

Ristorante Orso / ★★

737 W 5TH AVE, ANCHORAGE; 907/222-3232 This is one of the newest additions to the Anchorage restaurant scene. It's a cozy place, with warm lights, dark woods, and features Italian-prepared seafood specialty pastas. From the appetizer list, *caprese,* made with vine-ripened tomatoes, fresh mozzarella, and fresh basil is a popular choice. The applewood-grilled salmon or proscuitto-wrapped halibut are available at lunch or dinner. Ask about the featured wine. It's always Italian, and always a good value. Finish the evening with a risotto crème brûlée or mascarpone chocolate cheesecake made with Grand Marnier ganache, hazelnut florentine cookie, and raspberry sauce. And for a final touch, check out the bathroom's heated toilet seats. *$$$; AE, DC, MC, V; checks OK; lunch Mon–Sat, dinner every day; reservations recommended; between G and H Sts.*

Sacks Cafe and Restaurant / ★★★★

328 G ST, ANCHORAGE; 907/276-3546 OR 907/274-4022 Consistently adventurous food built with top-notch ingredients makes Sacks a welcome oasis. A knockout starter is baked garlic served with brie or gorgonzola and toast points. Chefs dream up a dish or two every night, centered on fresh Alaska fin fish graced with some exotic combination of favorites like pecans, pine nuts, Asian sauces, black beans, or ginger. Soups are standouts and include a slightly spicy African peanut, a cold cantaloupe soup kissed with cinnamon, and a hot salsa soup from south of the border. Locals love lunch here, returning for spinach salad with marinated Swiss cheese, the Thai chicken sandwich with spicy peanut dressing on a baguette, or the scrumptious vegetarian marinated olive sandwich. Always save room for dessert. The chocolate gâteau, ginger crème brûlée, and chocolate chip carrot cake with rum sauce are close to ethereal. *$$; AE, DC, MC, V; local checks only; lunch Mon–Fri, dinner every day, brunch Sat–Sun; beer and wine; reservations recommended; www.sackscafe.com; next to Artique on G St between 3rd and 4th Aves.* &

Simon and Seafort's Saloon and Grill / ★★★

420 L ST, ANCHORAGE; 907/274-3502 Part of a West Coast restaurant chain that has honed its art to a fine edge, Simon's is probably the most popular place in Anchorage for steaks, salads, and seafood. The consistency, the opportunity for a beautiful view of Cook Inlet, and the occasional flashes of greatness with fish and shellfish make going here a fun, warm, and pleasurable occasion. Even in the height of tourist season, you can usually get a table if you're willing to wait and munch in the bar. It's light and airy with a bustling and upbeat atmosphere. Wild Alaska salmon is good, with cracked black pepper and honey, served over greens with artichoke tartar sauce. Try the from-scratch margaritas, with fresh lime juice and without the blender treatment, or sample one of the largest selections of single-malt scotches in Alaska. Their Brandy Ice is a marvelous "sipping dessert"—rich vanilla ice cream blended with Kahlúa, brandy, and crème de cacao. *$$; AE, DC, MC, V; checks OK; lunch Mon–Fri; dinner every day; full bar; reservations recommended; main floor of an office building on L St and 5th Ave.* &

Southside Bistro / ★★

1320 HUFFMAN PARK DR, ANCHORAGE; 907/348-0088 This little restaurant is a neighborhood favorite, though takes a bit of effort to find. Walk in and head to the right if you want an elegant dining experience, turn left if the kids are with you or if you want to eat in the bar—still with white tablecloths. This is a good place to piece together a meal from the appetizer and soup and salad menu.

Fried crab and halibut cakes made with a corn flour crust and served with a cucumber salad and citrus rémoulade paired with a spinach salad dressed with almonds, proscuitto, shaved parmesan, and balsamic vinaigrette and followed by the cream of sundried tomato and roasted garlic soup can stand in for a meal, especially if followed by one the bistro's signature, hand-painted desserts. The entree menu features fresh-made pastas, a hazelnut-crusted halibut and pan-seared venison with melted gorgonzola, raspberry–green peppercorn sauce, and sweet onion jam. In the bar, order from the dinner menu or the bistro menu, which includes burgers and fries and wood-fired nachos. *$$$; AE, DC, MC, V; checks OK; lunch, dinner Tue–Sat; beer and wine; reservations recommended; www.southsidebistro.com; drive south on the Seward Hwy, exit at Huffman, turn right and go to the first light, turn right and go 1 block.*

Sullivan's Steakhouse / ★★★

320 W 5TH AVE, STE 100, ANCHORAGE; 907/258-2882 Tell 'em Joe sent you. Step through the doors into the speakeasy days of 1930 Chicago. Sleek, sexy, and trendy, Sullivan's slipped into Anchorage a few years ago and got the town hooked on martinis, steaks, and great live jazz. Ladies dress up; gents dust off their Panama hats. A spectacular bouquet of flowers adorns the center of a large, open room rich with mahogany and heavy white tablecloths. You are meant to see and be seen. The extensive cellar (more than 300 wines) is heavy into cabernets, reds, and merlots—all to complement those fabulous steaks. Talented bartenders move like lightning. While there are no vegetarian entrees, they do tip their hats to Alaska's rich seafood tradition with a sampling from the Pacific and Atlantic—halibut, salmon, grilled tuna, and lobster tail. *$$$; AE, DC, DIS, MC, V; local checks only; dinner every night; full bar; reservations recommended; corner of 5th Ave and C St in the Anchorage Fifth Avenue Mall.* ♿

Tempura Kitchen / ★★

3826 SPENARD RD, ANCHORAGE; 907/277-2741 This little oasis for Japanese cuisine in Spenard has been a popular and tasty destination for years. The sushi is superb. Alas, the rest of the menu is disappointing in comparison. Try the artful displays of the spider roll, decorated with sprigs of daikon sprouts and waving crab legs, or the *unagi* (grilled eel). Take all the side-striped shrimp you can when they're in season. (Shrimpers start pulling them from Prince William Sound in mid-April and continue until the end of July. There is a short fall season as well.) You can order them as sushi, with the heads deep fried on the side, or fried whole and served with a wedge of lemon. Try the sushi made with snapper and served with ponzu sauce, or simply trust the sushi chefs, who always know what's best. *$$; AE, DC, DIS, MC, V; local checks only; lunch Mon–Fri, dinner every day; beer and wine; reservations recommended on weekends; off Spenard Rd, south of 36th Ave.* ♿

Thai Kitchen / ★★

3405 E TUDOR RD, ANCHORAGE; 907/561-0082 In 1987, a young Thai couple, Ben and Sommay Kitchpanich, opened a small convenience market with two tiny tables in the back for Alaskans to sample authentic, delicious, home-cooked Thai food. "Thailand is so hot," says Ben. "We wanted to see the coldest place. Here, there are more adventurous eaters than in the Lower 48." Their kitchen became so popular around town that they added a table a year. Now there are 12, with cheerful batik tablecloths, and the store is gone. "The Boss" (Sommay) still does all the cooking with the help of her sister Orathay. Favorites include fresh spring rolls; "Popeye" chicken served with spinach and peanut sauce; garlic tofu; special eggplant sautéed with curry paste, coconut milk, and fresh basil; *tom yum kai* (lemon grass soup); and, of course, pad thai, the traditional thin rice noodles with peanuts, bean sprouts, and pork or shrimp. *$; MC, V; local checks only; lunch Mon–Fri, dinner every day; no alcohol; no reservations; www.thaikitchenalaska.com; in a strip mall off Tudor.* &

LODGINGS

Anchorage Hotel / ★

330 E ST, ANCHORAGE; 907/272-4553 OR 800/544-0988; FAX 907/277-4483 In the historic lodgings category, the Anchorage Hotel lays claim to being the city's oldest. Since its birth in 1916, many notables have stayed in its 26 rooms, including the famous painter Sydney Laurence, who once took up residence there. Guests step from busy E Street into a quiet, semiformal lobby with a fireplace and marble chess set. Renovated in the 1990s, the rooms are clean but lack the personality of the hotel's past. Some rooms face the street, and traffic noise carries. Rooms 301 and 303 overlook Fourth Avenue and E Street, a terrific viewpoint for watching the start of the Iditarod Trail Sled Dog Race when you don't care if the howling of the dogs, people, and vehicles wake you up early. All rooms have tea and coffee facilities and a minibar; bathrooms have nice amenities. A continental breakfast is served in the lobby each morning, and the staff is young, friendly, and accommodating. Rates are $209 summer ($129 winter), for single or double. *$$$; AE, DC, DIS, MC, V; checks OK; anchoragehotel@alaska.com; www.historicanchoragehotel.com; downtown, corner of E St and 4th Ave.* &

Bed & Breakfast on the Park / ★★★

602 W 10TH AVE, ANCHORAGE; 907/277-0878 OR 800/353-0878; FAX 907/277-8905 Hostesses Helen Tucker and Stella Hughton preside over this former log-cabin church on the Park Strip in downtown Anchorage. You cannot help but be charmed by this quaint historic inn, where the flower gardens get more beautiful every year. While peeling mangos for your breakfast, Tucker and Hughton will happily share tips on politics, gardening, old-time characters, or Chinese martial arts. They once owned the Willow Trading Post and made it an oasis on the way north to Denali National Park. The same delightful spirit pervades this abode. It's one of the best buys in downtown and a perfect location—quiet, but close to everything. The B&B has only five rooms, so book early. If you call their toll-free number direct, you get the lower per-night price of $100, double occupancy (otherwise it's $110 for a double). *$$; MC, V; checks OK; www.bedandbreakfastonthe park.net; downtown, between E and G Sts.*

Copper Whale Inn / ★★★

440 L ST, ANCHORAGE; 907/258-7999; FAX 907/258-6213 Something between a bed-and-breakfast and a country inn, the comfortable, Nantucket-styled Copper Whale is a rarity among Anchorage housing. It is charming and quaint, with an informal yet reserved staff. Most of the 15 rooms have beautiful picture-window views of Cook Inlet to the west (all but two with private bath). Redoubt is the nicest room in the inn, but you can't go wrong with any of them. Free Internet access. Summer daily rates run $120 to $175, single or double ($65–$95 in winter), with a hot breakfast; book early. If you rent a car, be aware that parking downtown is either an adventure or about $10 a day extra for a parking pass. *$$–$$$; AE, DIS, MC, V; checks OK; sometimes closed for a month in winter; cwhalein@alaska.net; www.copperwhale.com; downtown, corner of 5th Ave and L St.*

Hilton Anchorage / ★★

500 W 3RD AVE, ANCHORAGE; 907/272-7411 OR 800/245-2527; FAX, 907/265-7140 In the heart of downtown, the Hilton Anchorage is often packed with tourists and conventioneers. With 606 rooms, it's the biggest hotel downtown, and the lobby, which was remodeled in 2001, always feels more like Grand Central Station than a place for respite. But it's convenient. In the summer, the vendor-laden Saturday Market and the train to Denali are short strolls away. In the winter, the Iditarod Trail Sled Dog Race starts a block away, and the Fur Rendezvous festival happens all around the hotel block. Locals like the rooftop view and panoramic sunsets in summer from the bar in the Top of the World restaurant (dinner daily, summer; Tues–Sat, winter). Rooms are nicely appointed but small. Try for a corner room in the Anchorage Tower, the original section of the hotel. Rates are $280, double occupancy. *$$$; AE, DIS, MC, V; checks OK; www.hilton.com; downtown, corner of 3rd Ave and E St.* &

Hotel Captain Cook / ★★★★

939 W 5TH AVE, ANCHORAGE; 907/276-6000 OR 800/843-1950; FAX 907/343-2298 This is the hotel that two-time, former Governor Walter Hickel built, and it remains the top of the line for Anchorage. When the big-oil money was flowing in the 1970s and early 1980s, the Hotel Captain Cook and its elegant bars and restaurants (see Crow's Nest review, above) served as a backdrop for deal making and high-class partying. Towers Two and Three were renovated in the mid-1990s, so request a room in either tower. Ask for a view of Cook Inlet, available on the fifth floor and above, or a southwest corner room for a view of both water and mountains with morning and evening sun. It gets crowded with cruise ship tourists in summer. Summer rates are $280, double occupancy, but drop sharply in late September, once the ships sail south for the winter. *$$$; AE, DC, DIS, MC, V; checks OK; www.captaincook.com; downtown, corner of 4th and 5th Aves between I and K Sts.* &

Millennium Alaskan Hotel / ★★

4800 SPENARD RD, ANCHORAGE; 907/243-2300 OR 800/544-0553; FAX 907/243-8815 Formerly the Regal Alaskan, this hotel is located on Lake Hood, the busiest lake in Anchorage. Locals scramble to get to the deck on sunny days to drink local ale and watch the floatplanes vie for space with the ducks during take-offs and landings. The place is very Alaskan and has the feel of a finely appointed hunting lodge, with wildlife heads and full-size bears on display. In March, as dogs and mushers are racing from Anchorage to Nome, the hotel serves as the official Iditarod Trail Sled Dog Race headquarters, and guests can follow the progress of their favorite mushers on a frequently updated board in the lobby or from printouts issued every few hours from the computer room. The rooms are quite spacious ($290, double occupancy) and the hotel has a restaurant, the Flying Machine, that is open daily. The Sunday brunch is intense. *$$$; AE, DC, MC, V; checks OK; regal@ alaska.net; www.millennium-hotels.com; near the airport on Spenard Rd.* ♿

The Voyager Hotel / ★★★

501 K ST, ANCHORAGE; 907/277-9501 OR 800/247-9070; FAX 907/274-0333 In the heart of downtown, the Voyager is an unpretentious, comfortable little hotel with 38 large rooms (about 400 square feet each) with kitchenettes. Built in 1965, it is a low-rise, homey alternative to the big hotels. All the rooms are non-smoking and are a stone's throw away from the Coastal Trail. It has a loyal following and fills up fast. Best to get your dibs in early. Folks often stay several days, even up to two weeks. The location, friendliness, and prices ($169, double occupancy in summer—$40 less in winter) can't be beat. *$$; AE, DC, DIS, MC, V; checks OK; rsvp@alaska.com; www.voyagerhotel.com; kitty-corner from the Hotel Captain Cook, entrance on K St.*

BED-AND-BREAKFAST SERVICES

Decide whether you want to be in town, on the hillside near the mountain wilderness, or somewhere in between. There are some wonderful accommodations dotted around Anchorage in log homes, near water, or with mountain vistas. For more information on the range of B&Bs, try one of these services: **ALASKA BED AND BREAKFAST ASSOCIATION** (PO Box 242623, Anchorage AK 99524; 907/345-0923; www.anchorage-bnb.com), **ALASKA PRIVATE LODGING** (888/235-2148; www.alaskabandb.com), or **ALASKA SOURDOUGH BED AND BREAKFAST ASSOCIATION** (907/563-6244; www.alaskan.com/aksourdoughbba).

Palmer

Palmer, about an hour's drive northeast of Anchorage in the gorgeous mountain-rimmed Mantanuska-Susitna Valley (simply known as the "Mat-Su" around here), sits at the center of what little agricultural life Southcentral Alaska still has. This picturesque little town's roots were put down in the shadow of the towering, 6,400-foot Pioneer Peak during the Great Depression, when the federal government sent Dust Bowl farmers north. To this day, farmers still try to make the best of a short but intense growing season. Stop at any number of farmers' stalls along the highway for sweet carrots, lettuce, and a cabbage so big you'll have to buy it a separate plane ticket home.

EXPLORING

ALASKA STATE FAIR / The fair is a statewide party that dominates the tiny town of Palmer during the last week in August and the first weekend in September. The 10-day event is a cornucopia of music, rodeos, horse shows, carnival rides, food booths, and agricultural displays. Yes, they really do have 80-pound cabbages, 23-pound kale, and zucchinis as big as your arm. It's a good time. Everybody goes to the fair. *Mile 40 Glenn Hwy; 907/745-4827; www.alaskastatefair.org.*

MUSK OX FARM / In the 1940s, the prehistoric-looking musk oxen that populated Alaska's Arctic were disappearing. In 1954, efforts were made to domesticate the ox, one of the Arctic's oldest living species, and the result was the Musk Ox Farm, which is now located just outside of Palmer on the Glenn Highway. The musk ox produces a unique, downy-soft underwool that is shed every spring. The undercoat, or qiviut, is reportedly eight times warmer than wool, extra lightweight, and not scratchy. Native women formed a co-op and created a business knitting the fine wool into hats, sweaters, and neck gaiters (called smoke rings, or *nachaqs*). The hand-knitted apparel can be found at the farm's gift shop (as well as at a downtown Anchorage shop called Oomingmak). There's also a picnic area and museum. The private, nonprofit farm offers guided tours on the half hour in summer. Admission is $8.50 adults, $7 seniors or kids 13–18, $5.50 children 6–12. Children 6 and younger are free, with accompanying adult. *Open daily in summer 10am–6pm; 907/745-4151; www.muskoxfarm.org.*

RESTAURANTS

Vagabond Blues Coffeehouse / ★

642 S ALASKA ST, PALMER; 907/745-2233 With its warm wood floors and ambience, this is a delightful harbor for the gentle-hearted. Great cinnamon rolls, espresso, pastries, bread, pasta salads, and bagel sandwiches top the menu. Soups such as a creamy broccoli with large florets are homemade and served in a local artist's handmade pottery bowls. The strawberry pie alone is worth the drive from Anchorage. Live music featuring local talent can be found on weekends. Check out the new bookstore down the street, Fireside Books, which hosts occasional poetry slams. *$; No credit cards; local checks only; breakfast, lunch, dinner every day; no alcohol; Koslosky Center in downtown Palmer.* &

Girdwood

This woodsy, ski enthusiasts' oasis about an hour's drive south of Anchorage, with funky little cabins tucked into the hollows and expensive condos facing Mount Alyeska, has long been a mecca for downhill skiers. Summer brings a wealth of spectacular views, from hanging glaciers to mountains covered with blueberry patches. High on the ski slopes is one of the more elegant dining experiences in the region.

The town was started by a gold miner who staked a claim on Crow Creek. Today, Girdwood is a little village of about 1,200 that swells to some 3,000 when the snow

BEST WAYS TO DIE

Bears, moose, sightseeing flights, cruise ship gangplanks, halibut fishing, calving glaciers, icy rivers—you name it, and someone's died from it in Alaska. Even the most humbly adventurous traveler to Alaska must be aware of the state's natural dangers. While you might have the street savvy to avoid a mugger back home, such skills are useless when a city-bound moose is angry and looking right at you.

To that end, here's a little guide to the best ways to die in Alaska.

TRY TO GET CLOSE TO THE WILDLIFE. Both bears and moose can cover an amazing amount of real estate in a short time, and they're likely to be on any number of popular trails around Anchorage. In the summer of 1995, two local people out for a day's jog on McHugh Creek Trail, minutes away from downtown Anchorage, were killed by a grizzly. Earlier that winter, a moose trampled a man to death as he tried to enter a building at the University of Alaska Anchorage Sports Center. The rule is simple: don't feed them, don't pet them, don't hang around them, don't harass them, and don't surprise them. If you see a creature in the woods, back away slowly. Wear bells on your pack, clap, or sing to let bears know you're coming. Don't get between a moose and her baby, and don't try to go around a moose.

WALK ON THE MUDFLATS THAT SURROUND ANCHORAGE. That appealing shoreline is actually mud. And not just any mud. The consistency is more akin to wet cement or quicksand. You get a foot stuck and you'll have a hard time pulling it out. Matters get dicier if the tide is coming in or going out (and it's always doing one or the other four times a day). Anchorage has the second-highest tides in the world. Water levels can change several feet in a matter of minutes. People have gotten stuck and drowned while

falls. In winter, skiers try their hand at challenging Nordic routes or schuss down breathtaking Mount Alyeska in the abundant company of snowboarders; there are seven lifts and an aerial tram. You can plunge down powder-filled slopes while looking at the ocean below.

In summer, Girdwood is a good place for rafting trips, hikes, and live music featuring local performers. In fall, the hillsides are filled with berry pickers; in spring, the same hills offer rare black morel mushrooms and fiddlehead ferns. But beware: anytime but deep winter, when they're mainly snoozing, you'll find bears also roaming these valleys and hillsides.

EXPLORING

While driving from Anchorage to Girdwood along the **SEWARD HIGHWAY,** you enjoy wonderful views of Turnagain Arm, one of the most scenic drives in all the world. Watch for bore tides, Dall sheep, and beluga whales. A tasty place for dinner along the highway is the cozy **TURNAGAIN HOUSE** (907/653-7500), located in Indian, which has delicious seafood (try the silver salmon when it's in season or the

rescue workers tried to beat the tide. Don't go there.

DON'T WORRY ABOUT YOUR GEAR. Sure, that peak seems close enough to scramble up in an hour or two. Who needs water, good hiking boots, or emergency rations? You do. What was meant to be a short hike can turn into an overnight ordeal if you get lost or hurt. Remember, most of what surrounds Anchorage is wilderness. There are no park rangers or other hikers just around the bend. In all likelihood, you will be on your own. Basic emergency and survival gear should be tucked into your pack, including water, food, matches, fire starter, extra clothing, bug dope, a compass, a knife, a first-aid kit, and a topographical map.

DON'T RESPECT THE COLD. Cold can creep into any Alaska day, even in the summer. And if you add cold to the problems outlined above, you can easily lose your life. Hypothermia may set in quickly if you get dunked in one of the many glacial streams, or simply get rained on or caught out overnight. Dress for variable weather, and pack a space blanket and waterproof matches.

PANIC, ACT MACHO, AND DON'T FOLLOW YOUR INTUITION. Fear is a warning. It means something is unsafe. Listen to it. It's sort of like the adage about anything that sounds too good to be true. If it seems dangerous, it probably is.

DON'T DO YOUR HOMEWORK. Even in Alaska, knowledge is power. Check out guidebooks and talk to locals. Learn about how to stay safe in the woods, avoid avalanches, and handle a bear attack. The Alaska Public Lands Information Center (605 W 4th Ave; 907/271-2737; www.nps.gov/aplic), in downtown Anchorage, has a variety of free brochures covering much of what you'll need to know.

—*Kim Severson*

Alaska scallops and shrimp in basil-saffron cream sauce). It's often crowded in summer, but in winter it's a charming little dining room with a fireplace and view of the inlet.

At the base of Mount Alyeska in Girdwood, on the Alyeska Boardwalk, is the wonderful **BAKE SHOP** (907/783-2831), which has been catering to Alaskans for more than 20 years with its legendary sourdough bread, pancakes, farmer's breakfasts, tasty soups, and incredible sandwiches. Eat in, picnic out amongst the flowers, or pack a sandwich in your rucksack for a climb up the mountain.

If you want to see an old gold mine and pan for a little pay dirt in the creek yourself, bump 4 miles up Crow Creek Road in Girdwood to **CROW CREEK MINE** (follow the signs; www.crowcreekgoldmine.com). A working gold mine in winter, it's open to the public mid-May to mid-September and is quite peaceful and beautiful—no flotilla of tour buses here.

FESTIVALS AND EVENTS

GIRDWOOD FOREST FAIR / This folk-music festival held the first weekend in July includes an opportunity to buy all types of Alaskan crafts. This fair has grown quite popular, especially with the tie-dyed crowd, so be prepared to park a ways from the fair and hike. It features a beer garden and live music. *907/566-4702; www. girdwoodforestfair.com.*

RESTAURANTS

The Double Musky / ★★

CROW CREEK RD, GIRDWOOD; 907/783-2822 An old-time favorite among Alaskans, the Double Musky is known for its impeccable pepper steak and gargantuan Cajun portions. With remnants of Mardi Gras past hanging from the walls (as they say here, "Laissez les bon temps rouler"), the Musky is casual but expensive. The appetizer menu offers halibut ceviche, coconut salmon, and Cajun-spiced shrimp peelers. The dinner menu features mammoth steaks, seafood, and spicy Cajun and Creole dishes. Little loaves of bread, served with drinks, are studded with cheese and jalapeños, and the pepper steak is covered with a spicy coating of well-crushed peppercorns and Burgundy sauce. The fiery shrimp étouffée is flawless. For dessert, you can't go wrong with a slice of cool Key lime pie. Be advised: they don't take reservations, and sometimes the wait is long. *$$$; AE, DC, DIS, MC, V; no checks; dinner Tues–Sun (closed Nov); full bar; no reservations; www.double muskyinn.com; after the turnoff from the Seward Hwy to Girdwood, turn left on Crow Creek Rd (follow signs).* &

Seven Glaciers Restaurant and Lounge / ★★★

GIRDWOOD; 907/754-2237 OR 800/880-3880 Opened in 1994, this elegant restaurant—with friendly wait staff and stunning views of the mountains—sits high on Mount Alyeska. To get there, you take a Swiss-built tram to 2,300 feet. Fresh, local ingredients such as blueberries, oysters, and boletus mushrooms often grace the menu. Seafood and vegetarian dishes shine. Alas, in a setting of such natural beauty, it's a pity the architect was more visually enamored by the inner workings of the tram wheels than the mountains, glaciers, and ocean outside—there are few tables positioned with a really spectacular view. So take a short walk after dinner and drink in this exquisite location. *$$$; AE, DC, DIS, MC, V; local checks only; dinner every day in summer (closed Oct, winter hours vary); full bar; reservations recommended; take the tram from the Alyeska Prince Hotel.* &

LODGINGS

Alyeska Prince Hotel / ★★★★

ALYESKA SKI RESORT, GIRDWOOD; 907/754-1111 OR 800/880-3880; FAX 907/754-2200 The Alyeska Prince Hotel is a grand, chateau-style resort hotel that rises eight elegant stories at the base of Mount Alyeska. Cherry wood and granite accent rooms and lobby. The hotel was opened in 1994 by the Seibu Corporation of Japan, and many rooms are geared for the Japanese visitor. Most rooms have two double beds only (few kings, no queens), but elegant, small touches—such as towel warmers, bathrobes, and fresh roses on room-service trays in the dead of winter—

will win your heart. They'll even give you a wake-up call when the Northern Lights are visible. Rates start at $195, double occupancy. Two delicious restaurants are located in the hotel, the family-style Pond Café and a small fancy Japanese restaurant, Teppanyaki Katsura, where your chef grills your dinner of fresh seafood, meats, and vegetables while you watch, sipping hot or cold sake. The festive show is topped off with refreshing ginger ice cream and a huge almond cookie filled with crème brûlée. *$$$; AE, DC, DIS, MC, V; checks OK; www.alyeskaresort.com; at the base of Alyeska ski area.* &

BED-AND-BREAKFAST SERVICES
GIRDWOOD BED & BREAKFAST ASSOCIATION (907/222-4858; www.gbba.org) is a nonprofit, volunteer organization that can help you find a log home, lodging with a hot tub, a European ski chalet, or a romantic retreat. Most run $80 to $135 a night, for a single or double.

Chugach State Park

Chugach State Park, adjacent to Anchorage, is a standout in a state crammed with outstanding natural wonders—the park is so grand that in any other state it would be a national park, not just a state park. It offers visitors just about everything that draws people to Alaska—mountains, rivers, glaciers, wildlife, and the chance to roam in a countryside where you can stretch your legs and dream of adventure. Nowhere else does a major metropolis lie cheek-by-jowl with full-blown wilderness. Chugach is accessible to everyone and is visited in all seasons.

But the park isn't swarming with day-hikers and picnickers. While it receives a million visits a year—skiers, backpackers, mountaineers, photographers, kayakers, windsurfers, snowmobilers, and wildlife watchers—most people never venture more than a mile from the trailheads. Even by Alaska standards, Chugach is quite devoid of people once you get into it. When Alaskans utter the old bromide that "the best thing about Anchorage is it's close to Alaska," they mean Chugach.

The park is a half-million acres of raw, rugged terrain. Geologically young peaks loom tall and jagged—up to 8,000 feet. Valleys and rocks show ample evidence of scouring by not-so-ancient glaciers. One of the world's last remaining icefields lies 25 miles from downtown Anchorage, and the park is home to nearly every animal for which Alaska is known.

April, May, and June offer the least precipitation, while July and August are among the rainiest months. Many of the park's trails are snow-covered or muddy in April, but not the southern slopes facing Turnagain Arm. By June and July, most valley floors are lush as a jungle. But that's also the height of mosquito season (there's always a trade-off). September, although cooler, offers vivid fall colors, berry picking, rutting moose, fewer visitors, and a snow line steadily creeping down from the mountaintops.

Visitors should remember that, despite its accessibility, the park is rugged; it's an easy place to get killed. The causes are many—exposure, falls, avalanches, drowning, mauling by bears. People seem to die in the park almost every year.

Between 1973 and 1997, according to the *Anchorage Daily News,* 14 people lost their lives within a half-day's hike of a single trailhead, the popular Glen Alps.

Proximity to Anchorage offers only an illusion of safety. If you're going beyond the trailheads, be sure you have real outdoor savvy. And—even if planning just a short hike—take water, food, extra coat, pants for wind or rain, hat, gloves, map and compass, matches/fire starter, first-aid kit, and pocket knife. Maybe include insect repellent, sunglasses, and headlamp or flashlight (except in midsummer). And tell someone where you're going ahead of time.

Hunting for moose and sheep occurs in some parts of the park in the fall. For current hunting regulations, check with the Alaska Department of Fish and Game (907/465-4100; www.state.ak.us/local/akpages/FISH.GAME/adfghome.htm).

ACCESS AND INFORMATION

Chugach is accessible along two sides of its triangular rim. Of 30 access points, 15 offer a parking area and trailhead that can put visitors in touch with the most outstanding features. Although the park has more than 100 miles of trails and footpaths, nearly every valley is an untracked wilderness. Having to ford glacier-fed rivers and struggle through dense undergrowth while not getting lost deters many, but the rewards are grand.

To get to the park, you need a vehicle. If you have legs of iron, a bicycle will do, but within the park the use of mountain bikes is limited. Ditto for snowmobiles, all-terrain vehicles, and horses. For questions regarding any motorized or other use, check with the rangers at **PARK HEADQUARTERS** (907/345-5014), or visit them in the historic **POTTER SECTION HOUSE,** Mile 115 of the Seward Highway, south of Anchorage. Parking at Chugach State Park trailheads is $5 per visit or $25 for an annual pass. Nonprofit operators of two parking areas (Eagle River Nature Center—below—and the Alpenglow Ski Resort) charge their own fees, and the state's annual pass is not accepted.

The **EAGLE RIVER NATURE CENTER** (Mile 12, Eagle River Rd; 907/694-2108; www.ernc.org) is situated in one of the park's more spectacular valleys, operated year-round by a nonprofit organization. The center offers nature programs ranging from guided overnight hikes to talks on subjects from bears and birch syrup to edible mushrooms and orienteering. The center is 25 miles from downtown Anchorage and is open daily in summer months (call for winter hours). Public-use cabins and yurts, all within 2 miles of the center, are available (see Public-Use Cabins below).

Planning a visit has become even easier in recent years, thanks to the publication of the first comprehensive park map, "Chugach State Park: Chugach Mountains, Alaska" (Imus Geographics, PO Box 161, Eugene, OR 97440; www.imusgeo graphics.com), available for about $7 at sporting goods stores (like REI, see Adventures in the Anchorage section) or at park headquarters. The state Division of Parks and Recreation also maintains an informative Web site (www.alaskastateparks.org) that offers much data about Chugach and other parks.

Two recent books devoted solely to the Chugach are *50 Hikes in Alaska's Chugach State Park* (The Mountaineers Books, Seattle; $15) and *A Walk-About Guide to Alaska, Volume II: The Chugach Mountains* (Shawn R. Lyons, Anchorage; $18). The latter features first-person essays as well as guides to the trailheads and peaks. Both are excellent, written by people who have done plenty of hiking and adventuring in the Chugach, and both are available at local bookstores.

ADVENTURES

Most Chugach visitors come to day-hike and gawk at the scenery. They also pick berries, run hills, scramble up the peaks, ski, canoe, study nature, and watch the animals—**BIRDS, MOOSE,** and **BEARS** primarily. Grizzly and black-bear populations, which haven't been hunted in the area since the 1970s, have expanded to all corners of the park. Encounters can occur anywhere, so be bear savvy. Moose can be dangerous, too, and require an entirely different response. Fishing is limited. Windsurfing is for the experts. Ice climbers enjoy several frozen waterfalls, though none are high. Rock climbing is minimal—the rock is generally too friable—though adherents find outlets along the Seward Highway on Turnagain Arm.

The **SEWARD HIGHWAY,** one of America's National Scenic Byways, runs beside the southern rim of the park. Whether you're in a vehicle or on a bicycle, just riding alongside the park is prime use of your time. On one side of the highway is **TUR-NAGAIN ARM,** where, depending on the season, you may spot beluga or killer whales, windsurfers, and unusual bore tides. On the park side of the road, look for **DALL SHEEP** on the cliffs near **WINDY CORNER** (Mile 106.7). Be careful. When you want to rubberneck, pull off the winding highway into a turnout, or you may end up the kind of casualty that makes this one of the most hazardous stretches of roadway in the state.

Turnagain Arm offers a kaleidoscope of scenic thrills and recreation. **BELUGA POINT** (Mile 110.4) is a good place to watch for the whales in summer. The **MCHUGH CREEK PICNIC AREA** (Mile 112) offers interpretive panels, spotting scopes, and viewing decks, while the trailhead leads to both woodland and alpine hiking. Farther down the road, an interpretive overlook at **BIRD POINT** (Mile 96) juts into Turnagain Arm for lovely views.

TURNAGAIN ARM TRAIL—formerly known as "the old Johnson Trail"—runs along the mountain slopes parallel to the roadway. It was the mail and transportation route in the old days before the highway was built from Seward to Anchorage. It can be accessed at several trailheads. The section from Potter Creek (Mile 115) to McHugh Creek (Mile 112) is the easiest walking. From McHugh Creek to Rainbow (Mile 108.4) and on to Windy Corner (Mile 106.7) is more difficult but offers excellent views of Turnagain Arm and the Kenai Mountains across the water.

Those who want a strenuous climb (up to 4,000 feet elevation gain) but not the bother of a long approach should hike up **BIRD RIDGE** (Mile 101.7). **FALLS CREEK** (Mile 105.5) is another choice for a Turnagain Arm day hike that starts upward as soon as the car door is shut. Above tree line, visitors enter a beautiful alpine valley where they're almost sure to spot Dall sheep on the high escarpments.

Quick trips to the park alongside Anchorage provide beautiful city and mountain views and a way to get deeper into the park. There are three primary access points: **GLEN ALPS** (about 30 minutes from the airport), main gateway to Flattop Mountain and the Powerline Pass Trail; **PROSPECT HEIGHTS** (also about 30 minutes from the airport and equidistant from downtown), gateway to Near Point, Wolverine Peak, and the Powerline Trail; and the **ALPENGLOW SKI RESORT**

VIEWIN' BRUIN

The brown-bear viewing business in Alaska is booming.

For as little as $8 or more than $1,000, you can see this majestic symbol of Alaska wilderness. And this is exactly what Alaska visitors are doing. On the budget end, spend $8 and see black bears, brown bears, and a polar bear at the **ALASKA ZOO** on O'Malley Road in Anchorage. The zoo is almost certain to have an orphaned brown bear cub or two every summer. Spend $1,000 or more and book a night or two at a remote **WILDERNESS LODGE**. In between are opportunities to camp near state-managed bear feeding grounds or to fly to a remote stream for a day.

Because the standard, remote bear-viewing hot spots are operating at capacity, a whole new tourist business in Anchorage and on the Kenai Peninsula has been born. For $300 to $500, small **AIR TAXIS** that used to fly fishermen into remote areas are now ferrying binocular-toting tourists for a day of watching bears snatching spawning salmon out of streams. On one such stream across Cook Inlet from Anchorage, the air taxis flew in 2,200 bear viewers in 1999. That jumped to 6,000 viewers in 2000.

With the exception of the trip to the zoo, all of these trips involve getting in a plane or boat, so book ahead. Prime viewing times corresponds with salmon runs between June and September.

Here are some of the options:

MCNEIL RIVER STATE GAME SANCTUARY. This requires a permit, which the state of Alaska awards in a lottery every spring (see Southwest Alaska chapter). It involves flying to the sanctuary, 200 miles southwest of Anchorage, and camping in a designated area that has a wood-fired sauna. A cabin is available for cooking. It's a short hike to the

(40 minutes from the airport, 20 minutes from downtown), gateway to Rendezvous Peak and to Ship Creek Valley. All three are located on the front range facing Anchorage, and all take you above tree line to awesome views with minimal legwork.

FLATTOP is Alaska's most-climbed mountain. (It is also the most crowded, which means if you want a true Alaska experience, try something else.) Shaped as its name suggests, it rises 3,510 feet above sea level. You start from the Glen Alps parking lot and should allow 2–5 hours round-trip. Although popular, Flattop is no cakewalk. It is steep below the summit and people have died on its flanks. Wear good shoes and pay attention. Across the valley, **WOLVERINE PEAK,** facing Anchorage from the middle of the front range, is yet another easy-to-get-to mountain that offers moderate hiking through spruce forest, tundra meadows, and alpine ridges with beautiful views all around. Start from the Prospect Heights trailhead and plan on 6-9 hours for a round-trip.

Want to soak in exquisite natural wonders but don't want to walk very far? Drive northeast from Anchorage to **EKLUTNA LAKE**. The lake, largest in the park, was glacially carved and has saw-toothed mountains rising 6,000–7,000 feet around it.

feeding grounds, where bears munch on spawning salmon at McNeil Falls and neighboring Mikfik Creek. For more information, contact the Alaska Department of Fish and
Game, Division of Wildlife Conservation (333 Raspberry Rd, Anchorage AK 99518-
1599; 907/267-2182; www.state.ak.us/adfg).

KATMAI NATIONAL PARK AND PRESERVE. Fly from Anchorage for the day, or
spend a few nights. Stay at the campground or in one of the cabins. Expect to spend
about $500 for the day, more if you get a cabin. Either way, contact the park well
in advance (PO Box 7, King Salmon AK 99613; 907/246-3305; www.nps.gov/katm).
For cabin reservations, contact Katmailand (4125 Aircraft Dr, Anchorage AK
99502; 907/243-5448 or 800/544-0551; fax 907/243-0649; info@katmailand.com;
www.katmailand.com).

REDOUBT BAY LODGE. Located in the Lake Clark National Park and Preserve (see
Southwest Alaska chapter), this lodge recently expanded to handle the increased
bear-viewing traffic. The cost is about $350 for a day trip, or roughly $1,400 for a
three-night package (2525 Galewood St, Anchorage AK 99508; 907/274-2710;
www.withinthewild.com).

DAY TRIPS. From Anchorage try Rust's Flying Service (PO Box 190325, Anchorage
AK 99519; 907/243-1595 or 800/544-2299; www.flyrusts.com). From Soldotna try
Talon Air Service (PO Box 1109, Soldotna AK 99669; 907/262-8899; www.talonair.
com). Or from Homer, try Emerald Air (PO Box 635, Homer AK 99603; 907/235-
6993; www.emeraldairservice.com).

—*Natalie Phillips*

The **TWIN PEAKS TRAIL,** a strenuous hike from lakeside, can get you up high and
close to Dall sheep. Its southern exposure means it loses snow earlier than other
trails. Beyond Eklutna, a little farther down the road, you'll find the **PIONEER RIDGE
KNIK–GOOSEBAY RIVER TRAIL** climbing the back of mile-high Pioneer Peak, a dramatic mountain dominating the view from Palmer, a little town about an hour northeast of Anchorage. Both the Twin Peaks and Pioneer Ridge Trails rise directly from
the parking lot and quickly put the hiker/runner in possession of outstanding views.

For river runners, **EAGLE RIVER,** northeast of Anchorage, is the only river in
the park where there is any regular canoeing, kayaking, or rafting. An 11-mile seg-
ment can be managed by most experienced boaters. But unless you are experienced
and have scouted the rapids, do not go past the bridge on the highway. This can
be a deathtrap. For those who want a taste of the river but don't have a boat,
contact **LIFETIME ADVENTURES** (907/746-4644 or 800/952-8624; www.Lifetime
Adventures.net), which offers scenic rafting tours and white-water trips on this
extremely cold river for $70 per adult, $50 per child.

For those who desire a deeper drink of Chugach splendors, a 28-mile back-packing trek, the **GIRDWOOD TO EAGLE RIVER TRAVERSE,** crosses from Girdwood over Crow Pass and down Raven Creek to the Eagle River Trail. It cuts through the wilderness heart of the park, covering part of the historic Iditarod Trail that once carried travelers from Seward into the Interior before the advent of the railroad. Another fun alternative to the traverse is to go from **GLEN ALPS TO INDIAN** via Ship Pass and Ship Lake. It's 12 miles, but the middle section is off-trail and easy to navigate with experience. The route from Ship Pass down to the lake is steep but safe if you take your time. Take a hiking stick or ski pole. You can camp overnight at the lake or at Indian Pass or do it in a day. Both routes require vehicle shuttles or willing friends to drop you off and pick you up.

VEHICLE CAMPERS will find three developed campgrounds in the park. Each has wooded sites with fire rings and picnic tables, water, and latrines. Lifetime Adventures (see above) operates the **EAGLE RIVER CAMPGROUND,** 15 miles north from Anchorage, and takes reservations. Cost is $15 a night, plus the $5 parking fee. The state operates the **EKLUTNA LAKE CAMPGROUND** (about 40 miles north of Anchorage via the Glenn Highway) and **BIRD CREEK CAMPGROUND** (20 miles southeast of Anchorage), charging $10 a night (annual passes are available at $75). More information about the park's campgrounds is available by phone (907/269-8400, press zero) and online (www.dnr.state.ak.us/parks/units/chugach/facility.htm).

PUBLIC-USE CABINS

YUDITNA CREEK CABIN, about 3 miles from the Eklutna Lake trailhead, is far from luxurious, but it is wheelchair-accessible and can accommodate up to eight people snugly. Bring all your own gear and food, (a rule of thumb with all public-use cabins). Rent is $40 per night for a maximum of three consecutive nights and only one weekend a month per party. Reservations can be made in person, or by mail, fax, or online with a credit card (Alaska Department of Natural Resources Public Information Center; 550 W 7th Ave, Ste 1260, Anchorage AK 99501-3557; 907/269-8400; fax 907/269-8901; www.dnr.state.ak.us/parks/units/chugach).

SERENITY FALLS HUT, 12 miles from the Eklutna Lake trailhead along the Lakeside Trail, is a multiparty public-use hut that can fit up to 13. Expect to share the cabin with others. Bring all your own gear and food. Rental costs—for single or double bunks, or for a whole bay that sleeps three to five—range from $10 to $45 per night. It is possible to rent the entire hut, but only for one night, Sunday through Thursday; cost is $115. Reservations must be made in person at the Public Information Center (above).

For information on either cabin, call the Public Information Center (above) or visit state parks' comprehensive Web site at www.alaskastateparks.org.

EAGLE RIVER NATURE CENTER CABIN, managed by the nonprofit Friends of Eagle River Nature Center, is located 1¼ miles from the center, along the historic Iditarod Trail. The cabin accommodates up to eight on wooden platforms. Firewood is usually provided. The nature center also offers two yurts, or circular tents with stoves. The **RIVER TRAIL YURT,** 1½ miles down the trail from the center, sleeps four. The **RAPIDS CAMP YURT** is ⅕ mile farther and sleeps six. Maximum stay for all three is seven nights and costs $55 per night ($45 for members of the nature center), which includes parking for up to 4 vehicles. Reservations can be made up to a year in advance, by phone, mail, or fax. (32750 Eagle River Road, Eagle River AK 99577; 907/694-2108; www.ernc.org).

Hikers can rent a U.S. Forest Service hut near **CROW PASS**, a no-frills A-frame that can sleep 10 in an area that's a gateway to countless Chugach marvels. The pass is above tree line, so no woodstove. Because of avalanche hazard, the hut is available June 1–September 30 only, for $35 a night (for reservations, 877/444-6777; www.reserveusa.com).

Finally, along the park's extreme 40-mile Eklutna Traverse are three A-frame huts—**PICHLER'S PERCH, WHITEOUT, AND ROSIE'S ROOST**—that are free (no reservations required), sleep a dozen or more each, and have no woodstoves or amenities. These backcountry cabins were built by and are maintained by the Mountaineering Club of Alaska, and travelers are expected to share.

GUIDES AND OUTFITTERS

GREAT ALASKAN GOURMET ADVENTURES / Based in Anchorage, this outfit offers customized day hikes and multiday backpacking trips in Chugach State Park and elsewhere in the state, complete with gourmet meals. Day hikes cost $50–$75 per person; overnighters are $175 and up. Group rates available. Contact Jennifer Johnston. *11090 Hideaway Lake Dr, Anchorage AK 99516; 907/346-1087; fax 907/346-1356; jjohnston@hikealaska.com; www.hikealaska.com.*

LIFETIME ADVENTURES / These folks rent bikes and kayaks at Eklutna Lake and also gives boat rides for up to six people, for either day trips or overnight drop-offs around the lake. Perhaps their most popular offering, for $65 per person, is a kayak rental to the end of the lake (8 miles) and a bike rental back along the Lakeside Trail. Or bike to the end and paddle back. Either way, it'll take up most of your day (unless you're a triathalete). This outfitter also offers rafting tours on Eagle River (see Adventures, above). *907/746-4644 or 800/952-8624; info@Lifetime Adventures.net; www.LifetimeAdventures.net.*

FESTIVALS AND EVENTS

CROW PASS CROSSING / This 28-mile wilderness footrace held every July traverses the mountains from Girdwood to Eagle River. Winners complete the race in about three hours. Most backpackers, however, cover the same route in two or three days, parking a "getaway car" at one end, and then driving around in a second car to begin at the other trailhead.

WINTER AND SUMMER SOLSTICES / Visitors who chance upon Chugach in the third week of June or December may want to join solstice celebrations on 3,510-foot Flattop Mountain. Since the 1960s, solstice worshippers en masse have camped out on the peak's summit field. Festivities, which sometimes include bands playing to the glories of endless daylight, are sponsored by the Mountaineering Club of Alaska and take place on the Saturday closest to the solstice. Legend maintains that not a single solstice has been missed. In winter, not surprisingly, the numbers are fewer. One December, only one soul proved hardy enough to brave the severe cold and wind so that the record could remain unbroken.

PRINCE WILLIAM SOUND

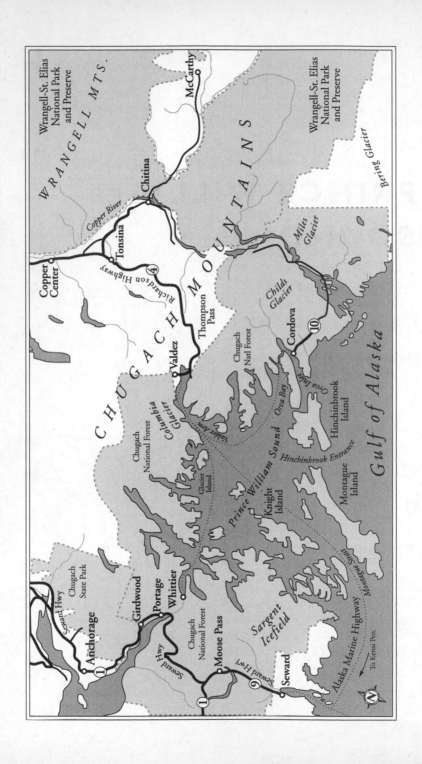

PRINCE WILLIAM SOUND

In the far northern Gulf of Alaska lies Prince William Sound, a marvelous wilderness of deep fjords, towering snowcapped mountains, rich blue seas teeming with wildlife, and chiseled tidewater glaciers. Only a few remote fishing towns and villages dot the coast of this vast array of forest, islands, and waterways. When the sun shines, there is nothing quite so exhilarating as kayaking through bobbing icebergs and curious sea otters, watching huge chunks of ice break off the face of glaciers, feeling the crisp breeze, and riding the swell of waves created by falling ice.

Almost all of Prince William Sound—its 3,500 miles of coastline and 150 glaciers—lies within the boundaries of **CHUGACH NATIONAL FOREST**, which was established by President Theodore Roosevelt in 1907 and today ranks as the second-largest national forest in the United States. (The first is the Tongass National Forest, which encompasses most of Southeast Alaska.)

The weather and seas in the Gulf of Alaska are legendary and tumultuous. But the waters of Prince William Sound are mostly protected from storms in the gulf by a series of islands. Standing guard at the entrance of the sound are the two largest—Hinchinbrook and Montague. On the east side are Orca Bay and the little fishing town of Cordova. Continuing northeast, you'll find Valdez Arm, a long, spectacular fjord leading through the Valdez Narrows to the head of the bay and the oil-boom town of Valdez. Anchoring the middle of the sound are three tiny islands named Naked, Peak, and Storey. Just south of them is lovely Knight Island, with its myriad coves and bays.

On the west side of the sound is the bunker town of Whittier, gateway to the railroad tracks and a new toll road that share a tunnel leading to the Seward Highway and to Anchorage. To the northwest, amid rafts of sea otters and seals, lie College and Harriman Fjords with glacier after glacier plunging into their waters. The 1899 Harriman Expedition named a number of glaciers here after the Ivy League and Little Ivy League colleges of the East Coast, such as Vassar, Smith, Harvard, and Yale.

When the great navigator Captain James Cook of the Royal British Navy first ventured into the sound in 1778, he named it Sandwich Sound for the Earl of Sandwich. But by the time Cook returned to England, the earl had fallen from grace, so the name was changed to Prince William Sound after the king's third son.

ACCESS AND INFORMATION

The state ferry, **ALASKA MARINE HIGHWAY SYSTEM** (800/642-0066; www.alaska. gov/ferry), can take you from Whittier to Valdez and Cordova, or from Seward to Valdez and Cordova, or vice versa. You can walk on, or take your car and drive the road system at your destination's end. Not only does the ferry provide transportation, but it's communal, fun, and a great way to view the remoteness of the sound.

There are only two places from which you can access the sound **BY ROAD**. Valdez on the east is at the beginning of the **RICHARDSON HIGHWAY,** and Whittier on the west is about an hour's drive south of Anchorage on the **SEWARD HIGHWAY.** From there, take the road to Portage Glacier and pay $15–$40 round-trip to drive the toll road that opened in 2000 and shares the railroad tunnel through the mountains. Tunnel drive-through times can be picked up on the radio at AM 1610 near Portage, or AM 530 in Whittier. You can also call ahead or check the Web (907/566-2244 or 877/611-2586; www.dot.state.ak.us/creg/whittiertunnel/). If you don't take the train or drive through the tunnel, you'll need to find a small plane to charter.

Dotted throughout the sound are about 25 **PUBLIC-USE CABINS** managed by the U.S. Forest Service (Chugach National Forest, 3301 C St, Ste 300, Anchorage AK 99503-3998; 907/743-9500; 877/444-6777 or www.reserveusa.com for reservations) and Alaska State Parks (550 W 7th Ave, Ste 1260, Anchorage AK 99501-3357; 907/269-8400; pic@dnr.state.ak.us; www.dnr.state.ak.us/parks/parks.htm). Ask the Forest Service for the 30-page *Public Recreation Cabins: Chugach National Forest Alaska* that describes each cabin and its location. The cabins go for about $40 per night.

Whittier

South of Anchorage and through the mountains at the end of the tracks, where the road and railroad meet the sea, Whittier is the launching point for many Prince William Sound adventures. But Whittier itself is not a place to linger. The same mountains that isolate Whittier also trap storms over the town, which gets about 15 feet of rain and 20 feet of snow a year. If the sun does happen to shine, you will find yourself surrounded by mountains dripping with glaciers. But too often it is gray and dreary in Whittier, so the trick is to keep the visit short.

Until World War II, there was no Whittier. This may explain the rather unusual look of the town, which today depends primarily on fishing and tourism. Created as a major logistics center and built to be a self-contained U.S. Army community, Whittier has a notable feature: two 14-story towers, left behind when the army pulled out in 1963. One of these war relics stands empty, its windows broken. The second one is home to many of the town's 200 residents in upper-floor condominiums, while the lower floors house government offices, the library, and many local businesses.

More than half of the state's population lives less than an hour away from the tunnel to Whittier. In days of yore, the mountain and train tunnel provided limited access to the sound and Whittier with its 300-boat harbor. But after years of debate and controversy, the state of Alaska built a toll road, which opened in 2002, to the tiny town. Some folks expected the improved access would open a floodgate of visitors into the town, straining public services, but that hasn't happened yet. So far visitor numbers have remained roughly the same at 200,000 each summer. This has locals and state officials wondering whether the toll is too high.

ACCESS AND INFORMATION
Whittier looks awfully close to Anchorage on the map, but a wall of mountains in between makes it seem remote. Your options are to **DRIVE THE TOLL ROAD,** near Portage Glacier and the Begich, Boggs Visitor Center (see sidebar) or get on the **ALASKA RAILROAD PASSENGER TRAIN** (907/265-2607) in Anchorage, which departs midmorning, returns in the evening, and costs about $55 round-trip. To drive from Anchorage, go south on the Seward Highway and take the turnoff to Portage Glacier. (For more information on the glacier, see the Kenai Peninsula chapter.) The toll road shares the tunnel with the railroad, but generally is open to

MORE THAN JUST A VISITOR CENTER

The Chugach National Forest covers 5.3 million acres in Southcentral Alaska, and is home to breathtaking alpine ridges, spectacular hanging and tidewater glaciers, and picturesque Alaska communities and Native villages.

Let's face it—you'll never see everything. But you can get a quick yet detailed overview of the area's history, flora, fauna, marine life, people, and culture with one stop at the **BEGICH, BOGGS VISITOR CENTER** (5 miles off Seward Hwy near Mile 79; 907/783-2326; www.fs.fed.us/r10/chugach; open all week Memorial Day through Sept, weekends in winter). And all for free.

When the center first opened in 1986, it was one of the state's top attractions, drawing as many as 600,000 visitors a year. Those numbers have settled at about 300,000 a year. One reason may be that during that period, Portage Glacier, which at one time could be seen from the visitor center, receded out of sight. Still, the center has magnificent views of Portage Lake, floating icebergs, and hanging glaciers. And a private company offers ferry rides on the lake for more up-close glacier viewing.

A couple of years ago, the U.S. Forest Service completed a $2.4 million overhaul of the 5,000-square-foot center, making it part information center, part interactive science center, and part museum. Computer, video, sound, and interactive exhibits have replaced old-fashioned still photography and printed text. It's the kind of place where you can take kids, go back repeatedly, and learn something new each time. The center offers nature walks and an information desk is available to help you plan trips, find maps, or reserve Forest Service cabins.

A wall-size map of Alaska with enough information to give you a sense of the state's true size greets you upon entering the building. From the main room, the center is broken into a half-dozen rooms with different themes; varied lighting reflects the seasons and captures different ecosystems within the forest. A round room features "Alaskans and their Stories," with 18 recordings sharing pieces of the state's history. There are profiles of people from the region as well as from people describing the 1899 Harriman Expedition, the famous scientific voyage to study the natural and cultural history of Alaska. Or listen to the Eyak raven story, a traditional Native legend that tells how Raven brought sun and moon to earth by tricking the chief. In a room called "The Wild Side: Animals in the Chugach," try on animal masks—a bee, a Sitka black-tailed deer, or a sea otter—and see the world from a different point of view.

To learn about glaciers and ice worms—check out their ice-worm safaris. Left intact after the renovations was the center's 200-seat theater, which shows the popular 20-minute feature film "Voices from the Ice" hourly. Tickets to the show are $1.

—Natalie Phillips

car traffic every half hour or so. You can call ahead or check the Web for times (907/566-2244 or 877/611-2586; www.dot.state.ak.us/creg/whittiertunnel). The toll is $15 round-trip for passenger cars and $40 round-trip for RVs.

Much is up in the air as Whittier adjusts to the new toll road. For the latest information on services, accommodations, and other visitor information, contact the **CITY CLERK'S OFFICE IN WHITTIER** (907/472-2327).

Note that kayak and recreational boaters have more than doubled in Whittier and western Prince William Sound since the 1989 oil spill; July is the busiest month.

GUIDES AND OUTFITTERS

ALASKA OUTDOOR ADVENTURES / Two experienced and talented young Alaskans, Rudi and Natasha von Imhoff, offer kayak paddling in the sound as part of an wide-ranging menu of outdoor adventures. Beginners or enthusiasts with limited time can take an early morning, two-hour paddle, or take a full-day kayak trip out of Whittier, watching for marine wildlife. Prices range from $70–$110 per person. If you're visiting in winter, these folks lead dog-mushing and snowmobiling expeditions. Other activities range from horseback riding to sailing trips. Stop by their office in Whittier at the small boat harbor. *DIS, MC, V; checks OK; 9400 Vanguard, Ste B, Anchorage AK 99507; 907/276-2628 or 888/414-7669; fax 907/222-1898; info@akadventures.com; www.akadventures.com.*

HONEY CHARTERS AND ALASKA SEA KAYAKERS / These two businesses have teamed up to offer custom taxi charters and tours from whale-watching to glacier viewing to guided kayak trips. The water-taxi service also provides drop-offs for kayak trips and overnight stays in remote cabins. The boat can carry small or large groups. Alaska Sea Kayakers rents boats and provides instruction to new paddlers. In summer, their offices are side-by-side in the Harbor Triangle in Whittier. *DIS, MC, V; checks OK; operates May to Sept; Honey Charters, PO Box 708, Whittier AK 99693; 888/477-2493; honeycharters@hotmail.com; www.honeycharters.com; Alaska Sea Kayakers, PO Box 770, Whittier AK 99693; 877/472-2534; alaska seakayakers@yahoo.com; www.alaskaseakayakers.com.*

LAZY OTTER CHARTERS INC. / Located near the East Ramp in Whittier, Lazy Otter provides a water-taxi service for groups up to six people plus gear and is also available for sight-seeing, photography, and drop-offs for kayakers, scuba divers, and campers. They will take you anywhere in western Prince William Sound. Perry Passage and southern Knight Island are good places for seeing orca and humpback whales. *MC, V; checks OK; PO Box 747, Whittier AK 99693; 907/472-6887 or 888/587-6887; info@lazyotter.com; www.lazyotter.com.*

MAJOR MARINE TOURS / This tour offers a six-hour round-trip out of Whittier to Blackstone Bay. The boat, which holds 150 people, stays in fairly calm waters and travels past three tidewater glaciers, some quite dramatic and active. The fare runs about $100 per person, $50 for children under 11, which includes an all-you-can-eat salmon and prime rib buffet. They sometimes offer beginning- and end-of-the-season specials. *AE, DIS, MC, V; local checks only; operates May to Sept; PO Box 101400, Anchorage AK 99510; 907/274-7300; www.majormarine.com.*

NATIONAL OUTDOOR LEADERSHIP SCHOOL / The Wyoming-based school has an "outpost" in Palmer and offers kayaking trips through the sound. These trips (two–four weeks) are not only paddling experiences but also are designed to train group leaders and teach outdoor skills. They're set up for different age groups, including a master's course for folks 50 and older. The two-week trip costs between $2,000 and $2,600. *MC, V; checks OK; operates June to Aug; PO Box 981, Palmer AK 99645-0981; 907/745-4047; admissions@nols.edu; www.nols.edu.*

PHILLIPS' CRUISES AND TOURS / The 330-passenger, high-speed, but smooth sailing, *Klondike Express* travels through protected waters in Harriman and College Fjords and offers a six-hour whirlwind tour of 26 glaciers. They've been in business for more than 20 years and have this trip down to a science. The $130 per person ticket includes lunch (it's about $10 cheaper in either May or September). *AE, DIS, MC, V; checks OK; operates May to Sept; 519 W 4th Ave, Anchorage AK 99501; 907/276-8023 or 800/544-0529; info@26glaciers.com; www.26glaciers.com.*

PRINCE WILLIAM SOUND KAYAK CENTER / In business since 1981, the center rents single and double kayaks at daily and weekly rates, offers guided day trips, or will provide an escort who serves as a group leader. But you're on your own as camp cooks. Prices run $45 per day to $275 per week, per person. Make reservations well in advance. *MC, V; checks OK; operates May to Sept; PO Box 622, Whittier AK 99693; 907/472-2452; pwskayak@aol.com; www.pwskayakcenter.com.*

SOUND ECO ADVENTURES / This charter is operated by retired marine biologist Gerry Sanger. He specializes in natural-history tours and whale-watching, but he also provides water-taxi services for kayakers or folks headed for remote cabins or campsites and has a boat that is designed for wheelchair access. *MC, V; checks OK; operates March to Nov; PO Box 707, Whittier AK 99693; 907/472-2312 or 888/471-2312; sea@alaska.net; www.soundecoadventure.com.* &

WILDERNESS ALASKA / In business since 1972, Wilderness Alaska began with trips into Alaska's Brooks Range and the Arctic National Wildlife Refuge. In recent years, the outfitters have responded to demands for trips to explore Prince William Sound. So the company added a range of sea kayaking trips that accommodate beginner to seasoned paddlers. Check the Web for their trip schedule. Trips generally range from 3 days ($795 per person) to 12 days ($1,900 per person). *MC, V; checks OK; operates May to Sept; PO Box 113063, Anchorage AK 99511; 907/345-3567; fax 907-345-3967; macgill@alaska.net; www.wildernessalaska.com.*

RESTAURANTS

Hobo Bay Trading Company / ★

I WINDY PL, WHITTIER; 907/472-2374 Babs has been running this little joint for nearly 25 years. She's a local renegade who usually can be found in the thick of local politics. Fishermen resupplying in Whittier will always treat themselves to a Babs Burger or a Buffalo Babs Burger made with real buffalo meat. Her burgers—beef or buffalo—have a bite. They come with a hot pepper on top. She also serves Alaska-made ice cream and pies. *$; No credit cards; checks "under protest"; lunch, dinner Thurs–Mon (closed mid-Sept to mid-May); no alcohol; near the harbormaster's steel blue building.*

Varly's Swiftwater Cafe / ★★☆

ON THE TRIANGLE, WHITTIER; 907/472-2550 In business for more than five years, this restaurant has become a favorite of locals and those passing through. This is the place to go for fresh Prince William Sound seafood, including halibut, side-striped shrimp, and rockfish. Everything is served deep-fried, fish-and-chips style. Don Varlamos also keeps fresh clam and seafood chowder on the stove. On Friday and Saturday nights he offers a smoked prime rib dinner. Wash it all down with one of 30 different kinds of pilsners and ales. *$; MC, V; checks OK ("good ones"); lunch, dinner every day, Apr to Sept; beer and wine; reservations recommended on weekends.*

Valdez

This little oil town is known as the Switzerland of Alaska because of its jagged, snow-capped peaks and emerald green mountain slopes. The name Valdez is Spanish. But to pronounce it correctly is to mispronounce it to most Alaskan's ears. Here you say "Val-deez." The town is home to 3,500 people, averages 26 feet of rain a year, and its record snowfall is more than 46 feet!

The town has seen its share of booms and busts. Around the turn of the century, Valdez was one port of entry to the rich goldfields in the Canadian Klondike. The gold route from Valdez to the Klondike was advertised all over the United States and drew about 4,000 hopeful gold seekers. A tent town sprang up and some of the miners stuck around. They later hacked a dogsled trail into the Interior, to the gold-rush town of Fairbanks, some 400 miles away. This was followed by a rough wagon route, which eventually became known as the Richardson Highway.

By the 1920s, the population was declining and stayed that way through the greatest earthquake ever recorded on the North American continent. The epicenter for that quake was in Prince William Sound. On the Friday before Easter in 1964, late in the afternoon, a terrifying force let loose, measuring 8.6 on the Richter scale. The ensuing tsunami created waves that swept over the dock and town. Thirty-two people died, including two people aboard a steamer tied to the dock.

In the late 1960s, the town's population began to swell again. Oil was discovered on the North Slope and Valdez was chosen to be the terminus for the 800-mile Trans-Alaska Pipeline. Work on the 48-inch diameter pipeline began in 1974 and, during construction, the town's population swelled to 10,000. When construction ended in 1977, the town's population plummeted to 3,500. It stayed there until 1989 when, ironically on Good Friday, exactly 25 years after the earthquake, disaster struck again. The *Exxon Valdez* oil tanker ran aground at Bligh Reef, spilling 11 million gallons of North Slope crude oil into the pristine waters of Prince William Sound. Alaskans were devastated. And yet, in one of those twists of fate that often occur, the ensuing massive cleanup effort ushered in another economic boom for Alaska's Switzerland.

But don't expect to roll into this industry town today and get the latest environmental statistics on Prince William Sound. Oil is still king here, so the spill is something most locals are not anxious to talk about. If you want to retrace a little history on your own, however, check out the Pipeline Club (see review below). It's the bar where Captain Joe Hazelwood of *Exxon Valdez* fame had that Scotch on the rocks before his ship ended up on the rocks at Bligh Reef.

Roughly 40 tankers are filled with crude at the Valdez terminal monthly; the pipeline's carrying capacity is 1.16 million barrels of oil a day. Touring the terminal used to be a popular tourist attraction, but the tour business was suspended indefinitely for security reasons following the September 11, 2001, terrorist attack on the East Coast.

ACCESS AND INFORMATION

The **DRIVE** from Anchorage to Valdez makes for a long day, but it is a beautiful one along the Glenn and Richardson Highways. **ALASKA AIRLINES** (800/252-7522; www.alaskaair.com) has regularly scheduled flights. Or you can take the train or drive the toll road (see Prince William Sound, Access and Information) through the mountains to Whittier from Anchorage and board the ferry to Valdez on the **ALASKA MARINE HIGHWAY SYSTEM** (800/642-0066; www.alaska.gov/ferry). This seven-hour trip through the sound passes near the Columbia Glacier.

The **VALDEZ CONVENTION & VISITORS BUREAU'S VISITORS INFORMATION CENTER** (907/835-2984 or 800/770-5954; info@valdezalaska.org; www.valdez alaska.org) is located at the intersection of Chenega and Fairbanks Drives. **ONE CALL DOES IT ALL** (907/835-4988; travel@ocdia.com; www.ocdia.com) is a co-op of bed-and-breakfasts and boat/plane charters that offers free reservation and information services.

EXPLORING

MAXINE & JESSE WHITNEY MUSEUM / Prince William Sound Community College opened the Whitney Museum in the summer of 1999 after it received a private collection of Eskimo art from the Whitneys, who arrived in Alaska in 1946. They started their own collection and for about 15 years ran the Eskimo Museum near Fairbanks. The displays include an extensive collection of ivory, trophy mounted wildlife, full-size kayaks, and skin boats called umiaks, and is reputed to be the largest private collection of Native Alaska art and artifacts in the world. *Call for hours; PO Box 97, Valdez AK 99686; 907/834-1690; www.uaa.alaska.edu/pwscc/museum/; at the Valdez Airport, 3.5 miles out of town.*

VALDEZ MUSEUM / The museum has relics of Valdez's past, starting with the gold-rush years. Open year-round, it features two restored fire engines, an 1896 hand pumper, a 1907 steam engine, and an exhibit on the history of oil. The new annex is open only during summer and focuses on the 1964 earthquake. Nominal admission fee. *9am–6pm Mon–Sat, 8am–5pm Sun (summer), shorter winter hours; 217 Egan St (main), 436 S Hazelet Ave (annex); 907/835-2764; vldzmuse@alaska.net; www.alaska.net/~vldzmuse/.*

ADVENTURES

BACKCOUNTRY SKIING / Skiing in the Thompson Pass area is booming. With miles of untracked powder, local entrepreneurs have figured out ways to get skiers up and down the mountains. **AIR CHARTERS**—both helicopter and fixed-wing planes on skis—can give you a lift to the top of a 1,000-foot run. This is steep terrain with tons of windblown snow. You need to be aware of avalanches. Be trained in assessing the dangers, know the precautions, and bring the appropriate gear. Try **ALASKA BACK-COUNTRY ADVENTURES** (907/835-5608, winter; 907/283-9354, summer; ski@ alaskabackcountry.com; alaskabackcountry.com). During the peak spring months for skiing, also try **VALDEZ HELI-SKI GUIDES** (907/835-4528; ski@valdezheliski guides.com; www.valdezheliskiguides.com) or **VALDEZ H20 HELI-ADVENTURES** (800/578-4354; dean@h2oguides.com; www.h2oguides.com;). For guided backcountry skiing or touring, call Matt Kinney with **THOMPSON PASS TREKS** (907/835-4817; chalet@alaska.net; www.alaska.net/~chalet).

COLUMBIA GLACIER / This is one of the most active tidewater glaciers in Alaska. It has been rapidly receding since 1978 and has lost about 6 miles of its once-spectacular face. The trip to Columbia takes you through the Valdez Narrows and out into the sound heading west. On the way, you pass two marine parks popular for camping and fishing. Outfitters who offer trips to the glacier include **PRINCE WILLIAM SOUND CRUISES AND TOURS** and **ANADYR SEA KAYAK ADVENTURES** (see Guides and Outfitters, below).

HIKING TRAILS / For information, find the **U.S. FOREST SERVICE VISITORS CENTER** on the edge of town. It's open only in summer (907/835-4680; in winter call 907/424-7661). Two popular hiking trails are the **SOLOMAN GULCH TRAIL**, which leads up from the fish hatchery to Soloman Lake, and the **GOAT TRAIL**, which follows the original road through Keystone Canyon to Valdez. The Goat Trail trailhead is at Horsetail Falls, about 13.5 miles out of Valdez. A newer 10-mile trail starts in Valdez and goes out to **SHOUP BAY STATE MARINE PARK** in the Valdez Arm. There, three state-park cabins are available to rent for overnight use through Alaska State Parks (550 W 7th Ave, Ste 1260, Anchorage AK 99501; 907/269-8400; pic@dnr.state.ak.us; www.dnr.state.ak.us/parks/).

THE RICHARDSON HIGHWAY / This road leads north out of Valdez toward the Alaska Interior. The road first winds up past Bridal Veil and Horsetail Falls through Keystone Canyon to Thompson Pass. About 30 miles from Valdez, **THOMPSON PASS** is spectacular and notable for holding most of the state's highest snowfall records. Near the top is the turnoff for **WORTHINGTON GLACIER STATE RECREATION AREA**. You can drive to the face of Worthington Glacier. All along the Richardson Highway to Glennallen, you will get glimpses of the Trans-Alaska Pipeline. The road cuts between the mountains of the **WRANGELL-ST. ELIAS NATIONAL PARK AND PRESERVE** (see The Roads North chapter). To the east are impressive Mounts Wrangell, Drum, Sanford, and Blackburn, some of Alaska's most picturesque summits. Just 30 miles shy of Glennallen is the community of **COPPER CENTER**. The tiny town, which sits on the banks of the **COPPER RIVER**, was founded in the gold-rush year of 1898. An old fish wheel still sits in the river.

GUIDES AND OUTFITTERS

ANADYR SEA KAYAK ADVENTURES / Anadyr offers an assortment of trips, from three-hour paddles out of Valdez to daylong trips to Shoup and Columbia Glaciers to lodge-based or mothership-supported, either sailboat or powerboat, multiday tours. In business since 1990, owner Hedy Sarney will also help you plan a longer, custom-designed trip and will rent kayaks to experienced boaters. Anadyr picked up the business of Alaska Wilderness Sailing and Kayaking recently when Jim and

Nancy Lethecoe retired. The Lethecoes, well-known authors on books about the sound, plan to continue to live aboard their sailboat in the sound and do guide training for Anadyr. Sarney now has their fleet of WindRiders, which are a hybrid kayak with outriggers and a sail. These very stable, fun little boats let you scoot around, in and out of coves effortlessly. *AE, DIS, MC, V; checks OK; Apr to Sept; 225 N Harbor Dr, PO Box 1821, Valdez AK 99686; 907/835-2814 or 800/TOK-AYAK (865-2925); anadyr@alaska.net; www.anadyradventures.com.*

KEYSTONE RAFT AND KAYAK ADVENTURES / This outfit has one of the most popular river trips—a thrilling ride down the Lowe River through Keystone Canyon with Class III rapids, costing $35–$60 per person. Two other popular half-day and day trips are down the Tasina River and the Tonsina River. They also offer multiday trips down the Copper River for about $875 per person. You can go by raft, or experienced whitewater kayakers can sign up for packages that include running a variety of nearby rivers. Keystone supplies the support. *MC, V; checks OK; May to Sept; PO Box 1486, Valdez AK 99686; 907/835-2606; keystone@alaska.net; www.alaska whitewater.com.*

PRINCE WILLIAM SOUND CRUISES AND TOURS / Formerly known as Stan Stephens Cruises, this business has been around for nearly 20 years. They offer a nine-hour trip to Columbia and Meares Glaciers, or a six-hour trip to Columbia Glacier. Both trips include a stop to see the Bull's Head sea lion haul out. Trip costs range from $80 to $120 per person. *AE, DIS, MC, V; checks OK; PO Box 1297, Valdez AK 99686; 800/992-1297; fax 907-835-3765; info@princewilliamsound. com; www.princewilliamsound.com.*

FESTIVALS AND EVENTS

EXTREME SKIING CHAMPIONSHIPS / For years, every spring some of the world's top extreme skiers—those daredevils who leap off of 45-degree slopes—gather in Valdez. The thrill seekers pick the steepest and most dangerous run down death-defying slopes around exposed rocks and over cliffs (a helicopter ferries competitors to the top). Called the **WORLD FREE SKIING CHAMPIONSHIPS**, judges award points in the event for aggressiveness, form, fluidity, and control. An umbrella event, the **CHUGACH MOUNTAIN FESTIVAL**, includes the skiing daredevils as well as mountain-bike races and orienteering competitions. Bring your binoculars. *Call Scott Matthews at 206/935-4464; www.xonet.org (click on the links).*

THE LAST FRONTIER THEATRE CONFERENCE / Sponsored by Prince William Sound Community College, the theater conference has been drawing hundreds of playwrights and theater buffs from around the country for a decade now. The "god-father" of the event is triple Pulitzer Prize winner Edward Albee. It's a wonderful chance for Alaska's own community theater organizers to rub elbows with New York City's finest. Held in mid-June at the Valdez Civic Center, the conference features workshops, critiques, and readings. Cost is about $100 per person for the five-day event. *Prince William Sound Community College, PO Box 97, Valdez AK 99686; 907/834-1612 or 800/478-8800; fax 907/834-1611; vntc@uaa.alaska.edu; www.uaa.alaska.edu/pwscc.*

RESTAURANTS

Alaska Halibut House

208 MEALS AVE, VALDEZ; 907/835-2788 This place is a favorite for locals because the food is cheap and fast, but it's not McDonald's. The restaurant features fresh Alaska halibut, a salad bar, and a variety of hamburgers. *$; MC, V; local checks only; breakfast, lunch, dinner every day (summer); lunch, dinner (winter); no alcohol; no reservations.* &

Mike's Palace Ristorante / ★★

201 N HARBOR DR, VALDEZ; 907/835-2365 Owner Mike Panagis's menu runs the gamut from steak and seafood to lasagna, pizza, and enchiladas. While the pizzas are alluring and come with thin, thick, or really thick crusts, many diners swear by the lasagna. It's a cozy restaurant with a view of the harbor. The walls, covered with old newspapers, tell the history of Valdez. *$$; MC, V; local checks only; lunch, dinner every day; beer and wine; no reservations; directly across from the harbor.* &

Pipeline Club Restaurant

112 EGAN DR, VALDEZ; 907/835-4891 This is where the tanker crews and fishermen head for steak and seafood dinners. The restaurant's specialty is Pipeline Pu Pu, created by a chef from the Hawaiian Islands. In Valdez, the dish is made with sliced steak sautéed with onion, bell pepper, soy sauce, tomato, and seasoning, and then served on a bed of rice. Stick your head into the bar next door, where Captain Hazelwood had that famous Scotch on the rocks. Or was it two? *$$$; DC, MC, V; local checks only; dinner every day; full bar; no reservations; in the town center, sandwiched between the Valdez Motel and the Westmark Inn.* &

LODGINGS

Blueberry Mary's Bed and Breakfast / ★★

810 SALMONBERRY WAY, BLUEBERRY HILL, VALDEZ; 907/835-5015 One of only two B&Bs located on the ocean. Each room (there are two) has a private entrance and ocean views, feather beds, and private baths. They share a kitchenette and sauna and go for $90, double occupancy. Mary serves a full breakfast, which most often includes blueberry waffles since blueberries in season grow all over the hillside. No smoking. *$; No credit cards; checks OK; open Memorial Day to Oct; bmary@ alaska.net; www.alaska.net/~bmary; about 1 mile from downtown.*

The Lake House Bed and Breakfast / ★★

MILE 6 RICHARDSON HWY, VALDEZ; 907/835-4752; FAX 907/835-9060 Like a country inn, far from the hustle of town, this home perched on a bluff has wide decks overlooking Robe Lake. In 2000, a former mayor and candidate for governor bought this B&B and did some remodeling. The setting is remote, yet only 10 minutes from downtown Valdez. Mountains can be seen from every window and all rooms have private baths. Prices, at $110 double occupancy, include a continental breakfast and a complimentary bottle of wine. *$$; MC, V; checks OK; open year-round; jhdvns@aol.com; www.geocities.com/lakehousevaldez.*

Thompson Pass Mountain Chalet / ★

MILE 19 RICHARDSON HWY, VALDEZ; 907/835-4817 This mountain chalet is north of town at Thompson Pass. Owner Matt Kinney guides backcountry telemark skiing, randonée skiing, and snowboarding trips. In the summer he leads hikes. The private chalet has a stocked kitchenette and private shower. It accommodates up to four people. Rates are $120 a night, double occupancy (family rates available). *$; No credit cards; checks OK; www.alaska.net/~chalet; chalet@ alaska.net; drive to Mile 19 on the Richardson Hwy—from there it is a ½-mile drive on a dirt road in summer or short ski or snowmachine ride in winter.*

Wild Rose's by the Sea B&B Retreat / ★★

629 FIDDLEHEAD LN, VALDEZ; 907/835-2930 This deluxe bed-and-breakfast has a spectacular view of Valdez Narrows and surrounding mountains. It's close to the new hiking trail that goes out to Shoup Bay. Rose has three guest rooms; the Guesthouse Room has its own living room and dining area and is quite private. One room also has a whirlpool. She does the full-breakfast routine, featuring fresh baked goods, fruit, and a hot dish, usually a soufflé. Double occupancy rates run $125–$140 a night. *$$; MC, V; no checks; rbm@alaska.net; www.bytheseaalaska. com; about 1 mile from town.*

Cordova

Isolated and quaint, this fishing community is the hidden gem of Prince William Sound. The docks are lined with weathered canneries. The harbor brims with a fat fleet of mom-and-pop commercial fishing boats. The streets and hillsides are dotted with sun-worn bungalows. It's the kind of place where stray mutts wander down Main Street and everybody knows them by name. You won't need a car; everything is within walking distance.

Out Cordova's back door is the Copper River Delta, an immensely lush and diverse ecosystem fed by six glacial rivers. The town's history is rich with stories of trade and conflict among Natives, Russians, copper miners, and oil explorers. Cordova is strategically situated amid enormous runs of salmon and a bounty of shellfish. It was fish that reeled in the first Americans, who came to build a cannery here in 1889.

Michael J. Heney, a brilliant engineer who also designed the White Pass & Yukon Railroad out of Skagway, showed up a few years later to direct the building of the Copper River and Northwestern Railway, which winds alongside the Copper River 200 miles to McCarthy and Kennicott, towns built on the fortunes of copper and nestled in the Wrangell Mountains. Until the 1930s, Cordova thrived as a supply depot for the copper mines there and for the oil fields at Katalla, about 45 miles southeast of Cordova on the Gulf of Alaska.

About 2,500 people live here year-round now, but the town nearly doubles when fishing starts in spring. It's an eclectic group of commercial fishermen, artists, intellectuals, Eyak Natives, and plain end-of-the-roaders. They live in bungalows clinging to steep slopes overlooking Orca Inlet or in old boathouses along Odiak

HEAD TO THE BEACH FOR SHOREBIRD FESTIVAL

Dunlins, western sandpipers, dowitchers, and godwits. They come by the millions every spring on their 2,000-mile journey from South America, the Pacific Islands, and Asia to their nesting grounds in western Alaska's Yukon-Kuskokwim Delta. And they can be spotted when they layover on the mud-rich tidal flats of Alaska's Southcentral coast to feed on small invertebrates and fly larvae.

It's a short visit, but for bird-watchers it is an event not to miss. There's about a two-week window in early May when thousands of these birds can be seen in two main locations in Alaska—Cordova and Homer. Each town offers a slightly different bird-watching experience, but each town hosts a shorebird festival that draws hundreds of avid bird-watchers to their waters' edges. (See Kenai Peninsula chapter for more on Homer's festival).

The **COPPER RIVER DELTA SHOREBIRD FESTIVAL** in Cordova (907/424-7260; cchamber@ctcak.net; www.ptialaska.net/~midtown/) is the state's oldest shorebird festival and has been held the first or second week of May for more than 13 years. As many as 5 million shorebirds, mostly dunlins and sandpipers, are estimated to pass through the Cordova area. The Copper River Delta is also home to trumpeter swans, dusky Canada geese, mallards, northern pintails, and shovelers. Homer's decade-old, mid-May festival is also a good bet, but Cordova offers a chance to see a greater variety of migrating birds, including Pacific golden plovers and surfbirds, according to Stan Senner, executive director of Alaska Audubon.

—Natalie Phillips

Slough. The town has a reputation for making room for just about anybody, but at the same time it can become fiercely divided over any political issue. Everyone has an opinion. Just mention "the road." You'll get an earful. There's a big debate—more than a decade old—about whether a road should be built to connect Cordova to the rest of the world.

Once upon a time, there were plans to build the Copper River Highway on top of the old railroad tracks that run up the Copper River to Chitina, where the road would link with the rest of Alaska. Construction began in the 1960s, but the 1964 earthquake buckled the Million Dollar Bridge, bringing the project to a halt. In recent years, there has been talk of renewing the project. Those who like the isolation of the surrounding mountains and the sea don't want the road. Those who want it say it will bring new blood and a more reasonable cost of living.

In late April and early May, the town bustles with bird-watchers. They are followed by a wave of commercial fishermen who fish 24-hour openings, and then return to Cordova, where you'll see them down in the harbor mending their nets and gearing up for the next opening. The season ends in late August, and the town is pretty quiet until spring rolls around again. But locals will tell you that since the

1989 Exxon Valdez oil spill, the town has been on a slow downward spiral. Fishing hasn't been the same, but it's hard to sort out how much of that has been caused by the spill, changing economies, or the naturally changing ecosystem. It's mild but wet here, with an average of 15 feet of rain a year. Don't expect the shops to stay open if it's sunny.

ACCESS AND INFORMATION

There are only two ways into Cordova, which is one of its beauties. You can fly in from Anchorage, Juneau, or Seattle on **ALASKA AIRLINES** (800/252-7522; www. alaskaair.com), or you can take the **ALASKA MARINE HIGHWAY** (800/642-0066; www.alaska.gov/ferry) ferry from Whittier or Valdez. From Whittier, it's about a seven-hour ferry ride. If you fly, the Mudhole Smith Airport, named for an early bush pilot, is located about 12 miles out of town and has a shuttle service.

On weekdays, the **CORDOVA CHAMBER OF COMMERCE'S VISITORS CENTER** (1st Ave downtown, PO Box 99, Cordova AK 99574; 907/424-7260; cchamber@ ctcak.net; www.ctcak.net/~cchamber) offers a wealth of information. Next door is **ORCA BOOK & SOUND CO.** (907/424-5305), also a good place for books, maps, and information. The sandwich shop in the back is a good place for a quick lunch.

EXPLORING

MOUNT EYAK SKI AREA / If the winter skies are clear and you can round up a group of six or so, the folks here will fire up the vintage chairlift to take you to the top of Mount Eyak. You'll have a spectacular view of Orca Inlet and miles beyond. Plus, you'll get to sit where Clark Gable and Marilyn Monroe once sat. This very same chairlift hoisted famous authors and movie stars such as Ernest Hemingway, Groucho Marx, Ingrid Bergman, Lucille Ball, and John Wayne to the top of the mountains in Sun Valley, Idaho, from 1936 to 1969. It's been in Cordova since 1974, and "you can't beat the view from here," says David Bradshaw, local chairlift historian. For more information, call 907/424-7766.

PRINCE WILLIAM SOUND SCIENCE CENTER / This independent, nonprofit research facility, housed down on the docks, is funded in part with settlement money from the 1989 *Exxon Valdez* oil spill. The work of the center focuses on the complex ecosystem of the sound. Interpretive signs have been installed on the decks that explain commercial fishing and explain where different hatcheries are in the sound. A second set of signs focus on the natural history of the area and include artwork by local artist Susan Ogle, whose husband can be found at the local bookstore. Tours are available during business hours upon request. *PO Box 705, Cordova AK 99574; 907/424-5800; www.pwssc.gen.ak.us.*

ADVENTURES

MOUNTAIN BIKES AND KAYAKS / For rentals and information on where to go, try **CORDOVA COASTAL OUTFITTERS** for just about any outdoor gear you can think of, ranging from kayaks and canoes to camping gear and fishing equipment. *PO Box 1834, Cordova AK 99574; 907/424-7424.*

CHILDS GLACIER AND THE MILLION DOLLAR BRIDGE / The bridge and glacier are 52 miles out of town, on the old Copper River Road. Impressive and close, the 300-foot wall of ice sits across the Copper River. Thunderous calving of ice off the glacier echoes from the steel beams of the bent bridge, which buckled during the 1964 earthquake. You can still walk across the bridge. To get there, call Becky at **COPPER RIVER NORTHWEST TOURS** (907/424-5356), hitch a ride, take a taxi, or rent a car.

COPPER RIVER DELTA / A rich, diverse ecosystem and breeding ground for all sorts of waterfowl, the Copper River flows 250 miles through the Chugach Mountains to the sound. It is a strong, turbulent river that produces highly prized red, or sockeye, salmon. Because of the firm, meaty flesh and layer of belly fat, Copper River salmon rank as the state's most delicious wild salmon. The best way to see the delta, including the glacier and the bridge, is to call Becky Chapek at **COPPER RIVER NORTHWEST TOURS** (see above). She runs bus tours to the delta as needed and when the cruise ships are in and offers a narrative on the area's history and wildlife with a snack thrown in. Hardy bike riders also can jump on for a one-way ride to the glacier, pedaling back at their own pace. Northwest Tours will do trail drops.

The U.S. Forest Service Cordova Ranger District maintains about 37 miles of **TRAILS** on the Copper River Delta and a dozen wilderness **PUBLIC-USE CABINS**, ranging from $25–$45 per night. For information and reservations, contact the ranger district (PO Box 280, Cordova AK 99574; 907/424-7661; 877/444-6777, reservations; www.reserveusa.com).

GUIDES AND OUTFITTERS

ALASKA WILDERNESS OUTFITTING COMPANY / Choose from fly-in fishing, adventure trips, hiking, kayaking, or wildlife viewing. This company has floating cabins in Simpson and Sheep Bays, cabins on shore, guided trips, and do-it-yourself trips where they'll set you up in a fully stocked cabin with a motorboat, and then leave you on your own; you bring only sleeping bags and fishing gear. Before dropping you off, they'll fly you over the best fishing streams in the area. (They do leave you with a radio, in case of emergency.) You can even opt for a combo trip—three days of saltwater fishing, then off to a remote camp in the Wrangell Mountains for freshwater rainbow- and lake-trout fishing. Costs for five-day trips run $1,200–$3,000 per person. *MC, V; checks OK; operates June to Sept; PO Box 1516, Cordova AK 99574; 907/424-5552; www.alaskawilderness.com.*

FISHING AND FLYING / These folks offer flight-seeing or drop-offs to the area's many remote Forest Service and state park cabins or their own fishing camps on the Katalla River and Tebay Lake. They also offer day flight-seeing trips to McCarthy. *AE, MC, V; local checks only; PO Box 2349, Cordova AK 99574; 907/424-3324.*

RESTAURANTS

Baja Taco / ★

NICHOLOFF ST AT THE HARBOR, CORDOVA; 907/424-5599 This funky red school bus serves a mean burrito and scrumptious fish tacos. Its menu, featured on a surfboard, stands next to the bus. The owners spend enough time in Mexico each winter to know how to keep the food spicy. *$; No credit cards; local checks only; lunch, dinner every day (closed Oct to Apr); no alcohol; PO Box 1748, Cordova AK 99574.*

Killer Whale Cafe / ★

507 1ST AVE, CORDOVA; 907/424-7733 This little deli and coffee shop in the back of Orca Book & Sound Co. is right in the center of town and a favorite espresso stop. It also serves hearty soups and bulky sandwiches. The cheesecake is a killer. The bookstore makes nice browsing, with its eclectic collection of fine literature and local art. *$; No credit cards; checks OK; breakfast, lunch Mon to Sat; no alcohol; downtown.*

Lighthouse Inn

CORDOVA HARBOR, CORDOVA; 907/424-7080 This new addition in Cordova was a welcomed one. Lisa Marie and Glenn Van Dyke specialize in breads made with freshly ground whole wheat, rye, or unbleached white flour and baked in a wood-fired brick oven. They also make fresh pastries and Danishes with real butter. They serve breakfast and lunch, including pizzas baked in the brick oven, but locals caution that service can be on the slow side. Upstairs they have four rooms ($90 for a double) that include private baths and cable television and views of the surrounding mountains or the harbor. *$; MC, V; checks OK; breakfast, lunch; closed Mondays; no alcohol; mamav@ctcak.net; www.cordovalighthouseinn.com.*

LODGINGS

The Blue Heron Inn / ★★

ORCA RD, CORDOVA; 907/424-3554 Another old cannery turned quaint bed-and-breakfast. You can rent the entire downstairs of this cannery, complete with kitchen, private entrance, and waterfall out back. There's also an upstairs suite. It's a short walk across the road to Fleming Spit and first-class salmon fishing. Either suite goes for $100, double occupancy; add $20 for each additional person. *$$; MC, V; checks OK; blueheron@ctcak.net; www.ptialaska.net/~heron/net; located north of the ferry terminal, 1½ miles north of downtown on Orca Rd.*

Cordova Rose Lodge / ★★

1315 WHITSHED RD, CORDOVA; 907/424-7673; FAX 907/424-3854 (CALL FIRST) Permanently dry-docked in Odiak Slough next to an operating lighthouse, the old barge (now lodge) is filled with nautical artifacts. Stay in the Captain's Quarters, the Officer's Quarters, or the Chief's Quarters. However, if you chose the Stowaway Room, the smallest and simplest, you're not allowed to complain. The joke is that they follow the rules of the sea here, and you know what happens to stowaways. Rates are $90 a night, single or double. Because the barge is on the slough, it is popular with bird-watchers. *$$; MC, V; checks OK; info@cordovarose.com; www.cordovarose.com; ¼ mile from downtown—go east on 1st, turn right on Whitshed.*

Orca Adventure Lodge

2 MILES NORTH OF TOWN, CORDOVA; 866-424-ORCA (6722); FAX 907/424-3759 This is a classic old cannery turned into headquarters for all sorts of outdoor adventures, from fishing and river rafting, to ice climbing and heli-skiing. Guests have access to the lodge's toys, including mountain bikes, fishing gear, kayaks, and canoes. The cost is $185 per night per person, but that includes all meals. Or you can arrange a package price that includes an adventure. *$$$; MC, V; checks OK; PO Box 2105, Cordova AK 99574; orca@ctcak.net; www.orcaadventurelodge.com.*

Reluctant Fisherman Inn

401 RAILROAD AVE, CORDOVA; 907/424-3272 OR 800/770-3272; FAX 907/424-7465 If it's predictability and the conveniences of a standard hotel you're looking for, stay here. Rates run from $105–$135, double occupancy. Ask for a room facing the harbor. You will pay more than you would for rooms without the view, but it's worth it. *$$; AE, DC, DIS, MC, V; checks OK; info@reluctantfisherman.com; www.reluctant@ctcak.net; 1 block from downtown.* &

KENAI PENINSULA

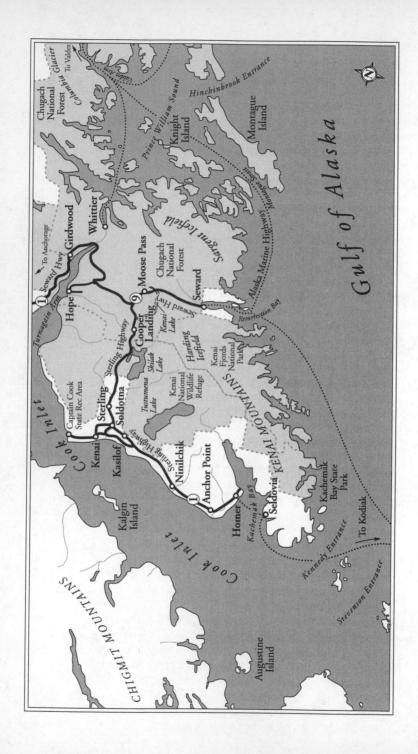

KENAI PENINSULA

The Kenai Peninsula dramatically extends from Alaska's southcentral shoreline into the northern reaches of the Gulf of Alaska. On the west, it is washed by the strong currents of Cook Inlet, named after British Captain James Cook, who explored the area in the 1700s. To the east is Prince William Sound. Nearly severing the peninsula from the mainland are Turnagain Arm's turbulent waters, where Captain Cook made his famous U-turn after realizing he had failed to find the Northwest Passage.

The peninsula's surface was carved over thousands of years by the slow grinding of advancing and receding glaciers. As the ice withdrew, humans moved in. The earliest inhabitants date back 8,500 to 10,000 years. Populations of Eskimos, Aleuts, and Athabascan Indians have made their mark, and the Kenaitze, a Dena'ina Athabascan tribe, can be thanked for giving the peninsula its name. Influences of Russian colonization during the 1700s can still be found in the names of families and villages. The onion-domed orthodox church in Ninilchik, silhouetted against the Chigmit Mountains' snow-covered volcanoes on the far shore of Cook Inlet, is a favorite subject for many photographers and artists.

Hunger for gold left its impact on the Kenai Peninsula, from Seward to Hope, and extending south to Homer. Rusted remnants of mining operations and the stories told by descendants of these early settlers add a sparkle to the area's history. Seeing land as the prize, rather than gold, others were drawn by homesteading opportunities. Carving a home out of the wilderness was as backbreaking as mining. Log homes provided shelter, gardens thrived during the long days of summer and provided fresh vegetables, and abundant wildlife kept meat on the table.

Until the late 1950s, commercial fish traps dotted the shores of Cook Inlet. Today, cork lines of set nets stretch out into the inlet's blue waters. The peninsula's fishing fleet reels out drift nets in the hope of catching salmon that make their way into the inlet, searching for the rivers of their birth. For many fishermen, this summer activity is a way of life that has been with their families for generations.

Then there's sportfishing. In 1985, Les Anderson caught a $97\frac{1}{4}$-pound king salmon in the Kenai River. Since then, crowds of single-minded enthusiasts line peninsula riverbanks or float the currents each summer to meet or beat Anderson's record. Fishing charter businesses offer opportunities to shove off from shore and drop a hook in fresh or salt water. With five species of Pacific salmon making the peninsula home, several communities host derbies. A halibut weighing over 400-pounds is another record begging to be broken. And a $1\frac{1}{2}$-pound, 8-inch long razor clam, preserved and displayed at Tustumena Lodge, has yet to be outdone.

More than once, Kenai Peninsula residents have risen from the ashes, thanks to their fiery neighbors across the inlet. Looking cool and calm beneath coverings of snow and ice are Mounts Spurr, Redoubt, Iliamna, Augustine, and Douglas, part of the Chigmit Mountains and the northern end of the Ring of Fire, a formation of volcanoes and active seismic areas that rim the Pacific Ocean. The most recent eruption, by 11,070-foot Spurr in 1992, forced the closure of the Anchorage airport. The last eruption of Redoubt, over a two-week period at the end of 1989, sent a cloud of ash 12 miles into the air and created a lightning storm that flash-danced along the horizon.

Wildlife abounds on the peninsula. Keep your eyes open for bear, caribou, and moose. Dall sheep and mountain goats defy gravity as they scale jagged mountain slopes. Venturing offshore, you may be rewarded with sightings of whales, including humpbacks, grays, orcas, fins, and beluga, as well as Steller's sea lions, seals, and otters. The sky is filled with winged visitors, such as the magnificent bald eagle and the Arctic tern that travels through on its way from the Arctic to the Antarctic.

Once a covering of snow softens the contours of the land, out come the snow machines, skis, snowboards, and snowshoes. You can ice fish on some frozen lakes. Dog mushing is a favorite sport. Beginners compete with champions in the Tustumena 200, a qualifying event for the world-famous Iditarod Trail Sled Dog Race.

All of this is set against a breathtaking backdrop of scenery, beginning with Portage Glacier positioned at the peninsula's doorstep. Its chilly welcome draws a half-million visitors every year and is the state's number one attraction. And from there, the welcome just gets warmer as the door opens into a treasure house of towering mountains, turquoise lakes, glacial green rivers, and rolling surf.

ACCESS AND INFORMATION

Traveling by **LAND, AIR, OR SEA** will bring you to the Kenai Peninsula. The Seward and Sterling Highways are favored routes. Commuter flights connect to Anchorage and several communities have air strips that accommodate smaller aircraft. Harbors in Seward, Seldovia, and Homer welcome cruise ships, Alaska state ferries, and private boats.

The **SEWARD HIGHWAY** runs from Anchorage to Seward. An hour and a half out of Anchorage is the turnoff to Hope, where a 17-mile drive leads to this small community founded as a mining settlement in 1896. After driving another half hour on the Seward Highway, you arrive at a "Y" in the road. Turning left, you'll continue another 36 miles on the Seward Highway, through Moose Pass, finally arriving in **SEWARD** on the shores of Resurrection Bay.

Turning right (west) will put you on the **STERLING HIGHWAY**. Driving through the Kenai Mountains, you'll arrive at **COOPER LANDING**, wind along the **KENAI RIVER**, eventually leave the mountains behind, drop onto the flats and continue through **STERLING** to **SOLDOTNA**, where another "Y" awaits. Continuing south on the Sterling Highway, you will visit the small communities of **KASILOF, CLAM GULCH, NINILCHIK**, and **ANCHOR POINT** before completing the two-hour drive to **HOMER** and **KACHEMAK BAY**. Turning right at the Soldotna "Y," a 10-mile drive on the Kenai Spur Highway leads to **KENAI**, at the mouth of the Kenai River, and another 36-mile stretch to the **CAPTAIN COOK STATE RECREATION AREA** on the shores of Cook Inlet.

The **ALASKA RAILROAD** (907/265-2607; www.alaskarailroad.com) connects Anchorage and Seward with daily trips aboard the Coastal Classic between mid-May and mid-September. A stop in Portage is included. The trip between Anchorage and Seward takes approximately four hours. A round-trip ticket is $90.

The **ALASKA PUBLIC LANDS INFORMATION CENTER** (605 W 4th Ave; 907/271-2737; www.nps.gov/aplic) in Anchorage is stocked with printed informa-

DRIVING TIPS

The drive down the Seward and Sterling Highways is spectacular in all seasons. But be aware that the word "highway" in Alaska really means "road" anywhere else. En route you will travel through park, forest, and refuge lands, and along glacially fed lakes and rivers. You'll curve around large bodies of salt water, through mountains and lowlands. Remember, too, that if you break down, you may be miles from any help. This is particularly important in the winter. Carry emergency survival gear with you in the car. This means flares, flashlight, warm clothes, warm shoes, a sleeping bag, extra food, and water. Double-check that you have tools for changing your own tires. Good footgear cannot be overemphasized. Pumps and hose won't get you very far if you have to walk for gas in the middle of winter. Winter or summer, day or night, drive with your headlights on. And watch for animals. Every year people slam into moose and bears, especially at night. If you see moose on the side of the road, slow down quietly. They are apt to bolt over the road right in front of you, and then get transfixed by your headlights.

—Nan Elliot

tion to help plan your stay. Knowledgeable staff will answer questions and help make your visit the best possible experience. Visitor centers and park, forest, and refuge headquarters also dot the peninsula.

Portage Glacier and the Seward Highway

As the Seward Highway begins its 126-mile route from Anchorage to Seward, it forms a dramatic border between the surging waters of **TURNAGAIN ARM** and jagged mountain cliffs, skirts the edge of Chugach State Park, weaves through Chugach National Forest, the second largest national forest in the United States, traverses mountain passes, and follows the shore of Kenai Lake before finally arriving in Seward, headquarters for Kenai Fjords National Park.

PORTAGE GLACIER, the state's top visitor attraction and one of 10,000 glaciers in the Chugach National Forest, is just 50 miles from Anchorage. A 5-mile access road to the **BEGICH, BOGGS VISITOR CENTER** (907/783-2326; www.fs.fed.us/r10/chugach) leads beneath the gaze of glaciers that hang from the towering Chugach and Kenai Mountains. (For more about the Begich, Boggs Visitor Center, see the Prince William Sound chapter.) To view the glacier up close between May and September, ice conditions permitting, take a one-hour **PORTAGE GLACIER CRUISE** (907/277-5581 in Anchorage; 907/783-2983 at the glacier). There are five sailings daily. Cost for adults is $25; $12.50 for children.

Circling around the end of Turnagain Arm, the Seward Highway climbs up to Turnagain Pass, an area favored by backcountry winter recreationists. The access road to Hope follows Sixmile Creek, an attraction for white-water rafters. Once bustling with mining activity, Hope marks the northern end of the

38-mile **RESURRECTION PASS TRAIL.** The southern end is on the Sterling Highway, near Cooper Landing.

After reaching the "Y" and turning left, toward Seward, you'll discover **MOOSE PASS** sitting quietly on the shores of Upper Trail Lake. Like many peninsula settlements, it dates back to the Alaska's gold rush. According to one local legend, this community's name honors a moose that stubbornly refused passage to a dog-sled-driving mail carrier.

Seward

Seward is the bookmark in Alaska's best-selling novel, the Kenai Peninsula. Rising sharply at its back is 4,063-foot **MOUNT MARATHON.** Sparkling at its front are the waters of **RESURRECTION BAY. KENAI FJORDS NATIONAL PARK** and the **ALASKA MARITIME NATIONAL WILDLIFE REFUGE** sit just outside Seward's front door. The town marks the southern terminus of the Alaska Railroad and the beginning of the Seward Highway. Cruise ships and Alaska state ferries find their way into Seward's harbor. And it marks the original beginning of the historic Iditarod Trail.

The city gets its name from William Seward, secretary of state under President Andrew Johnson, who negotiated the 1867 purchase by the United States of Alaska from Russia for $7.2 million. The acquisition of the new territory became known as "Seward's Folly," but it's the 3,000 residents who play host to thousands of visitors every year, summer and winter, who are having the last laugh.

ACCESS AND INFORMATION

The **SEWARD VISITOR INFORMATION CENTER** (Mile 2 Seward Hwy; 907/224-8051; fax 907/224-5353; chamber@seward.net; www.seward.net/chamber) is located at the Seward Chamber of Commerce, at the north end of town, and is open year-round. **THE KENAI FJORDS NATIONAL PARK VISITOR CENTER** (PO Box 1727, Seward AK 99664; 907/224-3175) is located at the small-boat harbor, close to the harbormaster; hours vary with the season.

EXPLORING

A leisurely stroll along the floats in the boat harbor reflects Seward's diversity. There are tour boats designed for comfort, sportfishing boats ready for play, commercial fishing boats meant for work, charter operators waiting to share their expertise, and a wide range of pleasure craft, from yachts to sloops. Seagulls swoop overhead. Otters roll in the calm, clear water. And occasionally a seal will poke its head above the surface to see what's happening. Along the boardwalk, you can book a fishing charter, reserve a spot on a whale-watching or glacier-viewing cruise, find gifts to take home, get your questions answered, chat with locals, and stop to catch your breath with a beverage or a bite to eat.

ALASKA SEALIFE CENTER / Perched on the edge of Resurrection Bay, the center is a balanced blend of public education, wildlife rehabilitation, and research. Through the center's "windows to the sea," you can catch the eye of a passing Steller's sea lion as he swims through the waters of his 162,000-gallon habitat resembling sea lion haul outs in Resurrection Bay. Watch seabirds "fly" beneath the sea.

Enjoy up-close views of wolf eels, octopus, salmon, and halibut. Live viewing of a Steller's sea lion rookery some 35 miles in the distance is also possible thanks to cutting-edge technology. One exhibit simulates activities beneath the harbor, while another lets you peer into the deep gulf environments of king crab and other seldom-seen creatures. The "discovery pool" allows some hands-on interaction, and be sure to ask about the possibility of behind-the-scenes tours. The 115,000-square-foot, $56 million facility, opened in 1998, was made possible through the *Exxon Valdez* oil spill settlement and funds from city, private, and corporate sponsors. Admission is $12.50 for adults; $10 for youth; children 6 and under are free. Family and group discounts are available. *Open daily 8am–8pm summers; reduced hours winters; 301 Railway Ave, PO Box 1329, Seward AK 99664; 907/224-6300 or 800/224-2525; fax 907/224-6320; visit@alaskasealife.org; www.alaskasealife.org.*

QUTEKCAK SHELLFISH HATCHERY / Also commanding a bay-side location, this is the only facility where cockles, rock scallops, and little neck clams have been spawned successfully, thanks in no small part to the clear, cold water brought in from Resurrection Bay. Also making their home in the tanks of varying sizes are oysters and geoducks at different life stages. Seed from the hatchery is shipped to shellfish farmers that dot Alaska's shoreline. The 7,500-square-foot, $3.2 million structure was built in 1996, and the Qutekcak Native Tribe opened it for operation in 1998. Visiting scientists and students frequent the hatchery and the staff will graciously give public tours if you call in advance. *101 Railway Ave; PO Box 369, Seward AK 99664; 907/224-5181; fax 907/224-5282.*

LOWELL POINT / Drive south of the hatchery and as the gravel road narrows and the wilderness closes around you, Seward's downtown disappears. Welcome to Lowell Point and its slower-paced, secluded environment. A thin gravel beach separates the bay's surf from the forest, which, in turn, gives way to steeply rising mountains. Scattered along the shore and nearly hidden beneath the thick, towering trees are a mixture of permanent residences, vacation cabins, B&Bs, and campgrounds. Some shine with the glow of modern architecture. Others appear to have been abandoned by the sea, their weathered exteriors perfectly matching the driftwood and beach rocks. The road ends at the trailhead for **CAINES HEAD STATE RECREATION AREA** (see Adventures, this section), with its reminders of World War II.

SHOPPING / Wander through the art, jewelry, and other eye-catching artistic expressions at **BARDARSON STUDIO** (1317 4th Ave; 800/478-7848; fax 907-224-5436; Bardarson@seward.net; www.bardarsonstudio.com). Satisfy your sweet tooth with delicious homemade fudge and other confections at **SWEET DARLINGS** (207 4th Ave; 907/224-7313; fax 907/224-2343; darling@seward.net; www.sweetdarlings.com). Hot soups, sandwiches, and the swirling smell of delicious fresh baked goodies satisfy a hungry crowd at **BAKERY AT THE HARBOR** (1215 4th Ave; 907/224-6091; fax 907/224-5159; eglofelty@alaska.com). In the heart of downtown, **THE RANTING RAVEN** (238 4th Ave; 907/224-2228; trailriver@hotmail.com) serves espresso, fresh coffee, and snacks that really are finger-licking good, like the coconut mocha coffee cake or their famous lemon cookies. While you're eating every last crumb, check out their selection of gifts. Comfortably at home in a renovated church is **RESURRECT ART** (320 3rd Ave; 907/224-7161; rezart@hotmail.com),

KENAI PENINSULA THREE-DAY TOUR

DAY ONE: Start out early in the morning from Anchorage, driving the Seward Highway to Seward. It's about a 3-hour drive if you drive straight through, but you're going to stop and spend a couple hours viewing the grandeur of **PORTAGE GLACIER** and exploring the **BEGICH, BOGGS VISITOR CENTER.** Time your arrival in Seward for a late lunch of deep-fried halibut at **HARBOR DINNER CLUB,** and then check into your artsy room at **RESURRECTION BAY GALERIE B&B,** where you made reservations weeks ago. You'll then have an hour or so to relax or explore (we suggest the **ALASKA SEALIFE CENTER**) before departing for your evening dinner cruise to Resurrection Bay in **KENAI FJORDS NATIONAL PARK,** with Kenai Fjords Tours. Or, if you'd rather and if time permits, take an abbreviated three-hour cruise with Kenai Fjords Tours in the afternoon and be back on shore by 5:30pm for dinner. Try relaxing with a glass of wine with Thai scallops at **RAY'S WATERFRONT.**

DAY TWO: Get up early; you've got a big day ahead. Grab some freshly brewed coffee and homemade pastries at either the **BAKERY AT THE HARBOR** or **THE RANTING RAVEN,** both on Fourth Avenue. Then get back in that car and hit the Seward Highway again, but this time turn onto the Sterling Highway instead of continuing back toward Anchorage. Stop for lunch in **COOPER LANDING** at Gwin's Lodge. If you like to fish, spend the afternoon with a charter on the **KENAI RIVER.** For those who'd rather hike, check out **CAPTAIN COOK STATE RECREATION AREA** or

where you can sample the menu of steaming hot or iced drinks, enjoy a snack, and gaze at the collection of Alaska art. Relax on pews resurrected as benches and arranged around the scattering of tables, or take your beverage and ascend to the choir loft for a higher perspective. Fine art is only part of the attraction at **RE-SURRECTION BAY GALERIE** (500 4th Ave; 907/224-3212; fax 907/224-5990; mabranson@wildbear.net; www.alaskafinearts.com). Owner Margaret Branson is the other part. A long-time Alaskan and former legislator, her stories are as fascinating as the original artwork and historic home in which she lives. And if the comfortable atmosphere makes you want to linger, her upstairs B&B awaits.

ADVENTURES

MOUNT MARATHON / The birth of the annual Fourth of July race up Mount Marathon, as well as the origin of the mountain's name are part of Seward's colorful folklore. According to the story, the event began in 1915 when Gus Borgan bet $100 that the mountain couldn't be run in an hour. James Walter was the first to win the 4,603-foot event, but his winning time put him two minutes over the limit. The challenge now draws more than 800 runners in separate divisions that run, crawl, slide, and frequently fall on the treacherous course. Olympic athlete Nina Kemppel holds the record for most wins, Bill Spencer holds the men's record in just over 43 minutes, and Nancy Pease holds the women's record of 50.5 minutes. Some 30,000 spec-

KENAI NATIONAL WILDLIFE REFUGE for an afternoon steeped in nature. You'll be tired after such a full day, so head to BED AND BREAKFAST COTTAGES in Soldotna for the night. If you went the fishing route, this B&B has a fish-cleaning station and grill, so you can eat your catch for dinner if you like. If not, head to MYKEL'S RESTAURANT AND LOUNGE and try the most delicious Bering Sea crab fondue.

DAY THREE: Take to the Sterling Highway early in order to spend most of the day in HOMER, a quaint slice of Alaska too good to miss. Spend the day strolling the downtown shops and galleries. Have lunch at CAFÉ CUPS downtown. Go BEACH-COMBING along the shores of Kachemak Bay. If there's time and you feel like halibut fishing, for which Homer is famous, call Rainbow Tours for a half-day FISHING CHARTER for the afternoon. If that doesn't strike your fancy, pick up a paddle and go KAYAKING with True North Kayak Adventures for a half- or full-day trip. Your evening will start when the *Danny J* departs for its evening jaunt to HALIBUT COVE, just across the water from Homer, where you'll dine at THE SALTRY, a wonderful little restaurant with ambiance and delightful meals. After dinner, stroll the boardwalks that make up Halibut Cove and visit the local art galleries, take photos, and drink in the view. When the *Danny J* takes you back to Homer, check into your cabin at ISLAND WATCH BED AND BREAKFAST, located in the hills above Homer. Soak in the outdoor hot tub, relax, and, the next morning, enjoy a hearty, homemade breakfast before heading out to your next adventure.

tators flock to Seward just to watch the excitement and celebrate in other holiday events. If you want to climb it on your own, a more reasonable goal is three to four hours. *Seward Chamber of Commerce; 907/224-8051; fax 907/224-5353; chamber@seward.net; www.seward.net/chamber.*

LOST LAKE / Begun in August 1992 with 55 runners, the Run to Lost Lake now attracts more than 500 participants who run a 16-mile U.S. Forest Service trail at Primrose Campground. The setting is gorgeous, complete with high-mountain lakes and sweeping vistas. Olympic athlete Nina Kemppel has called it "the most beautiful run in southcentral Alaska." The goal is raising funds to support cystic fibrosis research. A barbecue and awards await runners, the first of which crosses the finish line in less than two hours. Generous sponsors also kick in prizes that include cruises, airline tickets, fishing charters, hotel stays, and dinner certificates. *907/224-3537; www.lostlakerun.org.*

KENAI FJORDS NATIONAL PARK / Cradled within the towering mountains that rise from the park's 605,000 acres are tons of constantly moving ice that make up the 300-square-mile Harding Icefield. While the ice's tortoise pace prevents you from actually seeing it grind its way toward the sea, the icefield's booming voice echoing across the water and mountain faces lets you know movement is happening. Thanks to several day cruises into the park, you can witness slabs of blue ice calving or breaking free of the powerful force that moves ever forward. Sailing from Seward to the face of these icy monsters, you'll encounter thousands of seabirds that make their home in Resurrection Bay, the Alaska Maritime National Wildlife Refuge, and Kenai Fjords National Park. Mountain goats cling to steep slopes that drop sharply into the blue-green water. The curious or sleepy eyes of sea otters, Steller's sea lions, and harbor seals will monitor your presence. And keep your eyes peeled and your camera ready for the telltale dorsal fin of an orca whale or the silhouette of a humpback or gray whale's flukes. One of the oldest established tours into the park is **KENAI FJORDS TOURS** (907/276-6249, Anchorage; 907/224-8068, Seward; or 800/478-8068; fax 907/224-8934; info@kenaifjords.com; www.kenaifjords.com). **MARIAH TOURS AND CHARTERS** (907/224-8068, Seward; or 800/478-8068; info@kenaifjords.com; www.kenaifjords.com) has smaller boats for perhaps a more intimate view. **ALASKA RENOWN CHARTERS** (907/272-1961, Anchorage; 907/224-3806, Seward; or 800/655-3806; renown@alaska.com; www.renowncharters.com) takes passengers summer and winter, with the winter tours limited to Resurrection Bay. **MAJOR MARINE TOURS** (907/274-7300, Anchorage; 907/224-8030, Seward; or 800/764-7300; www.majormarine.com) has a national park ranger on board every cruise to serve as naturalist.

EXIT GLACIER / Water is not the only route into Kenai Fjords National Park. A 9-mile drive leads to the Exit Glacier Ranger Station and a series of trails that allow different viewing opportunities during the summer. An easy ½-mile path across glacial terrain is marked with signs measuring the rate at which the glacier has melted over the years. Other signs warn against chunks of ice that fall unexpectedly. Keep a safe distance and you'll be rewarded with views of deep blue crevasses and the feel of the glacier's chilly breath on your face as it descends 2,500 feet of the glacier's 3-mile length. A longer, more strenuous trail—7 miles round-trip, 3,000-foot gain—offers views into the Harding Icefield. For more information, check with the ranger station or at park headquarters in the Seward harbor area (907/224-3175).

DOG MUSHING / Catch dog fever at Mitch Seavey's Ididaride Sled Dog Tours. Seward and sled-dog mushing are linked by a history dating back to the early 1900s, when thousands of gold-hungry prospectors passed through this area on their way to the goldfields of Interior Alaska and Nome. In their wake, teams of sled-pulling dogs and their drivers delivered mail on what became known as the Iditarod Trail. In 1973, the inaugural Iditarod Trail Sled Dog Race was held, a 1,049-mile event between Anchorage and Nome, and Mitch's father, Dan, placed third. In 1988, Mitch entered the event. In 2001, Dan, Mitch, and Mitch's son, Danny, covered the course. And in 2001, Mitch's youngest son, Tyrell, placed first in the Junior Iditarod. In other words, the Seavey family is synonymous with sled-dog racing. Experience the thrill of touring the Alaska wilderness in the company of an enthusiastic team of dogs, examine the layers of protective gear worn by mushers and dogs, cuddle with puppies in the puppy pens, and photograph the sleek, hardworking canine heroes of "the last great race." Tours last 1½ hours. *May through Sept, winter tours by arrangement; PO Box 2906, Seward AK 99664; PO Box 735, Sterling AK 99672; 907/224-8607 in Seward; 907/260-3139 in Sterling; 800/478-3139; ididaride@wildbear.net; www.ididaride.com.*

FISHING / Drop a hook from shore or head for the deep blue sea with any of a number of charters for halibut and salmon fishing. The Silver Salmon Derby draws eager anglers in mid-August, with a wide range of daily and derby prizes including the $10,000 first prize and a tagged fish reward that can value up to $100,000, depending on the sponsors. If you want a little more time to catch a prize-winning fish, try the May-to-August halibut tournament that awards prizes of cash, dinners, overnight stays, dinner cruises, and fishing trips. The jackpot winner is determined at the end of the tournament. *Seward Chamber of Commerce, PO Box 749, Seward AK 99664; 907/224-8051; chamber@seward.net; www.sewardak.org.*

SEA KAYAKING / Keep your camera ready as you silently slip across the water's surface with only the sound of a paddle alerting wildlife to your presence. Guides with years of experience and an intimate knowledge of the area are your key to parts of Alaska few visitors experience. **SUNNY COVE KAYAKING COMPANY** (PO Box 332, Seward AK 99664; 907/224-8810 or 800/770-9119; kayakak@alaska.net; www.sunnycove.com) has guided adventures of Resurrection Bay and Kenai Fjords National Park from half day to 14 days starting at $59 per person. Working with **KENAI FJORDS TOURS** (see Kenai Fjords National Park, above), they will paddle with you around Fox Island, 14 miles from Seward, where you can enjoy the wildlife and a salmon bake on the island before day's end. **ALASKA KAYAK CAMPING COMPANY** (PO Box 1101, Seward AK 99664; 907/224-6056; kayakcamp@alaska.net; www.seward.net/kayakcamp) will take you out for evening trips, day trips, or multiday adventures with destinations that include Caines Head, Tonsina Creek, and Bear Glacier Lagoon. Beginning in 2002, owner Bob Ceeleen expanded the adventures he offers to include hiking, fishing, wildlife boat tours, and kayak rentals. Explore Kenai Fjords National Park with Jim Vermillion, of **KAYAK AND CUSTOM ADVENTURES WORLDWIDE** (323 3rd Ave, PO Box 2249, Seward AK 99664; 907/224-3960 or 800/288-3134; fun@kayakAK.com) and you benefit from his 30 years in Alaska. Half-day, full-day, and sunset trips begin at $55; kayak rentals start at $35.

THE COASTAL TRAIL / From Lowell Point, the Coastal Trail follows the shoreline south 4.5 miles to North Beach. A portion of the hike can only be done during low tide so be sure to consult a tide table and have the necessary gear for a possible overnight stay or to carry you through the 12-hour period between low tides. Continue another two miles south and you arrive at the abandoned remains of Fort McGilvray, set on a 650-foot cliff above Resurrection Bay. During World War II, this was a strategic spot to defend the port of Seward against possible attack. Get directions to the trail from the Seward Visitors Information Center (Mile 2 Seward Hwy; 907/224-8051).

MOUNTAIN TRAILS / Stretch those car-cramped legs by **HIKING, MOUNTAIN BIKING,** or **SKIING TRAILS** in and around Seward. **GRAYLING LAKE TRAIL** ascends gradually over 2 miles, taking you through forests and meadows. The 15-mile **LOST LAKE TRAIL** climbs 1,820 feet; you'll see snow even during summer. The steep **MOUNT MARATHON TRAIL** leads 3,022-feet above the city and can be slippery. **RESURRECTION RIVER TRAIL** is a 32-mile course that connects with the **RESURRECTION PASS TRAIL** to take you all the way to Hope, a distance of

72 miles. You can get a map and condition report from the Chugach National Forest Seward Ranger District (334 4th Ave, Seward, AK 99664; 907/224-3374).

PUBLIC-USE CABINS / Cabins are sprinkled throughout the Seward area, thanks to the Seward Ranger District of the Chugach National Forest, the Kenai Fjords National Park, and Alaska State Parks. The prices vary from $25 to $50 a night, but access can pose a challenge. Some are accessible by trail, some trails include ice bridges, and some cabins can only be reached by boat, kayak, or fly-in. There are cabins available only in the summer and others open in the winter. Information requests and reservations can be handled by contacting the Seward Ranger District (605 W 4th Ave, Anchorage AK 99501; 334 4th Ave, Seward, AK 99664; 907/271-2599, Anchorage; 907/224-3374, Seward; www.fs.fed.us/r10/chugach/), the National Reservation System (877/444-6777; www.reserveusa.com/), Kenai Fjords National Park (PO Box 1727, Seward AK 99664-1727; 907/224-3175; www. nps.gov/kefj), or Alaska State Parks (550 W 7th Ave, Ste 1260, Anchorage AK 99501-3557; 907/269-8400, Anchorage; 907/262-5581, Soldotna; pic@dnr.state. ak.us; www.dnr.state.ak.us/parks/).

RESTAURANTS

Apollo Restaurant / ★

224 4TH AVE, SEWARD; 907/224-3092 In the midst of glaciers, mountains, and frigid waters comes this Mediterranean influence, complete with columns, mythical gods, and music to remind you of other places and other times. The adventuresome diner can choose from a blend of Alaska seafood fixed Greek and Italian style, but the very American salmon and halibut fish-and-chips are done in a heavy batter that detracts from the taste. Pizza is a popular choice, especially the Chicken Supreme: charbroiled chicken breast, flavored with Mediterranean herbs, mushrooms, and onions served on a garlic-butter crust and sealed with mozzarella. *$$; MC, V; Alaska checks only; lunch (year-round), dinner (summer); beer and wine; no reservations; downtown.*

Harbor Dinner Club / ★

220 5TH AVE, SEWARD; 907/224-3012 Since the 1950s, this family owned restaurant has weathered changes and held its own. Slip in for a little peace and quiet while you test their halibut chunks deep fried in a batter whose ingredients are known only to the family. The menu also boasts of steaks seasoned and grilled to perfection and seafood fresh from Alaskan waters. *$$; AE, DC, DIS, MC, V; local checks only; lunch, dinner every day; full bar; reservations recommeded on weekends; downtown.*

Ray's Waterfront / ★★★

1316 4TH AVE, SEWARD; 907/224-5606 If you were any closer to the harbor, you'd be in it. And you'd miss the culinary currents that converge at Ray's Waterfront, bringing with them such dishes as Thai scallops and macadamia nut crusted halibut. Before you launch into the main meal, try the mussels sautéed with fresh ginger or the calamari. And if you're short on time and heading for a boat, take along one of Ray's deluxe box lunches. *$$–$$$; AE, DC, DIS, MC, V; checks*

OK; breakfast, lunch, dinner every day (closed Oct to Mar); full bar; reservations recommended for parties of 5 or more; at the Seward small boat harbor.

LODGINGS

Hotels, motels, lodges, cottages, cabins, hostels, and more than 100 bed-and-breakfasts await your arrival in the Seward area. Finding the right lodging can be a challenge. That's where Debra Hafemeister at **ALASKA'S POINT OF VIEW SUITE AND RESERVATION SERVICE** comes in (318 1st Ave, PO Box 312, Seward AK 99664; 907/224-5695 or 800/844-2424; www.alaskasview.com). Call Debra, let her know what you are looking for, your travel budget, and she will take it from there. Her service is free and comes with a discount on local tours. You might even decide to stay in one of Debra's two suites.

Hotel Edgewater and Conference Center / ★★

200 5TH AVE, SEWARD; 907/224-2700 OR 888/793-6800; FAX 907/224-2701 The lobby area is divided so guests can enjoy two distinct Alaska environments, one with the crackling warmth of a fireplace and one with cascading water, reminiscent of Seward's many waterfalls. Check your e-mails at the hotel's business center while sipping a beverage from the espresso bar. Stop by the concierge to find out more about the area, arrange tours, or reserve a fishing charter through the hotel's sister company Charter Option. The spa's exercise equipment, hot tub, and sauna have a view of sparkling blue water and snowcapped mountains. So do some of the 76 rooms. Others sit in the shadow of Mount Marathon. All of them have dataports. A complimentary breakfast is available and discounts are offered to return and special guests, such as runners in the Run to Lost Lake. Two meeting rooms are available and the hotel can arrange catering. Double occupancy rates during the peak season run $145–$180. $$$; AE, DIS, MC, V; checks OK; PO Box 1570, Seward AK 99664; edgewater@seward.net; www.hoteledgewater.com.

Sauerdough Lodging / ★★★

225 4TH AVE, SEWARD; 907/224-8946 OR 877/224-8946; FAX 907/224-8980 Colorful history is the order of the day and night when you stay in the historic Seward Commercial Company Building constructed in 1908 by William Sauer. What was once the warehouse and trading post have now become the lobby area, decorated to match the building's historic beginnings, and an interesting museum that will make duck fans, and you know who you are, feel right at home. The four private rooms, with arrangements of single and double beds, run $99 (including breakfast) peak season (mid-May through mid-Sept) and $59 the rest of the year (breakfast not included). Upstairs are five suites that vary in size, price ($149–$249), and charm. One has a claw-foot bathtub, and the largest, Madame's Suite, has a fully furnished kitchen, dining area, two double beds, and a single bed. A queen-size four-poster bed is separated by French doors. Breakfasts from host Gordon Turner's kitchen include monstrous cinnamon rolls, Belgian waffles, crepes, homemade yogurt, and all the fixings. Nonsmoking. $–$$; AE, DC, DIS, MC, V; checks OK; suites@ptialaska.net; www.sauerdoughlodging.com; downtown.

BED-AND-BREAKFASTS

DOWNTOWN / History and hospitality mix at **BALLAINE HOUSE LODGING** (437 3rd Ave, PO Box 2051, Seward AK 99664; 907/224-2362; www.superpage.com/ballaine/). Thanks to host Marilee Koszewski, the interior is in keeping with the home's 1905 beginnings; it is on both the State and National Historic Registers. Five rooms share one bathroom ($60 for a single; $84 for a double in summer; no smoking), there is a large, comfortable common area, and they serve a huge breakfast. Named for the nearby waterfall, **FALLS INN** (1103 2nd Ave, PO Box 2064, Seward AK 99664; 907/224-5790; fallsinnalaska@gci.net; www.fallsinnalaska.com), is hosted by Louis and Diane Bencardino. Mr. Bencardino is Seward's former mayor and chief of police. Guests here are within walking distance of the harbor, downtown Seward, and can take advantage of a 45-minute trail that begins just outside the door and winds through Two Lakes Park. For a truly artistic atmosphere, try the antique-decorated cozy red room with private bath tucked above the art gallery at **RESURRECTION BAY GALERIE B&B** (500 4th Ave, PO Box 271, Seward AK 99664; 907/224-3212; fax 907/224-5990; abranson@wildbear.net; www.alaskafinearts.com.

LOWELL POINT / Just off the deck at **ALASKA SALTWATER LODGE** (PO Box 695, Seward AK 99664; 907/224-5271; www.alaskasaltwaterlodge.com), Resurrection Bay surf rolls in and sea otter and sea lions swim past. There is a common area, with full kitchen, and suites perfect for large groups of fishing, hiking, and kayaking pals. Single rooms start at $85. Hosts Jim and Kathleen Barkley will arrange natural-history and wildlife tours, or fishing and kayaking trips. **OCEAN FRONT BED AND BREAKFAST** (PO Box 3322, Seward AK 99669; 907/224-5699; ocean@seward.net; www.seward.net/~ocean) began as the small cabin home of Butch and Gloria Sears. As their roots sank along the shores of Resurrection Bay, their home grew and now includes a room with separate entrance and deck so they can share their beachfront location with guests. Summer rates are $120 for a double; $70 in winter.

CABINS OR ALASKA-STYLE / The forest's solitude is more to some folks' liking. Towering trees and a cascading deck draw you into **ALASKA'S TREEHOUSE** (Mile 7 Seward Hwy, PO Box 861, Seward AK 99664; 907/224-3867; fax 907/224-3978; treehouse@seward.net; www.seward.net/treehouse), where hosts Al Lamberson and Sheila Morrow will thrill you with stories of adventures in Alaska and around the world. Hiking trails lead deep into the forest, but a bubbling hot tub draws you back, as will the changing breakfast menu. **BOX CANYON CABINS** (PO Box 1662, Seward AK 99664; 907/224-5046; fax 907/224-5074; young@ptialaska.net; www.boxcanyoncabin.com) is in the woods off the road to Exit Glacier. Three two-bedroom cabins are perfect for families, can sleep up to six, and have fully equipped kitchens. The fourth cabin, with a history all its own, is just right for two people. **CREEKSIDE CABINS** (Old Exit Glacier Rd, PO Box 1514, Seward AK 99664; 907/224-3834; creekside@seward.net) includes a cozy 1940s homestead cabin that can sleep two, four larger cabins, and a tent site tucked into the trees. The bathhouse is shared and the steaming sauna beckons at the edge of Clear Creek. **RENFRO'S LAKESIDE RETREAT** (27121 Seward Hwy, Seward AK 99664; 907/288-5059 or 877/288-5059; www.seward-alaska.com/renfros) is 8 miles from Moose Pass and

20 miles from Seward. Individual cabins sit on the edge of Kenai Lake or in thick forest. Each is fully furnished, with a kitchen. Your hosts are Sharon and Mike Renfro. At **STONEY CREEK INN B&B** (PO Box 1352, Seward AK 99664; 907/224-3940; fax 907/224-2683; www.stoneycreekinn.net; turn onto Lake Dr at Mile 6.5 Seward Hwy, watch for signs), hosts Kent and Lisa Rininger offer a home away from home in the woods, with the relaxing sound of a creek running past.

WILDERNESS LODGES

Kenai Fjords Wilderness Lodge

FOX ISLAND, SEWARD; 907/224-8068 OR 800/478-8068; FAX 907/224-8934 For a getaway that includes a cruise on Resurrection Bay, an island cabin, delicious meals, and glacier viewing combined with the convenience of running water (minus the distractions of a ringing telephone), book the special overnight package at Kenai Fjords Wilderness Lodge on Fox Island, 14 miles across the bay from Seward. For $329, enjoy the one-hour cruise from Seward, two-person cabin, meals, and a half-day glacier-viewing cruise. Owned and operated by Kenai Fjords Tours, the island is home to two lodges, one where lodge and cruise guests are served hearty meals, including an all-you-can-eat grilled salmon buffet. The second and smaller lodge is designed for no more than 18 overnighters seeking the seclusion of an island retreat and the relaxation of a kayak trip or a naturalist-guided hike. All meals provided and alcohol is available. *$$$; AE, DIS, MC, V; no checks; open June 1 to Sept 2; PO Box 1889, Dept SEW, Seward AK 99664; www.kenaifjords.com/content/lodging.*

The Sterling Highway

If you turned right, rather than left toward Seward, you are on the Sterling Highway and headed for the end of the road in Homer, some 226 miles south of Anchorage.

The highway threads along the edge of glacial-green **KENAI LAKE,** through the small community of **COOPER LANDING.** You'll cross where the lake empties into the **KENAI RIVER,** and then follow the upper portion of this 83-mile long river as it weaves its way to Skilak Lake. Keep your eyes open for anglers lining the shore or floating the swift river currents. Float trips that launch in Cooper Landing also are common on this portion of the river.

A 19-mile gravel loop, once part of the highway, swings off the main road and provides access to **SKILAK LAKE.** This 15-mile length of water separates the upper from the lower Kenai River. On Skilak, as on other large lakes such as the Kenai and the Tustumena, beware of winds that can appear suddenly and stir the frigid waters into dangerous whitecapped swells. For safety's sake, wear a life jacket and leave the alcohol on shore.

Breaking out of the mountains, the Sterling Highway descends into an area of muskeg and scrub spruce. On a clear day you will catch your first glimpse of two snow-covered volcanic peaks, **MOUNTS REDOUBT AND ILIAMNA,** on Cook Inlet's distant shore. The road continues through **STERLING,** to **SOLDOTNA,** and on to **HOMER.** Along the way, the inlet draws closer as the highway outlines the Kenai Peninsula's western coastline, leading you through the village of **NINILCHIK,** first settled by Russian pensioners and their Native wives in the mid-1800s, and **ANCHOR POINT**, where Captain Cook lost an anchor to strong tidal currents, and the most westerly point of the highway.

Cooper Landing

Nestled between Kenai Lake and the steeply climbing mountains that rim the shoreline, Cooper Landing claims the western end of the lake and the beginning of the Kenai River. It draws its name from Joseph Cooper, who discovered gold in the area in 1884. Stretching nearly 10 miles, it is home to numerous fishing charters, river rafting operations, campgrounds, hiking trails, and lodgings. An active group of civic-minded senior citizens deserves credit for Cooper Landing's recently completed community center. The Snug Harbor Road Snail-a-Thon is held in May to help raise funds for the local school. Watch out for the 100 slow-moving but dedicated walkers and bicyclers that compete for prizes. Along this area of the river, the U.S. Forest Service has coordinated archaeological digs with the Kenai Peninsula College, the Kenaitze (a tribe of Dena'ina Athabascans), and local school children. The setting and numerous outdoor opportunities make Cooper Landing a favorite summer spot, causing the population to swell dramatically beyond the 300-some year-round residents.

ADVENTURES

ALASKA WILDLAND ADVENTURES / Leave the flow of traffic behind and flow with the Kenai River instead. The seven-hour float includes lunch on the riverbank, with your guide as host. The last part of the trip is a cruise across Skilak Lake to the takeout area where a van awaits your arrival, ready to return you to Cooper Landing. A two-hour float also is available, but you'll miss the fun of the Class II rapids in Kenai Canyon. (See also Soldotna and Kenai, Guides and Outfitters, this chapter.) *16520 Sterling Hwy; 907/595-1279 or 800/478-4100; www.alaskariver trips.com.*

   HIKING / The 35-mile **RESURRECTION PASS TRAIL**, from Cooper Landing to Hope, leads deep into the Kenai Mountains, to a high point of 2,600 feet. There are **PUBLIC-USE CABINS** along the way; make reservations through the Chugach National Forest (605 W 4th Ave, Anchorage AK 99501; 334 4th Ave, Seward AK 99664; 907/271-2599, Anchorage; 907/224-3374, Seward; www.fs.fed.us/r10/chugach/) or the National Reservation System (877/444-6777; www.reserveusa.com/). A system of trails links **RUSSIAN LAKE**, **COOPER LAKE**, and the **RESURRECTION RIVER** and can be crowded with fishermen, depending on the season. From the viewing deck at **RUSSIAN RIVER FALLS**, watch salmon leap the falls on their way home. For more detailed information, pick up the terrific resource, *55 Ways to the Wilderness of Southcentral Alaska,* by Helen Nienhueser and John Wolfe Jr. (The Mountaineers Books, Seattle; $17).

RESTAURANTS

Eagle's Crest Restaurant / ★★

KENAI PRINCESS WILDERNESS LODGE, COOPER LANDING; 907/595-1425 OR 800/426-0500 Let the fire crackle in the fireplace, the Kenai River wind into the distance, and the eagles sail overhead while you sink into the warm rustic atmosphere. Sip an espresso or linger over a bowl of soup and a hot loaf of bread. The coconut prawns or smoked salmon appetizers are great starters, and the herb-crusted New Zealand rack of lamb is seasoned to perfection. The menu offers a wide range of selections for breakfast, lunch, and dinner and on special occasions, buffets spread across long tables. The seats fill fast. *$$–$$$; AE, DC, DIS, MC, V; local checks only; breakfast, lunch, dinner every day; full bar; reservations recommended for parties of 6 or more; www.princesslodges.com; in the main lodge, turn onto Bean Creek Rd at Mile 47.7 Sterling Hwy.*

Gwin's Lodge / ★

14865 STERLING HWY, COOPER LANDING; 907/595-1266 Since 1952, many a hungry traveler has filled up at this hand-built log lodge. The folks here take pride in their homemade food, including chili, salmon chowder, and cinnamon rolls that rival the size of Mount McKinley. They have 10 different varieties of hamburgers, and Gwin's macho nachos come with a homemade salsa that has a hint of Jose Cuervo. Winter staff of three swells to 50 hardworking summer employees who serve a meal every 80 seconds at the height of fishing season. *$$; DIS, MC, V; Alaska checks only; breakfast, lunch, dinner (open 24 hours in summer, shortened hours in winter); full bar; no reservations; gwins@arctic.net; Mile 52 Sterling Hwy.*

Sackett's Kenai Grill / ★★

MILE 47.4 STERLING HWY, COOPER LANDING; 907/595-1827 Nothing blocks your view of Kenai Lake's glacial waters except panes of glass and the plate of food sitting in front of you. The deck is glassed in, warmed either by the sun or a wood fire. The seafood chowder is delicious, with warm bread and a Caesar salad the perfect accompaniment. The halibut Caesar is a meal in itself and even self-professed local seafood experts keep coming back for the halibut dishes. Had enough seafood? Try the smoked prime rib, chicken, or pasta selections with a wine of your choice. Another bonus: they're open until midnight every day in summer. *$–$$; MC, V; checks OK; dinner daily (summer), breakfast, lunch, dinner daily (winter); beer and wine; no reservations.*

LODGINGS

Kenai Princess Wilderness Lodge / ★★★

MILE 47.7 STERLING HWY, COOPER LANDING; 907/595-1425 OR 800/426-0500 (RESERVATIONS) Its eagle perch above the winding Kenai River overlooks churning rapids and gazes at the wall of mountains embracing the valley. The vaulted ceilings, stone fireplace in the lobby, woodstoves in the bungalows, and the indoor and outdoor hot tubs create a warm hospitality on this 43-acre corner of Alaska wilderness. Conference facilities are available and the lodge's RV park has 29 sites, a small grocery store, as well as laundry and shower facilities. Owned by Princess Tours, the lodge is busy in the summer, but slows to a less hectic pace during the fall or winter. Double occupancy rates begin at $239. *$$-$$$; AE, DC, DIS, MC, V; checks OK; aklodges@princesstours.com; www.princesslodges.com/kenai.htm; turn onto Bean Creek Rd at Mile 47.7 Sterling Hwy.*

BED-AND-BREAKFASTS

Alaskan Sourdough Bed and Breakfast and Wedding Chapel / ★★

MILE 47.7 STERLING HWY, COOPER LANDING; 907/595-1541 Your welcome from hosts Willie and Lovie Johnson is made warmer by Willie's Yupik heritage and Lovie's Cajun roots. Accommodations with queen-size beds are separate from the main house and the Johnsons' original cabin has been remodeled to house groups of six to eight. The dining room's wraparound windows will tempt your eyes with views of the surrounding mountains, but Lovie's sourdough pancakes, homemade syrups, and omelets will keep your mind from wandering. Willie's talent on the accordion makes toes tap and faces smile. A retired minister, he also performs marriages or helps couples renew their marriage vows either at the Johnsons' wedding chapel or in any of the natural cathedrals in this picturesque area. Double occupancy rates are $105 if you pay cash; $115 for plastic. *$$; AE, MC, V; checks OK; PO Box 812, Cooper Landing AK 99572; sourdoughbb@arctic.net; www.alaskansour doughbb.com; turn onto Bean Creek Rd at Mile 47.7 Sterling Hwy.*

Soldotna and Kenai

Holding court along the lower Kenai River, it is no wonder **SOLDOTNA** has a fishing focus. The community spreads in two directions, from the "Y" south along the Sterling Highway and west along the Kenai Spur Highway toward Kenai. Local history is built on the hard work of homesteaders who arrived in the area after World War II. If you're looking for an upscale or humorous Alaska gift, stop in at **NORTH-COUNTRY FAIR** (35082 Kenai Spur Hwy; 907/262-7715), which is a short distance after you turn right at the "Y" toward Kenai. Or if you're in the mood for really good coffee and a friendly atmosphere, try **KALADI BROTHERS COFFEE COMPANY** (315 S Kobuk St; 907/262-5980), in the big turquoise building in Soldotna, or **CHARLOTTE'S AT RIVER CITY BOOKS** (43977 Sterling Hwy; 907/262-6620).

Turn right at the "Y" to get to **KENAI,** where the Kenai River flows into Cook Inlet, and the **CAPTAIN COOK STATE RECREATION AREA** at the end of the road, about 36 miles. Originally a Dena'ina Athabascan settlement, Kenai became a Russian post in the late 1700s, and finally the U.S. Army established Fort Kenay. The town takes its name from the Kenaitze Indians, a branch of the Dena'inas. In the mid-1950s, oil was discovered in the area; onshore and offshore drilling operations now ship the oil aboard large tankers. Kenai's population of 7,000 makes it the largest city on the peninsula and the sixth largest city in Alaska.

ACCESS AND INFORMATION

THE SOLDOTNA VISITOR INFORMATION CENTER (4790 Sterling Hwy; 907/262-1337; info@soldotnachamber.com; www.soldotnachamber.com) is open daily in the summer, Monday–Friday the rest of the year. Stop by to visit, get your questions answered, or take advantage of the stairway that leads to the edge of the Kenai River. **THE KENAI NATIONAL WILDLIFE REFUGE** (907/262-7021) has headquarters in Soldotna, and the **KENAI VISITORS & CULTURAL CENTER** (11471 Kenai Spur Hwy; 907/283-1991; info@visitkenai.com; www.visitkenai.com/) hosts rotating exhibits, speakers, and is filled with information. (See also Access and Information at the beginning of this chapter.)

EXPLORING

OLD TOWN / Atop the bluff overlooking the mouth of the Kenai River proved a choice location for the Dena'ina, whose subsistence lifestyle incorporated the rhythms of land and sea. The Russians chose it as a fur trading outpost in the late 1700s and when the focus of the fur trade shifted to southeast Alaska, a brick factory was constructed. In 1865, some 30,000 bricks were produced for chimneys, ovens, and building foundations. Although the factory is gone, the towering blue domes and golden crosses of Holy Assumption of the Virgin Mary Russian Orthodox Church remain as testimony to Russia's influence. After Russia sold its interest in Alaska to the United States in 1867, Fort Kenay was established, followed in 1898 with an agricultural experimental station. In 1930, the population numbered 286; today it numbers 7,000. A 45-minute **WALKING TOUR,** put together by the Kenai Visitors & Cultural Center (see Access and Information) leads to the parish house rectory. Built in 1881, the rectory is considered the oldest building on the Kenai Peninsula. Nearby are the orthodox church, a National Historic Landmark, and the chapel of St. Nicholas. Buildings from early American occupation, the homesteading era, and a collection of old civic and commercial buildings tell Kenai's historical tale. From one hand-hewn log structure wafts the enticing smells of espresso, luring you in to the warmth of **VERONICA'S COFFEE HOUSE** (907/283-2725). Choose from the menu of soups, sandwiches, and baked items and bask in the warmth emanating from the logs of Kenai's past.

RIVER CITY BOOKS / Owned by Peggy Mullen, the eldest daughter of homesteader Marge Mullen, this lovely little bookstore sits on a corner of the family's homestead property. Books range from best-sellers to a large selection of books on Alaska and a delightful array of children's books. Sharing the space is Charlotte's (see review below), where you can browse through your new book while enjoying something to eat or drink. *43977 Sterling Hwy, Soldotna AK 99669; 907/260-7722; fax 907/260-7447; peggym@alaska.net.*

ADVENTURES

CAPTAIN COOK STATE RECREATION AREA / Turn right at the Soldotna "Y," drive 36 miles, and this 3,500-acre playland awaits, complete with picnic spots, 52 campsites, and hiking trails. Stroll Cook Inlet shoreline, keeping your eyes open for agates. Raise your eyes and see the range of volcanoes staring back from the inlet's western shore. On a clear day, even the distant peak of Mount McKinley can be seen to the north. A launch on Stormy Lake opens the door to freshwater boating. *Alaska State Parks in Soldotna; 907/262-5581; www.dnr.state.ak.us/parks/units/captcook.htm.*

FISHING / Thousands of fishing enthusiasts flock to the **KENAI RIVER** every year, thus the somewhat unflattering but often accurate term you'll hear in reference to the river, "combat fishing." Some crowd for space along the shore. Others, relying on the expertise of several hundred guides, cruise the river in search of their guide's favorite fishing spot. The first run of salmon arrives in late May and averages 30 pounds in size. The second run, arriving midsummer, runs slightly higher in weight. July is the busiest month. Motor-powered boats dominate the lower Kenai, but drift boats bob in the currents of the upper Kenai, directed by the expert rowing of guides. With run sizes varying and a variety of species to be found, be sure to check fishing regulations and license requirements. The **KENAI RIVER SPORTFISHING ASSOCI-ATION,** a nonprofit organization committed to preserving this river famous for the salmon caught and the stories of those that got away, partners with the U.S. Fish and Wildlife Service and the Alaska Department of Fish and Game and other agencies to conduct fishery research in an effort to preserve the habitat. Fish and Game urges anglers to treat rivers with care, mindful that salmon young are frequently reared close to the bank, within the protective covering of vegetation and out of the strong current. Toward that end, anglers are urged to stay on developed trails, ladders, and boardwalks, use developed launch sites, avoid the discharge of fuel into the water, and refrain from trampling vegetation at the water's edge.

KENAI NATIONAL WILDLIFE REFUGE / More than 200 species of wildlife live or visit within the 1.9-million acre refuge, and more than 530,000 people stop by to view the wildlife and take advantage of year-round recreation opportunities, including camping, hiking, fishing, canoeing, boating, cross-country skiing, snow-shoeing, ice fishing, trapping, and hunting. Stop by **REFUGE HEADQUARTERS** (907/262-7021, Soldotna; from the Sterling Hwy, turn onto Funny River Rd by the Kenai River Bridge, turn right onto Ski Hill Rd, follow the signs) to sample what the refuge has in store, measure your hand against a grizzly bear paw print, and learn interesting animal trivia. Wildlife videos are shown daily during the summer, and you can stretch your legs on the "keen eye" nature trail.

GUIDES AND OUTFITTERS

There are 1,000 **FISHING GUIDES,** both saltwater and freshwater, on the Kenai Peninsula. More than 350 are permitted to fish the Kenai River alone, through Alaska State Parks at the Kenai River Center (907/260-4882). A federal permit is required to guide the upper portion of the river since it winds through the Kenai National Wildlife Refuge. Following is a sampling of top guides, most with 20 years of experience, who have been recognized for their concern for wildlife, the outdoors, and their client's enjoyment. **FLY-FISHING ON THE UPPER KENAI:** Try Andrew Szczesny, Alaska Fish and Float (907/262-9439; flyfisher@kenai.net; www.fly fishthekenai.com). For the **LOWER AND UPPER KENAI:** Gary and Val Early, of Early Fishing (907/262-6123; info@earlyfishing.com; www.earlyfishing.com); Randa's Guide Service (907/262-9494; dennis@randafishing.com; www.randafishing.com); Nick's Guide Service (907/262-3979; fishnick@alaska.net; www.alaska.net/~fish nick/); Alaska Rivers Company (907/595-1226; www.alaskariverscompany.com); Alaska Wildland Adventures (907/595-1279 or 800/334-8730; info@alaskwild land.com; www.alaskawildland.com); and Dan Meyers of Alaska Clearwater Sport-fishing (907/262-3797; meyerscl@alaska.net; www.alaskaclearwater.com).

LOWER KENAI ONLY: Laine Lahndt (907/262-3234); Larry Carlson of Larry's Guide Service (907/262-1815; lgs@olynet.com); Fred Pentt of Big Boy's Inc. (907/

262-2521; fishpent@techline.com; www.bigboyfishing.com); Jeff King's Budget Charters (907/262-4564 or 888/578-5333; info@jeffkingfishing.com; www.alaska. net/~lakerfsh/); Angler's Lodge and Fish Camp (907/262-1747 or 888/262-1747; anglers@alaska.net; www.alaska.net/~anglers/); Alaska Flagg's Kenai Charters (907/262-5426; akflaggs@alaska.net; www.alaska.net/~akflaggs/); and Sourdough Charters (907/262-5300 or 800/679-3473; vince@sourdoughcharters.com; www. akphil.com/sourdough/charters/).

ALASKA WILDLAND ADVENTURES / Strong supporters of ecotourism, Alaska Wildland Adventures has been creating opportunities for visitors to experience the wilderness in comfort for more than 25 years. They are ready to design an itinerary to fit your schedule and interests, including sportfishing, river rafting, mountain biking, hiking, or just sitting around the fireside at one of their lodges. Travel to tundra and high-country lakes, coastal areas, and inland rivers; photograph wildlife and sit at tables spread with delicious Alaskan fare. The Kenai Riverside Lodge, a small village of cabins, anchors their operations in Cooper Landing, where they launch guided rafting tours and drift fishing on the Kenai River. On the far side of Skilak Lake, hike with a naturalist, enjoy an evening kayaking, and a sumptuous dinner before relaxing in either a Yukon-style tent or a log cabin at the Kenai Backcountry Lodge. (See also Cooper Landing, Adventures, this chapter.) *16520 Sterling Hwy, Cooper Landing AK 99572; 907/783-2928 or 800/334-8730; info@alaska wildland.com; www.alaskawildland.com/lodges.html.*

RESTAURANTS

Charlotte's Bakery, Café, Espresso / ★★

 115 S WILLOW, STE 102, KENAI; 907/283-2777 Charlotte Legg knows how to serve variety and does it in a light-filled location that opens to the outdoors when weather permits. The breakfast menu includes locally familiar sourdough pancakes, but pulls in the influence of Mediterranean and chili seasoning for the omelets. Lunch soups and sandwiches have that same far-ranging influence, including Heather's Antipasto Veggie Sub, truly a sub of a different color. Variety is also the spice of tea time at Charlotte's; choose from blacks, greens, and reds, caffeinated or decaffeinated. Then there's the bakery case, tempting you with soft, chewy cookies, cream-cheese frosted confections, sour cream–laced goodies and berry-filled pastries to be enjoyed with tea or espresso. For the little folks, whose tastes run toward the uncomplicated, Charlotte's menu thoughtfully includes grilled cheese and peanut butter sandwiches. *$; MC, V; checks OK; breakfast, lunch Mon–Fri; no alcohol; no reservations; turn right onto Willow from the Kenai Spur Hwy.*

Mykel's Restaurant and Lounge / ★★

35041 KENAI SPUR HWY, SOLDOTNA; 907/262-4305 Step out of the nonstop Alaskan summer sun or the chill of winter, into the warm, intimate lighting of Mykel's and sink your teeth into some delicious Alaskan seafood. The steamer clams come directly from Kachemak Bay to find their place on the appetizer menu. A fondue of Bering Sea crab is blended with white wine, cheese, and just the right amount of seasonings to give it a little kick. The walnut-crusted salmon is a favorite of locals. And the secret ingredient in the ale-battered halibut comes from Homer Brewing. For those who prefer a seafood-free diet, there are plenty of other choices. *$$; AE, DC, DIS, MC, V; checks OK; breakfast Sat–Sun, lunch, dinner every day; full bar; no reservations; turn right at the "Y" in Soldotna.*

LODGINGS

Aspen Hotel / ★★

326 BINKLEY CIRCLE, SOLDOTNA; 907/260-7736 OR 888/308-7848; FAX 907/260-7786 Opened in 2002, the hotel is situated enviably near the bank of the Kenai River. In fact, the view of the river is the only telltale sign that you're on the Kenai Peninsula. Without that, you could be in any of the Aspen Hotels throughout Alaska. Guests' comfort rates high on Aspen's list, evidenced by the indoor swimming pool, Jacuzzi, workout area, and laundry facilities. Executive, spa, and family suites are available, as is a conference room. A continental breakfast awaits guests in the morning, a business center sits just off the lobby, and dataports and speaker phones are in each of the 63 individual rooms. A double goes for $149. *$$; AE, DC, DIS, MC, V; local checks OK; soldotna@aspenhotelsak.com; www. aspenhotelsak.com; turn left from the Sterling Hwy onto Binkley Circle.*

Bed and Breakfast Cottages / ★★

46700 E POPPY LN, SOLDOTNA; 907/262-7829 OR 800/582-7829; FAX 907/260-3576 Guests here have the option of completely furnished cabins with kitchens ($109, double) or B&B accommodations ($89, double), surrounded by a thick spruce forest. Bright flowers spill across the grounds, thanks to the green thumbs of hosts Lee and Carol Aley, who also own Poppy Lane Flowers. They will graciously arrange salmon or halibut fishing charters, and there's a cleaning station on site to clean your catch, grills and picnic tables to enjoy the fruits of your labor, or a freezer to preserve your bounty. *$–$$; AE, DIS, MC, V; checks OK; lcaley@alaska.com; www.alaskacottages.com/; take Kalifornsky Beach Rd from Sterling Hwy, turn right on East Poppy Ln.*

Harborside Cottages B&B / ★★

813 RIVERVIEW DR, KENAI; 907/283-6162 OR 888/283-6162; FAX 907/283-0906 Each of these five cabins faces a gloriously undisturbed view of Kenai River, Cook Inlet, and the volcanoes of the Chigmit Mountains in the background. The beautifully kept white cottages are surrounded by lawn, flowers, and trees that sway in the breeze rolling up the bluff from the inlet. Each cabin has a private bathroom, TV, and phone. Double occupancy rates are $150. *$$; AE, DIS, MC, V; local checks OK; cottages@ptialaska.net; www.harborsidecottages.com; on the bluff, near Kenai's Old Town.*

Soldotna B&B Lodge / ★★

399 LOVERS LANE, SOLDOTNA; 907/262-4779 OR 877/262-4779; FAX 907/262-3201 Watch the Kenai River flow past while you enjoy a full breakfast surrounded by the lodge's charming Swiss atmosphere. The local knowledge of hosts Steve Anderson and Monika Leiber make them valuable resources for hiking, berry and mushroom picking, skiing, snowmachining, ice fishing, and a list

of other activities. They work with local guides to arrange enjoyable fishing experiences made convenient by the lodge's private dock. Monika's multilingual abilities put Japanese and German guests at ease. In the summer, enjoy sunlight streaming through the glassed-in dining area; in the winter, let the heat from a fireplace draw you into the comfortably furnished, large common area. Each of the 16 nonsmoking rooms is warmly furnished and, though some share a bath, each has its own sink in the room. Rooms facing the river have private balconies. Double occupancy rates range from $147–$189, depending on river views. $–$$$; AE, DIS, MC, V; checks OK; monika@soldotnalodge.com; www.soldotnalodge.com; on the banks of the Kenai River, turn onto Lovers Lane from Sterling Hwy.

BED-AND-BREAKFASTS SERVICES

Let the **KENAI PENINSULA BED AND BREAKFAST ASSOCIATION** (PO Box 2992, Kenai AK 99611; www.kenaipeninsulabba.com) help you select a B&B. Organized in 1996, the goal is to assist peninsula innkeepers in providing quality accommodations. Members are inspected and licensed to ensure that health and safety standards are maintained. A list of their members can be found on their Web site; a printed version is available at the Kenai Visitors & Cultural Center (See Access and Information, above).

Between Soldotna and Homer

Stop by **TUSTUMENA SMOKEHOUSE** (Mile 101.4 Sterling Hwy; 907/262-0421; fred@tustumenasmokehouse.com; www.tustumenasmokehouse.com) and sample Alaska salmon smoked traditionally or with variations of brown sugar, lemon pepper, or Cajun seasoning. For a unique treat, try the salmon sausage. Crab and scallops harvested from Alaska's pristine waters and buffalo from the Interior are available for you to take home and fix to your liking.

Fifteen miles south of Soldotna, the Sterling Highway passes over the **KASILOF RIVER,** another hot fishing spot. Salmon runs arrive here prior to reaching the Kenai River, making this a popular area in June. Fish from the shore or charter a guide to take you down the river. Motorized boats are not allowed on the Kasilof, making the float pleasantly quiet. It took over 10 years, but **TUSTUMENA LODGE** (Mile 111 Sterling Hwy, Kasilof; 907/260-4216; suzieq@ptialaska.net) finally made it into the *Guinness Book of World Records*, thanks to a hat collection numbering more than 22,000 that covers the walls and ceiling. The lodge is also home to the Tustumena 200, a qualifying race for the Iditarod Trail Sled Dog Race. At either **CLAM GULCH STATE RECREATION AREA,** about 40 minutes south of Soldotna, or **NINILCHIK,** another 12 miles south, you can watch locals digging for razor clams on the low tides or get in on the action yourself after consulting the tide books and purchasing a license. You'll need a bucket, a shovel, and a fast eye.

Bed-and-breakfasts line the road between Soldotna and Homer, many offering more than a place to rest your head. When you call Katie Kennedy at **KENNEDY'S LOOKOUT B&B** (Mile 128 Sterling Hwy; 907/567-3482; liphook@ptialaska.net; www.charters.bizland.com), ask about fishing with her partner, Don Erwin, owner of Alaska Trophy Charters. Looking down on the Ninilchik River valley from the deck of **MEANDER IN B&B** (Mile 2.6 Oilwell Rd, Ninilchik AK 99639; 907/567-1050; meanderin@alaska.com; www.meanderin.net/), you will frequently see brown bears fishing in the slow-moving river and hosts Mike Schuster and Jodi Leah are available to take you rafting on the river. They also are avid anglers and clamdiggers and are happy to share their expert advice. **BLUFF HOUSE B&B** (PO Box 39327, Ninilchik AK 99639; 907/567-3605; bluffbb@alaska.net; www.alaska.net/bluffbb/) gets its name from an enviable perch above the mouth of Deep Creek, a busy fishing and clam-digging area in the summer. In the winter, hosts Terry and Margie Smith will show you another side of the Kenai Peninsula with snowmachine tours into the Caribou Hills.

BLACK WATER BEND ESPRESSO (Mile 161 Sterling Hwy, Anchor Point AK 99556; 907/235-6884 or 888/713-6432) is 10 miles out of Homer. Besides espresso, teas, and smoothies, owner Pat Ligenza makes sack lunches for fishing charters, offers assistance to motorists, and will even provide stock quotes from her computer to anxious visitors. Her coffee is delicious, her smoothies are made from fresh fruit, and her smile is a bright spot on a long drive.

Homer

Crest the top of the hill that overlooks Homer and you'll see the closing pages of this chapter of Alaska spread before you. The mouth of Cook Inlet opens wide onto the Gulf of Alaska. Augustine and Douglas, the two most southern volcanoes rimming the inlet, loom on the western horizon. Kachemak Bay sparkles in the distance. Snow-covered mountains and glaciers rim the bay. Small airplanes dot the sky, connecting the smaller communities on the bay's southern shore to Homer, on the northern shore. The 5-mile length of the **HOMER SPIT,** a naturally occurring sliver of land, extends into the bay. On a sunny day, the view is stunning.

Archaeologists have uncovered signs of early inhabitants on the bay's southern shore, where tiny inlets and fjords are protected from ocean storms. The elusive promise of gold drew settlers to the northern shore, and it is from one of them, Homer Pennock, that the city derived its name. Although the dream of gold blazed hot, the reality burned disappointingly cold and today's 4,000 residents depend heavily on the sea, either through commercial or sportfishing, and tourism.

The winds and currents have brought to Homer an interesting mix of people, blending artists, musicians, fishing crews, homesteaders, and activists for a wide range of causes. Pop singer Jewel's family were early homesteaders and author Tom Bodett, of Motel 6 "we'll leave the light on for you" fame, makes his home here.

Like a finger beckoning visitors, the spit bustles in the summer with license plates and accents from around the world weaving interesting threads into this already mixed basket of influences. Stroll the harbor or the boardwalk areas with their eateries, gift shops, fishing charters, and tour guides. Camp along the beach or slip into the shadowy quiet of the **SALTY DAWG SALOON** (907/235-9990), a pub of historic beginnings. In the winter, bald eagles swarm to the spit and photographers from across the planet follow, snapping photos of these majestic creatures. A volunteer effort, led by Homer's "eagle lady," Jean Keene, keeps the eagles fed with scraps of fish.

ACCESS AND INFORMATION

All **ROADS**, and the Sterling Highway is the only one, lead to Homer. If you're **FLYING**, your travel agent will make sure you're on the right plane. If arriving **BY SEA**, keep your eye on the nautical chart. If you thought about taking the train, think again. The train stopped in Seward. The community is spread out, so access to a vehicle is a good idea. Try **HERTZ RENT-A-CAR** (907/235-0734; fax 907/235-8414) or **ADVENTURE ALASKA CAR RENTAL** (907/235-4022 or 800/882-2808), which also rents fishing poles.

The **HOMER CHAMBER OF COMMERCE** (201 Sterling Hwy, 907/235-7740) is well stocked with maps, brochures, and information on lodging, restaurants, and activities. **CENTRAL CHARTERS** (4241 Homer Spit Rd; 907/235-7847; 800/478-7847) is a booking agency that can arrange just about anything, including fishing charters, kayaking trips, bear viewing, flight-seeing, water taxis, and stays at many B&Bs in town.

EXPLORING

PRATT MUSEUM / Local history, marine life, and art come together under one roof at the Pratt Museum, located on Bartlett Street in Homer's main business section. A solar cam mounted on Gull Rock, a rookery 8 miles from Homer, allows up-close viewing of the hundreds of seabirds that nest on the island. "Darkened Waters," a Smithsonian exhibit about the *Exxon Valdez* oil spill, brings excited chatter to a hush with sights and sounds of the 1989 disaster, which spilled 11 million gallons of crude oil into Prince William Sound. You can listen to the frightening announcement from the ship's Captain Joseph Hazelwood that he had run "hard aground." Admission is $6 adults, $5.50 seniors, $3 children ages 6–18. There's also a family rate of $20. The museum offers free guided walking tours in summer, including an historic harbor tour, on Thursdays, Fridays, and Saturdays. *3779 Bartlett St, Homer AK 99603; 907/235-8635; info@prattmuseum.org; www.prattmuseum.org.*

WALKS AND DRIVES / Homer's beachfront allows for miles of beachcombing. The **CENTER FOR ALASKAN COASTAL STUDIES** (708 Smokey Bay Wy; PO Box 2225, Homer AK 99603; 907/235-6667; cacs@xyz.net; www.akcoastalstudies.org; call for directions) has created a forest walk and forest-related activities for the family at the Carl E. Wynn Nature Center, located in the hills above Homer. The annual **KACHEMAK BAY SHOREBIRD FESTIVAL** (907/235-7740; homer@xyz.net; www.homeralaska.org/shorebird.htm) has been held around the second week of May for more than a decade to celebrate the more than 25 species of shorebirds from as far away as Asia, Hawaii, and South America that lay over in the Kachemak Bay area. According to festival organizers, the most commonly seen birds are western and least sandpipers; dunlins; short-billed dowitchers; greater and lesser yellowlegs; common snipe; and black-bellied, golden, and semipalmated plovers; Hudsonian, marbled, and bar-tailed godwits; and surfbirds.

SHOPPING / **BUNNELL STREET GALLERY** (106 W Bunnell Ave, Ste A, Homer AK 99603; 907/235-2662; www.xyz.net/~bunnell/) features solo and group shows in what was once the Inlet Trading Post. With an inside focus on cutting-edge Alaskan art, the gallery's exterior focuses on Kachemak Bay's Bishop's Beach. In the **FIREWEED GALLERY** (475 E Pioneer Ave, Homer AK 99603; 907/235-3411;

homerart@xyz.net; www.xyz.net/~homerart), the blue light reflected off ice shimmers from David Rosenthal's oil paintings. Dennis Anderson's photography captures the aurora, and artists' exhibitions change frequently. At **PTARMIGAN ARTS** (471 E Pioneer Ave, Homer AK 99603; 907/235-5345; homerart@ptialaska.net; www.ptarmiganarts.com) you'll find that the ceramics, jewelry, glass, photography, and watercolors are just some of the mediums displayed by local artists and craftspeople.

ADVENTURES

There is no end to ocean-related activities in Homer, thanks to Kachemak Bay. Whale-watching, salmon or halibut fishing, hiking, kayaking, and camping are all within reach, thanks to a host of guides and outdoor enthusiasts eager to share their appreciation for this pristine environment. If your tastes run toward berry picking, you can take your own bucket into the woods or sample some made from the local bounty.

BOAT TOURS / Have boat, will travel. To get across the bay to Halibut Cove, make reservations on the **DANNY J**, a converted fishing boat, through Central Charters (see Halibut Charter, below). The trip includes a stop at Gull Island (a bird sanctuary) and continues to the cove, where you'll have a couple of hours to explore this picturesque setting. Whale-watching tours are offered by **RAINBOW TOURS** (PO Box 1526, Homer AK 99603; 907/235-7446; rainbow@rainbowtours.net; www.rainbowtours.net). **ST. AUGUSTINE'S KAYAK AND TOURS** (PO Box 2412, Homer AK 99603; 907/235-6126; inletchr@ptialaska.net; www.homerkayaking.com) provides wildlife tours for small groups of 14 aboard the MV *Seabird*, as well as half- and full-day guided kayaking trips. Prices range quite a bit depending on what you do. An afternoon to Halibut Cove runs $44 per person, while a daylong whale-watching trip is about $125 per person.

HALIBUT CHARTER / Ready for a full or half day on the ocean? Call **CENTRAL CHARTERS** to reserve a spot aboard one of the many charter boats that depart daily from Homer's harbor. If the weather's calm, it can be a smooth and enjoyable ride to the fishing grounds, but if the water is rough, be sure to take along your sea legs; charter captains aren't known for making U-turns. Half-day rates are in the neighborhood of $85 per person; a full-day can run about $170 per person. Prices include fishing gear, bait, and cleaning your catch. *907/235-7847 or 800/478-7847.*

KAYAKING / A more personal approach to the water is offered by **TRUE NORTH KAYAK ADVENTURES**. Owners Alison O'Hara and Kevin Bell are experienced kayakers and instructors and have created daily guided trips with beginners in mind. Kayak rentals are available for experienced paddlers. Half-day guided tours start at $85 per person; full-day trips run $125 per person. Multiday trips range upward, depending on length and distance. *PO Box 2319, Homer AK 99603; 907/235-0708; kayak@xyz.net; www.truenorthkayak.com.*

RESTAURANTS

Boardwalk Fish & Chips / ★★

HOMER SPIT RD, HOMER; 907/235-7749 Like the name says, fish-and-chips are the house specialty. And the big windows on this corner location of the boardwalk give a sweeping view of Kachemak Bay, the islands, and far shore that is every bit as delicious to the eyes as the fish-and-chips are to the taste buds. It's hard to know which draws the biggest crowd, but lines are common so give plenty of time to get a seat. *$; MC, V; local checks OK; lunch, dinner (closed winter); beer and wine; no reservations; on the spit, across the road from the Salty Dawg Saloon.*

Café Cups / ★★★

162 W PIONEER AVE, HOMER; 907/235-8330 The whimsically decorated exterior, with its gigantic cups, is a clue to the artsy chic inside Café Cups. Dark woods, fresh flowers, cascading plants, and unique menus create tasteful warmth and charm, and the variety of items on the menu are just as unique and inviting. Steamed clams in pesto are a flavorful way to start a meal and halibut teriyaki, served on a bed of greens and drizzled with vinaigrette, is a perfect next step. For dessert, try Dave's Delight, a mouthwatering variation on cheesecake. *$$–$$$; MC, V; Alaska checks OK; lunch, dinner; beer and wine; reservations recommended for parties of 4 or more; downtown, across from the library.*

Captain Pattie's Seafood Restaurant / ★★

4241 HOMER SPIT RD, HOMER; 907/235-5135 Not only is the food good, but you can drop off your cleaned catch as soon as you finish a day of fishing and they will deep fry, charbroil, or bake it to your liking. The smoked-salmon stuffed mushrooms are a must on the appetizer menu. If the nautical motif doesn't let you know you're near the sea, the view from the windows definitely will. *$$–$$$; DIS, MC, V; Alaska checks OK; lunch, dinner; beer and wine; reservations recommended; on the boardwalk next to the hanging giant king salmon.*

The Fresh Sourdough Express Bakery & Café / ★★

1316 OCEAN DR, HOMER; 907/235-7571 The atmosphere is cheerful, the portions hearty, and there is a definite local preference, from potatoes to reindeer sausage to breads. Start your day with the Sourdough Joe, a yummy blend of salsa, cheeses, eggs, and sausage. Halibut finds its way into a lunchtime hoagie. They also offer vegan and vegetarian items. And the bakery case is stuffed with tempting treats. *$; MC, V; local checks OK; breakfast, lunch, dinner; beer and wine; www.freshsourdoughexpress.com; on the left side of Ocean Dr as you head toward the spit from downtown.*

The Homestead / ★★

MILE 8.2 EAST END RD, HOMER; 907/235-8723 After 10 years at the Homestead, Chef Sean Maryott has moved on to new horizons, but owners Lisa and Steve Nolan are striving to maintain the quality that Maryott, also the founding chef of Cups, brought to the restaurant. The log-cabin atmosphere is in keeping with the setting and there are new seafood specials nightly, depending on the season. *$$$; AE, MC, V; Alaska checks OK; dinner; full bar; reservations recommended.* &

Land's End Chart Room / ★★★

4786 HOMER SPIT RD, HOMER; 907/235-0406 OR 800/478-0400 Located at the end of the spit, you simply cannot beat the view here. In summer, you'll want to eat out on the deck. Fishing boats head in and out of the harbor and kayakers paddle to destinations across the bay. Sea otters bob off shore and shorebirds fill the sky. On wintry evenings, you'll want to stay inside and watch the aurora borealis dance above the mountains or experience the hush of falling snow. The crab and artichoke dip is considered an appetizer, but add a steaming loaf of bread and a salad topped with a dressing that hints of jalapeño, and you've got a meal. *$$$; AE, DC, DIS, MC, V; checks OK; breakfast, lunch, dinner; full bar; reservations recommended; at the end of the spit.* &

Two Sisters Bakery / ★

106 W BUNNELL, STE B, HOMER; 907/235-2280 This tiny hole-in-the-wall bakery and coffee shop whips up pastries, breakfast, and lunch pizzas and quiches that will make your mouth water. The rack for day-old and free bread is quickly emptied. Chairs outside extend the small quarters. *$; No credit cards; checks OK; breakfast, lunch; no alcohol; no reservations; in the same building as Bunnell Street Gallery.*

LODGINGS

Alaskan Suites / ★★★★

42485 STERLING HWY, HOMER; 907/235-1972 OR 888/239-1972 No other lodging in Homer can promise the elevation or the distance of view that these five cabins offer. Bald eagles glide just beyond your reach. In the distance, Cook Inlet joins the Gulf of Alaska. To the west, the volcanic cone of Augustine Island rises from the water. Hosts John and Sharon Bouman have spared no luxury. There are handcrafted beds, luxurious recliners, completely equipped kitchenettes, and DVD players with surround sound. Each cabin has a private deck facing the view. A gas grill stands ready for your freshly caught halibut or salmon. Tell the Boumans you're there for a romantic getaway, and they'll have the candles lit and soft music playing when you arrive. Rates are $195 for a double. *$$$; AE, DC, DIS, MC, V; checks OK; aksuites@alaska.net; www.alaskansuites.com; off Sterling Hwy, at the top of the hill.*

Bay View Inn / ★

2851 STERLING HWY, HOMER; 907/235-8485 (800/478-8485, IN-STATE); FAX 907/235-8716 The inn has proudly claimed this location since the 1950s and underwent a remodel several years ago, thanks to owner Dennis Novak. The 12 non-smoking rooms have separate entrances and some have kitchens. A private cottage sits separate from the inn. Chairs and picnic tables scattered along the surrounding lawn provide space for guests to enjoy the view of Kachemak Bay and inhale ocean breezes. A double goes for $99. *$$; AE, DIS, MC, V; checks OK; PO Box 804, Homer AK 99603; bayview@alaska.net; www.bayviewalaska.com; just off Sterling Hwy, below the overlook.*

Brigitte's Bavarian B&B / ★★

ON TERN COURT, HOMER; 907/235-6620 Hosts Willie and Brigitte Suter have created their B&B with a foot on the hillside, a face toward Kachemak Bay, and privacy guaranteed by the surrounding birch trees, vegetable garden, and an abundance of colorful, fresh flowers. The interior design, aided by Brigitte's carpentry skill, has turned the three cottages into wonderful getaways, as have furnishings picked up during the couple's travels. One of the cabins is attached to the main house, while two are separate. Each has its own entrance and private bath. Scents of freshly ground coffee, garden fresh herbal teas, homemade breads and jams, and other treats guarantee a full table for breakfast. Double occupancy rates are $105. *$$; No credit cards; checks OK; PO Box 2391, Homer AK 99603; akms.com/brigitte; turn left off East End Rd onto Bear Creek Loop, turn onto Steller's Jay, follow the signs.*

Chocolate Drop Inn / ★★★

57745 CLOVER AVE, HOMER; 907/235-3668 OR 800/530-6015; FAX 907/235-3729 Log construction surrounds you and the windows open onto a view across Kachemak Bay to "chocolate drop mountain." Five rooms, a family suite, a honeymoon suite with a private Jacuzzi, an outdoor hot tub, and a high-ceiling common area add to the attraction, but the frosting on the cake is owner Britney Gifford's cooking. When your mouth isn't too full, ask for her recipe for Sour Cream Cinnamon Coffee Cake or her Apricot Coffee Cake. She will gladly share. Double occupancy rates start at $115. *$$–$$$; AE, MC, V; checks OK; PO Box 70, Homer AK 99603; chocdrop@chocolatedropinn.com; www.chocolatedropinn. com; from East End Rd turn left onto Portlock, turn left onto Clover Ave, follow the signs.*

The Driftwood Inn & RV Park / ★

135 W BUNNELL AVE, HOMER; PHONE-FAX 907/235-8019 OR 800/478-8019 The lobby's beach-rock fireplace is inviting. Most of the 22 rooms are tiny, taking their design from ship's quarters, but they're clean, comfortable, and close to Bishop's Beach. Some share a bath, some have private baths, and some have private entrances. Rates range from $65–$130, double occupancy. In the common area, you'll find breakfast cereals, instant soups, snacks, fresh fruit, and hot beverages. Some rooms allow canine guests, and there is a coin-operated washer and dryer available for your convenience. The RV park has 22 spaces that go for $26–$29 a night (there are also weekly and monthly rates). Another plus: Two Sisters Bakery is just across the road. *$$; AE, DIS, MC, V; checks OK; driftinn@xyz.net; www. thedriftwoodinn.com; from the Homer Bypass, turn left on Main St, then left on Bunnell.*

Halcyon Heights / ★★★

61850 MISSION RD, HOMER; 907/235-2148; FAX 907/235-3773 The artistic flare and creative carpentry of owners Bob and Gail Ammerman add a special touch to this B&B, which has six rooms. Their warm smiles and colorful stories, drawn from the years they've lived in Alaska, will make you feel right at home. Be sure to ask about the paint design on the cupboard doors. The view is spectacular, the outdoor

Jacuzzi is waiting for you, and the pool table is ready for a game. Rates range from $100–$135, double occupancy. *$$; AE, DIS, MC, V; checks OK; PO Box 3552, Homer AK 99603; halcyon@xyz.net; www.ak-biz.com/halcyonheights/; take East Hill Rd off East End Rd, turn left on Mission Rd.*

Island Watch Bed and Breakfast / ★★

4241 CLAUDIA ST, HOMER; 907/235-2265 Whether you stay in one of the two private cabins, the two-bedroom suite, or one of the two B&B rooms in the main house, you'll be treated to a good taste of Alaskan hospitality, thanks to owner Eileen Mullen and her homesteading background. The path to the cabins is lined with flowers, and the cabins are situated near the horse paddock and only steps from the outdoor hot tub. Your day begins at the large dining table, where a full breakfast is served, plans for the day are made, and the view of Kachemak Bay, complete with islands, is spread before you. The cabins and suite are $140, double occupancy; the rooms in the house are $90. *$$; AE, DC, DIS, MC, V; checks OK; PO Box 1394, Homer AK 99603; island@xyz.net; www.islandwatch.net; take West Hill off Sterling Hwy, turn left on Claudia St, follow signs.*

Land's End Resort / ★

4786 HOMER SPIT RD, HOMER; 907/235-0400 OR 800/478-0400; FAX 907/235-0420 The location at the end of the spit is the biggest attraction at Land's End. Most of the 82 rooms have decks that face Kachemak Bay. Suites include the Starboard Bay Side Suite, with a sitting room, bedroom, and outside entrance, and two-story Midship Loft Suites. The spa and fitness center includes an eight-person outdoor Jacuzzi and an on-site massage therapist. At the tour desk, arrange your activities while in Homer. Meeting rooms for groups are available. Rates are $115–$203, single occupancy. Additional guests are $10 per person. *$$–$$$; AE, DC, MC, V; checks OK; landsend@alaska.net; www.lands-end-resort.com; end of the spit.* ௵

Old Town B&B / ★★

106 W BUNNELL, STE D, HOMER; 907/235-7558 Furnishings and decorations are charming and in keeping with the 1936 origin of the building. From the second floor vantage point (it's above the Bunnell Street Gallery and Two Sisters Bakery), guests in any of the three rooms have a view of nearby Bishop's Beach. The location can't be beat. Owner Asia Freeman's artwork decorates the walls. The stairway to the B&B leans a bit disconcertingly away from the building, but is nonetheless sturdy. Rates are $70–$85, double occupancy. And a special treat: guests are given coupons to get a scone at Two Sisters. *$–$$; MC, V; checks OK; oldtown@xyz.net; www.xyz.net/~oldtown/; corner of Bunnell and Main St.*

The Shorebird Guest House / ★★

4774 KACHEMAK DR, HOMER; 907/235-2107; FAX 907/235-5435 The privacy of this cabin, which can comfortably accommodate families or groups of six, puts you in a world of your own, with a view of the bay at your doorstep and stairs to the beach. The kitchen is completely furnished. Double occupancy rate is $120. *$$; MC, V; checks OK; open May to Sept; PO Box 204, Homer AK 99603;*

info@shorebirdcabin.com; shorebirdcabin.com/; at the base of the spit, turn left on Kachemak Dr, go 3 miles, look for sign on right.

Wild Rose Cottages

5440 EAST HILL RD, HOMER; 907/235-8780 Perched high above Homer and Kachemak Bay, these four cabins have a view of the bay and the log construction gives an Alaska-style comfort. The largest cabin has two bedrooms, some have full kitchens, and all of them have private bathrooms. Double occupancy rates range from $95–$125. *$$; MC, V; checks OK; PO Box 665, Homer AK 99603; wild rose@xyz.net; www.alaskaone.com/wildrose; drive 1 mile east on East End Rd, turn left up East Hill Rd for another mile, turn right at the sign.*

Halibut Cove

For a true taste of Alaskan tranquility, take the **DANNY J** ferry from Homer to Halibut Cove, a quaint community of artists and fishermen. No roads or parking lots here, just boardwalks, trails, and docks. Houses are built on pilings and perched on rocks. You'll feel the protective embrace of surrounding snowcapped mountains, the calm, deep green water of the cove, and the much slower pace of this laid-back community. Boardwalks and paths lead to the cove's three art galleries. **EXPERIENCE GALLERY** exhibits the work of 17 local artists. At Diana Tillion's **COVE GALLERY**, sepia tones reflect her work with octopus ink, which she harvests with the help of friends. A sign in **ALEX COMBS' GALLERY** invites you to touch the work he does with clay, whether it be bowls, cups, or intriguing pieces on the walls. There are two trips daily on the *Danny J*. If you depart Homer at noon, there is time to eat at the cove's wonderful little restaurant (see below) and explore before returning to Homer at 5pm. A shortened visit, just right for dinner, is available by leaving Homer at 5pm and returning that same evening.

RESTAURANTS

The Saltry / ★★★

ACROSS THE WATER FROM HOMER, HALIBUT COVE; 907/296-2223 This is Halibut Cove's only restaurant, and what a treat it is. Here the focus is on freshness, be it from the sea, the oven, or just-picked greens from the garden. Sit inside or, on a sunny warm day, take advantage of the covered deck that backs a rocky cliff and faces the cove. A fire pit adds warmth to the atmosphere, as do fresh flowers on the tables and pieces from the Combs' studio. Friendly servers are eager to make your visit an experience to remember. For a taste of the best the Saltry has to offer, try the combination seafood appetizer that includes ceviche with a wonderfully tart lemon flavor, pickled salmon, hot and spicy Korean shrimp poke, a creamy smoked salmon pâté, and norimaki. *$$; MC, V; local checks only; lunch, dinner every day; full bar; reservations required, call Central Charters, 907/235-7847 or 800/478-7847; www.centralcharter.com/; if you're in Halibut Cove, you can't miss it.*

LODGING

Quiet Place Lodge / ★★★

ACROSS THE WATER FROM HOMER, HALIBUT COVE; 907/296-2212; FAX 907/296-2241 If getting away from it all is the goal, the hushed atmosphere of the cove is the place. No more than eight guests are allowed at a time. The lodge's five waterfront cabins have shared baths. During your stay, boat, kayak, hike, fish, tour the cove's galleries, or just relax by the woodstove with a good book. Rates are $185 per person. *$$$; MC, V; checks OK; closed in winter; PO Box 6474, Halibut Cove AK 99603; quiet@xyz.net; www.quietplace.com.*

Kachemak Bay State Park

This state park, coupled with Kachemak Bay State Wilderness Park next to it, provides 400,000 acres of islands and shoreline, divided roughly down the middle by the Kenai Mountains. A network of trails offers you an up-close look at this remote and wild wonderland.

Whales ply the dark, shadowy depths, rising for air to the delighted surprise of visitors. Porpoises cut playful paths as they skim the water's surface. Seals, sea lions, and sea otters also inhabit this marine environment. The seabird population numbers in the thousands. Keep your eyes open for the telltale orange, black, and white coloring of puffins and black, long-necked cormorants. Kittiwakes and murrelets add to the numbers and circling overhead, as does the sharp-eyed and majestic bald eagle. And in the shaded woods, moose amble awkwardly and share the neighborhood with black bears and coyotes.

ACCESS AND INFORMATION

The road ends in Homer, but **WATER TAXIS** are waiting to take up the slack. Check with Central Charters (907/235-7847 or 800/478-7847) in Homer for reservations. For more information, visit or call the **DISTRICT RANGER STATION** (on Sterling Hwy as you enter Homer, PO Box 321, Homer AK 99603; 907/235-7024). They can provide you with maps, brochures, and answers to your questions. In the summer, a ranger station is open in Halibut Cove (907/235-6999).

ADVENTURES

HIKING / GLACIER LAKE TRAIL is an easy hike that can be made in a day. In 3.2 miles, you find yourself near Grewingk Glacier Lake, facing Grewingk Glacier. Ready for more adventure? Then take the **POOT PEAK TRAIL** up what some call "chocolate drop mountain." Your water taxi will drop you off at the trailhead in Halibut Cove Lagoon and what lies ahead can be enjoyed in a day. Better yet, take two days and overnight at the public-use cabin. In all, there are 90 some miles of trails, 21 remote campsites, and five public-use cabins ($50 per night). Check with the ranger (907/235-7024) for a list of the trails and trail conditions.

NATURAL-HISTORY TOURS / The **CENTER FOR ALASKAN COASTAL STUDIES** (PO Box 2225, Homer AK 99603; 907/235-6667; cacs@xyz.net; www.ak coastalstudies.org) has a half-day naturalist-guided tour they offer between Memorial Day and Labor Day. Sailing from Homer at 8:30am, view the seabird rookery on Gull Island, hike in the forest, and explore the tidal areas around the Peterson Bay Field Station. You'll be back in Homer by mid-afternoon. Adults $75; children under 12, $60; 2 years and under, free. Group rates are available for parties of more than 10. Bring warm clothing, waterproof footwear, and your lunch. Binoculars and cameras will ensure you don't miss any of the sights.

WILDERNESS LODGES

Kachemak Bay Wilderness Lodge

CHINA POOT BAY, NEAR HOMER; 907/235-8910; FAX 907/235-8911 Water transportation from Homer will deliver you across Kachemak Bay to this most exquisite lodge, situated on China Poot Bay. Owners and naturalists Mike and Diane McBride offer a wilderness experience that incorporates their philosophy of environmental responsibility. The lodge construction and design incorporates materials salvaged from wrecked ships, such as the unique chandelier in the dining room, crafted from a boat hull. Private cabins, with electricity and full baths, accommodate a dozen guests a week. A basket of fruit, wine, chocolates, and flowers awaits your arrival, and if you forgot to bring your fishing license with you, that can be purchased at the lodge. Glass Japanese floats and other beachcombing treasures have been worked into the decor. An outdoor hot tub can be enjoyed privately. And there are opportunities to fish, view wildlife, hike, and kayak. Rates for the Monday–Friday stay are $2,500 per person, and they will arrange for the transportation to the lodge via Rainbow Tours. *$$$; No credit cards; checks OK; open May to mid-Sept; PO Box 956, Homer AK 99603; wildrnes@xyz.net; www.xyz.net/~wildrnes/lodge.htm.*

Tutka Bay Wilderness Lodge

LITTLE TUTKA; 907/235-3905 OR 800/606-3909; FAX 907/235-3909 Tucked into the hidden waters of Tutka Bay and within the tiny community of Little Tutka, hosts Jon and Nelda Osgood have created a retreat along the shore and up into the forest's edge of an isthmus that connects Tutka and Little Tutka Bays. There are three cabins, as well as two guest suites on the second floor of the boat house. All accommodations have private baths. Trails into Kachemak Bay State Park begin nearby. Kayak, fish, harvest steamer clams and mussels, return the curious gaze of a sea otter swimming past, wave at a bald eagle swooping overhead, wander the beach in search of treasures to fill your pockets, ease your muscles with the sauna's penetrating heat, or simply snooze on the deck. If you must bring your laptop, there is electricity to keep it operable and an Internet hookup. The dining area is wrapped with windows, so the scenery is part of your dining experience. And you may have read *Gourmet* magazine's sterling recommendation of the food that fills the table and the satisfied guests. Sample menus and a recipe of the month are included on the lodge's Web site. Cost is $290 per night, per person, two-night minimum. Water taxi and excursions to view wildlife and fish are extra. *$$$; AE, MC, V; checks OK; open mid-May to mid-Sept; PO Box 960, Homer AK 99603; www.tutkabaylodge.com.*

Seldovia

This far-flung Kenai Peninsula community of some 300 residents was a bustling Russian fishing village in the late 1800s. In fact, the Russians named it Zaliv Seldevoy, or Herring Bay. Built in 1891 atop a rocky outcropping, **ST. NICHOLAS ORTHODOX CHURCH** steadfastly faces the entrance of the bay and is listed as a National Historic Site. Archaeological research has revealed artifacts of Athabascan Indian, Alutiiq, and Eskimo residence that date back to the 1400s and the Kenaitze name for the bay was Chesloknu.

A wooden boardwalk once served as the town's main thoroughfare, with buildings on either side supported by pilings and extending out over the bay. However, the land subsided 4 feet during Alaska's 1964 earthquake and the tides rose up and washed over the boardwalk and destroyed buildings along its edge. A small section of the boardwalk was left along Seldovia Slough, but the rest was replaced by a road. New buildings replaced the old, still perched on pilings with the bay underneath.

Berries grow in abundance, the beaches offer clamming, the calm waters of Seldovia Bay are perfect for exploring with a kayak, and trails are wonderful for hiking or mountain biking. Seldovia is the peninsula's smallest organized city; you can easily walk from one end to the other.

ACCESS AND INFORMATION

Playing on Homer's slogan as the city "at the end of the road," Seldovia takes pride in being "beyond the end of the road," with only sea and air as connecting links to Homer. The **ALASKA MARINE HIGHWAY**'s MV *Tustumena* (907/235-8449 or 800/642-0066; www.alaska.gov/ferry) provides service for passengers, vehicles, and freight. **RAINBOW TOURS** (907/235-7272) offers daily shuttle service to the Seldovia harbor and **JAKOLOF FERRY SERVICE** (907/235-2376; 907/235-6384, summer; www.jakolofferryservice.com/) delivers passengers from Homer to the Jakolof Bay public dock 11 miles from town. To see the views from the air, make the 15-minute flight with **SMOKEY BAY AIR** (2100 Kachemak Dr, Homer; 907/235-1511). The **SELDOVIA CHAMBER OF COMMERCE** (907/234-7612) will happily provide additional information.

EXPLORING

Flashy purple paint marks **THE BUZZ** (907/234-7479), the place to stop for espresso, quiche, soups, and pastries and to catch up on local news. The **MAD FISH RESTAURANT** (907/234-7676; madfish@alaska.net) is open daily for lunch and dinner, located directly across from the boat ramp. While the food is fine, the service can be less than friendly.

During berry season, watch the action at **ALASKA TRIBAL CACHE** (PO Drawer L, Seldovia AK 99663; 907/234-7898 or 800/270-7810; svt@svt.org; www.alaska tribalcache.com) where members of the Seldovia Village Tribe transform the berries into jams, jellies, and syrups. During the off-season, you can take home jars of the finished product. If you're looking for interesting and unique gifts to take home, stop at **HERRING BAY MERCANTILE** (907/234-7410). It is owned by local artist and author Susan Woodward Springer.

ADVENTURES

BOAT TOUR / Unless you decide to travel to Seldovia by air, you will enjoy two hours on the water, round-trip. For other boating adventures, go whale-watching with **RAINBOW TOURS** or a take a side trip to Halibut Cove with **JAKOLOF FERRY SERVICE** (for both, see Access and Information, above).

KAYAKING / Go kayaking with **KAYAK'ATAK** (in Herring Bay Mercantile, PO Box 109, Seldovia AK 99663; 907/234-7425; www.alaska.net/~kayaks), owned and operated by Kirby and Lynn Corwin. Day trips range from $80–$120 per person. Overnight trips start at $360 per person. They'll also custom-design an excursion for you. Kayak rentals are available for experienced paddlers at $50 the first day and $30 for each day after that.

MOUNTAIN BIKING / The road between the dock at Jakolof Bay and town is a great place to put your mountain bike to use. Or, instead of heading toward Seldovia, turn left and try the Jakolof–Rocky River Road. **MAIN STREET MARKET** (907/234-7633; fax 907/296-7461) rents mountain bikes for $10 for one hour, or $40 for 24. They only have a few so call ahead and reserve one.

WALKING AND HIKING / The **OTTERBAHN TRAIL** is a tribute to public participation and the outdoors. Its name spoofs the German Autobahn, but you'll want to take your time enjoying this pathway to the beach. The **TUTKA BAY TRAIL,** off Jakolof Bay Road, was originally built as back-up transportation for the Tutka Bay Salmon Hatchery. It winds through an area being logged by the Seldovia Native Association, so be careful to follow the signs. The **ROCKY RIDGE TRAIL** is a new, 2½-mile hike, built through the Alaska Recreational Trails Grant Program. It is moderately difficult, climbing to 800 feet. Your effort is rewarded with views of Seldovia, Cook Inlet, and Mount Iliamna.

LODGINGS

Across the Bay Tent & Breakfast Adventure Company / ★
JAKOLOF BAY RD AT KASITSNA BAY, SELDOVIA; 907/235-3633, SUMMER; 907/345-2571, WINTER It's summer camp revisited when you unroll your own sleeping bag inside one of these canvas-walled tents built on a deck. Hot showers are available, breakfast is included, and you have your choice of letting hosts Mary Jane and Tony Lastufka prepare your lunches and dinners with a seafood emphasis or you can bring your own food. They offer guided kayak tours or mountain bikes so you can strike out on your own to explore the surrounding shore and forest, or head for downtown Seldovia, some 8 miles away. You might want to consider this secluded and rugged environment for a retreat or conference. Tent and breakfast is $58; tent with all meals is $85; guided kayak tours are $95; mountain bikes rent for $25 a day (all prices per person). *$; MC, V; checks OK; closed Oct 1 to May 1; eco tours@ptialaska.net; www.tentandbreakfastalaska.com; 8 miles from Seldovia.*

Alaska Dancing Eagles B&B and Cabin Rental / ★★
CORNER OF MAIN AND WATER STS, SELDOVIA; 907/234-7627, SUMMER, 907/278-0288, WINTER Enviably situated on the shores of Seldovia Harbor and the end of the town's old boardwalk, the cabin, a remodeled boathouse built on pilings, sleeps six, has a fully equipped kitchen, and is perfect for families

and large groups. Bed-and-breakfast accommodations are located in the four-bedroom house that has an eastern exposure and is connected by a deck to the boathouse and the outdoor hot tub. Eat breakfast inside if you must, but the deck's fresh salty air is an invigorating option. The cabin rents for $175 per couple, per night, two-night minimum. Rates for the B&B are $65 per person or $110 for a double. *$$; No credit cards; checks OK; open May to Aug; PO Box 264, Seldovia AK 99663; dancingegl@alaska.net; www.dancingeagles.com; look for the signs at the beginning of the old boardwalk.*

Seldovia's Boardwalk Hotel

DOWNTOWN, JUST ABOVE THE HARBOR, SELDOVIA; 907/234-7816 OR 800/238-7862 The board- and batten-siding of the hotel can be seen at the harbor's edge. The no-frills rooms (there are 14 of them) are basic hotel design. Rates range from $89–$110 for a double, depending on the view (street or harbor). *$$; DIS, MC, V; checks OK; PO Box 72, Seldovia AK 99663; www.alaskaone.com/boardwalk hotel/.*

Seldovia Rowing Club / ★★

ON THE OLD BOARDWALK, SELDOVIA; 907/234-7614 Seldovia artist Susan Mumma has added her stamp of nautical Victorian charm to this delightful B&B located on a small remaining section of boardwalk, just around the corner from Alaska Dancing Eagles B&B (review above). It overlooks Seldovia Slough and the mountains beyond. There are two suites with sitting rooms and decks. One suite has a kitchen. The Stairway Gallery and Touch of Glass Antiques is open daily and features Susan's work. Besides being active in the local arts scene, she helps organize Seldovia's solstice folk festival, a fun two-day event that draws musicians from the world beyond. And when it comes to breakfast, you'll feel the benefit of her creative talents. Rates are $110 per night, per room. *$$; MC, V; checks OK; PO Box 41, Seldovia AK 99663; rowing@ptialaska.net; www.ptialaska.net/ ~rowing/.*

Swan House South Bed and Breakfast / ★★

175 AUGUSTINE AVE N, SELDOVIA; 907/234-8888, SUMMER; 907/346-3033, ALL YEAR; 800/921-1900, OUTSIDE ALASKA Indicative of a new Seldovia, rather than the historic buildings of the past, the location of this B&B has inspired the names for these five elegantly decorated nonsmoking suites. The Mountain View, Eagle Nest, Tree House, Garden, and Tidewater suites have mountain and water views, each has a private bath, and some have their own decks. Check the Web site for recipes used at the B&B and links to other valuable sites. Hosts Jerry and Judy Swanson will provide transportation from Seldovia's small airport and the harbor. They also own Swan House B&B in Anchorage. Rates are $139–$199 for a double. *$$$; AE, DIS, MC, V; checks OK; open May to Sept; swan1@alaska.net; www.alaska.net/~swan1; from town, cross the bridge over the slough and make the first right.*

KODIAK ISLAND

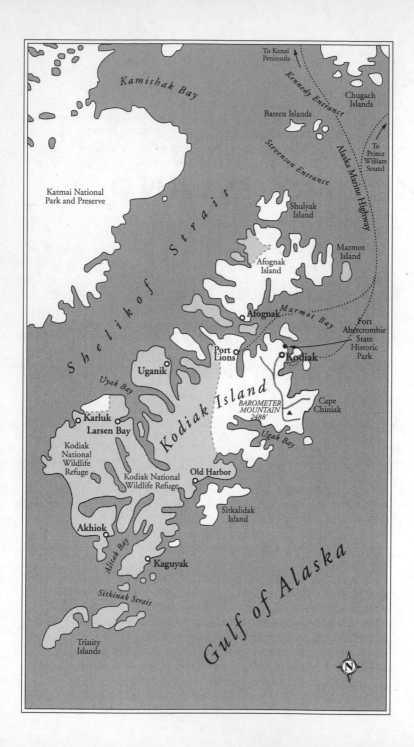

To Kenai
Peninsula

Kamishak Bay

Katmai National
Park and Preserve

Barren Islands

Kennedy Entrance

Chugach
Islands

Stevenson Entrance

To
Prince
William
Sound

Alaska Marine Highway

S h e l i k o f   S t r a i t

Shulyak
Island

Marmot
Island

Afognak
Island

Marmot Bay

Afognak

Fort
Abercrombie
State
Historic
Park

Port
Lions

Kodiak

Uganik

Uyak Bay

Kodiak Island

*BAROMETER
MOUNTAIN
2488'*

Cape
Chiniak

Karluk

Larsen Bay

Ugak Bay

Kodiak
National
Wildlife
Refuge

Kodiak National
Wildlife Refuge

Old Harbor

Sitkalidak
Island

Akhiok

Aliuk Bay

Kaguyak

Sitkinak Strait

G u l f   o f   A l a s k a

Trinity
Islands

N

KODIAK ISLAND

Kodiak Island is often one of the last places visitors to the state discover. Unlike communities on the road system or those served by Southeast Alaska's extensive ferry network, Kodiak isn't on the way to someplace else. Few people simply wander through. A trip here is a commitment, but one that can bring many rewards.

Anchored in the Gulf of Alaska, Kodiak is a 250-mile jet ride from Anchorage or a 10- to 13-hour ferry trip across the gulf from Homer or Seward. Remote as it is, you'll be surprised to find that Kodiak is a compact, bustling fishing port. Residents enjoy a cosmopolitan lifestyle with easy access to uncrowded beaches, extensive wilderness trails, and many mountain hikes. When you first arrive, snowcapped mountains rising out of the water like ships at sea immediately catch your attention. And the cool, moist salt air, often filled with sweet scents of summer wildflowers or pungent smells of fresh-caught fish, awaken your senses.

Kodiak is the **SECOND-LARGEST ISLAND** in the United States after the island of Hawaii, but it is mostly uninhabited. About 90 percent of the island is a refuge for the region's 3,000 Kodiak brown bears. Most of the island's 14,000 residents live in the small city of Kodiak and the nearby U.S. Coast Guard Base. Less than 100 miles of road serve the metropolitan area. The six Alaska Native communities, located on remote coasts throughout the Kodiak Island Archipelago, are accessible only by boat or plane.

Kodiak is home to a diverse wildlife population. More than 200 nesting pairs of bald eagles, about 200 other species of birds, 6 species of whales, sea lions, sea otters, porpoise, seals, deer, fox, land otter, and mountain goat thrive in the region, which boasts a mild maritime climate.

Called "Alaska's Emerald Isle" for its lush green beauty, Kodiak is home to the **ALUTIIQ PEOPLE,** who first came here thousands of years ago in sleek, well-designed skin boats. They lived in large, semisubterranean houses built of driftwood and covered with sod. They harvested marine mammals, including whales, sea lions, and seals. During the summers, they dried salmon for winter that they caught in the streams using nets and weirs. Ironically, Kodiak's abundance of marine life led to the Alutiiq's near collapse in the 1700s, when Russian hunters came for sea otters. After several fierce battles, the Russians overtook the Alutiiq and eventually used the men to harvest the sea otter. Meanwhile, many of the Alutiiq people died from foreign diseases the Russians brought with them. Later, Russian Orthodox priests arrived, establishing schools and religious training on the island, and the Alutiiq embraced the Russian Orthodox faith. Today, Russian-domed churches in Kodiak and the villages still dominate the landscape, as do Russian-named streets, geographic landmarks, and well-known family names.

Kodiak's ice-free harbors are home port to about 800 fishing boats and pleasure crafts. It consistently ranks among the top three fishing ports in the country. The fleet fishes all five species of Pacific salmon, which return in abundance every summer to spawn in the region's 800 streams. Fishing vessels also deliver halibut, herring, crab, cod, pollack, and rockfish to several waterfront fish-processing plants.

ACCESS AND INFORMATION

For **AIR TRAVELERS**, Alaska Airlines (800/252-7522; www.alaskaair.com) and Era Aviation (800/866-8394; www.eraaviation.com) fly several times daily from Anchorage. The city of Kodiak stretches along the coast, five miles end to end. Although public bus service is available, most visitors enjoy the freedom a **RENTAL CAR** affords. Avis (907/487-2264), Budget (907/487-2220), and Rent-A-Heap (907/487-4001) are all located at the airport. If you want to bring your own car or motor home to the island, make **FERRY RESERVATIONS** at least a month in advance with the Alaska Marine Highway (800/642-0066; www.alaska.gov/ferry). The state ferry MV *Tustumena* takes about 10 hours to sail from Homer to Kodiak and 13 hours from Seward to Kodiak.

SUMMERS in Kodiak are cool, with temperatures most often between 50–65 degrees. A thermometer reading of 75 degrees often tempts hardy locals to take a dip in Kodiak's frigid ocean and lakes. But in **WINTER**, Kodiak is one of the warmest cities in Alaska. Islanders often take delight in calling relatives in Mankato, Minnesota, who are shivering with subzero temperatures, to say they are enjoying a sunny, 45-degree day. But winters are not all fun. The island's famous hurricane-force winds can gust up to 100mph and drench low-lying areas with seawater.

A good source of information is the **KODIAK ISLAND CONVENTION AND VISITORS BUREAU**, at the ferry terminal (100 Marine Wy, Kodiak, AK 99615; 907/486-4782 or 800/789-4782; kicvb@ptialaska.net; www.kodiak.org). A **VISITOR CENTER** is also located at the ferry terminal and open year-round.

EXPLORING

The Great Alaska Earthquake of 1964, which was centered in Prince William Sound, created a tsunami that swept most of downtown Kodiak out to sea. Urban planners redesigned the city center around a series of closely spaced buildings known as "The Mall." Many of Kodiak's shops are located on The Mall and in the surrounding business hub. The two main drags, Mill Bay Road and Rezanof Drive, run parallel the length of Kodiak, and most other businesses are located on these two roads.

On The Mall, **NORMAN'S** (907/486-3315) and the **TREASURY** (907/486-5001) are good sources for books about Kodiak. Along the waterfront, **KODIAK MARINE SUPPLY** (412 Shelikof; 907/486-5752), also stocks a fine selection of Kodiak books and seafaring tales along with a great selection of outdoor gear. You can also gear up and buy nautical charts for navigating local waters at **SUTLIFF'S** (210 Shelikof; 907/486-5797), a hardware store across from the small boat harbor. While you're in the area, walk across the street and take a look at the informative harbor signs along the boardwalk overlooking the boat harbor. The collection of signs, produced by the emerging Kodiak Maritime Museum, explains everything about the fishing industry, from the types of boats and gear you see in the harbor to the species of fish that thrive in the region.

Other sources for books and artwork are the community's **DOWNTOWN MUSEUMS**. The Baranov Museum (101 Marine Wy; 907/486-5920; www.ptialaska.net\~baranov), is located in the oldest remaining Russian building on the West Coast. The museum is friendly, homey, and packed with history. The gift shop is best known for Russian lacquerware, icons, and samovars. Nearby, the Alutiiq Museum

KODIAK BROWN BEARS

Kodiak Island is roughly the size of Connecticut, but most of it is untamed wilderness. Established in the 1940s, the Kodiak National Wildlife Refuge encompasses about 90 percent of the island and is the domain of the Kodiak brown bear, the coastal relative of the grizzly and the world's largest carnivore. Each spring, the bears wake from their winter naps to graze on fresh spring grasses. As summer progresses, they congregate along the island's 800 streams to fish for salmon, which return to spawn after spending one to four years at sea. Bear attacks are very rare—only two people have been killed by a Kodiak bear over the past 100 years. Still, most locals make plenty of noise to avoid surprising a bear when they are hiking in bear country. If you encounter a bear, do not turn and run. Like a dog, the bear will think you are prey and chase you. And since they can clock 35mph going uphill, Kodiak bears will easily outrun you. Instead, let the bear know you are a human by yelling and waving your arms while slowly backing away.

—Sue Jeffrey

and Archaeological Repository (215 Mission Rd; 907/486-7004; www.alutiiq museum.com) focuses on the artifacts and traditions of the seagoing Alutiiq people, who arrived in Kodiak more than 7,500 years ago. The gift shop features Alaska Native artwork. Both museums have the same admission price—$2 adults; children under 12 free.

About a mile up the road from The Mall, **NORTHERN EXPOSURE GALLERY AND FRAME LOFT** (1314 Mill Bay Rd; 907/486-4956), offers a broad selection of prints and photographs by Alaska's leading artists.

If soaking up the culture makes you thirsty, there are plenty of options. In the early '80s, Kodiak was famous for its ubiquitous bars and liquor stores, but that scene has changed as espresso bars go head-to-head with saloons. **HARBORSIDE COFFEE AND GOODS** (216 Shelikof; 907/486-5862) could pass for a caffeine cache anywhere in Washington or California, except that a fishing fleet is tied up at its doorstep. **MONK'S ROCK** (202 E Rezanof; 907/486-0905) offers a unique window into Kodiak's Russian Orthodox community. You can pick up icons or peruse classical and religious books while waiting for your latte. Farther out of town along the "bike path," **MILL BAY COFFEE** (3833 E Rezanof; 907/486-4411) offers delectable fresh-baked pastries and occasional art shows. Across the street is Mill Bay Beach, a popular destination for joggers, bicyclists, local surfers, and anglers fishing for salmon.

Kodiak's roads are few, but the landscape they take you through is unparalleled in Alaska. Sheer cliffs emerge from the ocean and give way to lush green hillsides that Irish tourists swear look just like home. Puffins skim the water along wide sandy beaches while eagles circle overhead. To get a feel for the area, drive through the streets of Aleutian Homes—the city's first subdivision, which was built during World War II—to the top of Pillar Mountain. The stunning panoramic vista gives you a bird's-eye view of Kodiak and the outlying islands. The road is closed in winter and you may need four-wheel-drive after a long stretch of rain, but the view is worth it.

Within walking distance of downtown across the Fred Zharoff Memorial Bridge is **NORTH END PARK** on Near Island. An easy hike—ideal for families—takes you through dense spruce to tide pools and beautiful beaches. Also on Near Island, **ST. HERMAN HARBOR,** called "Dog Bay" by locals, is a scenic walk from the park. St. Herman Harbor and **ST. PAUL HARBOR,** right off The Mall downtown, provide an up-close view of a working waterfront with fishermen busy mending nets or offloading tons of fish from boats. Watch the sea lions and eagles scavenge scraps or strike up a conversation with a fisherman or two. Most are happy to explain what they do. Fishing is the passion and lifeblood of this town.

About five miles north of town is **FORT ABERCROMBIE STATE HISTORIC PARK** (907/486-6339; www.ptialaska.net/~kodsp/). The park includes campsites ($10 per night) and has well-maintained trails that take you along steep, rugged bluffs, through dense spruce rain forest, along a peaceful trout-stocked lake, and across hillsides carpeted with an amazing variety of wildflowers. The park is the site of a former World War II lookout and displays a cannon once mounted on a high bluff overlooking miles of open sea. To get an idea of what it was like to stand watch, step inside one of the small concrete pillboxes—mere turrets with slits facing seaward—built throughout the park. You also can take a tour of the **MILLER POINT BUNKER,** a former underground concrete residence for troops. Inside the bunker, the **KODIAK MILITARY HISTORY MUSEUM** (www.kadiak.org) displays a collection of military equipment, uniforms, and other relics.

Four roads branch off from Rezanof Drive, Kodiak's primary boulevard. To the north, Rezanof becomes **MONASHKA BAY ROAD** and ends 11 miles later at one of the island's rare white-sand beaches. (Most of Kodiak's beaches are composed of black slate sand.) A system of trails leads for several miles from "White Sands Beach" into a majestic Sitka spruce forest called **TERMINATION POINT.** Hikers will appreciate the spongy texture of the mossy forest floor.

To the south, Rezanof Drive becomes the **CHINIAK HIGHWAY** where the western edge of the island's spruce forest yields to alpine grasses and flowers. Before you head out the gravel road, let the folks at **FAIRWIND CAFÉ** (11206 W Rezanof; 907/487-4433) build you a gourmet sandwich on fresh-baked sunflower seed bread.

Motoring along the Chiniak Highway, you'll see jagged mountain ridges, winding seaside cliffs, and pastoral river valleys with grazing horses, cattle, and domestic buffalo. As you enter the Chiniak community, drop in at the **RAVEN'S NEST** for a look at Jane Van Atta's whimsical artwork of wire, beads, and driftwood.

Farther down the road overlooking beautiful Rosalyn Beach, take a break and visit the wine-tasting room at **KODIAK ISLAND WINERY** (907/486-4848; www.kodiakwines.com). The owners, a friendly couple, will let you taste the wines and champagnes they make from local rhubarb, salmonberries, blueberries, and raspberries while they regale you with tales of Kodiak. You also can buy local art at the winery's gallery and gift shop.

At the end of the road, you'll find the **ROAD'S END RESTAURANT AND LOUNGE** (907/486-2885). The popular greasy spoon is famous for its huge, hand-patted hamburgers served on French bread, deep-fried halibut sandwiches, and homemade pies. Road's End usually closes in February and opens in March at the first sighting of the northern migration of the gray whales, so call ahead during the winter months to make sure they're open. Road's End doesn't take credit cards, so plan ahead.

If you decide to take a right at the fork of the Chiniak Highway about 30 miles to the south of Kodiak, you'll be on **PASAGSHAK ROAD** heading south to the Pasagshak River and Pasagshak Bay. The area's wide, sandy beaches can be deeply peaceful on a calm day, but after a storm—surf's up! Kodiak is home to a tiny but hard-core band of surfers. (Wet suits, yes. Bikinis, no.)

Drive a few miles past Pasagshak and you'll find the **KODIAK LAUNCH COM-PLEX**. Operated by the Alaska Aerospace Development Corp., the site so far has put a NASA satellite in orbit and launched several military test vehicles over the Pacific Ocean. In stark contrast, the road past the space-age launch complex ends at ancient **FOSSIL BEACH,** a dream for rock hounds.

When you're heading back to town after a long day of fishing or exploring, stop by **THE RENDEZVOUS** (11652 W Rezanof; 907/487-2233) for a meal of fresh-caught fish. Owned and operated by local fishermen who recently bought the business, the roadside restaurant and bar is the newest place in town for live music and dancing.

If you only have time for a short road trip from town, take a right off W Rezanof Drive near the state airport. The gravel road runs along the salmon-laden Buskin River, snakes up between **BAROMETER** and **PYRAMID MOUNTAINS,** and then drops down 11 miles later to the shores of a long shallow inlet called **ANTON LARSEN BAY.** The protected bay is dotted with islets and is an excellent place to kayak. And it is so thick with salmon in the summer that you can see one jump about every five seconds. If your tastes run more to "birdies" than salmon, stop at the nine-hole **BEAR VALLEY GOLF COURSE** (907/486-7561 or 907/487-5108). The U.S. Coast Guard runs it from May through October. It has a driving range and all the rental gear you need.

All of Kodiak's outlying roads are unpaved, are often in rough condition, and don't have gas stations. So fill up before heading out and make sure you have a spare tire. Most of the undeveloped land on either side of the roads is privately owned—from Middle Bay to Cape Chiniak, the principal landholder is Leisnoi Inc. (3248 Mill Bay Rd; 907/486-8191), a Kodiak-area Native corporation. Leisnoi requests anyone hiking or camping on its land to carry a **FREE PERMIT,** which is available at the corporate office. Call for more information.

ADVENTURES

Kodiak has its share of creature comforts, but it's the vast wilderness—the island beyond the city—that draws many visitors here. And it's quick and easy to get into the backcountry. The tallest point on Kodiak is about 4,000 feet and the mountain peaks accessible by road are easily climbed in an afternoon. Near town is **BAROM-ETER MOUNTAIN** (2,488 feet). On a summer day, you can usually spot hikers against its green mountainsides as they make their way to the top for a view of the Pacific or the mainland's snowcapped volcanoes across Shelikof Strait. The local

THE CRAB FESTIVAL

An annual rite of spring, the Crab Festival is 45 years old and going strong. In the early days, it celebrated Kodiak's gigantic king crab harvests and hosted events such as seal-skinning contests for local hunters. You can still get a plateful of king crab legs but seal skinning has given way to ultra-marathon races and the famous Kodiak Fishermen's Wives Survival Suit Race.

The race is meant to simulate a real-life emergency and gives nonfishermen a taste of what the fishing fleet must be prepared to handle. Bulky, bright-orange neoprene survival suits are designed to insulate stranded mariners from the frigid waters of the North Pacific Ocean. Without such protection, a person can die from hypothermia within minutes. In the race, team members dash 100 yards down the St. Paul Harbor boat ramp to the water's edge. They stop and get into their suits—a difficult feat even when standing on solid ground—and then swim 300 yards to a life raft anchored in the harbor. The time clock stops when the last member of the four-person team is in the raft.

Before the Crab Festival is over, festival-goers also take time from the merriment to remember those lost at sea during the Fishermen's Memorial Service, held in front of Fishermen's Hall on Marine Way. A monument there lists the names of Kodiak fishermen lost at sea. The name of every man or woman who perished at sea that year is read as a bell tolls. The community waits for the year when the bell does not ring.

The Crab Festival (907/486-5557; www.kodiak.org) is held Memorial Day weekend, from Thursday through Monday, Memorial Day.

—Mark Gillespie and Sue Jeffrey

Audubon Society often leads backcountry hikes. Contact the visitor center (907/486-4782) for more information

Summer and early fall offers some of the best **SPORTFISHING** in the world. Many people prefer Kodiak's relatively unspoiled streams to the crowded, combative atmosphere on the mainland's Kenai River. And Kodiak salmon can be just as large as their Kenai Peninsula cousins, with king salmon sometimes weighing more than 100 pounds. The prize fish of the region is halibut, a flatfish that feeds on the bottom of the ocean and can top 300 pounds. Several charter-boat operators offer halibut, salmon, and rockfish trips, such as Eric Stirrup's MV *Ten Bears* (907/486-2200), or Chris Fiala's Kodiak Island Charters (907/486-5380 or 800/575-5380; urascal@ptialaska.net; www.ptialaska.net/~urascal). New charter operators pop up each year as Kodiak's visitor industry grows. **THE KODIAK CHARTER ASSOCIATION** (907/486-6363 or 888/972-6363), located in the lobby of the Best Western Kodiak Inn, maintains a list of available boats.

Several **AIR-TAXI** operators (contact the visitor center, 907/486-4782) provide flights over the stomping grounds of the famous Kodiak brown bear. Some operators actually guarantee that you'll see a bear on your flight. If you'd like a closer, longer look, visits to **BEAR-VIEWING LODGES** such as **ROHRER'S BEAR CAMP** (PO Box 2219, Kodiak AK 99615-2219; 907/486-5835), located within the bear refuge, provide guided viewing.

KAYAKING offers the quietest, most up-close wildlife viewing. Kodiak Kayak Tours (907/486-2722; fish2live@aol.com) and Mythos Expeditions (907/486-5536; mythosdk@ptialaska.net; www.mythos-expeditions.com) offer guided kayak tours near Kodiak. No experience is necessary and you're almost sure to spot whales, sea lions, sea otters, puffins, and fox.

Some of the best **WHALE-WATCHING** is in March and April, when migrations of gray whales skirt Kodiak's coastline. Kodiak marks the whale migration with "WhaleFest," including 10 days of lectures by local and off-island whale researchers, an art show, a poetry reading, and other whale-related events. Even the local paper, *the Kodiak Daily Mirror*, posts daily reports of whale sightings. Charter boats will take whale-watchers to prime viewing spots.

One of Kodiak's most unusual visitor opportunities is the chance to take part in an **ARCHAEOLOGICAL DIG**. Dig Afognak (907/486-6014; dig@afognak.com; www.afognak.com/dig) puts you to work at a field camp for weeklong sessions. No archaeological experience is necessary. Dormitory-style tents, family-style meals, and friendly hosts give Dig Afognak the aura of a summer camp for grown-ups. Day trips also are possible, depending on availability.

Although the snowpack may not amount to much in downtown Kodiak, the surrounding mountains provide excellent **CROSS-COUNTRY AND TELEMARK SKIING**, and **SNOWBOARDING**. Weather conditions vary from year to year, and access may be challenging, but the folks at Orion's Sports (1247 Mill Bay Rd; 907/486-8380) will have all the latest information.

If exploring the backcountry on wheels is more your speed, Tim at 58 Degrees North (1231 Mill Bay Rd; 907/486-6249) will rent you a **MOUNTAIN BIKE**, equip you with maps and a local bike-trail guide, and then send you on your way to enjoy a spectacular riding adventure.

NIGHTLIFE

The number of bars has dwindled in recent years, but it would be a mistake to say all of Kodiak's watering holes have dried up. Billing itself as "Alaska's Largest Navigational Hazard," **TONY'S** (907/486-9489) on The Mall—a favorite bar among fishermen and eight-to-fivers on Friday nights, is headquarters for the Pillar Mountain Golf Classic, a late-March, one-hole, par 70 cross-country golf event that has been featured nationally on *ABC Sports* and in *Sports Illustrated*. The rules specifically forbid the use of dogs to find lost balls or power tools to remove brush from the fairway. Also on The Mall, the **VILLAGE BAR** (907/486-3412) regularly brings live comedy acts to town, and the **MECCA LOUNGE** (907/486-3364) is the downtown dance joint.

RESTAURANTS

El Chicano / ★★★

103 CENTER ST, KODIAK; 907/486-6116 El Chicano's recently added a full bar, dance floor, and outdoor patio, but it still serves familiar Mexican dishes such as its "License-Plate Burrito," which really is as big as a license plate. *$$; AE, DIS, MC, V; checks OK; lunch, dinner Mon–Sat; full bar; no reservations.* &

Henry's Great Alaskan Restaurant / ★★★

512 MARINE WAY, KODIAK; 907/486-3533 It can be dim and smoky, but Henry's is where many Kodiak residents head for a good, reasonably priced meal. Steaks, gourmet hamburgers, sandwiches, pastas, and salads anchor the menu, along with daily specials such as prime rib or chicken-fried steak, and Wednesday's crawfish pie special. *$$; AE, DIS, MC, V; local checks only; lunch, dinner every day; full bar; no reservations; on The Mall.* &

King's Diner / ★★

1941 MILL BAY RD, KODIAK; 907/486-4100 While you bite into a bacon cheeseburger, you can watch bush planes land and take off through the big windows of this coffee shop overlooking the municipal airport runway. The atmosphere is "Kodiak casual" (Xtra Tuf rubber boots, sweat pants, and hooded sweatshirt—the perfect layer to wear between you and your damp rain gear), and the conversation at the counter is often spirited. The sourdough pancakes are a local favorite on weekend mornings. *$; MC, V; local checks only; breakfast, lunch, every day; no alcohol; no reservations.*

Mongolian Barbecue / ★★★

1247 MILL BAY RD, KODIAK; 907/486-2900 This Chinese American restaurant has something special—a barbecue buffet allows each diner to fill bowls with a choice of fresh meat, seafood, noodles, vegetables, and a variety of sauces. The brimming bowl is then tossed onto a giant grill and cooked as you watch, Benihana-style. The result is fast, tasty, and healthy, too—no oil or MSG is added. If you have small children with small appetites, they'll usually get a discount. Traditional Chinese meals also are on the menu. *$$; MC, V; local checks only; lunch, dinner every day; beer and wine; no reservations.* &

Peking Chinese Sizzler Burger / ★★★

116 W REZANOF, KODIAK; 907/486-3300 For a quick, tasty, full-course Chinese lunch or dinner or for an American burger and fries, Peking Restaurant is the place to go. The service is efficient and friendly and a bowl of their hot-and-sour soup really hits the spot on a gray, rainy Kodiak afternoon. *$; MC, V; local checks only; lunch, dinner every day; beer and wine; no reservations; downstairs.* &

2nd Floor Restaurant / ★★★

116 W REZANOF, KODIAK; 907/486-8555 Many locals think dining in Kodiak went up a notch when 2nd Floor Restaurant opened its Japanese sushi bar and restaurant. Try their excellent tempura dishes and the homegrown Kodiak Roll, sushi made from locally caught seafood. The restaurant offers a good selection of imported beers, including Japanese brands, and saki. *$$$; MC, V; local checks only; lunch Mon–Fri, dinner every day; beer and wine; reservations recommended; located upstairs, over the Peking Restaurant—look for the side door.*

LODGINGS

There are few bargains on this remote island. An alternative—typically less expensive and sometimes more luxurious—is one of Kodiak's bed-and-breakfasts. Most are in private homes, some with spectacular views of the water. The Kodiak Island Convention and Visitors Bureau (100 Marine Wy, Kodiak, AK 99615; 907/486-4782 or 800/789-4782; kicvb@ptialaska.net; www.kodiak.org), in the ferry terminal, maintains lists of bed-and-breakfasts and remote wilderness lodges. There are more than 40 lodges throughout Kodiak Island, and more spring up each year. They cover the full range of lodge experiences, with some catering to fishermen and hunters, while others are more geared to families or those who enjoy wildlife viewing, kayaking, or hiking.

Best Western Kodiak Inn / ★★

236 W REZANOF, KODIAK; 907/486-5712, 888/KODIAK-4 (563-4254), OR 888/563-4254; FAX 907/486-3430 Formerly known as the Westmark Hotel, the Kodiak Inn is in downtown Kodiak. Tours and charters may be booked in the lobby and the Chart Room Restaurant upstairs is one of the best spots in town for its killer view and wonderful steaks and seafood. Along the hallway outside the restaurant, take a look at the historic photos of the aftermath caused by the 1964 tsunami. Rates run about $149 for a double. *$$; AE, DC, DIS, MC, V; local checks only; kodiakin@ptialaska.net; www.kodiakinn.com.* &

Buskin River Inn / ★★

1395 AIRPORT WY, KODIAK; 907/487-2700 OR 800/544-2202; FAX 907/487-4447 The Buskin, as it is known locally, is an easy walk from the state airport. If you're on your way to a remote fishing or hunting camp or if you have a car, it is a convenient location and the on-site travel agency is a plus. Double-occupancy rooms go for $145. The Eagle's Nest restaurant is a worthy stop and looks out on the Buskin River. *$$; AE, DC, DIS, MC, V; local checks only; info@kodiakadventure.com; www.kodiakadventure.com.* &

Russian Heritage Inn / ★

119 YUKON ST, KODIAK; 907/486-5657; FAX 907/486-4634 This modest place is really a motel, not an inn. The rooms are simple, as you'd expect for $80 per night double occupancy. But its attraction is its location, in a quiet neighborhood in dowtown Kodiak. Some rooms have kitchenettes. *$; AE, MC, V; local checks only; www.ak-biz.com/russianheritage/.*

DENALI NATIONAL PARK AND THE PARKS HIGHWAY

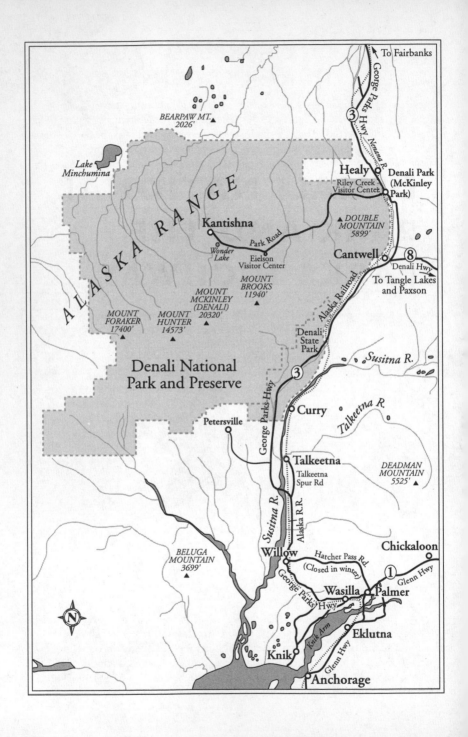

DENALI NATIONAL PARK
AND THE PARKS HIGHWAY

The George Parks Highway, named for an early 20th century territorial governor, stretches from the Glenn Highway, south of Palmer in the Matanuska Valley, to Fairbanks 324 miles to the north. The highway—referred to locally as the Parks—travels through a wide glacial valley as it parallels the Alaska Railroad and the Chulitna and Sustina Rivers, and is surrounded by Denali National Park and Denali State Park. Along the route, you'll encounter a multitude of lakes, stands of swamp spruce, wildlife, aging homesteads, trappers' cabins, rustic bars, roadhouses, and sleepy little towns. Traveling north provides spectacular views of distant mountains, including the Alaska Range, where the tallest mountain in North America, Mount McKinley (known as Denali among Native peoples), rises 20,320 feet above sea level.

Wasilla

The Wasilla you see today is a far cry from the tiny railroad village that supplied hard-rock and placer gold miners who worked mines near Mount McKinley and Talkeetna to the north. The town exploded as the Trans-Alaska Pipeline was constructed in the 1970s. Money flowed faster than aesthetics, as is common to boom-towns, and as the Parks Highway was opened in the early 1970s, Wasilla businesses prospered along the roadside. The old Alaska Railroad section house is now a National Historic Site and the Dorothy G. Page Museum and Visitors Center (323 Main St; 907/373-9071) offers a definitive history of the area and its people. The Matanuska-Susitna Convention and Visitors Bureau in a log cabin near the junction of the Parks and Glenn Highways (907/746-5000; www.alaskavisit.com) also has a wealth of information on Wasilla, Palmer, and the Mat-Su Valley.

ADVENTURES

THE NANCY LAKES STATE RECREATION AREA / At Mile 67.2 Parks Highway, this 22,685-acre recreation area is worth a stop for mild-adventure seekers. Paddle or ski through beautiful country with views of Mount McKinley. The Lynx Lake Loop is an 8-mile chain good for canoes and kayaks in the summer and cross-country skiing in winter. Thirteen cabins are available ($35 per night) or reserve a room at Denali View Chalet (907/333-9104), known locally as "Sepp's Cabin" for colorful owner Sepp Weber, and treat yourself to specialty German cuisine. For more information on the recreation area, call Alaska State Parks Mat-Su headquarters (907/745-3975). Or to reserve a cabin, log onto their Web site at www.dnr.state.ak.us.

SKY TREKKING ALASKA / These folks will take travelers who prefer bird's-eye views and wilderness experiences to remote streams and rivers to fish or kayak, or for a gourmet picnic. Design your personal itinerary and owner and chief pilot Lori Michels will fly you anywhere in Alaska. Package air tours, including a 12-day, checkpoint-to-checkpoint trip in March along the route of the Iditarod Trail Sled Dog Race, are also available. This trip runs about $5,200 per person. Costs for custom-designed trips vary substantially. *Located at Fiskehauk Airways,*

THE ALASKA RAILROAD

Heading north out of Anchorage on the Alaska Railroad toward the majestic peaks of the Alaska Range and its crown jewel, Mount McKinley, you'll travel along the broad Susitna River Valley and through the old railroad stops that motorists never see. Most were named by old gold prospectors. Their names alone reflect hope, nostalgia, and a hankering for home and warmer climes: Gold Creek, Sunshine, Colorado, and Honolulu. The view is especially dramatic in spring during breakup, when huge chunks of ice float down the Susitna River. Chances are good for seeing bald eagles, moose, and caribou, so keep a lookout.

The railroad, which extends from the ice-free port of Seward to the Interior gold-rush town of Fairbanks, was built in the 1920s to open up the rich Interior for development. Today, the railroad carries coal, gravel, logs, petroleum products, and half a million passengers every year. It is North America's last full-service railroad, offering both freight and passenger service.

In summer, the train runs daily between Anchorage and Fairbanks with a stop at Denali National Park. The Anchorage-to-Fairbanks run takes 12 hours; Anchorage to Denali takes 8. Package deals are available through the railroad (800/544-0552; reservations@akrr.com; www.alaskarailroad.com).

The railroad provides the last "flag-stop" service in the United States. "The Hurricane Turn," operating between Anchorage and Hurricane Gulch (170 miles north of Anchorage, where a dramatic bridge spans an even more dramatic canyon) in winter and Talkeetna and Hurricane Gulch in summer, is mainly for Alaska homesteaders, cabin dwellers, and wilderness folks. Officially, waiting passengers along the tracks are supposed to wave a white flag, but the train crew usually slows to a halt at the wave of a hand. The Hurricane Turn uses special, self-propelled silver cars that have their own engines so they don't need a locomotive to pull them.

Flag-stop service is available between Anchorage and Fairbanks, but only from October through May and only on weekends. Passengers include Alaskans traveling to their remote cabins or homesteads for a weekend or adventurers beginning multiday wilderness cross-country ski trips. Many enjoy a long weekend by riding the Hurricane Train out of Anchorage on Thursday, then catching the southbound train back to Anchorage on Sunday.

Other than the Hurricane Train, there is no flag-stop service in the summer. Regularly scheduled passenger trains, one northbound and one southbound each day, stop in Wasilla, Tallceetna, and Denali.

—Kris Capps

485 Pioneer Dr, Wasilla AK, 99564; 907/373-4966 or 907/357-3153; sky trek@alaska.net; www.skytrekkingalaska.com.

SNOWMOBILING / Alaska Snow Safaris offers half- or full-day guided expeditions. Prices range from $125 to $275 per person. Rentals are available for $175 per day. All necessary gear is provided. *907/783-7669 or 888/414-7669; www.ak adventures.com.*

FESTIVALS AND EVENTS

IDITASPORT EXTREME / The late Joe Redington Sr., founder of the Iditarod Trail Sled Dog Race, was also instrumental in founding the Iditasport. Held in early February, when daylight hours are becoming noticeably longer, the event is a consolidation of individual races. There is the Iditaski, a 210-mile ski along an historic gold-rush era trail, followed by the Iditashoe, a paltry 105-mile race on snowshoes. The event culminates with the Iditabike, where participants plow their way over 200 miles of snow-covered trail on mountain bikes. Couch potatoes need not apply—these events are for those who take the outdoors seriously. *907/345-4505.*

THE IDITAROD TRAIL SLED DOG RACE / The race begins on Fourth Avenue in downtown Anchorage on the first Saturday in March, but Alaskans know that ceremonial start, which runs to Eagle River, where it ends for the day, is just for show. The real race starts at the "re-start" in Wasilla the following day. Kept warm with hot chocolate and coffee, occasionally strengthened with adult additives to ward off the chill, sled-dog racing enthusiasts and the mildly interested make a day of attending this unique event. The dogs and the mushers are intent on leaving civilization behind and focusing on the 1,000-plus miles of wilderness that must be crossed before reaching the finish line in Nome. *Iditarod Trail Committee, Mile 2.2 Knik–Goose Bay Rd; PO Box 870800, Wasilla AK 99687; 907/376-5155, www. iditarod.com.*

DANCING BEARS DANCE CAMP / Dancing is good for the mind and body and this group loves to "dance 'til you drop." The Dance Camp kicks off the summer every Memorial Day weekend at King's Lake Fine Arts Camp off Wasilla's Fishhook Road with three days of square dances, clogging, swing, fiddle music, contras, and calling. Join musicians and callers from all over the United States for workshops and all-night music and dancing. Winter workshops are held monthly in Anchorage. *PO Box 200366, Anchorage AK, 99520-0366; 907/566-2327; www.alaska.net/~seb/ dbears.*

Knik

Visit the **IDITAROD TRAIL SLED DOG RACE HEADQUARTERS AND VISITORS CENTER** (Mile 2.2 Knik–Goose Bay Rd; 907/376-5155; open daily in summer) and immerse yourself in the history and future of the Last Great Race. Knik is home to many dog mushers and their kennels, and the historic Iditarod Trail passes through here. The visitors center can put you in contact with mushers who offer sled-dog trips year-round. They can also help if you are interested in becoming a volunteer dog handler for the race or if you prefer to vie for a $500 to $3,000 sled seat and a ride down Fourth Avenue on race day.

Swing for the mountains with moose and eagles at the **SETTLERS BAY GOLF CLUB** (Mile 8 Knik–Goose Bay Rd; 907/376-5466 or 800/478-7279). This 18-hole, daily-fee course has been listed in *Golf Digest*'s "Places to Play" guide and offers spectacular scenery with plenty of wildlife. Moose get to play through. At $30 per 18 holes, golfing doesn't get much better than this. Settlers Bay offers daily specials and half price for tee times after 6pm. Don't forget, summer days are long in Alaska; the last tee time is 8pm and you can play under the midnight sun. The clubhouse includes a snack bar and grill, beer, and wine.

Hatcher Pass

Where else in the world can you go from deciduous forest at sea level to an alpine environment in less than 20 miles? Travel east past Palmer, turn left on Fishhook Road, and follow 14 miles of newly paved road before curving sharply to the left where pavement turns to gravel. In a few miles you'll be at Hatcher Pass in high-country meadows dissected by streams of melting snow, surrounded by craggy peaks and the remnants of the Independence Gold Mine. The road continues across the pass and meets the Parks Highway near Willow. This is a beautiful summer drive, but be warned that the road is closed to Willow in the winter. Hatcher Pass seldom lacks for snow and is a popular area for early- and late-season cross-country skiing.

ADVENTURES

AVALANCHE EDUCATION / Heavy snowfall produces high avalanche hazard and avalanches have buried more than a few adventurers in recent years. Hatcher Pass is the venue for one of the nation's best avalanche education and training programs. The **ALASKA MOUNTAIN SAFETY CENTER** conducts weekend avalanche and mountaineering workshops in the winter. *9140 Brewsters Dr, Anchorage AK 99516; 907/345-3566.*

HIKING AND CAMPING / Pitch a tent in an alpine meadow and spend some time hiking the numerous trails, or make your own. The **REED LAKES TRAIL** is an excellent 9-mile round-trip day hike (2 miles up Archangel Rd from Mile 15 on Palmer-Fishhook Rd). Tents must be at least 100 feet from the road.

INDEPENDENCE GOLD MINE / This was one of Alaska's best producers during its 1930s heyday, and it produced $6 million worth of gold before it was closed in 1951. In 1974 it was entered into the National Register of Historic Places, and a few years later, 271 acres of land were donated to the state of Alaska for establishment of Independence Mine State Historical Park. Explore some of the old mining structures and learn about early mining in Alaska at the visitors center. Guided tours of the mine, offered twice daily during the week and three times daily on weekends and holidays, are $3 adults; $2 for children and seniors; children under 10 are free. *11am–7pm in summer (closed in winter); 907/745-2827; www.dnr.state.ak.us; from Parks Hwy at Willow, turn onto Hatcher Pass Rd and go approximately 38 miles to Hatcher Pass Lodge, turn left onto Fishhook Rd at T intersection, drive 1 mile; from Palmer, take the Palmer-Fishhook Rd about 22 miles to mine.*

LLAMA BUDDIES EXPEDITIONS / Learn to identify alpine flowers and plants, and then paint them. Llama Buddies Expeditions provides guided day and multiday tours, necessary botany and painting supplies, and llamas to carry them. A great trip for photographers and anyone interested in mountain flora and fauna. Day trips cost $175 per person; multiday expeditions start at $500. *907/376-8472; pam@llama buddies.com; www.llamabuddies.com.*

LODGINGS

Hatcher Pass Lodge / ★★

TALKEETNA MOUNTAINS, NORTH OF PALMER 907/745-5897; FAX 907/745-1200 Located at the base of the Independence Mine, 3,000 feet above timberline, the quaint A-frame lodge sits amidst spectacular peaks and alpine meadows. A haven for skiers in winter, Hatcher Pass Lodge offers three rooms in the main lodge and nine cozy A-frame cabins. Cabins are $115 a night for two; rooms in the lodge are $70, double occupancy. Pets will cost an extra $15. The small lodge has a back-country ambience with great food (breakfast, lunch, and dinner) and a full bar. Warm up after a day of skiing with a hot toddy and smoked halibut pizza. Home-made soups are a specialty and the lodge offers daily specials. Though only 18 miles from the Glenn Highway near Palmer, snow conditions can make the trip interesting in winter. Four-wheel drive is a good idea. *$–$$; AE, DIS, MC, V; local checks only; www.hatcherpasslodge.com; at Mile 14.5 Fishhook Rd—from Palmer, turn left on Palmer-Fishhook Rd, continue until it merges with Hatcher Pass Rd, and follow it all the way to the lodge and Independence Mine.*

Motherlode Lodge / ★★

MILE 14 FISHHOOK RD, HATCHER PASS; 907/745-6171 OR 877/745-6171; FAX 907/745-6004 Owner Jill Reese has turned this lodge, located 3 miles from Hatcher Pass on Fishhook Road, into "a very special celebration destination." Whether you are looking for a romantic getaway, wedding celebration, or a simple get-together with friends and family, Reese offers 11 rooms complete with a chef, bartender, and host, and twice-monthly live music all in a newly remodeled, nonsmoking environment. The lodge specializes in weddings, banquets, retreats, and meetings. Prices start at $99 per night, double occupancy, and dogs are welcome upon approval. Breakfast, lunch, and dinner are available for lodge guests (meals are extra and reservations are required), and there is a full bar; the menus change frequently, often featuring Alaskan cuisine. Reservations for meals are accepted after 3pm weekends for non-guests. *$$; AE, DIS, MC, V; out-of-state checks OK if paid 2 weeks in advance; www.motherlodelodge.com; from Palmer, turn left on Palmer-Fishhook Rd to Mile 14.*

Talkeetna

If you are tired of a life ruled by the clock, Talkeetna is the place to go. The 14-mile Talkeetna Spur Road is just past Mile 98 on the Parks Highway. The short trip from the Parks leaves ample time to do away with the wristwatch and prepare for Tal-keetna time. This laid-back village (pop. 500 including the surrounding area) situated on the bank of the Susitna River in the shadow of Mount McKinley, is a hodgepodge of aging hippies, bush rats, mountain guides, bush pilots, eclectic architecture, and people who prefer to set their own pace. Talkeetna is also the staging area for McKinley climbers. The land rises dramatically from 350 feet in town to the 20,320-foot summit of McKinley just 50 miles away.

As with many Alaska towns, Talkeetna has a history steeped in mining and mountaineering. The **TALKEETNA HISTORICAL SOCIETY** (907/733-2487) operates a Visitor Information Center on the single block downtown and a funky little museum detailing the town's mining history and the adventures of some of its most famous mountaineers and bush pilots. The museum houses a large topographic model of the McKinley massif where National Park Service rangers give detailed presentations on the mountain and its glaciers. The **NATIONAL PARK SERVICE** has a new ranger station and visitors center (907/733-2231) in town and offers a wealth of information, displays, and literature about the mountain, including weather updates.

ADVENTURES

D&S ALASKA TRAIL RIDES / For those who prefer relaxed sight-seeing, D&S offers one- to four-hour horseback rides on trails around the Talkeetna area. Prices start at $55 per person. *907/733-2205; www.alaskantrailrides.com; just off downtown near the river.*

MOUNT MCKINLEY / Talkeetna is home to some of the best glacier pilots in the world. These people fly hundreds of climbers to the Kahiltna Glacier base camp, at 7,000 feet, during the late spring and early summer climbing season. A sight-seeing flight around the mountain or a trip to the glacier is an incredible experience. For tour information check **HUDSON AIR SERVICE** (907/733-2321 or 800/478-2321; www.hudsonair.com); **DOUG GEETING AVIATION'S MCKINLEY FLIGHT TOURS AND GLACIER LANDINGS** (907/733-2366 or 800/770-2366; www.alaskaairtours. com); **K2 AVIATION** (907/733-2291 or 800/764-2291; www.flyk2.com); or **TALKEETNA AIR TAXI** (907/733-2218 or 800/533-2219; www.talkeetnaair.com). Flight-seeing costs start at around $110 per person and go up from there; trips with glacier landings start at about $225 per person.

If your desire is to stand on the summit of North America's tallest mountain or other peaks in the Alaska Range, experienced guides are available. **ALASKA MOUNTAINEERING SCHOOL AND DENALI GUIDING** (PO Box 566, 3rd St, Talkeetna AK 99676; 907/733-1016; climbing@alaska.net; www.climbalaska.org) offers mountain-climbing instruction and guided expeditions. Another respected high-country guiding outfit is **MOUNTAIN TRIP** (PO Box 111809, Anchorage AK 99511; 907/345-6499; mttrip@aol.com; www.mountaintrip.com). Expect to pay in the neighborhood of $4,000 for guided West Buttress climbs.

FESTIVALS AND EVENTS

TALKEETNA MOOSE DROPPING FESTIVAL / Talkeetna, and the rest of Alaska for that matter, needs little excuse to throw a party. The popular Moose Dropping Festival is held annually on the second weekend in July. See how far you can throw a moose dropping or enter the Mountain Mother competition. Enjoy a parade, Talkeetna style, arts and crafts, and plenty of good food and cheer.

BACHELOR AUCTION–WILDERNESS WOMAN CONTEST / It's tough being a wilderness bachelor, so the Talkeetna Bachelor Society has, for over 10 years, invited single ladies from all over the country to tough it out in the Wilderness Woman Contest, held the first weekend in December. The women vie for top honors in "firewood-hauling, water-fetching, snow-machining, fish-catching, moose-dispatching, beverage-opening, and other vital skills for daily living on the Last Frontier." The party culminates with the auctioning off of Talkeetna bachelors to the highest bidder. The only requirement is a sense of humor. Call 907/733-2323 or 907/733-2262 for information.

NIGHTLIFE

If you're looking for a lively good time, this little town can jump. The historic **FAIRVIEW INN** (907/733-2423; www.denali-fairview.com), on Main Street in the heart of downtown, is a haven for climbers and adventurers seeking relaxation. The Fairview's claim to fame is as the place where President and Mrs. Harding stayed in 1923 when they traveled north to drive the golden spike completing the Alaska Railroad. The town's lone parking meter is outside the inn. Portraits of climbers and famous glacier pilots adorn the walls of this frontier-style bar along with newspaper clippings detailing some of the town's more unique visitors. Enjoy live music most nights, including jazz on Sundays. Rooms upstairs share a bath, but if you're looking for a quiet place and a good night's sleep, this probably isn't the place.

Meet the locals and play pool at the **TALKEETNA MOTEL AND LOUNGE** (907/733-2323), locally known as the Teepee. The A-frame bar near the Denali National Park Visitors Center is a friendly beer-and-a-shot joint and a good place to learn more about the area from those who live there.

LATITUDE 62 LODGE (907/733-2262), on Main Street as you enter town, offers fine dining and a full bar. Though the volume of summer business leaves little room for live music, the pace picks up in the winter. Local musicians and many from the Lower 48 set up at the lodge, often on the spur of the moment.

LODGINGS

Enter Alaska Guesthouse

SECOND ST, TALKEETNA; 907/733-2111 Relax in a quiet private setting one block from downtown Talkeetna. Enter Alaska Guesthouse provides a full kitchen and dining room, bath, washer and dryer, and a yard with a deck, starting at $125 for three. The guesthouse can accommodate up to six people in a homey, comfortable atmosphere. Bring your own groceries or plan to eat out. $$; *Cash and checks OK; PO Box 583, Talkeetna AK 99676; www.enteralaska.net.*

Historic Talkeetna Roadhouse / ★★

MAIN ST, TALKEETNA; 907/733-1351; FAX 907/733-1353 The Roadhouse, located on Main Street in downtown Talkeetna, was built in 1917 by brothers Frank and Ed Lee. It was primarily used as a staging house for supplies earmarked for gold miners in the hills nearby. Today, the Roadhouse offers eight simple rooms with bathrooms down the hall (the upstairs bathroom has a claw-foot bathtub), ranging from $63 to $89 for a double. A bunk-room hostel with four twin beds goes for $21 per person. The location, near the park ranger station, museum, flight-seeing, gift shops, and local pubs, can't be beat. You'll wake up to the smell of freshly brewed coffee and fabulous cinnamon rolls. The cafe and bakery feature hearty fare in a family atmosphere. *$; MC, V; checks OK; PO Box 604, Talkeetna AK 99676; trisha@talkeetnaroadhouse.com; www.talkeetnaroadhouse.com.*

Talkeetna Lodge / ★★

MILE 12.5 TALKEETNA SPUR RD, TALKEETNA; 907/265-4501 OR 888/959-9590 Opened in 1999, the lodge, owned by the Native corporation Cook Inlet Region Inc., offers a dining deck where, on a clear day, unsurpassed views of Mounts McKinley and Foraker and a panorama of the Susitna Valley dominate the horizon. The lodge, 2 miles from beautiful downtown Talkeetna, has 201 rooms and four separate guest buildings that accommodate 12 each. Rates vary with the season, from $89 in winter to $199 in summer for a double. The lodge also offers a shuttle to town and the railroad station and transportation packages to Fairbanks and Anchorage. *$$$; All major credit cards OK; checks (with proper ID) OK; 2525 C St, Ste 405, Anchorage AK 99503; www.talkeetnalodge.com.*

Talkeetna Cabins / ★★

JUST OFF MAIN ST, TALKEETNA; 907/733-2227 OR 888/733-9933 These cabins, hand built and owned by carpenter Kevin Foster and his wife Peg, are situated at the edge of downtown, just off Main Street and a short walk from the river. The spacious cabins include queen beds and full kitchens. Rates start at $130 for a double. Foster also has a three-bedroom house for larger parties starting at $260 for four. *$$–$$$; MC, V; checks OK; PO Box 124, Talkeetna AK 99676; www.talkeetnacabins.org.*

Denali State Park

Denali State Park is one of Alaska's best-kept secrets because most travelers continue north to the more popular (and populous) Denali National Park. The state park is about half the size of Rhode Island and runs on both sides of the Parks Highway. On the east side, two ridges—Curry and Kesugi—provide the backbone of the park and run 35 miles north-south. They offer stupendous views of Mount McKinley and surrounding peaks. With a little effort, hikers can easily climb out of the thick vegetation (and crowds) and emerge onto beautiful alpine tundra ridges.

ACCESS AND INFORMATION

The **ALASKA PUBLIC LANDS INFORMATION CENTERS** in downtown Anchorage, Fairbanks, and Ketchikan are the best places for information on Denali State Park as well as on other parks and refuges throughout Alaska (in Anchorage: 605 W 4th Ave; 907/271-2737; in Fairbanks: 250 Cushman St, Ste 1A; 907/456-0527; in Ketchikan, 50 Main St; 907/228-6220; www.nps.gov/aplic). Or you can call **THE ALASKA STATE PARKS INFORMATION CENTER** in Wasilla (907/745-3975). To reserve state park cabins you can prepay at any one of the aforementioned information centers around Alaska or, in the summer, at the **DENALI STATE PARK VISITOR CONTACT STATION** (at the Alaska Veterans Memorial, Mile 147.2, George Parks Hwy). The Alaska Natural History Association (www.alaskanha.org) has a small bookstore here, which also sells maps.

ADVENTURES

BACKPACKING / LITTLE COAL CREEK TRAIL (Mile 163.8 Parks Hwy) is a short day hike or first stop for an overnight backpacking trip. It is also the quickest access to get above tree line in this section of mountains. Two miles into the hike on a clear day, enjoy a "forever" view of mountains and glaciers on the other side of the Chulitna River. If you're a strong hiker, you can get there in less than an hour. The trail is not particularly steep. Vegetation is thick en route, so make lots of noise to let bears know you're in the area—black bears are common.

FISHING AND CAR CAMPING / BYERS LAKE (Mile 147 Parks Hwy) is a great stop for car camping, especially for those folks with fishing poles in hand. Fish for grayling, burbot, rainbow trout, lake trout, and whitefish. The state campground has 73 sites and charges $10 a night. If you want to get a little farther away from civilization, pack your tent and hike or canoe to a more remote campground about 2 miles away. Black bears are common, so always keep a clean camp.

Farther north (Mile 162.7 Parks Hwy), the **DENALI VIEW NORTH CAMP-GROUND** offers spectacular views to the west for $10 per night. Large RVs can park here and scenic tent sites are tucked into the trees. There's an interpretive trail, spotting scope, and a short loop trail. Campsites are available on a first-come, first-served basis. Campgrounds are closed in winter.

RENT A CABIN / There are two cabins available for rent every day at Byers Lake. One is road accessible; the other is a half-mile walk or canoe to the other side of the lake and has a fantastic view of Denali. The $35-per-night fee must be prepaid (see Access and Information, above; www.alaskastateparks).

LODGINGS

Mount McKinley Princess Wilderness Lodge / ★★

MILE 133.1 PARKS HWY, DENALI STATE PARK; 907/733-2900 OR 800/426-0500; FAX 907/733-2904 Sister to the Denali Park Lodge right outside the national park entrance, this $20-million hotel is the first major hotel built along the south side of the park, which is still virtually inaccessible by road. Just 3 miles from the park border, overlooking the Chulitna River, the hotel boasts a spectacular view of Mount McKinley on a clear day, from the deck or from the floor-to-ceiling windows in the impressive Grand Room. A variety of activities are available, from flight-seeing and river rafting to hiking on state park trails. Rooms run $189 to $289, double occupancy, plus 5 percent tax in peak season. Off-season rates are cheaper. You can enjoy fine dining and drinks, not to mention panoramic views, in the Mountain View Restaurant. Or have a casual meal in the Cub Café. There's also Grizzly's Bar. *$$$; AE, DC, MC, V; closed Oct to May; 2815 2nd Ave, Ste 400, Seattle WA 98121; www.princesslodges.com.* &

Denali National Park and Preserve

Ah, the magic of Denali! It's no surprise thousands of people travel here every year. A wilderness area roughly the size of Massachusetts, this is home to some of the most magnificent creatures on earth. It is all framed by a range of breathtaking icy peaks leading up to the highest mountain on the North American continent—Mount McKinley. Memories here are not soon forgotten: the sight of a moose calf wobbling behind its mother, a wolf relentlessly digging for a ground squirrel, or a blond grizzly bear loping over the tundra. While most visitors will see bears and some will see caribou or a wolf, this is not a zoo. Sighting animals takes patience, persistence, and constant looking, looking, looking. Still, Denali is home to 163 species of birds, 37 species of mammals, and 450 species of plants, so you'll get your flora and fauna fix.

If weather cooperates during your visit, you may even see the top of Mount McKinley, rising 20,320 feet above sea level. During summer months, this imposing peak creates its own weather and may be clearly visible only a third of the time. When "the mountain is out," as locals like to say, there is no mistaking which peak is McKinley. It looms dramatically over every other mountain on the horizon.

A prospector dubbed the mountain "McKinley" in 1896, in honor of William McKinley of Ohio, who became the 25th president of the United States. Long ago, Athabascan Indians called it Denali, which means "the high one." Debate continues today over whether the name should be officially changed to Denali. Meanwhile, most Alaskans call it simply "The Mountain." More than 1,000 climbers attempt to scale McKinley every year. Only half succeed. To date, nearly 100 have died trying to reach the summit. Climbing McKinley is serious business and often can take 20 to 30 days. The mountain is not only high, but can be bitterly cold. Severe storms may hit without warning, and winds can gust to 150mph.

In 1922, only 22 tourists came to admire the wonders of this newly created park. By 1939, there were 2,200; in 1971, 44,528 visitors came; and in 2001, that number climbed to 360,190. The best season to come is May, when snow is still melting, through September, when the tundra turns red and gold. In between, the flowers bloom in June, mosquitoes attack voraciously in July, and the rains often hit in August. Snow may fall at any time, and each season holds its own charm.

ACCESS AND INFORMATION

Whether you're coming from Anchorage or Fairbanks, there are economical ways to get to Denali National Park if you're not driving your own vehicle. The **PARKS HIGHWAY EXPRESS** (907/479-3065 or 888/600-6001; info@alaskashuttle.com; www.alaskashuttle.com) is a shuttle bus that runs daily between Fairbanks and Anchorage. The trip takes 9 hours, but the bus will drop you off anywhere in between. One-way costs $74; round-trip, $139. The trip to Denali takes almost 6 hours from Anchorage ($54 one-way). It's 3 hours from Fairbanks ($39 one-way). **THE PARKS CONNECTION** (907/245-2000 or 800/266-8625; info@alaskacoach. com; www.alaskacoach.com) runs between Seward, Anchorage, and Denali National Park with two buses daily in each direction. Fare is $59 between Anchorage and Denali; children ride half-price. A special Denali Express does not stop in Talkeetna and is a good option if your time is limited. There are also air taxis that will fly you from the entrance into the park: Denali Air (907/683-2261; www.denaliair.com) and Kantishna Air Taxi (907/683-1223; www.katair.com).

If you arrive without wheels, you have a couple options for getting around. There is a **FREE "FRONT COUNTRY" SHUTTLE** service that runs between hotels in the general vicinity of the park entrance. Bus stops are clearly marked with schedules.

MCKINLEY "FIRSTS"

"To the summit!" was the rallying cry of Mount McKinley's first and most colorful guide. A boisterous Swiss American, Ray Genet made mountaineering history as part of the first successful winter expedition on McKinley in 1967. Three members—Dave Johnston of Talkeetna, Art Davidson of Rainbow, and Genet—reached the summit. But the next day on descent, winter storms scoured the slopes and hurricane-force winds dropped the temperature, with windchill, to minus 148°F. They were trapped for five days in a snow cave near the top. In the 11th hour, it was Genet who struggled painfully out into the winter gale to find a cache with cooking gas so they could melt snow for water. Davidson wrote a gripping account of that journey in his book *Minus 148°*.

In the fall of 1979, Genet climbed to the top of Mount Everest in Nepal, the highest mountain in the world. Beneath the summit, while on descent, he froze to death on a bivouac. But his legend lives on: Genet's son, Taras, at age 12, became the youngest person to summit McKinley in 1991.

McKinley is an arena of "firsts." Appropriately, the first to set foot on the top of the highest mountain in North America was a young Athabascan-Irish lad, Walter Harper, part of the Hudson Stuck expedition in 1912. Barbara Washburn, in 1947, was the first woman to climb McKinley and still holds the record for climbing both the North and South Peaks in a single expedition. In 1970, the famous Japanese world adventurer Naomi Uemura made the first successful solo ascent. In February 1984, Uemura returned to the mountain for the first solo winter summit bid. Tragically, he died upon descent. Following in Uemura's footsteps, mountain guide Vern Tejas in 1988 became the first to reach the summit alone in the winter and return alive.

—*Nan Elliot*

Check with your hotel. There is also a special **SAVAGE RIVER SHUTTLE** (cost $2, but expected to be free starting in 2003) to take visitors to and from Savage River in the park and the Visitor Access Center (see below). **CARIBOU CAB** (907/683-5000) can take you where you want to go. Cost is $4 per person (with $7 minimum) from the hotel/restaurant area known as "Glitter Gulch" to the train station and visitor center. You can also rent a car from **TERESA'S ALASKA CAR RENTALS** (907/683-1377; fax 907/683-1380; www.denalicarrental.com). Only one road leads into this magnificent wilderness, and private vehicle traffic is restricted (see Travel and Tours within the Park, below).

The **ENTRANCE AREA** of Denali National Park is changing dramatically. Visitors through 2004 should expect to encounter considerable construction, with lots of heavy-equipment traffic; quiet wilderness solitude will not be evident at or near the entrance area for several summers. The old park hotel was dismantled in 2002. In its place the National Park Service is building a Science and Learning Center and a new Visitor Center Campus. It will include a new theater, exhibits, art, and information about the park.

The soon-to-be former **VISITOR ACCESS CENTER** (907/683-1266, summer; 907/683-2294, winter) is located at Mile 1 on the park road, just after turning off the George Parks Highway. In 2003, this will likely be a Transit Center, where you can buy tickets for the bus into the park, get backcountry camping permits, and actually board the bus. Before you go into the backcountry, you'll be required to watch an orientation film, "Hiking the Denali Wilderness." Schedules here or at the new Visitor Center Campus will list daily ranger programs and ranger-led hikes. There is also a visitor center near the end of the park road at Eielson. The park's Web site is an excellent source for general information (www.nps.gov/dena).

In addition to campground fees and shuttle-bus fees to ride into the park, each visitor must pay an entrance fee; currently a seven-day pass for an individual is $10 and for a family, $20. But prices are expected to increase.

The park is divided into 43 units, and **BACKCOUNTRY PERMITS** are required for wilderness trips. To preserve the wilderness experience for backpackers, the number of people allowed into any given unit is limited. Sometimes units close due to wildlife activity, such as a curious grizzly bear. During the peak summer rush, they may be booked for days. Be flexible. Permits are issued one day in advance, no reservations.

July is the busiest time at Denali. Recreational vehicles that have driven north from the Lower 48 arrive in force by then, and campgrounds and hotels are usually booked. The "shoulder" seasons—May and September—are some of the best times to visit if you want to avoid crowds. Park workers begin plowing the park road in March and, in an average year, the road is open to the public as far as Savage River Bridge (Mile 15) in early April and as far as the Teklanika River rest stop and overlook (Mile 30.3) in early May. This is a great time to load up the bicycle, drive to either one of these spots, and enjoy a traffic-free bike ride on the park road. Expect cool temperatures—often below freezing—and be aware that the road could close again at any time due to snow.

TRAVEL AND TOURS WITHIN THE PARK / The primary way to experience the park is via the **PARK'S SHUTTLE BUS**. A trip into the park along the park road costs between $17 and $33, depending on how far you travel. Reserve a seat at the Visitor Access Center (see above; be aware that you may have to wait up to three days) or in advance through the reservation system (907/272-7275 or 800/622-7275; fax 907/264-4684). The buses leave from the Visitor Access Center every half hour, from early morning to late afternoon. They begin operating the Saturday before Memorial Day and end the second Thursday after Labor Day.

A special **CAMPER BUS** carries travelers, their backpacks, and camping gear to campgrounds inside the park, particularly Sanctuary, Igloo Creek, and Wonder Lake Campgrounds, which do not allow vehicles (see Camping, below). Backpackers with backcountry permits generally travel on this bus and stay in a campground their first night. Be sure to reserve and pay for a seat when you pick up your backcountry permit (907/272-7275 or 800/622-7275).

You can **DRIVE THE PARK ROAD** in your own vehicle as far as Teklanika, before the buses start running and after they stop running, if weather permits and the road is open. During summer months, most private-vehicle use is restricted beyond Savage River (Mile 14.8).

For four days each fall, beginning the second Friday after Labor Day, the park allows 400 private vehicles per day to drive the length of the park road. Permits are distributed through a **ROAD LOTTERY** and are contingent on weather and road conditions. To earn this privilege, mail a self-addressed, stamped envelope to the park headquarters (PO Box 9, Denali National Park AK 99755) between July 1 and July 31. List your choice of dates in order of preference. Permits are assigned by a drawing held in early August. Only one application per person allowed.

Denali Park Resorts (800/276-7234) offers **TWO NARRATED TOURS.** The Wildlife Tour goes to Toklat at Mile 53 or, if the mountain is out, to Stony Hill at Mile 62. A box lunch is provided for the seven-hour trip; cost is $74 adults, $36 children age 12 and younger. The Natural History Tour travels to Primrose Ridge at Mile 17 for an Alaska Native interpretive program. Other interpretive stops along the way include Savage Cabin, an historic patrol cabin. It's a three-hour trip, with a snack provided. The cost is $40 adults, $19 children.

Travel the length of the park road with an experienced naturalist guide and eat a buffet lunch at the Kantishna Lodge before returning the same day on a **KANTISHNA TOUR.** The special Kantishna bus leaves from park-entrance hotels at 7am. It arrives at Kantishna at noon, and you are allowed enough time for lunch, gold panning, relaxing, or exploring. Leave Kantishna at 3pm to return to the park entrance in time for dinner. Cost is $115 per person, reservations required (PO Box 81670, Fairbanks AK 99708; 800/942-7420; www.kantishnaroadhouse.com).

CAMPING / Camping permits are required to camp at any of the park's seven campgrounds except **MORINO BACKPACKER CAMPGROUND,** near the park entrance at Mile 1.9 (this campground will probably close in 2003, during construction). In addition to the campground fee, add the park entrance fee and a $4 reservation fee per site. The only campgrounds you can drive to are Riley Creek, Savage River, and Teklanika River. All others are reached by bus. **RILEY CREEK** is the first campground past the park entrance, open year-round. **SAVAGE RIVER** is at Mile 13. **SANCTUARY RIVER,** Mile 23, is for tents only. **TEKLANIKA RIVER,** Mile 29, has a number of sites for both tents and RVs. **IGLOO CREEK,** Mile 34, is for tents only (Igloo Creek was closed in 2001–2002 for wildlife management reasons). **WONDER LAKE,** Mile 85, is for tents only. Sanctuary River and Igloo Campgrounds are available by walk-in at the visitor center. Riley Creek, Savage River, Teklanika River, and Wonder Lake can all be reserved in advance through the park's reservation system (800/622-7275 or 907/272-7275).

EXPLORING
GOOSE LAKE STUDIO / Fine art by Alaskans is on display and for sale at Goose Lake Studio, run by one of Alaska's best-known artists, Donna Gates King, wife of Iditarod champion Jeff King. The log-cabin gallery offers one-of-a-kind artwork

including pottery, quilts, silk scarves, and paintings, as well as parkas with traditional fur ruffs. *Mile 239 Parks Hwy; 907/683-2904, mid-May to Sept; 907/683-2570, winter; in a log cabin at the Denali Princess Resort.*

GOOSE LAKE KENNEL / Three-time Iditarod champion Jeff King opens his Goose Lake Kennel to visitors three times a day during summer for Husky Homestead Tours. Meet the real champs—the dogs—and learn how they train. Half of the 90-minute narrated tour is spent outdoors meeting the adult dogs and puppies and learning about training and equipment. The other half is indoors, amid a display of mushing paraphernalia, art, and souvenirs. Although Iditarod commitments require Jeff King to travel regularly, he often is there in person. He or other Iditarod race veterans present the program about their Alaska lifestyle, the homestead, and the race itself. Cost is $39 adults, $19 children age 12 and younger. *907/683-2904, summer; 907/683-2570, winter; www.huskyhomestead.com; at the end of a winding gravel road off Mile 230 Parks Hwy.*

ADVENTURES

DENALI OUTDOOR CENTER / The center offers inflatable-kayak trips for full or half days, white-water instruction in hardshell kayaks, and raft trips down the nearby Nenana River. Participants need to bring warm clothes, polypropylene or wool (no cotton), and their enthusiasm. The center provides a full dry suit and paddling gear. The water is very cold—in the 40°F range—so it is important to dress appropriately. An experienced guide takes paddlers down the river, usually through Class II and III rapids. This is the only company offering inflatable-kayak trips, which even beginners can safely enjoy. The inflatable kayaks are stable and maneuverable, and they also are self-bailing, so water that sloshes in flows back out on its own. If you tip over, you just flip the kayak right side up again and crawl back in. Custom, multiday trips on the Nenana River and other rivers are also available. If you are a paddler new to the area and looking for either a paddling partner or information on Nenana River rapids, check in here, at what has become the center for white-water paddlers. Mountain bike rentals are also available. *Open May to Sept; PO Box 170, Denali National Park AK 99755; 907/683-1925 or 888/303-1925; docadventure@hotmail.com; www.denalioutdoorcenter.com; outside the park entrance, at Mile 238.5 on the Parks Hwy.*

DENALI RAFT ADVENTURES / This outfit has been running the Nenana River for more than 20 years and offers a variety of trips. You'll be outfitted in dry suits. Trips range from the scenic two-hour Mount McKinley Float to a thrilling two-hour trip down Wild Canyon Run, 11 miles of big waves and vertical canyon walls through rapids with names like Coffee Grinder and the Narrows. The four-hour Healy Express Run is a combination trip. *Drawer 190, Denali National Park AK 99755; 907/683-2234 or 888/683-2234; denraft@mtaonline.net; www.denaliraft adventures.com.*

THE PARK ROAD / A journey into Denali National Park is a journey into the heart of wilderness. From the time you board the bus at the visitor center until you reach Wonder Lake five hours later, you'll pass through forest and tundra and, if you're fortunate, see some of the animals that live here.

Most of the park is above timberline, which in Denali starts at 2,700 to 3,000 feet; you get above tree line about 10 miles into the trip. The trees on the tundra include dwarf birch, willow, and alder. The first 15 miles of road are home to many of Denali's **MOOSE**. By early fall, the bulls are showing off their massive antlers and butting heads to vie for the affections of cow moose waiting nearby. They can be spotted either in the forest along the road or as the trees give way to open tundra.

The first glimpse of **THE MOUNTAIN** comes just about 8 miles into the park as you pass from the forest into tundra. At that point, it looms large even 72 miles away. As the road dips and turns, you'll lose sight of it periodically. It will disappear when you drop into the **SAVAGE RIVER** drainage and come into view again 8 miles later at the top of a hill called Primrose Ridge, then again at Sable Pass. The first place you can see the full mountain, including its base, is at **STONY HILL** overlook at Mile 62. Here, McKinley is 37 miles away.

CARIBOU can be seen almost anywhere along the park road. They are usually moving or grazing on sedges and grasses. Sometimes they can be seen on snowfields, where they flee in order to escape harassing insects, particularly warble flies and nose flies. The easiest animals to find are **DALL SHEEP**, bright white spots on the mountain slopes. **IGLOO CANYON** is a good place for sheep viewing.

SABLE PASS, at Mile 39, is home to the Toklat **GRIZZLY BEAR**, and this area has been closed to hiking and camping since 1955. But grizzly bears can be seen anywhere along the park road, digging for roots, strolling through the tundra, or snoozing on a sunny hillside. Many are blond in color, easily blending in with fall's golden and red tundra.

The grandeur of the park is evident at the top of **POLYCHROME PASS**, Mile 45.9. There, you can revel in the spectacular view of a broad valley, lined with tendrils of glacial streams flowing from distant mountains. On the other side of Polychrome, you'll pass over the **TOKLAT RIVER**. Early conservationist Charles Sheldon lived on the Toklat during the winter of 1907–1908. His stay inspired him to campaign to preserve the area as a national park.

The road continues to undulate through valleys and over hills. At Mile 58.3 is **HIGHWAY PASS**, the highest point on the park road at 3,980 feet. Just a little farther is Stony Hill Overlook. From **EIELSON VISITOR CENTER** at Mile 66, named in honor of pioneer Alaska bush pilot Carl Ben Eielson, visitors can ogle McKinley from the warmth of the glass-enclosed building. This is also where you can change buses and continue on to Wonder Lake, if seats are available. Naturalists offer tundra walks here at different times each day. Just past Eielson, weather permitting, you can see the 1-mile-wide **MULDROW GLACIER**, the longest glacier on the north side of the Alaska Range. As the road heads west, it drops onto rolling tundra and the land becomes flatter and wetter.

You're getting closer to The Mountain, and at Wonder Lake Campground it's only 29 miles away. **WONDER LAKE** is 4 miles long and about 280 feet deep. It is home to lake trout, burbot, Arctic char, and lingcod. Beaver cruise along near shore, caribou wander by, and moose commonly wade in for an aquatic lunch. Beyond Wonder Lake lies **KANTISHNA**, once an active mining district, now home to four luxury resorts, open only to guests who make arrangements in advance.

FESTIVALS AND EVENTS

NENANA RIVER WILDWATER RACES / This 27-year-old festival of white-water rodeo, downriver, and slalom races on the Nenana River is usually held on the second weekend following the Fourth of July. This is a great spectator event. Contact the Denali Outdoor Center (see above) for information.

RESTAURANTS

Alaska Cabin Nite Dinner Theater

MILE 238.9 PARKS HWY, DENALI NATIONAL PARK; 907/683-2215, SUMMER; 907/276-7234, WINTER; 800/276-7234, YEAR-ROUND Definitely for tourists, but local folks love it. The 40-minute performance tells the story of Kantishna, an early mining town at the west end of the park road, through the lives of real-life pioneer Fannie Quigley and a cast of other characters. Dinner is delicious—Alaska salmon, barbecued ribs, side dishes, rolls, and dessert, all chuckwagon style. Dinner is also fun because the exuberant servers double as performers. Performances nightly at 5:30pm and 8:30pm; cost is $46, children 2–12 half-price. *$$; AE, DIS, MC, V; Alaska checks OK; dinner every day (closed Oct to May); beer and wine; reservations required; www.denaliparkresorts.com; down the hill from the McKinley Park Chalets, at Mile 238.9 Parks Hwy (follow the signs).* &

Black Diamond Grill / ★★

OTTO LAKE RD, JUST OFF MILE 247 PARKS HWY, HEALY; 907/683-GOLF (4653) This cheerful little restaurant is 10 miles north of Denali National Park but is worth the drive. Prices are reasonable, food is excellent, the atmosphere is delightful, and you can't beat the view of the Alaska Range. Fresh salads, sandwiches, pasta, or seafood and steaks are all available. You don't have to be a golfer to eat here, but if you are, you can step outside and play a challenging nine holes of golf at the Black Diamond Golf Course or 18 holes of minigolf, before or after your meal. *$$; AE, DIS, MC, V; Alaska checks only; breakfast, lunch, dinner every day (open Mother's Day to Sept 10); beer and wine; reservations accepted; www.black diamondgolf.com.; drive to Mile 247 Parks Hwy, turn onto Otto Lake Rd, drive 1 mile.* &

McKinley Creekside Café / ★★

MILE 224 PARKS HWY, DENALI NATIONAL PARK; 907/683-2277 A friendly spot right alongside Carlo Creek, this restaurant offers casual dining in a bright atmosphere. Menu items range from burgers to salmon and steaks. Get your espresso here. Some locals rave about breakfasts. One diner came away amazed that the cook made French toast better than her own mother. There's a play area for kids, making this a perfect stop for families. *$–$$; DIS, MC, V; local checks only; breakfast, lunch, dinner daily May to Sept; beer and wine; no reservations; cabins@ mckinley.com; www.mckinleycabins.com.* &

The Perch

MILE 224 PARKS HWY, DENALI NATIONAL PARK; 907/683-2523 OR 888/322-2523 This quiet restaurant on Carlo Creek is the place to get away from the busy hubbub of Glitter Gulch, the tourist strip more than 10 miles north. Locals come here to enjoy a peaceful meal with a lovely view. There's a good reason it's called the Perch—it sits atop a hillside, surrounded by mountains. Known for its bread—often baked for other eateries in the area—the Perch offers everything from halibut and salmon when they're in season to hamburger night once a week. This is one of the few Denali area restaurants that opens on weekends during winter months. Available for private parties anytime. *$$; AE, DIS, MC, V; checks OK; breakfast, lunch, dinner every day in summer; full bar; reservations required for groups of 6 or more only; the perch@yahoo.com; www.denaliperchresort.com.* &

LODGINGS

Denali Grizzly Bear Cabins & Campground / ★★

MILE 231 PARKS HWY, DENALI NATIONAL PARK; 907/683-2696 Jack and Ede Reisland homesteaded this chunk of land along the banks of the Nenana River back in 1958 and now welcome summer visitors. Cabins nestle in a birch and spruce grove; each one is unique. Fisherman Cabin has a pair of hip waders and a net nailed above the door. The Sourdough Cabin has a hand-painted scene of the northern lights. Some of the cabins date back to the early 1900s and are from Fairbanks. Jack dismantled them, and then reassembled them at the campground. Double occupancy rates start at $49 and go up to $120 for a cabin with a full bathroom. Cabins with a full kitchen are $125–$165. You also can stay in your own tent near the river, in surprisingly secluded settings, for $17.50 (up to four people; add $6 for electrical and water hookups). Recreational vehicles park on the other side of the campground, near the highway. Coin-operated hot showers are available for guests only. *$; DIS, MC, V; no checks; closed mid-Sept to mid-May; summer address: PO Box 7, Denali National Park AK 99755; winter address: PO Box 303, Healy AK 99743; www.AlaskaOne.com/dengrzly; across the highway from McKinley Village Lodge.* &

Denali Mountain Morning Hostel / ★★

MILE 224 PARKS HWY, DENALI NATIONAL PARK; 907/683-7503 (866/D-HOSTEL (346-7835), IN-STATE) Experience a quiet stay in the Denali area here, just 13 miles south of the park's entrance. As of this writing, this is the only hostel-style accommodation in the Denali National Park area, and it's a beauty. The owners are young, energetic Alaskans who know how to offer quality housing for low-budget travelers. Bunks are only $23 a night (two-night minimum) or $25 (one night). They also offer private rooms and private cabins. The deluxe private cabin ($100 per night for two people, two-night minimum stay) features a huge picture window with a grand view of Carlo Mountain. Two restaurants are right across the street, and shuttles to the park are available for $3 round-trip. *$; DIS, MC, V; checks OK; PO Box 208, Denali National Park AK 99755; akhostel@hotmail.com; www.hostelalaska.com.*

Denali Princess Lodge / ★★

MILE 238.5 PARKS HWY, DENALI NATIONAL PARK; 800/426-0500 This lodge has everything, including outdoor hot tubs overlooking the Nenana River. Rooms are clean and comfortable, and employees are friendly. Many people staying here are on package tours with Princess Cruise Tours (800/426-0442). Double occupancy rates run from $179 for a standard room to $189 for a riverside room. Family and bedroom suites go for $249 and $279, respectively. (Prices drop during the shoulder seasons, May and Sept). A large deck overlooks the river, and landscaped walkways line the bluff, a good spot for an evening stroll. If it's windy or too chilly, just move inside and enjoy the same view from the comfort of the lounge. There's also fine dining in the Summit Dining Room, with a full bar, as well as a cafe. *$$$; AE, DC, DIS, MC, V; checks OK; closed Oct to early Mar; www.princesslodges.com.* ♿

Earth Song Lodge / ★★★

MILE 4 STAMPEDE TRAIL, WEST OF HEALY; 907/683-2863; FAX 907/683-2868 If you want a real Alaska experience, away from buses and crowds, you will find it here where you are one step into the wilderness. Two longtime Alaskans operate this lodge year-round. There's a finely handcrafted main lodge and private cabins with private bathrooms. A new coffee house was added in 2002. Open tundra stretches to the nearby Alaska Range, and you can even see Mount McKinley 4 miles from the lodge. Standard cabins start at $115; large or two-bedroom cabins start at $135. *$$; DIS, MC, V; checks OK; PO Box 89, Healy AK 99743; koala@mtaonline.net; www.earthsonglodge.com; drive to Mile 251 Parks Hwy (17 miles north of Denali National Park), turn onto historic Stampede Trail, drive 4 miles.*

McKinley Creekside Cabins / ★★

MILE 224 PARKS HWY, DENALI NATIONAL PARK; 907/683-2277 OR 888/5DENALI (888/533-6254) Cozy cabins with private bathrooms overlook Carlo Creek or are nestled in the woods. This is a lovely place to stay, away from the crowds of Glitter Gulch, 14 miles north. There are picnic, barbecue, and fire pit facilities, a playground for kids, and mountain views right outside the door. And their cafe (see Restaurants, above) is right there for meals. Cabin prices start at $79. *$; DIS, MC, V; checks OK; PO Box 89, Denali National Park AK 99755; cabins@mckinleycabins.com; www.mckinleycabins.com.*

Motel Nord Haven / ★★

MILE 249.5 PARKS HWY, HEALY; 907/683-4500 OR 800/683-4501 This is by far the nicest commercial hotel in Healy, just 12 miles north of Denali National Park. It is clean, spacious, and in a quiet wooded setting off the highway. The new and bright Taiga Room can hold 40 people for meetings or dining; catering is available. A deck outside the room's sliding glass doors reaches into the taiga forest. Prices start at $115 single occupancy in summer, with lower rates in shoulder seasons and winter. Continental breakfast included in summer. *$$; AE, MC, V; PO Box 458, Healy AK 99743; info@motelnordhaven.com; www.motelnordhaven.com/.*

WILDERNESS LODGES

Camp Denali

DENALI NATIONAL PARK; 907/683-2290; FAX 907/683-1568 The first wilderness camp at Denali National Park was founded by Ginny Wood of Fairbanks and the late Celia Hunter. Both were World War II WASP pilots who flew to Alaska after the war. Originally outside park boundaries, Camp Denali became an island of private land when the park expanded in 1980. The camp has grown every year, with a lodge and permanent chalets eventually built to replace the tents. Today, it accommodates up to 40 guests in log or frame cabins, each with a view of McKinley. Cabins sleep two to six and come with small wood-burning stoves and propane lights. A gas hot plate for heating water is available in each building. Guests may use outhouses or a central bathhouse that is a short walk from each cabin. Resident naturalists lead a variety of hikes and teach natural history, and workshops feature visiting experts on all aspects of Denali. Camp Denali is also allowed day use of the park road, so guests can spend a long time observing wildlife. Cost is $375 per adult per day; $285 for children 11 and under. Prices include round-trip transportation from the park rail station, lodging, all meals, guided activities, natural-history interpretation, evening programs, use of bicycles or canoes, and park entrance fee. Family discounts available. *$$$; No credit cards; checks OK; closed mid-Sept to early June; Denali National Park Wilderness Centers, Box 67, Denali National Park AK 99755; info@campdenali.com; www.campdenali.com.*

Denali Wilderness Lodge

WOOD RIVER VALLEY, EAST OF DENALI NATIONAL PARK; 800/541-9779 OR 907/683-1287, SUMMER This fly-in-only lodge is not actually in Denali National Park, but rather lies a short flight east in the Wood River Valley. Once owned by a well-known Alaska hunting guide, the lodge has been transformed into a haven for tourists who want to shoot wildlife with a camera instead of a gun. Located on the scenic Wood River, the lodge features charming cabins with private baths, gourmet meals and a full bar, and an impressive wildlife museum. Naturalists lead hikes, and visiting experts present special evening programs. You won't see McKinley from here, but the country is spectacular. It is possible to fly out just for the day. Double occupancy at $340 per person per night includes accommodations, meals, and activities. Horseback riding costs extra: $30 for first two-hour ride, $60 additional two-hour ride. Flight-seeing and river rafting also available for a fee. Getting there is $90 round-trip from the lodge's airstrip near the park entrance. Guests can also arrange to fly out of Fairbanks. *$$$; AE, DIS, MC, V; local checks only; closed mid-Sept to mid-May; PO Box 50, Denali National Park AK 99755; info@denaliwilderness lodge.com; www.denaliwildernesslodge.com.* ♿

Kantishna Roadhouse

WESTERN EDGE OF DENALI NATIONAL PARK; 907/683-1475 OR 800/942-7420, SUMMER; FAX 907/683-1449 The historic Kantishna Roadhouse once provided comfort to miners and travelers in the early 1900s. When gold was discovered in the Kantishna Hills, so many miners flocked to the area that whole towns grew. They had names such as Glacier City, Diamond, Roosevelt, and Square Deal. Kantishna was once called Eureka and had a population of 2,000 in 1905, but gold fever ebbed by the mid-1920s. Today, Doyon Native Corporation owns the roadhouse and mines tourism, not gold. The lodge provides resident naturalists for guided hikes, natural-history programs, or activities such as panning for gold or mountain biking. Approximately $310 per person per night, double occupancy; two-night minimum; cost includes round-trip transportation from the park entrance area, all meals (full bar available), activities, and horse-drawn wagon rides. Group discounts. Singles add $100 per night. $$$; AE, DIS, MC, V; checks OK; closed mid-Sept to early June; PO Box 81670, Fairbanks AK 99708; info@kantishnaroad house.com; www.kantishnaroadhouse.com.

North Face Lodge

DENALI NATIONAL PARK; 907/683-2290; FAX 907/683-1568 A sister lodge to Camp Denali a mile away (see above review), this wilderness outpost rests near the remains of an old log cabin. Grant Pearson, an early superintendent of the park and the original owner of the lodge, staked out the property in 1957. The lodge has 15 guest rooms, private baths, and, of course, a view of McKinley. Arrivals and departures on Fridays and Mondays; daily rates are $375 per adult, $285 for children 11 and under (double occupancy). Family discount available. Prices include round-trip transportation from the park rail station, lodging, all meals, guided activities, natural-history interpretation, evening programs, use of bicycles or canoes, and park entrance fee. $$$; No credit cards; checks OK; closed mid-Sept to early June; Denali National Park Wilderness Centers, Box 67, Denali National Park AK 99755; info@ campdenali.com; www.campdenali.com.

The Denali Highway

(Note: Mile markers on the Denali Highway read east to west and west to east. We have chosen to take you east to west, from Paxson to Cantwell.)

The Denali Highway offers one of the most scenic drives in Alaska. From Paxson on the Richardson Highway it is 135 miles to Cantwell on the Parks Highway. The road is primarily gravel, except for the first 21 miles out of Paxson. The ride can be rough, dusty, and hazardous to your tires. Be sure to bring mounted spares. Potholes and other rough spots in the road require you to keep your speed well below 50mph and actually closer to 30mph. Four hours is a quick trip. Take your time and you will be rewarded with fabulous vistas and maybe wildlife sightings.

When the Denali Highway opened in 1957, it provided a route from the Richardson Highway to what was then Mount McKinley National Park, today Denali National Park. Before that, visitors could reach the park only by train, plane, or dog sled. The road that led from the entrance of the park to Wonder Lake was already in use, so visitors often sent their vehicles to the park via rail. After the Parks Highway was built, more than a decade later, the Denali Highway became a destination in itself.

ACCESS AND INFORMATION

In the summer, there are a few inns along the way that offer some amenities, but you should **COME PREPARED** with extra water and food for emergencies. Also be prepared for changes in weather. The day may start out sunny and warm and change dramatically to cold, rain, wind, and even snow, any month of the year. The road is not plowed in the wintertime.

You can camp anywhere along the highway. There are many beautiful spots. However, if you want a few extras, there are three Bureau of Land Management (BLM) campgrounds along the highway, with a total of 46 campsites. **TANGLE LAKES CAMPGROUND** (Mile 21.5) has a water pump, toilets, boat launch, and picnic area. This is the starting point for a three-day river trip (see Adventures, below). **TANGLE RIVER CAMPGROUND** (Mile 21.7) has a water pump, toilets, and boat launch. Take off from here for an extended wilderness canoe trip on the upper Tangle Lakes. **BRUSHKANA RIVER CAMPGROUND** (Mile 104) has fire pits, water pump, toilets, tables, trails, and 17 campsites.

ADVENTURES

TANGLE LAKES / On both sides of the highway, a series of beautiful lakes connected by the Tangle River are a popular destination. **ROUND TANGLE, LONG TANGLE,** and **LOWER TANGLE LAKES** are on the north side of the road, and **UPPER TANGLE LAKE** is on the south side of the road. The name Tangle comes from the maze of lakes and streams in this drainage system. The lakes offer good **FISHING**, even from shore. Catch trout, grayling, or burbot. Be sure to check state fishing regulations and have a fishing license in hand before you wet a line. The Tangle Lakes are also terrific for **BIRDING**. With a little luck you might see Arctic warblers, Smith's longspurs, gyrfalcons, or ptarmigan. Canoeists can paddle across any of the lakes and instantly find themselves in remote Alaska wilderness with tundra-hiking in any direction. Be sure to wear rubber boots, though, because some of that hiking is wet. You can rent a canoe from Tangle River Inn, Mile 20, or from Tangle Lakes Lodge, Mile 22 (see Lodgings, below).

RIVER TRIPS / Experienced paddlers looking for a longer trip can paddle across Round Tangle and Long Tangle Lakes to reach the Wild and Scenic **DELTA RIVER**. This 30-mile trip is best done in a leisurely three days, generally in a raft or canoe. At the end of Long Tangle Lake, you'll have to portage ½ mile around a waterfall. The 1½-mile section of river just below the falls is notorious for demolishing canoes, since the water moves swiftly and the river is very rocky. To paddle this section, you should know how to maneuver through Class III rapids. Takeout is at Mile 212 on the Richardson Highway.

Floating the **UPPER NENANA RIVER** is a classic wilderness canoe trip beginning at Mile 117 (or Mile 18 coming from Cantwell), where the Nenana River flows right next to the Denali Highway. Launch a canoe or raft here and spend the day floating swift but flat water through the Reindeer Hills. The river leaves the road and cuts through the mountains, making its way about 20 miles to the Parks Highway. Takeout is at the Nenana River Bridge north of Cantwell, at Mile 215.7 on the Parks Highway. The access road to the bridge is just south of there, at Mile 213.9 on the Parks Highway. The only disruptions to the peacefulness of the trip are jet boats or

235

air boats, which take visitors to the Bruskasna River vicinity. Boat pilots are generally courteous, however, and slow down when approaching canoes. The trip takes four to six hours, but may be faster at higher water.

ON THE HIGHWAY / The beauty of the Denali Highway is that views abound and you can take off hiking in any direction. As you drive west, on a clear day you'll have spectacular views the whole way. Keep a sharp eye on ponds and lakes. Swans and other migratory waterfowl nest in these areas and can be easy to spot.

Between Mile 17 and Mile 37, there are more than 400 archaeological sites. Designated the **TANGLE LAKES NATIONAL REGISTER ARCHAEOLOGICAL DISTRICT**, this area contains some of the earliest evidence of human occupation in North America.

The second-highest point on Alaska's road system is **MACLAREN SUMMIT**, at 4,086 feet. (The highest is 4,800-foot Atigun Pass on the Dalton Highway.) Just before Maclaren Summit, catch a panoramic view of the Alaska Range, including **MOUNT HAYES** (13,832 feet) and **MACLAREN GLACIER**. A short trail to Maclaren Summit takes off across the alpine tundra at Mile 37. Watch for ground squirrels and Arctic rodents called pikas.

At Mile 43.5, you might want to mountain bike or hike the **MACLAREN RIVER ROAD** as it follows along on the west side of the Maclaren River for 12 miles to Maclaren Glacier. After 4 miles, you must ford the West Fork of the Maclaren River, a glacial stream that can be dangerously high after heavy rains. That is followed by 5 miles of good trail, ½ mile of willow thicket, and another 3 miles of good trail.

Continuing on your route, you'll drive over the **SUSITNA RIVER**, a major drainage. Eventually, the Susitna turns west, flows through the Talkeetna Mountains, and empties into Cook Inlet. **CARIBOU** routinely migrate through the area past the Susitna River, so keep an eye peeled for bands of them. At Mile 93.8, a 5-mile trail leads to **BUTTE LAKE**, a popular local fishing hole with trout, grayling, and burbot.

LODGINGS

Gracious House

MILE 82 DENALI HWY; 907/822-7307, SUMMER (RADIO PHONE, SO LET IT RING); 907/333-3148, WINTER; 877/822-7307, YEAR-ROUND Gracious House has been serving travelers along the Denali Highway for 41 years. The name comes from the owner Butch Gratias's last name. Drivers can buy gas here, get flat tires repaired, or find a tow for disabled vehicles. If you're looking for a little adventure, Gracious House Flying Service offers scenic flights. Gratias is also a registered guide and offers guided hunts. The restaurant primarily serves short orders, but also has a full bar. A double in the motel with private bath goes for $105. *$$; MC, V; no checks; closed late Sept to May, but open for up to 40 (minimum 6) self-sufficient winter visitors with 2-week advance notice; summer address: PO Box 88, Cantwell AK 99729; winter address: PO Box 212549, Anchorage AK 99521-2549; Crhoa36683@ aol.com; www.alaskaone.com/gracious.*

Maclaren River Lodge

MILE 42 DENALI HWY, 40 MILES FROM NEAREST TOWN OF PAXSON; 907/822-7105 (RADIO PHONE) OR 888/880-4264 This Denali Highway lodge is open year-round. Snowmachiners and dog mushers visit regularly during the long winter months when the unplowed highway becomes a major winter trail. Competitors in the Iditarod Trail Sled Dog Race often train here early in the year and stop in to eat during their training runs. There are seven rooms in a separate building behind the lodge, three cabins, plus a bunkhouse, all of which can house about 51 people. There's a sauna with shower and a restaurant that serves breakfast, lunch, and dinner and has beer and wine. Summer rates are $65 for a room, $25 for a bunk; winter rates are $80 for a room, $30 for a bunk; and cabin rentals are $150 and $180. *$; MC, V; local checks only; PO Box 3018, Paxson AK 99737; Maclaren@starband.net; www.mclarenriver.com.* & *(main lodge and sauna only)*

Tangle Lakes Lodge / ★

MILE 22 DENALI HWY, PAXSON; 907/822-4202, SUMMER; 907/688-9173, WINTER Built in 1952 and originally known as Butcher's Hunting Camp, this lodge is now owned by Rich and Linda Holmstrom. It burned down in May 1998 and was completely rebuilt the following summer. Rich is a falconer, and you can see him working his falcon in the fall hunting season. The area is tundra with low bushes, so there are a lot of ptarmigan and spruce hens, which makes it a good area for falcons. "My wife calls it my $1.4 million ptarmigan camp," says Rich. The lodge has log cabins that sleep three people for $75 per night and new log cabin duplexes, about 10 units total. You can rent canoes for the Tangle Lakes ($3 per hour per person, or $30 for all day). Rich also can guide you to good fishing or hiking. Cabins with woodstove heat are available for rent in the wintertime. The restaurant features a full bar and serves breakfast, lunch, and dinner every day. *$; MC, V; checks OK; winter address: PO Box 670386, Chugiak AK 99567; tanglelakeslodge@starband.net; www.tanglelakeslodge.com; from Paxson, drive 1 mile past the end of the pavement.*

Tangle River Inn / ★

MILE 20 DENALI HWY, PAXSON; 907/822-7304 OR 907/822-3970, SUMMER; 907/895-4022, WINTER Overlooking Tangle Lakes, this inn features home-style cooking with breakfast, lunch, and dinner every day, and boasts the only karaoke bar along the Denali Highway (full bar). For about $65 per person, you can stay in one of the motel rooms or cabins. For $25 per person, stay in a log bunkhouse that sleeps 10 and is good for family reunions or parties who plan to float the Delta River the next day. Canoes available for rent at $3 an hour or $24 for 24 hours. The inn advertises the cheapest gas in 100 miles and guarantees that its lodgings are less expensive than any in the nearest towns—Delta Junction and Glennallen on the Richardson Highway. *$; MC, V; local checks only; closed Oct to Apr; Box 783, Delta Junction AK 99737; info@tangleriverinn.com; www.tangleriverinn.com.* &

FAIRBANKS AND
THE INTERIOR

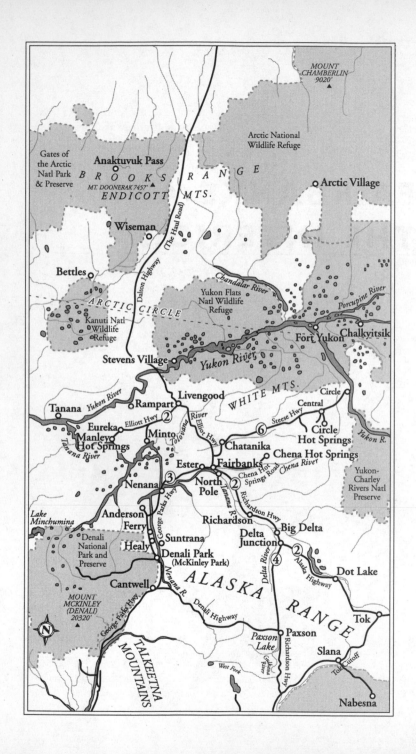

MOUNT
CHAMBERLIN
9020'

Arctic National
Wildlife Refuge

Gates of
the Arctic
Natl Park
& Preserve

Anaktuvuk Pass

B R O O K S   R A N G E

MT. DOONERAK 7457'

ENDICOTT   MTS.

Arctic Village

Wiseman

Bettles

(The Haul Road)

Chandalar River

Porcupine River

Yukon Flats
Natl Wildlife
Refuge

Dalton Highway

ARCTIC CIRCLE

Kanuti Natl
Wildlife
Refuge

Fort Yukon   Chalkyitsik

Stevens Village   Yukon River

Yukon River

Livengood   WHITE MTS.   Circle

Tanana   Yukon River   Rampart   (2)   Central

Eureka   Elliott Hwy   River   Steese Hwy   Circle

Manley   Minto   Elliott Hwy   (6)   Circle   Yukon R.

Hot Springs   Hot Springs

Tanana River   Chatanika   Chena Hot Springs

Ester   Fairbanks   Chena Hot   Chena River

Nenana   (3)   North   Springs Road

(2)   Pole   Yukon-
Charley
Rivers Natl
Preserve

Lake
Minchumina   Anderson   Richardson

Ferry   Richardson Hwy   Big Delta

Denali
National
Park and
Preserve   Healy   Suntrana   Delta
Junction

George Parks Hwy   Denali Park   (2)

(McKinley Park)   (4)   Dot Lake

Alaska Highway

Cantwell   A L A S K A   R A N G E

MOUNT
MCKINLEY
(DENALI)
20320'   Nenana R.   Denali Highway   Tok

N   George Parks Hwy   Paxson   Richardson Hwy

TALKEETNA
MOUNTAINS   Paxson
Lake   Slana

West Fork   Tok Cutoff

Nabesna

FAIRBANKS AND
THE INTERIOR

Lured first by gold in the 1890s, then by the opportunity for self-reliance, the "sour-doughs" of the Interior tend to be seasoned souls who'd rather take their chances carving a living out of the land than punching a time clock. They love elbow room. They hate regulations. They are miners, trappers, hermits, artists, scientists, climbers, dog mushers, and general wilderness junkies. You'll find condo dwellers whose idea of "the great outdoors" is the space between the front door and the carport. You'll find cabin dwellers whose idea of "the big city" is any place with a gas pump.

The land encourages individuality. There are rolling boreal forests as far as the eye can see, great meandering rivers, and ponds and lakes reflecting overcast skies like beads of scattered mercury. In the fall, the land shakes its subtle beauty and gets outright loud. Golds more gold than nuggets. Tundra the color of spawned-out salmon. Clear winter nights when the northern lights shimmer across the heavens in an ethereal dance. If you're driving when this happens, pull over to gawk.

The Interior comprises about a third of the state, with the Brooks Range at its northern border, the Alaska Range at its southern, and Fairbanks in the middle. More than 99,000 people live within the boundaries of this 192,660-square-mile region; 12 percent are Indian and Eskimo. That amounts to almost 2 square miles per man, woman, and child.

The major "highways" here are the rivers. The smaller ones, like the Chena running through Fairbanks, are the side streets. The larger ones—the Tanana, the Koyukuk, the Yukon—are the freeways. Native people have depended on these waterways for food and transportation for centuries. Today, these rivers still feed the people and connect their villages by boat in summer and by snow machine and dog team in winter.

In summer, the midnight sun is like an elixir. People get rejuvenated. You'll find them out gardening at midnight. Parents forget about bedtimes. The opposite problem occurs in winter. With less than four hours of daylight, the body slides into hibernation. Add weather inversions, dead car batteries, and cold trips to the out-house and you'll see why Interior winters aren't for everyone.

The highest temperature ever recorded in Alaska was in the Interior: 100°F in Fort Yukon on June 27, 1915. So was the lowest: it plummeted to minus 80°F at Prospect Creek, up the Dalton Highway, on January 23, 1971. Warm winter winds called "chinooks" can raise the temperature from minus 25°F to 25°F in a few hours. When you visit, dress in layers and be prepared for any of the region's moods.

Fairbanks

Athabascans were here first—living, hunting, and fishing up and down the banks of the Chena and Tanana Rivers. Then, in August 1901, a trader from Ohio named E. T. Barnette hired the steamer *Lavelle Young* because he wanted to establish a trading post along the trail from Valdez to Eagle on the Tanana River, far upstream from present-day Fairbanks. Barnette spent $20,000 on a shipment of food and supplies. The sternwheeler took what is now known as the Chena River in an effort to avoid the Tanana's shallow rapids. The plan was to rejoin the Tanana on a channel farther upstream off the Chena. But that didn't happen. Instead, the riverboat captain ran aground and was forced to turn back, leaving Barnette and his distraught wife Isabelle ashore, along with the trading goods, near the site of today's Cushman Street Bridge. Fortunately for Barnette, Italian immigrant Felice Pedroni, to become known in America as Felix Pedro, discovered gold in the nearby hills. Barnette set up shop.

The merchant exaggerated news of the strike, which led to a "false boom" that left many convinced the whole thing was a scam. But paying quantities of the precious metal were indeed mined as the summer of 1903 progressed. Pedro died of heart problems in 1910. A year later Barnette left in disgrace, blamed for the failure of the bank he founded and a $1 million loss to depositors.

By this time, Fairbanks was Alaska's most cosmopolitan city, while Anchorage was still muskeg and swamp. The U.S. Census counted 3,542 residents that year, with another 7,000, mostly miners, in camps nearby. The University of Alaska Fairbanks was founded in 1917 (called the Alaska Agricultural College and School of Mines), and both the army and air force eventually established military bases here. Fairbanks also is the northern terminus of the Alaska Railroad.

With the oil discovery on Alaska's North Slope, Fairbanks became a boomtown once again, this time as a staging ground in the mid-1970s for the 800-mile-long Trans-Alaska Pipeline from Prudhoe Bay to tidewater at Valdez. And the name? Fairbanks is named for Vice President Charles W. Fairbanks, who served under President Theodore Roosevelt.

ACCESS AND INFORMATION

You can get to Fairbanks by **DRIVING** the Alaska Highway, the Richardson Highway, or the Parks Highway. You can also take the **ALASKA RAILROAD** (907/265-2494; www.alaskarailroad.com) from Anchorage, or even quicker, you can fly. There are several scheduled flights a day, starting with **ALASKA AIRLINES** (800/252-7522; www.alaskaair.com). Or try the **PARKS HIGHWAY EXPRESS**, a bus that runs between Anchorage and Fairbanks (907/479-3065 or 888/600-6001; info@alaska shuttle.com; www.alaskashuttle.com). Once you get to town, there's a **PUBLIC BUS SYSTEM** (MACS, Metropolitan Area Commuter System; 907/459-1011) to transport you, as well as many local cab companies.

Stop first at the log cabin near the Cushman Street Bridge, the **FAIRBANKS VISITORS INFORMATION CENTER** (550 1st Ave; 907/456-5774 or 800/327-5774; info@explorefairbanks.com; www.explorefairbanks.com; open daily in summer, weekdays in winter). In addition to the usual, you'll find menus, the nightlife column from the local newspaper, and a board for posting messages such as "Looking for hitchhiker to split gas, costs to Prudhoe Bay."

At the **ALASKA PUBLIC LANDS INFORMATION CENTER** (250 Cushman St; 907/456-0527; www.nps.gov/aplic/center; open daily in summer, Tues–Sat in winter), located in the basement of the old Fairbanks Courthouse, you'll find maps, brochures, articles, and log books on hiking, rafting, canoeing, skiing, camping,

FAIRBANKS THREE-DAY TOUR

DAY ONE: You'll need to get up early to have enough time for breakfast at **SAM'S SOURDOUGH CAFÉ** (corner of University Ave and Cameron St; 907/479-0523) before your stern-wheeler leaves the dock at the **RIVERBOAT DISCOVERY.** The three-hour tour packed with Interior culture will leave you hungry, so head to the **THAI HOUSE** for a delicious and spicy lunch. Spend the afternoon at the **UNIVERSITY OF ALASKA MUSEUM** and, if the weather's nice, stroll through the **GEORGESON BOTANICAL GARDENS.** If time permits, head out to the university's **MUSK OX FARM** or take in a bit of shopping. For dinner, head out the Parks Highway to the little community of Ester, and the **ESTER GOLD CAMP DINING HALL & HOTEL,** where an all-you-can-eat buffet and a somewhat corny but fun musical revue in the **MALEMUTE SALOON** await you. You'll be tired after such a long day, so check into your train (that's right—this is no ordinary bed-and-breakfast) at **AURORA EXPRESS.**

DAY TWO: One of the best things about Fairbanks is it's so easy to get out of town and explore the vastness surrounding it. Grab some goodies and good, strong coffee at **BUN ON THE RUN** before heading up the Steese Highway. Bypass gold-mining attractions and go straight for the real thing, with a tour of the **FORT KNOX GOLD MINE.** Afterward, continue on the scenic Steese to your cozy cabin or room at **ARCTIC CIRCLE HOT SPRINGS,** where you'll spend the evening soaking in the natural hot springs and enjoying a quiet meal in the hotel's simple but pleasant dining room. Just call ahead, especially if you're visiting in winter, as the owners have closed the springs unexpectedly in the past.

DAY THREE: Another big day awaits. Get up early, eat breakfast at the hot springs, then drive the four hours back to Fairbanks in time for lunch downtown at **L'ASSIETTE DE POMEGRANATE.** You'll need to fill up on healthy, homemade fare because you're going to spend the afternoon in the **CHENA RIVER STATE RECREATION AREA,** hiking Angel Rocks Trail or perhaps doing a bit of fishing or river floating. All that activity will leave you starving, so drive back toward town to **TWO RIVERS LODGE,** where an elegant and delicious meal is sure to await you. After a relaxing evening, head a few miles more toward town on Chena Hot Springs Road to your beautiful log cabin or fully appointed room at **A TASTE OF ALASKA LODGE.**

photography, hunting, fishing, gold panning, scenic drives, and more. Parks, refuges, Wild and Scenic Rivers—all are featured here. Special programs and movies are also shown (call for programming schedule).

Check with the **NATIONAL WEATHER SERVICE** (800/472-0391; www.arh. noaa.gov/) for Interior forecasts, including aviation forecasts and hourly reports from every corner of the state online; for **LOCAL INFORMATION,** call 907/452-

3553. Our advice on bug dope: don't leave your room without it, June through August. The mosquitoes can be wicked. Hooded jackets made of mosquito netting, soaked overnight in repellent, are the ticket for serious bug territory. They're available at most sporting goods stores.

EXPLORING

ALASKA SALMON BAKE / The evening salmon bake offers an 18-ounce prime rib or all the salmon, halibut, and cod you can eat, along with all-you-can-eat salad bar and side dishes, for $24 (prime rib) or $23 (fish). Hot dogs and smaller fish portions are available for children. There are mining relics to look at, and you can eat either outside or inside. *Closed in winter; 907/452-7274 or 800/354-7274; beer and wine; www.akvisit.com; in a corner of Pioneer Park, off Airport Wy at Peger Rd.*

ALASKAN TAILS OF THE TRAIL WITH MARY SHIELDS / The first woman to finish the Iditarod Trail Sled Dog Race, Mary Shields is the author of five books and is the subject of the PBS film "Season of the Sled Dog," which has aired in 17 countries. In this two-hour tour she opens her Goldstream Valley home to visitors interested in taking a peek at how dog mushers live. She'll introduce you to Daisy, Clifford, Kiana, and others, as well as discuss training, racing, breeding, and the like. (Tip: Wear grubbies. Playing with sled dogs is fun, but sometimes dirty.) Cost is $25 adults; $20 children 8–12. No children under 8, please. Parks Highway Express (907/479-3065) will deliver you for $15 round-trip. *Closed mid-Sept to mid-May; 907/455-6469; www.maryshields.com; located 12 miles northwest of downtown Fairbanks, call for directions.*

CHENA LAKES RECREATION AREA / If you have children and you visit in summer, this spot is a must. Run by the Fairbanks North Star Borough, this park features a man-made lake leftover from gravel dredging for a massive public works project called the Chena Lakes Flood Control Project. For a $3 per vehicle entrance fee, you'll have access to picnic spots, the lake (good for fishing and swimming), a sandy beach, changing rooms, a playground, and bike trails. Overnight camping, everything from RV sites to tent sites on an island, is $10. There are also canoes and paddle boats for rent. In July, go to the U.S. Army Corps of Engineers' picnic area atop the Moose Creek Dam to see spawning salmon. In winter, bring your cross-country skis or snow machine, but watch for dog teams. *907/488-1655; drive 17 miles east of Fairbanks on the Richardson Hwy, left on Laurence Rd.*

CREAMER'S FIELD MIGRATORY WATERFOWL REFUGE / This is a gold-rush-era dairy farm. The buildings are historic, and the land now belongs to the birds. Each spring, snow buntings blaze the migration trail as early as mid-March, followed by Canada geese, trumpeter swans, pintails, golden plovers, sandhill cranes, peregrine falcons, and others. Some of the more rare sightings include snow geese and the Eurasian wigeon. The refuge has observation platforms, 3 miles of trails leading from the historic farmhouse through farm fields to forests and wetlands, and free guided nature walks. Bring binoculars and bug dope. Early mornings and late evenings are best for spying moose. In winter the Creamer's trail system connects with dog mushing trails off Farmer's Loop, for 40 miles of groomed cross-country ski trails. Trail guides and other information, as well as a small gift shop, are available at the Farmhouse Visitors Center. *Visitors center closed except Sat in winter;*

907/459-7307 or 907/452-5162; off College Rd, next to Fish and Game building—you'll see the big field and barn.

EL DORADO GOLD MINE / Nobody gets away without gold. They make sure you get at least a few specks by keeping their panning area stocked with pay dirt. But first, this two-hour tour takes you on a narrow-gauge train ride into a permafrost tunnel, where you learn about underground mining techniques and see prehistoric bones up to 30,000 years old. Back out in the daylight, Dexter Clark and "Yukon Yonda" explain how placer mining works and demonstrate what it's like to be stricken with gold fever. After a crash course in gold panning, visitors grab bundles of dirt and head to a panning shed. Train tours depart morning and afternoon; cost is $28 for adults, $20 for children 3–12. Children under 3 are free. *Closed mid-Sept to mid-May; 907/479-6673 or 866/479-6673; www.eldoradogoldmine.com; Mile 1.3 Elliott Hwy, just past the community of Fox.*

FIRST FRIDAY ART SHOWS / If you happen to be in Fairbanks the first Friday of the month, be sure to check out the latest art openings in a fun event known as First Friday. Several galleries host their openings on this day, and often feature hors d'oeuvres and wine as well as a chance to meet the artists. You can count on **WELL STREET ART CO.** (1304 Well St; 907/452-6169), **NEW HORIZONS GALLERY** (519 1st Ave; 907/456-2063), and **ALASKA HOUSE ART GALLERY** (downtown, corner of 10th and Cushman Streets; 907/456-6449; www.thealaskahouse.com) to participate. Other galleries, such as **ARTWORKS** (Campus Corner Mall, 3677 College Rd; 907/479-2563), often participate as well. The gallery hopping usually runs from 5pm–8pm. *Call David Mollett at Well Street Art, 907/452-6169.*

FORT KNOX GOLD MINE / This isn't just another tourist attraction—this is Alaska's largest operating gold mine, with the largest gold mill in North America grinding 40,000 tons of ore each day to extract the precious metal. The one-hour tour of the gold mine, located 25 miles north of Fairbanks, includes the excavation area, the crusher, gold-processing mill, as well as the chance to hold a 17.63-pound gold bar. Wear comfortable clothing and walking shoes. You'll be climbing some stairs and donning a hard hat, safety glasses, and earplugs. Daily tours are by reservation only. Cost is $21 adults; $17 for children 17 and younger. Children under 8 not allowed. *907/488-GOLD (4653), ext. 2800; tours@fairbanksgold.com; call for directions.*

GEORGESON BOTANICAL GARDENS / Do not leave town without visiting the veggies. Under the spell of the midnight sun, they grow into giants. While you're at it, check out all the other marvels of Alaska agriculture, including the brilliant, jumbo-size flowers. Since this is an experimental farm, there are new things in the garden every year. Free tours are available; call for times. Otherwise, just walk on through. *Closed winters; 907/474-1944; on Tanana Loop, 1 mile southwest of the lower University of Alaska Fairbanks campus.*

GOLD DREDGE NO. 8 / This is the best opportunity in Alaska to see an historic, five-deck gold dredge—or giant mechanical gold pan—in all its former glory. Between 1928 and 1959, this iron monstrosity gobbled up millions of ounces of gold from Goldstream and Engineer Creeks near Fairbanks. In addition to mining equipment and tailings, you'll see a collection of mammoth tusks and other prehistoric bones found in the area. Registered as a National Historical Site, Gold Dredge No. 8 is actually three museums constructed from the original miners' bunkhouse, bathhouse, and office. You can spend the whole day panning for gold if you like. Tour with gold panning and lunch is $32.50 for adults, $25 for children 6–12. Children under 6 are free. Or you can purchase a tour or gold panning separately at a lower cost. Tours begin every hour on the half hour, with the last one at 3:30pm. *Closed mid-Sept to mid-May; 907/457-6058 or 877/905-2905; www.golddredgeno8.com; from Steese Expressway north, left onto Goldstream Rd, left onto Old Steese, after about 1 mile watch for sign.*

LARGE ANIMAL RESEARCH STATION / This is more popularly known as the Musk Ox Farm. Musk oxen are stout, prehistoric-looking creatures. Yet beneath that shaggy exterior lies the softest and finest fiber produced by an animal. The underhairs, or qiviut, are warmer and softer than cashmere. Operated by the University of Alaska Fairbanks's Institute of Arctic Biology, this is home to the largest group of captive musk oxen and caribou in the world and draws researchers from all over. During summer months, viewing is best in early morning or late evening, after temperatures have cooled and the animals aren't hiding in shade. Bring binoculars. Guided tours are offered during the summer; $5 for adults and $3 for students; call for times. *907/474-7207; www.uaf.edu/lars; from the university, head north on Farmers Loop, left on Ballaine, left on Yankovich, farm is on the right.*

PALACE THEATRE & SALOON / The musical revue at the Palace, called Golden Heart Revue, features turn-of-the-century costumed performers telling tall tales laced with humor. The Alaska fashion show is a hoot. Greasy Carhartts. Breakup boots. Parkas adorned with glow-in-the-dark duct tape. In summer the show runs nightly at 8pm. Adults, $14; children 3–12, $7. Find a babysitter for younger children, as the show lasts a little over an hour and they likely won't sit still. *Closed in winter; 907/456-5960 or 800/354-7274; full bar; www.akvisit.com; in Gold-Rush Town at Pioneer Park, Airport Wy and Peger Rd.*

PIONEER PARK / This 44-acre pioneer theme park, formerly known as Alaskaland, was built to commemorate the 100th anniversary of the purchase of Alaska from Russia. While entrance to the park is free, some attractions come with a fee. Among them is the SS *Nenana,* the largest wooden-hulled stern-wheel river steamer ever built west of the Mississippi. You'll find a replica of a gold-rush town, historical cabins, art, aviation and history museums, a famous and posh railroad car, the Palace Theatre & Saloon, the Alaska Salmon Bake, two playgrounds, a historical carousel, train rides, picnic areas, and more. *Many attractions closed in winter; 907/459-1087; www.co.fairbanks.ak.us/parks&rec; off Airport Wy, at Peger Rd.*

RIVERBOAT DISCOVERY / While there are competitors that offer a choice for cruises on the Chena River, the best is still the Riverboat Discovery. You'll float past a fish wheel, a Native fish camp, and the home of four-time Iditarod champion Susan Butcher and her husband, Dave Monson, winner of the Yukon Quest International Sled Dog Race. Either they or their handlers give a sled-dog demonstration. Step ashore at a replica of an Athabascan Indian village. The late Capt. Jim Binkley, whose father was one of the original riverboat pilots during the gold-rush era, began the excursion business in 1950 with a 40-foot motor launch. The Binkley family now have three stern-wheelers, the largest being the *Discovery III,* a triple-decker capable of carrying more than 900 passengers. Cost is $40 for adults, $30 for ages 12 and under, with twice-daily departures. It's a bit more expensive than the alternatives, but it's worth it. *Closed in winter; 907/479-6673 or 866/479-6673; www.riverboat discovery.com; turn west off Airport Wy onto Dale Rd, follow signs.*

UNIVERSITY OF ALASKA MUSEUM / Perched atop a ridge overlooking the Tanana Valley, this museum is considered one of the best in the state. Its most famous exhibit is Blue Babe, a restored 36,000-year-old Ice Age bison, found in the permafrost by local miners. She was so well preserved that she even had most of her hide. The museum features exhibits on the natural history and cultural heritage of the Interior, Native arts and crafts, and the state's largest display of gold nuggets, some fist-size. Cost is $5 for adults, $3 for children aged 7–12. Children under 7 are free. A wonderful audio guide is available for $4 per person—you'll hear radio footage of the *Exxon Valdez* disaster as well as a variety of animal and nature sounds. And a much needed, $32 million expansion of the museum will get under way in spring 2003, regular programming through 2005 is up in the air; call for summer offerings. *907/474-7505; www.uaf.alaska.edu/museum; on the west ridge of the University of Alaska campus, from Geist Rd entrance, turn left and head uphill, then follow signs.*

SHOPPING

It may not look like it at first blush, but you can indeed find worthwhile shopping in Fairbanks. For unique gifts and interesting items, try **IF ONLY** (209 Cushman St; 907/457-6659). Within the souvenir genre, the downtown favorite is the **ARCTIC TRAVELERS GIFT SHOP** (201 Cushman St; 907/456-7080). If you're in the market for smoked salmon, stop by **SANTA'S SMOKEHOUSE** (2400 Davis Rd; 907/456-3885), home of the original salmon sausage and salmon hot dog, offering a variety of gift boxes. **BEADS AND THINGS** (537 2nd Ave; 907/456-2323) sells beads and things, but also some Native crafts on consignment—mukluks, porcupine quill earrings, ivory, soapstone carvings, birch-bark baskets, and much more. **ALASKA RAG CO.** (603 Lacey St; 907/451-4401) specializes in custom, handwoven rag rugs made of 100 percent recycled materials and discarded clothes. In addition, you'll find beautiful pottery and jewelry creations from Alaskan artists. For **ART GALLERIES,** check out a free copy of the 28-page *Fairbanks Arts Directory* at the log cabin visitors center, which lists everything from artists' studios to arts festivals.

At the **GREAT ALASKAN BOWL CO.** (4630 Old Airport Rd; 907/474-9663; www.woodbowl.com), you can watch craftspeople at work and create your own gift bowls, choosing from a variety of Alaska-made products, or you can bring in your own. And, if you're here in summer, don't miss the **TANANA VALLEY FARMERS MARKET** (1800 College Rd; 907/456-3276; www.tvfmarket.com), next to the Tanana Valley Fairgrounds. This is the homegrown, Alaska-made, seasonal market, offering everything from veggies to handcrafted soap made with melted snow, every Wednesday and Saturday from May to September.

With more than 40,000 titles of new and used books to paw through, including a healthy Alaskana section, **GULLIVER'S BOOKS** (3525 College Rd; 907/474-9574;

www.gullivers-books.com) is a local favorite. There's a great little cafe upstairs, with coffee drinks, soup, wraps, bagels, and other tasty treats. They also offer free Internet connection. If your visit coincides with winter, you might want to swing by **APOCALYPSE DESIGN** (intersection of College and Illinois; 907/451-7555). They custom sew outdoor gear and clothing, and they have a line of ready-made polar fleece jackets, mittens, hats, parkas, and other goodies to keep you toasty warm. Knitters must check out the **INUA WOOL SHOPPE** (907/479-5830; call for directions), which specializes in qiviut, or the soft undercoat of the musk ox, as well as other fine yarns from around the world.

Don't be alarmed if you start humming "Jingle Bells" as you pull up to **SANTA CLAUS HOUSE** (101 St. Nicholas Dr, North Pole; 907/488-2200; www.santaclaus house.com; off the Richardson Hwy, 14 miles south of Fairbanks) in neighboring North Pole. This is a town with a serious Santa fixation. Each holiday season, North Pole (pop. 1,600) gets deluged with children's letters to Santa, as well as grown-ups' letters requesting North Pole postmarks on their Christmas cards. Everywhere you look, there are establishments with a Christmas theme. Light poles resemble giant candy canes, and streets have names like Kris Kringle Drive and Rudolph Lane. The name of this city was no accident. Back in the early 1950s, when it was being incorporated, the townsfolk considered names like Moose Crossing and Mosquito Junction, but voted for North Pole instead. That sealed its fate as a theme town. The 30-foot Santa out front of the Santa Claus House is a clue you've arrived at Santa central.

If all the shopping makes you in need of a quick pick-me-up, there are a few good coffee houses in Fairbanks. Two of the best are **ALASKA COFFEE ROASTING CO.** (off Geist Rd near the university, inside the minimall next to a Pizza Hut; 907/457-5282) and the newly opened **COLLEGE COFFEEHOUSE** (Campus Corner Mall, corner of College and University; 907/374-0468).

ADVENTURES

BIKING / For getting around town, grab a copy of the free Fairbanks-area bike map at the log cabin visitors center and rent a bike from any of the outfits listed under Outdoor Rentals. The staff at **ALL WEATHER SPORTS** (907/474-8184) has good information, too. If you're a serious rider, check out the **FAIRBANKS CYCLE CLUB'S** Web site at www.fairbankscycleclub.org. It has maps, trail descriptions, and great info on upcoming events. Customized guided biking trips are available through **ALASKA OUTDOORS** (see Outdoor Rentals, below. They can do just about anything you want, depending on level of ability. Reservations required.

BOATING / The **ALASKA PUBLIC LANDS INFORMATION CENTER** (250 Cushman St; 907/456-0527; www.nps.gov/aplic) is an oasis of information for river travelers. In addition, there are river logs containing the comments of boaters who've made various trips. Ask for a copy of the BLM's *Alaska River Adventures,* which has descriptions of rivers, including Beaver Creek, Birch Creek, the Delta River, Fortymile River, Gulkana River, Squirrel River, and Unalakleet River. The National Weather Service's **ALASKA-PACIFIC RIVER FORECAST CENTER** (907/266-5160; aprfc.arh.noaa.gov) provides information on river conditions and water-level updates, from breakup to freeze-up, May through October. You'll find out about ice conditions the rest of the year.

FISHING / Rivers and lakes of the Interior are a fisherman's dream. You'll find Dolly Varden, Arctic char, pike, sheefish, Arctic grayling, rainbow trout, five different species of salmon, and more. You don't even have to go very far. The Chena River, which runs through downtown Fairbanks, offers salmon fishing and catch-and-release for grayling, which is usually good upriver, off Chena Hot Springs Road. For a recorded fishing report, call or stop by the **ALASKA DEPARTMENT OF FISH AND GAME** (1300 College Rd; 907/459-7385). Fish and Game stocks more than 70 lakes and sloughs within an hour or two of town, so ask about those too.

GOLF / NORTH STAR GOLF CLUB (330 Golf Club Dr, off the Old Steese Hwy; 907/457-4653; www.northstargolf.com) features 18 holes and certain wildlife hazards, such as moose, fox, and sandhill cranes. Or try **FAIRBANKS GOLF AND COUNTRY CLUB** (1735 Farmers Loop, near the university; 907/479-6555).

HIKING / For a short hike, try **ANGEL ROCKS TRAIL** (Mile 48.9 Chena Hot Springs Rd). This 3½-mile round-trip takes you along the North Fork of the Chena River, through the forest, and up into a maze of granite pinnacles that could pass as castle ruins. The highest point is 1,750 feet, atop a rock overlook. These outcroppings, called "tors," were formed millions of years ago when molten rock pushed upward but cooled and solidified before breaking ground.

For a longish hike, a local favorite is **GRANITE TORS TRAIL** (Mile 39 Chena Hot Springs Rd). You'll see lots of these outcroppings on the 15-mile loop. If you want, make an overnight trip of it—the camping is beautiful on top. For a longer option, try the **WHITE MOUNTAINS SUMMIT TRAIL** (Mile 28 Elliott Hwy). On a clear day, panoramic views of the Alaska Range, Minto Flats, and the White Mountains may find you bursting into a Julie Andrews impersonation. From the trailhead, the 20-mile trail climbs just under Wickersham Dome 7 miles in, follows ridges, drops into forest, and climbs to the highest point, 10 miles in, at 3,100 feet. The trail ends at Beaver Creek, where there's good fishing, camping, and even a cabin to rent. Call for reservations (907/474-2251) or for a recorded trail condition report (907/474-2372).

OUTDOOR RENTALS / If you know what you want to do and have the wherewithal to go it on your own, several businesses in town rent outdoor equipment. **INDEPENDENT RENTAL** (2020 S Cushman St; 907/456-6595) rents rafts, canoes, and lake boats. **ARCTIC 7 RENTALS** (4312 Birch Ln; 907/479-0751; gables7@ alaska.net; www.alaska.net/~gables7/7bridges.htm) rents canoes. **BEAVER SPORTS** (3480 College Rd; 907/479-2494; www.beaversports.com) rents bikes, snowshoes, cross-country skis, racquetball equipment, and trekking poles. **ALASKA OUTDOORS** (at Pioneer Park, near the Chena River; 907/457-2453; www.akbike.com or www.2paddle1.com) rents bikes, kayaks, and canoes. Rates vary depending on what you're renting and who you rent from, but for roughly $20 for either a bike or canoe, you're guaranteed a good time.

SKIING / Fairbanks is a cross-country skier's heaven. Try the groomed trails at **BIRCH HILL SKI AREA** (off Steese Hwy near Farmers Loop), **TWO RIVERS RECREATION AREA** (behind Two Rivers Elementary School, Mile 18 Chena Hot Springs

Rd), or miles of trails at the **UNIVERSITY OF ALASKA FAIRBANKS** (trailhead on the campus' west ridge, near the Arctic research building).

Downhill skiers can choose from **MOOSE MOUNTAIN SKI RESORT** (907/479-4732 or 907/459-8132 for conditions; www.shredthemoose.com; off Murphy Dome Rd in Goldstream Valley—call for directions) or **MT. AURORA SKILAND** (907/389-2314 or 907/456-SNOW (7669) for conditions and directions; www.ski land.org; on Cleary Summit).

VIEWS / For the best view of the city, head to Hagelbarger Turnout on Hagelbarger Road, off the Steese Highway. The best view of Mount McKinley (Denali) can be seen from the west ridge of the University of Alaska Fairbanks campus. For the best view—period—give a call to **MIDNIGHT SUN BALLOON TOURS** (907/456-3028). For $150 per person from mid-May through September, they'll take you up early in the morning or in the evening, when the winds are calmest. Reservations are necessary.

GUIDES AND OUTFITTERS

ALASKA FISHING AND RAFT ADVENTURES / This outfit owned by guide Logan Ricketts specializes in day trips, both fishing and scenic float trips, down the upper Chena River. He also offers "wade fishing" trips, in which you hike in and fish favorite spots from the riverbank. The upper Chena is mostly catch-and-release for Arctic grayling. Prices range from $105 to $180 per person, depending on the trip. The floats down the calm waters of the Chena ($95 per person) are great for families and children, and you may even see a moose or a bear. All of the trips feature a deli-style or gourmet lunch or dinner, depending on the time you go, fishing gear, transportation, and a licensed, professional fishing guide. Ricketts also can arrange a variety of multiday fishing trips, including one of his favorites, a four-night, five-day all inclusive trip on the Gulkana River in search of sockeye or king salmon ($1,195 per person). *MC, V; checks OK; 269 Topside Dr, Fairbanks AK 99712; 907/455-RAFT (7238) or 800/890-3229; www.aktours.net.*

ALASKA OUTDOORS / These folks will take beginners out for a guided, two-hour float along the Chena River for $117 per person (rates drop to $46 per person for parties of four to six). If you're a bit more bold, they'll drop you and a canoe off at the Nordale Bridge near North Pole for a relaxing four to six hour, do-it-yourself paddle down the Chena back to their site at Pioneer Park ($76 for two people, two boats). *Closed winters; 907/457-2453; www.2paddle1.com; at Pioneer Park, near the Chena River.*

ALEXANDER'S RIVER ADVENTURE / Wes Alexander, an Athabascan and certified master river pilot, picks you up in a heated, 28-foot jet boat in downtown Fairbanks and takes you 25 miles downriver to his family's fish camp. His wife, Mary, makes a hearty lunch of whatever is in season—fresh salmon, moose stew. You'll see the family's fish wheel and learn traditional ways of putting up food. You'll meet Alexander's mother, a delightful woman who makes moccasins and does lovely beadwork. Day and overnight trips are available, with hiking and other activities. The cost is $150 per person for the day (minimum two people) and $250 per person for overnights in a wall tent at camp (all meals provided). Parties of three or more get a $25 per person discount. *Closed winters; no credit cards; checks OK; PO Box 62, Nenana AK 99760; 907/474-3924; www.home.gci.net/~alexriveradv.*

DOG MUSHING / Several outfitters offer dog-mushing trips, everything from a simple 5- 10-mile ride to multiday backcountry expeditions to the Brooks Range, Alaska Range, Minto Flats—you name it. Two of the best are Leslie Goodwin's **PAWS FOR ADVENTURE** (PO Box 16046, Two Rivers AK 99716; 907/378-3630 or 800/890-3229; www.pawsforadventure.com) and Kathy Lenniger's **SLED DOG ADVENTURES** (PO Box 83601, Fairbanks AK 99708; 907/479-5090; www.sleddog adventures.com). Rates range from $45–$70 per person for short rides, up to $450–$500 per person for overnight trips. Expeditions go up from there, but every-thing—including arctic gear, food, dogs, and sleds—is included.

NORTH COUNTRY RIVER CHARTERS / If you're the serious fisher-type, Bill O'Halloran or one of his merry guides will take you out for half-day or full-day grayling trips ($95 or $165 per person, respectively); day trips out of Nenana for northern pike ($165 per person); as well as overnight trips that include two days of northern-pike fishing ($375 per person). There's also king salmon charters on the Chena River in July, as well as multiday trips in search of monster northern pike on the Yukon River. Those trips, which include round-trip airfare from Fairbanks to the nearby villages of either Ruby, Galena, or Tanana, range from $2,195 to $3,850 per person and include everything you'll need. *No credit cards; checks OK; 907/479-7116; www.ncrc.alaska.com.*

FESTIVALS AND EVENTS

YUKON QUEST INTERNATIONAL SLED DOG RACE / This is the epic of all sled-dog races. Blasting off in mid-February, competitors say this 1,000-mile, interna-tional race over gold-rush and mail routes is colder and tougher than the more well-known Iditarod Trail Sled Dog Race between Anchorage and Nome. Starting and ending points alternate each year between Fairbanks and Whitehorse, Yukon Territory. Check out the Quest's gift shop and mushing museum. *410 Cushman St; 907/452-7954; www.yukonquest.org.*

CHATANIKA DAYS / Witness people unwinding after a long, dark winter the second weekend of March. In addition to a pool tournament, a band, and general merrymaking, this celebration of spring includes an outhouse race from the Chatanika Gold Camp to the Chatanika Lodge. *Mile 28 Steese Hwy; 907/389-2164.*

NORTH AMERICAN SLED-DOG CHAMPIONSHIPS / This three-day event held the third week of March is known as the "granddaddy of all sprint races." These folks are serious—you'll sometimes see mushers hook up to 24 dogs on the gang-line, the rope that leads from the sled and to each dog in the team. Organizers use snow machines to hold the teams back as they inch toward their departure in the starting chute (most mushing races have competitors leave in two-minute intervals; times are adjusted later). The race has helped create mushing legends like George Attla, Roland "Doc" Lombard, and Roxy Wright. *907/457-MUSH (6874); www. sleddog.org.*

WORLD ICE ART CHAMPIONSHIPS / During this annual festival in March, carvers take huge blocks of clear blue ice and create a frozen art gallery, with some

PIPELINE LEAVES MARK ON FAIRBANKS

The frenzied atmosphere during the building of the Trans-Alaska Pipeline was like the gold rush all over again. During the three years of its construction, from 1974–77, the pipeline dominated life in Fairbanks, as the hurried project to tap North America's largest oil field with an 800-mile pipeline brought thousands of workers and millions of dollars into Interior Alaska.

As the largest settlement along the pipeline route, Fairbanks enjoyed some of the biggest economic benefits and the biggest social problems thanks to the unprecedented boom. Workers deserted low-paying jobs in town as cab drivers, postal workers, and store clerks. The turnover among tellers was such that bank presidents joked about giving seniority pins to those who were on the job for a month

Dispatched from Fairbanks union halls to jobs up and down the line, everyone from university professors to janitors joined the makeshift army of pipeline workers seeking lucrative jobs as laborers, housekeepers, truck drivers, and equipment operators. At the height of the mania, some people would quit one job and take another if they found the quality of the steaks or the Roquefort dressing inferior at a certain construction camp.

After nine weeks or more working on the pipeline, construction workers with thousands to spend flowed into the bars on Second Avenue for "rest and relaxation," willing players in a nightly spectacle of money, alcohol, drugs, and prostitution. A dozen-and-a-half bars in the city center featured standing-room-only crowds and rowdy atmospheres where everything was done to excess. Prostitutes openly solicited for customers along the thoroughfare the pipeliners dubbed "Two Street," and pimps circled the blocks on summer nights in their Cadillacs. To look at the street today, you would never know of its infamous past; most of the old watering holes are gone, replaced by a new hotel development and parking lots.

Aside from the crowds in the downtown bars, the population increase stretched the town's resources to the breaking point. The phone system barely worked and callers never knew if they'd be able to complete a phone call after picking up the receiver. A man who kept track on his watch once waited 26 minutes for a dial tone. Housing was almost impossible to come by, a shortage symbolized for many by the story of the two-bedroom rooming house that was home to 45 people in the spring of 1975. A local company had a standing classified advertisement in the newspaper about the "reasonable alternative to high-priced housing," urging people to buy its cozy, white canvas tents. A realtor sold a house to a man who bought it without going inside.

The building of the pipeline was like an earthquake, rattling the small town to its foundation. But, in keeping with its lively past, Fairbanks survived and the stories of the great oil rush took their place alongside stories of the famous gold rush.

—*Dermot Cole*

pieces so delicate you'd hate to sneeze. This international ice-sculpting competition draws sculptors from all over the world. Eighty to 100 teams participate. The temporary "ice park" off Phillips Field Road also includes a playground section for children, where everything—from pirate ships and swirling slides to fun mazes and round "spinners"—is sculpted from ice. If you miss the ice championships, you can get a glimpse of the art at the **FAIRBANKS ICE MUSEUM** *500 2nd Ave; 907/451-8222 or 907/451-8250; www.icealaska.com.*

MIDNIGHT SUN BASEBALL GAME / This annual baseball game, played on summer solstice (June 21), begins at 10:30pm and lasts until 2am, with no lights. The game, which features a college summer team called the Alaska Goldpanners, dates back to 1906, when it was originally played between the Drinks and the Smokes, so called because the local newspaper refused to identify their sponsors and give them free publicity. Incidentally, the Drinks won after 10 innings. *907/451-0095; www.goldpanners.com.*

Fairbanks Daily News-Miner **MIDNIGHT SUN RUN** / This 10K fund-raiser run brings characters out of the woodwork on the Saturday closest to summer solstice. In the costume category, entrants have run dressed as mosquitoes, cows, fish, and cans of insect repellent. One hardcore participant ran in a suit of armor. The audience gets crazy, too. Residents have been known to drag out couches, recliners, and floor lamps to the street to watch. The run begins at 10pm, but the party lasts well into the night—such as it is. *907/456-6661.*

GOLDEN DAYS / This festival in mid-July commemorates the founding of Fairbanks in 1902. The main event is the parade (always on a Saturday) through town, since there isn't one here on the Fourth of July. There's a Felix Pedro look-alike contest (Pedro being the prospector who struck gold), a hairy legs contest, a beard and mustache contest, a mock jail and pretend sheriffs who'll "arrest" you, and—a favorite with the toddler set—the Rubber Ducky Race, in which 6,000 rubber duckies are tossed into the Chena River. The first to reach the finish line downriver wins money for their ticket holders. *907/452-1105.*

WORLD ESKIMO-INDIAN OLYMPICS / You've never seen anything like it. For four days in mid-July, Native athletes, dancers, and artisans from around the state gather here to play traditional games, perform dances, and test their strength and skills in a variety of events, including high kick, knuckle hop, ear-pull, and others. The games originate from a lifestyle that demanded (and still demands) extraordinary skill and agility to survive. In addition, beautiful Native artwork is for sale. *907/452-6646; www.weio.org.*

FAIRBANKS SUMMER ARTS FESTIVAL / This is the art community's gift to the people of Fairbanks, held at the University of Alaska Fairbanks the last two weeks in July. The annual event is a study-performance festival, with up to 75 guest artists from around the world sharing their talents with more than 700 registrants in music, dance, theater, story telling, opera, theater, visual arts, and figure skating. There are five evening concerts, free daily "lunch bite" performances, as well as a variety of other events during the two weeks. *907/474-8869; www.fsaf.org.*

TANANA VALLEY STATE FAIR / Held each year in August, this weeklong fair features carnival rides, a rodeo, concerts, contests, vendors selling everything from funky clothing to pottery, a petting zoo, and kajillions of exhibits entered and judged by locals, including livestock, veggies, crafts, and foodstuffs. So what if it usually rains? The fair is always a blast. *907/452-3750; www.tananavalleyfair.org; off College Rd, next to Farmer's Market.*

ATHABASCAN OLD TIME FIDDLERS FESTIVAL / That's right: Athabascan fiddles, as in violins, played with an attitude. Along the Yukon River, 19th-century French, Canadian, and Scottish fur traders left behind a taste for old-time fiddle tunes and the dances they inspire. This November festival of performances and dances is one of the biggest winter gatherings in the Interior, with hundreds coming from outlying villages to perform, dance, and enjoy. *907/452-1825.*

FOLK FESTIVALS / Fairbanks hosts two music festivals each year for those who love folk, bluegrass, blues, Celtic, and more. One is indoors at the University of Alaska campus (Wood Center) on a Saturday in early February, when it's daylight for just a few hours a day and people are looking for something to help relieve cabin fever. The other is outside on a grassy field at Pioneer Park on a Saturday in June, when it's so beautiful you don't want to go indoors. Both festivals draw musicians from across the state and are extremely family friendly. Another bonus: they're free. *907/488-0556; fax 907/488-5666; www.alaskafolkmusic.org.*

NIGHTLIFE

THE BLUE LOON / Like to dance? Here's where you do it. In addition to local bands, the Loon has been the spot for such names as Bo Diddley, Laura Love, and Leo Kottke. It throws disco parties, swing nights, techno bashes, and folk fests—the place is eclectic. Don't like to dance? That's OK, too. The Loon shows movies most nights ($4 to $6 per person, depending on weekday or weekend). Munch on burgers and other tasty bar fare while you watch. *MC, V; Alaska checks OK; open daily; no reservations; 2999 Parks Hwy; 907/457-5666; www.theblueloon.com; 3 miles south of town, toward Ester.*

THE MARLIN / Under new management, this place is a cross between a cozy college bar and a basement jazz club, though you'll also hear about every other species of music here live most nights, including open mike on Wednesdays. The Marlin serves Guinness on tap and up to a dozen microbrews. Thursday is nonsmoking, bluegrass night. *MC, V; local checks only; 3412 College Rd; 907/479-4646; near the university.*

RESTAURANTS

Bun on the Run / ★★

COLLEGE RD, FAIRBANKS You walk up to the window of this pink-and-white food wagon; order a sandwich, a snack, or a cinnamon bun; and away you go. Bun on the Run. Get it? The business is the brainstorm of sisters Gretchen Petersen and Ingrid Herreid, who spent much of their childhood in the bush and learned to bake from their mom. No one delivers the goodies the way these two do. Their pastry lineup includes a variety of scones (the ham and cheese scone is a meal), sour-cream cakes and muffins, coconut bars, incredibly sinful crème de menthe brownies, and cinnamon rolls to die for. And if you like calzones, this is the place. Outdoor seating.

$; No credit cards; checks OK; breakfast, lunch Mon–Sat (closed winters); no alcohol; no reservations; in the parking lot between Beaver Sports and the Marlin.

Gambardella's Pasta Bella / ★★

706 2ND AVE, FAIRBANKS; 907/456-3417 OR 907/457-4992 This downtown Italian eatery has a surprisingly warm, urban atmosphere for a city full of establishments sporting moose antlers. Highly recommended for its aromatherapy value alone—it's filled with the smell of freshly baked bread and Italian spices. They make their own sausages here, too. Don't miss the focaccia with fresh garlic, olives, and fresh rosemary. The murals and artwork on the walls are by the owner/general manager sister team, Lisa and Laurie Gambardella. *$$; AE, MC, V; checks OK; lunch every day except Sun, dinner every day; beer and wine; reservations recommended; downtown.* &

Geraldo's Restaurant / ★★

701 COLLEGE RD, FAIRBANKS; 907/452-2299 This cozy little restaurant recently was nationally recognized for its halibut pizza, the most unique and tasty pizza you'll ever eat. They start with dough they make right there, topped with a white Dijon sauce, red bell peppers, broccoli, white onions, spinach, marinated halibut, and mozzarella and parmesan cheese. You can also find all your favorite Italian dishes, such as spaghetti, lasagna, and fettuccini (try the seafood fettuccini—its rich and flavorful). If you want a steak, they fix a great New York. Geraldo's also is well known for its "Geraldo's mix," a sauté of broccoli, cauliflower, onions, red peppers, and mushrooms in a garlic wine and lemon sauce, poured over your choice of pasta or even a steak. Do what the sign outside recommends, "Say yes to garlic." *$$; AE, MC, V; checks OK; lunch buffet weekdays, dinner every day; beer and wine; reservations recommended; www. geraldos.com.*

l'assiette de Pomegranate / ★

414 2ND AVE, FAIRBANKS; 907/451-7505 This is one of the newest eating establishments in Fairbanks, and it's delightful. Everything here is fresh and homemade—they even roast their own turkey and beef for their hearty and delicious sandwiches. They offer unique items in an ever-changing cast of specials, such as a sandwich made with roasted portobello mushrooms and imported fontina cheese, or the chicken breast breaded with foccacia crumbs, red onion, fresh mozzarella, tomato marinade, and lettuce. The salads are a refreshing mix of greens or perhaps a pasta or potato salad; the soups are wonderful and the cheesecake is tremendous. They serve espresso drinks and numerous baked goods for breakfast. The small tables and rack of magazines invite cozy gatherings; also a great choice if dining alone. *$; No credit cards; checks OK; breakfast, lunch, dinner every day; no alcohol; no reservations.*

Lavelle's Bistro / ★★

MARRIOTT SPRINGHILL SUITES, FAIRBANKS; 907/450-0555 Chef Kathy Lavelle and partner Frank Eagle opened this restaurant in 2001 to an already enthusiastic local crowd, as the two are longtime restaurateurs on the Fairbanks scene. A highlight of the bistro is its 3,000-bottle wine cellar—a literal "wall of wine" right smack in the middle of the place. Another outstanding feature is its diverse menu. If you're hungry, try the rack of lamb, sautéed and then baked with rosemary infused olive oil, with the kiwi-lime marmalade. Another favorite is the potato encrusted salmon. On the lighter side, Lavelle's has a wonderful tapas menu; our favorite is the build-your-own bruschetta with roasted peppers and garlic with boursin cheese. You won't want to miss "wine night," when Frank and Kathy offer ample samples of three featured wines ($12.50), along with a variety of specials to complement them. *$$; AE, DC, DIS, MC, V; checks OK; dinner every day, lunch Mon–Fri (summer); full bar; reservations recommended; info@lavellesbistro.com; in Marriott hotel, next to Cushman St bridge.* &

Pike's Landing

4438 AIRPORT WY, FAIRBANKS; 907/479-6500 This is a great spot on a warm, sunny day, as the deck is perched on the bank of the Chena River. Water-skiers, canoeists, river boats, and families of ducks pass by. Sitting inside is fine, too—the dining room is elegant. Reserve a table by the window. You'll find such entrees as Alaska king salmon, sautéed garlic prawns, and seafood baked en croute—crab, scallops, shrimp, and cheeses served in a puff pastry. There's also a decadent dessert tray. *$$; AE, DC, DIS, JCB, MC, V; checks OK; lunch, dinner every day, brunch Sun; full bar; dinner reservations recommended; on Airport Wy, about halfway between the airport and Fred Meyer.* &

Pump House Restaurant & Saloon

796 CHENA PUMP RD, FAIRBANKS; 907/479-8452 The exterior of this restaurant looks like a tin workshed because it once was one. The original Chena pump house, on the banks of the Chena River, was part of a vast system of pumps, sluiceways, ditches, and flumes built by the Fairbanks Exploration Co. to support its gold-dredging operations. Reconstructed as a restaurant and bar in the late 1970s, today the Pump House has the most colorful atmosphere of any restaurant in the city, with a solid mahogany bar and a pressed-tin ceiling. Seafood is your best bet here—they have fresh oysters and clams. *$$; AE, DIS, MC, V; local checks only; lunch, dinner every day, brunch Sun (summer); dinner every day, lunch Sat, brunch Sun (winter); full bar; dinner reservations recommended; www.pumphouse.com; Chena Pump Rd, off Geist near the university, watch for sign.* &

Thai House / ★★

526 5TH AVE, FAIRBANKS; 907/452-6123 This place practically has a cult following among the Fairbanks dinner crowd, particularly those who travel and know a good pad thai when they taste it. Among favorites are the red, green, and yellow curries; the leg of lamb marinated in a special blend of spices; and the Pa Ram Gai. All the important stuff is there: friendly service, consistently tasty food, and an assortment of hot oils and spices for turning up the heat when there's a request for "blistering hot." *$$; MC, V; local checks only; lunch, dinner Mon–Sat; beer and wine; reservations recommended; downtown.* &

Two Rivers Lodge / ★★★

 MILE 16 CHENA HOT SPRING RD, FAIRBANKS; 907/488-6815 Chef Tony Marsico knows how to make mouths water. The trouble will be making up your mind; we suggest the braised lamb shank, slow cooked in a red-wine sauce until the meat comes off the bone, served in a tureen with fresh vegetables; or the crispy duck with loganberry sauce, a semisweet glaze. While there are standard beef, seafood, and pasta options that you'd expect at any fine dining establishment, Marsico likes to offer seasonal surprises. There's an extensive wine list. You'll know you're in Alaska here—the log building is full of antlers and pelts. During sunny weather, the lodge's wood-fired oven on a deck overlooking a small lake produces delicious pizzas and foccacia, as well as other Mediterranean dishes. If you're into a more casual atmosphere, sit where the locals hang out, in the Trapline Lounge. *$$$; AE, DC, DIS, MC, V; checks OK; dinner every day; full bar; reservations recommended; www.tworiverslodge.com; from Steese Hwy, take Chena Hot Springs Rd exit, go 16 miles, you'll see it on the north side of the road.* &

Turtle Club / ★★

MILE 9 OLD STEESE HWY, FAIRBANKS; 907/457-3883 You can tell the popularity of this restaurant when you drive up and see the packed parking lot. You'll want to make reservations even in the middle of the week, and definitely on weekends. The Turtle Club has a somewhat limited menu, but what they do, they do extremely well. Prime rib dinners are their specialty (they come in three portions, ranging from to 10-ounce "foxy cut" to the 20-ounce "miner's cut") and they are mighty tender and tasty. They also serve halibut, crab, and prawns. *$$; AE, DIS, MC, V; checks OK; dinner, daily; full bar; reservations recommended; drive north on Steese Hwy until intersection with Fox, turn left, go about 1 block.*

LODGINGS

All Season's Inn / ★★

763 7TH AVE, FAIRBANKS; 907/451-6649 OR 888/451-6649; FAX 907/474-8448 This conveniently located B&B is within walking distance to downtown shops and features eight beautifully decorated rooms. It's immaculate, and the breakfasts for guests each morning include amaretto French toast, fresh fruit, sausage or bacon, and an egg pie with zucchini and red bell peppers. A small dinner theater, at $28 per person, is offered in the evenings to help tell the tale of Fairbanks. Double occupancy rates run $125–$160 in summer, $75–$95 in winter. *$$; DC, DIS, JCB, MC, V; no checks; www.allseasonsinn.com; downtown, off 7th Ave.*

Aurora Express B&B / ★★

1540 CHENA RIDGE, FAIRBANKS; 907/474-0949 OR 800/221-0073; FAX 907/474-8173 You won't find another place like this in Fairbanks. The Aurora Express is a train—a real train—sitting in Sue and Mike Wilson's front yard. The Golden Nellie, formerly Caboose 1068, has a golden ceiling, heavy velvet drapes, and original chairs re-covered in brocade. Sue added two Pullman sleeper cars and a water tanker, then two more cars, a locomotive, and a diner car, all on several hundred feet of winding track. The cars have been renovated with queen-size beds, private baths, and themes ranging from "the Bordello" to a wonderful family car with a Thomas the Tank Engine theme. Little boys will love it. The B&B is located on Chena Ridge, with views of the city and Tanana Valley. Double occupancy rates are $115, which include breakfast in the diner car. *$$; MC, V; checks OK; closed winters; www.aurora-express.com; 6.5 miles up Chena Pump Rd, watch for sign on the right.*

The Bridgewater / ★★★

723 1ST AVE, FAIRBANKS; 907/452-6661 OR 800/528-4916 There's something of a boutique and feminine feel to this cozy hotel, with each room fully appointed and sparkling private baths. The corner rooms facing the Chena River are the most spacious and have the best views (as well as tubs instead of showers). This hotel will pass any white glove test you give it—it's spotless. There's a cafe downstairs that serves a hearty breakfast buffet, but its convenient location to several fine restaurants downtown (some of which will let you charge your meal to your room) will make you want to get out and walk. The best thing about this hotel, though, is its staff—they are gracious, polite, and will treat you like royalty. Rooms (there are 94 of them) run $100–$140, double occupancy. Smoking rooms are thoughtfully kept to one floor. *$$; AE, DC, DIS, MC, V; checks OK; closed mid-Sept to mid-May; www.fountainheadhotels.com; downtown.*

Captain Bartlett Inn / ★

1411 AIRPORT WY, FAIRBANKS; 907/452-1888 OR 800/544-7528 (800/478-7900, IN-STATE) If you want a hotel that's truly Alaskan, look no farther. The main lobby of this cozy hotel is made of logs and decked with old photographs and rustic doodads. All 197 guest rooms and suites have hardwood furniture and warm-colored wallpaper throughout. Outside, there's a large patio and brilliant flowerbeds. The hotel restaurant, Musher's Roadhouse, has a huge stone fireplace, and serves breakfast, lunch, and dinner. The Dog Sled Saloon is popular with locals and visitors alike; you'll find free appetizers there from 5pm–7pm. Double occupancy rates start at $135 in the summer, $85 in winter. *$$; AE, DC, DIS, MC, V; checks OK on approval; www.captainbartlettinn.com; accessible from frontage road off Airport Wy.* &

Cloudberry Lookout / ★★★

310 YANA CT, FAIRBANKS; 907/479-7334; FAX 907/479-7134 It took Suzi Lozo and Sean McGuire eight years to build their three-story home on 40 acres. On a knoll overlooking a lake, surrounded by boreal forest, the Lookout is stunning. This log-frame home is loaded with glass and topped by an aurora borealis–viewing tower. To get there, you climb spiral steps notched into a nearly 200-year-old spruce log. Partway up is an aerial library stocked with natural-history and Alaska books. Another floor up is the aurorium. The Lookout also has a third-story outdoor walkway, a solarium on the south side of the house, and a music room with a grand piano (Suzi is a piano teacher). Skiing and nature trails are literally out your front door, and dog-mushing tours can be arranged. Rates run $95–$115, double occupancy; children over 8 welcome. Nonsmoking. *$$; AE, MC, V; checks OK; closed Nov to Feb; www.mosquitonet.com/~cloudberry; off Goldhill Rd, call for directions.*

Earthtone Huskies Bed & Breakfast / ★

MILE 17 CHENA HOT SPRINGS RD, FAIRBANKS; 907/488-8074 At Earth-tone Huskies, you'll find nature trails and berry picking in summer and dog mushing and aurora viewing in winter—all right outside your cozy, hand-hewn log cabin. There are two rustic cabins, with nearby outhouses, nestled amongst the trees on host Judy Cooper's peaceful, private grounds. You'll meet the likes of Blue, Rune, and Prince Caspian, several of Judy's 50 Alaskan huskies who live on the perimeter of her vegetable garden (the dogs are a great moose deterrent). A con-tinental breakfast is included. Dog-sled rides are available, and the B&B is close to dining and the neighborhood tavern, at Two Rivers Lodge, as well as a Laundromat, showers, hiking trails, and the fabulous Chena River State Recreation Area. For self-sufficient guests who don't mind roughing it a bit, you can't beat Cooper's rates at $50 for a double. *$; No credit cards; checks OK; open year-round; www.earthtone huskies.com; from Steese Hwy, drive 17 miles out Chena Hot Springs Rd, left on Wright Ln, left on Kanuti—the road dead-ends in Cooper's driveway.*

Fairbanks Princess Riverside Lodge / ★★★

4477 PIKES LANDING RD, FAIRBANKS; 907/455-4477 OR 800/426-0500; FAX 907/455-5094 You can count on Princess for a beautiful hotel. This tastefully deco-rated, 325-room hotel sits on the banks of the Chena River. A large, terraced river-side deck and lovely flowerbeds make it worth staying put on a warm, sunny day, watching canoeists and ducks paddle by. Extensive renovations in 2001 added a business center, as well as a new wing. Amenities include a health club, steam room, whirlpool, wireless Internet access, and a free airport shuttle. Dining lounges range from formal to casual, with all meals served and a full bar available. Standard room rates are $199 (double occupancy) in summer, dropping to $89 in winter. *$$–$$$; AE, DC, DIS, MC, V; checks OK; www.princesslodges.com; off Airport Wy, turn south at Pike's Landing, follow signs.* ⅄

Marriott SpringHill Suites

575 1ST AVE, FAIRBANKS; 907/451-6552 OR 888/287-9400 (RESERVATIONS); FAX 907/451-6553 If you're looking for familiar comfort and amenities offered by the Marriott line of hotels, this one is for you. All the rooms are minisuites, with kitchenettes and desks. There's a large continental breakfast available for guests, as well as small indoor pool, sauna, and exercise room. The riverside location down-town and the log cabin visitors center just across the street is what makes this a worthwhile place to stay, along with a great restaurant on its first floor, Lavelle's Bistro (see Restaurants, above). Double occupancy rates are $159 in summer, $89 in winter. *$$$; AE, DC, DIS, MC, V; checks OK; www.springhillsuites.com; right downtown, near the Cushman St bridge.* ⅄

Minnie Street Bed and Breakfast Inn / ★

345 MINNIE ST, FAIRBANKS; 907/456-1802 This immaculate B&B offers 10 rooms (all but 2 have private baths) with televisions, telephones, Internet service, and a large, airy common area where the hosts serve up full, hot breakfasts every morning. The best thing is the location—only two blocks from the Alaska Railroad depot and three blocks from downtown. Minnie Street is a rather busy thoroughfare, and there are no striking views to look at, but it's convenient and comfortable. Choose from a variety of rooms ($100–$175, double occupancy), offering everything from a classic B&B style room to a private suite perfect for families. *$$–$$$; AE, DIS, MC, V; checks OK; www.minniestreetBandB.com; on Minnie St near railroad depot, just off Illinois Ave.*

Pike's Waterfront Lodge

1850 HOSELTON RD, FAIRBANKS; 907/456-4500 OR 877/774-2400 This 180-room hotel is right on the water, and though it calls itself a "lodge," it's decor and furnishings are more typical of a nice hotel. Amenities include an exercise room, a business center, a sauna and steam room, and a deck overlooking the Chena River. Standard rooms are rather small, but a variety of suites and larger rooms are available following a remodel. Rates during the summer run from $190 for a double to $370 for the best suite. Off-season rates (mid-Sept through mid-May) are $79 to $250, double occupancy. It's conveniently located near the airport, too. The restaurant serves breakfast, lunch, and dinner, and there's a full bar. *$$$; AE, DC, DIS, MC, V; checks OK; www.pikeslodge.com.* &

River's Edge Resort / ★

4200 BOAT ST, FAIRBANKS; 907/474-0286 OR 800/770-3343; FAX 907/474-3665 These 86 cottages on the edge of the Chena River are perfect for families. Each light and airy unit is separate, so your children won't bother other guests. Instead of running up and down the hallway to work off that endless energy, the young ones can run up and down a pleasant little path along the river. There's kayaking and canoeing, fishing—you name it, the resort can help arrange it. The main lobby building has eight large rooms upstairs, and the same folks own the RV park next door, also on the river. There's also a restaurant. Rates are $173 for a double in summer but drop to a bargain $89 in winter. *$$–$$$; AE, MC, V; checks OK; reresort@alaska.net; www.riversedge.net; take Sportsman's Wy off Airport, go left and drive until you see the resort's signs.* &

A Taste of Alaska Lodge / ★★★

551 EBERHARDT RD, FAIRBANKS; 907/488-7855; FAX 907/488-3772 This wonderful log lodge and cabins, full of antiques and Alaska artifacts, are situated on a 280-acre family homestead, most of which was once an old potato and wheat farm staked in 1946. The 7,000-square-foot lodge overlooks the Alaska Range, with Denali in the distance, and in the winter offers great aurora viewing. The 10-acre field out front draws an occasional moose and sandhill cranes that stick around all spring and summer. Owners Debbie and Dave Eberhardt rent two beautiful cabins along with eight rooms in the lodge, which also can be rented for weddings and other special events. All rooms have private baths, and one of the cabins has a private hot tub. Gold panning, hiking, and hot-tubbing (separate from the one included in the cabin) are available, and a free gold-mine tour is included in the double occupancy rate of $150–$200. Sled-dog rides and other adventures can also be arranged. Buffet breakfasts (included in room rate) feature quiche, crepes, bacon, sausage, yogurt, fresh fruit, muffins, Danishes, granola, and more. Dinners (with entrees from $21–$35) are available with reservations, along with beer and wine. $$$; AE, MC, V; checks OK; www.tasteofalaska.com; 5 miles up Chena Hot Springs Rd, turn right on Eberhardt Rd. &

BED-AND-BREAKFAST SERVICES

The **FAIRBANKS VISITORS INFORMATION CENTER** (907/456-5774 or 800/327-5774; www.explorefairbanks.com) located in a sod-roofed log cabin next to the Chena River downtown, keeps an entire forest worth of brochures on local bed-and-breakfasts. It's open daily in summer and weekdays in winter. There are many bed-and-breakfasts in Fairbanks. While we've listed a few of our favorites, check also with the **FAIRBANKS ASSOCIATION OF BED & BREAKFASTS** (907/456-1802; fabb@ptialaska.net; www.ptialaska.net/~fabb).

WILDERNESS LODGES

Denali West Lodge

PO BOX 40, LAKE MINCHUMINA AK 99757; 907/674-3112 OR 888/607-5566 One hundred miles from the nearest highway, this stunning hand-hewn log lodge on the shore of Lake Minchumina is a visit to another world. It's not a seasonal outpost for Jack and Sherri Hayden; it's been their home for over two decades. They're located on the western border of Denali National Park and Preserve, with Mount McKinley practically in their laps. Guests stay in cozy log cabins with woodstoves and birch-log beds and have access to guided hiking, canoeing, wildlife photography, and birding excursions. You can fish for northern pike in front of the lodge, which accommodates 6 to 10 people. During winter, the Haydens offer sled-dog expeditions. The cabins have outhouses, but there's a guest bathhouse with a sauna and showers. All meals are included. A variety of multiday packages are available, from a four-day visit ($1,815 per person) to a nine-day Denali expedition ($6,550). $$$$; AE, DIS, MC, V; checks OK; closed Oct to Feb, mid-Apr to late May; info@denaliwest.com; www.denaliwest.com; fly-in only.

Ester

With two gold booms under its belt, Ester was quite the boisterous little miners' mecca in its day. The first boom came with the discovery of gold on Ester, Cripple, and Eva Creeks around the turn of the 20th century, which drew prospectors by the hundreds. The second came in 1936, when the Fairbanks Exploration Co. built Ester Gold Camp to support its nearby dredge operation. The camp shut down in the 1950s, and most of the miners moved on. Today, about 250 people live in houses and cabins scattered throughout the woods in the community fondly referred to as "The People's Republic of Ester." It may be the peace and quiet that attracts residents now, though it's only a few miles down The Parks Highway from Fairbanks. It's the town's former wild ways that lure tourists. The old gold camp has become one of the most popular tourist attractions in the Interior; be sure and visit one of the restaurant/saloons noted below for a bit of fun and a taste of history.

NIGHTLIFE

The **GOLDEN EAGLE SALOON** (Main St; 907/479-0809), just up the road from the Ester Gold Camp, is where the locals hang out. The appeal of this place isn't obvious the moment you walk in the door. Still, you're bound to meet some colorful folks. *No credit cards; local checks only; from Ester turnoff, turn right on Main St, and right again at the "T."*

RESTAURANTS AND LODGINGS

Ester Gold Camp Dining Hall & Hotel / ★★

MAIN ST, ESTER; 907/479-2500 OR 800/676-6925 On the National Register of Historic Places, the camp's big draw is an all-you-can-eat buffet and musical revue in the Malemute Saloon (complete with sawdust floor). The camp's hefty feed trough includes baked halibut, reindeer stew, and chicken ($16 per adult, $8 children; add Dungeness crab, $29 adult, $16 children). A musical revue heavy on Robert Service features costumes, songs, and stories from the gold-rush era ($14 adults; $7 children 3–12; lap children free). The camp offers free shuttle service from most major hotels and campgrounds. There's also a northern lights show at 6:45 and 7:45 nightly ($8 adult; $4 children). After all the fun you can sleep it off in the rustic charm of an old time hotel room ($70 double occupancy, shared bath). *$$; AE, DIS, MC, V; local checks OK; dinner every day (summer); closed mid-Sept to mid-May; full bar; from the Parks Hwy just south of Fairbanks, follow signs at the Ester turnoff.* &

Nenana

At the confluence of the Nenana and Tanana Rivers, 60 miles southwest from Fairbanks on the Parks Highway, this village of less than 500 folks was originally an Athabascan fish camp before its conversion to a transportation center. Now it's home port to a tug and barge fleet that supplies villages along the Tanana and Yukon Rivers.

The town's name comes from a Native word meaning "good place to camp between two rivers." These days, it's a good place to stop for gas, a bite to eat, and a stroll back in time. Look for fish wheels in action and their catches drying in the sun during salmon run season. The white crosses across the river mark graves at a Native cemetery.

It was in Nenana that President Warren G. Harding, the first U.S. president ever to visit Alaska, drove in "the golden spike," symbolizing the completion of the Alaska Railroad between the ice-free port of Seward and the Interior city of Fairbanks. The old Nenana Railroad Depot is on the National Register of Historic Places. There's a new cultural center on the bank of the Tanana River, with a salmon bake next door.

FESTIVALS AND EVENTS

NENANA ICE CLASSIC / The main attraction in town is the Nenana Ice Classic. A tripod is set up in the middle of the river after freeze-up, and participants guess the exact day, hour, and minute the river ice will start breaking up in the spring. The first stirring dislodges the tripod, which sets off a siren, which tips a meat cleaver, which

THE NORTHERN LIGHTS

The mystery of the night—the aurora borealis—may be the Interior's most alluring quality. Some nights there is only a single streak of green; other nights, the sky explodes with streamers of light like colorful confetti. They shimmer, spiral, and pulsate. They do the hula. They play crack-the-whip. The Interior is the ultimate domed theater, with the ideal latitude, enormous skies, and long, dark winters. Of all the skies Alaska has to offer, scientists from the University of Alaska's Geophysical Institute chose to set up shop here, 30 miles north of Fairbanks at Poker Flats, where they shoot rockets into the atmosphere to learn more about the aurora.

This polar phenomenon occurs when solar winds slam into the earth's magnetic field, causing electrons to react with atmospheric gases. The impact sends them into a major uproar, lighting them up like neon signs. This all happens 50 to 200 miles overhead. Color depends on the height of the interaction, due to the varying composition of atmospheric gas. Green, the most common color, comes when the impact is low, around 60 miles above the earth's surface. Reds occur around the highest impact zone. In the winter of 1958, the reds were so intense in the Fairbanks area that residents thought the surrounding hills were on fire.

Too bad there's a logical explanation. The legends are far more fun. One Eskimo tale says the lights are the pathway to heaven, lit by departed souls holding torches to the world beyond. In another, spirits are playing ball in the sky, kicking up colorful cosmic dust.

No matter how many times you may have seen this chorus line of lights, it never gets old. People will rouse each other from deep sleep without a hint of apology. The best time to see the aurora is on a clear dark night around 2am. The lights make dashing to the outhouse at 40 below a little more thrilling.

—*Debra McKinney*

cuts a rope, which pulls a cotter pin, which stops a clock, which determines the winner or winners. This annual event goes back to 1917, when Alaska Railroad surveyors pooled $800 in prize money to bet among themselves. Since then, the jackpot has grown to more than $330,000, divided among winners, the town till, and tax collectors. The earliest breakup was April 20, 1940, at 3:27pm; the latest was May 20, 1964, at 11:41am. *907/832-5446; tripod@ptialaska.net; www.ptialaska.net/~tripod.*

RESTAURANTS/NIGHTLIFE

On the drive from Fairbanks to Nenana, you'll see **SKINNY DICK'S HALFWAY INN** (Mile 328 Parks Hwy; 907/388-5770), a place notorious for its sleazy name, copulating bears logo, and raunchy jukebox tunes. It's a bar, not an inn. Dick is skinny and the place is about halfway between Nenana and Fairbanks. Just a few miles outside of Nenana, you'll find **THE MONDEROSA** (Mile 309 Parks Hwy; 907/832-5243), a roadside bar and grill that has a reputation with locals for having the biggest and best hamburgers in the Interior.

Chena Hot Springs Road

Chena Hot Springs Road heads east out of Fairbanks and bisects a 254,080-acre playground called the Chena River State Recreation Area (Mile 26 to Mile 53). The park is made up of marshes, sloughs, rolling boreal forest, alpine tundra, and turretlike granite pinnacles. Within its boundaries are some of the region's best hikes, as well as opportunities for rock climbing, horseback riding, river running, fishing, and wildlife viewing in summer months, and ski touring, dog mushing, snowmaching, and snowshoeing in winter months.

ADVENTURES

The **CHENA DOME TRAIL** (Mile 50.5) is a 29-mile loop that circles the Angel Creek drainage and is mostly on tundra ridgetops. The highest point is Chena Dome, a flat-topped ridge at 4,421 feet. On a clear day, the views are awesome. There are six cabins for rent in the rec area for $25–$40 a night, depending on the cabin. Make reservations through **ALASKA STATE PARKS** (907/451-2705; www.alaskastate parks.org). Two of them are right along the road; three are best for winter camping, perfect for skiing, snowmachining, or dog mushing. There are also several campgrounds at Mile 27, 39, and 42.8. (For more about hikes in the rec area, see also Adventures, Fairbanks).

LODGINGS

Chena Hot Springs Resort / ★★

MILE 56.7 CHENA HOT SPRINGS RD, FAIRBANKS; 907/451-8104 OR 800/478-4681; FAX 907/451-8151 This is a favorite spot among locals—close enough to get to within an hour or so, yet far enough away that the word "resort" really does fit. Perfect for warming up on freezing winter nights, the resort has a variety of pools and tubs (kept within 102–104°F), from several standard hot tubs inside to an outdoor rock pool with a cascading water fountain in its center. There's another larger hot tub on a redwood deck outside. Inside there's also a regular swimming pool, but it's kept a bit warmer so parents won't freeze while the kiddies are splashing about. New owners have made improvements, but the biggest drawback remains the tiny dressing rooms. The dining room, with log walls and a stone fireplace, specializes in beef, seafood, and pasta and has a full bar. Activities include cross-country skiing, dog mushing, guided snowmobile rides, horse-drawn sleigh rides, ice skating, and aurora borealis watching in winter; summer activities include horseback riding, hiking, rafting, and mountain bike rentals. Several local tour companies, as well as the resort, can arrange transportation. Rooms vary from rustic cabins ($65–$200) to full hotel-style rooms ($135–$175, double occupancy, winter peak season; summer rates are cheaper, $105–$145). All rooms come with pool passes; if you drive out from Fairbanks for a one-day visit, adult passes are $10.

There's also a campground ($20 per night). *$$; AE, DC, DIS, JCB, MC, V; Alaska checks only; www.chenahotsprings.com; dead end of Chena Hot Springs Rd.*

The Steese Highway

Built in 1927 to connect Fairbanks with Circle on the Yukon River, this mostly gravel road has been open year-round since 1984, though some maps won't tell you that. The first 44 miles are paved, with some nasty frost heaves. The gravel stretch is in better shape, although it can get a little muddy around **TWELVEMILE** and **EAGLE SUMMITS** (907/451-5204 for a recorded road report). There's fishing, gold panning, rustic lodges, and great hikes, as well as a motley mix of roadside attractions.

Opportunities for fishing abound between Mile 29 and Mile 40 on the **CHATANIKA RIVER**. At Mile 85.6, you'll reach Twelvemile Summit, elevation 2,980 feet. Then on to Eagle Summit, 3,624 feet, about 20 miles up the road. Winds can be strong enough here to rip up road signs, so watch your hat. Down the other side, the mountains give way to hills, which give way to the Yukon Flats. When you hit a slab of pavement, you'll know you've reached the town of **CENTRAL,** hub of the Circle Mining District, one of the oldest and most active in the state. This hard-working, no-sniveling type of town is home to miners, homesteaders, and others with little use for city ways.

A hard right takes you to **ARCTIC CIRCLE HOT SPRINGS**. If you continue straight, the road narrows, gets windier, and finally dead-ends at the **YUKON RIVER** in Circle (pop. approx. 95), which began as a mining supply town in 1887 and was so dubbed because it was thought to be on the Arctic Circle.

ADVENTURES
CAMPING / The **WHITE MOUNTAINS NATIONAL RECREATION AREA** offers several campgrounds at Mile 57 and Mile 60, but call for road conditions as spring thaws have been known to wash out roads and campsites (907/474-2372). The U.S. Creek and Nome Creek Roads offer access for put-in floating of Beaver Creek, a Wild and Scenic River, at the Ophir Creek Campground. For winter trails and camping, the McKay Creek trailhead (Mile 42) is another entrance point into the recreation area (see also Elliott Highway section, below).

PINNELL MOUNTAIN NATIONAL RECREATION TRAIL / This trail offers stunning views of the Alaska Range to the south and the Crazy Mountains and Yukon Flats to the north. The entire trail follows treeless, tundra-clad ridgelines for 27.3 miles, starting and ending on the Steese Highway at Eagle Summit (Mile 107.3) and Twelvemile Summit (Mile 85.6). The trail is defined by wooden posts and cairns. Allow at least three days and be prepared for summer temperatures that can range from 20°F to 80°F and high winds that can whip up anytime. Keep your eyes open for caribou and the occasional moose or bear. Wildflowers are jamming from mid-June to mid-July. The terrain is a little kinder if you begin at the Eagle Summit trailhead. Water can be a problem on this trail, especially later in the season. Call for a recorded trail-condition update (907/474-2372); two small cabins, 10 miles from each trailhead, are available on a first-come, first-served basis.

LODGINGS

Arctic Circle Hot Springs / ★★

MILE 8.3 CIRCLE HOT SPRINGS RD, CENTRAL; 907/520-5113; FAX 907/520-5116 At this hot springs, there's nothing between you and the stars but your bathing suit. As the story goes, the hot springs were "discovered" in 1893 by a hunter tracking a moose. When the hotel first opened in 1930, miners could get a bed, three square meals, and a hot bath for $3 a day. Today, you can get much more than that—your gracious host Laverna Miller will see to it. In the winter, there's a network of trails for cross-country skiing and snowmaching; sled-dog rides can be arranged. Summer attractions include fishing, hiking, berry picking, and mountain biking on old mining trails. There is also an Olympic-size pool, massage therapy, tavern, and a cozy library. The dining room is homey and serves breakfast, lunch, and dinner. The resort has 24 rooms in the old hotel and 14 cabins for rent. Hotel rates are $100 for a double; suites are $125. Cabins run $85–$125, depending on the season and their size. Attic hostel space is $20 (bring your own sleeping bag); additional people $15 extra. *$$; MC, V; checks OK; php.indiana.edu/~kurichte/achshome.html; 134 miles northeast of Fairbanks—in Central, turn right at Crabb's Corner, drive until you see the springs.* &

Chatanika Gold Camp / ★

MILE 27 STEESE HWY, CHATANIKA; 907/389-2414 Built in 1921, this old gold camp is on the National Register of Historic Places. For 30 years, the complex provided room and board to miners. Now it does the same for travelers and Fairbanksans escaping the city. There's a bunkhouse, cabins, a bar, and an Alaskana restaurant with an enormous antique woodstove. Ten rooms upstairs in the main lodge share a bath ($55, double occupancy), while two rooms in each of the nearby log cabins also share a bath ($75, double occupancy). Dining features rack of lamb, prime rib, halibut, and a full bar. During winter months the camp offers dog mushing and snow-machine rides. *$–$$; AE, MC, V; Alaska checks OK; restaurant closed Mon and Tues, winter hours vary; www.fegoldcamp.com; 27 miles up the Steese Hwy, just before Chatanika Lodge.* &

Chatanika Lodge

MILE 28.5 OLD STEESE HWY N, CHATANIKA; 907/389-2164; FAX 907/389-2166 You'll find this rustic log lodge decked to the teeth with quintessential Alaskana— diamond willow, moose antlers, totem poles, and a satellite dish. You'll find all kinds of things inside to gawk at, too, including the best salt-and-pepper shaker collection in all of Alaska and donated dollar bills coating the walls. No-frills rooms with shared baths are $60 for a double. Breakfast, lunch, and dinner are offered, as well as a full bar. Friday and Saturday nights feature all-you-can-eat halibut and catfish dinner ($18 adults, $7.75 children). *$; MC, V; local checks only; 27 miles up the Steese Hwy, just past Chatanika Gold Camp.* &

The Elliott Highway

It may seem like all roads out of Fairbanks lead to hot water, and it's almost true. This former gold trail dead-ends at Mile 152 (mileage begins in Fox) at the community of Manley Hot Springs (pop. about 100). Alas, the hot springs resort has closed. This tidy old trading-post town is what you're likely to envision when you think of bush Alaska. It has log cabins surrounded by great gardens, houses made of salvaged building materials huddled among the trees, and an historic roadhouse serving as the town's community center. You'll meet mushers, miners, trappers, fishermen, and other folks carving a living out of the land. There's fishing for northern pike in the Manley Hot Springs Slough and for salmon in the Tanana River. Built in 1906, **THE MANLEY ROADHOUSE** (PO Box 1, Manley AK 99756; 907/672-3161) offers room and board and a lot of antiquities, including some of the bar's regulars. At a separate location, hot tubs with the natural hot springs water are available for one-hour rentals (907/672-3231).

Before heading out on the Elliott, stop about ¼ mile out of Fox and fill your water bottles at **FOX SPRINGS,** which has pure artesian springwater that runs year-round. This is where many locals living without running water come to fill their jugs. For the hugest heap of breakfast in the Interior, stop at **HILLTOP TRUCKSTOP** (Mile 5.5 Elliott Hwy; 907/389-7600); it's famous for pies, too.

The first 28 miles of the highway are paved; the remaining 124 are not. Watch for moose and other wildlife, including spruce hens attempting self-sacrifice in the middle of the road. The road is wide and hard-packed up to its rendezvous with the Dalton Highway (see Arctic chapter), west of Livengood. From then on, it narrows and gets into a little roller coaster action.

In addition to hot springs, the Elliott offers access to fishing spots, hikes in the White Mountains National Recreation Area, a local rock-climbing spot called Grapefruit Rocks at Mile 38.5, and a side trip at Mile 110 to the Athabascan village of Minto, at the edge of Minto Flats State Game Refuge.

ADVENTURES

TOLOVANA HOT SPRINGS / These reservation-only hot springs offer a rustic but peaceful getaway for people with the ability to get there. It's at least an 11-mile hike, ski, snow-machine or dogsled ride from the main trailhead to the springs, though longer trails at different departure points will get you there as well. Traveling to the springs is part of the experience, and the reward of soaking in the wilderness under the northern lights is well worth it. There are two simple cabins—one sleeps eight while the other sleeps four. The cabins have outhouses, propane lights, and cook stove, sleeping pads on bunks, and a woodstove for heat. Propane, firewood, and a fully equipped kitchen are provided, but you'll need to bring just about everything else. There are two tubs with the natural hot springs water—you can cool them down if necessary by piping in cold stream water. The smaller cabin goes for $30 per night on weeknights and $60 per night on weekends; the larger cabin is $60 per night on weeknights and $120 per night on weekends. Rates are higher over certain holidays, so check first. You'll get a map once you make reservations. *No credit cards;*

checks OK; Mile 93 Elliott Hwy, PO Box 83058, Fairbanks AK 99708; 907/455-6706; www.mosquitonet.com/~tolovana.

WHITE MOUNTAINS NATIONAL RECREATION AREA / This 1-million acre area, just 30 miles north of Fairbanks between the Elliott and Steese Highways, offers fantastic recreational opportunities, both summer and winter, but mostly winter. It's pure heaven for dog mushers, skiers, skijorers (a dog-powered skier), and snowmachiners. The Bureau of Land Management maintains 200 miles of winter trails, with 10 remote and rustic public-use cabins available for rent ($20–$25 per night) by permit only. An 11th cabin, the Blixt Cabin, is right off the road (Mile 62 Elliott Hwy), so it's great year-round. Many of the trails are too wet for comfortable hiking in summer, though some aren't bad. The trailheads are at Miles 28 and 57 Elliott Hwy. *Bureau of Land Management, 1150 University Ave, Fairbanks AK 99709; 907/474-2251 or 800/437-7021; 907/474-2372 for trail conditions; www. ndo.ak.blm.gov/whitemtns.*

THE ARCTIC

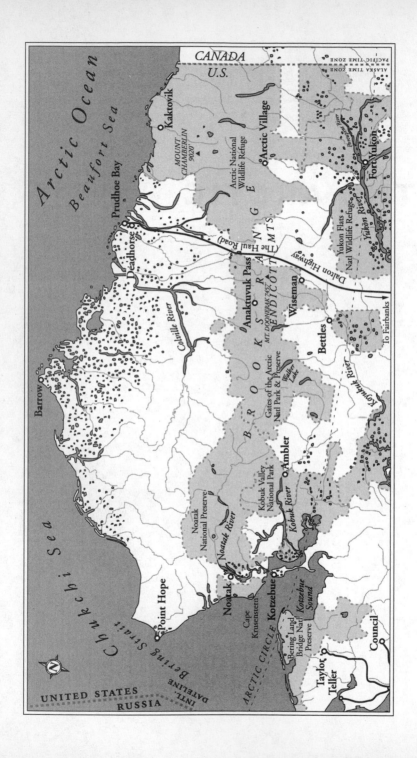

CANADA
U.S.

PACIFIC TIME ZONE
ALASKA TIME ZONE

Arctic Ocean

Beaufort Sea

○ Kaktovik

MOUNT
CHAMBERLIN
9020'

● Arctic Village

● Fort Yukon

Arctic National
Wildlife Refuge

Porcupine River

Prudhoe Bay ○

Yukon River

Deadhorse ○

The Haul Road

Colville River

Yukon Flats
Nat'l Wildlife Refuge

Dalton Highway

Anaktuvuk Pass ●

B R O O K S   R A N G E

E N D I C O T T   M T S.

MT. DOONERAK 7457'

Wiseman ●

To Fairbanks →

Barrow ○

Bettles ●

Walker
Lake

Gates of the Arctic
Nat'l Park & Preserve

Kobuk River

Koyukuk River

Ambler ●

Noatak
National Preserve

Kobuk Valley
National Park

Noatak River

Kobuk River

Chukchi Sea

Noatak ○

Cape
Krusenstern

Kotzebue ○

Kotzebue
Sound

ARCTIC CIRCLE

Point Hope ●

Bering Land
Bridge Nat'l
Preserve

Council ○

Bering Strait

INTL. DATELINE

Taylor ○
Teller ○

N

UNITED STATES
RUSSIA

THE ARCTIC

Stretching north of the Arctic Circle (66° 33' north latitude) is a wilderness of spare taiga, which means "land of little sticks," and tundra, "flat or rolling, treeless plain." The Brooks Range, that "range of blue light" described by early explorer Robert Marshall, sweeps across the Arctic, separating the forests from the 80,000 square miles of tundra known as the North Slope. Rivers south of the mountains flow into the Yukon River, which empties into the Bering Sea; northern rivers flow into the Arctic Ocean.

The Arctic is a frigid zone, with cold winters and short, cool summers. With less than 10 inches of precipitation per year, it is really a cold desert. Temperatures range from 80 degrees in summer to 60 degrees below zero and colder in winter. Permafrost underlies much of the region, in places to a depth of up to 3,000 feet. These frozen soils account for the countless lakes and ponds that dot the coastal plain. Thirty percent of its surface is covered by fresh water. Pingos, steep-sided mounds with ice cores, and polygons, patterned ground caused by ice wedges, are distinctive surface features related to permafrost.

Arctic, from the Greek *arctos* for bear, refers to the two constellations Ursa Major (Great Bear) and Ursa Minor (Little Bear) that rotate around Polaris (the North Star), the one fixed point in the northern sky. These constellations contain the easily recognized Big and Little Dippers. As one travels north, the bears loom higher and higher in the night sky. The seasonal change in daylight, which limits available energy, is the single most important physical characteristic of the polar region.

On June 21, summer solstice, the day when the sun is at its greatest distance from the equator, the sun does not set at the Arctic Circle and, due to refraction, appears not to set for four days. In Barrow, the northernmost American city, the sun does not set for 84 days, from May 10 to August 2. On winter solstice, December 21, the sun does not rise at all at the Arctic Circle. In Barrow the sun remains below the horizon for 67 days, from November 18 to January 24.

No large cities and only a few large villages dot this vast region. Barrow is the largest community and a regional trade center. Prudhoe Bay is the industrial center, with its oil wealth and jobs flowing out statewide. Most communities are small and isolated, with subsistence-based economies. The 414-mile-long Dalton Highway, built as the Trans-Alaska Pipeline haul road from Fairbanks, bisects the Arctic north to south and parallels the pipeline. All other access to the region is by aircraft.

Inupiat Eskimos are the predominate culture here. Nunamiut Eskimos—"The People"—live in Anaktuvuk Pass. Gwich'in Athabascans also live just north of the Arctic Circle in Arctic Village and across the Yukon River valley into Canada.

Seasonal abundance of wildlife is characteristic of a region marked by long, hard winters. Much of the region's wildlife is migratory and transient. Two large herds of caribou, the Western Arctic Caribou Herd and the Porcupine Caribou Herd, attract wildlife watchers from around the world. The smaller Central Arctic Caribou Herd sometimes frequents Prudhoe Bay and the Dalton Highway corridor.

The Arctic is the last great stretch of wilderness on the face of the earth. As Justice William O. Douglas said in 1960, "The Arctic has a call that is compelling. The distant mountains make one want to go on and on over the next ridge and over the one beyond. This last American wilderness must remain sacrosanct."

ACCESS AND INFORMATION

One road takes you from Fairbanks into the Arctic—the **JAMES DALTON HIGHWAY,** or "Haul Road" (see below). Alaska Airlines (800/252-7522; www. alaskaair.com) has **JET SERVICE** to Barrow, Deadhorse/Prudhoe Bay, and Kotzebue. Cape Smythe Air (907/852-8333), in Barrow, can take you to coastal villages and other destinations. 40-Mile Air (907/474-0018), at Fairbanks International Airport, offers scheduled flights as well as charters and North Slope tours; Frontier Flying Service (907/474-0014 or 800/478-6779 in-state; www.frontierflying.com), in Fairbanks, regularly flies to Anaktuvuk Pass, Bettles, and Kaktovik. Fairbanks-based Larry's Flying Service (907/474-9169) flies to Anaktuvuk Pass and Arctic Village. Warbelow's Air Ventures (907/474-0518 or 800/478-0812), also in Fairbanks, goes to Ambler, Kobuk, and Shungnak and also flies charters and tours. Wright Air Service (907/474-0502), also in Fairbanks, flies to Anaktuvuk Pass, Arctic Village, and Bettles, with charters to bush destinations.

Those who fly strictly **AIR CHARTERS** are Fairbanks-based Arctic Air Alaska (907/488-6115), to all Brooks Range destinations; and Yukon Air Service (907/662-2445), in Fort Yukon. Other charter operators located in the Brooks Range include Bettles Air Service (907/692-5111) and Brooks Range Aviation (907/692-5444), both based in the village of Bettles; and Coyote Air (907/678-5995) out of Coldfoot on the Dalton Highway. Remember, a typical trip may include one or two days waiting on fog and weather, so allow extra time.

Ambler Air Service (907/445-2157) is the very best **SMALL-TOWN AIR SERVICE,** especially if you are flying to Kobuk National Park. It is located in the small Inupiat village of Ambler. David Rue has been running this flight service since 1976 and knows the area along the Kobuk River as well as anyone. His pilot, Scott Jones, is affable and unflappable, just the qualities that make for a good bush pilot. These folks fly on floats, wheels, and skis and do a lot of support work for river rafters, fishermen, and government agencies. They charter and also have limited scheduled service to Kobuk River villages and Fairbanks, and have competitive rates too.

Note: Many bush villages **BAN ALCOHOL** importation and possession. Check with air carriers and your outfitter before transporting alcohol in any quantity.

ADVENTURES: RIVER FLOAT TRIPS

EASTERN ARCTIC / Float trips in the Arctic National Wildlife Refuge (ANWR) have exploded in popularity over the last decade. Two outstanding trips are down the **KONGAKUT** and **HULAHULA** Rivers. Both, depending on the timing of the trip, offer exceptional views and encounters with the Porcupine Caribou Herd, which roughly numbers 150,000. Visitors commonly encounter Dall sheep, bears, golden eagles, waterfowl, and small mammals, as well as musk oxen. Neither trip is particularly hazardous, but experience in wilderness travel is essential. Guided trips are recommended for novices and the inexperienced. Access is via air from Kaktovik and Arctic Village.

CENTRAL NORTH SLOPE / The **COLVILLE RIVER** flows north to the Arctic Ocean past cliff-nesting falcons, hawks, and eagles; fossilized remains of Pleistocene mammals visible in sloughing permafrost bluffs; and tundra mammals, large and small. The 428-mile-long Colville, the seventh-longest river in the state, begins in the De Long Mountains of the Brooks Range and runs to the coast. Except for one or two rapids, it is slow moving and easy to run, but is extraordinarily remote. The town of Umiat is about 230 miles from the headwaters. Travelers need to be prepared and experienced in wilderness trekking. Access is via Barrow, Bettles, Umiat, or Deadhorse.

CENTRAL BROOKS RANGE / It is difficult picking the best float trip because Gates of the Arctic National Park offers many great excursions on wonderful rivers north and south of the Continental Divide. Perhaps the best choice for a family trip is the **JOHN RIVER** float, from its Hunt Fork tributary to its confluence with the Koyukuk just below Bettles. This five- or six-day trip passes through spectacular mountains before wending through the spruce thickets near its terminus. Generally a peaceful run that requires no extraordinary boatmanship, the trip requires common sense and camping experience.

WESTERN BROOKS RANGE / A float down the Wild and Scenic **NOATAK RIVER** through the Noatak National Preserve begins near Mount Igikpak and, if desired, can terminate almost 400 miles later in Kotzebue Sound. From the headwaters to the village of Noatak takes about 15 days or so, but shorter trips are possible, depending on pickup or drop-off points. The mountains around the headwaters are spectacular, as is the only slightly hyperbolic Grand Canyon of the Noatak. There are several Class II rapids along the river, but altogether it's a fairly easy float. Again, this is a remote wilderness river, and the inexperienced should consider a guide service. The river is becoming an ever more popular destination. Access is via Bettles for the headwaters and via Kotzebue for the lower river.

ADVENTURES: FLIGHT-SEEING TRIPS

EASTERN BROOKS RANGE / Circumnavigate Mounts Chamberlin and Michelson. These are some of the only glaciated peaks in the eastern Arctic, and on a summer "night" they glow with golden rays of the midnight sun. It's an expensive flight from almost all access points, notably Kaktovik and Arctic Village; therefore, it's best arranged as an adjunct to another backpacking or float trip in the area.

CENTRAL BROOKS RANGE / Two trips to recommend: the **ARRIGETCH PEAKS**, just west of the Alatna River, and **THROUGH THE GATES OF THE ARCTIC**. The granitic, Teton-like spires of the Arrigetch are a favorite visitor attraction, but our personal favorite is a flight up the North Fork of the Koyukuk River and by Frigid Crags and Boreal Mountain to Mount Doonerak. Inspiring country at any season, but indescribable at the peak of fall colors. Bettles is the most economical place to begin a flight. Road travelers can ask at Coldfoot for charter service.

WESTERN ARCTIC / Fly from Kotzebue, early or late in the day, along the coast 10 miles to Cape Krusenstern. From altitude, the traveler can best appreciate the starkness of the Chukchi Sea coast and landscape. An early-morning or late-evening flight best reveals the folding beach terraces. Flying services in Kotzebue offer flight-seeing here, as well as around Kotzebue Sound and to local villages.

MOSQUITOES

The Arctic from mid-June to early August is a good place to avoid if you fear mosquitoes. Mosquitoes are often thought of as tropical, but some of the densest concentrations are found in northern regions. Permafrost traps water on the surface, providing prime insect hatcheries. How bad are the mosquitoes? In July 1995, one scientist near Toolik slapped the back of another, killing 270 mosquitoes in a single blow!

A biologist estimated that the North Slope's summer mosquito population outweighs the biomass of all its other living creatures. At least 27 species of mosquito are found in Alaska, measuring from an eighth- to a quarter-inch long. Only female mosquitoes bite; males buzz around looking for mates. The constant humming of mosquitoes, beating their wings more than 300 times a second, disturbs some people more than actual bites. Mosquitoes are capable of flying 30mph but are fragile and easily grounded, even by a light breeze. Cold weather also grounds or kills them. Warm, still mornings and evenings are prime time for mosquitoes.

Female mosquitoes need blood protein to manufacture eggs. They home in on their prey by using their twin antennae to sense warm, moist air rising from the body. When they bite, they inject saliva that contains a chemical to prevent blood clotting and improve blood flow. It is the victim's allergic reaction to the saliva that makes mosquito bites itch. Once her abdomen is full, the female mosquito flies off—often before the victim can feel the bite. She then rests for several days, digesting the meal, before laying between 75 and 500 eggs. In summer, campers, hikers, floaters, and fishermen will

GUIDES AND OUTFITTERS

Not all guides are a good match for all clients. One client may swear by one guide, while another may swear *at* that same guide. Check references and clearly spell out your individual desires and expectations. Some of these guides offer similar trips but have different perspectives on the same areas and adventures. This list is not to be considered inclusive. Some great guides work for large organizations. Veteran Arctic guide and photographer Wilbur Mills, for example, sometimes guides for the Sierra Club.

Airfare from Fairbanks into the bush is not always included in the price of a trip—be sure to ask about this in advance. Arctic air travel is not cheap. Because trips must be planned well ahead of time, provisions and supplies purchased, logistics secured and paid for in advance, most wilderness guides and outfitters often require large deposits—anywhere from 30 to 50 percent—at the time of booking. Final payment may be required as much as 90 days in advance of the trip. This is standard procedure, but individual arrangements can be made.

ABEC'S ALASKA ADVENTURES / Ramona Finnoff has been guiding river travelers for more than 20 years and has extensive experience in white-water kayaking, rock and ice climbing, skiing, dog mushing, and mountaineering. Three special offer-

have intimate contact with mosquitoes, but even those on group tours to places such as Barrow, Kotzebue, and Prudhoe Bay will encounter at least some biting insects.

Mosquito sprays, lotions, and pumps containing the active ingredient DEET (short for N,N1-diethyl-m-toluamide) are the most effective and widely used repellents in Alaska. However, formulas containing 100 percent DEET may pose some neurological risk to humans, especially children and infants. Experts are divided on the actual risk. Many health experts recommend using only repellents with formulations of less than 30 percent DEET. DEET-free repellents made from citronella are growing in use. Naturapel is a popular alternative. Some people swear by Avon's Skin-So-Soft bath oil, which contains pennyroyal. Mosquito coils made of pyrethrum, Buhach powder, and citronella candles are also widely used. "Bug jackets," or bug suits, are the choice of a few trekkers. Head nets, gloves, and long-sleevedT shirts offer time-tested protection.

Casual travelers to larger villages or destinations need to take along nothing more than a small bottle of repellent or perhaps a lightweight head net. However, no one should venture cross-country without ample protection. Mosquitoes are capable of "hearing" and detecting motion as well as sensing warmth and moisture. Hot, sweaty backpackers staggering across uneven tundra or through brushy terrain are ideal targets. On one such trek, a friend took a picture of me in a "fur coat." The "coat" was made of bugs.

—*Tom Walker*

ings are a **RAFT AND BACKPACKING COMBINATION TRIP** during the caribou migration in the Arctic National Wildlife Refuge; a backpack in the pristine headwaters of the Nigu/Alatna Rivers; and Ramona's favorite, the Noatak River float and backpack. All three are good bets for folks who will make only one trip to the wilderness of arctic Alaska. *No credit cards; checks OK; 1550 Alpine Vista Ct, Fairbanks, AK 99712; 907/457-8907 or 877/424-8907; fax 907/457-6689; abec@abec alaska.com; www.abecalaska.com.*

ALASKA WILDTREK / Alaska Wildtrek specializes in adventures especially suited for European travelers or anyone interested in wildlife viewing, rafting, hiking, and wilderness camping. One offering is called "The Arctic Parks," **A BACKPACK AND RAFTING ADVENTURE** to three parks: Gates of the Arctic, Kobuk Valley, and Noatak. The multilingual owner, Chlaus Lotscher, also leads climbing adventures to places like Mount Chamberlin and Mount Michelson in the Arctic National Wildlife Refuge. An internationally published photojournalist, Lotscher will assist photographers in obtaining high-quality images. *No credit cards; checks OK; PO Box 1741, Homer, AK 99603; 907/235-6463; aktrek@xyz.net; www.alaskan.com/ alaskawildtrek.*

ALASKA PERIMETER EXPEDITIONS / Born and raised in Alaska, Henry D. "Te" Tiffany IV is a professional, registered, big-game guide and outfitter offering **TRA-DITIONAL FAIR-CHASE HUNTS** from comfortable tent camps established in the Brooks Range and the Koyukuk River valley. Tiffany stresses quality over quantity and books only a small number of hunters. The warm, friendly atmosphere brings clients back year after year. *No credit cards; checks OK; PO Box 329, Ester, AK 99725; 907/456-4868 or 907/223-3226; fax 907/456-3412; apehunt@ptialaska. net; www.alaskanperimeter.com.*

ARCTIC TREKS / This family-run business has been leading trips into Alaska's arctic regions since 1979, specializing in small-group backpacking and rafting. Under the guidance of owners Carol Kasza and Jim Campbell, guests of Arctic Treks learn to walk lightly on the land yet at the same time glory in the experience of minimal impact. *No credit cards, checks OK; PO Box 73452, Fairbanks, AK 99707; 907/455-6502; fax 907/455-6522; arctreks@polarnet.com; www.arctictreks adventures.com.*

ARCTIC WILD INC. / This company and their guides have been operating in the Brooks Range for over 30 years. They also specialize in trips to the Arctic National Wildlife Refuge. Operating from late May through early September, they offer a range of possibilities, from backpacking only to backpacking/river trip combinations. Prices vary greatly as the trips are custom made, but they range from about $1,700 to $3,500 per person, including all transportation from Fairbanks to the wilderness and back, as well as food, boats, and other equipment. They can also rent personal gear. The owners, David and Jennifer van den Berg, have a true love of the Arctic, with a low-impact, "leave no trace" philosophy toward the land. They also donate a portion of their income each year to the Fairbanks-based Northern Alaska Environmental Center, a nonprofit organization dedicated to preserving wild spaces. *Checks OK; PO Box 80433, Fairbanks AK 99708; 907/479-8203 or 888/577-8203; www.arcticwild.com.*

WILDERNESS ALASKA / Macgill Adams's goal is to see and visit *all* of the Arctic National Wildlife Refuge; his guided treks, therefore, are not limited to "the same old routes." Each trip offers some portion that is unique as well as open to flexibility. The refuge's great glory lies in the opportunities to observe wildlife in undisturbed settings. Adams, ably assisted by Dee Dee Van Vliet, works hard to ensure that Arctic novices learn to appreciate not only the smack-in-the-face beauty of the Brooks Range, but also the glorious subtleties of the plain and coastal lagoons. Trips offered throughout the Brooks Range. *No credit cards; checks OK; PO Box 113063, Anchorage, AK 99511; 907/345-3567; fax 907/345-3967; macgill@alaska.net; www.wildernessalaska.com.*

WILDERNESS BIRDING ADVENTURES / Lisa Moorehead has been a wilderness guide for over 20 years and holds a master's degree in cultural anthropology. Bob Dittrick, a biologist, has been guiding 20 years and birding for over 30 years. Together, they offer **BIRDERS** the chance to explore via raft and to backpack wilderness areas missed by most serious birders. Two special offerings are a raft/hike in the Arctic National Wildlife Refuge during the caribou migration and a Nome beach birding trip suitable for both beginning and experienced birders. Also offered are trips designed to locate uncommon or rare species. An example: a four-day back-pack trip in the Arctic Refuge to see grey-headed chickadees. *No credit cards; checks OK; 5515 Wild Mountain Rd, Eagle River, AK 99577; phone-fax 907/694-7442; wildbird@alaska.net; www.wildernessbirding.com.*

The James Dalton Highway

The Arctic's sole highway, the Dalton Highway, was built in 1974 as the haul road for construction of a portion of the 800-mile Trans-Alaska oil pipeline from Prudhoe Bay to the port of Valdez. Until recently this dusty gravel road has served mainly the oil industry; watch for potholes and mud.

The road begins in forested rolling hills at **MILE 73 ON THE ELLIOTT HIGHWAY,** crosses the inclined bridge over the Yukon, and runs 414 miles from the Yukon River over the Brooks Range to Prudhoe Bay on the Arctic coast. The highway was named for James William Dalton, an engineer involved in pioneer Arctic oil exploration. The only services and fuel stops between the Elliott Highway and Prudhoe Bay are **YUKON VENTURES ALASKA** (907/655-9001), located at the Yukon River Bridge, Mile 56, and **SOURDOUGH FUEL/SLATE CREEK INN** (907/678-5201), at Coldfoot, Mile 175, where you'll find the best truck stop—albeit the only truck stop—north of the Arctic Circle.

Road travelers should be well prepared for emergencies and carry food and sur-vival gear, two *mounted* spare tires, extra gasoline, and spare parts. Mishaps or breakdowns can have painful financial consequences. Towing companies charge $5 per mile, both directions. Drive slowly and with headlights on at all times. Give way to large trucks. Watch for flying rocks and tire blowouts! Winter use is not advised for casual travelers.

The road north from Coldfoot traverses the Brooks Range and the North Slope tundra and has phenomenal vistas of mountains, tundra, and wildlife. Moose are commonly seen south of the mountains, Dall sheep in Atigun Pass, and caribou, griz-zlies, musk oxen, waterfowl, and occasionally wolves in the north. Even though the Dalton opened to the public in 1995, streams along the road have long been over-fished. Fish in frigid Arctic waters grow slowly and are never in abundance. One lake trout caught near Toolik was 46 years old, and it was a midget by Alaska standards.

Interesting stops north of Coldfoot are numerous and include **WISEMAN,** turnoff at Mile 188.6, a historic mining town and a community of about 25 whose heyday was in 1910. Many log buildings from the 1920s are still in use, one of which is a museum of area history. The sheer granite rock faces of the south side of **MOUNT SUKAPAK** are impressive, but a peaceful lakeside view of the more slanting north side is available from Mile 205. It is believed this mountain marks the traditional boundary between Eskimo and Athabascan territories. **CHANDALAR SHELF,** Mile 237.1, offers views of the Chandalar River headwaters and 6,425-foot Table Moun-tain. **ATIGUN PASS** (4,800 feet), Mile 244.7, is not a pass at all in the true sense, but a cut in the mountains through which the pipeline and road passes. A marvel of engineering, it also marks the Continental Divide and the break to the true North

Slope of Alaska. You can regularly see Dall sheep here. From the first **ATIGUN RIVER** crossing at Mile 253.1, the road passes through gorgeous alpine tundra and mountain vistas. Tree line is far behind and the open country offers views of Galbraith Lake, the pipeline, caribou, grizzly bears, and even wolves. **SLOPE MOUNTAIN** (4,101 feet), just west of the road at Mile 305, is another excellent place to see Dall sheep. A side road runs behind the Sag River Highway Camp and gives access to the river. Musk oxen are sometimes seen here. Watch for wildlife all the way to Prudhoe Bay.

The last 90 miles into Deadhorse are often rocky and dusty; drive with care. **DEADHORSE/PRUDHOE BAY** is the end of the line, where the road meets the ice of the sea. Oil companies tightly control access to the fields at Prudhoe Bay and Kuparuk. You may find accommodations at the **PRUDHOE BAY HOTEL** (907/ 659-2449), which also may be able to give updated information on tours to the Arctic Ocean.

Although people have argued that the pipeline paralleling the road is Alaska's greatest eyesore, one has to admire the 800-mile-long, $8 billion project as an engineering marvel. On average, over one million barrels of oil pass through the pipeline each day.

GUIDES AND OUTFITTERS

NATUREALASKA TOURS / Alaska's oldest nature, wildlife, and birding tour company, NatureAlaska Tours blends adventure travel with education and conservation. With 35 years in the business, the company is a pioneer in arctic tourism via the Dalton Highway. They specialize in custom-designed tours for small groups of bird-watchers and photographers, and for museum and zoo groups. Tour leaders are Alaskan scientists, educators, and wilderness guides. Prices vary greatly depending on what you want. *No credit cards; checks OK; PO Box 10224, Fairbanks, AK 99710; 907/488-3746; dwetzel@alaska.net; www.NatureAlaskaTours.com.*

NORTHERN ALASKA TOUR COMPANY / This company offers several small-group Arctic Circle adventures. One tour takes you on a one-day guided journey along the Dalton Highway to the Arctic Circle. This trip offers travelers an opportunity to look at the arctic tundra, visit a trading post, and make a ceremonial crossing of the Arctic Circle. Another tour offers a one-day guided drive up the highway combined with a flight to the Nunamiut Eskimo village of Anaktuvuk Pass. Also offered is a three-day/two-night driving and flying trip to Prudhoe Bay, as well as many other natural history and cultural tours. Most tour prices range from $130 per person to $400 per person, depending on the tour (the longer Prudhoe Bay tour goes for $749). *MC, V; checks OK; PO Box 82991, Fairbanks, AK 99708; 907/474-8600 or 800/474-1986; fax 907/474-4767; adventure@northernalaska.com; www. northernalaska.com.*

Barrow

More than 300 miles above the Arctic Circle, this is the northernmost settlement in the United States. Take a ride out to **POINT BARROW** and you've gone as far north as dry land will allow. The 1,300 miles still separating you from the North Pole is ocean, clogged with ice and populated by polar bears, whales, walrus, seals, and other critters of near mythic stature. This is not just the end of the road—it's the absolute edge of the planet.

Visitors to Barrow encounter reminders of this marginal planetary location at every turn. Satellite dishes seem to point at the ground as they track communications satellites in orbit over the Lower 48. Tour companies issue parkas to arriving guests in mid-July. Even the concepts of "day" and "night" must be renegotiated out here on the edge. When you're sitting on top of the world, 84 days pass between a single sunrise in May and the next sunset in August.

Barrow (pop. 4,500) usually makes the national news when the sun sets in November, not to rise again until the end of January. But in 1998, *The Wall Street Journal* did a story on the town's penchant for America's number-one sport: baseball. Well, up here, softball. The story, "Batters Shiver, Bears Lurk," reported that, contrary to the hot-weather version the rest of the country recognizes, games here often are canceled on account of fog alerts, high-wind advisories, subzero temperatures (in summer!), or even polar bears loping into town.

The **INUPIAT ESKIMOS** have inhabited the Arctic coast for more than a millennium. Even with the advent of a cash economy, hunting remains an essential cultural activity. The most important hunt of all occurs in the spring and fall, when bowhead whales migrate along the coast. Contact the Alaska Eskimo Whaling Commission (907/852-AEWC (2392)) for more information. The **NALUKATAQ FESTIVAL** in June celebrates a successful and safe spring whaling season. The Inupiat equivalent of Christmas, Nalukataq (pronounced nah-loo-ka-tahk), or blanket-toss festival, attracts relatives from the outlying villages and can last for several days. There also can be more than one Nalukataq in one season. Contact the North Slope Borough Public Information Office (907/852-0215).

The Inupiat have pursued economic development with the same aggressive pride that keeps their traditional customs and language alive. In response to the discovery of America's largest oil field at Prudhoe Bay, the Inupiat formed a regional government, the North Slope Borough, to guarantee their voice in development decisions.

EXPLORING AND ADVENTURES

THE INUPIAT HERITAGE CENTER / This museum, which celebrates the past and present-day life of the Inupiat Eskimo peoples of the North Slope, opened in 1999. There is a major exhibit on the bowhead whale, hunting, and the importance of the whale in the life of the Native people. The philosophical foundation of the heritage center is based on the ancient *qargi,* or community house, where village activities traditionally occurred. Ilisagvik College runs the heritage center, which has a museum and a traditional workshop where craftsmen carve walrus ivory, etch baleen, and refurbish (during the months of February, March, and early April) the *umiat,* the small whaling boats made from the skins of *ugruk* (bearded seal). *8:30am–5:00pm, closed noon-1pm, Mon–Fri, closed weekends winter, during summer open every day; 907/852-4594 or 800/478-7337; fax 907/852-4224; INUP_Interpretation@nps.gov; www.nps.gov/inup/.*

KIVGIQ / This event is held in January and February (though not annually, so you need to check to see if your visit coincides with the celebration) and brings Inuit from

AMONG THE PEOPLE

First-time travelers to the bush are often surprised by conditions in rural communities. Dilapidated cabins stand next to modern houses; satellite dishes sprout next to racks groaning under the weight of walrus meat; yards seem full of junk snowmobiles and rusting barrels. But it is the lack of fresh, clean water and modern sanitation that most shocks tourists: "Honey Buckets? Gross!"

An Inupiat guide in Barrow once said that the hardest question she has to answer from tourists is "Why is this community here?" They see a lack of industry, agriculture, and trade. They notice the pockets of poverty and unemployment, and the incredibly high cost of goods and services. Born and raised in Barrow, the guide has no satisfactory answer for visitors—other than, it's just home.

Alaska Natives have a rich and varied cultural heritage tied to the land. Until a very short time ago (a few decades, really), the people lived in small family bands or tribal groups and moved seasonally from one choice subsistence site to another. Some followed caribou; others relied on marine mammals. They all collected and cured furs, fish, berries, roots, and plants. Starvation, privation, and hardship were facts of life.

Life began to change forever around the turn of the century when European adventurers, prospectors, whalers, and missionaries began arriving. Change was rapid and, in many cases, devastating. People began to settle near missions and whaling stations. Traders brought modern implements, a cash economy, religion, and science. Disease, alcohol, deceit, and prejudice were also part of the package.

across the North Slope, Russia, and Canada together to renew ties and share traditions. Known as the "messenger feast," it is a three-day celebration of dance, song, and bartering. Contact the North Slope Borough Public Information Office (907/852-0215) for more information.

PIURAAGIAQTA / This is a weeklong "spring" festival (we say that in quotations because there's still plenty of snow on the ground and cool temperatures in the air) in April. There's usually a parade, races, igloo building, dog mushing, and geese-calling contests, snowmachine races, golf on the ice, and other activities. Contact the City of Barrow (907/852-5211) for more information.

HIKING / Depending on your fitness level (as well as personal adventure barometer), there are several possibilities. One is to walk along the road leading to **FRESH WATER LAKE**, one of the village's original sources of drinking water. You'll stroll by Imiqsaun Cemetery, where ancestral remains previously excavated by archaeologists have since been properly put to rest. Along the Chukchi Sea coast, adventuresome souls can trek or rent a four-wheeler the 13 miles (one-way) to the site where the nation's beloved humorist **WILL ROGERS**, along with pilot **WILEY POST**, crashed their small aircraft and were killed in 1935. In town, identification tags from the

The raison d'être for the existence of Barrow, as well as other villages "next-to-nowhere," may elude some visitors, but in reality the same question can be asked of many towns and cities in decline in the rest of the country. Gone are the mills, factories, and trade routes that caused many such places to spring up. Perhaps only in the stark reality of the Arctic is the incongruity of location so obvious.

Permafrost and remoteness are major, almost insurmountable hurdles to sewage treatment, safe water distribution, and trash and garbage disposal. Everything costs much more in remote places. Unemployment is high, with poverty as the result. Nutrition, health care, and education suffer in isolation. A subsistence way of living may not mean life or death to the people now, but it renews cultural pride and adds immeasurably to the quality of life in places where a can of soup costs $6.

While many villages offer cultural performances for visitors, village life is not a tableau enacted for the tourist season. Things seen are often not what they seem. One person's "yard full of junk" may be another's collection of spare parts. Hauling drinking water by hand is both a necessity and hard work, not a photo opportunity. The lined face of an aging Nunamiut woman may clearly convey wisdom and strength of character, but she isn't a photographer's model who can be rudely approached. No matter how humble, village homes and property should be respected by visitors and not stared at as if they were part of some Disney-ish "Arcticland." Poverty does not mean quaint. Uniqueness does not mean carte blanche for photographic intrusion. The people of the Arctic have survived in a cold land of darkness and hardship for centuries. They deserve respect.

—Tom Walker

plane can be viewed at the old Whaling Captain's station, in a section of town known as Browerville. There's also a monument near the Cape Smythe air terminal, next to the visitors center. Be prepared with proper clothing, food, and water for any hike, and make sure you let the North Slope Borough Police Department (907/852-6111) know of your plans before you leave.

GUIDES AND OUTFITTERS

ALASKAN ARCTIC ADVENTURES / Run by the father-son team of John and John Tidwell, Alaskan Arctic Adventures will take you out to Point Barrow, 12 miles from town and the most northerly point in the United States, to view polar bears mid-October to mid-March. Or take the birding tour (250 species of birds migrate here each spring and summer) and look for snowy owls, eiders, gulls, arctic terns, and loons. Also see arctic fox, whales, and seals. Either way, the trip runs $60 per person and takes about two hours, sometimes longer, and are especially geared toward photographers. (The elder Tidwell is a photographer himself, so he knows what appeals to shutter bugs.) If snow's on the ground, and it is more often than not this far north, you can go on a dog mushing tour with the younger Tidwell, for $85 per person.

THE ARCTIC

907/852-3800; info@arctic-adventures.com; www.arctic-adventures.com (the King
Eider Hotel, see below, also has a good link for the tours at www.kingeider.net).

RESTAURANTS

Arctic Pizza

125 APAYAUQ ST, BARROW; 907/852-4222 About a half mile from the Top of the
World Hotel (see Lodgings), this restaurant could be more aptly named Arctic Pizza,
Italian, Mexican, Steak, Seafood, and Sandwiches. Even the pickiest eater could find
something to like on their extensive menu—a pleasant surprise for such a far-flung
village. Should you have the chicken-and-shrimp Cajun jambalaya pasta? a grilled
New York steak topped with sautéed spinach, mushrooms, and blue cheese? or "halibut à la Arctic," the famous flatfish charbroiled and topped with lemon and fresh
garlic? There's even a children's menu, free delivery, and everything is reasonably
priced. Take a seat upstairs for a view of the Arctic Ocean. $–$$; MC, V; lunch and
dinner every day; no alcohol; no reservations; just down the road from the Top of
the World Hotel.

Brower's Cafe

WATERFRONT, BROWERVILLE; 907/852-5800; FAX 907/852-2100 For a good view
and sense of history, stop in at Brower's Cafe, located in an historic building on the
far side of town in an area called Browerville. It's the site of the whaling and trading
station operated before the turn of the century by Charles Brower, a Yankee whaler
who settled here in 1882, learned the language, married a local woman, and established what has become one of the largest Eskimo families in Barrow. Brower's Cafe
has a nice ocean view, and after your meal you can photograph the arched whale
jawbones and umiak (traditional seal-skin whaling boat) out front. $$; MC, V;
checks OK; lunch, dinner every day; no alcohol; no reservations; PO Box 626,
Barrow, AK 99723.

Pepe's North of the Border Restaurant / ★

1204 AGVIK ST, BARROW; 907/852-8200 A stop here is de rigueur. Mexican and
American food are on the menu, but the real pizzazz at Pepe's is its owner, Fran Tate.
Approaching the age when most folks retire, Fran is a dynamo in a miniskirt. She's
also a consummate promoter of Barrow, which landed her on the Tonight Show a
number of years back. During her 15 minutes of fame, she presented an oosik to
Johnny Carson. "What's an oosik?" Johnny asked, as he beheld the 2–foot–long
bone. Fran replied, "Let's just say every male walrus has one." $$; DC, MC, V; local
checks only; breakfast, lunch, dinner every day; no alcohol; no reservations; PO Box
403, Barrow, AK 99723; located in town.

LODGINGS

King Eider Inn

1752 AHKOVAK ST, BARROW; 907/852-4700 (888/30-EIDER (888/303-4337), IN-
STATE RESERVATION LINE); FAX 907/852-2025 This nonsmoking hotel is considered the "new kid on the block," having opened its doors in 1998. The hotel features
a guest sauna, a beautiful stone fireplace in the lobby, and a presidential suite. The

rooms are spacious and have pine log furniture. These folks work closely with Alaskan Arctic Adventures (see Exploring and Adventures, above) and can help arrange a custom tour of the Barrow area. Summer rates range from $195, double occupancy, to $300 for the presidential suite, which features a vaulted ceiling, full kitchen, king-size canopy pine log bed, Jacuzzi tub, and stone fireplace. Lower rates in winter, as well as business and senior discounts. *$$$; AE, MC, V; checks OK (if secured with credit card); PO Box 1283, Barrow, AK 99723; eider@barrow.com; www.kingeider.net; at the Barrow Airport.* &

Top of the World Hotel

1200 AGVIK ST, BARROW; 907/852-3900 OR 800/882-8478 (800/478-8520, IN-STATE) It's not the only hotel in town, but it has the best location and serves as the hub of visitor activity. Ask for a room in the new wing. Better yet snag oceanside rooms, like 246, 248, or 250, for the best views. Walking maps and lists of activities are available at the front desk. The hotel operates local sight-seeing excursions year-round through Tundra Tours (907/852-3900), and in the summer months hosts a daily Inupiat cultural presentation of song, dance, games, and crafts in a large tent at the Inupiat Heritage Center. A package Tundra Tour along with the cultural presentation goes for $65 per person, though that price may change. Even if you're fairly independent, the hotel package is still the best way to get oriented. There are different room rates for pleasure, business, or government, ranging from $109 to $185 per person. *$$–$$$; AE, DC, DIS, MC, V; checks OK; PO Box 189, Barrow, AK 99723; tow@asrc.com; www.topoftheworldhotel.com; Barrow business district.* &

Kotzebue

A regional service hub, Kotzebue (pop. 3,000) is located on a 3-mile-long spit jutting into Kotzebue Sound. This predominately Inupiat village serves as the trade center for 10 northwestern villages. Summer visitors see Eskimo blanket tosses and other cultural activities. The Northwest Arctic Native Association's (NANA) **MUSEUM OF THE ARCTIC** (907/442-3747) in Kotzebue is a highlight. The best large museum anywhere north of the Arctic Circle, it features Northwest Coast Inupiat cultural history, displays, dioramas, and live performances unmatched statewide. From the beach you can watch the midnight sun arc above the Bering Sea.

If time permits, walk out to **KOTZEBUE'S "NATIONAL FOREST"**—one black spruce growing on the tundra, about three-quarters of a mile from town inland. Fishing buddies stationed at the Kotzebue Air Force Base planted the tree in 1958 as a seedling. Withstanding the fierce winds of the coast, permafrost, and subzero temperatures, the tree is now 11 feet tall. **CAPE KRUSENSTERN NATIONAL MONUMENT,** 10 air miles northwest of town, is made up of 114 beach ridges, each an archaeological mother lode. Humans have hunted and lived here for over 9,000 years. Camping and boating along this windswept shoreline will build an appreciation for the hardy people who lived—and continue to live—along this remnant of the Bering Land Bridge.

ACCESS AND INFORMATION

AIR CHARTERS and **SCHEDULED FLIGHTS** provide access to Kotzebue, surrounding villages, the eastern Brooks Range, Kobuk Valley National Park, Noatak National Preserve, Cape Krusenstern National Monument, and Selawik National Wildlife Refuge. The best tours are with **NANA TOUR ARCTIC** (907/442-3301).

The best place to stay, in fact the only hotel in town, is the **NULLAGVIK HOTEL** (AE, MC, V; local checks only; PO Box 336, Kotzebue, AK 99752; 907/442-3331; fax 907/442-3340; www.nullagvik.com.)

The Brooks Range

Stretching from the Yukon border almost to the Chukchi Sea, these mountains separate the muskeg and forest of Interior Alaska from the treeless tundra expanses of the Arctic coast. The peaks and valleys of this northern extension of the Rocky Mountains—with elevations from 4,000 to 9,000 feet—spawn numerous spectacular rivers and streams, flowing both north and south, and support fish and wildlife in, at times, astonishing numbers.

Impressive peaks include **MOUNT IGIKPAK** (8,510 feet), the highest point in the western Brooks Range; and **MOUNT CHAMBERLIN** (9,020 feet) and **MOUNT MICHELSON** (8,855 feet), the two tallest peaks, which are located in the eastern Brooks Range and within the Arctic National Wildlife Refuge. The **ARRIGETCH PEAKS**, along with **MOUNT DOONERAK** (7,457 feet), are impressive spires in the central range. **BOREAL MOUNTAIN** and **FRIGID CRAGS**, rising on either side of the North Fork of the Koyukuk River, are explorer Robert Marshall's "Gates of the Arctic."

Temperatures vary from about 85 degrees in summer to 60 degrees below zero in winter. Summer offers 24 hours of daylight, wind, and mosquitoes. Winter offers 24 hours of darkness, wind, and ice. This is real wilderness, with miles of great, uninhabited expanses. Bush travelers should be self-reliant and skillful in the outdoors. Those who come prepared can choose from a plethora of activities, ranging from river rafting to mountain climbing (see Adventures and Guides and Outfitters at beginning of chapter).

Entire books have been written about Arctic and Brooks Range parks, rivers, and refuges and the exquisite country that surrounds them. In this chapter is a small sample of some of the most popular places and excursions. But popular doesn't mean crowded; it will be a rare day when you see any other people.

ACCESS AND INFORMATION

The best places to obtain initial information on the Brooks Range and the Arctic's national parks and wildlife refuges are the **ALASKA PUBLIC LANDS INFORMATION CENTERS** in Anchorage (605 W 4th Ave, Ste 105; 907/271-2737) and in Fairbanks (250 Cushman St, Ste 1A; 907/456-0527). In summer, stop in or call the **COLDFOOT VISITORS CENTER** in Coldfoot (907/678-5209 late May–early Sept).

The community of Bettles on the south–central slope of the range is a prime jumping-off point for travel into the heart of the wilderness. It is served by **CHARTER AND SCHEDULED FLIGHTS** from Fairbanks (see Access and Information at the beginning of this chapter). Contacts in Bettles include Bettles Lodge, which runs Bettles Air Service (907/692-5111 or 800/770-5111), Sourdough Outfitters (907/692-5252), Gates of the Arctic National Park and Preserve (907/692-5494), and Kanuti National Wildlife Refuge (907/692-5555).

LODGING

Bettles Lodge

PO BOX 27, BETTLES, ALASKA 99726; 800/770-5111; FAX 907/692-5655 Built in 1948, and a designated National Historic Site, this lodge serves travelers heading out into the Brooks Range from the village of Bettles. Here you'll find all the usual amenities including a restaurant, tavern, supplies, gifts, and cozy rooms. A special two-day, one-night tour goes for $486 per person. Bettles Air, owned and operated by the lodge, provides transportation throughout the Brooks Range either with float- or wheel-equipped aircraft. *$$; MC, V; checks OK; Bttlodge@alaska.net; www.alaska.net/~bttlodge.*

Gates of the Arctic
National Park and Preserve

Astride 200 miles of the central Brooks Range, this park covers about 8.4 million acres of mountains, valleys, and rivers, an area four times the size of Yellowstone National Park. Access is **VIA PLANE** from Bettles, Fairbanks, or Kotzebue. **LIMITED ROAD ACCESS** is via the Dalton Highway.

Established in 1980, Gates of the Arctic is unique from other national parks in that it is completely undeveloped. There are **NO VISITOR FACILITIES** of any kind within the park. Visitors must seek their own trails and adventures. But those who do will enjoy pristine territory in which to camp, canoe, climb, fish, photograph, river raft, and view wildlife. Winter activities include cross-country skiing and dog mushing.

Hiking is difficult. The tundra is covered with grass tussocks and knots of Arctic cottongrass that twist and turn under foot. Good hikers can average 2 to 2½mph, with the rigors of walking making four to five hours a long enough day. River crossings can be dangerous and difficult. Frostbite in winter and hypothermia in summer are real threats. It is important to check in with park rangers in Bettles, Coldfoot, or Fairbanks before embarking. Consult with those who have local knowledge, such as lodge owners and pilots, for trip suggestions. And **FILE A TRIP PLAN**—you'll be glad you did should a search-and-rescue operation be necessary. Expect to see Dall sheep, ptarmigan, maybe caribou, and to encounter grizzly bears, perhaps even wolves. For more **INFORMATION**, contact Superintendent, Gates of the Arctic National Park and Preserve (PO Box 74680, Fairbanks, AK 99707; 907/456-0281; www.nps.gov/gaar).

LODGINGS

Iniakuk Lake Wilderness Lodge

PO BOX 80424, FAIRBANKS, AK 99708; 907/479-6354 OR 877/479-6354 In 🏃 its 30th year, this beautiful lodge on the shores of Iniakuk Lake is the best in all the Arctic. A maximum of 12 guests enjoy fishing, hiking, canoeing, river rafting, wildlife watching, flight-seeing, birding, massage therapy, and photography—or simply relaxing in the handcrafted lodge. Longtime Alaskan and owner Pat Gaedeke offers gourmet meals and fresh baked goods. One highlight is "whirlwind adventures"—spur-of-the-moment excursions that take advantage of the best the wilderness has to offer at each changing light. Another is "Dinner at the Continental Divide"—a flight-seeing trip into the Brooks Range that culminates in dinner and champagne at the divide. Pat also offers guided stays at two well-maintained cabins on the Alatna River within Gates of the Arctic National Park. The lodge is accessible by a 30-minute flight from Bettles. Daily rates are $450 per person at the main lodge, $295 for guided cabin stays, and $195 for unguided river cabin stays. Airfare is not included. A special three-day, all-inclusive stay, including airfare from Fairbanks, is $3,225 per person. *$$$; MC, V; checks OK; info@gofarnorth.com; www.gofarnorth.com.*

Peace of Selby Wilderness

PO BOX 86, MANLEY HOT SPRINGS, AK 99756; PHONE-FAX 907/672-3206 Because of its location along Selby/Narvak Lake within Gates of the Arctic National Park, Peace of Selby offers a chance to explore the wilderness of the Brooks Range in comfort. This lodge, owned and operated by Art and Damaris Mortvedt, specializes in small groups with custom adventures that may include hiking, wildlife photography, fishing, bird-watching, river trips, and lake canoeing. In winter enjoy snowshoeing, ice fishing, cross-country skiing, and aurora watching. The handcrafted main lodge, built of white spruce logs, includes dining room, kitchen, library, bathroom, and loft. Meals include fresh vegetables and fruit flown in with each party. Arrangements can be made to use one of four remote rustic cabins in sheltered, unvisited areas, for a self-catered experience. Lodge rates are $300 per day per person. Do-it-yourself cabins are $150 per person per day. Discounted weekly rates. *$$$; No credit cards; checks OK; Peaceofselby@compuserve.com; www.alaska wilderness.net.*

Kobuk Valley National Park

The Kobuk River flows through a wide, forested valley between the Baird and Waring Mountains. The river meanders through spruce, birch, and aspen forests and past several Inupiat villages before emptying into Kotzebue Sound. The boundaries enclose 1.7 million acres of undeveloped parkland.

Just 75 miles east of Kotzebue, this park boasts two **WILD AND SCENIC RIVERS**—the Kobuk and the Salmon. Villagers along the river are dependent on subsistence hunting and fishing for much of their livelihood, so visitors often are surprised to find that hunting continues within park boundaries. Private property along the river should be respected. Sportfishing for grayling, pike, char, and sheefish is often outstanding. The vast Western Arctic Caribou Herd crosses the Kobuk in early September en route to southern wintering grounds. Floaters have found themselves amid large herds swimming the river.

You can design a personalized Kobuk River **FLOAT TRIP** lasting anywhere from one to four weeks depending on take-out location. Most floaters put in at 14-mile-long Walker Lake in the eastern end of Gates of the Arctic National Park and float downstream to one of the native villages—Kobuk, Shungnak, Ambler, Kiana, or Noorvik. Except for three very dangerous rapids—up to Class V—and chutes in the first 30 miles below the lake, the river is placid and easily navigated. Below the Lower Kobuk Canyon the river becomes Class I, considered the easiest water. To skip the white-water adventures, bush pilots drop floaters here instead of at the lake. Check for current conditions.

The **GREAT KOBUK SAND DUNES,** which cover 25 square miles inland from the south bank of the river, are the park's most notable feature. These dunes, up to 125 feet high, would look more at home in an Edward Abbey novel than they do in arctic Alaska. Travelers can hire local guides with boats, float down the Kobuk on their own, or be dropped off by plane. The dunes are accessible from the river by a short hike up Kavet Creek. Watch for bears. For **INFORMATION,** contact Superintendent, Kobuk Valley National Park (PO Box 1029, Kotzebue, AK 99752; 907/442-3890; www.nps.gov/kova).

Arctic National Wildlife Refuge

Truly America's Serengeti, the 19.6 million–acre Arctic National Wildlife Refuge (ANWR) has become the center of a heated debate in developing a national energy policy because of its suspected value for oil. The argument comes down to this: some people want to open up the refuge's coastal plain to oil exploration, and some people are fighting fiercely to protect it.

The coastal plain is the calving ground for thousands of **CARIBOU,** as well as prime habitat for millions of **MIGRATORY BIRDS.** Indeed, the refuge is a priceless treasure. Rivers flow clear and pure. The land embraces musk oxen, moose, polar bears, black and brown bears, wolves, and the great Porcupine Caribou Herd. Part of the refuge is mountainous with limited tree cover, but much of it is tundra and marsh. Refuge winters are long and severe, summers short and intense. The brief summer growing season, with its attendant insect plague, supports minimal plant growth. A white spruce tree growing at the northern tree line may take 300 years to achieve a base diameter of 5 inches. Both Inupiats and Gwch'in subsist off refuge lands.

Visitors enjoy summer float trips, hiking, photography, climbing, fishing, and hunting. (See Adventures and Guides and outfitters at beginning of this chapter.) The main lure for many people is viewing the spectacular caribou migrations and post-calving aggregations. For **INFORMATION,** contact Refuge Manager, Arctic National Wildlife Refuge (101 12th Ave, Room 236, Box 20, Fairbanks, AK 99701; 907/456-0250; www.r7.fws.gov/nwr/arctic).

NOME

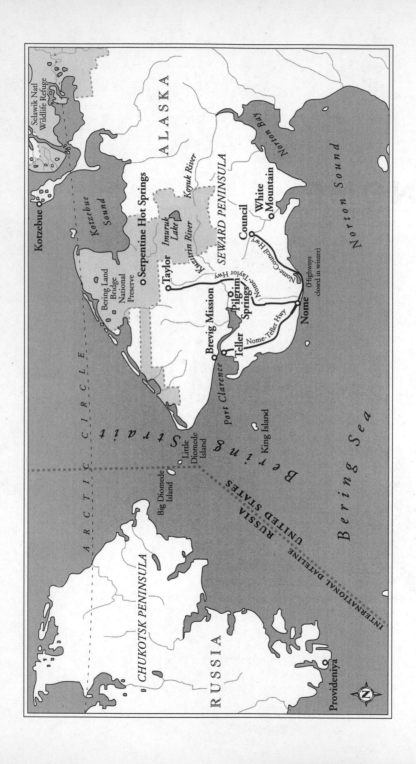

NOME

Born in the late 1800s as a gold-boom town and best known today as the finish line of Alaska's Iditarod Trail Sled Dog Race, Nome retains its frontier image in everything from its rough-hewn buildings to its residents' unabashedly rowdy, fun-loving ways and raucous festivals.

At first glance, Nome may seem a bit disheveled, even homely. But it may be best to think of the town as unpretentious. Everything serves a purpose. In a place where fierce storms blow off the Bering Sea and winter temperatures drop to 50 degrees below zero or colder, function rules. And although they inhabit one of the farthest reaches of the continent, people here do not feel isolated. As one bemused resident explained, "We are smug in the shared belief that Nome is really the center of the universe."

Nome is on the Seward Peninsula, 102 miles below the Arctic Circle, with its back to the hills and its face to the sea. People work hard here; the land demands it. They play hard, too, in their unique Alaskan way. During summer solstice, for instance, they dig out bathing suits and plunge into the icy Bering Sea. In fall, they race down Front Street in bathtubs on wheels. In March, during Iditarod Days, they host a golf tournament on the sea ice.

The people of Nome know how to have a good time. They celebrate with wild abandon. Any excuse will do—anniversaries, divorces, their birthdays, their dogs' birthdays, the bars being open—it doesn't matter. As reported once in *The Wall Street Journal*: "Every night is Friday night in Nome, Alaska. Except Friday night—which is New Year's Eve."

Today, this city of 3,500 people is the hub of Northwest Alaska. Yet only a little more than a century ago, it was only desolate, windswept tundra. Then, in 1898, three prospectors known as the "Lucky Swedes" found gold in the black sands of Cape Nome. Within months, a tent city of 20,000 hopeful gold seekers rose from the tundra. It was known as the "poor man's gold rush," because gold lay all over the beaches just for the taking. Gamblers, con men, prostitutes, and other B-movie type characters flocked to the north. The legendary lawman and gunslinger Wyatt Earp even owned a saloon here. At one time, Nome had a French lingerie shop and piano-moving businesses. Although fires and storms have wiped out nearly all remnants of this colorful era (a devastating blaze in 1934 destroyed 90 percent of the historic buildings), Nome still identifies heavily with its past.

There is no road to Nome. But there are about 300 miles of roads in and around the community. The city is located 539 air miles north of Anchorage, and the only way to reach it is by air or sea or sled-dog team, as dozens of Iditarod mushers do each March in yet another celebration of Nome's gold-boom days.

ACCESS AND INFORMATION

Regularly scheduled **FLIGHTS** to Nome are available only on Alaska Airlines (800/252-7522; www.alaskaair.com). Frontier Flying Service (907/474-0014 or 800/478-6779, in-state; www.frontierflying.com) will do charters from Fairbanks. Nome also has taxicabs (including service to the Eskimo village of **TELLER**, 72 miles to the northwest), and several businesses that rent vehicles (see Adventures, below).

Located at 301 Front Street, the **NOME CONVENTION & VISITORS BUREAU** (PO Box 240, Nome, AK 99762; 907/443-6624 or 800/478-1901, in-state; fax 907/443-5832; www.nomealaska.org/vc) has bird lists, pamphlets on fishing and wildlife, and information on lodging and tours. The staff is knowledgeable and friendly and can help you get set up to do any of the activities highlighted below.

Nome's daytime summer **TEMPERATURES** range from the low 50s to the mid-70s, and in the winter, it can range from about 20 degrees above to 50 degrees below zero. If you plan to visit in summer, be prepared for rainy weather and occasional chilly winds. The best time to visit may be September, when the tundra changes to colors as vibrant as any New England hillside. That's also the time when the ubiquitous summer mosquitoes are gone.

SHOPPING

There are a half-dozen gift shops on Front Street (Nome's main roadway) selling Native ivory carvings and other Alaskana. Especially good are the **ARCTIC TRADING POST** (907/443-2686; arctictrading@gci.net; www.arctictradingpost. com), **MARUSKIYA'S** (907/443-2955), and the **BOARD OF TRADE IVORY SHOP** (907/443-2611). Harder to find, but worth the effort, is the **CHUKOTKA-ALASKA STORE** (514 Lomen St; 907/443-4128). Manager Victor Goldsberry packs this small shop with a multitude of mementos from the Chukotka region of Russia, directly across the Bering Strait from Nome. You'll see traditional Russian designs as well as Siberian and Alaskan Yup'ik handicrafts and furs.

The "Grand Poobah" and former mayor of Nome is Leo Rasmussen, who owns **RASMUSSEN'S MUSIC MART** (103 Federal Wy; 907/443-2798; leaknome@nook. net). Rasmussen has had a hand in almost every unusual and silly summer event that has evolved in Nome over the last 30 years. Located just off Front Street, his store is a pleasant jumble of all those things you never thought you might need; Leo himself is a pleasant jumble of anecdotes and facts about this place. He's also president of a nonprofit corporation that manages fund-raising and development for the Iditarod National Historic Trail, the route of the famous dog race.

ADVENTURES

ROAD TRIPPING / In the summer, Nome offers a rarity in bush Alaska: the chance to travel deep into the country by road. The Nome area has more than 300 miles of well-maintained **GRAVEL ROADS** to explore, with opportunities for hiking, mountain biking, fishing, skiing, boating, birding, wildlife viewing, and other adventuring. Birding is big, with more than 180 species found on the Seward Peninsula from late May through July, including Asiatic birds rarely seen in North America.

The roads are generally open May through October, depending on snowfall, and maintained during summer and fall. Cars may be rented from **STAMPEDE CAR RENTALS** (907/443-5598; www.aurorainnome.com) and **ALASKA CAB GARAGE** (907/443-2939). If you don't want to rent your own vehicle, Nome has three local cab companies that will drive you around town or even to the village of Teller: **CHECKER CAB** (907/443-5211), **VILLAGE CAB** (907/443-2333), and **NOME CAB** (907/443-3030).

Three major roads, plus one short drive, lead out of Nome and are outlined below. There are no services—no gas, no food, no lemonade stands—once you leave the town. Keep your eyes open for reindeer, musk oxen, bears, and foxes, as well as abandoned gold dredges. And be prepared to do battle with mosquitoes.

Head out on the **NOME-TELLER HIGHWAY,** and about 40 miles northwest of Nome you'll see another road (about 7 miles long) wandering off toward the sea to **CAPE WOOLLEY,** a fish camp formerly used by King Island Natives during summer months. The main road dead-ends 72 miles northwest of Nome in the Inupiat Eskimo village of **TELLER,** a community of about 300 people located on the sea between Grantley Harbor and Port Clarence. During summer, many Teller families head upriver, through Imuruk Basin and up the meandering Kuzitrin River, to fish camps at Mary's Igloo. **GRANTLEY HARBOR TOURS** (Box 586, Teller, AK 99778; 907/642-3682 or 800/478-3682, in-state; fax 907/642-3681; www.grantleyharbor. com), run by Kenneth and Emily Hughes, offers cultural and sight-seeing tours of Teller and the chance to meet local artists, including ivory carvers.

The **NOME-TAYLOR HIGHWAY** is more popularly known as the **KOUGAROK ROAD.** Originally intended to lead to Taylor, a privately owned gold-mining operation, the highway project was stopped at the Kuzitrin River Bridge, 85 miles from Nome (it's another 25 miles, by trail, to the mine). Eight miles out of Nome, there's good fishing in the **DEXTER VALLEY.** About 38 miles out, **SALMON LAKE** is a beautiful spot for camping or picnicking. At Mile 53, take the left-hand turn to reach **PILGRIM HOT SPRINGS,** 7 miles off the main road. The hot springs is an interesting historical site with a wooden hot tub for soaking (traditionally it's been free to use, but its caretakers say that may change). A Catholic mission, boarding school, and orphanage were established here during the flu epidemic of 1918, to help Native children who'd lost their families. The Jesuits ran the orphanage until it closed in 1941. Pilgrim Hot Springs is now owned by the Roman Catholic Church's northern diocese, but the property has been leased for possible geothermal energy development. Before you explore the area or take a dip in the springs, contact caretaker Louie Green (907/443-5583) for permission.

The **NOME-COUNCIL HIGHWAY** follows the coast for about 30 miles before wandering inland toward Council, 72 miles northeast of Nome. **CAPE NOME,** about 13 miles out, has a sweeping view of the Bering Sea. About 34 miles out is the **GHOST TOWN OF SOLOMON.** Just before Solomon you'll see the old gold-rush train, "The Last Train to Nowhere." About 65 miles out, you'll see a rare sight for the Seward Peninsula—trees! Council is another former gold-rush town turned fishing camp with a summer population of 40.

The **ANVIL MOUNTAIN ROAD** is a 5-mile jaunt out of Nome that takes you to the top of Anvil Mountain and offers a view of Nome and the Bering Sea. Take Bering Street north to the Nome-Beltz Highway. Once you pass Icy View, Nome's one and only suburb, you'll see a right-hand turn. Take it. About 2 miles up, turn left and continue until you reach the top where four giant antennae stand. This used to be part of the U.S. Air Force DEW Line system, a first line of defense against anticipated Soviet attack during the Cold War days. And, it should go without saying but we'll say it: please respect private property on either side of the Anvil Mountain Road.

DOG MUSHING / Aaron Burmeister, an Iditarod veteran, can take you on a halfhour sled-dog ride or arrange lessons and longer rides through **FLAT DOG KENNELS**

THE IDITAROD TRAIL SLED DOG RACE

Often called the "Last Great Race," the Iditarod is Alaska's own version of March Madness. From its ceremonial start in Anchorage on the first Saturday in March, until the final sled-dog team has crossed the finish line in Nome some 2 to 2½ weeks later, the Iditarod is given center stage throughout Alaska.

The trail that gives its name to the race is an historic route that once connected the coastal community of Seward with the gold-rush town of Nome. Some portions of that route were used for centuries by Eskimos and Athabascan Indians; but without question, the Iditarod Trail's heyday was during the Alaska Territory's gold-rush era, from the 1880s through the 1920s. Primarily a winter pathway, the trail acted as a transportation and communication corridor that connected mining camps, trading posts, and other settlements that sprang up during the gold rush. One of those was a remote gold-boom town named Iditarod (derived from the Indian word *haiditarod*, meaning "a far, distant place"). Actually a network of trails, the entire system measured more than 2,200 miles, including side branches. Some people walked the trail; others traveled on horse-drawn sleds or even bicycles. But most people, by far, used sled dog teams.

By the mid-1960s, both the Iditarod Trail and the mushing culture so closely associated with it were in danger of disappearing. Enter Joe Redington Sr. and Dorothy Page. Together, the so-called Father and Mother of the Iditarod race helped to revive a sport and bring new attention to the trail. Redington and Page staged a two-day, 50-mile race

(PO Box 1103, Nome, AK 99762; 907/443-2958). In the summer, the sled dogs pull you on wheels rather than runners. If you happen to be in town during the Iditarod, there is also an amateur **BUSINESSMAN'S SLED DOG RACE,** where local mushers give newcomers a brief training session and send them out on a 3-mile race. Pay a $50 entry fee to the Nome Kennel Club to get in on the action. Contact the Nome Convention & Visitors Bureau, 907/443-6624.

GOLD PANNING / Pick up a pan at one of the local stores and hit the beach. Gold panning is allowed on a 2-mile stretch east of Nome, between town and the Fort Davis Roadhouse. Contact the Nome Convention & Visitors Bureau 907/443-6624 if you want to gold pan as part of a tour.

TOURS TO PROVIDENIYA, RUSSIA/ A Bering Air Piper Navajo was the first American aircraft to fly through the "Ice Curtain" between the United States and Russia in May 1988. Now, hundreds of flights later, **CIRCUMPOLAR EXPEDITIONS** offers a three-day, two-night whirlwind tour of Nome's sister city of Provideniya in the Russian Far East. It's advised that you check into the current political situation in the Chukotka region of Russia before you travel, and make your plans well in advance because of all the paperwork. You also will need a valid passport. Circumpolar Expeditions, which can also schedule fishing and kayak tours in the Chukotka region, will help make arrangements for required invitations and visas. The cost is

along the Iditarod Trail in 1967, to celebrate the centennial of America's purchase of Alaska from Russia. Enthusiasm for that event soon waned, but Redington began to promote a thousand-mile race from Anchorage to Nome. Critics called his proposed race an "impossible dream," but in 1973, Joe Sr. made the dream a reality. Thirty-four mushers signed up for the first-ever 1,049-mile Iditarod Trail Sled Dog Race. (Redington knew the race was at least 1,000 miles long and he intended the "49" to symbolize Alaska, the 49th state. In reality, the race course is more than 1,100 miles long.)

The winner of that first race to Nome was a little-known musher named Dick Wilmarth, of Red Devil, Alaska. His winning time: just over 20 days. Overall, 22 of the 34 mushers who began finished the race and the top finishers split $51,000 in prize money. The race has grown steadily—with a few rough episodes along the way—ever since. For well over a decade now, the Iditarod has earned national and international credibility and fame. Dozens of journalists from throughout the United States and overseas have reported from the trail and through the Iditarod's first three decades, and entrants have represented 16 foreign countries. The speed record has fallen under nine days and the purse has increased to more than $500,000. Along the way, the race has produced legends: five-time winner Rick Swenson; four-time champions Susan Butcher, Doug Swingley, and Martin Buser; and the first woman to win the race, Libby Riddles. Yet those most closely associated with the Iditarod agree the real heroes of this race across Alaska are the dogs that continue Alaska's mushing legacy.

—Bill Sherwonit

$1,149 per person. 907/272-9299; fax 907/278-6092; wallack@arctictravel.net; www.arctictravel.net.

NOME DISCOVERY TOURS / Former Broadway showman Richard Beneville gives a lively, well-informed tour of Nome and its environs, with an emphasis on the gold rush and Inupiat history of the region. Beneville caters to independent groups, and his presentation is peppered with his trademark expression, "Hello, Central!" once used by party-line telephone operators. PO Box 2024, Nome, AK 99762; phone-fax 907/443-2814; discover@nome.net.

GUIDES AND OUTFITTERS

NOME TOUR AND MARKETING / Wiley E. Scott's guided tours include a sled-dog demonstration at a kennel owned by Iditarod veteran Mike Weber; a visit to a reindeer corral; a trip to the Little Creek Mining camp; and opportunities to touch the Bering Sea and pan for gold. Front St, PO Box 430, Nome, AK 99762; 907/443-2651; fax 907/443-3887.

SUBARCTIC WILDERNESS TOURS / Lee and Regina Zimmerman run custom tours that range from birding trips to photo safaris, tundra hikes, backpacking trips, and flight-seeing. PO Box 427, Nome, AK 99762; 907/443-4895; fax 907/443-4895; www.subarctictours.com.

FESTIVALS AND EVENTS

IDITAROD TRAIL SLED DOG RACE / This world-famous race across Alaska begins in Anchorage the first Saturday of March and ends in Nome some 2 to 2½ weeks later, when the last sled-dog team passes beneath Front Street's famed burled arch. As the finish line for the race, Nome draws mushers, media, and fans from all over the world. Iditarod time is something to behold, with everything from Native dancing and drumming to golfing on the frozen Bering Sea. You'll also find a whole ream of sports going on, from the 3-mile Businessman's Sled Dog Race (see Adventures, above) to Iditabasketball tournaments, drawing teams from all over the state. The Iditarod Awards Banquet is usually held on the Sunday following the winner's arrival. Because of all this activity, March is the best time to visit Nome. Accommodations fill up quickly at Iditarod time, so book early. Once everything is full, a call goes out to the community for spare rooms; even floor space is for rent. *Iditarod Trail Committee, PO Box 870800, Wasilla, AK 99687; 907/376-5155; www. iditarod.com.*

BERING SEA ICE GOLF CLASSIC / Held mid-March at Iditarod time, this six-hole fund-raising tournament sponsored by the Bering Sea Lions Club is played on the frozen Bering Sea, with bright-orange golf balls and coffee cans sunk into the ice as holes. Golfers tee off outside the back door of one of the bars after the prerequisite number of drinks. (See Nome Convention & Visitors Bureau, under Access and Information, above.)

MIDNIGHT SUN FESTIVAL / Nome revels in the ancient tradition of celebrating the summer solstice, and with good reason. The longest day of the year here doesn't end in night. The sun never goes down. The Midnight Sun Festival is a hodgepodge of small-town parades, races, and events spread over a number of days, including a softball tournament and polar-bear swim. At high noon on the solstice, a half-dozen residents stage a mock robbery at the local Wells Fargo branch. Evening events include the **SOLSTICE FOLK FEST**, featuring local Celtic and bluegrass band Land Bridge Toll Booth. On the Sunday closest to solstice, the **NOME RIVER RAFT RACE** begins at Mile 13 of the Kougarok Road. Homemade rafts—basically anything that floats—race downriver. The victorious team claims the distinctive trophy, a fur-trimmed honey bucket, a polite term for a bucket sometimes used in the bush in lieu of a "loo." (See Nome Convention & Visitors Bureau, above, under Access and Information).

ANVIL MOUNTAIN RUN / Now more than a quarter-century old, this Fourth of July event begins at 8am in downtown Nome. Entrants run from city hall—not much higher than sea level—to the top of 1,134-foot Anvil Mountain and back, a distance of 17 kilometers or 12½ miles. *Leo Rasmussen at Music Mart, PO Box 2, Nome, AK 99762; 907/443-2798; leaknome@nook.net.*

THE GREAT BATHTUB RACE / The annual Labor Day spectacle, with bathtubs mounted on wheels rattling down Front Street, is a sight not to be missed. The rules state the tubs must be full of water and bubbles and that the "bather" must wield a bar of soap, a towel, and a bath mat while being propelled by teammates down the course. Tubs must have at least 10 gallons of water left at the finish line to win. Contact Leo Rasmussen, above.

RESTAURANTS

Fat Freddie's / ★

50 FRONT ST, NOME; 907/443-5899 The food here is solid family fare: cheeseburgers with lots of grease, sandwiches off the grill, homemade soup and chowder, and hearty meat-and-potato dinners that include New York steaks and prime rib. Broad windows offer a nice view of the Bering Sea. Fat Freddie's is a popular Nome hangout, and during Iditarod time many racers can be found here enjoying a hot meal after their 1,049-mile trek. *$–$$; AE, MC, V; local checks only; breakfast, lunch, dinner every day; full bar; no reservations; located next to the Nugget Inn on Front St, across from Nome City Hall.* &

Polar Cub / ★

234 FRONT ST, NOME; 907/443-5191 Here's another spot that's popular with locals, who like to linger while sharing coffee and conversation. The Polar Cub serves standard American diner food, from omelets to steaks to seafood. Views of the Bering Sea, good prices, and friendly service add to the restaurant's appeal. *$–$$; AE, MC, V; checks OK; breakfast, lunch, dinner every day; full bar; reservations recommended, especially during the Iditarod; on Front St in downtown Nome.*

LODGINGS

The Aurora Inn / ★★

302 E FRONT ST, NOME; 907/443-3838 OR 800/354-4606; FAX 907/443-6380 Nome's newest entry into the hotel business is also its most posh. The rooms are spacious and most have a sweeping view of the Bering Sea. Four types of rooms are available, from the basic double at $125 per night in the summer to $180 per night for an "executive suite" with a full kitchen. A sauna is available to chase away the chill. The inn's front desk is also a good place to rent pickup trucks or cars from Stampede Vehicle Rentals. *$$–$$$; AE, MC, V; local checks only; aurorainn@ gci.net; www.aurorainnnome.com; on E Front St, next to the National Guard Armory.* &

Chateau de Cape Nome / ★

1105 E 4TH AVE, NOME; 907/443-2083 This could be one of the biggest houses on the Seward Peninsula—a two-story, 4,400-square-foot home with a stretch limousine parked in the garage. Former Nome police chief-turned-wilderness-and-hunting guide Bob Kauer and his wife, Cussy, the city comptroller, run their B&B off and on throughout the year in a home full of gold-rush memorabilia and hunting trophies—that is, when they aren't too busy guiding bear hunters. You're most likely to find rooms available June through early September and mid-October through March. Breakfasts range from sausage and eggs to blueberry pancakes with hand-picked berries. Guests can also pet and feed the Kauers' pet reindeer, Mr. Moses. *$; No credit cards; checks OK; cussy@nome.net; 4 blocks from Front St at the east edge of town.*

Nome Nugget Inn / ★

FRONT ST AND BERING AVE, NOME; 907/443-2323 OR 888/443-2323; FAX 907/443-5966 The Nugget, in the heart of town, has both character and class. The famous burl arch for the finish line of the Iditarod stood for many years right outside. During the race, it's like Grand Central Station. The Gold Dust Lounge—with friendly bartenders, gold-rush character, and a view of the Bering Sea—is a pleasant place to trade stories and wild rumors of mushers and the trail. Plus, it's the only no-smoking saloon in town. The inn also features Dusty's Gold Mine, touted to be one of the world's finest collections of Arctic art. Room rates are $149 for a double. *$$; AE, DC, DIS, MC, V; no checks; annie@nugget-inn.com; www.nugget-inn.com; downtown at the intersection of Nome's two main streets.*

Bering Land Bridge National Preserve

This national preserve is one of the most remote and least-visited parklands in the country. Yet it is the remains of an ancient First People's highway. Today, Siberia is 55 miles across the Bering Sea. But during the Pleistocene Ice Age, much of the earth's water was locked in ice. The level of the seas fell, exposing a broad bridge of land—1,000 miles wide—between Asia and North America. Many anthropologists believe this is how the First Peoples came to Alaska thousands of years ago.

The Bering Land Bridge is a primitive landscape, with extensive **LAVA FLOWS, LOW SAND DUNES,** and **VOLCANIC CRATERS** that have since become lakes (called **"MAARS,"** they are the largest of their kind in the world). Yet for all its barren appearance, the preserve is home to some 250 species of flowering plants and is seasonally inhabited by more than 100 species of birds, which come here in spring from around the world. The area is also home to musk oxen, grizzly bears, moose, caribou, wolves, wolverines, and foxes. In winter, polar bears cruise the coastline and sometimes come ashore.

You can get to the preserve by boat or bush plane in the summer or by ski plane, snow machine, or dog team in the winter. Be forewarned it has **MINIMAL VISITOR FACILITIES** (four shelter cabins with woodstoves and bunks are intended primarily for emergency use) and no roads.

ADVENTURES

SERPENTINE HOT SPRINGS / A natural hot springs within the preserve is surrounded by an otherworldly landscape. The steaming hot springs are circled by granite spires, called "torrs." Once a place of power used by shamans for training in traditional medicines, the hot springs area has been used by Inupiat Eskimos for more than 5,000 years. There's a short airstrip, a World War II era bunkhouse that's been renovated and is available on a first-come, first-served basis, and a small bathhouse with a wooden pool. It's free and open to the public. In winter, access is by snow machine or dog team. The springs are about 40 miles beyond the end of the Taylor Highway and about 125 miles by snow machine or dog team north of Nome. *Bering Land Bridge National Preserve, PO Box 220, Nome, AK 99762; 907/443-2522; www.nps.gov/bela.*

SOUTHWEST ALASKA

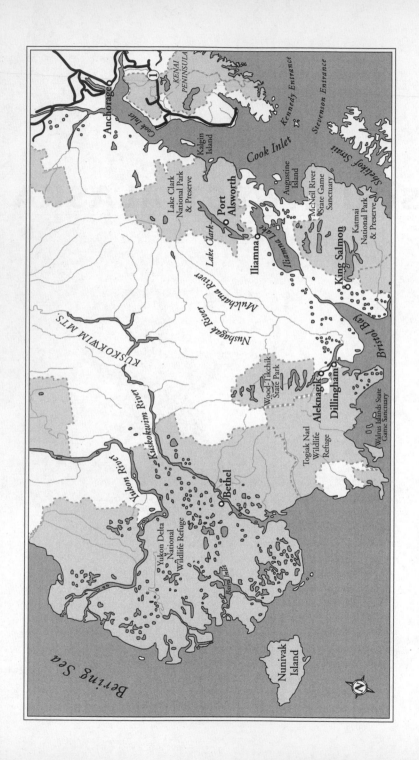

SOUTHWEST ALASKA

Southwest Alaska is best defined by its wildness and biological diversity. The region stretches from Lake Clark down to Bristol Bay, then up the coast to the Yukon-Kuskokwim Delta. It is North America's largest nesting and breeding area for migratory waterfowl. The world's densest population of brown bears and greatest salmon runs are also here. More than 60 communities dot the landscape, most of them **SMALL, REMOTE VILLAGES** whose Athabascan and Yup'ik residents continue to lead subsistence lifestyles heavily dependent on the region's abundant wildlife. Most villages have fewer than 200 people. There is only one paved "highway," 15½ miles long. Few other roads connect villages. Access is by air, boat, or snow machine in winter. Scheduled airlines serve only four of the region's towns: Iliamna, King Salmon, Dillingham, and Bethel; local air taxis fly to villages. Fishing is the main work. Bristol Bay, the world's largest sockeye salmon fishery, generates millions of dollars each summer.

This is an **ANGLER'S PARADISE**—salmon country and rainbow heaven. For the well-to-do, there are luxury fishing lodges (up to $6,000 or more per week). If you're not so flush, do what most Alaskans do—pack your gear and go camping. There's a wealth of areas from which to choose: two national parks, two national wildlife refuges, several Wild and Scenic Rivers, two state game sanctuaries, and the largest state park in the country. Not only do these water-rich habitats sustain incredible salmon migrations, but they also support two of the world's great gatherings of brown bears—at McNeil River State Game Sanctuary and at Brooks River and Falls in Katmai National Park and Preserve—with regional densities of up to 1.4 brown bears per square mile, greater than even Admiralty and Kodiak Islands. The Yukon Delta National Wildlife Refuge is seasonal home to one of the world's largest nesting populations of geese, ducks, and swans. And thousands of male walrus gather on islands and remote mainland beaches within Bristol Bay.

Though overshadowed by the region's wildlife and fisheries, several of Alaska's most fascinating landscapes occur here. There are two separate lake regions—Lake Iliamna and Lake Clark in the east and the lakes of Wood-Tikchik State Park farther west. Katmai National Park in the south includes 15 active volcanoes and the Valley of Ten Thousand Smokes, site of the largest volcanic eruption in Alaska's recorded history. To the extreme west on the edge of the Bering Sea lies the remote Yukon-Kuskokwim Delta. In summer, visitors can expect wet, cool weather with temperatures around 55 degrees, overcast skies, and occasionally fierce storms.

Iliamna

Iliamna is an Indian word meaning "big ice" or "big lake." With a surface area of more than 1,100 square miles, Iliamna Lake is Alaska's largest lake and gives its name to the town on its shores. About 100 people live here year-round. In summer, anglers from around the world come to fish for salmon, Dolly Varden, and especially rainbow trout. The Kvichak River, which flows out of Iliamna Lake, is famous for the largest rainbow trout in the world. The Iliamna-Lake Clark watershed is considered the most important spawning habitat for sockeye salmon in the world and is the major contributor to Bristol Bay's commercial sockeye fishery. Fishing and hunting lodges have operated in the Iliamna Lake region since the 1930s.

ACCESS AND INFORMATION

Located about 100 miles from King Salmon and 225 miles southwest of Anchorage, Iliamna is reached only **BY AIR.** Scheduled passenger service is provided year-round by Iliamna Air Taxi (907/571-1248 or 907/571-1245; fax 907/571-1649; iliamna airtaxi@starband.net) and in summer by Era Aviation (907/266-8394 or 800/866-8394; fax 907/266-8483; www.eraaviation.com). Iliamna Air Taxi also does charter flights throughout much of Southwest Alaska.

Iliamna is a short flight from both Lake Clark and Katmai National Parks. A gravel road connects Iliamna to the neighboring Native village of **NEWHALEN,** as well as the Newhalen River, a popular sportfishing stream. Individuals and Native corporations own much of the land surrounding Iliamna Lake. **ILIAMNA NATIVES LTD.** allows camping on its land, but charges a fee. For information, contact **ILIAMNA VILLAGE COUNCIL** (PO Box 245, Iliamna, AK 99606; 907/571-1246; fax 907/571-1256; ilivc@aol.com).

LODGINGS

Gram's Lodging and Dining / ★

¼ **MILE ROADHOUSE STRIP, ILIAMNA; 907/571-1463; FAX 907/571-1509** For those who cannot afford the thousands of dollars for a fishing lodge, here is a moderately priced option, for this remote part of the state. Built in the mid-1990s, Gram's has seven guest rooms, each with its own bathroom and satellite TV. The price ($300 for a double) includes lodging, plus all meals and transportation to and from the airport. Owner Myrtle Anelon (Gram) runs a cafe-style restaurant next door, with nightly dinner specials that range from steaks or pork chops to salmon or shrimp. *$$$$; MC, V; checks OK; www.gramscafe.com; 3 miles from the airport and ¼ mile from Lake Iliamna.*

WILDERNESS LODGES

Iliaska Lodge

PO BOX 228, ILIAMNA, AK 99606; PHONE-FAX 907/571-1221, MAY–SEPT; 907/337-9844, OCT–MAY Iliaska caters particularly to fly fishers. On the edge of Lake Iliamna, the lodge has private guest rooms for 12 people who come to fish from three to seven days. Guests are flown out daily with experienced guides to the best fishing for rainbows, salmon, grayling, and arctic char. Chief pilot, guide, and owner Ted Gerken has been flying for more than a quarter century and tying flies for over 41 years. Cost is from $2,500 per person for three days to $5,800 for a week. *$$$$; No credit cards; checks OK; open early June–late Sept; lodge@iliaska.com; www. iliaska.com; winter address: 6160 Farpoint Dr, Anchorage, AK 99507; on the edge of Lake Iliamna, 4 miles from the airport.*

Lake Clark National Park and Preserve

Located on the western side of Cook Inlet, this park and preserve is the quintessential Alaska parkland. Here, wilderness seems to stretch forever, rich with mountains, glaciers, wildlife, wildflowers, forests, tundra, lakes, rivers, and rugged coastal cliffs. There are two active volcanoes, including **MOUNT REDOUBT** (10,197 feet), visible from Anchorage, which last erupted in 1989. The Aleutian and Alaska Ranges join to form rugged peaks, still mostly unclimbed and unexplored. Several major rivers and lakes offer world-class sportfishing for rainbow trout and all five species of Pacific salmon. **LAKE CLARK,** a narrow, 42-mile-long body of water, is the sixth-largest lake in Alaska and the jewel for which the park was named. It is one of the state's least-known and least-appreciated national parks, in large part because access is only by air. There are no campgrounds, no maintained trails, and no visitor centers. But of wildness, there is plenty.

ACCESS AND INFORMATION
From Anchorage, Lake Clark Air (907/781-2211 or 800/662-7661; fax 907/781-2215; grasrjr@aol.com; www.lakeclarkair.com) provides daily commuter flights. Once in Port Alsworth, travel is by foot, boat, or air taxi to outlying areas. For **INFORMATION,** contact Superintendent, Lake Clark National Park and Preserve (4230 University Dr, Ste 311, Anchorage, AK 99508; 907/271-3751; fax 907/271-3707; www.nps.gov/lacl).

Field headquarters for the park is at **PORT ALSWORTH,** a small community (pop. 104) on Lake Clark's southeastern shore. Among the first settlers were bush pilot Leon "Babe" Alsworth and his wife, Mary, who homesteaded 160 acres, built an airstrip, and gave this tiny town its name. The park has no other public facilities, although rangers may be seasonally based at Twin, Telequana, and Crescent Lakes. Visitors exploring the backcountry should plan to be totally self-sufficient and understand how to behave around bears.

FLOAT the Tlikakila, Mulchatna, or Chilikadrotna Rivers (each of them officially designated a Wild and Scenic River). **FISH** for salmon, rainbow trout, or Dolly Varden. Beautiful lakes to explore by **KAYAK** are Lake Clark and Telequana, Turquoise, and Twin Lakes. **BACKPACK** from Turquoise to Twin Lakes.

Rimmed by rugged peaks and fed by glacial rivers and clearwater streams, **TUXEDNI BAY,** along the coast, is also quite beautiful. **LAKE ILIAMNA,** Alaska's largest lake and another area known for world-class sportfishing, is located just south of the park. Much of the **MULCHATNA** and **CHILIKADROTNA,** two popular fishing and floating rivers, lie outside park boundaries. They feed into the **NUSHAGAK RIVER,** also a popular river-trip destination.

GUIDES AND OUTFITTERS
ALASKA ADVENTURES (907/345-4597; www.ak-adventures.com) specializes in guided river floating and fishing trips. **NORTHWARD BOUND** (907/243-3007; fax 907/243-9559; harrower@alaska.net) primarily guides hunters but also outfits mountaineering, backpacking, and hiking trips. **OUZEL EXPEDITIONS** (907/783-2216; fax 907/783-3220; paul@ouzel.com; www.ouzel.com) provides fishing and

river trips. Park headquarters (see above) has a complete list of Lake Clark's guide and travel services.

WILDERNESS LODGES

Alaska's Wilderness Lodge

WILDERNESS POINT, PORT ALSWORTH, AK 99653; PHONE-FAX 800/835-8032 Nestled among the aspen and spruce on the shores of Lake Clark at Wilderness Point, this lodge run by Jay Sessler specializes in fly-out fishing adventures with guided trips into the park and surrounding areas. Guests stay in private cabins. Gourmet meals are served in the main lodge. No more than 12 guests at a time for weeklong visits. The cost is $5,950 per person for the week with fly-out fishing included. $$$$; MC, V; checks OK; open June–Sept; fishawl@att.net; www.alaskas wildernesslodge.com; winter address: PO Box 700, Sumner, WA 98390.

The Farm Lodge

BOX I, PORT ALSWORTH, AK 99653; 907/781-2281 OR 800/662-7661; FAX 907/781-2215 The Farm Lodge was built on Lake Clark's Hardenberg Bay by homesteaders Babe and Mary Alsworth in the 1940s and has been operated as a lodge since 1977 by their son Glen and his wife, Patty. The main lodge (also their home) originally resembled a big red barn, but now is cedar-sided. Home-cooked meals feature wild game, salmon, and vegetables from their garden. The Alsworths also provide flying services (through Lake Clark Air), guided fishing, backpacking drop-offs, and river trips. Full lodging with three meals a day is $85 per person; bed-and-breakfast rates are $65 per person. $; DIS, MC, V; checks OK; grasrjr@aol.com; www.lakeclarkair.com.

Koksetna Wilderness Lodge

GENERAL DELIVERY, PORT ALSWORTH, AK 99653; 800/391-8651, YEAR-ROUND; 907/781-2227, JUNE–AUG; 530/458-7446, SEPT–MAY Located on Chulitna Bay, on the shores of Lake Clark, guest accommodations include the main lodge, two cabins with woodstove for heat, two bathhouses, and a steam bath. Accessible by plane, the lodge is a family affair, hosted by Jonathan, Juliann, and Drew Cheney. During the six-day, five-night stay ($1,525 per person), activities range from fishing, bird-watching, and wildlife viewing to boating and hiking. Guests also may stay in the cabins and provide their own meals at a lower cost. $$$–$$$$; No credit cards; checks OK; open June–Aug; swingfishd@hotmail.com; come.to/koksetnawilderness lodge; winter address: 1425 5th St, Colusa, CA 95932.

McNeil River State Game Sanctuary

Created in 1967, McNeil River State Game Sanctuary, located 200 miles southwest of Anchorage, is intended to protect the world's largest gathering of brown bears. The main focus is McNeil Falls, where bears come to feed on chum salmon returning to spawn. During the peak of the chum run (July to Aug) dozens of brown bears congregate at the falls. More than 100 bears, including cubs, have been observed along the river in a single day. No more than 10 people a day, always accompanied

MCNEIL RIVER BEARS

Brown bears—the coastal equivalents of grizzlies—are solitary creatures by nature. For them to gather in large numbers and close quarters, as they do at McNeil Falls within McNeil River State Game Sanctuary, is exceptional. That they do so while viewed by humans is even more remarkable.

Larry Aumiller, the sanctuary manager since 1976, attributes this phenomenon to several factors: (1) the presence of salmon, an abundant and reliable energy-rich food source; (2) the lack of other good fishing nearby; (3) the presence of McNeil Falls, which acts as a barrier to the chum salmon, making them easy prey for the bears; and (4) the region's high bear density.

The final piece of the puzzle is people management. Visitors are told: "The bears come first at McNeil River. All human use is of secondary importance." That philosophy led to the sanctuary's highly successful permit system, limiting the number of people at the falls each day. Since the state enacted visitor restrictions in the early 1970s, the number of bears visiting the falls has increased dramatically. Even more significant: no bears have been killed in self-defense, and no humans have been injured by bears. This despite thousands of bear-human encounters, often at close range.

"It's widely assumed that bears and people don't mix," says Aumiller. "But here, we've shown that they can mix, if you do the right things. To me, that's the most important message of McNeil: humans can coexist with bears. The first day people come here, many are fearful because of things they've heard or read about bears. But after they've seen a few bears up close and the bears go about their business, people begin to relax. The transformation is almost universal." Instead of irrational fear, visitors learn tolerance and healthy respect. They also learn to understand what Aumiller means when he says, "McNeil is an example of what could be."

A summary of bear-safety tips is available in a free brochure, "Bear Facts." Pick one up at the Alaska Public Lands Information Centers in Anchorage, Fairbanks, Ketchikan, or Tok. Another excellent source is Stephen Herrero's book *Bear Attacks: Their Causes and Avoidance.*

—*Bill Sherwonit*

by one or two state biologists, are allowed to visit bear-viewing sites during the permit period, June 7 through August 25. Because demand is so high, there is an annual drawing to determine permit winners.

The bears begin to arrive at the sanctuary in late May or early June, along tidal mudflats, where they graze on sedges. From mid- to late June they also feast on sockeye salmon that spawn in Mikfik Creek, a neighboring stream of McNeil River, also within the sanctuary. June visitors make daily guided visits to Mikfik to watch the bears. Mikfik's salmon run ends in late June, and the action shifts to McNeil Falls, where humans are restricted to two gravel viewing pads. Located about a mile above the mouth of the river, the falls are actually a series of small waterfalls, pools, and white-water rapids. One of the great thrills is to watch these magnificent creatures close at hand. It's not uncommon for the most tolerant bears to eat salmon, take naps, or even nurse cubs within 10 to 20 feet of the falls' viewing pads.

ACCESS AND INFORMATION
Located near the northern end of the Alaska Peninsula, along Cook Inlet's western shore, McNeil is accessible by either boat or plane, but nearly all visitors fly into the sanctuary on **FLOATPLANES**. Most arrange for air-taxi flights out of Homer, a coastal community on the lower Kenai Peninsula. The most commonly used is Beluga Lake Floatplane (907/235-8256; fax 907/235-0541; berryman@xyz.net), but the **ALASKA DEPARTMENT OF FISH AND GAME** can provide a complete list. Once in the sanctuary, all travel is on foot. For information, contact Alaska Department of Fish and Game, Division of Wildlife Conservation (333 Raspberry Rd, Anchorage, AK 99518-1599; 907/267-2182; www.state.ak.us/adfg).

PERMIT APPLICATIONS are available from Fish and Game. They must be postmarked no later than March 1 and be accompanied by a $25 nonrefundable fee. The permit drawing occurs on March 15 of each year. Permits are for four-day periods. As many as three people may apply as a group. Visitors pay an additional user fee for the sanctuary—$150 for Alaskans and $350 for nonresidents.

All visitors stay in a designated tent-camping area that also has a wood-fired sauna. Food is stored and cooked in a cabin. Bring sturdy camping gear and be prepared for **WILDERNESS CONDITIONS**. Note that the hike to the falls is 4 miles round-trip and is strenuous. Visitors spend approximately six to eight hours viewing bears each day. **WEATHER** at McNeil River Sanctuary is often foggy or rainy, and coastal storms are common. Visitors should be prepared for travel delays when planning their trip.

King Salmon

King Salmon was a U.S. Air Force base during World War II and remained a major military installation until 1994, when the base closed down. Now, only a skeleton maintenance crew of nonmilitary people remains. But the community that grew up around the base continues to do just fine, thanks to the superior runway. People stop here en route to other villages or backcountry destinations in nearby parks and refuges.

Fewer than 450 people live here year-round (about 15 percent are Alaska Natives). Most are employed by government or transportation agencies, such as the Alaska Department of Fish and Game, U.S. Fish and Wildlife Service, National Park Service, National Weather Service, and Federal Aviation Administration.

The nature of the town changes dramatically in summer, when seasonal workers arrive to work in Bristol Bay's fishing or tourism industries. From June through September, thousands of tourists come here from around the world, bound for fishing, hunting, wildlife viewing, river floating, and backcountry trekking adventures in nearby wilderness areas.

ACCESS AND INFORMATION

Located along the Naknek River, about 20 miles from Bristol Bay and 290 miles from Anchorage, King Salmon has **AIR SERVICE** year-round with Peninsula Airways (907/243-2323 or 800/448-4226; fax 907/243-2026; www.penair.com). Alaska Airlines (800/252-7522; www.alaskaair.com) flies to King Salmon from late April through late October.

Once in King Salmon, it's possible to rent a car, catch a cab, or walk. Most everything in town is within walking distance. Several **AIR-TAXI** operators offer transportation to outlying villages, as well as nearby parks and refuges. **CHARTERS** can be arranged with Branch River Air Service (907/246-3437; fax 907/248-3837; bras@alaska.net; www.branchriverair.com), C-Air (phone-fax 907/246-6318; attt@bristolbay.com), Egli Air Haul (907/246-3554; fax 907/246-3654), and King's Flying Service (907/246-4414; fax 907/246-4416; kingair@bristolbay.com). For those going to **BROOKS CAMP** and **RIVER** in Katmai National Park (see below), Katmai Air Service (907/243-5448 or 800/544-0551; fax 907/243-0649; info@katmailand.com; www.katmailand.com) offers regularly scheduled summer flights. Located at the airport, the **KING SALMON VISITORS CENTER** (PO Box 298, King Salmon, AK 99613; 907/246-4250; fax 907/246-8550; angie_terrellwagner@fws.gov) is open daily in summer and Monday–Friday from October through May.

Make **RESERVATIONS** for airlines and hotels well in advance. King Salmon's three hotels are often filled in summer. The same is true for flights.

A paved road connects King Salmon with the village of **NAKNEK** (15 miles away), as well as Naknek Lake, which offers boat access into Katmai National Park and Preserve. Boats can be rented locally.

RESTAURANTS

Quinnat Landing Hotel / ★

ALONG THE NAKNEK RIVER, NEAR THE AIRPORT, KING SALMON; 907/246-3000 OR 800/770-FISH (3474), SUMMER; FAX 907/246-6200 With large windows looking out at the Naknek River, the restaurant offers the most formal and elegant dining experience in King Salmon. White tablecloths, wine lists, gourmet meals, daily specials—everything you'd expect in a big city. It's also seasonal, open only in summer. Fresh fish and other seafood are served daily, in both appetizers and entrees. $$–$$$; AE, DC, MC, V; checks OK; breakfast, lunch, dinner every day; closed Oct–May; full bar; no reservations; PO Box 418, King Salmon, AK 99613; quinnat@bristolbay.com; www.quinnat.com; a 10-min walk from the airport, along King Salmon's main street. &

WILDERNESS LODGES

Mike Cusack's King Salmon Lodge

MILE 1, NAKNEK RIVER RD, KING SALMON, AK 99613; 907/246-3452 OR 800/437-2464, SUMMER; FAX 907/563-7929 Located on a grassy bluff that overlooks the Naknek River, this has evolved into one of the region's premier fishing lodges. Gourmet meals include fresh salmon, Alaska king crab, filet mignon, duck, pheasant, or quail, plus a selection of premium wines. The dining room has views of both the Naknek River and Mount Katmai. Guests may choose to participate in guided fishing trips. Anglers are flown out to world-class fishing streams and lakes anywhere within a 200-mile radius. The lodge offers five-night and seven-night packages for $4,750 and $6,500, respectively, per person. *$$$$; AE, MC, V; checks OK; open mid-June–Sept; info@kingsalmonlodge.com; www.kingsalmonlodge. com; winter address: 3601 C St, Ste 1350, Anchorage, AK 99503; along the Naknek River, a short distance from the airport. &*

Katmai National Park and Preserve

Declared a national monument in 1918 to preserve the "living laboratory" of a violently explosive 1912 volcanic eruption, Katmai—upgraded to national park status in 1980—is perhaps now best known for its abundance of brown bears. The park's premier attractions are the **VALLEY OF TEN THOUSAND SMOKES** and **BROOKS FALLS,** where up to two dozen bears may be observed fishing for sockeye salmon. The salmon start arriving in early July, bound for spawning grounds in Brooks Lake. As they near the end of their journey, they face one final obstacle: 6-foot-high Brooks Falls. Following the salmon to the falls are brown bears, the coastal equivalents of grizzlies. As many as 60 brown bears inhabit the Brooks River drainage in July, although only rarely do more than a dozen fish the falls at any one time.

The bears, in turn, attract humans. Hundreds of people come daily from mid-June through mid-September to Brooks Falls and nearby **BROOKS CAMP,** which is a park field station, campground, and wilderness lodge. They come to see bears and to fish. The Valley of Ten Thousand Smokes, however, makes an interesting side trip; it was formed by the giant volcanic eruption of Novarupta and subsequent collapse of Mount Katmai in 1912.

Despite the monument's volcanic wonders, Katmai received little attention until the 1940s, when entrepreneur and early bush pilot Ray Petersen established five remote sportfishing camps. The largest was Brooks, which remains the focal point of Katmai tourism. Largely overshadowed by Brooks' bears is the rest of Katmai National Park and Preserve, which includes hundreds of miles of rugged, pristine coastline, 15 active volcanoes belonging to the Pacific Ring of Fire, two officially designated Wild and Scenic Rivers—the Nonvianuk and Alagnak—and a series of large, connected lakes that form a kayak and canoe route called the **SAVONOSKI LOOP.**

ACCESS AND INFORMATION

Located at the northern end of the Alaska Peninsula, Katmai National Park and Preserve is 300 miles southwest of Anchorage. Most visitors fly into the park through **KING SALMON** (see charters under Access and Information, King Salmon).

Prime-time bear viewing is in July and September. For more **INFORMATION** about the bears or other park attractions and facilities, contact Katmai National Park and Preserve (PO Box 7, King Salmon, AK 99613; 907/246-3305; fax 907/246-2116; www.nps.gov/katm). There's a campground, visitors center, and ranger station at Brooks Camp, as well as viewing platforms to watch the bears at Brooks Falls and the lower Brooks River. The remainder of the park, however, is undeveloped (with the exception of a few privately owned lodges). Camping is by **PERMIT** only, within 5 miles of Brooks Camp. Sites at the Brooks campground must be reserved in advance (800/365-2267). Wilderness travelers may camp anywhere in the park but are asked to pick up a backcountry permit at the King Salmon headquarters, located a short walk from the airport. Clean camping is particularly important in bear country.

With the notable exception of Brooks Camp and a 23-mile gravel road to an overlook of the Valley of Ten Thousand Smokes, Katmai is wilderness with no public facilities. Visitors going beyond Brooks must be self-sufficient and prepared for wilderness travel. A brochure, "Traveling the Katmai Backcountry," is available from park headquarters. The Katmai region has one of the world's highest densities of brown bears, and visitors should understand the dos and don'ts of bear encounters.

At Katmai, the main activity is, of course, watching bears. You can also attend **NATURALIST PROGRAMS,** staged nightly at Brooks Camp; fish for salmon and rainbow trout; **BACKPACK** through the Valley of Ten Thousand Smokes; or explore remote, seldom-visited mountains and valleys. **DUMPLING MOUNTAIN** (2,440 feet) makes a good day hike and is accessible from Brooks Camp. Possibilities on the water include **CANOEING OR KAYAKING** the Savonoski Loop, floating the Non-vianuk and Alagnak Rivers, or kayaking along Katmai's remote outer coast.

GUIDES AND OUTFITTERS

GUIDED HIKING and/or **RIVER-RUNNING TRIPS** are offered by **ALASKA RIVER ADVENTURES** (907/595-2000 or 888/836-9027; fax 907/595-1533; info@alaska riveradventures.com; www.alaskariveradventures.com) and **ALYESKA WILDER-NESS GUIDES** (phone-fax 907/345-4470; awg@alaska.com; www.akwild.com), while **OUZEL EXPEDITIONS** (907/783-2216; fax 907/783-3220; paul@ouzel.com; www.ouzel.com) does river floating and fishing trips. For wildlife viewing and photography trips, contact **KATMAILAND** (907/243-5448 or 800/544-0551; fax 907/243-0649; info@katmailand.com; www.katmailand.com) and **TRAVELWILD EXPEDITIONS** (206/463-5362 or 800/368-0077; fax 206/463-5484; www.travel wild.com). **LIFETIME ADVENTURES** (907/746-4644; fax 907/746-4648; info@Life timeAdventures.net; www.LifetimeAdventures.net) offers biking, bear viewing, kayaking, and climbing packages.

Three dozen companies and lodges offer **GUIDED FISHING SERVICES,** including **ALASKA TROPHY ADVENTURES** (907/246-8280; aktrophy@aol.com; www.alaska trophyadventures.com), **FOX BAY LODGE** (phone-fax 907/246-6234, summer or 800/555-7444, year-round; fax 541/878-0990, winter; fox_bay@hotmail.com; www.foxbaylodge.com), and **MORRISON GUIDE SERVICE** (907/246-3066; morrison@bristolbay.com). A complete list of guide services and air-taxi operators is available from Katmai park headquarters.

WILDERNESS LODGES

Katmailand

4125 AIRCRAFT DR, ANCHORAGE, AK 99502; 907/243-5448 OR 800/544-0551; FAX 907/243-0649 Katmailand operates three fly-in lodges within Katmai National Park, billed as "Anglers Paradise Lodges." Brooks Lodge was built in the 1940s as a fishing camp, though today most of its guests come to see the brown bears that fish for salmon at nearby Brooks Falls. The lodge looks out over Naknek Lake, with 16 small cabins around it that sleep four guests each. Visitors fish for salmon or rainbow trout, watch and photograph bears, or take the day trip to the Valley of Ten Thousand Smokes. The lodge operates from June to September. Prices vary depending on the number of people staying in a cabin; the per-person rates range from $673 for a one-day tour to $1,103 for three days, including airfare from Anchorage. Kulik Lodge, on the Kulik River, offers premier fishing for rainbows and salmon. The spruce-log lodge has a large stone fireplace and bar. Multiday packages include transportation from Anchorage and range from $2,025 and $4,100 per person. Grosvenor Lodge, on the stream that connects Colville and Grosvenor Lakes, is another sportfishing lodge. There is room for only six people in three guest cabins with shared bathhouse. Prices range from $1,900 to $3,075 per person, depending on the length of stay. *$$$$; No credit cards; checks OK; open June–mid-Sept for Brooks Lodge, June–early Oct for the others; info@katmailand.com; www.bearviewing.net or www.katmailand.com.*

Katmai Wilderness Lodge

PO BOX 4332, KODIAK, AK 99615; 907/486-8767 OR 800/488-8767; FAX 907/486-6798 On property owned by the Russian Orthodox Church, this lodge is located on Kukak Bay along Katmai's remote outer coast. Brown bear viewing is the main attraction; other activities include sea kayaking and fishing for halibut or salmon. Up to 12 guests stay in the lodge's six log cabins. The three-night "wilderness package" costs $2,000 per person, including round trip from Kodiak, lodging, meals, guided bear viewing, and fishing. *$$$$; MC, V; checks OK; open May 15–Sept; katbears@ptialaska.net; www.katmai-wilderness.com.*

Dillingham

Commercial fishing has been the heartbeat of this town for more than a century. Bristol Bay's first cannery was built in 1884 at the site of present-day Dillingham, and several more were constructed over the next 17 years. Dillingham's population more than doubles in summer with the arrival of Bristol Bay's world-famous salmon runs. The harbor holds more than 500 boats, and the city-run dock handles more than 10,000 tons of fish and freight annually. Traditionally a Native village, Dillingham's year-round population (2,470) includes a mixture of Eskimos, Aleuts, Athabascans, and non-Natives. About 55 percent of the population is Native. Residents live subsistence lifestyles that include hunting, fishing, trapping, and berry picking. The largest community in the Bristol Bay region, Dillingham has eight churches, a hospital, a health clinic, a public library, a community college, a lumberyard, several hotels and bed-and-breakfasts, five restaurants, a handful of taxi companies, nearly a dozen air-taxi operators, and some 200 businesses. The region's climate is maritime, and the weather is often foggy, windy, and wet.

ACCESS AND INFORMATION

Alaska Airlines (800/252-7522; www.alaskaair.com) and Peninsula Airways (907/243-2323 or 800/448-4226; fax 907/243-2026; www.penair.com) have regularly scheduled flights from Anchorage, which take about an hour. Several local **AIR-TAXI OPERATORS** offer access to the region's parks, refuges, and villages. Among them are Bay Air (907/842-2570; fax 907/842-2470; bayair@nushtel.com), which specializes in big-game hunting and transport, Tucker Aviation (907/842-1023; fax 907/842-2600), Mulchatna Air (907/842-4500 or 907/842-5677; fax 907/842-3677; mulchat@nushtel.com), Shannon's Air Taxi (907/842-2735; fax 907/842-2545), and Tikchik Airventures (907/842-5841; fax 907/842-3211; grant@nushtel.com).

For **INFORMATION,** contact Dillingham Chamber of Commerce (PO Box 348, Dillingham, AK 99576; 907/842-5115; fax 907/842-4097; www.dillingham chamberofcommerce.com).

EXPLORING

Dillingham is a jumping-off point for many backcountry destinations, including Wood-Tikchik State Park, Togiak National Wildlife Refuge, Round Island, several streams popular with river runners, and numerous fishing lodges. A 22-mile gravel road connects Dillingham with **LAKE ALEKNAGIK,** the lowermost lake in the Wood River chain. Located in the library building, the **SAMUEL K. FOX MUSEUM** (907/842-5115) features contemporary and traditional Native arts, crafts, and artifacts, and occasionally hosts traveling exhibits (limited hours).

Wood-Tikchik State Park

Despite its inland setting, this is a water-based park dominated by the Wood River and the spectacular Tikchik Lakes. Snowcapped mountains, low tundra, and interconnected clearwater lakes, some 45 miles long, characterize the region. Everything from grizzlies and moose to porcupines, river otters, and loons inhabits the park's forests and tundra, but best known are the fish. Lakes and streams here provide critical spawning habitat for the five species of Pacific salmon. They also support healthy populations of rainbow and lake trout, arctic char, grayling, and pike. This has long been known as a fisherman's paradise. Today it is becoming increasingly popular with water adventurers, such as kayakers and rafters, who travel its interconnected river and lake systems.

ACCESS AND INFORMATION

Located in the Bristol Bay region, 325 miles southwest of Anchorage, Wood-Tikchik is easiest to reach **BY PLANE** through Dillingham. Among those flying into the park are Bay Air (907/842-2570; fax 907/842-2470; bayair@nushtel.com), Tikchik Airventures (907/842-5841; fax 907/842-3211; grant@nushtel.com), and Freshwater Adventures (907/842-5060; fax 907/842-4231; freshh2o@citlink.net; www.fresh-h2o.com). Contact the park for a complete list of air-taxi services (see contact information below). Once in the park, the easiest way to get around is by boat via the Wood River and Tikchik Lakes systems.

Managed as a wild area, Wood-Tikchik has no maintained trails and only a few very primitive campsites. For general **INFORMATION**, contact Wood-Tikchik State Park (summer: PO Box 3022, Dillingham, AK 99576; 907/842-2375; Oct–May: 550 W 7th Ave, Ste 1380, Anchorage, AK 99501; 907/269-8698; www.dnr.state. ak.us/parks/index).

ADVENTURES

You can **FLOAT** either the Wood River or Tikchik Lakes systems and **FISH** for rainbow trout and salmon. The park's most popular fly-in float trip is the 90-mile journey from Lake Kulik to Aleknagik, a Yup'ik Eskimo village north of Dillingham. Though it can be done in less than a week, paddlers are advised to give themselves at least 10 to 14 days. The other popular trip begins at Nishlik Lake and ends at Tikchik Lake, a distance of about 60 miles. Those who float the Nuyakuk River below Tikchik Lake should use extreme caution; portages are necessary to get past the Nuyakuk Rapids and Nuyakuk Falls.

GUIDES AND OUTFITTERS that operate within Wood-Tikchik include Alaska River Adventures (see Guides and Outfitters, Katmai National Park and Preserve, above), which does guided river and fishing trips; and Tikchik State Park Tours (907/243-8450; fax 907/248-3091; info@tikchik.com; www.tikchiklodge.com), which rents kayaks and rafts and flies people into the park's northern and more remote Tikchik Lakes system.

WILDERNESS LODGES

Royal Coachman Lodge

SUMMER: PO BOX 450, DILLINGHAM, AK 99576; 907/868-6033; FAX 907/868-6032 YEAR-ROUND: 1062 W RIDGE RD, CORNVILLE, ME 04976; 207/474-8691; FAX 207/474-3231 A floatplane-accessible fishing lodge in the heart of the nation's largest state park, Gary Merrill's Royal Coachman Lodge lies at the outlet of Tikchik Lake, on the Nuyakuk River. Guests stay in comfortable cottages. Experienced fishing guides take guests to streams and lakes throughout the Wood-Tikchik State Park and Togiak National Wildlife Refuge, but there's also excellent fishing right at the lodge. No more than 12 guests at a time are hosted for a week's stay. Cost is $6,000 per person per week, which includes transportation from Dillingham, lodging, meals, and guide services. Gary and Heather Merrill also operate Lower Nushagak King Salmon Camp and Kanektok Wilderness Camp, one of only two fishing camps in the Togiak Refuge wilderness. *$$$$; AE, MC, V; checks OK; open June–Sept; gmerrill@somtel.com; www.Royalcoachmanlodge.com.*

Tikchik Narrows Lodge

PO BOX 220248, ANCHORAGE, AK 99522; 907/243-8450; FAX 907/248-3091 Located on a narrow peninsula between Nuyakuk and Tikchik Lakes, Bud Hodson's lodge has a view of the ruggedly beautiful Kilbuck Mountains. More than 50 miles from the nearest road and accessible only by floatplane, it sits deep within Wood-Tikchik State Park. Guests stay in modern cabins. The main lodge has a stone fireplace and a panoramic view of the surrounding park. Meals include freshly baked breads and pastries, and entrees ranging from Alaska king crab to filet mignon. Guests fish the waters of this parkland, as well as neighboring Togiak National Wildlife Refuge. The weeklong stay includes daily guided fishing trips and costs $5,950 per person. *$$$$; No credit cards; checks OK; open mid-June–Sept; info@ tikchik.com; www.tikchiklodge.com.*

Walrus Islands State Game Sanctuary

Each year, in spring and summer, thousands of male walrus gather on this group of seven islands in Bristol Bay. The females and young travel north to spend their summers in the Bering and Chukchi Seas. Scientists still aren't sure exactly why males stay behind. However, what is clear is that the walrus bulls use these islands as resting places in between food binges. Because of their importance to these creatures, the seven Walrus Islands and adjacent waters were given special protected status in 1960. The centerpiece of the sanctuary is **ROUND ISLAND**, a small (2 miles long by 1 mile wide) and rugged piece of ground where thousands of walrus congregate in spring as the pack ice begins its annual retreat. For the next seven months, these huge fellows (some weigh up to 2 tons) spend their time alternately gorging on invertebrates such as clams and snails, and then hauling out on the rocks and resting up for the next binge.

ACCESS AND INFORMATION

Round Island is located about 30 miles from the mainland. Most visitors get there by **CHARTERING A BOAT** ride from the village of Togiak with Terry Johnson's Walrus Island Expeditions (phone-fax 907/235-9349; walrus@ptialaska.com; www.alaskawalrusisland.com). Several **AIRLINES** and **AIR-TAXI OPERATORS** fly between Dillingham and Togiak, including Peninsula Airways (907/243-2323 or 800/448-4226; fax 907/243-2026; www.penair.com), Mulchatna Air (907/842-4500 or 907/842-5677; fax 907/842-3677; mulchat@nushtel.com), and Tucker Aviation (907/842-1023; fax 907/842-2600). The boat ride takes one to three hours from Togiak, depending on the seas.

Once at Round Island, visitors are met by sanctuary staff, who assist in transferring people and gear to shore. Travel on the island is entirely by foot. Round Island has by far the largest gathering of walrus of all the islands. The best time to visit is June through August. Only 12 people at a time are allowed to camp on Round Island. Permits for a five-day block of time are issued on a first-come, first-served basis. **APPLICATIONS** must be sent to the Alaska Department of Fish and Game, Division of Wildlife Conservation (PO Box 1030, Dillingham, AK 99576-1030; 907/842-2334; fax 907/842-5514; www.state.ak.us/adfg), accompanied by a $50 fee.

Round Island is a rugged, often stormy place, and anyone who goes there should be in good physical condition, prepared for **WILDERNESS CONDITIONS**. Visitors should also anticipate weather delays when making travel plans. Visitors are required to bring their own camping gear. Tents should be expedition quality, capable of withstanding 60mph winds. Two wildlife technicians are stationed on the island to conduct research and enforce sanctuary regulations, but they are not tour guides. Visitors should be prepared to fend for themselves. Visitors are expected to stay on the island's trail system and within designated viewing areas. Beaches are off-limits to minimize disturbances to resting walrus.

Bethel

This is not the picture-book part of Alaska with green forests and snowcapped mountains, nor is it part of the popular tourist circuit. The Yukon-Kuskokwim Delta is flat and almost treeless. But the longer you are there, the more extraordinary you'll find its beauty.

This is the home of the most traditional Native population in Alaska—the Yup'ik Eskimos. From Platinum to Kotlik, from Stony River to Tuntutuliak, from Grayling to Emmonak, they live in 46 villages scattered over 76,000 square miles. It is a vast, wet expanse of land with twisted, convoluted rivers and streams, myriad lakes, and soggy tundra. For anyone outside the culture, the names of many of the villages are often unpronounceable—words such as Chuathbaluk, Kwigiumpain-ukamiut, and Mamterillermiut. The last is the original Eskimo name for the town we know today as Bethel.

Bethel (pop. 5,500) is the hub of the region—a ramshackle assortment of buildings on the western bank of the Kuskokwim River. Next to the Yukon River, the Kuskokwim is the second-longest river in Alaska. This is bird country, and subsistence fishing is a way of life. In 1885, the Moravian Church sent missionaries to the area to establish a church and school here. They took the name Bethel from the Holy Scriptures. In Hebrew, it means "House of God." But, once here, the missionaries ignored the advice of the local shaman about where to site their mission. He warned them that the riverbank would fall away underneath their home and the water would sweep it downstream. The missionaries thought this was only superstition. But, rather, it was the forces of nature—weather, wind, and water—correctly interpreted. Consequently, over the past 100 years, Bethel residents have been dragging their homes away from the banks of the river on a consistent basis, and the town has moved farther and farther inland.

Until about 1984, the most modern attempt at controlling this erosion was to take junked cars and push them over the bank to make a type of bulwark. It, too, ultimately failed. But the sight of 1959 Ramblers and Willys jeeps tilted on the bank at 50-degree angles, as if some phantom were about to drive them into the river, made an unforgettable picture. The present seawall, constructed by the Army Corps of Engineers, is sturdier, but Bethel lost some of its charm with the departure of the junkers.

The river defines the way of life here. Most Native folks spend time at fish camps along its banks in the summer, go duck hunting on the delta in spring, pick berries in the fall, and take their skiffs upriver to hunt moose for the winter. People here still wear traditional clothing, such as caribou- and squirrel-skin parkas with wolf or wolverine ruffs, as well as caribou- and seal-skin boots called mukluks.

ACCESS AND INFORMATION

Regularly scheduled daily **FLIGHTS** are available, winter and summer, to Bethel on Alaska Airlines (800/252-7522; www.alaskaair.com), while Peninsula Airways (907/243-2323 or 800/448-4226; fax 907/243-2026; www.penair.com) flies from Anchorage into the Kuskokwim River village of Aniak.

Information on Bethel can be obtained by contacting the **CITY OFFICE** (PO Box 388, Bethel, AK 99559; 907/543-2047; fax 907/543-4171; www.ci.bethel.ak.us). The **YUPIIT PICIIYARAIT CULTURAL CENTER** (907/543-1819; joan_hamilton@ avcp.org; www.avcp.org) opened in 1995 and showcases artifacts and artwork of three Native cultures: Athabascan, Cup'ik, and Yup'ik. Its three galleries spotlight historic and prehistoric treasures, from masks and statues to carvings in ivory, baleen, and whalebone. The center is well worth a visit and is open afternoons Tuesday through Saturday. The gift shop has many local arts and crafts of the region.

GUIDES AND OUTFITTERS

LAMONT ALBERTSON / A warm-hearted, no-nonsense, burly fellow, and former mayor of Aniak, Lamont Albertson is the best sportfishing guide in the Aniak-Bethel-Kuskokwim region. He has fished, lived, raised his family, and taught school in this part of Alaska for more than 30 years. His guided fishing trips have a natu-ralist/educational bent to them with strong emphasis on catch-and-release. He also does bird-watching and other naturalist activities. Albertson's tent camp, 45 miles up the beautiful little Aniak River, is reached by jet boat from the village of Aniak. All five species of Pacific salmon and the northernmost population of naturally occurring rainbow trout in the world swim here, as well as Dolly Varden, arctic char, and grayling. Bears, moose, and caribou wander close to camp—sometimes right through. Lamont's wife, Sheryll, does the cooking and you'll eat like a king— salmon, king crab, wild game, and a vast array of local blueberry dishes. Fishing is good mid-June to September. Cost is $250 to $500 per person per day. *PO Box 91, Aniak, AK 99557; 907/675-4380, Apr–Sept; 352/498-0225, Oct–Mar; trout@ arctic.net or trout@svic.net.*

FESTIVALS AND EVENTS

THE KUSKOKWIM 300 / Held every year at the end of January, this is one of the most popular sled-dog races in Alaska and a qualifier for the Iditarod Trail Sled Dog Race. It starts in Bethel, runs a course up the Kuskokwim River, turns around in Aniak, and dashes back. With a purse of $100,000, it is the second-richest long-distance dog race in the world, next to the Iditarod. For more information, contact head-quarters near race time (907/543-3300; www.k300.org).

CAMA-I DANCE FESTIVAL / Held the first weekend of April, this is a regional festival of special importance that celebrates the renewal of spring and preserves the Yup'ik tradition of dancing. In the Yup'ik language, *cama-i* means "hello." Despite the efforts of missionaries to suppress this traditional form of expression, it never disappeared in Southwest Alaska. In the past 15 years, it has seen resurgence, with many villages sponsoring youth dance groups led by village elders who teach the songs, drumming, and movements. The festival also includes arts and crafts shows, quilting exhibits, and dinners, and takes place in Bethel High School, which is filled to capacity during the three days and nights of dancing. Each village gets a half-hour to perform; two or three groups from outside Alaska join local groups. These are not actors pretending to demonstrate a culture; this is the real thing. Contact the Bethel Council of the Arts for more information (907/543-2321; fax 907/543-1507; www.bethelarts.com.)

LODGINGS

Bentley's Porter House Bed and Breakfast / ★

624 IST AVE, BETHEL; 907/543-3552; FAX 907/543-3230 Bentley's overlooks the Kuskokwim River and is a block from downtown. From the second floor, you can see the famous Bethel seawall, the river, and the start of the Kuskokwim 300, if you're there in the right season. A big, friendly, two-story inn with 25 rooms, encompassing the main house and three smaller homes, Bentley's serves family-style breakfasts, with good food and plenty of it. The inn's downstairs once housed a newspaper operation, but has since been remodeled. Choose rooms upstairs in the main house for the best views and light. Room rates range from $103 for a single to $138 for the plushest double. *$$; AE, DIS, MC, V; checks OK; PO Box 529, Bethel, AK 99559; downtown, on the river.*

Pacifica Guesthouse / ★

1220 HOFFMAN HWY, BETHEL; 907/543-4305 This hotel is a mile or two out of town, on the way in from the airport. There's a simple, northern European feel to it. There are 30 rooms, half of them with private bath. If you really want to be luxurious (by bush standards), stay in one of their 10 suites ($150 for a double). Each has a private bath and sitting room with furnishings that years ago graced the Lake Tahoe Hilton. A single room with shared bath is $95 and a double room with shared bath is $110. The hotel also has a conference room for meetings and its owner runs a restaurant next door, Diane's Café (no alcohol). Housed in a solarium setting, Diane's serves gourmet meals that range from Alaska salmon and halibut to steaks and vegetarian dishes. *$$; AE, DIS, MC, V; checks OK; PO Box 1208, Bethel, AK 99559; dianes@alaska.com; 1½ miles from the airport, toward downtown.* &

Yukon Delta National Wildlife Refuge

Each spring, millions of birds return to the Yukon-Kuskokwim Delta, where they nest and raise their young on the wetlands. Birds come from all over North America as well as from continents that border the Pacific Ocean. Most notable are brant, geese, ducks, and swans. This is the nation's largest refuge. Most of it is tundra, interwoven with countless ponds, lakes, sloughs, marshes, and meandering streams, including Alaska's two longest waterways: the **YUKON AND KUSKOKWIM RIVERS**. One-third of the refuge's acreage is water. Not surprisingly, given the abundance of fish, birds, and other wildlife, the delta has been home to Yup'ik Eskimo people for thousands of years.

ACCESS AND INFORMATION

The only companies with permits to operate **AIR TAXIS** in the refuge are Yukon Aviation (907/543-3280; fax 907/543-3244; yukonaviation@alaska.com) and

Ptarmigan Air (907/543-5225 or 888/868-8008), both based in Bethel. Also offering transportation from Bethel to outlying villages are Craig Air (907/543-2575; fax 907/543-3602) and Hageland Aviation (907/543-3800; fax 907/543-4156).

There are **NO VISITOR FACILITIES** within the refuge itself. For further **INFORMATION,** contact Yukon Delta National Wildlife Refuge (PO Box 346, Bethel, AK 99559-0346; 907/543-3151; fax 907/543-4413; www.r7.fws.gov).

The prime time to visit the delta is **MID-MAY TO LATE JUNE,** when the weather is best and breeding season is at its peak. Fishing and river floating are best from June to September. Outfits that provide guided hunting, birding, or wildlife viewing/photography **TRIPS ON REFUGE LANDS AND WATERS** are Nunivak Island Experiences (907/827-8512) and Spud's Transporting (907/827-8065).

Some of the Yukon Delta's villages are starting up **CULTURAL TOURS** that may eventually include trips into the refuge. Contact the refuge for more information. **MOSQUITOES AND BITING INSECTS** can sometimes be intolerable, especially in lowland areas, during midsummer.

Besides the Yukon and Kuskokwim, other rivers popular with boaters, anglers, and wildlife watchers are the **KISARALIK RIVER,** a Kuskokwim tributary, and the **ANDREAFSKY RIVER,** a Yukon tributary. Nunivak Island offers opportunities to see musk oxen, reindeer, marine mammals, and birds.

ALASKA PENINSULA AND ALEUTIAN ISLANDS

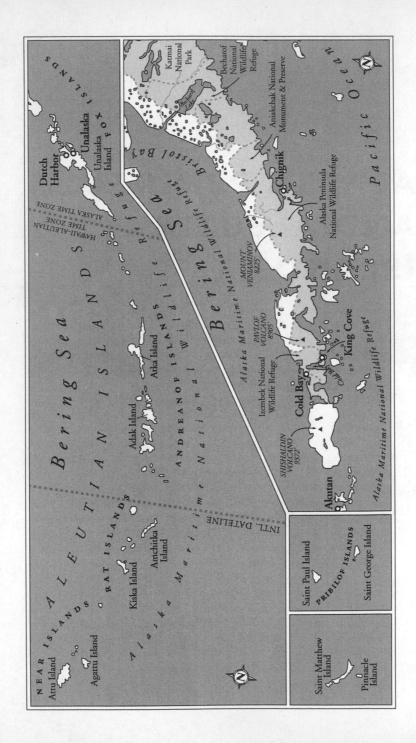

NEAR ISLANDS

Attu Island

Agattu Island

Bering Sea

ALEUTIAN ISLANDS

RAT ISLANDS

Kiska Island

Amchitka Island

Alaska Maritime National

INTL. DATELINE

Adak Island

ANDREANOF ISLANDS

Atka Island

Alaska Maritime National Wildlife Refuge

Range

HAWAII-ALEUTIAN TIME ZONE

ALASKA TIME ZONE

FOX

Unalaska Island

Unalaska

Dutch Harbor

ISLANDS

Bering Sea

Bristol Bay

SHISHALDIN VOLCANO 9372'

Izembek National Wildlife Refuge

PAVLOF VOLCANO 8905'

MOUNT VENIAMINOF 8225'

Cold Bay

King Cove

Akutan

Katmai National Park

Becharof Lake

Becharof National Wildlife Refuge

Aniakchak National Monument & Preserve

Chignik

Alaska Peninsula National Wildlife Refuge

Pacific Ocean

Alaska Maritime National Wildlife Refuge

Saint Paul Island

PRIBILOF ISLANDS

Saint George Island

Saint Matthew Island

Pinnacle Island

ALASKA PENINSULA
AND ALEUTIAN ISLANDS

Sweeping away from Alaska's mainland, the Alaska Peninsula and Aleutian Island Chain stretch more than 1,500 miles toward Siberia, separating the North Pacific Ocean from the Bering Sea. Mere dots in the vast waters of the Bering Sea are the Pribilof Islands, a tiny volcanic archipelago whose geologic origins are tied to the peninsula and the Aleutian Chain. All are part of the Pacific basin's Ring of Fire.

The region encompasses some of Alaska's most remote, inaccessible, and **RUGGED COUNTRY**. Volcanoes, earthquakes, wind, and oceans carve the landscape. From a seismic and volcanic perspective, this is one of the most turbulent regions in the world. More than 70 volcanoes have been identified, many of them active. Among the most active are Akutan, with 27 eruptions; Shishaldin, which has erupted 28 times; and Pavlof, with 41 eruptions within the past 225 years. Pavlof is on the lower Alaska Peninsula, while the other two are in the Aleutians. The most recent mountain to erupt was Chuginadak Island's Cleveland Volcano, in February and March 2001. The Aleutian and Pribilof Islands are actually the tops of large, submerged mountains. Among the most spectacular volcanic landforms in the region are the Aniakchak Caldera, Ukinrek Maars (craters), the Aghileen Pinnacles, Pavlof Volcano, and Mounts Veniaminov and Peulik.

This is the traditional home of the **ALEUT PEOPLE,** distant cousins of the Eskimos. Many still supplement their income with subsistence lifestyles, dependent on the harvest of wild game, berries, fish, and other foods from the sea. There are few roads (all of them local and isolated, and none more than 50 miles long) and no paved highways. Of the region's two dozen villages, 15 have fewer than 200 year-round residents. The largest community, Unalaska/Dutch Harbor, has a population of 4,280 people.

Biologically, the waters of the North Pacific, the Bering Sea, and Bristol Bay are among the richest on earth. They support a billion-dollar fishing industry, though a growing number of scientists, conservationists, and Native people fear overfishing is taking its toll on the region's sea life. A few coastal villages boom dramatically in summer, as fishermen and cannery workers from Outside arrive for the lucrative salmon and bottomfish harvests. King Cove's population more than doubles during the fishing season. Egegik, on the shores of Bristol Bay, jumps from 120 residents in winter to more than 1,000 in summer. Until recently, when downsizing caused the closure of bases, the other main employer since World War II had been the military. (The Aleutians were the site of one of the bloodiest battles in the Pacific.)

WILDLIFE ABOUNDS in this region in spectacular numbers, all dependent on the ocean's bounty. Forty million seabirds are seasonal residents. The coastal cousin of the grizzly—the brown bear—grows to enormous proportions on a high-protein diet of salmon, which spawn in vast numbers in the peninsula's clear lakes and streams. The sea coast boasts an abundance of marine mammals—sea lions, seals, otters, whales, and porpoises—yet there are distressing signs that even the rich North

Pacific–Bering Sea ecosystem is under stress. Three once-plentiful species—sea lions, sea otters, and harbor seals—have experienced dramatic declines in recent decades.

ACCESS AND INFORMATION

The principal means of travel is **BY AIR**. Peninsula Airways (907/243-2323 or 800/448-4226; fax 907/243-2026; www.penair.com) provides regularly scheduled passenger service to Chignik, Cold Bay, Sand Point, Adak, and the Pribilof Islands. Costs range from about $700 to $1,200 round-trip, depending on the destination. Both Peninsula Airways and Alaska Airlines (800/252-7522; www.alaskaair.com) fly into Dutch Harbor and Pen Air also flies to other peninsula and island communities out of Dutch Harbor and Cold Bay.

The **STATE FERRY** MV *Tustumena,* known as "The Trusty Tusty," provides service between Homer and the Aleutians from April through October. The trip takes two to four days one-way, depending on your destination, so a flexible schedule is a must. Ferry stops include Chignik, Sand Point, King Cove, Cold Bay, False Pass, Dutch Harbor, and Akutan. Contact the Alaska Marine Highway System (800/642-0066; www.alaska.gov/ferry) for information and reservations.

Anyone traveling to this region must be prepared for **WEATHER DELAYS,** sometimes lasting several days. Weather often can be violent and stormy. **BROWN BEARS** are abundant throughout much of the Alaska Peninsula; take precautions to avoid unwanted encounters. Boil or filter water before drinking to prevent giardiasis, an intestinal disorder caused by a waterborne parasite. Parks and refuges within this region generally have **NO VISITOR FACILITIES**. If you plan to explore the backcountry, come well prepared for wilderness camping and travel.

Unalaska/Dutch Harbor

The history of this far-flung community mirrors Alaska's history. More than 8,000 years ago, the ancestors of the Aleuts arrived in this new land. Much, much later, in the 18th century, Russian fur hunters discovered a rich treasure chest here in the soft, black, velvety fur of the playful sea otter. By the turn of the 20th century, whales and gold had lured waves of fortune hunters and ships to sail north along this coast.

For a long time, the village of Unalaska on Unalaska Island, with its charming onion-domed church, was the main town on the Aleutian Chain. During the goldrush era, Unalaska and her little neighbor, Dutch Harbor, swelled with thousands of hopeful gold seekers on their way north. Some called her "the bawdy queen of the Alaska Gold Coast." As the gold began to taper off, though, Unalaska was left almost a ghost town. Business boomed again during World War II, when it became a strategic naval base. After the war, it again sat deserted. Not so today. Beginning with the rich and dangerous king crab industry, which took off in the 1960s, the pendulum of history has swung back. Only today, fortunes are mined from beneath the sea.

The big money is in fish and crab. The city of Unalaska and the International Port of Dutch Harbor (Unalaska/Dutch Harbor) are the number-one fishing port in the United States, measured in both pounds of fish processed and total dollar value delivered. Unalaska is a working town with an international flavor. On any given day,

HALIBUT, "THE OLD WOMAN OF THE SEA"

Unalaska is one of the best-kept secrets of big-game fishermen. The icy Bering Sea off the town's shore is home to some of the largest halibut in the world, measuring more than 8 feet in length and tipping the scales at 400-plus pounds. These monsters are so big fishermen call them "barn doors," because that's what it feels like when you're pulling one off the bottom of the ocean.

Halibut from Unalaska made headlines in the summer of 1995 when fishermen landed three whoppers, ranging from 347 to 439 pounds. The next summer, a world record was set with a 459-pounder hauled out of Unalaska Bay.

Fishermen out here say it's only a matter of time until someone sets another world record. The visitors bureau is even banking on it. They put up a $100,000 prize in the local halibut derby, held annually from June through September, to lure some lucky fisherman on to glory. All you have to do is top the record halibut of 459 pounds as well as have a derby ticket in your pocket. It's tricky, though. Rules of the International Game Fish Association demand that the fish be gaffed, not shot, before landing. Trying to wrestle a 400-pound fish into your boat is more than challenging. The 1996 derby winner, fishing from a small skiff, solved that problem by towing his 459-pound catch to shore rather than swamping his boat.

If you're fishing for dinner, the tastiest halibut are actually in the 20- to 60-pound class. Because the largest and oldest fish are the females and thus produce generations more halibut (that's why Native fishermen respectfully called the halibut "the old woman of the sea"), charter owners often will encourage you to release those that aren't derby-winning size. But Unalaska fishermen have dreams that go beyond the derby. They all swear that somewhere out there is "The Ultimate Halibut," a fish that will break the 500-pound mark. Perhaps, she's waiting for you.

—*Carol M. Sturgulewski*

Russian, Japanese, and Korean vessels are waiting in the harbor to pick up fish products and cargo to freight back home.

For many visitors, the area's military aspect is perhaps the most interesting. There's a partially sunken war ship left over from World War II in one of the bays. Old trails zigzag up the sides of the mountains, leading to former defense garrisons. (The zigzagging was to avoid strafing by Japanese warplanes.)

Wind, water, fog, and ferocious gales characterize the area's weather. Clear blue skies on average happen perhaps 10 days out of the year. During the war, American forces in the Aleutians lost two men to weather and frostbite to every one killed by enemy gunfire! As the soldiers stationed out here used to say, "It doesn't rain in the Aleutians. It rains in Asia and blows over."

The town is divided into two sections by a bridge known locally as "The Bridge to the Other Side." The Unalaska side, on massive Unalaska Island, is home to the original village site, most homes, businesses, and city offices. The Dutch Harbor side, on neighboring Amaknak Island, is the site of the state airport and most industry. Mariners long ago incorrectly christened the whole community Dutch Harbor, after the place they dropped anchor, and that's what airline schedules and many Outsiders call it, but locals know the city officially as Unalaska. The Chamber of Commerce compromises by calling it "Unalaska/Dutch Harbor"—so, take your pick!

ACCESS AND INFORMATION

For information on fishing excursions, birding, sight-seeing tours, historical tours, flight-seeing, hotels, restaurants, and special events, visit the **UNALASKA/DUTCH HARBOR CONVENTION & VISITORS BUREAU** (907/581-2612 or 877/581-2612; fax 907/581-2613; updhcvb@arctic.net; www.unalaska.info). See also the Access and Information section at the beginning of this chapter.

EXPLORING

CHURCH OF THE HOLY ASCENSION / A National Historic Landmark, this Russian Orthodox cathedral has been a symbol of Unalaska and part of its distinctive charm since its construction in 1895. The first church here was built under the sharp eye of Father Veniaminov in 1826. Later canonized as Saint Innocent, he was a singularly impressive fellow who mastered the baidarka (an early form of kayak) so that he could paddle a thousand miles through the Aleutians to tend his flock. A recently completed church restoration has brought new luster to the largest collection of Russian Orthodox artifacts in Alaska, including some that date back to Veniaminov's time. Work still continues on restoring church icons and the neighboring Bishop's House. Tours of the church are available through the local convention and visitors bureau. *907/581-2612 or 877/581-2612; fax 907/581-2613; updhcvb@ arctic.net; www.unalaska.info; on Broadway Ave, in the heart of downtown Unalaska.*

MUSEUM OF THE ALEUTIANS / Opened in 1999, this museum is the first ever to exclusively feature the Aleutian and Pribilof Islands. Many collections that have been scattered at museums around the world are gradually being brought home. Exhibits begin with Aleut prehistory dating back 9,000 years and follow the Russian occupation, gold rush, World War II, and the fisheries of the past century. The museum also sponsors summer **ARCHAEOLOGICAL DIGS**, which you can join for an hour, a week, or a month. No experience is necessary. If you'd rather work indoors, the museum also welcomes volunteers to work with the laboratory and collections. *907/581-5150; fax 907/581-6682; aleutians@arctic.net; www.aleutians.org; at Salmon Way near the Grand Aleutian Hotel.*

REMNANTS OF WORLD WAR II / Bunkers, pillboxes, tunnels, the remains of old Quonset huts, zigzag trails all over the hills, and a sunken ship in the harbor are visible reminders of the military presence here and the fierce battle for the Aleutians. Hike up **BUNKER HILL**, visit **MEMORIAL PARK**, walk along **UNALASKA LAKE**, and note where modern Unalaska has converted military leftovers into homes and businesses. There's even a pillbox next to the school playground. An **ALEUTIAN WORLD**

WAR II NATIONAL HISTORIC AREA (visitor center, 907/581-9944; www.nps. gov/aleu/) has been established north of the airport to preserve and celebrate the area's military legacy.

ADVENTURES

HIKING THE MOUNTAINS / On Unalaska Island there are no bears, no trees to block your view, and sea breezes tend to blow away bugs. The island does have, however, a lot of bald eagles and red foxes and a profusion of wildflowers, birds, and berries. Salmonberries are ripe in August, followed by blueberries, which can be picked as late as November some years. MOUNT MAKUSHIN (6,680 feet), a steaming volcano, is the highest mountain on the island. Some of the popular hikes close to town are PYRAMID PEAK (2,136 feet), rising to the south, and MOUNT BAL-LYHOO (1,589 feet), on the Dutch Harbor side. They say the famous writer Jack London named this mountain on his way to the Nome gold fields around the turn of the 20th century. Every July there's a rigorous scramble up to its summit called the BALLYHOO RUN.

The Native people privately own most of the land on the island. In order to hike, ski, bike, or camp on the land, you must first obtain a PERMIT from the Ounalashka Corporation (907/581-1276; fax 907/581-1496; www.ounalashka.com) on Salmon Way, near the Grand Aleutian Hotel. Topo MAPS (as well as an espresso bar) are located at NICKY'S PLACE (907/581-1570; fax 907/581-2837; abi@arctic.net) on the Front Beach Road. Nicky's also features works by local artists, a surprisingly large and talented pool for such a small community. Open every day, with the exception of "especially sunny days," Nicky's also will open after hours "for coffee emergencies and for those who work late or fish hard."

FISHING / The ILIULIUK RIVER, which runs out of Unalaska Lake into Iliuliuk Harbor, teems with salmon in the summer. As it flows past the cathedral's onion-shaped domes, it is in full view of bald eagles sitting atop the spires, watching their dinner passing by on the fin. The really big fish here, though, are HALIBUT. Unalaska is home to the International Game Fish Association's world-champion halibut, weighing in at 459 pounds. Local charter operations make an art of going after the big ones. Fishing licenses may be purchased at local grocery or fish supply stores.

GUIDES AND OUTFITTERS

Bobbie Lekanof's EXTRA MILE TOURS (phone-fax 907/581-6171; xmitours@ arctic.net) gives customized tours that range from bird-watching to hiking, visits to World War II sites, and Aleut cultural history. Patricia Lekanof-Gregory's ALEUT TOURS (phone-fax 907/581-6001; akaleut@arctic.net) offers a two-hour tour with an emphasis on Aleut and Russian history. DAN PARRETT PHOTOGRAPHY (907/581-5175; parrett@arctic.net) and Scott Darsney's MOUNTAIN WORLD IMAGES (907/581-1312; fax 907/581-5408; scott@mountain-world.com; www. mountain-world.com) both assist camera bugs in Aleutian photo safaris, and Darsney's also does some mountain guiding. ALEUTIAN ADVENTURE SPORTS (907/581-4489 or 888/581-4489; advsports@arctic.net; www.aleutianadventure. com) provides guided backpacking and sea kayaking trips around Unalaska and neighboring islands. VOLCANO BAY ADVENTURES (907/581-3414; volcano@ arctic.net; www.volcano-bay.com) offers guided salmon and trout fishing, halibut

THE PRIBILOFS, "ISLANDS OF THE SEALS"

Five tiny volcanic islands in the Bering Sea make up the Pribilof Archipelago. The two largest, 40 miles apart, are inhabited—**ST. PAUL** (pop. 530) and **ST. GEORGE** (pop. 150). Most residents are Aleut. In the late 1700s, Russians forcibly moved several hundred Aleut people here to harvest northern fur seals. When the United States purchased Alaska in 1867, relatively little changed out here except the flag. The Aleuts were considered wards of the state. It was only on October 28, 1983, on the long coattails of the civil rights movement, that the Aleuts gained total autonomy, and that is the day they celebrate. Though their lives have revolved around the fur seal harvest for nearly 200 years, residents are now dependent on two other industries: tourism and commercial fishing. The fur seal harvest today is for subsistence only.

Located 300 miles from mainland Alaska and nearly 800 miles from Anchorage, St. Paul and St. George are as remote as you can get, but their treasure chest of wildlife is rich indeed. Part of the **ALASKA MARITIME NATIONAL WILDLIFE REFUGE** (907/235-6546; alaskamaritime@fws.gov; www.r7.fws.gov/nwr/akmnwr/), the islands annually attract hundreds of visitors, who come mainly to watch seals and birds. Nearly all visitors travel here by air on Peninsula Airways (see Access and Information at beginning of this chapter.) St. Paul is home to the largest northern fur seal colony in the world; more than 800,000 seals gather here annually. St. George has a smaller seal population than St. Paul, but nearly a quarter of a million fur seals still arrive on its shores every summer.

The seals spend their winters at sea, and begin arriving in the Pribilofs in May. Large male "beachmasters," weighing about 600 pounds, show up first, quickly establishing

charters, and bird-watching. **FAR WEST OUTFITTERS** (907/581-1647; fwo@arctic. net) specializes in marine tours, fishing charters, and sight-seeing. Other local fishing charters include **SHUREGOOD ADVENTURE CHARTERS** (phone-fax 907/581-2378 or 877/FSH-4FUN (877/374-4386); shurgood@arctic.net) and **DAN MAGONE'S** 32-foot commercial fishing boat *Lucille* (phone-fax 907/581-5949; lucille@arctic. net; www.unalaskahalibutfishing.com).

RESTAURANTS

The Chart Room / ★★★

498 SALMON WY, DUTCH HARBOR; 907/581-3844 OR 800/891-1194 Located in the Grand Aleutian Hotel (see Lodgings) with windows overlooking Margaret Bay, the Chart Room is quite posh and no more expensive than a nice restaurant in Anchorage, but you'll rarely see anyone in a tie or high heels. Get a happy start to your evening with a drink by the fireplace in the Cape Cheerful Lounge. It's no big surprise that from this island's vantage point, facing out to the

their territories and building their harems (sometimes up to 100 females). Pregnant females don't arrive until June. They usually give birth to a single pup within 48 hours, and then mate again within a week, while still nursing their newborn.

Though they've been nicknamed "Islands of the Seals," the Pribilofs could just as easily be called "Islands of the Birds." This remote archipelago is widely recognized as a birder's paradise, with more than 200 species identified. Some birds migrate from as far away as Argentina, while others are year-round residents. Of special note to birders are the rare Asian "vagrants" such as the Siberian rubythroat and Eurasian skylark, rarely seen elsewhere in North America. Blown to the Pribilofs by strong western winds, the "fall-out" of Asian species most commonly occurs from mid-May to mid-June, the prime-time period for birding trips. Seals can be seen from May through August and the wildflower bloom peaks from late June through mid-July.

The majority of Pribilof visitors go to St. Paul on a package or guided tour and stay at the **KING EIDER HOTEL** (contact Tanadgusix—TDX—Native Corporation, 907/278-2312 or 877/424-5637; www.alaskabirding.com), but it's possible to explore the islands on your own, if you plan well in advance. St. George is much less frequently visited, because no package tours go there; and while it has a hotel (St. George Tanaq Hotel, 907/272-9886), there is no restaurant. There is a kitchen available for use and one store. No camping is allowed anywhere on St. Paul or St. George Islands.

One final note: The Pribilofs are known for their wet, cool, foggy, and windy weather, so visitors should bring high-quality foul-weather clothing and be prepared for weather delays, both coming and going.

—Bill Sherwonit

ocean with the Bering Sea in its backyard, halibut, salmon, shrimp, squid, and other fish and shellfish are star players in the Chart Room's North Pacific Rim cuisine. The wine selection is quite good and reasonably priced. Locals crowd in for the lavish Sunday brunch and Wednesday evening seafood buffet. *$$–$$$; AE, DC, DIS, MC, V; local checks only; dinner every day, brunch Sun; full bar; no reservations; in the Grand Aleutian Hotel on the Dutch Harbor side.* &

Tino's Steakhouse

11 N 2ND ST, DUTCH HARBOR; 907/581-4288 Tino's is an example of the Unalaska melting pot. Its menu includes American steaks, seafood dishes, and hamburgers, but for locals the big draw is the Mexican side of the menu. Nachos, burritos, tostadas, and chile specialties cover the plates, in hefty servings designed for hard-working, hungry fishermen. *$$–$$$; AE, MC, V; local checks only; breakfast, lunch, dinner every day; beer and wine; no reservations; tinos@arctic.net; downtown at the corner of 2nd St and Broadway.*

LODGINGS

Carl's Bayview Inn / ★

606 BAYVIEW, UNALASKA; 907/581-1230 OR 800/581-1230; FAX 907/581-1880
On the Unalaska side of town, a stone's throw from the Russian Orthodox church, this is a roomy and comfortable inn with homey touches and a well-connected host. Carl Moses is a 10-term state legislator in the Alaska House of Representatives, with a district that covers Bristol Bay through the Aleutian Islands. With a view over Iliuliuk Bay (when it's not too foggy), the inn is next door to Carl's general store, where you can buy anything from a fishing boat to a thimble. The inn has about 30 rooms. Prices vary, from a single room with shower for $90, to the best suite in the house for $175. For a couple, add $20. The inn also has a live band, playing country and rock 'n' roll, five nights a week in its lounge with a full bar. And right next door is Tony's Italian Restaurant, which boasts the best pizza in town. *$$–$$$; AE, DIS, MC, V; checks OK; bayview@arctic.net; in downtown Unalaska, near the Russian Orthodox church.* ♿ *(one room only)*

The Grand Aleutian / ★★★

498 SALMON WY, DUTCH HARBOR; 907/581-3844 OR 800/891-1194; FAX 907/581-7150 Some call it "The Grand Illusion"—a fancy hotel seemingly at the end of the world and in another time zone. But it is fancy without pretension and certainly the most comfortable place in Unalaska. From its opening in 1994, it quickly became the hangout for all the local movers and shakers. Here's where you'll find the big muckety-mucks in the fish business. It's also perfect for tourists who want familiarity. Live music and dancing are found most nights in the bar during peak fishing season. All rooms have a view of Margaret Bay, Unalaska Bay, or Mount Ballyhoo. The standard room rate for two is $175; double-room suites cost $245 for two. The hotel's tour operation—Grand Aleutian Tours—offers a selection of excursions, such as charter fishing, birding, nature hikes, island tours, marine tours, and mountain biking. It also offers a special package for those wishing to work on the Museum of the Aleutians archaeological dig during the day and relax over gourmet meals at night. *$$$; AE, DC, DIS, MC, V; local checks only; www.grandaleutian.com; 5 minutes from the airport on Airport Beach Rd at Margaret Bay on the Dutch Harbor side.* ♿

Aniakchak National Monument
and Preserve

This is one of the nation's wildest and least-visited parklands. On the Alaska Peninsula, 450 miles southwest of Anchorage, its principal feature and attraction is the **ANIAKCHAK CALDERA.** Six miles across, the caldera (crater) was created thousands of years ago by the collapse of a large volcano, following an eruption geologists say was much larger than the one at Mount St. Helens in 1980. Still active, Aniakchak last erupted in 1931.

When first viewed from a plane, the caldera looks like a moonscape, bleak and desolate. But, surprisingly, with a closer view, one finds a myriad of life—bushes, wildflowers, mammals, and birds. Sockeye salmon swim up the Aniakchak River into the caldera through a break in the crater wall called "The Gates." They then spawn in the blue-green waters of Surprise Lake.

Even in midsummer, weather in the Aniakchak Caldera may become violent. The caldera creates its own microclimate, and its interior is subject to severe windstorms and heavy rains. Campers have had their tents ripped apart by 100mph gales, and high winds can stir up volcanic ash clouds to an elevation of 6,000 feet.

ACCESS AND INFORMATION

If you visit the caldera, you're likely to have it all to yourself. Fewer than 100 people visit it annually (not including flight-seers). Because of its remote location and fly-in access, Aniakchak is expensive to reach. Park staffers discourage solo travel. All visitors are advised to file a trip plan with the National Park Service at **PARK HEAD-QUARTERS** (PO Box 7, King Salmon, AK 99613; 907/246-3305; www.nps.gov/ania). For **GENERAL INFORMATION** on the park, you also can contact the Alaska Public Lands Information Center (907/271-2737; www.nps.gov/aplic) in Anchorage.

AIR TAXIS serving the monument include Branch River Air Service (907/246-3437; fax 907/248-3837; bras@alaska.net; www.branchriverair.com), Egli Air Haul (907/246-3554; fax 907/246-3654), King's Flying Service (907/246-4414; fax 907/246-4416; kingair@bristolbay.com), and Katmai Air, c/o Katmailand (907/243-5448 or 800/544-0551; fax 907/243-0649; info@katmailand.com; www.katmailand.com). Ouzel Expeditions (907/783-2216 or 800/825-8196; fax 907/783-3220; paul@ouzel.com; www.ouzel.com) in Girdwood offers wilderness float trips down the Aniakchak River as well as other guided trips in Alaska.

The best things to do are to explore the caldera; **HIKE ACROSS CINDER PLAINS; CLIMB VENT MOUNTAIN** (3,350 feet), a splatter cone formed 1,500 years ago; or **FLOAT THE ANIAKCHAK RIVER,** which flows out of Surprise Lake within the caldera and offers Class II to Class IV white water as it rushes past sharp volcanic boulders in its upper 13 miles. Officially designated a Wild and Scenic River, the Aniakchak offers easier floating and excellent salmon fishing in its lower 14 miles, before emptying into the Pacific Ocean. Floatplane pickups can be made along the coast.

Alaska Peninsula and Becharof National Wildlife Refuges

These two refuges stretch along the Alaska Peninsula and encompass towering volcanic mountains, broad valleys, rugged coastal fjords, rolling tundra, and glacially formed lakes. Fourteen major volcanoes are located here, including nine that have erupted in historic times. **MOUNT VENIAMINOV** last erupted in 1995. The refuges are best known for sportfishing and trophy hunting. **BECHAROF LAKE,** 35 miles long, is Alaska's second-largest lake (next to Lake Iliamna) and is the nursery for one of the world's largest runs of salmon. **MOUNT PEULIK, UKINREK MAARS,** and **GAS ROCKS** offer a glimpse into the region's volcanism. **UGASHIK LAKES** are famous for salmon and trophy grayling (the world-record grayling, nearly 5 pounds, was caught at Ugashik Narrows in 1981). The coastline offers rugged scenery and abundant wildlife, although it's often stormy or shrouded in fog. The land is dense with brown bears, and caribou migrate through here annually.

ACCESS AND INFORMATION

Most visitors fly in from King Salmon, located about 10 air miles from Becharof's northern corner. (See air taxis, under Access and Information for Aniakchak National Monument and Preserve).

Two of the top wilderness lodges for hunting and fishing in the refuges are **BLUE MOUNTAIN LODGE** (907/688-2419; fax 907/688-0491; bluemtn@alaska.net; www.bluemountainlodge.com), in the Ugashik Lakes region, and **PAINTER CREEK LODGE** (907/344-5181; fax 907/344-6172; www.paintercreeklodge.com), which is exceptional for sportfishing—rainbows, salmon, arctic char, Dolly Varden, and grayling.

For **GENERAL INFORMATION** on the refuge, contact the Alaska Public Lands Information, (907/271-2737; www.nps.gov/aplic) in Anchorage. For **IN-DEPTH INFORMATION,** contact the Refuge Manager, Alaska Peninsula and Becharof National Wildlife Refuges (PO Box 277, King Salmon, AK 99613; 907/246-3339; www.r7.fws.gov). Be advised you often will get a recording in summer, though.

Izembek National Wildlife Refuge

An international crossroads for migrating waterfowl and shorebirds, Izembek is Alaska's smallest national wildlife refuge. It's also one of the oldest. Visitors normally fly into the town of **COLD BAY** on regularly scheduled flights with Peninsula Airways (907/243-2323 or 800/448-4226; fax 907/243-2026; www.penair.com) then arrange transportation into the refuge. Fall is the most spectacular season in the refuge for wildlife viewing.

The heart of the refuge is **IZEMBEK LAGOON,** 30 miles long, which contains one of the world's largest eelgrass beds. Hundreds of thousands of waterfowl converge on the lagoon each fall, including the entire world population of black brant, which feed on Izembek's eelgrass before heading south to warmer climates. Brown bears fish salmon-rich streams. Caribou feed on tundra plants. Among the year-round residents are **TUNDRA SWANS,** the only nonmigratory wild population of this species in the world.

Two of the most prominent features of the land are **FROSTY PEAK** (6,000 feet), accessible from the Cold Bay road system, and **AGHILEEN PINNACLES,** a series of volcanic spires (up to 4,800 feet)—an extreme mountaineering challenge.

Make sure you bring rain gear as it rains frequently in the summer. Contact **IZEMBEK NATIONAL WILDLIFE REFUGE** (PO Box 127, Cold Bay, AK 99571; 907/532-2445; www.r7.fws.gov) for more information.

YUKON TERRITORY

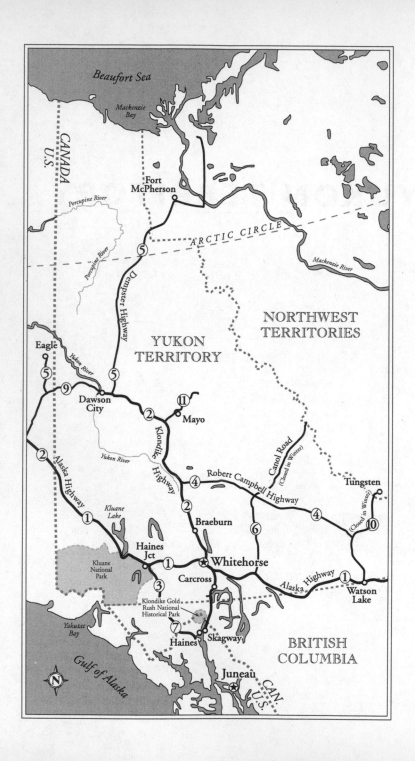

YUKON TERRITORY

A vein of gold has linked Alaska and the Yukon Territory for over a century, following the Klondike Gold Rush of 1898. Before the gold rush, both the Canadian and United States governments considered the North nothing more than a useless wasteland.

It was not, of course. Indigenous peoples lived off a land rich in wildlife and beauty for centuries. Their skills and willingness to share them were instrumental in aiding those who ventured into the territory much later. Natives in the Yukon, now called First Nations people, are divided into eight major groups: the Gwich'in, who live in Old Crow, north of Dawson City on the Porcupine River; the Han, from Dawson to Eagle; the Northern and Southern Tutchone, widely spread from Burwash Landing, across Whitehorse and up to Pelly Crossing; the Kaska, in the surrounding region of Watson Lake; the Upper Tanana, of Beaver Creek near the Alaska border; and the Tlingit, in the Carcross and Teslin area to Skagway, Alaska (and throughout the Southeast).

The Gwich'in called the Yukon River *Yu-kun-ah,* meaning "great river." And it is. All 1,920 miles of it. Swelled by glacier-fed lakes and streams of the White Pass above Skagway, the Yukon River snakes through lakes to Whitehorse, north to Dawson City, across Alaska, and empties into the Bering Sea. The Yukon is the longest river in Alaska, and the third largest in the United States. For the people who live on its banks, it is their highway—by water in the warm months, on ice in the winter.

At first it was whales in the Alaska Arctic and furs in northwest Canada that drew the white man up here, but the dull yellow metal lured so many more fortune seekers that both countries finally recognized the region's valuable resources.

In August 1896, George Carmack, a Californian hooked on gold rushes, and his two Tagish Indian brothers-in-law, Dawson Charlie and Skookum (meaning strong) Jim, were panning for color on Rabbit Creek, off the Klondike River a few miles upstream from Dawson City. In exposed bedrock, they found gold that was "thick between the flaky slabs, like cheese sandwiches," Carmack later said. Each of their original claims would produce more than a million dollars. Appropriately, they renamed the creek Bonanza Creek.

A year later in July, the steamships *Excelsior* and *Portland* chugged into San Francisco and Seattle carrying enough gold aboard to ignite the world's imagination and jump start the Klondike Gold Rush. The *Portland* held more than a ton of gold, and 5,000 people crowded, open mouthed, on the dock to watch miners drag battered suitcases and satchels full of the stuff down the gangway.

Gold fever swept round the world. From every walk of life, men and women left their jobs bound for the Klondike to strike it rich. They had no idea where they were going or what hardships they would endure. Escaping a depressed economy, they carried with them the fervent hope of a more prosperous life. Only a few ever found gold or got rich, and many who did squandered it away.

What the stampede for the Klondike actually did accomplish was to swell the North's population enough to force both governments to provide an infrastructure—

TIPS FOR AMERICANS CROSSING THE BORDER

The border between Alaska and Canada tightened mightily after September 11, 2001, the day suicide hijackers rammed jets into the World Trade Center in New York and the Pentagon in Washington, D.C., killing several thousand people. Take absolute proof of citizenship: a passport, birth certificate, and/or Social Security card, and make sure to have picture identification. Be prepared with enough paperwork to satisfy the most officious gatekeeper. That goes for the kids, too. If you're divorced, carry proof-of-custody papers or a letter from your former spouse. Children under 18 years old, when not accompanied by a parent, should have a letter of permission.

Driving with your headlights on is mandatory, as visibility on roads to the Yukon is often limited by blowing snow or dust-covered windows. You must also wear a seat belt in Canada. Once across the border, you will be faced with what Americans have avoided for decades: the metric system. Gas is in liters (about a quarter gallon) and distances are in kilometers (0.621 mile).

You will hold a different lucre in your hands. In addition to paper bills in denominations similar to the U.S. currency, you'll notice "loonies," the Canadian one-dollar coin with a loon on the back, and "twonies," the two-dollar coins with a copper center. They're both big and heavy. Pennies, nickels, and dimes are about the same as U.S., but Canadian coins will not work in U.S. vending machines and vice versa. However, U.S. nickels and dimes will work in parking meters in Canada. Go figure. In recent years, the

the inevitable bureaucracy. The Northwest Mounted Police, with their distinctive red uniforms and strict code of honor, became the stuff of legends. They patrolled the mountain passes during the stampede and turned back all who were not carrying at least one ton of provisions in order to prevent starvation during the long winter ahead.

Some people who did make money supporting the miners' lives in some way—grocers, restaurateurs, outfitters, and "Good Time Girls"—took their profits and returned home. But many stayed because of their love of this wild place and the rewards of a life lived amid such overwhelming beauty. Some of their descendants are still here, and you'll get to meet them.

Like Alaska, the Yukon Territory has few people and a lot of land—a population of 32,000 spread across 186,000 square miles. Alaskans and Yukoners share many similarities. They'll greet you with an open and ready warmth and take you for who you are; they work hard and play hard; and watch out—these folks can party! Just try to keep up.

While there are still active gold mines in the Yukon, today's real bonanza is tourism. Museums, cultural centers, adventure tours, and visitor accommodations have popped up to meet the demand.

Canadian dollar has been weak next to the American dollar. Exchange rates fluctuate, but take roughly a third off your purchase and you have the U.S. equivalent.

The Canadian government also has a refund program on the 7 percent Goods and Services Tax (GST). To qualify you cannot be a Canadian resident. You must spend more than $100 CDN on goods purchased and/or accommodations, and there's a $500 cap per person. You must take the goods out of Canada within 60 days of purchase, and you must present your original receipts (credit card slips are not acceptable). You also must have the receipts stamped on your way out of Canada at Canadian Customs. Mail a completed application form within a year to Visitors Rebate Program, Summerside Tax Centre, Canada Customs and Revenue Agency, 275 Pope Rd, Suite 104, Summerside, PE, C1N 6C6, Canada.

Handguns are prohibited in Canada. Whether or not you are carrying one is one of the questions you are invariably asked by border guards. Don't lie. They've seen it all and they can see it in your eyes. Hunting firearms are allowed, but they need to be declared at the border in writing (Canadian Firearms Centre; 800/731-4000). If you intend to use them while in Canada, you must have a hunting license. There is a waiting period, so call the Department of Renewable Resources (867/667-5221; www.renres.gov.yk.ca). There's no waiting period for fishing licenses—they are sold at sporting goods stores or other commercial facilities.

—Dimitra Lavrakas

ACCESS AND INFORMATION

The Yukon, like Alaska, has few roads. The **MAJOR ROADS** from the United States and southern Canada are the **ALASKA HIGHWAY** (also known as the Alaska-Canada Highway, or Alcan), starting in Dawson Creek, British Columbia; the **STEWART/CASSIAR HIGHWAY** from Prince Rupert, British Columbia; and the **TAYLOR/DEMPSTER HIGHWAY,** which runs east from Alaska to Dawson City and then north to above the Arctic Circle, dead-ending in Inuvik, Northwest Territories.

The **ALASKA MARINE HIGHWAY SYSTEM** (800/642-0066; www.alaska.gov/ferry), the state ferry service, carries passengers and vehicles from Bellingham, Washington, and docks in Haines and Skagway, both in Alaska. From either port you can drive to the Yukon via the **HAINES HIGHWAY,** out of Haines, or the **KLONDIKE HIGHWAY,** out of Skagway. From Skagway the route winds through spectacular White Pass and a glacially created high alpine plateau.

Canada provides 24-hour **ROAD REPORTS** for the Yukon highways (867/667-8215), the British Columbia section of the Alaska Highway (250/774-7447), and the Stewart/Cassiar Highway, from Prince Rupert (604/771-3000).

The main airport for the Yukon is in Whitehorse, which has **LIMITED JET SERVICE.** You can catch a plane from Anchorage on **ERA AVIATION** (800/866-8394; www.eraaviation.com), through Fairbanks on **AIR NORTH** (800/764-0407, in the United States or 800/661-0407, in Canada; www.airnorth.yk.net), or connect through Vancouver, British Columbia, via **AIR CANADA** (888/247-2262; www.air canada.ca). **CONDOR GERMAN AIRLINES** offers a weekly flight from Germany (www.condor.de).

An excellent source of information is the tour planner, "Yukon: Canada's True North," from **TOURISM YUKON** (Government of the Yukon, PO Box 2703, Whitehorse, YT Y1A 2C6; 867/667-5340; www.touryukon.com).

Whitehorse

Situated on the banks of the **YUKON RIVER,** Whitehorse is the largest city in the territory (pop. 23,000). Named by stampeders for a series of tumultuous rapids that looked like the flowing manes of dozens of wild, white horses, the town sits in a bowl surrounded by hills. The gold seekers of 1898 had to maneuver those rapids in their crudely built boats, and many didn't make it. A hydroelectric dam tamed the river's wild horses in 1958. Eight years earlier, Whitehorse had become the territorial seat of government, usurping the position Dawson City once held. It was an act of convenience—a road now connected Whitehorse to the rest of the country and the Lower 48. After the bombing of Pearl Harbor during World War II, the U.S. Army built the **ALASKA-CANADA HIGHWAY,** or Alcan. Strategically located in the Pacific arena, the Alaska road was designed to supply operations there during the ensuing war years. But the road also brought many Americans north and an infusion of money that Whitehorse sorely needed at the time. Sadly, with the Yankees came disease—influenza and measles—against which Native peoples had no immunity. All along the route north, villages were deeply affected, and many people died.

The road made Whitehorse a destination. The support services brought prosperity. People still come in from remote areas to buy supplies and enjoy a movie or a night on the town.

ACCESS AND INFORMATION
The **YUKON VISITOR RECEPTION CENTRE** (Hanson St and 2nd Ave; 867/667-3084; fax 867/393-6351; www.touryukon.com) is lovely, with light streaming through stained-glass windows. Staff will point you in the right direction and offer plenty of excellent brochures on what to see and do.

EXPLORING
SS KLONDIKE NATIONAL HISTORIC SITE / The largest and most modern sternwheeler of its time (launched in 1937), the SS *Klondike* is dry-docked on the west bank of the Yukon River in Whitehorse. It is a living museum and tribute to the important job stern-wheelers performed in transporting people and supplies up and down the Yukon River during the gold rush. By 1899, 60 steamboats, 8 tugs, and 20 barges plied the waters of the Yukon between Whitehorse and Dawson City. With the building of the Alaska Highway in 1942, the old stern-wheelers faded into history. Maintained by Parks Canada, tours are offered every half hour, and it's open May through mid-September. For information, call Canadian Heritage (867/667-3910).

MACBRIDE MUSEUM / The "Rivers of Gold" exhibit here features the largest collection of Yukon gold anywhere. Covering half a city block, the museum is chock-full of exhibits on the prehistory and history of the Yukon. Great gift shop. *Open daily in summer, call for winter hours; 867/667-2709; fax 867/633-6607; www. macbridemuseum.com; at 1st Ave and Wood St.*

YUKON BERINGIA INTERPRETIVE CENTRE / If you're a prehistory buff, just look for the giant, plastic mastodon on the Alaska Highway, next to the **YUKON TRANSPORTATION MUSEUM,** and you'll find the Beringia Interpretive Centre. Here you'll find all the details on the Yukon's Ice Age history. *Open daily, May–mid-Sept; 867/667-8855; fax 867/667-8854; info@touryukon.com; www.beringia.com.*

ADVENTURES

TAKHINI HOT SPRINGS / A most welcome respite to weary travelers, Takhini Hot Springs is north of Whitehorse at Mile 6.2 on the **TAKHINI HOT SPRINGS ROAD,** just off the North Klondike Highway. Owned by a consortium of Whitehorse families who love the place, it has wooded tent sites and an RV park, laundry, excellent cafe, and sauna. Bring a towel and a bathing suit to swim in the outdoor pool (108° Fahrenheit; 30° Celsius). In the winter there are sleigh rides and cross-country ski trails. *867/633-2706; fax 867/668-2689; hotsprings@yknet.yk.ca; www.Takhini hotsprings.yk.ca*

CARCROSS / An abbreviation of "Caribou Crossing," this is a small Tlingit Native village (pop. 431) an hour's drive south from Whitehorse along the South Klondike Highway. Early morning you may catch a coyote sniffing down breakfast as it lopes along Lake Bennett. **THE CARIBOU HOTEL** (867/821-4501) is the oldest business in the territory. **THE CARCROSS BARRACKS** (867/821-4372) sells locally made Native crafts, ice cream, and fresh-baked goods in summer.

ATLIN / The town of Atlin, on the shores of beautiful Atlin Lake, just over the border into British Columbia, is an old gold-mining town that still has several active claims. It's a three-hour drive from Whitehorse. At the end of the Klondike Gold Rush, it attracted a number of stampeders. Between 1910 and the mid-1920s it was a tourist destination from Skagway by train and then by steamship. One old steamship, the **MV TARAHNE,** still sits on the shore.

FESTIVALS AND EVENTS

YUKON QUEST INTERNATIONAL SLED DOG RACE / Temperatures in February can dip into serious below-zero weather when mushers take off on "the toughest sled-dog race in the world." Each year, Whitehorse alternates with Fairbanks, Alaska, as the start or finish of this grueling 1,000-mile sled-dog race, which runs along the Yukon River through Dawson City, and then traverses trails once used by miners and trappers over peaks much higher, and more numerous, than those found on the more famous Iditarod Trail Sled Dog Race from Anchorage to Nome. No matter how frigid the temperatures, fans always turn out to watch them doggies run. And a full complement of veterinarians, dog handlers, and race officials follow the race from checkpoint to checkpoint to ensure both canine and human well-being. *867/668-4711; www.yukonquest.net.*

FROSTBITE MUSIC FESTIVAL / This event brings in the best national and local talent. Performances, workshops, dances, and an acoustic stage encompass all types of music, from jazz to folk. Held in Whitehorse in mid-February when everybody has the winter blues, it lifts the spirit. *867/668-4921; www.frostbitefest.com.*

YUKON SOURDOUGH RENDEZVOUS FESTIVAL / The city's gold rush past is remembered with games and events for the entire family the last week in February. Don't be alarmed to see your bank teller costumed as a can-can dancer! Toe-tapping fiddling happens at the Yukon College Arts Center, and out on the streets there's heavy competition in the flour-packing and whipsaw contests. *867/667-2148; www.rendezvous.yukon.net.*

YUKON RIVER QUEST CANOE RACE / If you can't come north in winter for the dog-sled races, come north in June for this race—a tribute to the early stampeders. Canoeists paddle from Whitehorse to Dawson City—a distance of 460 miles! There's a healthy purse for the winners. *867/668-4711; www.polarcom.com/~riverquest.*

ANNUAL GOLD RUSH BATHTUB RACE / In the third week of August, you can participate in one of the wackier races on the Yukon—the world's longest and toughest bathtub race, from Whitehorse to Dawson City. The winners make it in about 48 hours; all others must finish in at least three days. Organized by the folks at Sourdough Rendezvous, the tubs compete for prize money of $5,000 CDN. *867/667-2148; www.rendezvous.yukon.net.*

KLONDIKE TRAIL OF '98 INTERNATIONAL ROAD RELAY / If you like to race on terra firma, there's the grueling relay run from Skagway, Alaska, to Whitehorse in September. This 161-mile race goes up and over White Pass, closely following one of the routes of the Klondike Gold Rush. Teams split the mileage by running different legs of the journey—in the foggy mists at the top of the pass, they appear as apparitions. Teams come up with imaginative names like Chocolate Claim Jumpers, Medicine Chests (women who work at the clinic), Trial Runners (a lawyers' team), and Klondike Keystone Kops (members of the Royal Canadian Mounted Police). *867/668-4236.*

RESTAURANTS

Bäckerei Kaffee Haus / ★★

 100 MAIN ST, WHITEHORSE; 867/633-6291 Locals embrace this new cafe, and rightly so. The bread and pastries are very European—nice heavy crust you can really sink your teeth into, and a dense texture. The homemade soups are remarkable for their spicy, lively flavor. Overall, there is an enjoyable meeting of European, North African, and Middle Eastern flavors here. Tables on the sidewalk offer a view of the bustle on Main Street. *$; MC, V; local checks only; open year-round; no alcohol; no reservations; east end of Main St at 1st Ave.*

The Moose Cafe / ★

4220 4TH AVE, WHITEHORSE; 867/667-2527 OR 800/661-0454 This is your basic meat-and-potatoes place with hearty, solid meals to refuel you and send you up or down the Alaska Highway. The waitresses are attentive, and will refill your coffee until you float away. The breakfasts are excellent, often with specials that have a south-of-border theme. This may, of course, be a form of winter daydreaming. *$$; AE, DIS, MC, V; no checks; open year-round; beer and wine; no reservations; www. yt-biz.com/moosecafe; a mile off the Alaska Highway on 4th Ave at the Yukon Inn.*

LODGINGS
New hostels in town offer free Internet service, private or bunk rooms, board games, lockers, and more: **BEEZ NEEZ BAKPAKERS HOSTEL** (867/456-2333; hostel@klondiker.com; www.bzkneez.com) and **HIDE ON JECKELL GUESTHOUSE** (867/633-4933; hide_on_jeckell@hotmail.com; www.hide-on-jeckell.com).

A Country Cabin Bed and Breakfast / ★★

MILE 5.5, TAKHINI HOT SPRINGS RD, WHITEHORSE; 867/633-2117 A short drive out of town, three cozy log cabins with wrought-iron bedsteads, kerosene lamps, and woodstoves sit peacefully in the woods—a perfect place to unwind from the road. A dip in nearby Takhini Hot Springs will unkink your driving knots. Listen for the hoot of an owl and the swish of its wings as it chases down a snowshoe hare in the night. There are outhouses and a quaint pitcher and bowl for washing up. In the morning, owner Bona Cameron-Lambert leaves a breakfast basket full of homemade muesli, yogurt, dried fruit, muffins, and coffee or tea. *$; No credit cards; local checks only; off the Klondike Hwy heading to Dawson City, look for Takhini Hot Springs Rd.*

Hawkins House Bed & Breakfast / ★★
303 HAWKINS ST, WHITEHORSE; 867/668-7638; FAX 867/668-7632 A bright, cheerful home with Victorian charm located a few blocks from the Yukon River and Main Street shops of downtown Whitehorse, Hawkins House has four guest rooms with private balconies, bathrooms, and work tables with computer jacks for business folks. Rooms are tailored colorfully along cultural and historical themes. Breakfast (an extra $7 CDN) is a sumptuous affair, including homemade moose sausage, crepes, waffles, jams, and salmon pâté, and also features themes from French Canadian to First Nations. Room rates range, winter to summer, from $100 to $150 CDN (double occupancy). The proprietors speak both French and German. *$–$$; MC, V; no checks; cpitzel@internorth.com; www.hawkinshouse.yk.ca/; downtown.*

Dawson City

Dawson City was the epicenter of the Klondike Gold Rush, and every time you turn a corner you'll be reminded of it. Stroll down **WOODEN BOARDWALKS** and into restored historic buildings. The streets are still unpaved—frost heaves make asphalt roads too expensive to repair.

Dawson City throws open the doors and rolls out the welcome mat for tourists from mid-May through mid-September. In winter, the pace slows and there are fewer places open. Wintertime population is about 2,000. For the locals, it's a welcome breather from the hustle and bustle of summer.

THE MIGHTY YUKON

The mighty Yukon River is the fifth-longest river in North America, flowing 1,920 miles from its headwaters in the Yukon, through Dawson City, and across Alaska into the Bering Sea. Its headwaters are the glacier-fed lakes and streams of White Pass on the border of Canada and Alaska.

The Gwich'in called the Yukon River *Yu-kun-ah*, meaning "great river." For the people who live along its banks, it's a daily thoroughfare—by boat in summer and by dog sled or snow machine in winter. In some places in Alaska, like Bethel, they even drive taxis on it!

To paddle the Yukon is every river lover's dream. From Whitehorse to Dawson City, following in the footsteps of the 1898 stampeders, it takes about 7 to 10 days. The river flows about 6mph and every bend offers surprises—maybe a bear, moose, or wolf. Keep your eyes peeled!

Whitehorse outfitters will guide, rent gear, and pick you up wherever you pull out of the river. Contact **KANOE PEOPLE** (867/668-4899; fax 867/668-4891; kanoe people@yknet.yk.ca; www.kanoe.yk.net). **EXPERIENCE YUKON INC.** (867/863-6021; fax 867/863-6021; expyukon@yknet.yk.ca) in Carmacks, 104 miles north of Whitehorse, offers a Yukon riverboat tour to Five Finger Rapids and Fort Selkirk. Canoe rentals are also available. For those who like being on the water but don't want to paddle, there are float trips through Miles Canyon near Whitehorse. Call **GOLD RUSH FLOAT TOURS** (867/633-4836) in Whitehorse.

—*Dimitra Lavrakas*

ACCESS AND INFORMATION
To reach Dawson City, turn off the Alaska Highway, west of Whitehorse, onto the Klondike Highway. Or approach from the Taylor/Dempster Highway off the Alaska Highway near Tok, Alaska, at Teslin Junction. The **GEORGE BLACK FERRY** will carry you and your vehicle free of charge across the Yukon River (May–Sept, 24 hours a day, except Wed mornings, 5am–7am). Dawson is served from Whitehorse by **AIR NORTH** (800/764-0407 in the United States or 800/661-0407 in Canada; www.airnorth.yk.net). There's also ready help at your fingertips by calling the **KLONDIKE VISITORS ASSOCIATION** (867/993-5575; fax 867/993-6415; KVA@ Dawson.net; www.dawsoncity.org).

EXPLORING
BRAEBURN is a small settlement on the way to Dawson City from Whitehorse. It has a gas station and lodging. Best of all it has the **BRAEBURN LODGE** (Mile 43.8 on the Klondike Highway) that serves Frisbee-sized cinnamon buns. Their sandwiches are equally large, made with fresh bread baked on the premises.

DIAMOND TOOTH GERTIE'S CASINO in Dawson City has three nightly music and dance performances, as well as gambling. You can play blackjack or poker, spin the wheel, or become mesmerized for hours at the one-arm bandit at Canada's oldest gambling hall. Enjoy the **GASLIGHT FOLLIES,** a vaudeville-style show at the **PALACE GRAND THEATRE.** The **DAWSON CITY MUSEUM** (867/993-5291; fax 867/993-5839; dcmuseum@yknet.yk.ca; www.gold-rush.org) is open during the summer season and holds a treasure trove of Klondike Gold Rush and Han Native people artifacts with good interpretive exhibits. **KLONDIKE NATIONAL HISTORIC SITES** (867/993-7200; fax 867/993-7299) offers a city walking tour and other historic sites. The **COMMISSIONER'S RESIDENCE** (867/993-7200; fax 867/993-7299), a splendid old turn-of-the century building, holds polite Victorian teas June–mid-September.

Literary types can go to **ROBERT SERVICE'S CABIN,** where daily readings of the "Bard of the North" are held. Jack London's original cabin—well, half of it—is also here. The other half is in Jack London Square in Oakland, California. The cabin features daily readings from London's work, as well as an account of London's life. The **BERTON CABIN** is the boyhood home of Pierre Berton, who wrote *Klondike Fever* and many other popular books on the Klondike.

FESTIVALS AND EVENTS

YUKON GOLD PANNING CHAMPIONSHIP / Open to cheechakos and sourdoughs alike. All events are timed—see how fast you can pan! Always held on July 1, Canada Day. Contact the Klondike Visitors Association (see Access and Information, above).

DAWSON CITY MUSIC FESTIVAL / In the third week of July, Dawson is overrun with music lovers. Headline acts from all over North America come to play. There are special workshops, as well as events for children. Tickets go fast. *867/993-5584; www.dcmf.com.*

GREAT KLONDIKE INTERNATIONAL OUTHOUSE RACE / Canoes, bicycles, skis, bathtubs, outhouses—Yukoners will race in or on anything! During the first week of September, teams race fancifully decorated outhouses through downtown streets. Watch out for flying TP. Contact the Klondike Visitors Association (see Access and Information, above).

RESTAURANTS

Klondike Kate's / ★★

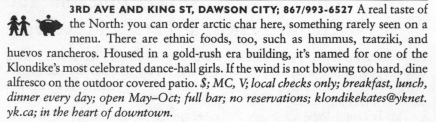 **3RD AVE AND KING ST, DAWSON CITY; 867/993-6527** A real taste of the North: you can order arctic char here, something rarely seen on a menu. There are ethnic foods, too, such as hummus, tzatziki, and huevos rancheros. Housed in a gold-rush era building, it's named for one of the Klondike's most celebrated dance-hall girls. If the wind is not blowing too hard, dine alfresco on the outdoor covered patio. *$; MC, V; local checks only; breakfast, lunch, dinner every day; open May–Oct; full bar; no reservations; klondikekates@yknet. yk.ca; in the heart of downtown.*

LODGINGS

Bombay Peggy's Inn and Pub / ★★★

SECOND AND PRINCESS STS, DAWSON CITY; 867/993-6969; FAX 867/993-6199 Named after the building's former owner—a madame and bootlegger—this lovingly restored Victorian inn and pub opened in 1999. It's a place for adults only, and there is no smoking in the rooms, only in the pub downstairs. *$–$$; MC, V; traveler's checks or cash; open year-round; PO Box 411, Dawson City, YT Y0B 1G0; bombaypeggys@yknet.yk.ca; www.bombaypeggys.com; smack in the middle of town.*

Dawson City River Hostel / ★★

ACROSS THE RIVER, DAWSON CITY; 867/993-6823 Welcome to Dieterland. This is Dieter Reinmuth's own hostel that he built by hand. Look around at the unique use of old bicycle parts and recycled junk. A fertile mind put this all together. As in any sovereignty, there are laws. Don't worry, you won't have to memorize them—they're posted everywhere. You can camp here or rent a cabin for two–four people. It's a fairly basic setup with outhouses, a "prospector's bath house," and plans for a wood-fired sauna. Campers come here in droves for the Dawson City Music Festival. Dieter also offers bicycle and canoe rentals. *$; No credit cards; checks OK; open mid-May–Sept; PO Box 32, Dawson City, YT, Y0B 1G0; yukonhostels@yahoo.ca; www.yukonhostels.com; take the George Black Ferry from Dawson City over to the hostel.*

White Ram Manor Bed and Breakfast / ★★

7TH AVE AND HARPER ST, DAWSON CITY; 867/993-5772; FAX 867/993-6509 It's hard to miss. Look to the hillside above the city for a pink building within walking distance of downtown. The White Ram is bright, cozy, and squeaky clean. You can either share a bathroom or have one of your own, depending on your budget. There's Internet access, a laundry, barbecue area, a big kitchen, and a hot tub out back. The chalkboard out front lists the rooms available. You write down the one you want, after checking it out. Full breakfast (eggs and pancakes) is included. *$; MC, V; no checks; open year-round; Box 302, Dawson City, YT Y0B 1G0; pbarthol@yknet.yk.ca; www.bbcanada.com/white rammanor.*

Haines Junction and Kluane National Park and Reserve

Nestled into one of the world's most dramatic settings, Haines Junction is a small town of 800, located in the Yukon at the junction of the Haines and Alaska Highways (see Haines and Skagway chapters). Whitehorse in the Yukon is 100 miles east on the Alaska Highway from Haines Junction.

This beautiful little crossroads is located on the eastern border of **KLUANE NATIONAL PARK AND RESERVE**. The park was established first as a game sanctuary in the 1940s and formally as a national park in the 1970s. Together with bordering **WRANGELL-ST. ELIAS NATIONAL PARK** in Alaska, these two parks represent extraordinary wilderness, including some of the highest mountains on the continent (Mount Logan at 19,500 feet is the highest mountain in Canada and the second-highest in North America after Mount McKinley in Alaska), huge glaciers, remote bush areas, and abundant wildlife. In 1980, the parks were declared by the United Nations to be a joint World Heritage Site. The **KLUANE NATIONAL PARK AND RESERVE VISITOR RECEPTION CENTRE** (867/634-7207 or 867/634-2345; fax 867/634-7208; www.parkscanada.gc.ca) has interpretive displays, schedules of guided hikes, and more. It's located just off the Alaska Highway, about a quarter mile east of the junction with Haines Highway. It's open every day in summer and Monday through Friday the rest of the year. The pale glacial blue waters of Kluane Lake are most spectacular in June when the deep purple and blue lupine flowers bloom and in September when the trees turn golden.

Haines Junction is also headquarters for the Tatshenshini-Alsek Wilderness Park, international protection for the wilderness surrounding two spectacular rivers—the "Tat" and the Alsek.

RESTAURANTS AND LODGINGS

The Raven / ★★★

ALASKA HWY AT VISITOR CENTRE ACCESS, HAINES JUNCTION; 867/634-2500
Surrounded by the spectacular St. Elias Mountains, on the border of Kluane National Park, this wonderful little European oasis offers gourmet dining and lovely, spacious, clean rooms. They're all nonsmoking and pets are not allowed. The hosts, Christine and Hans Nelles, are German and serve a variety of European and German specialties. Even if you can't stay, make a point to stop for one of their elegant dinners. *$$; AE, MC, V; no checks; open Apr 1–Sept 27; beer and wine; Box 5470, Haines Junction, YT Y0B 1L0; www.yukonweb.com/tourism/raven.* ᕒ *(one room only)*

ALASKA CRUISES

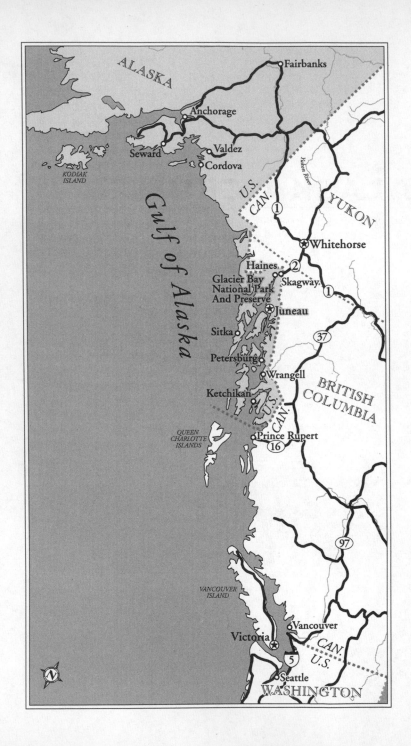

ALASKA CRUISES

Alaska has a staggering 34,000 miles of shoreline, including all of its many islands and inlets. That's twice as much as the Lower 48. From point to point, the state's coastline alone stretches 6,640 miles. Throw in glaciers too numerous to count (covering 29,000 square miles), and whales, walrus, seals, porpoise, bears, bald eagles, and other wildlife, and you could argue that Alaska is best seen from the deck of a boat.

Alaska is a top request among cruise ship travelers and the market has responded—you'll have a wide array of lines and ships to choose from if you decide to visit the 49th state via this mode of transportation. And what a mode it is. After watching whales breach or glaciers calve, you can adjourn to a luxurious cabin or savor a gourmet meal. You don't have to worry about hotel reservations or gamble on which restaurants are decent in any given town—everything is taken care of for you. Once onboard, you don't even have to worry about where to go next—the decisions have all been made and the itineraries set.

That's not to say you don't have options. Even if you depart Vancouver, British Columbia, aboard a 2,000-passenger mass-market ship, you'll have different opportunities in port, with various shore excursions to suit your personal style. Some cruise lines offer pre- or post-cruise land tours (combined with the cruise, these are called "cruisetours") that include numerous possibilities, such as Denali National Park, Canada, the Arctic, and the Interior. Or you could top off your cruise with your own do-it-yourself land tour.

But first, understand something about cruises in Alaska: you won't be alone. The number of cruise passengers to the state has doubled since 1993, topping off at around 600,000 visitors annually. Often there are several (we've seen as many as six) cruise ships in the harbors of towns like Juneau, Ketchikan, or Sitka—all at the same time. In some of the smaller towns, a single cruise ship can double or even triple the population temporarily.

Alaska towns have struggled to keep up with an exploding industry, one that unfortunately has been called on the carpet for doing such things as dumping wastewater into the pristine waters of Southeast Alaska, as well as violating air-quality standards with dirty smokestack emissions. While state officials have taken steps to curb the pollution, the cruise lines themselves are cleaning up their act by opting, for instance, to plug into electrical grids rather than run their engines while in port. These efforts are crucial in some areas, where cruise ships and their accompanying swarm of passengers and crew have worn down the welcome mat. Alaskans are a friendly and generous bunch, but you might find a few tight-lipped smiles near the end of the season. A couple of tips: Don't walk in the middle of the street. You may think this is obvious, but you'd be surprised how many visitors seem to forget they're in real towns and cities. The roads are for cars, not for tourists trying to snap a pretty picture for their albums back home. Also, keep in mind that residents, while happy to give directions or other quick information, may not have time to provide lengthy suggestions of what to do in port.

It's no surprise that cruises in Alaska are so popular—they are a convenient and very comfortable way to travel. Many of the ships spare no luxury for their guests, and the lines, along with their bevy of shore excursions (most of which cost extra), allow visitors to glimpse more of the state than they ever could on their own in the same amount of time. Cruises can also be quite affordable. Trips in the off-peak months of May and September are sometimes discounted, for those who don't mind if the weather is a bit chillier than it is during the height of summer. (Let's face it: even in July, you can't guarantee pleasant weather in Alaska.) Discounts are also often available for last-minute bookings, a good option if your schedule is flexible. The cruise lines would rather fill their cabins than leave the dock with empty staterooms.

One note about rates: They are highly volatile and confusing, sometimes even more so than airline tickets. Hardly anyone, especially on the large ships, pays the full brochure price. You may find a great deal during May or September (expect to pay up to several hundred more for peak-season voyages). Early-booking discounts are also often available (about six months in advance), and are sometimes published in brochures. Depending on the market, you could even find a deal as late as several weeks before departure. But if your schedule doesn't allow for that kind of spontaneity, make sure not to wait until the last minute to book—you could find yourself out of luck.

Quoted cruise prices are always per person and based on double occupancy. Singles or extra people in a cabin will cost more. Inside rooms (no windows) are less expensive than outside cabins facing the ocean. Some cabins have balconies, but not all. Also, keep in mind that published rates don't include certain taxes or extras, such as visits to the spa or shore excursions. Meals in main dining rooms are always included in the fare, but it will cost you extra in many cases if you dine in one of the numerous "alternate" restaurants that many of the cruise lines now feature. Bar tabs are usually not included in the cruise price; the notable exceptions are on some of the smaller "yacht" cruises. Generally, airfare is not included in cruise prices.

WHEN TO GO

With the exception of perhaps a few late-April sailings, departures are limited to May through September. Even if it's sunny and it's officially the season known as summer, understand that temperatures in the coastal areas of Alaska often don't rise above the mid-50s, even in mid-July. September is notorious for rain, but it can and does rain in Southeast Alaska year-round. (It is a rain forest, after all.) If you come in early May, the landscape won't be as green as it will be later in the spring and summer, but that can have its advantages too—wildlife is easier to spot without the lush foliage. Early- or late-season sailings are often less crowded, both onboard and on shore, than they are during the height of the season.

While you will be more likely to hit good weather during June and July, don't limit your wardrobe to classic summer garb. Go ahead and bring shorts, but don't be surprised if you never wear them outside the ship's gym. Do bring a bathing suit though—most ships have pools. In addition to some dressy evening attire suitable for the onboard nightclubs, bring a sensible raincoat, waterproof walking shoes, and layers of clothing for a range of temperatures.

CHOOSING AND BOOKING YOUR CRUISE

Deciding which cruise is right for you isn't as hard as you might think, so long as you have done your homework. Start off by asking yourself the following questions: What can I afford? How much time do I have? Do I want an active itinerary or a more sedentary cruise? Are gourmet meals and a plush cabin important to me, or would I rather paddle in remote coves by myself in a kayak and show up for dinner in jeans and a sweatshirt? Do I appreciate the camaraderie of a group, or would I rather call the shots on my own terms? Do I want a large ship with a great variety of restaurants, lounges, and entertainment, or am I satisfied with more modest accommodations and the quiet benefits of fewer fellow passengers?

While the larger ships offer amenities galore, such as pools, spas, shopping, entertainment, lounges, and restaurants, the smaller ships are physically more agile—they can get to places the big ships can't, such as Misty Fjords near Ketchikan. These are the kinds of spots where you're more apt to see wildlife, and since you'll be at sea level (versus several stories up, as you would in a large cruise ship), you'll get a better look at the whales, porpoise, bears, and other wildlife. Smaller ships generally have a greater emphasis on educating passengers about what they're seeing. In addition, these smaller ships can avoid the crowds at Alaska's usual ports of call and stop in at remote coves or small villages. Smaller ships also have the flexibility to adjust their itineraries to their passengers' preferences, spending the afternoon whale-watching or taking rafts ashore for beachcombing instead of adhering to a rigid sailing schedule.

Small-ship cruising is generally more expensive than trips on larger vessels, although unlike the bigger ships, the price of some shore excursions is often included. Also, the smaller ships lack the onboard shops that make retail sales to a captive audience.

All of the cruise lines have Web sites, and several allow you to book online. But we recommend you find a trusted travel agent with experience in Alaska cruises, or at least an agent with a solid grasp of the lines serving Alaska. One of the best Alaska travel agencies for helping you decide which cruise line is right for you is the **ALASKA CRUISE CENTER** (907/874-3382 or 800/977-9705; info@akcruises.com; www.akcruises.com). Another good online source is **WWW.TRAVANTS.COM** (type in "cruises" and "Alaska" to narrow your search).

A word about wheelchairs: While most ships have wheelchair-accessible staterooms, off-ramps at most ports often include stairs, and passengers in wheelchairs will need help negotiating them. Also, when ports are crowded, ships often must anchor in the harbor and ferry passengers back and forth on small boats. Passengers in wheelchairs will need some assistance in getting ashore.

SHORE EXCURSIONS

Shore excursions are organized outings to see the sights and enjoy various activities while in port. These are the types of things listed under the Exploring, Adventures section of each port town listed in this book (see those individual sections for contact information). Shore excursions are most often run by independent operators, who may or may not have operating agreements with your ship. In many cases you

A FEW TIPS ON TIPPING

When planning and budgeting for your dream cruise to Alaska, make sure you figure in enough money for onboard tips. You'll have cabin stewards, dining room servers, assistant waiters or busboys, the maître d', table captain, and an assortment of other staffers. They'll all be waiting on you, attending to your every need. And they will, naturally, expect and deserve tips.

An increasing number of cruise lines have lessened the confusion—or even embarrassment—some passengers feel about tipping the crew by instituting gratuity programs, in which tips are automatically added to your onboard account. The bill almost always amounts to the industry-wide recommendation of $10 in tips per passenger, per day. This means $140 for a couple on a seven-day Inside Passage cruise. Even with the automatic gratuity programs, you can tip the crew extra if you feel they have gone above and beyond the usual call of duty. Likewise, you can decrease the crew's tip, should you feel that action is necessary. On some lines you may also tip in advance.

If you decide to tip individual crew members on your own, or if your cruise line doesn't figure tips automatically, you can generally use these guidelines (per passenger, per day): $3–$4 for the cabin attendant (also called the cabin steward or stewardess); $3–$4 for the waiter or server; $1.50–$2.50 for the assistant waiter or busboy; and 50 cents to $1 for the hostess or maître d'. Bar tabs are billed separately for the entire cruise, and they may or may not include a gratuity, so be sure to ask. It's usually noted on the bill. Spa tips are usually 15 to 20 percent the cost of the service, whether it be a massage or mud bath.

can book these in advance when you book your cruise. Usually these cost extra, but they may be included so be sure to ask.

There are some advantages to booking shore excursions through your ship versus booking with tour operators on your own. First off, you'll be assured that the tour operators who work directly with the cruise ships will get you back to the ship on time! And if there's any chance you do run late, a ship is more likely to wait a few extra minutes for a group of passengers booked through one of "their" operators. Arranging trips through your cruise line also allows for convenient, one-stop shopping. On the other hand, tours booked independently are often less expensive than those affiliated with your ship. That's because they don't have to give the cruise line a cut of their profits in exchange for a solid customer stream. Most cruise lines also require their tour operators to have a certain amount of insurance or bonding. Just be sure to thoroughly check out a company if you decide to book independently (See Exploring and Adventures sections for contact information for the ports your ship visits).

Another point worth noting: Heli-tours, boat tours, and especially dog-sledding tours on the Juneau Icefield can only take a limited number of passengers during a

Each ship or cruise line usually has its own tipping guidelines, and travel agents with cruise experience can be particularly helpful. Here's an overview for most of the lines serving Alaska. All tip suggestions are per passenger, per day:

- Carnival: automatic gratuity program, $9.75
- Celebrity: stateroom attendant, $3.50; waiter, $3.50; assistant waiter, $2; maître d', 75 cents; head housekeeper, 50 cents; butler (suites only), $3.50. Bar bills have a 15 percent gratuity included. Spa tips are 10 percent of the service, automatically added.
- Crystal: waiter in main dining room, $4; assistant waiter, $2.50; butler (penthouse only), $4; additional $6 per meal for alternate restaurants. Bar bills have 15 percent tip included. Advance tipping allowed.
- Holland America: has a no-tipping required policy, and does not like to recommend amounts, but notes passengers may tip if they want. Bar bills do not include a gratuity.
- Norwegian: automatic gratuity program, $10. Bar bills have a 15 percent tip included.
- Princess: automatic gratuity program, $10. Bar bills have a 15 percent tip included.
- Radisson Seven Seas: officially has a no-tipping policy, but tips are allowed if passengers feel the service warrants it.
- Royal Caribbean: waiter and steward, $3.50 each; assistant waiter, $2; headwaiter, 75 cents. Passengers may tip automatically by arranging with the purser when they board. Bar bill has a 15 percent tip included.

Small cruise yachts and adventure ships often use the standard $10 per passenger, per day tipping recommendation, but check in advance.

—Kate Ripley

ship's time in port. If your cruise offers advance booking for these types of trips (many do), it's a good idea to pre-book in order to avoid disappointment.

If you're the athletic type, you might want to consider a cruise with one of the smaller "adventure" ships, such as Glacier Bay Cruiseline or Lindblad Expeditions (see Small Ships, below). These ships have kayak and Zodiac shore explorations as a steady part of their cruising diet, as well as hiking and beachcombing (all included in the fare). But kayaking, hiking, and other athletic shore excursions can be arranged if you're traveling aboard one of the megaships as well. We know some passengers who simply hiked the local trails for their shore excursions while in port, a truly inexpensive way to go, and great exercise to boot. (For information on hiking trails within the Tongass National Forest, which encompasses nearly all of the Southeast, check out www.fs.fed.us/r10/tongass, click on "recreation," and follow prompts to a listing of individual trails).

If you choose to pass on the shore excursions and instead wander the storefronts through town, the savvy shopper could be disappointed. While many of the ports of call offer quaint shops with beautiful artwork and crafts made by extremely talented locals, you'll also find T-shirt shop after T-shirt shop, along with tired little stores offering a bevy of knickknacks and cheap curiosities. In this book's other chapters, read the individual town Shopping listings for tips on the best places to buy. A word of caution: you'll hear talk on some ships of "approved" stores while in port, versus those that are not. All this means is that certain stores have a marketing arrangement with certain cruise lines (in other words, paid advertisements). Check out these businesses if they interest you, but be sure to follow your own nose and sense of adventure as well.

CRUISETOURS

If you hear someone refer to "cruisetours," they're talking about a package land tour/cruise that includes the Inside Passage or Gulf Coast, as well as noncoastal parts of the state, such as the Interior, Denali National Park, the Arctic, or Canada's Yukon Territory. By far, the leader in the cruisetour business is Princess Cruises, which owns five hotels in Alaska (they like to call them lodges, but they're really hotels), including a new one just outside the remote and wild Wrangell-St. Elias National Park. Princess also owns passenger cars on the Alaska Railroad, as well as a fleet of tour buses. Several other cruiselines, most notably Holland America, also have railcars and buses, but tour participants stay in affiliated hotels, offering more variety—and more inconsistency—than you'll find with the Princess chain of hotels. Several other lines offer cruisetours as well, including Royal Caribbean, Celebrity, Crystal, Glacier Bay, and Cruise West (see reviews, below).

The most popular cruisetour, which can typically add anywhere from three to seven days to your cruise, includes Denali National Park. For example, Holland America offers a seven-day northbound cruise of the Inside Passage/Gulf of Alaska, landing in Seward. Cruisetour passengers then take a bus (called a "motorcoach") to Anchorage, where they can take in a few popular sites and then stay overnight in a local hotel. The next day, cruisetour participants board the Alaska Railroad in Holland America domed cars and ride the train to Denali National Park. After typically taking another bus tour into the park, cruisetour participants stay the night at a hotel near the park entrance. The next day, they take either the train or motorcoach to Fairbanks, where they might have time to take in a few attractions such as the University of Alaska Museum or the Riverboat Discovery. Then they fly back home from the Fairbanks airport.

These cruisetours can add as little as $700–$800 per person to your cruise price. But check the fine print. Sometimes entire cruisetours are discounted, but other times you'll find the land portion adds a hefty chunk to a cruise that would have been a great bargain otherwise. Armed with the knowledge gained from reading this book, you might consider booking your own pre- or post-cruise land tour. A good travel agent could help with the arrangements. One benefit of taking this independent route, beyond saving some money, is that it could steer you away from the crowds, as well as give you the flexibility to visit sights that aren't on the typical list of stops.

LUXURY LINES
CRYSTAL CRUISES / Crystal's 940-passenger *Crystal Harmony* is perhaps the most luxurious ship available in Alaska. The line's reputation for fine dining is unmatched, with the choice of elegant dining in the Crystal Dining Room; in Kyoto, a Japanese restaurant; or in Pergo, an Italian-themed restaurant. *Crystal Harmony* has received "best" awards from *Travel and Leisure, Condé Nast,* and Fielding's travel guides. The show lounge features incredible entertainment, plus there's a Caesars Palace casino, with 80 slot machines. The 790-foot *Crystal Harmony* has one of the highest per-passenger space ratios of any cruise ship. Its cabins are large and attractively decorated—every attention to detail has been made. Passengers like to dress up, typically are well-off financially and usually well-traveled, and most are in their 40s through 60s. A 10-day Inside Passage trip, leaving from San Francisco, goes for as low as $2,875 per person. *2049 Century Park E, Ste 1400, Los Angeles CA 90067; 800/820-6663; www.crystalcruises.com.*

RADISSON SEVEN SEAS CRUISES / Radisson's *Seven Seas Mariner* offers a beautiful choice for cruising, right up there with Crystal or perhaps a notch or two below. The all-suite and all-ocean-view layout of the ship's cabins, which range from 301 square feet to 1,173 square feet, give nearly every passenger a luxurious, well-appointed cabin. The *Mariner* is a 709-foot, 700-passenger ship, with four restaurants (one of which is overseen by chefs of the famous Cordon Bleu of Paris). There are lavish spas, sparkling entertainment, and numerous guest lecturers. While the atmosphere onboard is impeccable, these ships lean more toward "resort casual" than, say, the *Crystal Harmony*. Typical passengers are high-income, yet low-key, around age 50 and up. Seven-night north- and southbound cruises between Vancouver, British Columbia, and Seward start at $2,345 per person. *600 Corporate Dr, Ste 410, Fort Lauderdale FL 33334; 800/477-7500; www.rssc.com.*

LARGE SHIPS
CARNIVAL CRUISE LINES / Carnival likes to call its fleet of 18 vessels "fun ships." But only one, *Carnival Spirit,* cruises Alaska. The ship is 963 feet long and holds up to 2,124 passengers, with four swimming pools, a wedding chapel, conference center, formal dining room, casual buffet restaurant, and a "crow's nest" restaurant sitting up near the ship's smokestack. The ship also has a gym, balconies on many of the cabins, and two decks full of bars, lounges, and nightspots. "Camp Carnival" ensures plenty of activities for children. This line has perhaps the youngest demographic in the industry, attracting a good share of families, children, and single folks under 50. Carnival offers seven-day north- or southbound cruises. We saw one rate as low as $799 per person. *3655 NW 87th Ave, Miami FL 33178; 800/CARNIVAL (800/227-6482); fax 305/406-5607; www.carnival.com.*

CELEBRITY CRUISES / Celebrity's *Mercury, Infinity,* and *Summit* all ply Alaska's waters, and all are finished in wood, marble, etched glass, and polished granite. The *Infinity* and *Summit* are sister ships, both at 965 feet, 11 decks, and a capacity of 1,950 guests. The slightly smaller *Mercury* (866 feet) is a favorite in the large-ship category, with its bright décor, 10 decks, and a 1,870-passenger capacity. While there's less of a "party boat" atmosphere than you might find on Carnival or Princess (also in the Large Ship category), Celebrity's line of ships offers a variety of things to do, from cultural lectures and stage shows to sporting events such as trapshooting or volleyball. Children's counselors supervise a camp-style program for the little ones, called "Fun Factory," broken down by age group (included in your fare). Along with Holland America (below), the Celebrity line boasts the largest cabins of vessels cruising Alaska. The ships' cuisine is under the direction of master chef Michel Roux, one of the top French chefs in the world. The spas are also top-notch, but cost extra. The passenger profile runs the gamut, from young families with children to retirees. The prices, for such luxury and beautiful design, are quite affordable, starting at $890 per person. *1050 Caribbean Wy, Miami FL 33132; 800/437-3111; fax 800/437-5111; www.celebritycruises.com.*

HOLLAND AMERICA LINE / If you're looking for solid tradition and class in Alaska cruises, Holland America has what it takes. Their ships (there are six of them that sail Alaska's Southeast and gulf waters) offer classic, dignified cruising. Their seven-day round-trip Glacier Bay Inside Passage Cruise leaves nothing wanting as they highlight Southeast Alaska's most popular ports: Juneau, Skagway, Ketchikan, and, of course, a full-day on Glacier Bay. A new seven-day round-trip Alaskan Explorer Cruise from Seattle features Saturday departures, scenic cruising on Puget Sound, the Queen Charlotte Islands, Stephens Passage, Hubbard Glacier, Vancouver Island, the Strait of Juan de Fuca, and ports of call in Juneau, Sitka, Ketchikan, and Victoria, British Columbia. And the seven-day Glacier Discovery Cruise goes all the way to Seward, adding Sitka and Valdez to the itinerary. Holland America's children's program, Club HAL, keeps the children up to age 17 busy. Cabins on all of their ships are among the roomiest. Typical Holland America passengers are retiree age, but expanding children's programs has resulted in a younger demographic. Early-season bookings can go for as little as $899 per person, but expect to pay in the $1,449 range in many cases. *300 Elliott Ave W, Seattle WA 98119; 206/281-3535 or 800/426-0327; fax 206/281-7110; www.hollandamerica.com.*

NORWEGIAN CRUISE LINE / Like many of the other big lines, Norwegian has ships all over the globe. Three of them do the Alaska cruises: the 853-foot *Norwegian Sun,* which accommodates 2,000 passengers; the 853-foot *Norwegian Sky,* for up to 2,000 passengers; and the 754-foot *Norwegian Wind,* which holds 1,748 guests. All make seven-day cruises through the Inside Passage to Glacier Bay or Sawyer Glacier, ending in either Seattle, Washington, or Vancouver, British Columbia. The *Sun* has 15 decks, 36 suites, and 107 "minisuites" complete with balconies, as well as typical staterooms. The *Sky* has 12 decks, seven restaurants, a library, casino, numerous shops, and 13 different lounges and bars, including a coffee bar and Internet cafe. The ship also has an eight-story-high atrium midship. Staterooms are well-appointed, but storage space is limited. The *Wind* has five restaurants, 12 bars and lounges, two pools, and a sports deck with basketball, volleyball, a golf-driving net, and table tennis, and the sailing itinerary is much the same as the *Sky.* Norwegian cruises also feature flexible dining (traditional cruise dining typically offers two seatings; flexible dining allows you to eat whenever you feel like it). All three of the ships visiting Alaska feature Norwegian's "Kids Crew" program for children ages two to seventeen. Typical passengers are often retiree age, but the line has attracted a larger portion of the family market in recent years. Cruises on the *Sky* and *Sun* start at $949 per person; those on the *Wind* start at $799 per person. *7665 Corporate Center Dr, Miami FL 33126; 800/327-7030; fax 305/448-7936; www.ncl.com.*

PRINCESS CRUISES / Remember that 1970s television series, *The Love Boat*? That was a Princess ship (but that particular vessel has long since been retired). There are six Princess ships cruising the Inside Passage and Gulf of Alaska. In addition to the cruise ships, the company's five Princess lodges, a fleet of tour buses, and cars aboard the Alaska Railroad make this company the largest cruise and tour operator in the state. Despite the "chain" aspect of the line, Princess ships consistently offer high quality. The sister ships *Dawn* and *Sun* (1,950 passengers each); *Island* and *Coral* (1,950 passengers each); and the *Star Princess* (2,600 passengers) all have what cruising enthusiasts would expect—numerous restaurants and lounges, entertainment, especially large children's playrooms, libraries, and the like. There are many onboard activities, as well as flexible dining (eat whenever you want).

The cabins are average size for the industry. Many passengers fall into the 50–65 age group, but an emphasis on children's programs has added a younger clientele. A seven-day cruise from Vancouver, British Columbia, to Seward can go for as little as $799 per person. *24844 Ave Rockefeller, Santa Clarita, CA 91355; 800/PRINCESS (800/774-6237); fax 661/284-4744; www.princess.com.*

ROYAL CARIBBEAN INTERNATIONAL / Royal Caribbean has three casual, well-run ships in Alaska—the 962-foot *Radiance of the Seas* (2,500 passengers); the 915-foot *Vision of the Seas* (2,435 passengers); and the 867-foot *Legend of the Seas* (2,076 passengers). These ships have all the usual features of large-ship cruising, including spas, pools, numerous restaurants and lounges, solid children's programs, casinos, Internet cafe, theaters, and a variety of cabins from which to choose. The entertainment is lavish and high-tech. The *Radiance of the Seas* is an excellent choice for sports enthusiasts, with a rock-climbing wall, full-size basketball court, and golf simulator. This line has a fairly young demographic, with typical passengers in the 30–60 age range, plus a good share of families with younger children. A sample seven-night Inside Passage cruise aboard the *Legend of the Seas* starts at $800 per person. *1050 Caribbean Wy, Miami FL 33132; 305/539-6000 or 800/327-6700; www.rccl.com.*

MEDIUM SHIPS

EMPRESS OF THE NORTH / This unique 236-passenger stern-wheeler is scheduled to make its 2003 cruising debut in Alaska with 11-night north- or southbound cruises between Seattle, Washington, and Juneau. The *Empress of the North,* still under construction as of press time, will offer 112 staterooms, with all but seven featuring private balconies. A main dining room, lavish show room, Paddlewheel Lounge, bar and grill, gift shop, and library round out the ship's amenities list. The ship's operator, American West Steamboat Co. of Seattle, also promises a shore excursion in each port of call, to be included in the brochure rate of $4,949 per person. The ship is a bit too large to be included in the traditional "small ship" category, but small enough that it doesn't fit with the megasize ships either. The company expects to attract passengers 50 years old and up, and since there are no

"CRUISING" ON THE CHEAP: COME ABOARD A BLUE CANOE

If cruise ship sailing isn't your style and you can't afford the price tag of a small adventure cruise but like the idea of exploring by boat, then you might consider hopping aboard one of the sturdy vessels of the state-owned **ALASKA MARINE HIGHWAY SYSTEM** (6858 Glacier Hwy, Juneau AK 99801; 800/642-0066; www.alaska.gov/ferry).

Only two communities in Southeast Alaska, Haines and Skagway, are connected to the rest of the world by road. Yet coastal towns are integrally linked by culture, family, economics, and social events such as high-school basketball—a staple sport on the Panhandle—and their communication pathway is the water. Beginning in 1963, the young state of Alaska launched its "marine highway" transportation system, known fondly to locals as **THE BLUE CANOES.** Though it's a perennial political battle for adequate cash to operate the system (some lawmakers from "up north" don't think state ferries along the coastal regions are comparable to roads elsewhere), the Alaska Marine Highway chugs along, hauling about 360,000 passengers each year.

A fleet of nine vessels serves 16 communities in Southeast; 10 communities in the Prince William Sound/Kenai Peninsula area; and 7 communities on the Alaska Peninsula and Aleutian Chain. The largest and newest vessel, the MV *Kennicott,* launched its maiden voyage in 1998 and can hold 748 passengers. The smallest ship, the MV *Bartlett,* can take only 190 passengers and has no staterooms (it's used for shorter voyages).

You won't find plush accommodations on the state ferries, but they are quite comfortable and offer the visitor a chance to see Alaska's coastal communities as the locals do. While there are sometimes Forest Service rangers or other experts onboard offering short educational lectures and programs, you are, for the most part, on your own to whale-watch, read, or daydream. There aren't exciting floor shows in glitzy lounges, but there are bars and plenty of interesting fellow passengers to chat with. Dining is cafeteria style and extremely casual. The fare served up is, unfortunately, not that great—locals tend to bring their own groceries.

If you're really on a budget and don't mind communal living, you can even bypass staterooms, opting for a sleeping bag on the floor or lounge chair in the solarium. The fresh sea air coupled with the hum of the ferry's engine will lull you to sleep like a baby. Most vessels also have showers available, and there are towels, blankets, and pillows for rent.

Ticket prices vary, depending on the route. A one-way ticket between Juneau and Haines is about $26 per person (walk-on, no stateroom), while a one-way Bellingham-to-Juneau (walk-on) fare costs $253 per person (add another $273 for a two-person stateroom with private bath). While walk-ons usually can hop aboard without advance reservations, if you want to drive your vehicle onboard you should make reservations as far in advance as possible. Staterooms also are extremely limited, so if this amenity is important to you, early reservations are a must.

Another thing you should know about state ferry travel: it's slow, and departure and arrival times are often in the middle of the night. Also, unlike cruise ships, the ferries don't stay "in port" for much longer than a few hours. If you want to see the sights, you'll need to get off with your baggage, stay in hotels or campgrounds for a day or so, and then book passage on another ferry to your next destination. In some towns, such as Sitka, you could have a several-day wait until the next ferry. We recommend you enlist the help of a good travel agent. One suggestion is **VIKING TRAVEL** in Petersburg (907/772-3818 or 800/327-2571; www.alaskaferry.com), which specializes in ferry travel. You may actually find that, once all your costs are factored in, it could actually be cheaper to take a cruise aboard one of the large lines.

—Kate Ripley

children's programs in the works, it likely won't draw much of the family market. *2101 4th Ave, Ste 1150, Seattle WA, 98121; 800/434-1232; www.empressofthe north.com.*

SMALL SHIPS

AMERICAN SAFARI CRUISES / This Washington-state based company has three yachts designed for those who want to experience the wilderness of Alaska without sacrificing comfort. Each luxury yacht holds only 12 to 21 passengers each and has large staterooms with private baths, and hot tubs, kayaks, mountain bikes, and a shore boat. One crew member for every two guests ensures that you'll be pampered. Be as active as you want, or stay onboard and enjoy your favorite book on the deck. Fine cuisine, premium beers, wines, and liquors are all included, as well as all shore excursions, including flight-seeing. The company offers 7-, 10-, and 14-night cruises through the Inside Passage, with varying ports of call, most often remote coves or small villages. Passengers tend to be well-off financially, and range from about 45–60 in age. Most are couples. Rates start at $3,695 per person, though there are sometimes early-booking discounts. *19101 36th Ave W, Ste 201, Lynnwood WA 98036; 425/776-4700 or 888/862-8881; fax 425/776-8889; www.amsafari.com.*

CLIPPER CRUISE LINES / With its *Yorktown Clipper* and *Clipper Odyssey* (138 and 128 passengers, respectively), this line offers seven-night Inside Passage cruises between Juneau and Ketchikan, as well as longer Inside Passage voyages in the spring and fall. They also offer a Bering Sea and Kenai Peninsula cruise. The size of these ships allows visitors to experience daily life in smaller communities without invading them. The public rooms are slightly larger than those aboard similar-size ships, and all cabins are located on the outside of the ship. Other than those at the lowest level, all cabins have large windows. The top suite on the *Odyssey* has a private veranda

Typical passengers are in their 50s and above, and financially successful. Pricing for the seven-night "hidden fjords and glaciers" tour starts at $2,410, and it sells out quickly. *11969 Westline Industrial Dr, St. Louis MO 63146; 314/655-6700 or 800/325-0010; fax 314/655-6670; www.clippercruise.com.*

CRUISE WEST / This company has over 50 years in the business, with its founder, Chuck West, considered the "father of tourism" in Alaska. The 294-foot *Spirit of Oceanus* is the company's flagship, with room for 114 passengers in 57 cabins, all on the outside of the ship. The ship has two main lounges, several smaller bars (including a piano bar), a small library, medical clinic, as well as an elevator to the five guest-level decks. It also has a large hot tub on an outdoor terrace. While this ship is oceangoing and can cross the Gulf of Alaska between the Inside Passage and Prince William Sound, it's still small enough to hug shorelines and to explore nooks and crannies that the bigger ships can't. Prices start at $5,599 per person, including an overnight in Anchorage. The *Oceanus* also does several unique Bering Sea trips, starting at $7,199 per person. Several itineraries on the company's different vessels are available. (The Cruise West fleet totals eight; *The Sheltered Seas* is the smallest boat and the *Spirit of Oceanus* is the largest.) Three- and four-night Prince William Sound cruises start at $949. Other cruises range from $1,399 (for the 70-guest daylight yacht, *The Sheltered Seas;* passengers stay in hotels at night) to $3,399 per person on the other vessels. Cruise West also has a nine-day Inside Passage voyage (one-way, northbound, or southbound) between Seattle and Juneau or between Ketchikan and Juneau with varied ports of call costs $3,399. Early-booking and early-pay discounts are available. Cruise West attracts active, financially secure travelers (most often couples traveling without young children) who would rather watch whales in Fredrick Sound than spend the afternoon at a ship casino. *2401 4th Ave, Ste 700, Seattle WA 98121; 206/441-8687 or 800/426-7702; fax 206/441-4757; www.cruisewest.com.*

GLACIER BAY CRUISELINE / This is the only Native-owned cruise line operating in the state, and you'll appreciate the emphasis on Native culture and history. Their focus is on "soft adventure," with wilderness trips that feature kayaking, beachcombing, and hiking. This casual line has three small ships they like to call "sport utility vessels"—the *Wilderness Adventurer* offers a backcountry wilderness cruise and a seven-night Juneau-to-Ketchikan trip. The utilitarian *Wilderness Explorer* specializes in five-night wilderness trips. The *Wilderness Discoverer* does a Juneau-to-Sitka, seven-night trip. A pre- and post-season, 10-day Inside Passage cruise, beginning or ending in Seattle, is also available. The ships range from 104–169 feet and accommodate 32–94 passengers. Regular-season cruises have shore excursions included at every port, and a visit to Glacier Bay National Park and Preserve is included in every cruise. Passengers tend toward the younger set. Cruises start at $1,780 per person for the five-night trip; the seven-night trip starts at $2,520 per person. Early-booking and early-pay discounts are available. *107 W Denny Wy, Ste 303, Seattle WA 98119; 206/623-7110 or 800/451-5952; fax 206/623-7809; www.glacierbaycruiseline.com.*

LINDBLAD EXPEDITIONS / Lindblad specializes in expedition-style cruising with its twin 70-passenger ships in Alaska, the *Seabird* and the *Sealion*. The company focuses on exploration and education, featuring lectures by naturalists with a good depth of knowledge about the region and its wildlife. The cruises offer a Zodiac boat for shore exploration, an attentive staff, and fresh, healthy meals. Lindblad touts their flexibility, which follows the opportunities that Mother Nature provides. They can make a 180-degree course change to watch breaching humpback whales or linger at a remote beach to enjoy a sunset. Cabins are utilitarian, and public spaces are limited to a sun deck, the bow, dining room, and observation lounge, often the spot for group talks and gatherings. One sample cruise starts at $3,690 for seven nights between Juneau and Sitka. Typical passengers are aged 55 and over, physically active, and financially stable. *720 5th Ave, New York NY 10019; 212/765-7740 or 800/397-3348; fax 212/265-3770; explore@expeditions. com; www.expeditions.com.*

Index

We Stand By Our Reviews

Sasquatch Books is proud of *Best Places Alaska*. Our editors and contributors go to great lengths and expense to see that all of the restaurant and lodging reviews are as accurate, up-to-date, and honest as possible. If we have disappointed you, please accept our apologies; however, if a recommendation in this 3rd edition of *Best Places Alaska* has seriously misled you, Sasquatch Books would like to refund your purchase price. To receive your refund:

1. Tell us where and when you purchased your book and return the book and the book-purchase receipt to the address below.
2. Enclose the original restaurant or lodging receipt from the establishment in question, including date of visit.
3. Write a full explanation of your stay or meal and how *Best Places Alaska* misled you.
4. Include your name, address, and phone number.

Refund is valid only while this 3rd edition of *Best Places Alaska* is in print. If the ownership, management, or chef has changed since publication, Sasquatch Books cannot be held responsible. Tax and postage on the returned book is your responsibility. Please allow six to eight weeks for processing.

Please address to Satisfaction Guaranteed, *Best Places Alaska*, and send to:
Sasquatch Books
119 South Main Street, Suite 400
Seattle, WA 98104

Best Places Alaska Report Form

Based on my personal experience, I wish to nominate the following restaurant, place of lodging, shop, nightclub, sight, or other as a "Best Place"; or confirm/correct/disagree with the current review.

_____

_____

_____

_____

REPORT

Please describe food, service, style, comfort, value, date of visit, and other aspects of your experience; continue on another piece of paper if necessary.

_____

_____

_____

_____

_____

_____

I am not concerned, directly or indirectly, with the management or ownership of this establishment.

_____

SIGNED

_____

ADDRESS

_____

_____

PHONE   **DATE**

Please address to Best Places Alaska and send to:
SASQUATCH BOOKS
119 SOUTH MAIN STREET, SUITE 400
SEATTLE, WA 98104
Feel free to email feedback as well: **BOOKS@SASQUATCHBOOKS.COM**